SECOND EDITION

PERSONALITY THEORIES

DEVELOPMENT, GROWTH, AND DIVERSITY

BEM P. ALLEN
Western Illinois University

Allyn and Bacon

Boston   London   Toronto   Sydney   Tokyo   Singapore

To my best friend and colleague
Charles R. Potkay

Vice President, Social Sciences: Sean Wakely
Senior Editor: Carolyn Merrill
Editorial Assistant: Alyssa Dorrie
Marketing Manager: Joyce Nilsen
Editorial Production Service: Chestnut Hill Enterprises
Manufacturing Buyer: Megan Cochran
Cover Administrator: Linda Knowles

Library of Congress Cataloging-in-Publication Data

Allen, Bem P., 1940–
    Personality theories : development, growth, and diversity / Bem P.
Allen. — 2nd ed.
      p.   cm.
    Includes bibliographical references and index.
    ISBN 0–205–19993–3 (hardcover)
    1. Personality.   I. Title.
BF698.A3614   1996
155.2—dc20   96–27648
                                                    CIP

Printed in the United States of America

10   9   8   7   6   5   4   3   2   1   01   00   99   98   97   96

Photo credits: 3 (Jung): National Library of Medicine; 4 (Adler): The Granger Collection, New
York; 5 (Horney), 8 (Erikson), 9 (Rogers), 10 (Maslow): UPI/CORBIS-BETTMAN; 13 (Susa
Anthony): National Archives; 14 (Skinner), 15 (Murray): AP/WIDE WORLD Photos; 15 (T/
© by John Coletti

BRIEF CONTENTS

Preface   xvii

1 Introduction   1

2 The Psychoanalytic Legacy: Sigmund Freud   21

3 Personality's Ancestral Foundation: Carl Jung   49

4 Overcoming Inferiority and Striving for Superiority: Alfred Adler   73

5 Moving Toward, Away From, and Against Others: Karen Horney   99

6 Personality from the Interpersonal Perspective: Harry Stack Sullivan   123

7 The Seasons of Our Lives: Erik Erikson   147

8 The Sociopsychological Approach to Personality: Erich Fromm   173

9 Every Person is to be Prized: Carl Rogers   199

10 Becoming All That One Can Be: Abraham Maslow   225

11 Marching to a Different Drummer: George Kelly   251

12 The Social–Cognitive Approach to Personality: Julian Rotter and
        Walter Mischel   281

13 Thinking Ahead and Learning Mastery of One's Circumstances:
     Albert Bandura   309

14 It's All a Matter of Consequences: B. F. Skinner   337

15 Human Needs and Environmental Press: Henry A. Murray   367

16 The Factor Analytic Approach to Personality Traits: Raymond Cattell
     and Hans Eysenck   393

17 Personality Development and Prejudice: Gordon Allport   425

Glossary   457

References   483

Name Index   525

Subject Index   535

CONTENTS

Preface   xvii

1 Introduction   1

Preliminary Definition of Personality   1
    Implications and Cautions   2
Methods of Studying Personality   3
    The Case History Method   3
    The Correlational Method   4
    The Experimental Method   9
Personality Tests: Personologists' Tools   10
    Reliability and Validity   10
    Projective and Objective Tests   11
*Testing and Theorizing about Personality in a World of
    Human Diversity   13*
A Final Word about "Science"   14
Chapter Sections   14
    Introductory Statement   14
    The Person: Biographies   14
    View of the Person: General Philosophical Orientation   15
    Basic Concepts: The Heart and Soul of a Theory   16
    Evaluation: Placing a Theory in Perspective   16
Occasional Sections   17
Conclusion Section   18
E-mail Interaction   18
Summary Points   18

Essay/Critical Thinking Questions   *19*
E-mail Interaction   *20*

2 The Psychoanalytic Legacy: Sigmund Freud   21

Freud, The Person   *21*
Freud's View of the Person   *23*
Basic Concepts: Freud   *24*
    Personality Structure: Three Interacting Systems   24
    Personality Development: Five Sequential Stages   28
    A Basic Diversity Issue: Freud's View of Females   34
Evaluation   *36*
    Contributions   36
    Supporting and Qualifying Evidence   39
    Limitations   41
Conclusions   *45*
Summary Points   *46*
Essay/Critical Thinking Questions   *47*
E-mail Interaction   *48*

3 Personality's Ancestral Foundation: Carl Jung   49

Jung, The Person   *50*
Jung's View of the Person   *51*
Basic Concepts: Jung   *52*
    Consciousness and Unconsciousness   52
    Archetypes   54
    Dreams as Messages from a Wise Unconscious   59
    Personality Typology   60
    Personality Development   61
Evaluation   *63*
    Contributions   63
    Limitations   67
Conclusions   *68*
Summary Points   *69*
Running Comparison   *70*
Essay/Critical Thinking Questions   *71*
E-mail Interaction   *71*

4 Overcoming Inferiority and Striving for Superiority: Alfred Adler   73

Adler, The Person   *74*
Adler's View of the Person   *76*
    Basic Orientation   76

Humanitarian Approach: Diversity as It Concerns Women and
   All Kinds of People Everywhere   77
Basic Concepts: Adler   78
   Developing Social Feeling: Society, Work, and Love   78
   Style of Life   78
   Future Goals Versus Past Events   79
   Overcoming Inferiority   80
   Striving for Superiority and the Superiority Complex   81
   Family Influences on Personality Development   82
Evaluation   84
   Contributions   84
   Limitations   93
Conclusions   94
Summary Points   94
Running Comparison   96
Essay/Critical Thinking Questions   96
E-mail Interaction   97

5 Moving Toward, Away From, and Against Others: Karen Horney   99

Horney, The Person   99
Horney's View of the Person   101
Basic Concepts: Horney   104
   Basic Anxiety: Infantile Helplessness in a Parental World   104
   Coping by Way of Ten Neurotic Needs   105
   Moving Toward, Against, and Away from People   105
   Developing an Idealized Versus a Real Image of Self   108
   A Basic Diversity Issue: The Psychology of Women   110
Evaluation   111
   Contributions   111
   Some Research Support   118
   Limitations   118
Conclusions   119
Summary Points   119
Running Comparison   121
Essay/Critical Thinking Questions   122
E-mail Interaction   122

**6 Personality from the Interpersonal Perspective:
Harry Stack Sullivan   123**

Sullivan, The Person   124
Sullivan's View of the Person   126
   Significant Others and the Self   126
   A Need for Tenderness   127

Basic Concepts: Sullivan   128
   Empathy, Anxiety, and Security   128
   Three Modes of Experience and Six Stages of Development   128
Evaluation   138
   Contributions   138
   Limitations   142
Conclusions   143
Summary Points   144
Running Comparison   145
Essay/Critical Thinking Questions   146
E-mail Interaction   146

7 The Seasons of Our Lives: Erik Erikson   147

Erikson, The Person   148
Erikson's View of the Person   150
   Freudian?   150
   On the Tasks and Polarities of Life   152
Basic Concepts: Erikson   152
   Infancy   153
   Early Childhood   154
   Play Age   155
   School Age   156
   Adolescence   156
   Young Adulthood   158
   Adulthood   159
   Old Age   160
Theoretical and Empirical Support for Erikson's Point of View   162
   Levinson: The Midlife Crisis   162
   Sheehy: Women are Different   163
   Empirical Support: Research Confirming Erikson's View   164
Evaluation   166
   Contributions   166
   Limitations   167
Conclusions   168
Summary Points   168
Running Comparison   170
Essay/Critical Thinking Questions   170
E-mail Interaction   171

8 The Sociopsychological Approach to Personality: Erich Fromm   173

Fromm, The Person   174
Fromm's View of the Person   176
Basic Concepts: Fromm   177

Existential Needs   177
Individual and Social Character   184
Evaluation   191
Contributions   191
Limitations   193
Conclusions   194
Summary Points   195
Running Comparison   197
Essay/Critical Thinking Questions   197
E-mail Interaction   198

9 Every Person is to be Prized: Carl Rogers   199

Rogers, The Person   199
Rogers's View of the Person   203
Basic Concepts: Rogers   206
Actualization   206
The Importance of the Self   207
Personality Development: Some Favorable Conditions   210
Procedures for Changing Personality: Client-Centered Therapy   213
Evaluation   214
General Contributions   214
Caring about the Person in Human Relationships   215
Rogers's Scientific Contributions   216
Limitations   218
Conclusions   220
Summary Points   220
Running Comparison   222
Essay/Critical Thinking Questions   223
E-mail Interaction   223

10 Becoming All That One Can Be: Abraham Maslow   225

Maslow, The Person   226
Maslow's View of the Person   229
The Evolution of a Theorist   229
The Gestalt Influence   230
Motivation   231
Basic Concepts: Maslow   232
Not by Bread Alone: Five Basic Human Needs   232
Human Nature is Born, Not Made   236
Self-Actualizing Persons: Superior Personalities   236
Needs and Values beyond the Pale and Experiences from
    the Mountaintop   238
Evaluation   238

Contributions   238
Supporting Evidence   241
Limitations   243
Conclusions   246
Summary Points   247
Running Comparison   248
Essay/Critical Thinking Questions   248
E-mail Interaction   249

11 Marching to a Different Drummer: George Kelly   251

Kelly, The Person   251
Kelly's View of the Person   254
Basic Concepts: Kelly   255
Personality as a System of Constructs   255
Relations among Constructs   260
Personality Development   262
Predictability   262
Dependency Constructs   262
Role Playing   263
Choices: The C-P-C Cycle   263
Evaluation   264
Contributions: Supporting Evidence and Practical Applications   264
Limitations   272
Conclusions   274
Summary Points   276
Running Comparison   278
Essay/Critical Thinking Questions   278
E-mail Interaction   279

12 The Social–Cognitive Approach to Personality: Julian Rotter and Walter Mischel   281

Rotter, The Person   282
Rotter's View of the Person   283
Basic Concepts: Rotter   285
Reinforcement Value, Psychological Situations, and Expectancy   285
Locus of Control: Internals and Externals   286
Characteristics of Internals and Externals   288
Changing Externals   290
Other Generalized Expectancies   291
Evaluation   292
Contributions to Controlling Our Lives   292
Limitations   293
Conclusions   294

Mischel: A Challenge to Traits   294

Mischel, The Person   295
Mischel's View of the Person   296
Basic Concepts: Mischel   298
   Supporting Evidence   300
   Mischel Summed Up: Consistency of Cross-Situation
      Behavioral Patterns   302
Evaluation   303
   Mischel's Contributions   303
   Limitations   305
Conclusions   305
Summary Points   305
Running Comparison   307
Essay/Critical Questions   308
E-mail Interaction   308

**13   Thinking Ahead and Learning Mastery of One's Circumstances:
Albert Bandura   309**

Bandura, The Person   309
Bandura's View of the Person   311
   Observational Learning and Reciprocal Determination   311
   Person Factors, Behavior, and the External Environment   311
   Free Will, Personal Agency, and the Power of Forethought   313
   Learning   313
   "Social" and "Cognitive" in "Social Cognitive Theory"   314
Basic Concepts: Bandura   314
   Models and Modeling   314
   Goals and Self-Regulation   316
   Self-Efficacy: Avenue to the Correction of Harmful Behavior   316
   Other Things We Learn from Models, Besides Behavior   318
   Rewards   319
   Defensive Behaviors   321
Evaluation   321
   Supporting Evidence   321
   Implications of Social Cognitive Theory for Moral Functioning   327
   Limitations   331
Conclusions   332
Summary Points   332
Running Comparison   334
Essay/Critical Thinking Questions   334
E-mail Interaction   335

14 It's All a Matter of Consequences: B. F. Skinner   337

Skinner, The Person   338
Skinner's View of the Person   340
    Environmentalism: The Importance of Consequences   340
    "Beyond Freedom and Dignity"   341
Basic Concepts: Skinner   343
    Operant Conditioning   343
    Positive Reinforcement   344
    Negative Reinforcement and Punishment   346
    Schedules of Reinforcement   347
    The Development of Humans: Language, Personality,
        and Child-Rearing   352
Evaluation   358
    Contributions   358
    Limitations   360
Conclusions   361
Summary Points   362
Running Comparison   364
Essay/Critical Thinking Questions   364
E-mail Interaction   365

15 Human Needs and Environmental Press: Henry A. Murray   367

Murray, The Person   368
Murray's View of the Person   371
    Early Exposure to Psychology   371
    Why did Murray Become a Psychologist?   372
    Developing a Unique Approach to Understanding People   372
Basic Concepts: Murray   374
    Postulates   374
    Definition of Needs   375
    Varieties of Needs   376
    Strength of Needs, and Interactions among Them   378
    Need Integrates (Complexes)   379
    Environmental Press   381
    Thema   381
Evaluation   382
    Contributions   382
    Limitations   388
Conclusions   389
Summary Points   390
Running Comparison   391
Essay/Critical Thinking Questions   392
E-mail Interaction   392

16 The Factor Analytic Approach to Personality Traits: Raymond Cattell and Hans Eysenck   393

Cattell, The Person   *394*
Cattell's View of the Person   *396*
  Cattell's Approach to Understanding the Person   396
  Personality Defined   397
  Nature and Nurture   397
  The Econetic Model   397
  Factor Analysis   397
Basic Concepts: Cattell   *398*
  Data Types   399
  Data Collection Techniques   399
  Traits   400
  Intelligence   402
  The Personality of Nations   402
Evaluation   *403*
  Contributions   403
  Limitations   405
Conclusions   *409*

Eysenck: 16 = 3—Conceiving of Personality in Three Dimensions   410

Eysenck, The Person   *410*
Eysenck's View of the Person   *411*
Basic Concepts and Contributions: Eysenck   *412*
  Traits and Types in Eysenck's Theory   412
  Biological Determinism   412
  Toward a Scientific Model of Personality   413
  Researching Traits and Types   414
  Measuring and Describing E, N, and P   414
  Supporting Evidence   416
Limitations   *418*
  Arousal and E-I   418
  Genes and Controversy   418
  The Bell Curve: Race and Environment   419
  Big 5 or Big 3?   420
Conclusions   *420*
Summary Points   *420*
Running Comparison   *422*
Essay/Critical Thinking Questions   *422*
E-mail Interaction   *423*

17 Personality Development and Prejudice: Gordon Allport   425

Allport, The Person   426
Allport's View of the Person   428
  Humanism?   428
  Emphasis on Unique Traits and Behavioral Variability   428
  De-emphasizing the Freudian Unconscious   429
Basic Concepts: Allport   429
  Personality Defined   429
  Traits   431
  Cardinal, Central, and Secondary P.D.s   432
Personality Development   434
  The Proprium and the Seven Stages of the Developing Self   434
  The Mature Personality   436
Personality and Prejudice   440
  Prejudice Defined   441
  Social Distance   442
  "Race" Differences   444
  Stereotypes   445
  Painting the Picture of the Prejudiced Personality   447
Evaluation   449
  Contributions   449
  Limitations   450
Conclusions   452
Summary Points   452
Running Comparison   454
Essay/Critical Thinking Questions   454
E-mail Interaction   455

Glossary   457

References   483

Name Index   525

Subject Index   531

PREFACE

The second edition of *Personality Theories* has added a subtitle that highlights emphases of theme and content, including changes from the first to the current edition. *Development, Growth, and Diversity* reflects strengthening of the first edition's themes and cultivation of new foci. In terms of human personality development, almost all texts, including the first edition of this one, recognize the contribution of Freud's and Erikson's stage theories. More uncommon is the coverage of developmental stages and other aspects of development found in this book's treatment of Jung, Adler, Horney, Sullivan, Kelly, Skinner, and Allport. Jung, Sullivan, and Allport present stage theories that are well covered in the current edition, but neglected elsewhere. Horney's, Kelly's, and Skinner's theories have strong implications for personality development which are explicit in the case of Horney (e.g., basic anxiety) and Kelly (e.g., dependency constructs), but must be "read between the lines" of Skinner's writings. All of these contributions to understanding personality development are "writ large" in the pages of this text. Further, some other contributions are teased from the writings of additional theorists (e.g., Mischel's "delay of gratification" and Bandura and colleagues' work on gender identity in children).

The humanistic perspective and its orientation to growth is more emphasized in the second edition. Horney's alleged pessimism about humans has been de-emphasized in favor of accentuating her humanistic inclination, reflected in the notion of "real self." This more humanistic position characterized her late in life. Fromm's role as a pioneer in the humanistic movement is brought out more in the second edition. Allport's humanism is also brought more into focus, especially in regard to his concern for religious issues (religion itself is more often mentioned). I point out in this edition that some people have even managed to fit Skinner into the humanistic picture. Finally, the core humanistic chapters (Rogers and Maslow) have been strengthened. All in all, there is more emphasis on what people can become.

"Diversity" is quite the buzz word these days. Text authors are injecting it into their books as "the latest thing." To me it is much more than that. Beginning about ten years ago, a few colleagues and I started to develop a diversity curriculum at our university. Through persistence, we have overcome initial resistance and have instituted a diversity requirement for all our students. In the process we have developed a core diversity course, which I have taught several times. I have also written several articles about diversity and have made presentations at several national, state, and local diversity conventions, as well as in other contexts. I am currently developing a diversity course so that our graduate students can meet state and national requirements that mental health professionals have a background in diversity studies.

Obviously, I believe diversity is here to stay. In fact, it is my belief that our students' ability to prosper in the future depends in part on their grasp of diversity issues. Accordingly, every chapter in the second edition devotes significant space to diversity. Students should come away from this booklong consideration knowing what diversity *is* (no single definition, even one several pages long, can do justice to the term) and what *it is not* (it is not something just for "minorities" and women; it is for everyone).

But, one may still wonder, why all this emphasis on diversity in a personality theories book. If "individual differences" is a core personality consideration, and obviously it is, "diversity" is a natural companion to the study of personality theories. Actually, I cannot think of a better place to put coverage of diversity issues.

Of the theories attempting to explain psychological phenomena, those applied to understanding personality are among psychology's oldest and most enduring sets of theories, with origins dating back to the ancient Greeks. Despite being "long in the tooth," these venerable points of view are still being pursued by modern theorists, researchers, and practitioners. In fact, few groups of theories focused on a single, complex phenomenon have survived so well as theories of personality. For example, while personality theories have gained many new advocates, theories of conditioning (instrumental and classical) have recruited relatively few new enthusiasts.

Why the longevity of these notions? They have served psychology well in terms of generating fruitful new ideas, leading to means of helping people with psychological problems, and providing the grist for psychological researchers' scientific mills. Thus, one basic assumption behind this book is that personality theories are central to psychological thinking. I have woven this assumption into the fabric of the text.

A second basic assumption is wrapped up in the answer to the question, "At what level of difficulty can a broad range of college students be expected to function successfully?" Personality theories do not have the reputation for difficulty and arcane structure by which physicists' theories of time and space are known. They do, however, involve complexities and abstractions that can be quite challenging. Nevertheless, the question can be answered in an optimistic fashion: Typical students attending every kind of school, including community colleges and Ivy League universities, can learn even intricate and daunting material, provided it is presented in a manner that will excite their imaginations and relate to their lives. Therefore, I have worked hard to make each personality theory come alive by showing how it relates to the personality of the individual who composed it, by indicating how solutions to life's puzzles may be better approximated through understanding it, and by using it to inspire some insightful thoughts that most students have yet to think.

A third basic assumption of *Personality Theories—Development, Growth, and Diversity* involves notions of objectivity. Although perfect objectivity is probably unobtainable, even-handedness can be achieved. *Personality Theories* assumes that students should come away from a thorough consideration of personality theories with a sense that each has its merits and deficiencies and none can be reasonably called "the best" or the "the worst." Allowing students to achieve this goal entails taking the perspective of each theorist as I write about her or his theory, while also maintaining an informed, balanced point of view so that merits and deficiencies are seen in relation to the field of personality as a whole. These two complementary orientations allow me to write about theorists' major contributions with great enthusiasm, sometimes bordering on zealousness, while being able to step back and caution students about the apparent weaknesses of even the most laudable ideas and about holes in theories left by failures to entertain important matters of personality.

Personality Theories—Development, Growth, and Diversity is designed for undergraduate students, regardless of level. It is written to be easily read. However, it does include sentences of moderate complexity/length and it contains many words that are not common. Although some students may be advised to occasionally use a dictionary, care is taken so that context usually defines uncommon words. These practices will ensure that students who are unintimidated by any readings, even the most difficult, will find that *Personality Theories* holds their interest. At the same time, students who are not so widely read can manage this text without undue trouble and can improve their ability to read more challenging literature.

Organization

The organization of the chapters in *Personality Theories* is unique and consistent throughout the book. All chapters are written using basically the same format, allowing students to quickly learn what to look for—a lesson that will make reading more comfortable and rapid. I have seen many comments about the first edition by students at my university and elsewhere that clearly indicate great appreciation for *Personality Theories'* organization (more generally, student reaction to the text has been very favorable). Because the organization is so important to students, it is detailed in the first chapter where they will not miss it. Here, I have provided only a brief rationale for the various chapter sections constituting the organization. Readers of the Preface who want more information are referred to chapter one.

An *introductory statement*, designed to link a given chapter to preceding ones, is followed by a *biography* of the theorist under consideration. Here each theorist is humanized and groundwork is laid for linking his or her personality to the theory in question. These biographies provide students with "memory hooks" upon which to hang components of theory.

A *view of the person* section follows and orients students by providing them with the philosophical underpinnings of each theory. This section answers such questions as "To what degree is the theory scientific?" "Does the theory attempt to understand the person by reference to the past, present, or future?" "Are external or internal determinants of psychological functioning emphasized?" and "Do inborn or acquired determinants explain personality?"

The *basic concepts* section lays out the fundamental constructs of each theory. These critical elements of each theory are linked so that students may understand their interrelationships and, where possible, are organized according to some familiar schema. For example, if a theory fits the "stage theory" mold, its concepts are presented within the framework of its sequential stages. In any event, an effort is made to begin with more global concepts, where they can be identified, and proceed to more specific ones.

Evaluation of each theory is organized into "contributions" and "limitations" subsections. Two broad categories of criteria applicable to both subsections are used to assess aspects of each theory. A given criterion may be used for one theory to illuminate contributions, and for another to point out limitations. Alternatively, a theory may meet a given criterion to some degree, therefore revealing a contribution, or fail to meet the criterion to some degree, indicating a limitation. None of these criteria are relevant to every theory; thus, a given one may be used to evaluate one theory but not another. One of these broad categories is "science criteria." These criteria address such questions as "Is the theory constructed in logical fashion?" "Are the concepts well interrelated?" "Do the concepts tend to be distinct or are they overlapping?" "Are common labels for concepts used or are obscure labels used?" "Does each label give precise meaning to its concept or does it have multiple meanings?" "Do concepts imply testable predictions?" and "Do research studies support the validity of concepts." "Non-science criteria," the other category, raise such questions as "Does the theory inspire psychologists to experience new insights and clarify their thinking?" "Does the theory lead to a useful method of therapy?" and "Have the theorist's writings been interesting and helpful to laypersons?"

Content and Chapter Organization

Personality Theories—Development, Growth, and Diversity is comprehensive. A first step in developing a plan for the book was to informally survey the range of theories apparently deemed most central to instructors of personality theory. Every theory that has been of interest to even a substantial minority of personality instructors is included in this text. Few if any other texts cover as many theories and none cover a better representation of mainstream theories. It is, therefore, likely that most personality instructors will find the theories they want to cover within the pages of *Personality Theories*.

The chapters are grouped in representative clusters and ordered within clusters in popular fashion. For example, chapters 3 through 8 are devoted to theorists who use Freud's point of view (Chapter 2) as a point of departure for developing their own theories. Theorists most closely linked to Freud are considered in early chapters of this cluster (Jung and Adler) and those more removed from direct influence by him are considered in later chapters (Horney, Sullivan, Erikson, and Fromm). Consideration of Fromm, who should be regarded as an early humanist, provides a bridge to the second cluster—chapters on modern humanists, Rogers and Maslow. A chapter on the cognitive approach (Kelly) is followed by chapters on the social/cognitive point of view (Rotter/Mischel and Bandura). Next, come the ideas of self-proclaimed anti-cognitive theorist, Skinner. Then a chapter on Murray's theory links early-chapter traditions to the humanistic, cognitive, and behavioral orientations, and lays the groundwork for the trait theories. Cattell's and Eysenck's theories are next and emphasize modern approaches to the study of traits. Finally, ending the book is Allport's more humanistic and socially flavored theory of traits that focuses on personality development and prejudice.

Alternative Uses of the Book

I have always found comprehensive texts more attractive than ones with specialized content because they invariably include the chapters I want to cover. Only some of them, however, are written so that I can "unplug" the chapters I want to consider without concern that I have eliminated material essential for understanding covered chapters. In composing *Personality Theories* I have taken great care to interrelate chapters, while, at the same time, making sure that each chapter can stand alone should a given instructor wish to consider only a subset of all chapters. I believe that personality instructors will find they can readily skip some chapters of *Personality Theories* and focus on others without fear that students will be unduly troubled by lack of exposure to eliminated material.

Special Features

Each chapter begins with some "teaser questions" which are designed to alert students to critical issues considered in the chapter and to arouse their curiosity regarding the theory. The presence of these questions at the beginning of each chapter primes students to entertain new material that is dissimilar to that discussed in previous chapters. The questions are always answered in the text of the chapter.

Immediately following the text for each chapter, students will find some *Summary Points* that will allow them a quick review of the chapter. These "points" are synopses of ten major considerations. They are not an attempt to reiterate the entire chapter. Students can expect that the "points" will trigger their memories concerning major issues in the chapter and the details surrounding them, **if they have carefully read the text**. The "points" are not a substitute for perusal of the chapter.

All too often some students will read a chapter—or more likely, a set of chapters on which they are to be tested—and then forget about chapter content as soon as they will no longer be evaluated based on their knowledge of it. The *Running Comparison* that follows the "points" is constructed so that students are continually reminded of material in earlier chapters. It is expanded in the Second Edition. This goal is accomplished by comparing the theory currently under consideration with theories of previous chapters. Also, the "comparison" helps students anticipate future theories by occasionally comparing the current theory with ones yet to be considered. Should instructors wish to give a comprehensive, final exam, the "comparison" will help students greatly, because it will ensure that they are continually reviewing material from all chapters. In addition, the comparison further sharpens students' understanding of a given theory by contrasting it with other theories.

The next section in each chapter is designed to promote critical thinking. While these *Essay/Critical Thinking* questions can be used as essay-test items, alternatively, they can be used as a basis for class discussions. In addition they are good review questions, but more important, they can be used by students to expand their thinking by conjuring up implications of theories that reach far beyond the text. Many of these questions will be challenging even to the best students, partly because they require analysis, not "rote memory."

A complete *Glossary* of all concepts composing covered theories is presented at the end of the book. The listing is alphabetical and each entry clearly specifies its concept. Concepts are also listed (with text-page numbers) under each theorist's name in the subject index. I have had my students make multiple copies of the subject index so they can more easily prepare for essay questions that ask them to compare theorists.

The last section of each chapter is a listing of questions students can address to me personally via E-mail. Of course, they may also send me their own questions. Instructors are invited to join students in addressing questions to me by E-mail. I hope adopters of this book will encourage students to interact with me in this modern internet way, not just for their further education in personality, but also because they will benefit by using a mode of communication that will characterize their future. I look forward to relating to student-users of my book in a more personal way than is allowed by most text authors.

A comprehensive test-item file is available. Multiple choice items thoroughly cover each chapter's material. Many of these items have been battle-tested. Having used many of them for my own tests, I have been able to eliminate questionable items, rewrite others for clarity, and create new ones that are easily understood by today's students. There are an average of more than 75 items per chapter providing instructors with in the order of 1300 items total, more than enough for several during-the-semester tests and a final exam. In addition, I have placed some *Extra Items* (25% more) at the end of each item file so that adopters will have a separate pool for make-ups and finals. As I have years of experience in contributing multiple choice items to text manuals, instructors can be assured that items are carefully and professionally done. Alternatives such as "all of the above," "none of the above," and "both *a* and *b*" are avoided because they confuse students. Each item, therefore, has only one correct alternative. All incorrect alternatives are written to be highly plausible so that students must make thoughtful choices. They are often statements true of other aspects of a theory, but incorrect in terms of the main body of the question. These alternatives require students to discriminate among concepts of a theory. Concepts from other theories are also sometimes used so that inter-theory discrimination can be assessed.

I have always believed that tests are learning experiences, not just occasions for evaluation. Accordingly, items are written to engage students in analytic thinking. Most require that students employ their reasoning powers, rather than merely recognize the correct alternative. Items are written so that correct alternatives follow logically from main bodies of questions, a process that will sharpen students' logical thinking. They are also written to be interesting in and of themselves. A computerized file for MAC and DOS machines is now available.

The Instructor's Manual accompanying this text is constructed so that instructors may institute interesting and edifying classroom discussions and exercises to complement the lectures. As a member of a national college teacher's organization, and a frequent participant in its conventions, I have become convinced that spending the entire class period lecturing is not ideal for either students or instructors. Students can obtain basic information from the text. Class time can be used to get students excited about the course content, to go over difficult material, to provide the latest hot-off-the-press information about course content, and to cover issues about which the instructor is expert in greater depth than text space allows.

The Instructor's Manual for each chapter also contains an outline of the chapter so instructors can orient themselves regarding chapter content, chapter objectives which may provide further orientation and which can be passed on to students, a list of readings for lecture support, and a list of readings for students, (they can be placed on library reserve lists). Also, the Instructor's Manual contains a film/video list and the Case of Estella Monroe, an additional experience in diversity that will allow instructors to engage students in the application of all theories to a single case history (the case of Estella Monroe is considered further in Chapter 1).

Acknowledgments

Sincere thanks are due Executive Editor Sean Wakely for his insights, sensitivity, and suggestions during the planning and much of the writing of *Personality Theories* (2nd Edition). Carolyn Merrill, Senior Editor, was brand new at Allyn and Bacon when she took on *Personality Theories*. Her fresh insights have been very useful and her support much appreciated.

These colleagues are much appreciated for their constructive and thoughtful reviews during the writing of *Personality Theories:* Christina Frederick, Southern Utah University; Robert Johnston, College of William and Mary; William Scott, College of Wooster; James Calhoun, University of Georgia; Michael F. Shaughnessy, Eastern New Mexico University; Paul R. O'Brien, University of Massachusetts/Boston; Michael Botwin, California State University/Fresno; Gerald Hilyard, Curry College; Joseph Horvat, Weber State University; James J. Johnson, Illinois State University; Eugenio Galindro, El Paso Community College; Jim Amirkhan, California State University/Long Beach; C. George Boeree, Shippensburg University; Constance DiMaria-Kross, Union County College; and Ruth Reese, Arizona State University West.

1

INTRODUCTION

- How is personality defined?
- How is personality measured?
- If two factors are correlated, does it mean that one causes the other?
- Are personality researchers scientists?
- What kinds of tests do personality psychologists use?

One goal of this first chapter is to give you an answer to the question "What is Personality?" by providing a preliminary definition. Another is to consider how personality is studied and the kinds of tests **personologists**, psychologists who study personality, use. A final goal is to lay out the logic behind the structure of chapters. To facilitate reading chapters and comparing one with another, all the chapters have the same sections.

Preliminary Definition of Personality

The preliminary definition of personality has several facets, including individual differences, behavioral dimensions, and traits. **Individual differences** is a key psychological phrase generally referring to the observation that people differ in a variety of ways. In the study of personality, the important differences involve **personality traits**, internally based psychological characteristics that often correspond to adjectives such as *shy, kind, mean, outgoing, dominant*, and so forth.

Each trait corresponds to one end of a **behavioral dimension**—a continuum of behavior analogous to a yardstick. Just as one end of a yardstick is anchored by 0 inches and the other end by 36 inches, one end of a behavioral dimension is anchored by one behavioral extreme and the other end is anchored by the opposite extreme. For example, affiliativeness, assertiveness, and conscientiousness are labels for behavioral dimensions. The behavioral dimension for assertiveness can be represented as follows:

assertive:1:2:3:4:5:6:7:unassertive

One end of the assertiveness dimension is anchored by **assertive**, the tendency to stand up for one's rights and to say no when it seems appropriate to do so. The other end is anchored by **unassertive**, the tendency not to defend one's rights and to say "yes" when one wants to say "no". For the sake of convenience and simplicity, the diagram has only seven degrees. In reality the number of degrees of a dimension is difficult or impossible to determine. In any case, only behaviors falling near the extremes of dimensions have much meaning for personality. Only if a person's behavior can be represented on the assertiveness dimension by a degree close to the anchor *assertive* can it be inferred that she possesses the trait assertive.

Putting the facets together, an individual's **personality** is a set of degrees falling along many behavioral dimensions, each degree corresponding to a trait. Note that, although some people may share a particular trait, there are individual differences in possession of the trait. Some people have it and others do not. However, sharing does not apply to entire personalities. There are individual differences in the sets of traits that people possess such that no two personalities are exactly alike.

Implications and Cautions

There is a coincidence of personologists' beliefs about personality and the common sense notions held by nonprofessionals or laypersons. First, many personologists and laypersons believe that an individual is quite consistent across different situations (his behavior is at about the same point or degree along the assertiveness behavioral dimension in one situation as it is in the next). This point of view may constitute the most basic assumption of the preliminary definition of personality. Second, where single dimensions are involved, individuals can be very similar or even identical. That is, two or more people can, on the average, exhibit about the same degree of a behavior, and thus possess the same trait. Third, the overriding agreement between personologists and the people they study is the shared belief in individual differences (Lamiell, 1981). Because there are individual differences along every behavioral dimension, given enough dimensions, personalities must differ. One respected estimate put the number of traits and corresponding dimensions at 17,000+, thereby guaranteeing that each individual's personality is different from that of other persons and, thus, each person has a unique personality (Allport and Odbert, 1936).

My experience reading personality publications and reviewing them for various publication outlets tells me that the preliminary definition is implicitly, if not explicitly, adopted by more personologists than any other. It fits the theories of Murray, Cattell, Eysenck, and Allport rather well. All of them to some degree, at least implicitly, adopt its most basic assumption: A person behaves consistently from one situation to the next. These "trait theorists" must make the consistency assumption. Otherwise they would not be able to infer a trait from observations of a person's behaviors that fall along a dimension such as assertiveness. If a person is assertive in one situation and not in the next, how could anyone draw an inference about whether he has the trait "assertive"?

The consistency assumption, while widely adopted, is nevertheless not without its critics. Some theorists, such as Rotter and Mischel, reject it outright. I also have serious reservations about it. Other deficiencies of this preliminary definition include inattention to physiological and developmental processes. In view of these shortcomings, consider the preliminary definition to be a sort of benchmark against which to compare the various theorists' definitions that are considered in this book. You will find that each theorist has her or his own definition, in some cases fitting the preliminary definition fairly well, but not in other cases.

Methods of Studying Personality

First, before considering methods for studying personality, there is a need to specify a set of criteria for evaluating those methods. Science provides the needed criteria. The minimum requirement for a research method to be called **scientific** is that it involve unbiased observations that are quantified so that systematic analyses can be performed (Allen, 1990). Methods can properly be called scientific if 1) they allow researchers to make observations without regard to their personal biases, and 2) they permit the assignment of numbers to those observations so that systematic analysis is possible. By contrast, users of unscientific methods base selection of observations on convenience—whatever happens to be handy is observed. Or observations are based on personal bias—the researchers arbitrarily believe that selected observations are more important than other observations they might make. In addition, users of unscientific methods may draw conclusions about what they have observed based solely on personal inclinations. However important such efforts may be for some purpose or another, the methods involved would not ordinarily qualify as scientific.

The Case History Method

The **case history method** involves collecting background data *about* and making intensive observations *of* a single individual in order to discover how to treat that person or to obtain information that may apply to other people (Rosenhan & Seligman, 1995). The case history method may be scientific in that observations can be unbiased. It is possible for psychologists to lay aside their own personal biases concerning personality functioning. However, unbiased observations may be difficult for them because the person under observation may be a patient with whom they are personally involved. Also, observations made on a single individual may not be applicable to other persons. A given individual may be quite unusual and, therefore, not at all representative of other people. Further, although it may be possible to assign numbers to observations, systematic analysis may be difficult or impossible. For example, a psychologist may give personality tests to an individual and then derive some scores. Still, systematic analysis may be difficult because scores from more than one person are ordinarily needed to conduct a meaningful analysis.

Despite these shortcomings, case histories may sometimes qualify as scientific. It is possible to give the subject of a case history personality tests and then compare her/his scores to norms or average scores derived by testing large populations of people. In this way, how the case history subject's scores compare to those of "people in general" can be determined, and, thus, whether his/her score is unusual or like most people's can be stated.

Further, there have even been whole books written on using a single case as the source of data for a statistical analysis in a scientific study (Davidson & Costello, 1969). Charles Potkay and I have actually used a single case to illustrate research results for our entire sample of research subjects (Allen & Potkay, 1973).

While the case history method does not typically qualify as scientific, information derived from it may be useful in many ways. Reports based on observations of single individuals often are valuable as illustrations of personality functioning. At a number of points in this text, real and, occasionally, contrived cases will be used to concretely illustrate some aspect of personality functioning. Bearing these cases in mind will help you remember some of the important patterns that relate to personality theories.

Case histories found in the book that you will probably find intrinsically interesting include the following: Little Hans, the boy who feared horses (Freud chapter); characters in horror movies (Jung chapter); Anna, a delightful and mischievous little girl (Jung chapter); an analysis of Frankenstein and his monster based on the actual story by Mary Shelley (Adler chapter); the case of Clare, a clingingly dependent woman madly in love with a self-centered man (Horney chapter); Hitler as a necrophilous (death-loving) character (Fromm chapter); Becky and Dennis, Catholic and Protestant, coming to know one another in war-torn Northern Ireland (Rogers chapter); Jim and Joan, two college friends trying to resolve Jim's conflict with a professor (Kelly chapter); a baby reared in a box (Skinner chapter); dreams about the kidnapping and murder of the Lindbergh baby (Murray chapter); an analysis of a disturbed college student (Murray chapter); and a school-girl case of mass hysteria (Cattell/Eysenck chapter). In addition, every theorist's life story constitutes an often fascinating case history that begins every chapter.

In addition, your professor has a comprehensive case history in her or his Instructors' Manual that accompanies *Personality Theories*. The case history subject, Estella Monroe, is a young Latina mother who has survived a divorce and is "moving up the corporate ladder." Estella's relations with her son, her ex-husband, her new romantic partner, her co-workers, and her parents reveal material suitable for analysis by all the theories covered in this book.

The Correlational Method

The correlational method involves variables. The term **variable** refers to a variation in quantity specified by numbers. The numbers associated with a variable are called values. Weight is a variable, because it can take on different values. Some people weigh 100 lbs., some weigh 200 lbs., others 140 lbs., and still others 250 lbs. For adults, weight can vary from well under 100 lbs. to well over 500 lbs. Likewise, height is a variable. Adults vary in height from under three feet to well over seven feet. Anxiety, intelligence, and kindness are also variables. In each case, observations can assume values that vary over some range.

The correlational method is used to determine whether variations in certain variables tend to occur together. Any two variables are said to be **correlated** if variations in one correspond to some degree with variations in the other. To illustrate the correlational method, consider a hypothetical example. Suppose some researchers are interested in the relationship between just two variables, the number of alcoholic drinks some people consume per day and the number of psychological complaints they register per day. Assume that for the researchers' sample of people (called "subjects"), the greatest number of drinks consumed per day, averaged over a ten-day period, was 20, and the least was none. Thus, for the variable "number of drinks per day," values varied from 0 to 20. The list of psychological complaints that subjects could check off included "felt anxious," "felt irritated," "felt depressed," "felt worthless," "felt lonely," "felt humiliated," "felt stupid," "felt unmotivated," "felt pressured," and "felt persecuted." For the variable "psychological complaints," values could vary from 0 to 10 (complaints were also averaged over 10 days). Table 1.1 shows the number of drinks per day and the number of complaints registered per day (the numbers presented are whole numbers in order to keep things simple). Figure 1.1 depicts a plot of the relationship

TABLE 1.1   Positive Correlation

Subject's Initials	# Drinks/Day	# Complaints/Day
JJ	2	1
PC	6	4
RM	3	2
LD	15	9
RC	2	1
MP	10	7
IN	4	2
MA	7	5
BC	9	6
KI	5	3
MZ	11	8
PS	6	4
CC	16	9
BT	3	1
LL	8	6

between number of drinks per day and number of psychological complaints per day. Look at them before going on.

In Table 1.1, notice that the variation in number of drinks closely matches the variation in the number of complaints. For a given subject, if the number of drinks per day is high, the number of complaints also tends to be high. If the number of drinks is low the number of complaints is low. You can clearly see this pattern in Figure 1.1.

When using the correlational method, researchers are usually interested in the degree to which the variables they are investigating are related in straight-line or linear fashion. In the example shown in Table 1.1 and Figure 1.1, the relationship is quite linear.

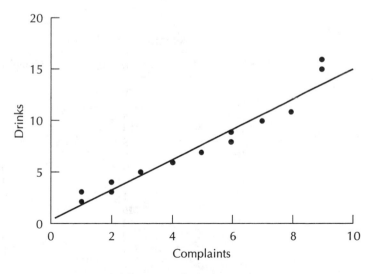

FIGURE 1.1   Positive Correlation

Relationships that tend to fit a straight line can be represented by a **correlation coefficient**—an index, designated by the letter *r*, of the degree to which a relationship is linear. Correlational relationships conform to one of two patterns. Two variables are said to be **positively correlated** when high values on one variable correspond to high values on the other, and low values correspond with low values, as in Table 1.1 and Figure 1.1. For positive correlations, the coefficient varies from 0 to 1.00. In this example case the correlation coefficient is r = +.975.

The second pattern, shown in Table 1.2, involves different assumptions. On the one hand, variation in number of drinks corresponds closely with variation in the number of complaints, therefore, the relationship is approximately linear. On the other hand, Figure 1.2 shows that the relationship is inverse, rather than direct, as in the positive correlation. The line in Figure 1.2 is almost perpendicular to the one in Figure 1.1. A given subject who has only a few drinks a day reports many complaints. One who reports few complaints has many drinks per day (remember that this relationship is hypothetical). This case illustrates a **negative correlation**—high values on one variable correspond to low values on the other variable. The correlation coefficient is r = −.968.

Variables may fail to relate in a way that fits either type of linear pattern. Table 1.3 displays such a case. It is not true that as the number of drinks goes up the number of complaints goes up. Nor is it true that as the number of drinks goes up the number of complaints goes down. Figure 1.3 depicts this circumstance. Notice that the line drawn to represent the values is nearly parallel to the axis for complaints. Whenever the line is parallel to an axis, the correlation is nil. The correlation coefficient for the data in Table 1.3 and Figure 1.3 is nearly zero, r = −.045.

The correlational method can qualify as scientific. Observations can be unbiased. Generally, bias is avoided by selecting subjects, and therefore observations, at random. If you pursue the "drinking and complaints" example a bit further, you find that random selection

TABLE 1.2   Negative Correlation

Subject's Initials	# Drinks/Day	# Complaints/Day
JJ	10	3
PC	4	8
RM	5	7
LD	14	1
RC	8	4
MP	5	8
IN	2	10
MA	11	3
BC	1	10
KI	16	1
MZ	3	8
PS	12	3
CC	7	6
BT	5	7
LL	10	2

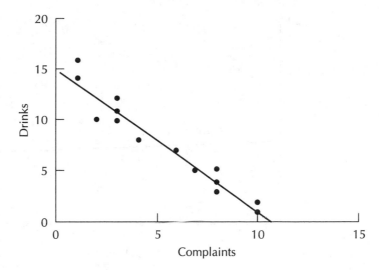

FIGURE 1.2   Negative Correlation

prevents getting too many alcoholics or too many people with serious psychological problems in a subject sample. Either one of these two biased selections would obviously make results difficult to interpret (if the sample had mainly people with serious psychological problems, results might apply only to such people).

The correlational method also involves quantification and systematic analysis. In this example, numbers are associated with both the observations of drinking and the observations of complaints. These numbers were plotted to depict the relationship between variables and the degree of relationship was represented by a correlation coefficient.

TABLE 1.3   Nil Relationship

Subject's Initials	# Drinks/Day	# Complaints/Day
JJ	10	10
PC	9	1
RM	15	2
LD	8	7
RC	7	9
MP	9	3
IN	6	8
MA	16	10
BC	4	2
KI	1	10
MZ	1	10
PS	2	4
CC	5	3
BT	18	9
LL	2	10

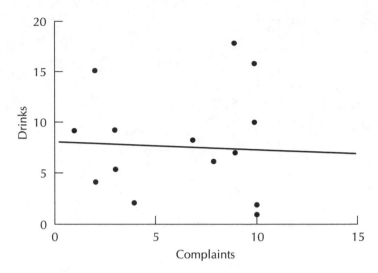

FIGURE 1.3   Nil Correlation

While the correlational method can readily qualify as scientific, like the other methods, it has its problems. Chief among them is the fact that, while it can indicate whether there is a relationship between two variables, it cannot indicate whether one variable determines variation in another. This weakness is best expressed in the statement "correlation is not causation." That is, just because two variables are correlated does not mean one "caused" variation in the other. A few examples will illustrate the point. There is a high, positive correlation between the inseam length of pants and the height of wearers, but buying longer jeans will not make a person taller. Nor will increases in height cause jeans to grow. Similarly, a researcher once found a high, positive correlation between the amount of rainfall in Arizona and the rate of suicide in Canada. Obviously, no one was willing to argue that rain in Arizona "causes" suicides in Canada, or vice versa.

It often happens that when one of two correlated variables seems to have caused variation in the other, a third or fourth variable actually is a more likely candidate as the "cause." In another country, there was a high correlation between the presence of storks on roofs during one winter and the births of babies the following summer and fall. Assuming that storks do not bring babies, something else accounted for the obtained relationship. Consider this alternative account. The storks roosted on the roofs near chimneys to keep warm, and the people, having no TV and tiring of card games, resorted to other forms of evening recreation. "Escaping the cold" both led the storks to the chimneys and confined the people inside where the possibilities for enjoyable entertainment were limited.

Even with new, sophisticated techniques, it is accurate to say that the correlational method generally cannot reveal which variables determine variation in which other variables. Nevertheless, the correlational method can be very useful. First, sometimes it does not matter which of two variables "causes" variation in the other. If intelligence is highly, positively correlated with doing well in school, college recruiters will not care whether high intelligence "causes" doing well in school or doing well in school "causes" high intelligence. They may go about the business of recruiting those who score high on some intelligence test and rest easy in the belief that these people will succeed in college. Second, correlational methods may suggest a causal relationship between variables, thereby alerting researchers to apply other methods to confirm causality. The persistent positive correlation between cigarette smoking and lung cancer certainly suggests that smoking causes lung cancer. Use of another kind of method has confirmed that, indeed, cigarette smoking is a primary cause of lung cancer.

That method is considered next, but first it is worth mentioning that a sophisticated technique built on correlation—called factor analysis—is very important to the study of personality. It will receive considerable attention in the chapter on Raymond Cattell and Hans Eysenck.

The Experimental Method

The variables that psychologists deal with when they use the experimental method are classified into two categories. **Independent variables** have variation that is arranged by the person who uses the experimental method, called the *experimenter*. Through certain manipulations, the experimenter assigns values to independent variables, thereby dictating their variation. **Dependent variables** have values that are free to vary so that they are open to influence by the independent variables. The experimental method involves performing an **experiment,** a procedure whereby an experimenter first sets the variation in some independent variable(s) and then ascertains whether variation in some dependent variable(s) is influenced. In contrast to the correlational method, with use of the experimental method it may be possible to assert that, when variation in two variables corresponds, variation in one determined or "caused" variation in the other. The claim is possible because the experimenter, not some third variable, dictated the variation in the independent variable that, in turn, corresponds with variation in the dependent variable. With the correlational method, there is no prior manipulation of one variable followed by verification of whether the other variable was influenced.

An interesting experiment by William Perry and colleagues Sprock, Schaible, Mc-Dougall, Minassian, Jenkins, and Braff (1995) illustrates the experimental method. These researchers wanted to find out whether the famous Rorschach (1942/1951) inkblot test would be sensitive enough to detect anxiety generated by a drug. This familiar test consists of ten cards on which there are inkblots, five in black and white and five in color. The inkblots were originally created by spilling some ink onto the middle of sheets of paper and then folding the papers in half. This technique produced random configurations that can be interpreted in an indefinite number of ways (see Figure 1.4 on page 12; this test is described further in a later section).

The experimenters created variation in the independent variable by giving three different doses of a drug known to cause anxiety-like symptoms—dextro-amphetamine—to three different groups of subjects. One group got a mild dose of amphetamine (16.5 milligrams or mg). Subjects in a second group received a mild-to-moderate dose (29.2 mg). A third group got capsules that looked like those ingested by subjects receiving amphetamine, but their capsules contained only an inert substance (zero mg). Please note that the mg numbers are averages for each of the two groups of subjects receiving amphetamine, as each subject's dose was adjusted to fit his unique body weight.

The Rorschach inkblots were presented to subjects three hours after amphetamine capsules were ingested, enough time to ensure that the amphetamine had reached maximum levels in the subjects' blood (those receiving the inert substance also waited three hours). Subjects looked at the inkblots and described what they saw (on seeing the blots, people often make simple responses like "butterfly" or "flower" and then they elaborate). These responses were scored for anxiety content. Results showed that there was no difference between the two amphetamine groups in the amount of anxiety imagery reflected in their responses. However, the difference between anxiety shown by subjects receiving some amphetamine and anxiety displayed by those who got no amphetamine was **statistically significant**—the difference between groups was so large that it was unlikely to occur solely by chance. Thus, experimenter-generated variation in the independent variable, amount of amphetamine ingested, was related to variance in the dependent variable, amount of anxiety imagery reflected in responses to Rorschach inkblots. It is legitimate to state that amphetamine determines anxiety in responses to Rorschach inkblots.

While the experimental method may be the most powerful scientific procedure, it too has its problems. Its most serious fault may be that, in order to have control, researchers need to carry out manipulations of independent variables. These manipulations require that experiments be performed in laboratories or other artificial settings. As a result, experimental outcomes must be generalized to real life with considerable caution. Experiments conducted under stale laboratory conditions may sometimes reveal little about how real people behave, feel, and think in real life. Consistent with this complaint against experimentation, and indirectly against an overemphasis on science, some of this book's theorists have condemned the experimental method. Murray must have had it in mind when he blasted "scientism," as did Cattell when he derogated "brass instrument" psychology. Many humanists also have grave reservations about "science" as represented by the experimental method.

Because it is generally assumed that behavior corresponding to traits is consistent across situations, experiments are a relatively rare form of personality research. Why manipulate circumstances to create different situations if behavior is not going to be differentially affected by those situations? Nevertheless, experimental research is done by some personologists, such as Albert Bandura and Hans Eysenck. They show that behavior corresponding to traits is affected by experimental manipulations that amount to the creation of different situations. Further, one theorist, George Kelly, even used the experimental method in psychotherapy to help people get a better grip on their lives.

Personality Tests: Personologists' Tools

Reliability and Validity

Like other scientists, personologists also have their instruments. Their tools, or assessment tests, come in a variety of forms, all of which are evaluated on two important dimensions. First, tests must demonstrate **reliability**, the degree to which test results are repeatable. When people take a test on one occasion and then again a short time thereafter, *test–retest reliability* is demonstrated if the scores on the two occasions are highly similar. Should people score similarly on two forms of the same test *reliability of parallel forms* is demonstrated. Second, tests must demonstrate **validity**, the degree to which a test measures what it was designed to measure. A test can be said to have *content validity* if its items actually sample the behaviors of interest, such as typing skills or arithmetic computation. A test of shyness should have items such as "Do you tend to blush and look away when people introduce themselves to you?" (a reference to shyness, the trait of interest) rather than "Is your room neat and clean?" (a reference to conscientiousness, a different trait). *Predictive validity* refers to a test's capacity to make predictions about people's behavior. A test of the trait aggressiveness in children that accurately predicts pushing and shoving on the playground would have this kind of validity. *Construct validity* is the degree to which a test measures a defined concept. If a test measures the construct honesty, several of its items should be highly intercorrelated and, together, represent honesty. Example items would be "I frequently lie," "I never cheat on tests," and "I never steal," all rated on agree–disagree scales. Finally, a valid personality trait test should correlate positively with tests of dissimilar format that assess the same trait (*convergent validity*), but not at all with tests of similar format that assess different traits (*divergent validity*). A multiple-choice test of "helpfulness" and a true/false test of the same trait should be positively correlated, but two true/false tests, one measuring "helpfulness" and the other "ambition," should be uncorrelated.

Projective and Objective Tests

Most personality tests fall into one of two categories. **Projective tests** present people with test items that are unstructured, ambiguous, or open-ended, thus allowing them a wide range of freedom in making responses. A prime example of the projective test are the inkblots (Rorschach, 1942/1951) used in the amphetamine experiment. Because the inkblots result from spilling some ink in the middle of sheets of paper and then folding the sheets together, they are inherently unstructured, ambiguous, and, thus, interpretable in various ways. (see Figure 1.4). People "project" their psychological selves onto the "blank screens" represented by the inkblots, thereby revealing their individual backgrounds, perceptions, thoughts, feelings, and fantasies (Frank, 1939). Responses are scored in several ways based on what a person said about the inkblot: what part of it is emphasized, what shape is seen, whether the person's response is typical of what other people say or original, how organized responses are, how the person uses color, and whether what the person says about the blots relates to factors like anxiety. Scoring is rather subjective: It is up to the peculiar interpretation of the particular psychologist who looks at the responses. Consequently, agreement between interpreters who make judgments on the same occasion is rather low, as is test-retest reliability (Potkay, 1971). Whenever reliability is low, validity is difficult to demonstrate, as it has been for the Rorschach test.

The Thematic Apperception Test (TAT) developed by Henry A. Murray, one of the theorists covered in this book, has also been popular. Because the TAT is considered in detail later, for now it is sufficient to say that the test consists of twenty cards, each containing a black-and-white drawing, painting, or photograph of a human situation, such as a boy playing a violin. An individual is asked to look at each card and make up a short story about it, which the personologist writes down. These stories are analyzed to identify dominant themes that are important for understanding the individual's personality and relate to in-

FIGURE 1.4   Ink Blot

ner needs and external pressures. In other kinds of projective tests respondents are asked to complete partial sentences, add an ending to a story, or draw a picture such as "your house" or "a man."

Because projective tests, being inherently ambiguous, generate responses that can be viewed differently by different scorers, it is very difficult to show that they are valid. Nevertheless, validity is sometimes shown, as in the amphetamine experiment. Despite validity problems, the Rorschach, TAT, and other projective tests still have many advocates who find them useful for gaining a more intuitive sense of the patient's mental processes than is allowed by the type of test considered next.

The second type of personality test is **objective tests**—highly structured paper-and-pencil questionnaires, usually true/false or multiple-choice, each with a single score-key, reflecting the fact that there is general agreement on scores. They are considered "structured" because they allow people very little freedom of response in answering items. People are typically instructed to read a number of statements and indicate which best applies to them or which are true of them and which are false. A sample item on an objective personality test might be "When I go to a party (check the statement that best applies to you) (1) "I am a wallflower"; (2) "I am the life of the party"; (3) "I just blend in with the others"; (4) "I tend to throw a wet blanket on other people's fun." Alternatively an item might simply be "I am the life of the parties I attend (indicate true of you or false)." There is a way to appreciate the difference between objective and projective techniques that will be familiar to you. Contrast true/false and multiple-choice examinations on format as well as freedom to choose your own response with the format and freedom that characterizes open-ended essay exams.

The scoring of objective tests is straightforward. Each possible response can be regarded as factually correct or contrary to some facts. Thus, an item can be assigned some numerical value and the values of items are simply totaled to yield an overall score. Because objective tests, being highly structured, can be quantified in a concrete, nonarbitrary fashion, they show high reliability and validity relative to projective tests. There are several examples of objective personality tests in this book.

Testing and Theorizing about Personality in a World of Human Diversity

Human **diversity** refers to the numerous cultures, along with gender and sexual orientations, that characterize the population in the United States and other countries. There has always been great diversity in the United States and Canada. Diversity now characterizes much of Europe. Always more than half of these populations have been female. Always gays, lesbians, bisexuals and indigenous people have been present. In Canada and the United States people from Asia are present in increasing numbers and people of African heritage have been present for hundreds of years. Diversity is here. People need to acknowledge and embrace it if they are to survive and prosper at work, at school, and in their neighborhoods.

In this edition of *Personality Theories*, diversity considerations are brought to the forefront. This emphasis seems particularly appropriate because personality theories, and the tests that arise out of them, have been based primarily on observations of European American males. Usually, the theories can be readily generalized to other groups, such as females and Latinos. However, in many cases it is spontaneously suspected, or entirely obvious, that some theories and some tests do not apply well to some groups.

Progress has recently been made in addressing how diversity relates to personality theory and testing. Most of these advances have been in the area of testing. For example, Whitworth and McBlaine (1993) have shown that the famous objective personality test, the Minnesota Multiphasic Personality Inventory (MMPI) and its successor the MMPI-2, yield similar overall scores for Anglos and Latinos; however, they found that the two groups did respond differently on four scales. Rogers, Flores, Ustad, and Sewell (1995) compared the Spanish Personality Assessment Inventory (PAI) with the corresponding English version, using some bilingual Mexican Americans; and some who spoke only Spanish. Bilingual subjects' responses to the Spanish and English versions corresponded reasonably well and two administrations of the Spanish version revealed good test-retest reliability. However, there was evidence of variation in responding across the two language forms and across administrations of a form.

Despite these recent efforts, inattention to diversity when personality theories and tests are considered remains a problem. Thus, when diversity issues are explicitly mentioned in the present edition, or simply implied, you can help your classmates and your instructor by initiating or promoting discussion. The more personologists take diversity into account, the better their tests and theories will be and, more important, the richer and more successful people's social and professional lives will be.

A Final Word about "Science"

All this talk of science should not leave you with the impression that it is good and other approaches are bad. It is neither good nor necessarily better than other orientations; science just is. However, because personality psychologists generally claim to have scientific theories, it is reasonable to use scientific criteria to evaluate those theories. Therefore, those criteria will be applied to the theories covered in this text. Some covered theories will meet the scientific criteria better than others. Theories that fail to meet these criteria well will be subjected to appropriate criticism—so will more scientific theories that are flawed in other ways. But no theories will be dismissed solely on the basis of failure to meet scientific criteria. There are good reasons to include theories that do not meet scientific criteria well. In fact, strengths in the nonscientific realm may make these theories more valuable than some more scientific theories. Sometimes a well-thought-out philosophical position, though it is too abstract to be tested scientifically, can have more merit than a "hard science" point of view. For these reasons, nonscience criteria will also be used to evaluate theories.

Chapter Sections

The chapters of this book have virtually the same sections. After you have read a few chapters, you will know what to expect from the rest. The remainder of this introduction is devoted to familiarizing you with the chapter format.

Introductory Statement

Brief introductory sections at the beginning of each chapter are designed to provide a transition from the previous chapters to the current one. Contrasts between previous theorists and their theories and the theorist/theory presently under consideration will allow you to "shift gears" in preparation for a new orientation. How you may expect to benefit from the chapter is also often a part of this first section.

The Person: Biographies

Just as oppression suffered during his youth led former Supreme Court Justice Thurgood Marshall to pursue racial justice throughout his illustrious career, psychological interests born of theorists' peculiar backgrounds have sometimes influenced the development of their personality theories. Some theorists covered in this book suffered personal difficulties during childhood, adolescence, or young adulthood that influenced which personality issues interested them. Others had highly positive experiences that drew them to certain personality issues rather than others. In turn, how they framed their ideas about those issues was determined by their own reactions to their important experiences. Knowing something about a theorist's life can tell you something truly meaningful about where that person "is coming from."

In addition, knowing about the life of a theorist can transform a sometimes alien name and a curious picture in the text into an image of a fascinating person. Indeed, by any standard, many of the theorists covered in this text are remarkable individuals. Some have overcome enormous obstacles to win fame and make lasting contributions. Others are notable for devoting themselves to making other people's lives better, not only through their theories, but also through their personal efforts, including freely donated time and money. Some theorists escaped from territories controlled by the Nazis, others overcame the handicap of poverty, and still others conquered psychological disorders or the aftermath of childhood trauma.

All this information will provide you with "memory hooks." People often have no trouble remembering details of individuals' personal lives, but sometimes they do have some difficulty remembering abstract theories. After grasping a theorist's personal background and how it may relate to her or his theory, you can more easily get a grip on that person's basic ideas. Ideas are like articles of clothing that lie around in disarray if there is nothing to "hang them on," but become easy to organize and relate one to another if an "apparel rack" is available with hooks of various sizes and shapes. Extending the analogy to advances in brain science, if you have a "neurological network" containing information about computers, it is a memory rack on which you can "hang" newly encountered ideas relating to computers. Should you lack such a network, you are forced to use cumbersome and inefficient rote memory.

Memory hooks come from more than just details of theorists' lives. Very often the personality traits of theorists play a large role in determining their personality theories and, thus, can provide a rack for hanging ideas about their theories. One theorist's personality may dictate the assumption that conflict in interpersonal relations is the rule, not the exception. Another theorist's personality may give rise to the assumption that harmony characterizes interpersonal relations. Some theoretical ideas about personality hang easily on the network of a theorist's personality characteristics.

View of the Person: General Philosophical Orientation

Before getting into theorists' basic concepts or other elements of their theories, it is beneficial to consider their underlying assumptions. Without knowing a theorist's orientation to people and how their personalities function it is difficult to understand basic concepts of her or his theory. Trying to absorb a theory without grasping the theorist's orientation is a little like going to the polling booth without knowing politicians' positions on critical issues.

There are a number of questions one needs to answer to discover a theorist's orientation. Is a theory founded on the belief that all people can solve their own problems if offered adequate support? Is a theory predicated on the presumption that normal and abnormal personality are on the same continuum or that the two are quite separate so that the theory deals with one or the other, but not both? Does the theorist believe in free will or determinism? Is the theorist a "scientist" who quantifies personality data so that correlational and experimental methods can be used, or a "nonscientist" who relies solely on intuition and qualitative information? Does the theorist look to the person's *past* in attempting to understand her or his personality, or to the *present* (or to the *future*)? Does the theory assume that personality can be understood only by examining circumstances outside the person or by looking at processes *inside* the individual? Does a theorist assume that genetic coding determines personality, or that events after birth shape personality? The *view of the person section* will tackle these and other questions, so that you can get into the mind of the theorist you are considering before you entertain his or her theory.

Basic Concepts: The Heart and Soul of a Theory

The *basic concepts* section is the centerpiece of each chapter. It contains a presentation of a theory's elements fitted into the structure of the theory. Whenever possible, the theory's framework, which may take the form of trait categories or stages of personality development, is used to organize concepts. If appropriate, the description of a given theory is constructed pyramid fashion, with more global concepts at the top and more elemental concepts forming the foundation. In any case, connections among concepts are emphasized so that understanding relations among concepts is the learning mode, not memorizing disconnected ideas.

Evaluation: Placing a Theory in Perspective

Each evaluation section is divided into contributions and limitations subsections. It is sort of a "pluses and minuses" organization. Various criteria are used to evaluate theories. Because not all criteria are relevant to all theories, only some are used in the examination of a given theory. These criteria are organized into two categories.

Science Criteria

For a theory to be scientific, it must be structured in a logical fashion. Concepts must bear a definite relationship to one another: some may be seen as more central than others and some may build on others. Thus, one criterion for evaluating theories can be stated as: "Is the theory coherent, so that the relationship among concepts is clear and overlap among them is minimal or is the theory chaotic so that some concepts are disconnected from others while some overlap?" Some theories may be tightly bound networks with each concept having a definite place relative to others. Conversely, some may be a collection of isolated concepts or a group of minitheories, each not well related to the others.

Are labels for concepts common terms, each with several meanings, or are they words, common or not, that have precise and specific meanings? Words with several meanings, such as *hot*, *cool*, or *gay*, are a nuisance when used as labels for concepts. When trying to relate such labels to those of other concepts, the irrelevant meanings get in the way. By contrast, words with precise and specific meanings are easy to grasp and relate one to another, because there are no irrelevant meanings that one must ignore.

Words that can be easily given different meanings by different people can also be problematic. *Experience*, a word often used by personologists, may be a confusing label for a concept because, invariably, each theorist defines it differently. Also, nonprofessional people use it in different ways. *Competency*, on the other hand, is a helpful word, because it always refers in some way to a person's skills, talents, or abilities.

Generally, the fewer the concepts the better. This statement is the first rule of parsimony. The essence of efficient explanatory power is simplicity. Whenever redundant terms can be collapsed into one another, a helpful act of parsimony has been performed.

Another axiom of science is that if two notions account for something equally well, choose the simpler one. This statement is the second rule of parsimony. Concepts with short definitions that are "given away" by their labels are to be preferred to those with lengthy definitions seemingly unrelated to their labels. *Positive-self-regard* is an example of a label preferable to *sizothymia*. The latter word roughly means "reserved," though most people would not know why. *Sizothymia* brings up another issue. Theorists may resort to Greek or Latin words to avoid multiple meanings, but in so doing, enshroud their concepts in unnecessary mystery. A well-known word is best, so long as it does not have multiple meanings.

Do concepts imply definite predictions that can be confirmed or disconfirmed by some method or another, or do they yield no clear expectations that can be evaluated through systematic observation? If a theory cannot be falsified as well as supported, it is beyond the pale of science. On the one hand, high *self-efficacy* refers to confidence in one's ability to perform some feat and predicts a high level of performance. If one has high self-efficacy for handling a snake, it is predicted that one can unhesitantly pick up the reptile and, perhaps, even hold it close. On the other hand, *proprium* is "me as felt and known," but what predictions can be derived from the concept?

Does a theory have a body of data to support it, or is there little observable evidence to confirm implications of its concepts? To modify the rule offered earlier, if two theories are equally coherent and equally simple, choose the one that is most strongly supported by evidence. Some of the theorists covered in this book have inspired many researchers to produce much current data that supports their theories, but others' theories suffer from lack of evidential support. Those theories that catch the attention of each new generation of researchers are more likely than the others to maintain a place in future books like this one.

Non-Science Criteria

In tune with the contention that science is not everything, there are criteria for evaluating theories that are not strictly scientific. Theorists may inspire not just researchers, but others as well. If second generation theorists or practitioners make careers of pursuing a given theory, the impact of the theory will be ensured. Some theories covered in this book have failed to stimulate a great deal of research. Still, among them are theories of such great interest to professionals that they have generated a lively discourse in journals devoted solely to them. Psychotherapies derived from some of these same theories have been embraced by thousands of practitioners.

In turn, these same practitioners have used the theory-based therapies to help thousands of people. Nevertheless, therapies arising from theories are not the only ways that theorists' ideas may have positive impact on people. There are personality theorists who have written books that have been read by thousands of people, many of whom have experienced increased understanding of themselves and increased fulfillment as a result of exposure to the theories. Some theorists covered in this book have a large following among laypeople, if not among researchers and other theorists.

Occasional Sections

Aside from the sections that occur in every chapter, there are a couple that appear only in some chapters. A separate section entitled **Supporting Evidence** will appear in chapters devoted to theories that have generated important, current research. Several theories merit a separate section on **Personality Development** because they include especially strong ideas relating to that issue.

Conclusion Section

If a theory did not have more positive than negative features, it would not have the following that dictates its representation in books like this one. The conclusion section states why entries in the evaluative ledger are writ large in the assets column.

E-mail Interaction

Sometimes it is hard to sit down and write someone a letter. We feel like we have to "say" quite a lot and write at least a page. However, as most of you who use e-mail can testify, we tend not to show "writing inhibition" when we boot up the e-mail server. It takes an instant to type in someone's e-mail address and only a moment more to rattle off a message a few sentences long. It is kind of like leaving a note for a friend. We don't worry so much about how much or what we write.

So why not e-mail the text author? All you have to do is type in "mfbpa@wiu.edu." You can ask anything or state whatever is on your mind. Not only is it OK for the message to be short, brevity is preferred. And be assured, I certainly will not look at your message with an English teacher's eye.

Just in case you want to say something, but cannot think of what to say, at the end of each chapter I will list a few possible questions or statements you may wish to forward. My e-mail address will be there also, so you will not have to look it up. Alter my suggested questions and statements in any way you wish, or perhaps one of them will inspire an original query on your part. Whatever. Just do it. I promise to respond.

Summary Points

1.   The working definition of personality includes the assumption that people differ in a variety of ways. Individual differences can be attributed to the possession of specific traits, internal characteristics that correspond to labels such as *shy* and *kind*. These traits are related to behavioral dimensions, or continua, which are like yardsticks. Personality, therefore, is a set of points falling along several behavioral dimensions, each corresponding to a trait.

2.   The scientific method involves quantification of observations. The case study method involves intensive observations of a single person. Unbiased observations may be difficult, because the observer, often a psychotherapist, is frequently involved with the individual observed. Also, the person observed may be atypical and a meaningful analysis is difficult to conduct on the data of one person. Nevertheless, it is possible and has actually been done. Many interesting case histories illustrate aspects of various theories covered in this book. One, that of Estella Monroe, illustrates aspects of all the theories.

3.   A variable assumes different values. Two variables are correlated if variation in one closely corresponds to variation in the other. They are positively correlated when high values on one correspond to high values on the other and they are negatively correlated when high values on one correspond to low values on the other. When the relationship

between variables reflects neither of the two patterns, it is called nil. With random selection of observations, the correlational method can be scientific, but correlation does not mean causation.

4.   In an experiment, variation in an independent variable(s) is set, and it is ascertained whether variation in a dependent variable(s) is influenced. Perry and colleagues gave subjects two different doses of amphetamine or no dose (independent variable) and observed what effect their manipulation had on anxiety reflected in subjects' responses to Rorschach inkblots (dependent variable).

5.   Personality tests must demonstrate reliability (repeatability), and validity (actually measure what they are designed to measure). Reliability can be determined by the test-retest or the parallel forms techniques. Methods for determining validity include content validity, criterion related validity, and convergent versus divergent validity. On projective tests, people respond to ambiguous, unstructured, or open-ended stimuli. With the Rorschach test, people describe what they see in some inkblots. Scoring is rather subjective, so reliability and validity are difficult to demonstrate. With use of the TAT, people view ambiguous pictures and tell stories about them. Testing and theorizing must take diversity into account: people's ethnicity, gender, and sexual orientation.

6.   Objective tests employ multiple choice or true/false formats and, thus, are highly structured. They have relatively high reliability and validity. The several sections of each chapter begin with an introductory statement that ties the theory(s) to be covered to previously considered theories. A biography section forms a link between a theorist's personality and background and her or his theory. Knowing about the lives of theorists makes them real. It also provides "memory hooks" on which to hang theoretical principles.

7.   Getting to know the philosophical orientation of a theorist lays the groundwork for understanding his or her basic concepts. Does the theorist believe people can solve their own problems? Is she or he scientific or intuitive? Does she or he believe in free will? Is the past emphasized or the present? Is what matters "inside" or "outside"? Is nature more important or nurture? With answers to these questions, basic concepts can be fitted into a theoretical framework such as stages of development.

8.   Scientific criteria for evaluating a theory include: Is it structured in a logical fashion? Do labels for concepts each have many common meanings, or highly specific meanings? Do the labels "give away" the meanings of the concepts? Are the rules of parsimony obeyed? Do the concepts imply definite predictions that can be confirmed or disconfirmed? Have theorists' ideas inspired researchers to produce supportive data?

9.   Nonscientific criteria include: Have second generation theorists and practitioners been inspired to pursue the theory? Have lay readers of the theory embraced its principles and bettered their lives? Occasional sections include "supporting evidence" and "personality development." Conclusions sections state the overall merit of each theory. An e-mail interaction section contains questions and statements to send the author.

Essay/Critical Thinking Questions

1. What did the term "personality" mean to you before you encountered the preliminary definition? What do you think that it means to most people?

2. Could you make up some behavioral dimensions that seem relevant to you and "score" yourself on them?

3. Prior to encountering a formal definition of *scientific* what did it mean to you? What do you think it means to other people?

4. Could you do a case study of someone you know well?

5. If you found that the correlation between physical attractiveness and grade point average was positive and high, what would you conclude?

6. Could you design a simple experiment to determine whether high versus low self-esteem influences performance on some task? (Hint: you must manipulate self-esteem.)

7. If you developed a personality test, how would you go about showing that it was reliable and valid?

8. Could you conceive of a format for a projective test that is different from any mentioned in the text?

9. Could you build an argument that science <u>does not</u> provide the most appropriate criteria for the evaluation of personality theories? Mention some shortcomings of the scientific method that are not covered in the text.

10. You will be evaluating the personality theories covered in the pages to follow (whether you intend to or not!). What criterion would you consider to be the most important for a theory to meet if it is to be acceptable to you?

E-mail Interaction

(Write the author at mfbpa@wiu.edu)
Forward one of the following questions or phrase your own.

1. What did your training in psychology emphasize?
2. Why did you decide to write the book?
3. What are your biases concerning "what makes a theory good"?
4. Tell me what to do to make an "A" (no kidding!)?
5. Will this book help me solve my problems?

2

THE PSYCHOANALYTIC LEGACY: SIGMUND FREUD

- To what degree can people control their behavior, thoughts, and feelings?
- How much of what is commonly called the "mind" is unconscious?
- Do profound childhood experiences affect later personality development?
- Is the unconscious revealed in our dreams?
- Can a "talking therapy" change personality?

Sigmund Freud

When asked questions about personality, Sigmund Freud responded in a tone usually reserved for the revelation of timeless truths. Some of his answers are important contributions to understanding personality. Others, offered with equal certainty, have been less helpful. However, Freud clung to all of his ideas with great tenacity. He was suspicious of those who disagreed with any of his notions. During a speech at Clark University in Massachusetts, Freud accused his most esteemed student, Carl Jung, of being interested in archeology—the discipline that often studies long-dead cultures—because of an unconscious wish that Freud would die. Jung and many other early followers soon split with Freud as their ideas began to deviate from his. Nevertheless, all were influenced by him, whether they admitted it or not. More importantly, it is possible that none of them would have developed meaningful theories had Freud's ideas not provided stimuli for their own.

Freud, the Person

Sigmund Freud was born on May 6, 1856, in Moravia, a Germanic area that is now a part of the new Czech Republic. He was the oldest of Amalie and Jakob Freud's eight children. Amalie, Jakob's second wife, twenty years his junior, bore her "golden Sigi" at age twenty-one. She had a lively personality and sharp-witted mind. Jakob, a wool merchant, was devoted to his wife. He had a good sense of humor and was a liberal thinker. They were Jewish.

Sigmund was scarcely ten when he entered high school and only seventeen when he entered medical school at the University of Vienna (1994 materials from the Freud Museum, Vienna). There he used his photographic memory to excel as a student of neurology. Young Freud was most influenced by professor Ernst Brucke, a respected and disciplined physiologist with an uncompromising spirit and a stare that could terrorize students. Brucke believed that the only active forces in living organisms were physical–chemical ones interacting in a closed energy system, a viewpoint that later influenced Freud.

During medical school, Freud was preoccupied with becoming well-known and economically secure by making some important discoveries (E. Jones, 1953; Parisi, 1987). His research as a student included: (1) dissecting 400 male eels to show, for the first time, that they had testes; (2) discovering new characteristics of neurons (nerve cells) in fish; and (3) developing the first gold-chloride technique of staining nerve tissue. It is also noteworthy that Freud's notion of "contact barriers" anticipated the concept "synapse," the space between neurons (Parisi, 1987). His discovery that cocaine could be used as an anesthetic may also have been motivated by the desire for fame and economic security (Parisi, 1987). Notably, his observations of cocaine's effects were made on himself. He was twenty-five when he received his MD degree (1994 materials from the Freud Museum, Vienna).

Freud lived seventy-eight years of his life in Vienna, where he established a private practice for the treatment of nervous disorders (1994 materials from the Freud Museum, Vienna). His home and offices were located at Berggasse 19, now a world famous address and a museum in his honor. He enjoyed his role as father to three girls and three boys (1994 materials from the Freud Museum, Vienna). Anna, the youngest, became an important psychoanalyst, specializing in the treatment of children. Shortly after the Nazi invasion in 1938, Freud had to be persuaded by friends to leave Vienna because of the oppression of Jews. In fact, he was never an avid believer in Judaism and considered all religion an illusion used by civilization to cope with feelings of infantile helplessness. At the time of his departure, the Gestapo (Nazi secret police) attempted to obtain an endorsement from him. Freud declined. Nevertheless, they allowed him to migrate to England, probably because denial of the great man's wish to leave Nazi territory would adversely affect world opinion of Hitler's regime. Box 2.1 contains more information about his tragic relationship with the Nazis.

Freud survived only a year and a summer after he migrated to London on June 4, 1938. He died from cancer of the jaw and mouth on September 23, 1939. The malignancy undoubtedly stemmed from his lifelong addiction to cigars, which he chain-smoked from early morning to late evening. You may find this addiction quite interesting when you read about Freud's theory of orality.

During his last years he experienced pain, fatigue, and difficulties in speaking and eating caused by repeated surgery and a mechanical device that separated his nasal cavity from his mouth. Essayist Stefan Zweig (1962), who delivered one of several eulogies offered at Freud's funeral, wrote of Freud's "gloomy" perspective, which became all the more evident during the autumn of his years: ". . . So long and so abundantly has Sigmund Freud been a physician that he has gradually come to look upon mankind at large as ailing. His first impression, therefore, when he looks forth from his consulting-room into the outer world, is a pessimistic one . . ." (p. 208). However, Freud valiantly fought his disability and the Grim Reaper: "I prefer a mechanical jaw to no jaw at all. I still prefer existence to extinction"

BOX 2.1   Freud: Target of Nazi Persecution

They burned his books, stole much of his fortune, drove him from his home country, and sent three of his four sisters to the infamous gas chambers (a fourth sister died of internal bleeding, probably due to starvation suffered while in a concentration camp; Leupold–Loewenthal, 1989). Anna Freud was briefly arrested during this time. Ostensibly, the Nazis persecuted Freud because he was Jewish. Indeed Hitler distrusted everything Jewish, even the theories of Einstein, a mistake that helped to hasten his defeat (Shirer, 1960). However, one can speculate about other reasonable possibilities. Freud taught that people are controlled by inner forces that are beyond their access or control. Hitler, by contrast, believed in the "triumph of the will." Willpower could dominate one's mental

processes, behavior, and environment, given, of course, that one is a member of the mentally superior "master race" rather than a Jew or a person of color. Just as he could not tolerate Jehovah's Witnesses, a religious sect that refused to submit to the power of the state, Hitler could not permit the presence of or countenance the writings of someone who held that mysterious internal forces control people (Toland, 1976). Such an individual and his writings could corrupt the people and make them weak. Also, Hitler felt rather uncomfortable with sexuality. He kept his affair with Eva Braun a secret partly because he did not want the German people to think of him as sexually involved. A theory that was popularly considered to be founded on sex was probably alien to him.

(quoted in Golub, 1981, p. 195). That he may have committed suicide when pain and incapacity became overwhelming is an unsubstantiated rumor.

Freud's View of the Person

Probably you are already familiar with some of the fundamental notions of Freudian theory. Freud painted a vivid portrait of human nature as dominated by instinctual, unconscious, and irrational forces. To him, the human organism is selfish, at war internally and externally, aggressive and sexual, even during the supposed innocence of childhood. Determined by events outside of conscious control, the person is covered with a thin crust of civilization, but exists in a constant state of frustration. These aspects of people's nature preempt free will. Therefore, humans were considered incapable of dealing with their own psychological problems. They turn to religion in the vain hope of gaining some control over their wanton urges and of procuring absolution for their compulsive pursuit of pleasure. But their efforts to gain control, or explain the lack of it, come to naught.

Throughout his life, Freud never ceased self-analysis, using the last half-hour of each day to explore himself. He was surprised and consternated when he was unable to understand someone else's behavior in terms of himself. Arguably his most important book, *The Interpretation of Dreams* (1900/1958), was based largely on analyses of his own dreams. Freud believed that dreams allow people to experience the wish fulfillments that evade them in real life (Dement, 1976). His *Psychopathology of Everyday Life* (1901/1965) also was derived from self-analysis and dealt with the psychological meanings of apparent "mistakes" in memory, speech, reading, and writing. Both works assumed the influence of **psychological determinism**, a belief that nothing about human behavior occurs by accident or chance. For Freud, everything about personality is "determined" or has a psy-

---

BOX 2.2   Do You Know Someone Who. . .

For each of the descriptions below write down a self-generated code (nickname) for the name of a person you know personally who fits the description. Use a different name-code for each description (avoid real names or risk the wrath of those named).

A person who spends a lot of time in the bathroom.

A person who is always eating, sucking on, or chewing something.

A man who is frequently attracted to women resembling his mother.

A woman who is attracted to older men, about the age of her father.

A woman who is constantly cutting men down and trying to best them.

A man who is constantly afraid that he will injure his genitals.

---

chological cause. One need only uncover these causes and examine them. However, contrary to a popular belief, he was not an advocate of biological determinism (Parisi, 1987). In fact, in attempting to discover why people do what they do, Freud emphasized psychological rather than biological determinism. He wrote, "consciousness knows nothing of . . . neurons" (quoted in Parisi, 1987, p. 240). He meant that while consciousness could not exist without nerve cells, what emerges from the neurons transcends them and cannot be explained solely by reference to them.

During his self-analyses, Freud confronted his personal experiences, secrets, and conflicts as he traced his behaviors back to their hidden origins. He was a theoretical pioneer who was able to overcome intense personal fears even as he explored the closeness of his relationship with his mother, as well as hostile feelings toward his father. In fact, Freud's explorations of his own childhood experiences were important contributors to his belief that boys want to "kill" their fathers in order to "marry" their mothers. Among Freud's earliest memories, "one was of penetrating into his parents' bedroom out of [sexual] curiosity and being ordered out by an irate father" (E. Jones, 1953, p. 7). Consistent with his theory, these feelings toward his father may have created guilt when Jacob died during Freud's fortieth year. About the time of the funeral, he wrote his friend Wilhelm Fliess: "By one of those dark pathways behind the official consciousness the old man's death has affected me deeply . . . I now feel quite uprooted" (quoted in Bronfen, 1989, p. 963).

Complete the exercise in Box 2.2. It will prepare you for the consideration of Freud's basic concepts. It will also serve to prime you for a later exercise designed to help you evaluate Freud's point of view.

Basic Concepts: Freud

Personality Structure: Three Interacting Systems

Structure refers to how something is put together. Most things have a readily definable structure: atoms, dormitories, families, and business organizations. For Freud, personality also has a definable structure with three basic components. One can be thought of as the personality's biological side, a second represents the psychological side, and a third reflects society's contribution to personality. These are not "parts" of personality in a physical sense, nor do they have any specific, physical location in the person. Rather, they are processes or systems of the mind. Their "job" is to organize mental life and interact with one another in a dynamic way so that personality is influenced and changed.

Id

For Freud, the origin of personality is the id, the most basic of the three systems. **Id** is beyond conscious awareness and is composed of whatever is present at birth, including everything that relates to the satisfaction of physical drives, such as sex and hunger, or primitive psychological needs, such as for comfort and for protection from danger. Id operates according to what Freud termed the **pleasure principle**, the achievement of pleasurable feelings as quickly and immediately as possible through the reduction of discomfort, pain, or tension. Id satisfies its needs through the **primary process**, a continual flow of events involving infantile images and wishes that demand immediate and direct satisfaction. It demands satisfaction of its needs without consideration of what is right or wrong or "good" for the person.

Among its other important functions, id is the reservoir of **instincts**, inborn forces with characteristics that are both physical (bodily needs) and psychological (wishes). In Freud's writings, id and the other two systems were described as powered by **libido**, an energy variously described as "psychical desire," "erotic tendencies," "sexual desire in the broadest sense," and the "motive forces of sexual life" (Freud quoted in Rychlak, 1981, p. 54). After career-long deliberation, Freud (1940/1949) assumed the existence of only two basic categories of instincts, those of life and those of death. Instincts toward life, called **Eros**, represent energy for preserving oneself (love of self) and one's species (love of others). In other writings, Freud subsumed the several meanings of libido under "love," thereby tying libidinal energy to eros.

Thanatos is the instinct toward destructiveness and death that is aimed at returning living things to their original lifeless state. The promotion of aggressiveness is the most important function of Thanatos. Life and death instincts may fuse together or work against each other, giving rise to "vicissitudes" or frequent changes in a personality, as well as to individual differences among personalities.

To understand the operation of id, think of the behaviors of a baby just a few days old. It sleeps, it awakens, it cries for milk and comfort, it urinates and defecates, it fusses, or its hand finds its mouth. However, it does nothing at all for its parents, or anyone for that matter, at least not intentionally. Since the baby's personality is dominated by id, its preoccupation is with itself and its primarily physical needs and comforts. The behavior of the infant corresponds with a popular song lyric, "I want what I want when I want it."

Ego

The infant's behaviors are one-sided and preoccupied with inner states of tension, because id has no means of directly establishing contact with the world outside itself. While able to detect changes in internal tension, such as hunger or cold, it has no way of relieving them. It experiences only pain/discomfort and pleasure, but it is isolated from external sources of relief and satisfaction.

It should be obvious that humans equipped only with ids would have difficulty surviving. It is dangerous to satisfy a need as soon as it arises with whatever apparently gratifying object happens to be available. For example, hungry babies who are a few months of age will stuff anything into their mouths that appears edible and is within reach, including poisonous or otherwise dangerous objects. There is a clear need for another structure that will satisfy id needs without getting the baby in trouble (Freud, 1923).

Ego is a coherent organization of mental processes that develops out of id energy, has access to consciousness, and is devoted to contacting reality for the purpose of satisfying id needs. Ego strives to adapt personality to the world outside itself. Id is subjective, directed internally toward itself in its wants and demands. By contrast, ego is objective, or directed outside itself. Ego has the task of satisfying id needs in a manner that promotes self-preservation. The term has become equated with the "I" or "me" that gets things done in the best interest of oneself.

Whereas id is governed by the pleasure principle, ego operates according to the **reality principle**: ego has the capacity to delay satisfaction of id's demands until an appropriate object is found that will allow gratification without harmful side effects. Ego is guided by a higher level of mental functioning, called **secondary process**, which includes intellectual operations, such as thinking, evaluating, planning, and decision-making, that test reality to determine whether certain behaviors are beneficial. Ego thus serves as a bridge to reality. It plans for actions in the real world that will satisfy id. Unlike id, ego has the capacity to appreciate the difference between food-producing breasts or bottles and ineffective objects such as thumbs or dangerous ones such as objects with sharp edges. The functions of ego increase the likelihood that id will experience satisfaction of its demands while avoiding the dangers associated with choosing an inappropriate real-world object.

While ego has contact with reality, it is not totally conscious (see Figure 2.1). It also "suffers" from secondary status: it is an arm of the id rather than an independent entity. Ego's operations on both the conscious and unconscious levels, along with its secondary status, make it vulnerable to the stresses of dangers both internal and external. For this reason, ego is constantly walking a tightrope. External dangers include insufficient food, water, and physical comfort to sustain life, as well as threats of physical or psychological injury, and loss of parental love. Internal dangers include uncontrollable increases of instinctual energies, particularly sex and aggression. Freud (1923) liked to use the metaphor of a horse and rider: the superior strength of the horse (id) must be held in check by its rider (ego).

Ego's reaction to threatening surges of instincts is to experience **anxiety**, a state of extremely unpleasant emotional discomfort. To minimize anxiety, ego calls upon various **defense mechanisms**—internal, unconscious, and automatic psychological strategies for coping with or regaining control over threatening id instincts. Defense mechanisms keep unacceptable urges or ideas from reaching conscious awareness.

The most important defense mechanism is **repression**, a selective type of memory mode in which threatening material is unavailable for recall, because it has been pressed down into the unconscious. Repression protects the personality by allowing ego to be conscious only of those thoughts and urges that it deems to be "safe" or that do not relate too closely to threatening material. Other defense mechanisms can be called upon as well. **Projection** protects individuals from threat by allowing them to literally project their own unacceptable traits onto other people—"Those filthy Abagarians; unlike me, all they can think about is sex!" **Rationalization** allows people to excuse their threatening and unacceptable behavior and thoughts—"So what if I stole from my employer; they don't pay me enough." Other mechanisms allow them to *deny* whatever is too hard to bear by refusing to think

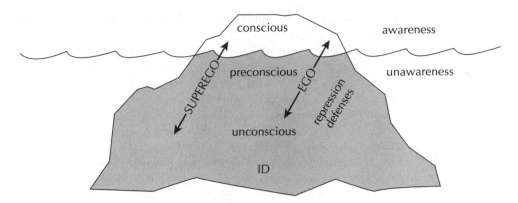

FIGURE 2.1 **Personality as an iceberg: Only the tip of the psychic iceberg is above the "waterline," which represents the part of the psyche that is available to awareness. Part of the psyche that is below the waterline is available with effort—the preconscious—but most is unavailable—the unconscious.**

about it or otherwise address it. People **intellectualize,** talk and think at an intellectual rather than an emotional level, about what they do or contemplate that is threatening to them (smoker says, "The link between cancer and smoking is unproven; I've seen the studies."). They may also attempt **undoing** "bad" behavior by displaying behavior designed to reverse the effects of the undesirable acts ("Forgive me for hitting you! Let me grovel at your feet, and proclaim my undying love for you, and buy you flowers."). Freud's daughter Anna is often credited with developing the defense mechanisms.

Freud believed that exaggerated use of such defense mechanisms results in **neuroses,** anxiety-driven patterns of abnormal behavior related to over-control of instincts. One such pattern is **hysterical neurosis,** in which a person who displays no medical signs of a physical disorder develops symptoms of the disorder to avoid experiences too painful or threatening for conscious consideration. For example, a person who feels angry may develop a "paralyzed" arm to lessen the chances of hitting someone. These neuroses; often assume metaphorical form (White, 1989). One of Freud's patients who felt "stabbed in the heart" by important persons in her life developed chest pains in the heart region. Another who experienced lack of feeling in the face declared that her husband's remarks were ". . . like a slap in the face" (p. 1042).

Superego

The third major force in personality is **superego,** the representation of society in personality that incorporates the norms and standards of the surrounding culture. As children strive to identify with and thereby become like their parents, a pursuit considered in detail later, they adopt their parents' renditions of their society's rules, regulations, and codes of right and wrong. The specific mechanism through which superego receives its content is called **introjection,** a process by which personality incorporates the norms and standards of its culture through identification with parents or other admired persons in society (Freud, 1977).

The superego may be thought of as operating according to a **morality principle,** a code that concerns society's values regarding right and wrong. One of its aspects is equivalent to **conscience,** the internal agent that punishes people when they do wrong. Like ego, super-ego develops from id energy. Superego's most important function is to help control id impulses by directing energy toward entirely inhibiting id's expression of its sexual and aggressive instincts. Thus, the superego, like the ego, addresses id needs, but the superego seeks to suppress those needs rather than satisfy them.

Superego can become a relatively independent and dominating force that makes the personality excessively conforming to social norms. The result is patterns of anxiety-driven behavior such as illogically striving for 100 percent perfection in absolutely everything one does. It can observe and influence ego directly, taking it to task, giving it orders, or correcting it. Superego can also threaten ego with unpleasant emotional experiences when perfectionistic, parental standards—represented by its "conscience" aspect—are not being met. These unpleasant emotions include **guilt,** an intense feeling of regret over having done something wrong and evaluations of oneself as an undeserving, inadequate person. It is as if the maturing personality never outgrows the role "child of one's parents." As young children grow toward maturity they gradually replace the verbal punishment once meted out by parents with internal self-scolding: "That's a bad feeling. It's wrong to think that. Always do what is right. Be perfect in everything." Through this process the voices of one's parents, speaking of right and wrong, move inside oneself and become one's own inner clarion call of righteousness.

On the other hand, superego can offer the personality favorable emotional experiences when another of its aspects comes into play. The superego can result in feelings of pride and self-respect through the influence of the **ego ideal,** positive standards in the form of internal representations of idealized parental figures (Freud, 1920/1977). These favorable feelings can take the form of statements about oneself that substitute for parental statements: "You're a good child. You make your parents proud and happy. They love you."

Freud conceived of personality as an internal battleground where the combatants are id, ego, and superego. Id, ego, and superego constantly struggle to dominate the personality. One of the spoils of this war is energy captured from one of the three systems by another. The victor can use this plundered fuel for its own purposes. Sometimes there is a temporary truce: one system forms an alliance with another. The ego may "say," in effect, "Superego, let me satisfy this aggressive need; then you may have your revenge." Table 2.1 compares the three major structural systems of personality identified by Freud.

Personality Development: Five Sequential Stages

Development, processes by which something grows from a beginning state to a later one, is seen in plants, animals, and even solar systems. Personality also develops over time from an immature beginning state to a later mature state. Freud hypothesized a series of five sequential stages of personality development. Four of the stages are closely associated with **erogenous zones,** sensitive areas of the body from which instinctual satisfactions can be obtained (Freud, 1920/1977). These zones, in chronological order of appearance, are the mouth, anus, penis or clitoris, and penis or vagina. Freud assumed the clitoris to be a miniature penis, because both structures are outer sexual organs that become erect during sexual stimulation.

Freud defined "sexual" very generally to encompass any pleasurable feeling associated with stimulation of any one of the erogenous zones. Libido was often used as a substitute

TABLE 2.1   Comparisons of Freud's Three Systems of Personality

	Id	Ego	Superego
Nature	Represents biological aspect	Represents psychological aspect	Represents societal aspect
Contribution	Instincts	Self	Conscience
Time Orientation	Immediate present	Present	Past
Level	Unconscious	Conscious and unconscious	Conscious and unconscious
Principle	Pleasure	Reality	Morality
Purpose	Seek pleasure Avoid pain	Adapt to reality Know true and false	Represent right and wrong
Aim	Immediate gratification	Safety and compromise	Perfection
Process	Irrational	Rational	Illogical
Reality	Subjective	Objective	Subjective

term for sexual cravings, which also are reflections of Eros, the instinct toward life. One example of libidinous satisfaction is the release of tension and stimulation of the anus associated with defecation. Manipulation of the lips and tongue is another. Given this general view of sexuality, it is easy to see why Freud referred to the developmental epochs as **psychosexual**, stages conceived of as "sexual" only in the broadest sense of the word, because some stages involve organs ordinarily seen as "sexual" and other organs not popularly regarded as "sexual."

Freud's statement that "the child is father to the man" represents his firm belief that every person's basic personality is established by the age of five. In short, important psychological aspects of the personality you have today are basically the same as those you had when you were just entering kindergarten. This idea is grounded in Freud's unique notion of determinism, which allows little room for free will, conscious purpose, or routine changes in one's personality or behavior.

Suppose you were asked to think of the name of a person, any person. You may think you were making a free choice about the name you came up with, but Freud would say you are a victim of an illusion. To Freud, every decision you display during your lifetime—your "choices" of hobbies or a mate—results from influences present in your unconscious.

Oral Stage: Phase One

During the **oral** or **narcissistic (self-centered) stage**, which begins at birth, the organism's psychic activity focuses on satisfying the needs of the mouth and digestive tract, including the tongue and lips (Freud, 1920/1977; 1977). Narcissus is a Greek mythological figure who saw his reflection in a pool of water and fell in love with himself.

Eros' aim of self-preservation is facilitated by the production of energy, made possible by nourishment received through the mouth. Whatever promotes self-preservation is likely to generate pleasure. Likewise, whatever is related to the self-preservation promotion process, even if it is not a direct contributor, produces pleasure. Thus, sucking provides the infant with pleasure. "Thumbsucking shows that the pleasure gained from breast or bottle is based not alone on the gratification of hunger but on the stimulation of the erogenous oral mucous membrane as well; otherwise the infant would disappointedly remove his thumb, since it produces no milk" (Fenichel, 1945, p. 63).

The importance of stages in understanding adult personality is manifested in Freud's concept of **fixation**, the impairment of development at a particular stage because its satisfactions are frustrated, resulting in permanent investment of libidinal energy in the stage. When under stress the fixated person is likely to show **regression**, retreating to behaviors, feelings, and thoughts characteristic of the earlier fixated stage (a twelve-year-old frightened by a dog begins to suck his thumb).

Freud referred to two personality types related to fixation at the oral stage. The **oral-receptive** personality type is derived from childhood pleasures of receiving food in the mouth and ingesting it. Persons with this trait form relationships characterized by dependency on others, who are expected to care for them. Such persons are more suggestible and gullible than others. It is as if they are willing "to swallow" anything. They are also interested in receiving information and knowledge and acquiring material goods. Persons especially fond of candy, others sweets, smoking, and oral sex, and those who are obese, are often identified in psychoanalytic literature as oral-receptive.

The **oral-aggressive** type is also derived from childhood pleasures associated with the mouth, food, and eating, but with greater chewing, biting, and use of teeth (Freud, 1977). Persons of this type would be expected to favor rock candy and jawbreakers to gumdrops and marshmallows, and hard-stemmed pipes to cigarettes. They are orally aggressive in their relationships with others, as if "to bite the hands that feed them." Their manner of talking is sarcastic and argumentative. They also seek to hold firmly onto others, as if to possess them or even to incorporate them internally.

Anal Stage: Phase Two

During the **anal stage** (approximately two–three years of age) sexual gratification occurs when defecation relieves the tension of a full bowel and simultaneously stimulates the anus. "There are many people who retain a voluptuous feeling in defecating all through their lives and describe it as being far from small" (Freud, 1920/1977, p. 316).

An important aspect of the anal stage is toilet training, which involves children and parents in issues of interpersonal interaction and conflict. From the parents' point of view, the issue is control: "Will my child 'go' on the toilet as I desire or not?" For the child, on the other hand, the issue is power: "Should I do what I want to do or what they want me to do?" Individual differences are shown in the behavioral manifestations of the way parents and children answer these questions. Some parents are rigid and demanding, expecting their child to "Go right here! Now!" These interactions can lead to a contest of wills, with the child experiencing conflict and pressure to perform for Mommy and Daddy. Such experiences can carry over to later situations in life, even building to rebellion against other authority figures in society—schoolteachers, principals, police, and bosses. On the other hand, some parents are highly permissive in accepting their child's preferences and personal schedule, reacting favorably to the child's personal needs and self-expressions: "Take as long as you want. Oh, you did it! Good for you." Such reactions can foster positive self-esteem.

Fixation at the anal stage may produce the **anal-retentive** adult personality type, which is characterized by delay of final satisfactions to the last possible moment, a constipated orientation. Individuals who fit this personality type constantly "save" for the future, whether the reference is to money or gratification of some need. They delay gratification and retain objects for future use just as once, at the behest of their parents, they retained their feces until an appropriate receptacle was found. Other characteristics include orderliness, stinginess, and stubbornness. In a famous case study called *The Wolf Man*, Freud (1963) traced an adult's interests in gifts and money to childhood defecation experiences.

In contrast, the **anal-expulsive** type involves an inclination to disregard widely accepted rules of cleanliness, orderliness, and "appropriate behavior, a "diarrhetic" orientation. Anal-expulsive people react against others' attempts to restrict them by doing whatever they want, just as, during childhood, they defecated whenever and wherever they wanted. Characteristics of these people include messiness—their adult lifestyle is sloppy and slovenly—and "messing their pants" like rebellious children. They may also show aggressive destructiveness, temper tantrums, explosive emotional outbursts, and even sadistic cruelty.

Phallic Stage: Phase Three

During the **phallic stage** (approximately four–five years of age), satisfaction is gained primarily by stimulation of the penis or clitoris, through masturbation (Freud, 1920/1977). The phallic stage is central to Freud's theory for several reasons:

1. It is the last of the infantile stages of psychosexual development.
2. It provides the context in which two important complexes, formations having ideational content, develop and the critical issues of castration anxiety and penis-envy become relevant.
3. It forms the basis of psychological and social identification for all children.
4. It results in psychological and sex-role differences between boys and girls.
5. It determines the development of superego.

Physical and fantasy pleasures experienced through masturbation are important aspects of the phallic stage. However, satisfaction of libidinous needs is only one part of this developmental experience, because the phallic stage is dominated by the realization that boys have penises whereas girls do not.

The question then becomes, "Why don't girls have penises?" According to Freud, answers to this question are accompanied by fear in boys, jealousy in girls, and changes in all children's relationships with their parents. He theorized that boys, at this stage of development, have feelings of possessive love for their mothers and see their fathers as rivals. His thinking was influenced by the Greek myth of Oedipus Rex, immortalized by Sophocles. In this tragedy, fate determines that Oedipus will kill his father and marry his mother. To Freud, the scenario reflects an internal psychological process characteristic of everyone. Freud termed this process **Oedipus complex**, the constellation of feelings, desires, and strivings revolving around the boy's desires for his mother and his fearful/hateful orientation to his father. The corresponding dynamic for girls, involving love of father and hatred of mother, is called the **Electra complex**. The significance Freud attached to issues surrounding "complex" is evident in his famous assertion that "if psychoanalysis could boast of no other achievement than the discovery of the repressed Oedipus complex, that alone would give it a claim to be counted among the precious new acquisitions of mankind" (1940/1949, p. 97).

Freud saw boys as experiencing **castration anxiety**, a generalized fear that they might lose their penises, their highly prized organs of pleasure (Freud, 1977; see Box 2.3). They "reason" that "if Father discovers I want to love Mother the way he does, he might cut 'it' off." Girls, on the other hand, supposedly display **penis envy**, feelings of inferiority over not having the male organ and compensatory wishes to someday obtain one of their own. They may blame their mothers for their lack of a penis—"after all she doesn't have one either . . . maybe in a fit of jealousy she cut mine off so we'd be alike."

At this point the foundations of socialization are set. The boy is faced with a fantasized dilemma: either he loses his penis or gives up his desire to have "Mama the way Daddy does" in favor of a safer but more distant relationship to her. He chooses the latter. Boys react to the imagined threat of castration by accepting their father's dominant status and power. They identify with father, becoming "just like Dad" for safety's sake. Just as tigers attack members

---

BOX 2.3   The Case of Little Hans

Freud's (1909/1963) case study of Little Hans provided the cornerstone for his ideas about the Oedipus complex. Hans was a five-year-old boy who was afraid to go outdoors because of a particular *phobia*, an exaggerated fear that a horse would bite him. Freud agreed that Hans was afraid, but not of horses. For Freud, the origin of all phobias is fear that has its source in the unconscious. He believed Hans had resorted to the ego defense mechanism of **displacement**, finding a new target for some feelings, one that is less threatening than the original. The boy's fear had been redirected away from its original source, father, onto horses. Freud hypothesized that "Hans was really a little Oedipus who wanted to have his father 'out of the way,' to get rid of him, so that he might be alone with his handsome mother and sleep with her" (1909/1963, p. 148). He supported this hypothesis with the following observations:

1. Hans said he wanted to sleep in his mother's bed, caress her, be married to her, and have children "just like Daddy."
2. Hans experienced castration anxiety. His parents had told him that if he continued to play with his "widdler" (penis), it would be cut off. Hans saw that his younger sister had no "widdler."
3. Hans wanted his mother all to himself, was jealous of his father, and feared that his mother would prefer father's bigger widdler, which was "like a

horse's." Hans had dreamed of two giraffes, a "big" one and a "crumpled" one. Freud inferred that Hans had a death wish regarding his father. Hans' dream is a good example of wish fulfillment through dreams (Dement, 1976).
4. Hans showed greatest fear of horses with black muzzles, reminiscent of his father's black mustache.
5. Horses were symbolic substitutes for Hans's father. When Hans saw a horse fall down, he sensed his own aggressive wish that his father would fall down and die, an idea too threatening to be consciously recognized.

Psychoanalysis reportedly helped remove Hans' phobia. Unconscious fears were brought into the open, and through the process of insight, the unconscious was made conscious.

It should be noted that Freud's analysis of Little Hans was based on information provided by the boy's father, who was biased in favor of Freud's theory. Several alternatives to Freud's interpretation of Little Hans have been suggested. Marsha Garrison (1978) observes that Hans seemed to fear castration more from his mother than from his father. Joseph Wolpe and Stanley Rachman (1960) concluded that Hans's "cure" was simply desensitization, a way to modify behavior that depends on repeated discussions of his obvious fear, horses.

of other species, not their own, the boy reasons that if he becomes like his father, his father will not attack him. Also, if he becomes like his father, it is almost as if he is his father. Therefore, when his father possesses and physically loves his mother, so does he. Finally, if he becomes like his father he will adopt the masculine characteristics that are apparently pleasing to his mother. In this process of becoming "like Dad," he also *introjects* the father's values and rules. Thus, the superego is formed out of the father's rendition of society's rights and wrongs. The formation of the superego is the final step in resolving the Oedipal complex.

Failure to identify appropriately and, thus, failure to resolve the Oedipal complex, has important implications for the male, adult personality. The male who is fixated at the phallic stage may become a Don Juan as an adult, devoting his life to sexual promiscuity in a quest for the sexual gratification denied him as a child. Alternatively, he may fail to take on the masculine characteristics due to weak identification with the father. The result could be a feminine orientation and possibly attraction to men. Libidinous feelings toward mother, the first object of childhood phallic pleasure, must be entirely eliminated. Otherwise they will be kept buried deep in the unconscious through action of the automatic ego defense mechanisms outlined earlier.

Freud saw the socialization process as different for girls. On the average, they resolve their complex less completely than boys. Boys are motivated to work through their complex by castration anxiety, but girls, lacking a penis, lack the appropriate motivation. Girls do identify with the same-sex parent and do so for roughly the same reasons as boys, but there are two reasons why identification is more difficult for them. First, girls experience ambivalence toward their mothers. Pre-Phallic love may be eclipsed by Electra hostility, because the girl may blame her mother for "taking off my penis" and devalue her mother for lacking a penis. Mothers, therefore, are not so attractive as objects of identification. The probability daughters will identify with their mothers is further lowered by their jealousy of their mothers' closeness to their fathers. Second, the girl's Electra complex turns her toward father in the hope of indirectly obtaining the missing penis from him, perhaps by having all of him for herself. This motivation lowers the likelihood that girls will fully identify with their mothers. These difficulties in completing the process of identification led Freud to believe that females' superegos would, on average, develop less completely than males'. Further, fixation at the phallic stage, accompanying incomplete resolution of the Electra complex, ensures that women will have, on average, less **ego-strength**, the ability of the ego to interact successfully with reality on behalf of the id and inhibit id impulses until "safe" satisfactions are found (Freud, 1977). Deficient ego-strength results because fixation ties up libidinal energy, leaving less of it available to the ego for use in its attempts to deal with reality.

Latency Stage: The Fourth Phase

Freud's fourth stage of psychosexual development is notable for its absence of a dominant erogenous zone and readily visible events or outcomes. As its name implies, **latency** is a quiet period around ages six to twelve during which children lay aside their attraction to parents and become sexually disinterested. Libidinous instincts are reduced in intensity or deeply buried in the unconscious through repression. They are transformed through **sublimation**—a process that reorients instinctual aims in new directions that are more personally and culturally acceptable. For example, an adolescent fixated at the anal stage might become interested in sculpting with clay, an acceptable substitute for earlier desires to play with his feces.

Genital stage: The Fifth Phase

Freud's final stage of development, **genital**—the phase of mature sexual love—begins at puberty, and includes directing both feelings of lust and of affection toward another person. The difference between this more mature stage and the first three stages revolves around **cathexes**, attachments of libidinous energy either to real external world objects or to fantasized inner world images. Pregenital-stage cathexes are typified by self-centered maximizing of bodily pleasures accompanied by "me first" relationships with parents or peers. In contrast, genital stage cathexes are directed less toward bodily pleasures and self-enhancement and more toward relatively altruistic relating to others.

These externally directed energies are represented by two psychoanalytic ideals of mature, normal personality functions: love and work. Thus, loving and caring relationships with others develop during adolescence and young adulthood, along with interests and activities related to productive, cooperative work. The successful pursuit of these goals contributes to the fulfillment of Eros's instinctual aim, preservation of self and species. People unable to make psychological attachments during their early years will show abnormal personality patterns during this later stage: immaturity, sexual deviation, and neurosis.

Another characteristic of this stage is the final resolution of the phallic stage identification difficulties theorized for women. Supposedly, to mature successfully, women must be able to accept the absence of a penis and identify with the vagina. With this change to "femininity," the clitoris "should wholly or in part hand over its sensitivity, and at the same time its importance, to the vagina" (Freud, 1901/1965, p. 118). This view supported Freud's belief in vaginal orgasm as the standard of mature, normal, sexual experience for women.

Table 2.2 summarizes the five stages of psychosexual development identified by Freud.

A Basic Diversity Issue: Freud's View of Females

Because of the different socialization processes for girls and boys, Freud believed girls are more dependent on the defense mechanism of repression. Further, because of their assumed weaker superego development, "for women the level of what is ethically normal is different from what it is in men" (Freud, 1925/1959, p. 196). That is, Freud thought that, on average,

TABLE 2.2   Summary of Freud's Stages of Psychosexual Development

Stages	Ages	Zones	Activities	Task
Pregenital (infantile)				
Oral	0–1/2	Mouth	Sucking Biting	Weaning
Anal	2–3/4	Anus	Expelling Retaining	Toilet training
Phallic	4–5/6	Penis Clitoris	Masturbating	Identifying
Latency	6–12/13		Repressing	Transforming
Genital	13+	Penis Vagina	Being sexually intimate	Loving another Working

BOX 2.4 Phyllis Freud

Recently journalist Gloria Steinem (1994) asked "what if Freud had been a woman?" Here is a summary of "Phyllis" Freud's biography, a tongue-in-cheek paraphrasing of Sigmund Freud's biography, "with only first names, pronouns, and anything else related to gender changed in order to create a gender-reversed world" (p. 50).

When Phyllis was a girl in mid-1800's Vienna, women were considered superior because they could give birth. Due to the power inherent in the birth process, men were afflicted with womb envy. Women's right to dominate was at the heart of Western matriarchal society. With no prompting, women of the day would argue that men could never be great artists, musicians, or poets, because they lacked the true source of creativity, the womb. They might manage family meals, but having only "odd, castrated breasts that created no sustenance" (p. 50), their deficient knowledge of nutrition precluded ever attaining the title "chef."

Men were allowed to dress themselves and even design their own clothes, but a preference for certain patterns rendered their "creations" rather monotonous. "Thus, the open button-to-neck 'V' of men's jackets was a recapitulation of the 'V' of female genitalia; the knot in men's ties replicated the clitoris while the long ends of the tie took the shape of labia; men's bow ties were the clitoris erecta in all its glory" (p. 50). Every woman knew that men, not being subject to the monthly menses, were out of tune with time, the tides, the stars and the seasons. Little wonder they were no good at mathematics, engineering, and science.

Many of Phyllis Freud's ideas have a timeless quality. Phrases like "womb envy" and "anatomy is destiny" were constantly on the lips of even uneducated men. One concept, however, was the source of special fascination. "Testyria" was particularly intriguing to people, because it is, in today's phraseology, weird. Men show mysterious symptoms—blindness though there is nothing wrong with their eyes—that seem traceable to the testes. After all, mostly men show these strange symptoms. Therefore, they must be laid at the door of what is unique to men, the testicles (it could not be the penis, because women have that too, the clitoris). Early treatments in use before Freud developed her theory seem abhorrent to us now: ". . . electric shock . . . removal of the testicles . . . cauterization of the penis . . ." (p. 51). Shunning these barbaric measures, Freud, in collaboration with

Dr. Josephine Breuer, used hypnosis. While in a trance, men talked out their fantasies of seduction by their mothers. Even this more humane method had its shortcomings: its effects were temporary. Undaunted, Freud marshaled the imposing forces of her legendary genius and discovered that, if Testyrics "talked out" while fully awake, effects were permanent.

Among Freud's most endearing qualities was a rarity for women of her time. She was able to listen to men for hours on end and take them seriously. Even though laywomen and professionals alike marveled at this astonishing ability, masculinists, though not so shrill as the modern versions, nevertheless charged her with "androphobia" (p. 52). It seems that nothing Freud did could redeem her in the eyes of the masculinists, as long as she continued to insist that men's anatomy doomed them to inferiority.

When confronted with such irrationality, Freud always pointed to the scientific facts. For example, if harassed because she asserted that "men possess a weaker sexual instinct" (p. 52), Freud reminded critics that only women were capable of multiple orgasms. She added, how could women's sexual superiority be doubted when the sexual act produces a pack of puny sperm all pathetically fighting for union with the massive ovum, only to be immediately swallowed up by it. And why is the clitoris superior? Obviously it has only a single function, while the penis is burdened with dividing its energies to accommodate dual function: "excretion of urine and sperm delivery" (p. 53). Not only was the duality of the penis a problem with regard to basic physiological functions, it also reared its ugly head on a more psychological level. "Immature penile orgasm had to be replaced by lingual or digital ones" (p. 54).

Of course, not everything was right in Freud's theoretical world. No account of her theory would be complete without bringing up an early change of critical assumptions. When Freud first heard her young male patients indicate they were sexually abused by their mothers, she may have been skeptical, but she soon experienced a revelation. They were telling the truth! However, after later allegedly reflecting on public reaction, and contemplating implications for mothers—even her own (Phyllis had brothers)—letters to very close friend Wilimina Fliess documented Freud's abrupt switch to the "fantasy" theory. Some claim it was an honest change of heart; others doggedly continue to question her intellectual integrity.

women function at a lower moral level than men. The fact that this opinion is still around is evidenced by an unflagging interest in the work of leading moral development theorist Lawrence Kohlberg, who allegedly also consigned women to a relatively low level of moral functioning (Kohlberg, 1981). Continued interest in attempts by Carol Gilligan, (1982) to defend female morality against the Freud/Kohlberg position also attests to the currency of this issue (see Allen, 1990).

Elisabeth Young–Bruehl (1990) outlined the reasoning behind Freud's view of women in her book concerning "Freud on women." Her point was that Freud did not wish to confine women to the status of lesser men. Rather, he wanted to account for his observation that women were "innately bixsexual" (p. 22). Freud reasoned that to be sexual young females had to be masculine. Thus, girls engage in sex like boys: They actively manipulate the clitoris just as boys stroke the penis. But at about adolescence they must come to accept their femininity and the lack of a penis by renouncing clitoral stimulation and embracing the passive sexual mode: penis in vagina. By this "logic," females are first masculine and then feminine, therefore, bisexual. In turn, the switch accounts for their greater tendency to neurosis: Females experience greater internal turmoil because they must abandon one set of needs, masculine, and then, while still in the throes of the loss, embrace another, feminine. Thus, concluded Young–Bruehl, the negative traits Freud assigned to females arose out of the necessary transition from masculinity to femininity dictated by their anatomy, not out of female inferiority per se. However, a reviewer of Young–Bruehl's book declared that "Her unconvincing introduction to this chronologically organized anthology of Freud's essays, case material and letters reads like" an apology (Stuttaford, 1990, P. 54). Allegedly, Young–Bruehl merely reiterated Freud's point of view, offering nothing new. She does not effectively rebut critics of Freud's view of women; she simply offers a plea for a different interpretation.

Assume that gender bias is actually the source of Freud's conception of women, in that he viewed women from his masculine vantage point. It follows that it should be possible to rewrite his theory from a feminine perspective and preserve all its concepts and basic assumptions, except one. Male inferiority would replace female inferiority. Box 2.4 constructs that logical sequence.

If Freud were alive today, he would almost surely not retreat from his position on women. His final pronouncement on the subject was that he refused "to be deflected from [my conclusions about women] by the denials of the feminists, who are anxious to force us to regard the two sexes as completely equal in position and worth" (1925/1959, p.197).

Evaluation

Contributions

To talk of unconscious aspects of personality is one thing; to observe or measure such phenomena is quite another. How can psychologists possibly get at something that, by definition, is not directly available to consciousness? Freud suggested a number of avenues to the unconscious: free association, slips of the tongue, certain events occurring during psychoanalytic therapy, waking fantasy, and interpretation of dreams.

Free Association

Freud's primary assessment technique for getting at the unconscious was **free association**, in which the person adopts a mental orientation that allows ideas, images, memories, and feelings to be expressed spontaneously. It allows patients to experience **catharsis**, a process by which inner feelings are openly expressed in words or behaviors. If one idea—apple— suggests an associated idea—worms—one is free to pursue thoughts about worms. The fundamental rule of free association is to allow expression of anything and everything that comes to mind, no matter how senseless, illogical, trivial, embarrassing, unpleasant, or absurd it may seem. Free association is important because it provides Freudian therapists with clues about the person's unconscious.

Interpretation of Dreams

According to Freud (1900/1958), dreams are "the royal road to . . . the unconscious . . ." (p. 608). It is not simply dreams in and of themselves that are important, but their interpretation. Freud believed that the **manifest content** of dreams, what the dreamer remembers about the dream when awakened, is deceptive and should not be taken at face value. Dreams originate in unconscious, primary processes of the id. Id forces gain strength during sleep, when conscious suppression is less than during wakefulness. Ego deals with this problem by distorting and modifying id instinctual impulses and images that are represented in dreaming, thereby lessening the threat they pose. It uses such mechanisms as censorship and symbolic substitution. Consequently, the true content of dreams is seldom what it appears to be on the surface; everything is in disguise and mysterious. Skilled interpretation is required to get at **latent content**, the underlying meaning of each dream.

Freud assumed that every dream has a meaning that can be interpreted through decoding representations of unconscious materials. Symbolic interpretation focuses on the dream as a whole and seeks to replace disguised manifest content with some reasonable latent parallel. For example, in a biblical account from Genesis, a Pharaoh dreamed of seven plump ears of corn on a single stalk, followed by seven diseased ears that devoured the first seven. Joseph offered a symbolic interpretation of this perplexing dream: The ears of corn symbolically represented seven future years of good harvest for Egypt, followed by seven years of famine.

A **dream symbol** is dream content that represents some person, thing, or activity involved in unconscious processes. Freud believed that symbols can sometimes have common meanings for people in general. Table 2.3 illustrates this point. However, he believed even more strongly that symbols are often highly personal rather than universal. All symbols must be interpreted individually, because they are determined by unconscious forces in the individual's unique personality: "The same piece of content may conceal a different meaning when it occurs in various people or in various contexts" (Freud, 1900/1958, p. 105).

Freud preferred an alternative to general symbolic interpretation. He used a decoding method in which each part of the dream is analyzed separately from the others. Correct analysis deciphers all dream elements, including symbols, that are then put together to uncover each dream's hidden meaning. The final result is certain to involve the discovery of some wish-fulfillment for the dreamer, which Freud saw as the primary purpose of dreaming (Dement; 1976).

TABLE 2.3   Some Freudian Dream Symbols

Dream contents	Symbolic meanings
Knife, umbrella, snake	Penis
Box, oven, ship	Uterus
Room, table with food	Woman
Staircase, ladder	Sexual intercourse
Water	Birth, mother
Baldness, tooth removal	Castration
Left (direction)	Crime, sexual deviation
Children playing	Masturbation
Fire	Bed-wetting
Robber	Father
Falling	Anxiety

Psychoanalysis

Free association quickly became the basic technique of Freud's "talking treatment" (Breuer & Freud, 1895/1950). This technique was embedded in **psychoanalysis**, Freud's systematic procedures for providing a patient with the insight necessary to rid the personality of its neurotic conflicts. The recall of childhood experiences is central to these procedures, especially recollections of sex and aggression involving one's parents. Through **insight**, personally unacceptable and socially "taboo" experiences buried in the person's unconscious can be made conscious.

Free association substituted for Freud's earlier use of hypnosis as a treatment technique. Freud tried hypnosis before the turn of the century when working with Josef Breuer (1994 materials from the Freud Museum, Vienna; Nathan & Harris, 1975). They showed that patients will abandon neurotic symptoms while in the hypnotic trance. However, Freud became discouraged with hypnosis when the symptoms often returned after the trance was removed. Consequently, he sought a more permanent solution.

Unlike the supposedly unconscious "trance" state, free association enabled patients to consciously comprehend everything they said while they were saying it. One reason Freud decided to use a couch in psychoanalysis was that it helps patients settle into the mental state needed for effective free association (see the picture of the couch at the beginning of the last chapter). Use of the couch led patients to adopt a passive posture and relaxed attitude for experiencing a more preconscious-like state than usually occurs during normal wakefulness. Freud sat behind his patients, away from their direct view, partly to minimize his influence on their psychological explorations. He wanted to be like "a neutral, blank screen," so that his patients would feel free to verbalize their associations without looking for his facial reactions or fearing criticism and disapproval. Eventually, patients would project their unconscious images onto Freud, "the mirror." They would also display **transference**—they relate to the psychoanalyst as if he were some other person from their past with whom they were continuing to experience psychological conflict. The origin of these unrealistic transformations is the patient's unconscious. It is as if the patient needs to remake the analyst in the image of the patient's father, mother, or some other significant person in order to work through the psychological problems left over from childhood. Use of the couch partly contributed to transference by fostering a dependent, childlike relationship with the parent/psychoanalyst. **Countertransference** occurs when analysts project their own unconscious needs onto their patients.

Supporting and Qualifying Evidence

Empirical support for Freud's ideas has accumulated over the years, although it has often been qualified. J. McVicker Hunt (1979) assessed evidence from different lines of investigation flowing from Freud's ideas. He found that the studies "lent support" to Freud's general proposition about "the special importance of early experience" (p. 119), but not to the specific psychosexual experiences that Freud hypothesized. Salvatore Maddi (1968) reviewed the research literature and concluded that there was qualified support for two Freudian concepts. First, while not all behavior is defensive, the general concept of ego defense is "tenable," supported by a "rather convincing" number of studies related to repression. Second, "there is more evidence of castration anxiety among men than women" (p. 392).

Lloyd Silvermam (1976) summarized two ten-year research programs bearing on specific Freudian concepts. Results of these independent, laboratory studies support the relationship between certain types of abnormal behavior and certain types of unconscious conflict over libidinal and aggressive wishes. One series of studies involved thirty-nine groups, some comprised of stutterers, others of depressives or schizophrenics. Subjects were asked to view flickers of light through the eyepiece of a tachistoscope, a machine that exposes visual stimuli for fractions of a second. Visual information relevant to the participants' psychological conflicts was presented to subjects subliminally, that is, below their level of conscious awareness (Dixon, 1971). Psychoanalytic Theory (PT) predicts that information relevant to a particular fixation or inner conflict would affect persons with that fixation/conflict, but information related to other kinds of fixations/conflicts would have no effect on them. The prediction was generally confirmed. Persons with oral-aggressive conflicts were made anxious by the message "Cannibal eats person" but not by "Murderer stabs victim." Persons with oral-receptive conflicts showed decreased anxiety with the wishful message "Mommy and I are one" but not with "I am losing Mommy."

A number of research studies on castration anxiety in men and penis envy in women have been reported. Blum (1949, 1950, 1962) assessed psychosexual fantasies in college students who were asked to tell stories about a series of cartoon pictures of a dog named Blacky. In the 1962 study, men who were high and low in castration conflict told contrasting stories in response to a picture of Blacky watching as a knife falls toward sibling Tippy's tail. An example of a "low castration anxiety" response follows:

> *Tippy, Blacky's little brother, is about to have his tail chopped off unknowingly. Blacky is about to bark and warn him of his danger. Physically there is nothing he can actually do, but he will also try to push him away from the block (p. 135).*

The following is a contrasting example of a "strong castration anxiety" response:

Blacky doesn't like the looks of this at all, and he's very conscious of his big black tail out behind him ... The expression on Tippy's face is worried, and Blacky's beginning to think that way (p. 135).

In a study by Hall and Van de Castle (1965), three groups of college students, 20 men and 20 women per group, recorded their dreams as part of a class project. All of the 1,909 dreams were scored by two judges to determine the presence of castration anxiety (CA), castration wishes (CW), and penis envy (PE). Male dreamers tended to have high CA scores compared to females, and female dreamers tended to have higher CW and PE scores compared to males. Zero CA scores were observed for 50 percent of the women but only 13 percent of the men. Findings were replicated using an additional sample of men aged 37–54, suggesting a stable rate of castration anxiety from young adulthood to middle age. However, Hall and Van de Castle's research has been severely criticized because of the procedure they used and because more efficient explanations of their results may be provided by non-Freudian theories (Daly & Wilson, 1990).

Raskin and Shaw (1988) reported research outcomes that could be interpreted as evidence for Freud's narcissistic or oral stage. People fixated at this stage might continue to be self-centered just as they were during infancy. In confirmation of that possibility, subjects whose tape-recorded monologues reflected heavy use of first person singular pronouns ("I" and "me") scored high on a narcissism test of tendency to be self-centered and self-absorbed.

Gabriel, Critelli, and Ee (1994) examined positive illusions of intelligence and physical attractiveness among people administered a narcissism test. Positive illusions were excess self-perceptions of intelligence and attractiveness after actual intelligence and attractiveness were measured and statistically removed. High narcissism was associated with high positive illusions of intelligence and attractiveness for both males and females. Males tended to significantly over-estimate both their intelligence and attractiveness but females significantly overestimated only their intelligence. Males tended to be higher than females on narcissism. Consistent with this observation, they showed greater positive illusions of attractiveness and intelligence than females.

The first convincing experimental evidence for Freud's "transference" has been made available recently. DeAngelis (1994) reported on research by Susan Anderson and colleagues in which subjects described a significant other and then were exposed to characterizations of fictional others including one who was partially like a significant other. On a subsequent memory test, subjects tended to falsely "remember" certain features of a significant other as belonging to the partially similar fictional other, even though the features were not part of the characterization with which they had been provided. These results show that we have mental images of significant others from early life that we project as a whole onto people we encounter later in life who resemble the significant others. As Freud would agree, if we encounter a person partially resembling father, mother, or another significant other, we tend to see the partial replica as wholly like the significant other. Other work by Anderson and colleagues suggests that emotional reactions consistent with our feelings about the significant other may become attached to persons resembling the significant other.

Much of the research has attempted to support Freud's most central idea, the unconscious. Freud found evidence for the existence of the unconscious in **slips of the tongue,** verbal errors that seem to replace neutral words with ones that supposedly emanate from the unconscious. However, researcher Michael Motley (1985; 1987) believes that most such slips are usually due to the misfirings of the brain and its verbal mechanisms. For example, consider the following scenario: young man approaches an attractive woman with whom he has plans to spend the evening and exclaims, "I'll pick you up at sex. . . . I mean six!" According to Motley, the most efficient and verifiable way to explain this error is in terms of word retrieval mechanisms. The words *six* and *sex* share two of three letters, and are thus probably stored in the same neural network. Therefore, the young man's brain "went looking for" the word *six*, but "found" *sex* instead, because their structural near-identity caused them to be stored "close to" one another.

Motley believes, however, that traditional notions about the unconscious are not entirely without merit. In fact, his work has shown that sometimes the unconscious actually may rear its ugly head, much to our embarrassment. In one of his studies, he and his colleagues tested three groups of college men. One group were fitted with electrodes and warned that they would receive an electric shock at some point in the experiment. A second group performed in the presence of a provocatively dressed female experimenter. Both groups and some control subjects were asked to speak a set of word pairs designed to elicit verbal foul-ups that Freudians would interpret as spill-over from the unconscious. Males threatened with electric shock tended to say "damn shock" for "sham dock" and "cursed wattage" for "worst cottage" rather than commit sexual slips. The group in the presence of the provocative female experimenter tended to make mistakes like "fast passion" for "past fashion" and "nude breasts" for "brood nests." Control subjects were no more likely to make sexually than electricity-related slips. Thus, when the environment contains cues relating to certain motivations that we tend to harbor in our unconscious minds, words that represent these forbidden motivations may pop out.

More generally, it can now be asserted that there is an unconscious (see the *American Psychologist*, v. 47, #6, 1992). That unconscious, however, may not be the analytic, manipulative, and smart entity that Freud assumed. Instead, it may be simple, straightforward, and unanalytical compared to consciousness (Greenwald, 1992).

Limitations

The Uncertain Status of Psychoanalytic Theory (PT)

Freud's view of psychoanalytic theory (PT) as "a new science" may have been partly justified during psychology's youth at the turn of the century. It certainly was Freud's intent to make PT the basis of a scientific psychology that would integrate, once and for all, the psychological and physical events of mind and body. However, after three quarters of a century, the scientific potential of PT has not been realized, despite occasionally supportive research and attempts to integrate PT with other areas of psychology such as learning (Dollard & Miller, 1950), development (Wolff, 1960), and cognition (G. Klein, 1970). Because of the problems to be covered next, PT cannot be considered a fully scientific theory.

As you have seen, there is considerable, qualified support for some of Freud's ideas, but it is not great considering the large number of researchers who have tried for so many years to confirm his concepts. One reason is that the concepts of PT, even when clearly defined, are not open to direct observation (Stanovich, 1989; Daly & Wilson, 1990). Thus, they are hard to test scientifically. How is a researcher to quantify energy that is "psychological" or get at events that are "unconscious" and "repressed"? Unfortunately, the answer is "indirectly, uncertainly, and often not at all."

Taking into account the large number of attempts to support PT, it has shown little ability to predict behavior. PT concepts work best when applied backward, accounting for an individual's past behavior after the facts have been gathered (Stanovich, 1989). They seldom are able to predict the person's future behavior. You will have more appreciation of this point after doing the exercise in Box 2.5.

The primary setting for gathering data relevant to PT has been the clinic, not the laboratory. In the clinic, events that are irrelevant to diagnosis and treatment act on patients and analysts but cannot be controlled: interruptions, chance moods of patient and analyst, temporary health status of both, events in the setting (baby crying next door), and unknown events occurring just before the session (a lover's quarrel). One of Freud's patients, a psychiatrist, wrote that during treatment sessions Freud's dog was "sitting quietly. . . . at the foot of the bed . . . a big chow" (Wortis, 1954, p. 23). Obviously, it did not occur to Freud that the presence of this possibly threatening, at least distracting, animal may have affected his patient's thoughts, verbalizations, and behaviors, and, in turn, Freud's interpretations. If Freud thought this patient's discomfort was due to touching on sensitive, unconscious material, he might have been incorrect.

Analysts, as observers, influence what they observe (Joseph, 1980). Requiring analysts to undergo psychoanalysis may lessen this influence by allowing them to see from the patient's perspective how analyst/observers have impact on diagnosis and treatment. However, total objectivity, never fully achieved in any setting, is especially unlikely in the clinician's office where the observer and subject share the therapist–patient relationship.

BOX 2.5

Would you bet $1000 that among the people you know there are some who will show the characteristics listed below at some time in their lives (it is charitably assumed that you have a thousand to bet)? Use the name-code method employed in Box 2.2. For each characteristic, list a person you know (well enough to be privy to their childhood experiences) who you would bet will show the characteristic at some time in the future.

A man who is not now but will become a Don Juan.

A macho man who is not now regarded as gay by anyone but who will prove to be gay in the future.

A slim person from a slim family who will become obese.

A woman who now shows no inclination to leadership or business acumen who will become a high-level business executive.

You will probably recognize that there should be some people you know for whom, based on knowledge of psychoanalytically significant events in their childhoods, you should be able to predict the listed behaviors. Indeed, you may have been able to come up with some names, but how confident are you in your predictions? It is always more difficult to predict an event than to "explain" it after it occurs (see Allen, 1978). The problem for PT is that it may have more difficulty predicting future outcomes than other psychological theories.

The clinic subject samples often used by Freud and other psychoanalysts are unrepresentative of people in general. One source of unrepresentativeness is that, unlike most people, clinic subjects have serious psychological problems. Further, Freud's major case studies were of persons seen in Victorian Vienna (probably 100 percent) between the years 1889 and 1900 (50 percent) who showed abnormal behaviors (50 percent hysterical neuroses; Brody, 1970). Further, the sample was upper-class (100 percent) women (67 percent) between the ages of 18 and 20 (75 percent) who were single (75 percent). Selective sampling may have biased theory development and limited the generalizability of Freud's observations.

Freud's ideas relied heavily on people's early childhood experiences. However, Freud actually had few child patients (Daly & Wilson, 1990). He obtained most of his information about children through everyday experience, reading, his own recollections of his childhood, and the recollections of adult patients.

A number of Freud's assumptions about children have been called into question (Daly & Wilson, 1990). In two separate studies, only 50 percent of children between 4 and 6 years of age showed knowledge of differences between the sexes' genitals, and those who did showed little evidence of emotional trauma (Conn & Kanner, 1947; Katcher, 1955). According to Kohlberg (1966), a more plausible alternative to castration anxiety is the general childhood fear of bodily injury, not the specific fear of losing the sex organ. Social-learning explanations involving sex roles also have offered alternatives to Freud's overemphasis on physical anatomy as the basis of gender differences (Rohrbaugh, 1979).

Finally, the very foundation of psychoanalytic theory has been attacked (Daly & Wilson, 1990). Critic Jeffrey Masson (1984) was fired from his post as projects director of the Sigmund Freud Archives because of his assault on PT. With the reluctant cooperation of Anna Freud, Masson examined Freud's correspondence with an eye to publishing his exchange of letters with Wilhelm Fliess (only excerpts had been previously published). Comparing these letters with an 1896 lecture to the Society for Psychiatry and Neurology in Vienna led to an "alarming discovery." In that lecture, Freud confidently presented the **seduction thesis**, his belief that his early patients actually had been sexually molested in early childhood, and that repressed memories of these traumas were the source of their adult hysterical neuroses. Less than two years later, he wrote Fliess that he had abandoned the seduction thesis. Among his reasons for the change was ". . . in all cases, the father, not excluding my own, *had to be accused* of being perverse . . ." (Freud quoted in Masson, 1984, p. 108; emphasis added). He went on to express his belief that the frequency of such "perversion" would have to be improbably high to account for all the observed cases of hysteria, as many cases of seduction would not lead to hysteria.

On the basis of Freud's letters, Masson concluded that Freud changed his "real abuse" assumption to what was later to become the "fantasy abuse" assumption not for objective, scientific purposes, but for personal reasons. If Masson's interpretations are correct, Freud may be guilty of intellectual underhandedness and submission to fear of censure by colleagues (his 1896 "seduction" lecture was received in icy silence, according to Freud). He may also be accused of insensitivity to the suffering of sexually abused children who, over time, number in the millions. On the theoretical side, if Masson is correct in implying that, contrary to Freud's change of heart, early patients were actually molested, Freud's theory, in its final form, may be wrong. The theory is based in large part on the idea that young children are attracted to the parent of the opposite sex and desire to possess that parent sexually. The "fantasies" of seduction supposedly confirm this desire and, according to Freud's theory, the remainder of children's psychological development rests largely on the existence of the alleged desire. If the molestations of Freud's early patients were real, the fantasy notion becomes suspect and, if it is rejected, support for the claim that children desire their parents sexually collapses. Remove that claim and Freud's entire theoretical structure is in danger of tumbling down.

Other commentators have not accepted Masson's position, believing that Freud had an honest change of heart. Anna Freud agreed with them. Some others believe that Masson was inaccurate in his description of the whole affair: Early patients never overtly claimed they were seduced as he implies (Esterson, 1993). It is important to acknowledge that when Freud believed his patients actually had been seduced (1896) he based his belief on his interpretations of what he regarded to be symbolic representations of repressed material they presented to him. Had Freud indicated that patients overtly claimed they had been seduced, he would have undermined the theory he held at that time. Incidentally, Freud may never have completely dismissed the possibility that his early patients were actually seduced (Hanly, 1987).

Russell Powell and Douglas Boer (1994) have yet another proposal. They argue that what is important about Freud's flip-flop was not that he changed his mind about whether his patients were actually seduced; rather it was that he had *suggested* the seduction scenarios to patients and then changed his interpretation of the information he had planted in patients' minds. This account of Freud's change draws parallels between Freud's early cases and current court cases involving the "false memory syndrome" (see Loftus, 1993). In sensational court cases, several adults have claimed they suddenly "remembered" that, during childhood, they had been abused by a parent or significant other. Very frequently these memories occurred during sessions with therapists who believed that most current problems stem from childhood abuse.

Based on examinations of Freud's writings, Powell and Boer (1994) contended that Freud placed heavy pressure on his early patients to report memories of childhood seduction. They cite a letter to Fliess in which Freud describes a patient as being "dishonest" and tells of threatening "to send her away" because she did not adopt, as her own belief, his assumption that she had been abused. Further, they point to Freud's writings in which he admits that he frequently had to coerce his patients into believing that they had been seduced. The pressure was so great that patients would sometimes make comments like "Something has occurred to me now, but you [Freud] obviously put it into my head" (Freud, quoted in Powell & Boer, p. 1287). Finally, they cite a passage by Freud written many years later in which he seems to admit that he may have been guilty of forcing seduction scenarios onto his early patients: ". . . [memories of seduction] which I myself had perhaps forced on them" (Freud quoted in Powell and Boer, p. 1286). In a more recent article, Powell and Boer (1995) report additional evidence that Freud, in later years, developed a strong bias toward regarding certain types of incest allegations as fantasies rather than cases of real abuse.

Even more damning is a contention by Allen Esterson in his fascinating book *Seductive Mirage* (1993). Esterson asserts that whether Freud "changed his mind" or implanted suggestions is moot, because few if any of his early patients provided any information pointing to molestations in early childhood. Instead of early patients' comments interpretable as abuse stories, there were only Freud's preconceived analytic reconstructions that he tried to coerce patients into accepting. Esterson supports his position by showing that Freud's early "seduction" cases were not what he described them to be in writings published many years later. First, when Freud wrote about the Oedipal complex in 1925, he either suffered from such severe memory loss that his competency should have been questioned or he was disingenuous. At this later time Freud wrote that the early cases involved fathers seducing daughters, when in fact his early writings indicated that the "accused" had been mostly brothers or non-relatives, not fathers. Recall that in his letter to Fliess in which he announced his disenchantment with the seduction thesis, Freud indicated that "fathers" "had to be accused" not that any were being accused. He must have known then, as well as later, that a preponderance of abusive fathers, whether parties to the early cases or fantasized as he asserted in 1925, did not exist. Second, Esterson argued that no matter what patients may or may not have said in therapy, Freud typically concocted an interpretation that fit his current theory, whatever that happened to be.

Esterson notes that Freud was a lover of analogies. In constructing his analogies, he often implied that psychoanalysts could ignore patients' testimony in favor of other "evidence": Just as a physician can look at a patient's symptoms and determine the patient's disorder, no matter what the patient says, a psychoanalyst can look at a patient's symptoms and determine what his or her underlying, childhood trauma had been, regardless of what the patient might have said. First the argument is circular—the patient is hysterical; therefore it must be that she fantasized seduction by her father; hence her hysteria is explained by the fantasy seduction. Second, Esterson sees a serious breach of scientific protocol. Freud assumed the validity of his theory, then "collected evidence" by creating a fit between what his theory would dictate and what he attributed to the patient. The irony of ignoring what patients explicitly said in therapy, while acting as if their testimony was the primary basis of psychoanalytic interpretations, is seen in Freud's acknowledgments that patients often stubbornly refused to accept his interpretation of what they said to him.

Freud used the analogy method for another purpose, to rebut critics who attacked the subjectivity of his theory. Rather than responding to criticisms with facts, he would draw an analogy in compelling fashion and then act as if he had performed a successful refutation.

These allegations that Freud either suggested seduction scenarios to his patients or constructed them himself are not new. As far back as 1974 Frank Cioffi published a paper with the tabloid title, "Was Freud a liar?" in which he made similar allegations to those of Powell/Boer and Esterson, though in skeletal form. In 1982, Robert Steele made some of the same points as these current commentators are now making, though he was less forceful and provided less supportive documentation than they. The assault on Freud seems to be intensifying.

Conclusions

The intensity, number, and perhaps convincingness of the assaults on Freud's theoretical fortress may seem to have increased so much over time that its walls appear sure to come tumbling down soon. However, there is another perspective. Detractors, though increasing in number, may be a mere platoon compared to the vast army of psychological professionals who either explicitly support Freud or imply support by making his ideas central to their own. I did a computer search of psychological literature titles and abstracts to determine who among the theorists covered in this book was most often mentioned between January 1990 and March 1995. There were 3265 mentions about half of which (1624) were of Freud's name. The closest competitor was Carl Jung at 332 mentions. Apparently any speculations about the impending demise of Freud's ideas are greatly exaggerated.

Three of Freud's global conceptions have had profound impact on psychology. First, more than anyone else, Freud has taught us not to take literally people's behaviors and their expressions of thoughts and emotions. Rather we can understand people better if we look beyond the blatantly obvious to the more challenging and meaningful subtleties. Second, his ideas about the identification process through which children become like their parents have influenced most theories of human development (Mussen, Conger, & Kagan, 1979). Third, while it may not be quite what Freud thought it was, even some of the most tough-minded experimental psychologists now acknowledge the existence of Freud's most central idea, the unconscious. Further, they assign a significant role to the unconscious in the lives of people (*American Psychologist*, vol. 47, #6, 1992).

Freud's vast writings are still being mined to discover new fuel for thought. For example, Freud was ahead of his time with regard to attitudes toward gay people. Years ago he wrote: "We surely ought not to forget that . . . the sensual love of a man for a man, was not only tolerated by a people so far our superiors in cultivation as were the Greeks, but was actually entrusted by them with important social functions" (quoted in Young–Breuhl, E.; 1990 p. 14). Although he has been gone for nearly sixty years, Freud still has much to teach us.

Freud was one of the most influential thinkers of the late nineteenth and early twentieth centuries, along with Charles Darwin and Albert Einstein. The ideas he developed have had major impact on the fields of psychiatry, social work, psychology, literature, and history. One cannot claim to be an educated person without possessing knowledge of Freudian thought.

Summary Points

1.   Freud was born (1856) of Jewish parents in the Germanic area of Moravia. He made a number of notable discoveries while a young medical student. *Interpretation of Dreams* (1900) set the tone for later break-through concepts, such as libido. Freud was banished from Vienna by the Nazis and died in London of cancer in 1939.

2.   Freud pictured humans as under the control of instincts that fall into two categories: Eros and Thanatos. Consistent with this orientation, he posed a primitive first structure of personality, id, that operates according to the pleasure principle and the primary process. The ego holds the id in check with its reality principle and secondary process. It protects itself with the defense mechanisms. The superego operates according to the morality principle and comes into existence through the process of introjection.

3.   The oral stage involves pleasure from stimulating the mouth area. Fixation can lead to either oral-receptive or oral-aggressive adult personality types. During the anal stage, pleasure is achieved by dispelling the feces. Adult personality types can be anal-retentive or anal-expulsive.

4. During the Phallic stages, boys lust after their mothers. Fear of their fathers takes the form of castration anxiety. They resolve their Oedipal complexes by identifying with their fathers, a process that leads to superego development if it succeeds and overuse of defense mechanisms as well as adult promiscuity or feminization if it fails.

5. The girl lusts after her father and hates her mother, but her lack of castration anxiety, due to lack of a penis (penis envy), makes resolution of her Electra complex difficult. As a result she may have lowered ego-strength and superego development relative to males. An apologist for Freud contends that he did not intend to degrade women; negative traits of women are attributable to women's anatomy which, in turn, dictates a change in sexual expression. A transformation of Sigmund to Phyllis, however, suggests gender bias.

6. The latency stage involves no focal, genital area, but entails the process of sublimation. The genital stage involves cathexes that are more altruistic and less self-centered than earlier ones. Freud's psychoanalytic free association technique depended on use of a couch that induced patients to cathartically pursue insight. It replaced hypnosis and involved transference and countertransference. Freud examined dreams for both manifest and latent content.

7. Freud felt people are controlled from within, by primitive, unconscious forces, a position that challenged popular notions. Some research results that support Freud include evidence for the importance of early experience, and evidence confirming ego defense, oral-aggressive and oral-receptive types, castration anxiety in men but not women, narcissistic tendencies, transference and the operation of the unconscious when cued by the environment.

8. Problems with his psychoanalytic theory include concepts that are difficult to measure, relatively low predictive validity, use of uncontrolled clinical settings, difficulties because the analyst/observer participates in observations, over-reliance on case studies, sampling bias, and limited experience with children.

9. Challenge to Freud's ideas in recent years includes Masson's accusation that Freud, for personal reasons, abandoned an earlier seduction theory in favor of a fantasy position. In addition, Powell and Boer charge that Freud suggested seduction scenarios to patients who incorporated them into memory. Esterson asserted that patients' reports to Freud contained nothing regarding seduction; rather Freud consciously or unconsciously invented the seduction scenarios.

10. Freud is clearly the most cited personality theorist. His timeless contributions include inspiring us to look beyond the obvious, the identification process, and the unconscious. Because Freud's writings are so vast, he may yet teach us more.

Essay/Critical Thinking Questions

1. What was it about the era in which Freud lived that so shaped his point of view?

2. Freud wrote of the Oedipal and Electra complexes as if we are all predisposed to these conditions from birth. Can we inherit ideas and tendencies to fantasies? Explain.

3. Hysterical neuroses are rather strange. Come up with two that are not discussed in the text and specify an origin for each.

4. There are descriptions of the oral-receptive and oral-aggressive adult types in the text. Expand on the text and provide a more complete description of these types; this could involve coming up with additional traits that are implied by the text.

5. What would Phyllis Freud say men should be better at than women?

6. "Sublimation" is an interesting concept. Invent some unacceptable needs or desires on the part of some hypothetical people and indicate how they might sublimate those needs or desires. (Hint: How about artists and athletes?)

7. Pick a concept not emphasized in the text and argue that it is Freud's most important concept.

8. Based on Freud's point of view analyze a dream that you have had recently (or one someone has told you about).

9. Sketch a scenario in which an analyst displays countertransference.

10. What is a Freudian contribution, possibly implied by the text, but not actually covered in it, that might be influential in years to come.

E-mail Interaction

(write the author at mfbpa@wiu.edu)
Forward any of the following questions/requests or write your own.

1. Do you think that Freud lied?
2. Is Freud dying? (Is his point of view fading?)
3. Did Freud really believe that females are inferior?
4. Tell me what to concentrate on in my studies of Freud.
5. Tell me why people are so fascinated with Freud.

3

PERSONALITY'S ANCESTRAL FOUNDATION: CARL JUNG

- Did you inherit your mind?
- Are you an introvert or an extravert?
- Where is the "self" located?
- Sensing, feeling, thinking, intuiting, which is you?
- How do UFO reports reveal the workings of the unconscious?

Carl Jung

On the occasion of his former mentor's death, Carl Jung described Freud's work as "surely the boldest attempt ever made . . . to master the riddle of the unconscious psyche. For us young psychiatrists, it was a source of enlightenment . . ." (quoted in Wehr, 1989, p. 29). These words were written despite the fact that Freud's view of Jung had changed from that of a loving father to one of a betrayed patriarch. In the early years of their collaboration, Freud pleaded with Jung, "My dear Jung, promise me never to abandon the sexual theory. That is the most essential thing of all. You see, we must make a dogma of it, an unshakable bulwark" (p. 34). Later he wrote, to his "number one man, the 'crown prince' " (p. 34): "I therefore don once more my hornrimmed paternal spectacles and warn my dear son to keep a cool head . . . I also shake my wise gray locks . . . and think: Well, that is how the young folks are; they really enjoy things only when they need not drag us along with them . . ." (p. 36). But, unfortunately for Freud, Jung could not endorse dogma nor could he drag along someone else's theoretical baggage. He had his own ideas including a conception of an unconscious that is dominated by the ancestral past of humans, not sexuality, however broadly defined. It was the beginning of the end when Jung's interest in paranormal phenomena led him to declare his "father" wrong. While in Freud's presence, Jung had a curious sensation in his diaphragm which was followed by a loud "detonation" in a nearby bookcase. When he labeled the experience a "catalytic exteriorization phenomenon" and Freud responded "sheer bosh," Jung exclaimed, "You are mistaken Herr Professor" (p. 35). Then Jung proceeded to add insult to injury by successfully predicting a second "detonation."

By 1913, such insubordination had become too much for Freud. He wrote Jung suggesting "that we give up our private relationship altogether. I lose nothing by this, since . . .

I have been bound to you only by the thin thread of . . . previously experienced disappoint-ments . . . Assume complete freedom and spare me the supposed 'duties of friendship' " (p. 39). The thread had indeed worn thin, as Jung wondered whether he was ever really a stu-dent of Freud. Thereafter, he went his own way.

Jung, The Person

Carl Gustav Jung (1875–1961) was born in Kesswil, Switzerland, the son of a minister and the grandson of a professor and a clergyman (Wehr, 1989). One of those grandfathers was rumored to be the bastard son of Goethe, the famed German author of *Faust*, a play about a magician who sold his soul to the devil in return for magic powers (Lebowitz, 1989). Jung nurtured this rumor because he liked to view himself as a person with ties to mysticism.

Jung suffered through some painful experiences as a boy (Feldman, 1992). Perhaps re-lated to the absence of his mother during a period of his childhood, he experienced numer-ous "visions." Reflecting on this time, he recalled a dark and dreary funeral during which men in black clerical gowns lowered a coffin into a deep hole and repeated the phrase "Lord Jesus" over and over. This phrase scared him thereafter. He called the experience a trauma. Another event, a recurrent dream also involving a dark hole, haunted Jung for years.

> *I ran forward and peered into it . . . I saw a stone stairway . . . At the bottom was a doorway . . . closed off by a green curtain . . . I pushed it aside [and] saw a rectangular chamber . . . a red carpet ran from the entrance to a low platform. On this platform stood a . . . golden throne . . . something was standing on it . . . It was a huge thing, reaching almost to the ceiling . . . it was made of skin and flesh, and on the top was something like a rounded head with no face and no hair. On the very top of the head was a single eye, gazing motionlessly upward (Lebowitz, 1989, p. 13).*

Jung could still recall this dream even in his later years. One can only wonder whether the obvious phallic symbolism of this dream so intrigued Jung that it led him to Freud's door.

Jung spent much of his youth by himself, in "extreme loneliness," talking out his in-nermost thoughts to a small mannequin he had carved and secreted away under the floor-boards of the family's "forbidden attic."

> *I am a solitary, because I know things and must hint at things which other people do not know, and usually do not even want to know [Jung, 1963, p. 42]. Loneliness does not come from having no people about one, but from being unable to communicate the things that seem important to oneself, or from holding certain views which others find inad-missible (p. 356).*

Following medical training at the University of Basel, Jung became aware of Freud's work and began to defend him from critics (Wehr, 1989). When Jung's *Studies in Word As-sociation* was published in 1905, he sent a copy to Freud, only to be informed that the fa-mous psychoanalyst had, "out of impatience," already acquired a copy. Freud's blunt message arrived in April of 1906. Seven years later, the two had exchanged 350 letters. Freud had looked on Jung as heir apparent to the psychoanalytic throne. Jung's presence at Freud's side would assure an intolerant world that psychoanalysis was not a Jewish movement. Around the time Freud ended their relationship, Jung experienced a period of soul searching and psychological upheaval. Visions of apocalypse overwhelmed him. "I saw a monstrous flood covering all the northern low-lying lands between the North Sea and the Alps. . . . I realized that a frightful catastrophe was in progress. I saw the mighty yellow waves, the floating rubble of civilization, and the drowned bodies of uncounted thousands. Then the whole sea turned to blood" (Wehr, 1989, p. 41). That was October 1913. The next year, World War I broke out.

The "bloody war" premonition must have shaken Jung, because it was followed by, in his words, a struggle with the "building blocks of psychosis" (p. 44). The turmoil within him would not cease. His mind was flooded with images and fantasies, many of them containing mythological symbols and figures. One day, when gripped with the feeling that he was in the "land of the dead," Jung glimpsed two human forms (p. 45). One was an elderly sage, "Elijah," and the other was a blind beauty who called herself "Salome." It was the beginning of his unique conception of the unconscious. He would later transform these Biblical figures into important components of the collective unconscious, "wise old man" and "seductive woman."

Jung's View of the Person

Jung and Freud did share ideas and even theoretical concepts. Like Freud, Jung talked about the psyche, ego, consciousness, and unconsciousness. Jung's theory included analogies to id and "insight." Their theories even share some of the same shortcomings. But the common ground ended there. Although they used some of the same terms, Jung's definitions were different from Freud's. Further, Jung offered alternative explanations for "penis envy" and viewed dream content quite differently than Freud. Jung's conception of maternal and paternal influences on children was markedly different. He also believed that the human organism's physical and psychological functions were more teleological— characterized by purpose —than did Freud: "Life is teleology per excellence; it is the intrinsic striving toward a goal, and the living organism is a system of directed aims which seek to fulfill themselves" (Jung, quoted in Rychlak, 1981, p. 196.). Finally, Jung's rejection of Freud's sexualism guaranteed that his theory would be fundamentally different.

Jung's orientation to people was different not only from Freud's, but also that of other theorists covered in this book. There are some ironies in the contrast of the two. Freud was controlling as a therapist in comparison to Jung, who sometimes participated in therapy sessions as a partner with the patient. Freud never did, but he would allow patients to "free associate." In contrast, Jung frequently offered less freedom during association sessions and in some ways provided more structure. On some occasions, Jung would even suggest what patients should think and talk about.

Jung's greater trust in people's ability to contribute to their own "cure" was evidenced in his willingness to suggest that they "self-analyze." His greater trust in other points of view was reflected in his occasional use of other people's ideas and methods. Further, he felt that people's minds were not limited by the size of their craniums, but could expand beyond their skulls into the mental spaces of other people. He believed that there is connectedness between the minds of people and that minds could communicate with other minds. In addition, as implied by Jung's claims to have anticipated "detonations," minds can communicate with nonhuman entities. Because of these beliefs, Jung was labeled a "mystic," which lowered his status among some of his colleagues, but may have raised it among the public.

Perhaps the label "mystic" was not entirely misapplied. Despite the existence of Christian religious figures among his ancestors, Jung may have felt ideologically closer to the Eastern religions. Oriental religious notions of transcendence above materialism and reincarnation resonated with Jungian thought.

Jung anticipated other theorists' ideas about people when he abandoned Freud's rather pessimistic conception of humans in favor of a refreshingly optimistic position. He believed that people are capable of being more than they are. In fact, to Jung, one of the major tasks of life is to develop the "self" so that all aspects of the psyche are acknowledged. In this developmental process people are able to become all they potentially can be. They can relate more completely to others and to realms of experience that are beyond our restricted and meager physical reality.

To Jung humans are multifaceted beings who, if they wish to be whole beings, have to accept all aspects of themselves, the foreboding as well as the pristine, the selfish as well as the altruistic, and the physical as well as the spiritual. People have to reconcile the opposing forces in their psyches. In fact, the very essence of human mentality is the clash of opposites. Jung believed that for every facet of our mental life there is a contrasting face. In every male there is femaleness; in every female there is maleness. Consciousness opposes unconsciousness and feeling opposes thinking. A nonviolent person will dream of violence; a chaste person will dream of sexual wantonness. If we acknowledge these opposing forces and coordinate their expression, we can become fulfilled, complete persons.

Basic Concepts: Jung

Consciousness and Unconsciousness

For Jung, unconsciousness refers to two distinct entities. His **personal unconscious**, which "is made up essentially of contents [that] have at one time been conscious but which have disappeared from consciousness through having been forgotten or repressed . . . ," did bear some resemblance to Freud's unconscious (Jung, 1959a, p. 42). As with the Freudian unconscious, each individual's personal unconscious is unique to him or her. Jung also wrote of "complexes"—though, as you will see, differently than Freud—and located them in the personal unconscious. However, he devoted the lion's share of his attention to the **collective unconscious,** a storehouse of ancestral experiences dating to the dawn of humankind and common to all humans. This unconscious belongs to the collective, not just to a single person. It has "never been in consciousness, and therefore [has] never been individually acquired, but owe[s its] existence exclusively to heredity" (p. 42).

Jung's conception of the collective unconscious crystallized as he pursued scholarly interests in a variety of fields: archeology, history, religion, mythology, and even alchemy, a now discredited precursor of chemical science that was prevalent during the Middle Ages. In addition, his affinity for anthropology led him to the United States for explorations of culture. During these pursuits he was struck by the remarkable consistency with which certain themes emerged from a colossal array of cultures, religions, literary works, and art forms, spanning thousands of years. Despite differences in time, geography, culture, and historical development, people everywhere seemed to express their life experiences in highly similar ways that encompassed many forms of human experience: attitudes, ideas, feelings, actions, fantasies, and dreams. Jung saw much of human experience as being communicated through common, age-old symbols, artistic figures, myths, legends, fairy tales, and folklore. These images would crop up century after century, even among cultures isolated from those that had previously displayed these universal symbols of human experience. Jung attributed the consistent appearance and reappearance of these ancient motifs and figures to the mechanisms of the collective unconscious.

Like Freud, Jung wrote of a **psyche** or total mentality, all of consciousness and unconsciousness. But **ego** is what one thinks of as oneself, the genuine me, and is the "centre of the total field of consciousness" (Jung, 1959b, p. 3). While not Freud's servant of unconscious urges, the ego does have communion with the collective unconscious. That Jung's ego is not entirely equivalent to consciousness is confirmed by the existence of another facet of consciousness, **persona**, or mask, the identities we assume because of the socially prescribed roles we play. Jung wrote:

> *Every calling or profession, for example, has its own characteristic persona. It is easy to study these things nowadays, when the photographs of public personalities so frequently appear in the press. A certain kind of behavior is forced on them by the world and professional people endeavour to come up to these expectations. Only the danger is that they become identical with their personas, the professor with his text-book, the tenor with his voice (Jung 1959a, p. 122–123).*

Rychlak (1981) dubbed persona the "collective conscious" because we all share knowledge of the prescribed behaviors that are associated with the various roles people play. In a sense, personas are stereotypes associated with various roles: the dumb jock, the nurdy student, the straightlaced accountant.

Consciousness and unconsciousness may be welded into a unified whole by the development of the **self**, the "total personality," the unifying core of the psyche that ensures a balance of conscious and unconscious forces (Jung, 1959b, p. 5). When properly and fully developed, it is a fulcrum located at the center of the psyche, balancing conscious and unconscious like the centered device that balances the playground teeter-totter. However, the self is a potentiality that may not become actual. In the poorly developed self, the balance of the conscious and unconscious is disrupted. The result could be various psychological ills.

Jung often wrote in terms of balancing opposing forces or opposites. Like Freud, he referred to **libido**—psychic energy which he imbued with less sexual meaning than Freud. Libido is subject to the principle of **equivalence**—energy consumed to accommodate one intention - "be benevolent," is balanced by energy fueling an opposite intention, "be hostile." **Entropy** is the equalization of differences in order to bring about a balance or equilibrium. Balancing maleness with femaleness is an example.

BOX 3.1   A Theory That Revels in Diversity

If there is a virtue that Jung's theory exudes more than others covered in this book, it is pan-culturalism. Jungian psychology applies to all cultures. In fact, it honors all cultures. If it were "to show more interest in" some cultures than others, it would be drawn to the so-called "primitive" cultures. People indigenous to various areas of the world, such as Native Americans and Australian Aborigines, who have somehow managed not to be assimilated, may be regarded as closer to the basic humanity embedded in the collective unconscious. The artifacts of their cultures as well as their rituals and customs reflect more openly and clearly such basic human themes as an awe-struck reverence for nature, the life/death cycle, and the transitions of every human life. In contrast, it would have less "interest in" so-called "civilized" cultures, as these more recent cultures have submerged or lost contact with ancient propensities and expressions.

Given Jungian theory's recognition of each culture's uniqueness as well as the commonality of cultures, participants in any culture could embrace it as a means of communication with their culture. People of African heritage could examine Egyptian culture in search of its unique expressions of all humanity's basic themes. Does the perfect geometry of the pyramids reflect the inherent attraction of humans to numerical precision? People of Native American heritage could examine the ancient Pueblos of Southwest North America for implications of human community. Those of Chinese ancestry could examine the recently unearthed precise ranks of ancient horsemen for evidence pertaining to the orderliness of human relations. People of Northern European ancestry could investigate their Viking past for evidence of humans' need to explore beyond the confines of their own locales.

Archetypes

The contents of the collective unconscious are called **archetypes** or ancient types, preexistent forms that are innate and represent psychic predispositions that lead people to apprehend, experience, and respond to the world in certain ways (Jung, 1959a). Jung explains their nature as analogous to Freud's biological instincts, but more psychological. The existence of archetypes is due exclusively to heredity. Therefore, the mind of the newborn infant is not a tabula rasa, or blank slate, but is imprinted with forms from the past experience of humans. What is inherited are not specific ideas or images but predispositions to recognize and appreciate certain general ideas and images. They are potentials rather than actuals. They often may be cast in terms of human forms, but many are most accurately perceived by the mind's eye if pictured as nonhuman symbols, such as numbers representing "order." They may be thought of as magnets that attract ancestral experiences that all relate to a common theme. For example, the mother archetype draws together ancient experiences common to all humans such as nurturance, warmth, love, protection, and other experiences related to motherness.

One prominent archetype comes as close to Freud's id as Jung gets. The **shadow** is the underside of the personality, the inferiorities of the person that are emotional in nature and too unpleasant to willingly reveal (Jung, 1959a). Jung believed that the shadow is a moral problem for the ego because it may resist moral control. This resistance may be bound up in projection—the person sees some of their unsavory qualities in other people. Jung was sometimes evasive when writing about the shadow. Although he refused to clearly indicate that its contents included Freud's primitive, biological instincts, it does apparently contain the physical urges. However, there is more to it. The shadow is manifested as the crude, bumbling, immature, incomplete side of us. It is the worst of us; it is what causes us to do what we do when "the devil made us do it." But the shadow is important. If the self is to evolve from potential to actual, it must fully acknowledge and deal with the contents of the shadow, as well as the ego and persona.

The archetype **anima** is the representation of woman in man. It is the accumulation of men's ancestral experiences of relating to women. Jung conceived of this archetype in terms of genetics as it existed in his day. "It is a well-known fact that sex is determined by a majority of male or female genes, as the case may be. But the minority of genes belonging to the other sex does not simply disappear. A man therefore has in him a feminine side, an unconscious feminine figure—a fact of which he is generally quite unaware" (Jung, 1959a p. 284). **Animus** is the corresponding man in woman. It is a constellation of ancestral experiences concerning women relating to men. Anima is to Eros (sexual allure) as animus is to Logos (rational thinking). In women, animus may "show up" in argumentativeness, opinionation, and insinuation. In men, anima may make an appearance in the form of faithlessness, sentimentality, and resentment. When the two archetypes "meet" they clash: "the animus draws his sword of power and the anima ejects her poison of illusion and seduction" (Jung, 1959b, p. 15). Ageless assumptions about differences between the genders are evident in these archetypes.

The result of a man's anima meeting a woman's animus can be quite humorous. Initially the man, under the influence of anima, may be seductive. When the woman, at the behest of animus, counters with arguments, he may become resentful. In turn, she may make insinuations. According to Jung "no man can converse with an animus for five minutes without becoming the victim of his own anima. Anyone who still had enough sense of humour to listen objectively to the ensuing dialogue would be staggered by the vast number of commonplace, . . .misapplied truisms [and] clichés . . ." (p. 15). On the positive side, anima gives men a sense of relatedness to others that may help them interact with people more smoothly. Animus provides women with the capacity to reflect and deliberate, which may help them understand their natural surroundings. By extrapolation, it seems reasonable to assume that the presence of woman in man and man in woman allows each to better understand the other.

While Jung believed that there is an indefinite number of archetypes, he did consider several in addition to shadow, anima, and animus. Table 3.1 lists a sample of these.

TABLE 3.1 Some Jungian Archetypes

Name	Qualities
Trickster (also clown)	characterized by unconsciousness and ability to change forms
Child	beginning and the end; invincible
Mother	sacred motherness (as in the Virgin Mary)
Father	dynamism, form, and energy; like the cerebrum
Wotan	warrior–god
Animal	horse or snake
Quarternity	squared circle with cross: fourfold division of ideal completeness
Order	Number; the numbers 3, 4
Hermaphrodite	Union of opposites

Jung likened the process by which archetypes affect us to the experience of "love at first sight." Love "can suddenly seize you." Imagine that a person has been carrying "a certain eternal image" of a potential partner, without necessarily knowing it. Another person then appears who fits that inner image and "instantly you get the seizure; you are caught" (Jung quoted in Evans, 1964, p. 51). Archetypes may seize you in a similar fashion. You may find yourself in their clutches when you are strolling through a museum and happen upon a suit of armor that was worn by a medieval warrior. One may sink its talons into you as you show unusual interest in a pregnant woman. You may experience the vice-like grip of an archetype when you gaze at a symbol rendered in stone or wood—such as a representation of the quarternity—even though you have never encountered it before.

It will be déjà vu: you will feel that you have been there before. Indeed Jung would say you have, or rather your ancestors have. Thus, the roots of your shared experience are embedded in your collective unconscious in some archetypal form.

Jung (1978) speculated that twentieth-century interest in saucer-like unidentified flying objects (UFOs) may reflect the workings of the archetype for wholeness or totality. He noted that the sightings of flying saucers began toward the end of World War II, a time of intense conflict and strife. The psychic basis of these sightings is a splitting apart, which is then projected outward. The opposite of splitting apart is wholeness, as symbolized by a **mandala** or magic circle, a round object often including an inner spiral that draws the eyes to the center of its surface. Therefore, the "many thousands of individual testimonies" involving round flying bodies may be a *compensation* on the part of the collective unconscious as it seeks to bring about order and "heal the split in our apocalyptic age by means of the symbol of the circle" (Jung, 1964, p. 285). UFOs are often reported as luminous disks that come to earth from another planet (the unconscious) and contain strange creatures (archetypes) (Hall & Nordby, 1973).

Archetypes are not merely invoked to explain perceptions of alien presence. They creep into even the most modern expressions of culture, including the movies. James Iaccino (1994) has produced an enjoyable and edifying new book on archetypes in horror movies. His argument seems to be that the horror movie genre is inspired by, even founded on, archetypes and would not exist without them. Examples are plentiful. Mother archetypes are often the theme of horror movies. In *Aliens*, "a gigantic Queen Bee protect[s] her revolting larvae" (p. 5). The mother archetype also rears its sometimes ugly head by forming the core of a "mother complex" which, in turn, plagues a movie's central character. Complex victim Norman Bates of the classic *Psycho* movies is an outstanding example. Manifestations of the "invincible" child archetype abound as well. *The Exorcist*, *Omen*, and *Children of the Corn*, as well as other Steven King works, center on children possessed by evil and endowed with the power to make the devil reign. Shadow archetypes in movies are so numerous that Iaccino breaks them down into categories. He places Dr. Jekyll and Mr. Hyde in a category of disguised forms. Here the shadow is masked, but reveals itself periodically (often when the moon is full). Obviously, the various werewolf and Dracula movies fit: normal people become shadowy monsters after dark. Shadow motifs can become inflated to "bigger than big" (p. 8), a second category. *Them!* and the *King Kong* movies are examples. Irrational, avenging shadows form the third class. Monsters in this case are the dead coming back to life. *Night of the Living Dead* and *Tales from the Crypt* show zombi-like creatures bringing havoc to the living.

No account of the Jungian themes in horror movies would be complete without consideration of animus and anima. Animus manifestations are seen in any movie where women show masculine aggressiveness and dominance. *The Bride of Frankenstein*, *The Cat People*, and *She-Wolf of London* provide good illustrations. Anima, cases where the woman in men comes out, are amply represented in the classic *Some Like It Hot* and the maybe classic *Mrs. Doubtfire*.

Other archetypes include the mad magician, fully exploited by the *Frankenstein* movies, and the wise old man, manifested by the Merlin character in the King Arthur movies. Obe Won Kanobe of the *Star Wars* series is also an excellent example. Finally, any of the shapeshifting movies would fit the trickster archetype. The *Howling* series is illustrative, as well as the more contemporary *Terminator II*.

Archetypes seem present always and everywhere in the psyche. While predominantly emotional, they also have intellectual elements. However, no archetype has itself ever been present in any individual's consciousness (Jung, 1959a). Archetypes manifest themselves only secondarily, through symbols, images, and behavior. Their pure form is not concrete. They exist as potentials or dispositions, similar to genetic dispositions. When they are manifested in consciousness, they are not themselves, but some representation of themselves that is manufactured by consciousness. For example, if one has a dream or daydream of the Christ Child, the archetype of the child has not entered consciousness. Rather a manifestation of it has been developed by consciousness into a recognizable form. It is possible for archetypes to become so powerful that they constitute a separate personality system, as sometimes occurs in certain mental disorders.

An archetype may manifest itself in one's experience and, at about the same time, in an external event. To explain this phenomenon, Jung introduced **synchronicity**, the simultaneous occurrence of two happenings that are correlated but have no direct cause-and-effect connection. Jung sought to understand coincidences and connections that are meaningful because each forms a pattern that cuts across chains of causally linked events. There is the appearance of communication between external and internal events, not causal connection. He used the concept of synchronicity to explain, without implying causality, simultaneous occurrences of inner images and outer events relating to some archetype. Inner images may be manifested in dreams, visions, forebodings, and hunches. Outer events may include any observable occurrences from the past, present, or future. Here are a few everyday examples: "It's weird that you telephoned about the birth of your baby, because I was talking about babies with my wife"; "Grandfather had flashbacks of his World War I experiences just as he turned on the radio to hear that World War II had begun"; "I dreamed of the Devil last week and the next day a friend offered me her copy of *Faust*."

Jung also linked synchronicity to parapsychology, a subfield of psychology in search of acceptable scientific explanations for extrasensory perception (ESP) phenomena such as mental telepathy and clairvoyance. That he made this connection is not surprising in view of the fact that his parapsychological roots run deep in his family history (Las Heras, 1992). You may be experiencing ESP when you have the same thought as someone else (telepathy: "I was thinking about Michael Jackson just as you began to talk about his failed marriage to Lisa Marie Presley") or successfully predict a future event (clairvoyance: you have a feeling that a relative is coming to visit and he or she shows up shortly thereafter).

BOX 3.2   The Case of Little Anna

"About the time when Freud published his report on the case of 'Little Hans,' I received from a father who was acquainted with psychoanalysis a series of observations concerning his little daughter, then four years old" (Jung, 1954, p. 8). So Jung introduced his analysis of a bright little girl who was virtually obsessed with what the casual observer might view as the age-old childhood question, "Where do babies come from?"

Anna's curiosity was stimulated by the impending arrival of her new sibling. Before Anna was told that her brother had been born, she was asked, "What would you say if you got a little brother tonight?" She promptly answered, "I would kill it." This seemingly shocking response might have been interpreted by Freud as indicating that Anna was showing natural jealousy of her new brother's anatomy, or "worse," if he were dead, maybe she could take his penis. However, Jung characteristically had a much milder interpretation: Anna did not mean "kill it" literally, but "just get rid of it," perhaps because she was jealous of the attention it would receive or maybe because it was something new and new "things" are nuisances with which one must cope.

Some of Anna's behaviors and experiences did seem "Freudian." She saw some carpenters working and then dreamed that one of them cut off her genitals. A game she played in the tool house involved "getting rid of mother." Seeing the gardeners and her father urinating outdoors made her very curious. Jung's response to the "sliced genitals" comment was a reference to Anna's curiosity regarding the purpose of her genitals. "Getting rid of mother" was merely to keep her from interfering with the children's games (they enjoyed defecating in the corner of the tool house, a practice that Mother wished to terminate). However, watching the men urinate had greater significance, but not in the Freudian sense.

To Jung, Anna was curious about the men urinating because she had a burning interest in how babies are formed, how they "get out" of mothers, and more relevant to the present concern, what role fathers play in all of this. She wanted to know "what fathers do," that is, how do fathers contribute to the birth of babies. The interest was not mere childish curiosity. Anna's collective unconscious was at work. The ancient and never-ending cycle of birth and rebirth was manifesting itself in her consciousness.

Anna was fond of her uncle and once asked if she could sleep with him (think of what Freud would make of that!). While making this request she was clinging to her father's arm as her mother often did. Later she dreamed that she crept into her uncle's and aunt's bedroom and peeked under the covers to discover ". . . Uncle lay on his stomach, and joggled up and down on it" (p. 31). Still later she frequently crawled into her father's bed, lay on her stomach—arms and legs stretched out—and joggled back and forth while exclaiming "this is what father does" (p. 32). According to Jung all this was in pursuit of knowledge concerning what "father does" in the whole process of birth and death.

Evidence of rumblings in the unconscious regarding the life–death cycle were more clearly displayed when Anna asked whether her mother would die when the baby was born. This question suggests that death is exchanged for life. The cycle is also evident in a conversation Anna had with her grandmother:

"Granny, why are your eyes so dim?

"Because I am old."

"But you will become young again?"

"Oh dear, no. I shall become older and older, and then I shall die."

"And what then?"

"Then I shall be an angel."

"And then you will be a baby again?" (p. 9)

To Jung, many childhood games have meaning related to the collective unconscious. When, like children of today, Anna stuffed pillows under her clothes and incessantly queried adults about "where babies come out," she was not just playing games or satisfying childish curiosity. Nor was she being controlled by psychosexual urges when she spoke of "joggling back and forth" in bed like "father does." She was under the spell of the collective unconscious.

Dreams as Messages from a Wise Unconscious

Jung was highly respectful of dreams and fantasies. Dreams were a primary tool used in his approach to therapy. "I have spent more than half a century in investigating natural symbols, and I have come to the conclusion that dreams and their symbols are not stupid and meaningless" (Jung, 1964, p. 93). He was convinced that dreams contained important messages from the "wise" unconscious. The task was to decipher these messages, a job that was much more straightforward than Freud thought.

Jung did not distinguish between "manifest" and "latent" content of dreams as did Freud. He wrote "The 'manifest' dream-picture is the dream itself and contains the whole meaning of the dream. When I find sugar in the urine, it is sugar and not just a facade for albumen. What Freud calls the 'dream-facade' is the dream's obscurity, and this is really only a projection of our own lack of understanding" (Jung quoted in Rychlak, 1981, p. 246). To Jung, the symbols of the collective unconscious are undisguised in a dream, ready for interpretation. Nevertheless, interpretation may be difficult because of the complex and abstract nature of the symbols, each of which has at least two meanings. However, one need not dig through some protective crust to get at those symbols. They are naked, out in the open, and in plain sight.

One type of message, mentioned earlier in relation to flying saucers, is **compensation**—the balancing of a conscious experience with an opposing unconscious representation as in observations that a dream's meaning is often just the opposite of the person's conscious experience. In this sense, the collective unconscious represents the second of "two sides to every story," each side reflecting an autonomous function that compensates for the other. As you have seen and will see again, the balance of opposites is a constant theme in Jung's writings. Jacobi (1962) offers an example and interpretation of a compensation dream:

> *Someone dreams that it is spring, but that his favourite tree in the garden has only dry branches. This year it bears no leaves or blossoms. What the dream is trying to communicate is this: Can you see yourself in this tree? That is how you are, although you don't want to recognize it. Your nature has dried up, no green grows within you. Such dreams are a lesson to persons whose consciousness has become autonomous and overemphasized. Of course the dreams of an unusually unconscious person, living entirely by his instincts, would correspondingly emphasize his "other side." Irresponsible scoundrels often have moralizing dreams while paragons of virtue frequently have immoral dream images (p. 76).*

Another type of message is **prospective** or anticipatory, through which dreams may "foretell" future events and outcomes. A friend of mine told of a dream he had during his high school years. He was riding a bicycle, with his brother on the handlebars, when a hole suddenly opened in the street, toppling both of them. Two days later, the mishap of the dream occurred in real life. Jung's favorite example illustrates how dreams may prepare a person for the future . . . if they pay attention to dream-meaning. A friend of Jung's described a dream about climbing a steep mountain and experiencing exhilaration upon reaching the top. When Jung advised caution in the future, the friend scoffed. Later he fell to his death during a climb.

Personality Typology

Two Psychological Attitudes: Extraversion and Introversion

After twenty years of observing people "of all classes from all the great nations," Jung theorized that human beings could be divided into two groups based on "two fundamentally different general attitudes," extraversion and introversion (Jung, 1921/1971, p. 549). He defined **attitude** as "a readiness of the psyche to act or react in a certain way" to experience (p. 414). He defined **type** as a habitual attitude, or a person's "characteristic way." Although extraversion and introversion are discussed at length later in this book, it would be remiss not to introduce Jung's version of these two psychological types which many psychologists consider his best-known contribution to understanding personality (Evans, 1964).

According to his theory (1921/1971), **extraversion** is an "outward-turning" of libido that involves a positive movement of interest away from one's inner experience toward outer experience. The extravert is characterized by

> *interest in the external object, responsiveness, and a ready acceptance of external happenings, a desire to influence and be influenced by events, a need to join in and get "with it," the capacity to endure bustle and noise of every kind, and actually find them enjoyable, constant attention to the surrounding world, the cultivation of friends and acquaintances, none too carefully selected, and finally by the great importance attached to the figure one cuts, and hence by a strong tendency to make a show of oneself (p. 549).*

Introversion is an "inward-turning" of psychic energy and involves a negative movement or withdrawal of subjective interest away from outer objects and toward one's inner experience. Jung, a well-documented (Dolliver, 1994) and self-acknowledged introvert, believed that introverts have more problems with social relations than extraverts (Lebowitz, 1989). The introvert

> *holds aloof from external happenings, does not join in, has a distinct dislike of society as soon as he finds himself among too many people. In a large gathering he feels lonely and lost. The more crowded it is, the greater becomes his resistance. He is not in the least "with it," and has no love of enthusiastic get-togethers. He is not a good mixer. What he does, he does in his own way, barricading himself against influences from outside. He is apt to appear awkward, often seeming inhibited . . . His own world is a safe harbour, a carefully tended and walled-in garden, closed to the public and hidden from prying eyes. His own company is the best. He feels at home in his world, where the only changes are made by himself. His best work is done with his own resources, on his own initiative, and in his own way (Jung, 1921/1971, pp. 550).*

Four Psychological Functions: Thinking, Feeling, Sensing, and Intuiting

Jung also theorized that there are four orientations, or basic psychological functions, in personality: sensing, intuiting, thinking, and feeling. The first and second are considered "rational," while the last two are "irrational." These functions, when combined with

---

BOX 3.3   What Combination Are You?

The attitudes and functions combine as follows: ex-traverted–thinking, extraverted–feeling, extraverted–sensing, extraverted–intuiting, introverted–thinking, introverted–feeling, introverted–sensing, intro-verted–intuiting. Carefully go over each of the eight possibilities. Put together the attitude and function definitions of each attitude/function combination, referring back to the text as needed. Then determine which combination best fits you. Later your choice will become even more meaningful as you read about a famous test that classifies people as you have done with regard to yourself.

---

introversion/extraversion, make eight possible permutations. **Sensation** determines that something is present; it is the same as sensory perceptions of sight, sound, smell, taste, and touch. The sensation function is especially characteristic of children, with emphasis placed on actual observations or "facts." **Thinking** determines what is present and interprets its meaning; it connects ideas with one another to form intellectual concepts or reach solutions. **Feeling** evaluates how experiences strike us, whether they are suitable to us or not; it is a kind of judgment that is entirely subjective. Feeling imparts a definite value, of accep-tance–rejection or of like–dislike. It also includes mood. **Intuition** suggests where some-thing seems to have come from and where it may be going. It is a kind of "instinctive apprehension" having an unconscious origin and no tangible basis. You display intuition when you understand something but cannot explain how or why you understand it.

It should be noted that Jung was not primarily interested in classifying people into dis-tinct categories. His aims were to (1) understand dimensions of individual differences, (2) guide research, and (3) aid clinical evaluation of patients.

Personality Development

Individuation

For Jung, the direction of personality development is **individuation**, "the process by which a person becomes a psychological 'in-dividual,' that is, a separate, indivisible unity or 'whole'" (Jung, 1959a, p. 275). It is a process of self-realization in which the totality called "self" is differentiated from the various parts of the personality, including the collective un-conscious.

It is union of opposites represented by the archetype Hermaphrodite. It is confronting what we are not as well as what we are. Through individuation animus is balanced with an-ima and conscious with unconscious. This bringing together of opposites has a name, **tran-scendental function**, the process of rising above what we are through our tendency "to combine consciousness and unconsciousness into a balanced whole" (Rychlak, 1981, p. 218). Thus, individuation may be thought of as the process by which the self emerges from the psyche through the operation of the transcendental function.

At first, the person refuses to accept the unconscious within. However, the person may eventually begin to accept what is within as part of his or her personality, rather than "pro-jecting" it outside the self, onto others, as "not me." In this process, personality development is expressed through the archetypes, as the person comes to terms with each, in sequence (Hogan, 1976). The proposed steps are as follows: (1) the persona dissolves when the person recognizes the artificiality of society's goals; (2) the shadow is integrated with other psychic units when there is awareness of one's selfish and destructive "dark side"; (3) acceptance of the anima or animus is achieved by recognition of opposite-sex components in one's personality; and (4) commitment to an archetype that is symbolic of spiritual or creative meaning allows one to tackle the final stage of individuation.

Recognition of unconscious contents leads to synthesizing archetypes to consciousness, a process of blending conscious and unconscious into a whole resulting in self-knowledge (Freud's "insight"). Recognition does not mean consciously entertaining material that was formerly unconscious. Rather it means that the personality acknowledges previously neglected unconscious contents and acts to blend them with consciousness. Recognition allows projections to be withdrawn from the external world, thereby releasing energy for use in continued personal development.

The process of individuation proceeds slowly, in stages covering the entire life span. Fulfillment of individuation is "a favor that must be paid for dearly." Archetypes need to be recognized every step of the way, which is no easy task. However, the process is not simply one of struggling with the collective unconscious, but a continuing adaptation to it. Think of a plant that must first be able to grow in soil (recognition of the collective unconscious) before it can unfold its own particular fullness (development of the self). In its ultimate adult form, individuation shows characteristics not found during childhood: definiteness, completeness, and maturity. As you will see, the notion of individuation of the self anticipates Carl Rogers's ideas about self-acceptance and Abraham Maslow's thoughts about self-actualization.

Four Stages of Life-span Development

Jung discussed four stages of personality development: childhood, youth, middle age, and old age (Hall & Nordby, 1973).

Childhood (birth to adolescence) is a relatively problem-free period that is dominated by instincts, dependency, and a psychological atmosphere provided by parents. Development of an ego occurs gradually, as does one's separation from the protective "psychic womb" of home that occurs when schooling starts. The infant has no real ego, or separate identity, and is almost totally dependent on its parents. The infant's unconscious is not personal, only collective.

Youth (adolescence through young adulthood) begins at puberty, at which time physiological changes are accompanied by "psychic revolution." The demands of life dictate that people make their own decisions. At the same time young people find it difficult but necessary to give up the illusions and fantasies of childhood. "Psychic birth" occurs as the psyche begins to take on its own character, although experiences of sexuality and inferiority may create problems. The person begins to establish vocational, marital, and community roles. A major developmental task of this time is turning outward and engaging life (Kelleher, 1992).

Middle age (age 40 to old age) brings with it the task of building a whole personality. Jung observed many of his adult patients dealing with issues of lost zest and meaning in life. Their focus was on inner, spiritual values, rather than earlier adaptations that were more external and materialistic. A main goal of maturity is to achieve an integrated personality by establishing an interrelationship between conscious and unconscious aspects of the self (Kelleher, 1992). Contemplation becomes more important than activity. Opposite psychological processes, such as introversion–extraversion or feeling–thinking, may be synthesized. This blending process may be stimulated by a symbol that represents ascendency of the spirit above worldly matters. One example involves the symbol of yin and yang which may be interpreted as the female-like and male-like forces in nature, according to ancient Oriental philosophy. Appreciation of this symbol may lead to synthesis of the male and female aspects of the person.

The period of *old age* parallels childhood because of a return to submersion in the unconscious. The figure of a snake biting its own tail is symbolic of life coming full circle. Death is as important as birth. Jung found belief in a hereafter so universal that he considered it to be a manifestation of the unconscious (see Campbell, 1975). Perhaps psychic life does not end with bodily death because the psyche continues an endless quest for self-realization. Again, this theme of reincarnation is in tune with Jung's possible greater affinity for Eastern as opposed to Western religion.

A Different View of Maternal and Paternal Influence

One aspect of Jung's view of interpersonal relationships differs quite markedly from those of Freud and other theorists to be considered later. Jung saw individuals as relating psychologically to others more on the basis of universal inner archetypes than on others' individual external characteristics. Jung attributes only "limited [causative] significance" to a child's personal mother and father. The influences mothers reportedly have on their children "do not come from the mother herself, but rather from the archetype projected upon her" (1959a, p. 83). In effect, children respond less to their parents than to the archetypes they have of "mother" and "father." The mother archetype is a composite of humans' experiences with all mothers down through the ages. It has "an almost infinite variety of aspects": mother, grandmother, stepmother, mother-in-law, nurse, governess, "good" mother, "bad" mother, Mother of God, Great Mother, fertility, fruitfulness, cooking vessels, rose, cow, witch, dragon, deep water, and so on. On the other hand, parents do have an influence on the child's development of other archetypes. A boy's interactions with his own mother and father affect the functioning of his anima and shadow, respectively. Similarly the girl's relationship with her own father and mother affects the functioning of her animus and shadow, respectively.

Evaluation

Contributions

Jung's Psychological Types

Later in this book I will return to introversion/extraversion and the literally hundreds of studies that support this important contribution by Jung. Here the concentration is on the combination of this central dimension with the four functions. This eight-fold typology has been the focus of a number of research studies.

A particularly good example of research on the typology matrix was an investigation by Gorlow, Simonson, and Krauss (1966). The subjects were 98 introductory psychology students at the Pennsylvania State University, two-thirds of whom were male. The results supported the hypothesis that subjects using a self-report technique would order themselves into the eight types postulated by Jung. However, extraverted types emerged much more clearly than introverted types in the sample studied. Evidence was strongest for the extraverted-feeling type. The data supported Jung's assertion that this type of personality is more commonly female than male. Second most prominent was the extraverted–thinking type ("a man . . . who make[s] all his activities dependent on intellectual conclusions, which in the last resort are always oriented by objective data . . ." Jung, 1921/1971, p. 346).

The most popular psychological measure of Jung's typology matrix is the Myers Briggs Type Indicator (MBTI) (Myers, 1962). The MBTI is a self-report questionnaire that has been used in at least 400–500 studies (Carlyn, 1977; Carskadon, 1978). Strong interest in the MBTI and issues related to it continues into the mid-1990s (Harvey & Murry, 1994).

Carskadon (1978) has used the MBTI to predict the quality of contributions made by students to discussions in undergraduate psychology classes at Mississippi State University. Carskadon noticed that self-described MBTI extraverts made "very infrequent discussion contributions," whereas introverts made "frequent and thought-provoking contributions." However, this pattern seemed to be related less to the extraversion–introversion dimension than to the sensation–intuition dimension. Carskadon tested the hypothesis that the best classroom contributions come from intuitive types. At the end of a semester, 65 students in three psychology courses were asked to rate every class member on quality of discussion contributions during the course. A 3-point rating scale was used (3 = excellent, 2 = good, and 1 = fair to poor). Carskadon also rated the students independently. The correlation of .84 between class means and instructor ratings was statistically significant. Results for both sets of rating data also proved significant. Students with high intuitive scores obtained the highest discussion ratings, while students with high sensation scores obtained the lowest discussion ratings. Other comparisons were nonsignificant, indicating that intuiting/sensing was critical to contributions to class discussion compared to extraversion–introversion in combination with the functions. By way of general advice to instructors, Carskadon noted, "Too many extraverts can give all action but little thought; too many introverts all thought and no action. Too many thinking types can use all logic and no human values; too many feeling types, all subjective values and no critical analysis" (p. 141).

In sum, research showed that extraversion emerged more clearly than introversion, but evidence presented later in this book supports both extremes. Use of the MBTI shows that it is introverts, not extraverts, who contribute most to discussions and that a better understanding of discussion processes may be achieved by attention to the four functions than to introversion–extraversion. Clarifying ambiguities in these results may await the resolution of controversies surrounding MBTI scoring (Harvey & Murry, 1994).

Jung's Analytic Psychotherapy

Jung's approach to therapy was flexible, open-minded, and eclectic, showing a willingness to use whatever methods seemed most workable with individual patients (Hall & Nordby, 1973). Freud's and other theorists' methods were considered right along with his own when he was selecting procedures for dealing with psychological problems (Rychlak, 1981). He was even known to send his Catholic patients to confession as he thought their knowledge of that "method" might lead them to use it effectively in ferreting out unconscious influences. Further, unlike Freud and other theorists, Jung maintained a more or less equal relationship with his patients. As you will see, he sometimes participated in some types of therapy right along with the patient. This innovation may have influenced Carl Rogers and some other psychotherapists.

Roazen (1974) writes that Jung "successfully pioneered short-term psychotherapy" and promoted the development of self-help programs like Alcoholics Anonymous (p. 284). Initially, he might see patients four times a week. Then he would cut back to one to two hours a week. Finally, he would encourage patients to do self-analysis and would serve only as their consultant (Rychlak, 1981).

Jung also was a pioneer in the use of projective tests, like the ones discussed in the first chapter. He often encouraged patients to express their experiences through drawing and painting, a technique that has been adopted by others, especially therapists who work with children. The waking-imagery techniques he developed have become popular with current-day professionals working with terminally ill cancer patients (Achterberg & Lawlis, 1978; Simonton & Simonton, 1975).

Jung tended to see older patients than Freud (Rychlak, 1981). Of course, he wished to help them toward individuation and the further development of the self. Often, however, they were troubled in such a way that individuation was arrested. A major source of these troubles were **complexes**, mental contents in the psyche that agglutinate or stick together like the clumping of red blood cells and eventually take up residence in the personal unconscious. For example, a person's strong religious faith may lead to the agglutination of religious beliefs into a complex that may overwhelm the identity of the person. Complexes may be thought of as clogs in the pipeline of the psyche that block commerce between the conscious and collective unconscious. A frequent goal of Jungian analytic psychotherapy was to identify these complexes and "dissolve them"—in the sense of decentralizing them—so that the conscious and collective unconscious might better relate to one another.

An illustrative case involves a mother complex (Jung, 1959a). The core of this complex might be the mother archetype. As the complex develops it migrates from the collective unconscious, the realm of the archetype, to the personal unconscious where experiences with the person's mother agglutinate to it. A boy with this complex, for example, may unconsciously seek his mother in every woman he encounters.

The existence of the mother complex may be confirmed by one of the first personality tests used in clinical settings, an instrument developed by Jung (1910). The **Word Association Test** involved instructing people to say the first word that comes to mind after hearing each of 100 words from a standardized list. These associations then were analyzed according to content, commonness or uniqueness, time lapse between list word presentation and patient's response, later recall, and accompanying behavior (facial expressions, postural shifts, voice changes, laughing, crying). He paid particular attention to responses given to emotionally arousing words, such as *mother*. Strong reactions to the word *mother* would inform Jung that a mother complex may exist. An analyst's knowledge that a mother complex exists, however, may do little by way of solving the patient's problem. For dissolution of the complex to occur, the patient must have *insight*. This critical event will likely require deeper probing all the way to the heart of the matter, in this case, the mother archetype. Other techniques are needed for this plunge into the depths of the collective unconscious.

Interpreting Dreams in a Series

Unlike Freud, Jung generally saw dreams as having little to do with worldly concerns and much to do with the meaning of life. Jung's approach to dream interpretation was one of **amplification**, broadening and enriching dream or other image content through a process of directed association (Rychlak, 1981). Jung's interpretations were guided by images and analogies related to the dream's emotional nucleus or hub. His method differs from Freud's free association in three ways: (1) Instead of deducing meaning by working backward from present to past, Jung sought to understand meaning by progressing forward, from present to future; (2) Jung provided dreamers with his vast knowledge of universal archetypal symbols and meanings, orienting them in certain directions and actively guiding their interpretations (in our example, he would introduce the patient to symbols of "mother"); and (3) Jung offered his own associations to dream content, sometimes simultaneously engaging in the association process with the patient. The goal was to aid patients in deriving the meanings of symbols themselves. Once they are acquainted with those meanings, dissolution of troublesome complexes becomes possible.

Amplification could also occur apart from the exploration of dream content. In this case Freud's free association would be used, except that "freedom" was restricted by Jung's interventions to keep a patient oriented to a particular image or to join in the associations.

Jung did not use any standard, cookbook approach to interpreting dream symbols. His approach was also highly individualized, taking into account different personalities, circumstances, and contexts. For example, while for some individuals sexual intercourse might signify lustful needs, for a particular person it might well symbolize union with another human being. He sought to increase his patients' ability to interpret dreams by encouraging them to keep a log of all dreams and interpretations, and to pursue their own interpretations whenever possible.

Jung was the first theorist to investigate large numbers of dreams in succession, or **dream series** (Jacobi, 1962). Jung did not find interpretations of single dreams generally representative of the dreamer, but he did find later dreams helpful in correcting misinterpretations of earlier ones. He also recognized that the meaning of dreams in a sequence is not necessarily chronological, but radial. Imagine a wagon wheel having spokes that extend outward from a central hub. Different dreams would be represented by the spokes, but all would be related to the hub which could be a complex of the dreamer.

Waking-Dream Fantasy

Another technique frequently used by Jung was **active imagination** through which patients are encouraged to simulate dream experiences by actively engaging in imagination while fully awake (Watkins, 1976). For example, a patient may be asked to close his eyes in a darkened room and imagine himself descending a succession of stairways. While so doing (symbolically going down into the unconscious), the patient is also asked to detail his sensations, perceptions, experiences, thoughts, and behaviors as vividly as possible. It frequently happens that the patient finds himself next to water, perhaps a lake, the most common symbol of unconscious psychological spirit. To pursue our example further, "deep water" is a mother symbol.

Limitations

Jung's theory shares several shortcomings with that of Freud. Many of his concepts are not amenable to scientific testing. How does one get at an archetype so that some hypothesis regarding it can be tested? How does one understand a Jungian symbol when each symbol has at least two meanings? What is the real meaning of each?

Another problem also lowers the scientific status of Jung's theory. Some of Jung's notions seem mixed up with others. The anima and the shadow sometimes get mixed up in his writings, as do the shadow and the trickster. In fact, his writing is sometimes perplexing: For example, some concepts are never clearly defined—complex is a case in point—and others are defined in obscure fashion or defined differently in different writings—individuation is an illustration (Rychlak, 1981). Even the central concept "collective unconscious" is sometimes treated ambiguously. It is not entirely clear whether there is initially anything in the collective unconscious except archetypes. Jung (1959a) does mention simple unconscious elements in the collective unconscious—such as fire and water—but does not make it clear whether these elements stand alone or exist only as parts of archetypes.

These problems are relatively minor compared to Jung's ideas concerning how the collective unconscious comes into being. Like Freud, Jung was influenced by Charles Darwin's contemporary, Chavalier De Lamarck, who believed that animals and plants can change their forms during their lifetimes in adapting to their environments and these changes can be passed on to future generations. In other words, Lamarck believe in the inheritance of acquired characteristics. If a seagoing animal loses its front feet and that loss helps it survive better in the sea, the lack of feet might be passed on. Unfortunately Lamarck's ideas are not scientifically sound.

Broadly speaking, the "mind" (psyche) can be thought of as composed of "ideas" (ideas can include thoughts and feelings relating to experiences). There are problems with associating "inheritance" and the "mind." First, inheritable traits are usually thought of as physical, but the mind and its contents are not physical. Second "ideas" are acquired during people's lifetimes and, in view of the way the scientific community regards Lamarck's infamous notion, are not properly thought of as inheritable.

There is a strong flavor of "inherited ideas" in Jung's notion that the collective unconscious consists of elements that originated in the experiences of ancient humans and then were genetically passed to the present generation. He writes, "We must assume that [mythological types] correspond to certain collective (and not personal) structural elements of the human psyche in general, and, like the morphological elements of the human body, are inherited" (Jung, 1959a, p. 155). At least later in his life, Jung knew the claim that any characteristic can be acquired during a lifetime and then passed on to future generations was discredited along with its advocate, Lamarck. In an attempt to defend the acquisition of collective unconscious content against the "acquired characteristics" charge, Jung argued that what is inherited are not ideas per se and certainly nothing concrete, but "experiences" that are merely dispositions. These dispositions may ready a person for certain experiences, but never are present themselves in any observable form (remember, archetypes appear in consciousness only as transformed representations). Yet, the problem remains: an experience, however defined, occurs to somebody at some point in time, and anything occurring during a lifetime would rarely if ever qualify as "inherited." Jung was never able to get around this problem. Accordingly, the stigma of "inheritance of acquired characteristics" remains branded on notions of the collective unconscious and may be the most serious weakness of Jung's theory.

Like Freud, Jung's character and intellectual integrity have been attacked. From time to time Jung has been accused of being anti-Semitic and sympathetic with the Nazi movement (Neuman, 1991; Samuels, 1993). He has also been accused of "lying" about the scientific origins of the collective unconscious (New York Times Service, 1995). Richard Noll, in his book *The Jung Cult: Origins of a Charismatic Movement* (1994), contends that Jung's account of the "scientific" origins of the collective unconscious is suspect. Noll is a German-speaking Jung scholar who has had access to Jung's personal papers and frequently travels to Switzerland for research. According to Noll, Jung claimed he collected his first objective data supporting the collective unconscious from the hallucinations reported by one of his patients during some 1906 therapy sessions. This patient had visions of the Sun Phallus: an image of the sun with an erect penis extending from its surface. A book published in 1910 confirmed that the Sun Phallus was indeed a symbol from humans' ancient history as told in mythology. Because the Sun Phallus Man, as he was dubbed, had his visions before the book's publication, Jung argued his patient could have had no prior knowledge of the Sun Phallus. Thus, Jung claimed the Sun Phallus visions must have come from the patient's collective unconscious. But Noll charges that Jung prevaricated about some important facts. First, the patient was not his, but was in the charge of his student, Honegger. Second, Honegger did not begin working with the patient and recording the Sun Phallus visions until 1909. Third, the 1910 book was clearly marked as a second edition; the first edition was published in 1903, making it the possible source of the Sun Phallus Man's visions. Further, contrary to Jung's elitist belief, uneducated people like the Sun Phallus Man had access to the symbols of mythology through the popular press of the day. Given these allegations are true, according to Noll, the evidence Jung considered his most important support for the collective unconscious is tainted. While these charges are serious, they are neither as long-lived nor forceful as those lodged against Freud. Only time will tell whether they are sufficiently valid to be a matter of great concern.

Conclusions

Although Jung's contributions to the psychology of personality have had less impact than those of Freud, appreciation of his ideas is increasing over time. Jung was not a theorist "in the right place at the right time." He was often overshadowed by the dominating presence of Freud, a circumstance he shared with others considered in this book. Following his break with Freud, Jung (1963) found even his professional acquaintances dropping away—"I was a mystic, and that settled the matter" (p. 167). However, the breadth of Jung's perspective on personality remains unrivaled. It encompasses the collective unconscious of antiquity as well as futuristic ideas about synchronicity and extrasensory perception.

If one lays aside science criteria and views Jung's theory as more philosophical, many of its problems evaporate. Regardless of the "science" question, it was Jung who introduced the timeless notion of introversion–extraversion—now a part of our language—and popularized the central idea "self." Further, as you will see in subsequent chapters, his openness to the use of many different kinds of procedures in therapy and his willingness to participate in therapy with patients set precedents that are still being followed today. More specifically, several theorists have endorsed Jung's assumptions about dream-series interpretation (Perls, 1969), self-realization (Horney, 1950), the holistic nature of human experience (Rogers, 1961), and the biological origin of spiritual meaning (Maslow, 1967).

Clinically, Jung worked more with normal persons than did Freud. Unlike Freud, his therapy clientele covered the full range of the life span, including adults undergoing midlife crises. Also, his therapeutic work was undertaken not only with neurotic patients but with more seriously disturbed people. Thus, ideas derived from his clinical experience have the aura of more general representativeness than those of Freud. In addition, thanks in part to the great variety of patients contributing to his clinical experience, his theoretical notions are broader, spanning not just childhood and adolescence, but also adulthood and old age.

Experimentally, there is support for Jung's concepts of introversion and extraversion, the four functions, and for applications of the Word Association Test (Cramer, 1968). Although Jung's popularity may be greater in Europe than the United States, a journal devoted to his view, *The Journal of Analytical Psychology*, has an American as well as a British version.

Like Freud's writings, Jung's twenty-volume collected works contain many undiscovered insights. His orientation to the mystical and to the past history of humans may have more appeal to young people of today than to the youth of Jung's own time. That you can expect increased interest in Jung during the next century is evidenced by the observation that Jungian therapists are thriving and Jung's ideas are moving into the sphere of popular literature (DeAngelis, 1994). As the latter, witness the success of Latina author and Jungian therapist Clarissa Pinkola Estes' *Women Who Run with Wolves*, an exploration of the wild woman archetype.

Summary Points

1. Jung was born (1875) in Kesswill, Switzerland, the son of a minister and possibly the great-grandson of Goethe. As a lonely, reclusive boy, he had many visions, including one of a phallic symbol. These mystical interests carried over into adulthood as indicated by the theme of his post-M.D. research and his interest in Eastern religions. His break with Freud was traumatic, but was associated with creative visions and experiences. He believed in the balance of opposites, including entropy, and that libido is subject to equivalence. Jung's theory is pan-cultural and can be embraced by people of any culture.

2. Jung's personal unconscious is different for different people, but his collective unconscious is the same for all people. The psyche is all of mentality. The ego is associated with consciousness. Persona is the mask that corresponds to any one of the roles that society thrusts upon us. The self is the core of the psyche. The collective unconscious contains the archetypes.

3. Jung emphasized the archetypes shadow, anima, and animus. Archetypes can suddenly "seize you" and have been used to explain reports of UFOs. Archetypes are plentiful in horror movies and may be manifested in synchrony with external events and synchronicity is a concept in tune with ESP.

4. Little Anna was obsessed with "where babies come from." She sometimes displayed behaviors that appeared to support Freud's notions of psychosexuality. However, Jung discounted Freudian explanations in favor of Anna's archetypical obsession with the cycle of

birth and rebirth. Unlike Freud, Jung did not distinguish between latent and manifest dream content—the symbols of the collective unconscious and its archetypes are displayed directly in dreams. Dreams anticipate the future and compensate for a conscious process by manifesting its unconscious opposite.

5. Jung's most enduring contributions are "extraversion" and "introversion." Also important are his four psychological functions: thinking, feeling, sensing, and intuiting. Individuation is the "process by which a person becomes a psychological in-dividual." It differentiates the self from the psyche with the aid of the transcendental function. Jung postulated four stages of development. He viewed the impact of relations between children and their parents differently than Freud.

6. Some research regarding Jung's psychological types seems to indicate clearer support for extraversion than introversion, and, in the case of classroom discussion, stronger support for the importance of his four functions than for introversion/extraversion. Jung's analytic psychotherapy is unique in that patient and therapist have relatively equal status, therapy tends to be relatively short-term, and different techniques associated with different theories are seen as relatively equivalent.

7. Jung pioneered the use of projective tests and helped popularize the concept "complex." Dissolving troublesome complexes was a main goal of psychotherapy. A boy with a mother complex is a case in point. Jungian therapeutic and diagnostic techniques include the Word Association Test, dream and waking amplification, dream series analysis, and active imagination.

8. Jung's limitations are much like Freud's: his concepts are often poorly or ambiguously defined, some of his concepts are mixed up with others, some concepts are defined differently in different writings, and the contents of the collective unconscious are not clearly specified. Those faults lower the scientific status of the theory.

9. The most serious problem with Jung's point of view is that assumptions behind the collective unconscious have the flavor of "inheritance of acquired characteristics." Jung has been accused of prevaricating in regard to his claims for evidence in support of the collective unconscious. Jung's impact may have been less than Freud's because he stood in the "master's" shadow and was identified with mysticism.

10. Jung's innovations, such as extraversion–introversion and self, as well as his flexibility and contribution to others' theories, make him a major contributor. Undoubtedly, Jung's vast writings will yield new insights when they are more fully examined. In the meantime, his more mystical point of view may receive increased attention as time passes, especially among young people. He is even moving into the sphere of popular literature.

Running Comparison

Theorist	*Jung in Comparison*
Freud	Jung also used psyche, ego, consciousness, unconsciousness and analogies to id and insight. He and Freud even shared shortcomings. But Jung rejected sexualism, criticized penis envy, made no distinction between latent and manifest dream content, and viewed the impact of parents differently.

Carl Rogers	Jung anticipated Rogers's concern with self-acceptance and his more equal status relations with patients.
Abraham Maslow	Jung anticipated Maslow's concern for self-actualization.

Essay/Critical Thinking Questions

1. Can you argue that the mystical, magical, parapsychological orientation is, as Jung would have it, an important part of understanding personality?

2. List and describe three personas that are not mentioned in the book. How does each impede the development of persons who manifest it?

3. Can you make up an archetype different from any discussed by Jung? Choose it from the mythology of an ancient culture. For example—but not for your use—the swastika is an ancient Germanic and Native American symbol.

4. Can you reconsider the case of Little Hans and reinterpret it in Jungian terms?

5. Can you write four items for a test of introversion–extraversion, two that would be endorsed by introverts and two that would be endorsed by extraverts?

6. Reconsider a series of your own dreams, briefly describe them, then analyze them in Jungian terms.

7. Are you a sensation, thinking, feeling, or intuiting type (or none of the above)? Indicate why you are one or more of the four function types and not the other types.

8. Pretend that you are a Jungian analyst hunting for a complex that is troubling a patient. Can you describe the complex, how you would confirm its existence, and what you would do to dissolve it?

9. Several contributions of Jung are described in the book. Can you come up with one missed by the author and indicate why it is important?

10. Several criticisms of Jung's ideas and methods are described in the book. Can you come up with one missed by the author and indicate why it is important?

E-mail Interaction

(Write the author at mfbpa@wiu.edu)
Forward any of the following or phrase your own questions.

1. Do you believe in parapsychology?
2. Do beings visit from other planets or from the collective unconscious?
3. Are you an introvert or an extravert?
4. Was Jung really a Nazi sympathizer?
5. Tell me what is the most central part of Jung's theory.

4

OVERCOMING INFERIORITY AND STRIVING FOR SUPERIORITY: ALFRED ADLER

- Are people prone to feel inferior?
- Does it matter whether you are born first, second, middle, last, or are an only child?
- Are people destined to be social beings, or do they have to work at it?
- Is your life style temporary—forced on you by your current circumstances—or does it have deeper meaning?
- Do the earliest memories that you can recollect say anything about you as a person?

Alfred Adler

Although Freud stands apart from other theorists in pioneering new ideas and methods for understanding personality, one of his continuing contributions has been to inspire others concerning new ways to think about personality. It was not just a matter of the content of Freud's ideas—what to think. It was also a matter of procedure—how to think. Some of Freud's psychiatric followers adhered closely to his orthodox tradition (Deutsch, 1945; Fenichel, 1945). Others, like Jung, shared many ideas with Freud, but deviated from his position. Still others began to elaborate entirely new concepts, to question and even abandon some of the tenets of classical psychoanalysis. These *neo-Freudians* include the theorists covered in this and two subsequent chapters: Alfred Adler, Karen Horney, and Harry Stack Sullivan. That Erik Erikson and Erich Fromm were also neo-Freudian is questionable because they ventured too far from Freudian thought. In fact, you may have difficulty seeing Horney, Sullivan and, perhaps, especially Adler as neo-Freudian. Freud is well hidden in their points of view. Although these theorists were influenced by Freud, all departed from his ideas. In effect, they reacted against Freud's ideas in developing their own. All, in varying degrees, abandoned Freud's "overemphasis" on infantile sexuality and elaborated new concepts about parent–child relationships, social experiences, and cultural patterns of behavior.

Jung's split with Freud was painful and not really desired by either party. Mutual respect and personal warmth had characterized their relationship. By contrast, Alfred Adler's fatal

73

rift with Freud was more due to a clash of wills. When Adler brazenly refused to embrace Freud's sexual instinct, and openly rejected the Oedipus Complex, he came to be regarded as a renegade. Adler even saw Jung as deviating little from Freud's "sexualism" (Kaiser, 1994). At the urging of his close followers, Freud decided to force Adler out of the psychoanalytic camp. As both individuals were editors of a psychoanalytic journal, Freud devised a showdown. He wrote the journal staff a "him or me letter": He would resign if Adler remained on the editorial board. Adler promptly quit and thereafter became the enemy. During the period that followed, some of Freud's communications with Jung were diatribes against Adler.

Adler, The Person

Alfred Adler was born in Vienna in 1870 to a middle-class Jewish family. Because he did not grow up in a Jewish neighborhood, he never developed a strong identity as a Jew. Accordingly, he converted to Protestantism in his youth and thereafter considered himself a Christian.

The fact that he was the second of six children was to have a profound affect on Adler. He felt that he would always be in the shadow of his successful older brother. Despite some successes of his own, Adler regarded his childhood as rather unhappy. His childhood illnesses, however, proved to be assets. He suffered from rickets during infancy, and nearly died of pneumonia at age five. Following a miraculous recovery, young Adler vowed to become a physician and save others. Later he was to theorize about the implications of being an invalid.

In a lecture given when he was more than sixty years old, Adler talked about the importance of his early physical ailments:

> *I was born a very weak child suffering from certain weaknesses, especially from rickets which prevented me from moving very well. Despite this obstacle, now, nearly at the end of my life, I am standing before you in America. You can see how I have overcome this difficulty. Also, I could not speak very well early in my life; I spoke very slowly. Also, though you are probably not aware of it in my English, I am supposed to be a very good orator in German. I have also overcome this difficulty (Stepansky, 1983, p. 9).*

Adler was more of a father's son than a mother's boy. The fact that he felt closer to his father may in part explain why he found Freud's Oedipal Complex so alien. A boy who cherishes his father and is somewhat distant from his mother is not likely to accept the belief that boys wish their fathers would disappear so they could be in sole possession of their mothers.

Adler did not distinguish himself as a student. In grade school he was average. The University of Vienna did grant him a medical degree in 1895, but he failed to impress any professor enough to develop the close mentor–student relationship that Freud experienced. During this period he flirted with Marxism and became something of a student revolutionary. Among the rebellious youths who shared his socialist inclinations was an intellectual revolutionary from a wealthy Russian family who especially interested him. She eventually became Raissa Adler.

Adler began his medical career as a general practitioner. Among his typically impoverished patients were some who showed outstanding physical abilities. For example, some were acrobats. What intrigued Adler the most was his observation that some of these strong performers had been victims of physical weakness or accidents as children. Coupled with his own experience of childhood weakness, it appeared that early handicaps can, through compensation, lead to adult accomplishments.

Adler had a strong social conscience. His tendency to support the underdog may explain his initially friendly overtures to Freud and his ideas. Like Jung, at first Adler defended Freud. Despite the irreconcilable differences they developed later, Adler never totally rejected all of Freudianism. Even after his resignation from the joint editorship with Freud, Adler recommended that his students become thoroughly acquainted with Freud's "meritorious" theory of dreams (Adler, 1964). Like Jung, he was more open to Freud than Freud was to him.

Unlike Jung, the formation of Adler's major ideas followed rather than preceded his split with Freud. It was after serving as an army physician during World War I that Adler framed perhaps his most useful concept. During this period he witnessed firsthand the suffering of wounded soldiers and the despair of children damaged by war. These human tragedies and some people's altruistic responses to them led him to theorize about *Gemeinschaftsgefuhl*, development of a deep-seated concern for others and a need to associate with them (Ionedes, 1989). Later it was translated as "social interest," a concept that was to become central to his theory.

After he established his own point of view, Adler endured rebellion among the socially conscious radicals he attracted. He also suffered the deprivations that came with serving the "common folk" rather than the "well-to-do" who gathered in Freud's waiting room. These difficult experiences probably increased his interest in overcoming adversity and also his identification with those who suffer calamities during their lives.

Adler was probably the only well-known personality psychologist who held political office (Rychlak, 1981). As vice-chairman of the workers committee in Vienna, he gained some influence with the Social Democrats. Using the leverage associated with this post, he and his students installed Adlerian clinics in the thirty state-run schools of Vienna. These mental health facilities prospered from 1921 until 1934 when they were closed by the Nazis. The clinics scored many successes. For example, the Viennese delinquency rate dropped during the clinics' existence.

Later, Adler's emphasis on adult education established him as a pioneer in applied psychology. After a first visit in 1926, the United States became his home when in 1934 he and his wife fled Nazi-infested Austria. Here Adler became known as an "indefatigable lecturer" to parents and teachers, as well as a "constant advisor" to child-guidance clinics (Alexander & Selesnick, 1966). These characteristics clearly confirm his tendency to extraversion, especially relative to Freud and Jung (Dolliver, 1994). His remaining life combined great energy, enjoyment, and capacity for work. You will learn in later chapters that he had significant influence on other personality psychologists during his time in the United States.

Adler has been described as "a most democratic, friendly, hospitable person with a love for informal sociability, music, and all the arts, including gardening" (Ansbacher 1964, p. xxii). Two of his four children, Alexandra and Kurt, became psychiatrists in their father's tradition. Like their father, they were devoted to helping people overcome handicaps and enjoy life more fully.

Adler's View of the Person

Basic Orientation

As you may have already gathered, Adler did not like to think of humans as collections of ids, egos, and complexes. Rather he saw the person as a whole individual with aspects that are too interconnected for meaningful examination apart from one another. The lives of people were seen as flowing from immaturity to maturity without the discrete breaks that characterized Freud's stages of psychosexual development. From his perspective, people decided for themselves what direction their lives would take—sometimes wisely, sometimes not. Whatever direction people's lives took, Adler saw them as striving for "perfection" as they conceived of the term.

Unlike Freud, Adler changed his view of the person over the years (Ansbacher & Ansbacher, 1964). At first he emphasized natural feelings of inferiority that supposedly appear very early in life and require compensation thereafter. Eva Dreidurs Ferguson (1989) called this orientation the first stage in the development of Adler's thinking. She defined a second stage that emphasized striving for power and superiority. Finally, more near the end of his career, "Adler made it explicit that humans as a species strive to belong and that the goal ... is to contribute to human welfare" (p. 354).

Dinkmeyer and Sherman (1989) list five principles that might be regarded as basic Adlerian assumptions about people and their psychological functioning. Understanding them will move you closer to appreciating Adler's view of the person.

1. *All behavior has social meaning.* A social group, such as a family, has its own social system, including methods of relating and ways by which power is communicated. "All behavior has meaning inside this social context. Behavior can best be understood and changed when seen within the social context" (p. 148).
2. *All behavior has a purpose and is goal-directed.* Adler firmly believed that all behavior is **teleological** or performed with a purpose. He also believed that people are always moving toward some significant goal. To understand a person's goal is to take a giant step toward understanding that person.
3. *Unity and pattern.* As indicated already, Adler was a pioneer in viewing people holistically. He saw people as unified, indivisible wholes, each with his or her unique pattern of behaviors that are designed to reach a goal (Kern & Watts, 1993).
4. *Behavior is designed to overcome feelings of inferiority and to move toward feelings of superiority.* "We are continuously working from a feeling of being less, toward to a feeling of being more. This is the striving for significance" (p. 149).
5. *Behavior is a result of our subjective perceptions.* "We all create unique meanings for our experiences. We actually create our script, produce, direct, act and act out our roles" (p. 149). The way we see ourselves in relation to others is from our own unique perspectives.

These principles may seem to embrace conflicting goals. On the one hand, individuals strive to perfect themselves. On the other hand, they are supposedly embedded in and dedicated to the social group. How does one devote oneself to the group and at the same time pursue personal goals? Kurt Adler (1994) provides an answer. He argues that when a person develops well, he or she forms such a strong synthesis of self-interest and social interest that whatever is done for the group is also done for the individual.

Humanitarian Approach: Diversity as It Concerns Women and All Kinds of People Everywhere

A section of the *Psychologists for Social Responsibility Newsletter* was devoted to Adler's contribution to the cause of world peace and just treatment of all people. Rudmin and Ansbacher (1989) indicated that "Adler was a social activist in theory and practice. He opposed violence of all forms and promoted social interest in the individual and in the group. To him mental health implied 'socially affirmative action' . . . and social responsibility was fundamental to the practice of psychology . . ." (p. 8). Adler himself was quoted as saying: "The honest psychologist cannot shut his eyes to social conditions which prevent the child from becoming a part of the community and from feeling at home in the world, and which allow him to grow up as though he lived in enemy country. Thus, the psychologist must work against nationalism . . . against wars of conquest . . . against unemployment which plunges people into hopelessness; and against all other obstacles which interfere with the spreading of social interest in the family, the school, and society at large" (Adler quoted in Rudmin and Ansbacher, 1989, p. 8).

In 1928 Adler, along with such notables as Mohandas Gandhi, contributed an article to *Violence and Non-violence: A Handbook of Active Pacifism*, edited by Franz Kobler on behalf of War Resisters International. In this piece he proved to be ahead of his time in appreciating diversity. Believing that people who are different from those in power should not be subjected to oppression made him an advocate of women's rights. He wrote: "War is not the continuation of politics with other means, but the greatest social crime against the solidarity of humanity . . ." (Adler quoted in Rudmin and Ansbacker, 1989, p. 8). Later he expanded this point of view to include a sympathetic reference to women. "He theorized that it was war, with its high valuation on physical strength, that led to the original subjugation of women, and he claimed that the 'inequality of women is greater in warlike countries' " (Adler, quoted in Rudmin and Ansbacher, 1989, p. 8).

Though a socialist, Adler was vehemently anti-Communist. The reasons were twofold. First, the Bolsheviks, Soviet Communists, embraced violence and sought power for its own sake. He wrote of them: "The rule of Bolshevism is based on the possession of power. Thus its fate is sealed . . . the intoxication of power has seduced them . . . Cheap reasons are given to justify action and reaction. Fair becomes foul, foul becomes fair!" (Adler quoted in Rudmin and Ansbacher, 1989, p. 8). "He likened Bolshevism to a puppet without a soul, and argued that it will be worthless if it succeeds . . ." (Rudmin and Ansbacher, 1989, p. 8). His words were obviously prophetic. Bolshevism has failed.

His second reason for hating the Communists was the arrest of his daughter Valentine during the Stalinist purges of 1937 (she had fled to the Russia of her mother to escape the Nazis). In April of the same year he wrote that "Vali" caused him sleepless nights and that he did not know whether he could endure the thought of her incarceration. Later, when he had exhausted his last means of freeing Vali, he reported that he could neither eat nor sleep for worrying about her. At about this time he was on a trip to Scotland as a part of his 1937 speaking tour. While on an after-breakfast walk he suffered a heart attack and died. Adler was sixty-seven years old.

Basic Concepts: Adler

Developing Social Feeling: Society, Work, and Love

Alfred Adler's commitment to "individual differences" is seen in the label he affixed to his point of view, **individual psychology**, an attempt to conceive of a unique human being as an interconnected whole, biologically, philosophically, and psychologically (Adler, 1971). Given this uniqueness and wholeness, the same situations, experiences, and life problems have different meanings for and effects on different people. While recognizing the existence of inborn differences among people, Adler warned against overstressing them: The important thing is "not what one is born with, but what use one makes of that equipment" (1956, p. 176). He viewed the basis of individual differences as more psychosocial than hereditary. The psychosocial factor of ultimate importance to civilization is **social feeling**, concern for the community and the need to associate/cooperate with people (Adler, 1964).

The cornerstone of individual psychology is Adler's belief that there are three unavoidable problems each person must address in life: *society*, *work*, and *love*. The solution to all three problems requires childhood preparation for **social interest**—individuals' efforts to develop social feeling (Rychlak, 1981). Although "social feeling" is a potential and "social interest" involves efforts to make it actual, Adler often used the terms interchangeably (Rychlak, 1981).

First, social feeling relevant to *society* is revealed in the individual's capacity to develop and maintain friendships. It involves preparation for cooperation in school, sports, and choice of a partner. Also the development of interest in state, country, and humanity is involved. Second, the individual must show an ability to be interested in *work*. Here social feeling takes the form of cooperative activity for the benefit of others. Individuals who perform useful work not only provide themselves with a livelihood but obtain a sense of what society values, for example, industry over laziness. It is through work that individuals assist in the progress of their developing community. Third, is an interest in *love*, the ability to be more concerned for a partner than for oneself. Here social feeling is focused on a task that requires the cooperation of two persons, as both help perpetuate the human species by caring for offspring. Prerequisites of love include childhood preparation for a two-person task, continuing consciousness of the equal worth of both partners, and a capacity for mutual devotion.

Style of Life

According to Adler, an individual's attitudes toward society, work, and love are summarized in a **style of life**, the individual's unique but consistent movement toward self-created goals and ideals developed beginning in childhood (Adler, 1964). The style of life is an original, psychological orientation that contains the individual's relatively permanent **law of movement**—the direction taken by the person that originates in his or her ability to exercise free choice in fully exploiting personal capabilities and resources (Adler, 1933a).

You have likely noticed the coincidence of style of life and "lifestyle," a currently popular phrase. "Lifestyle" probably originates from Adler's "style of life." It is another example of how our language has been influenced by the major personality theorists.

Adler illustrated style of life by reference to a couple of pine trees, one growing in a valley and one growing on a mountaintop. Although they are of the same species, each shows a distinct style of life, with individuality "expressing itself and molding itself in [a unique] environment" (1956, p. 173). In human terms, the style of life is the medium through which each of us interprets the facts of our existence and through which our lives unfold. It dominates personal experience and guides dreams, fantasies, games, and recollections of childhood. It even selects images to serve its own ends and it determines thinking, feeling, and behaving.

In forming a style of life, we are not passively molded by our environment. Personality results from the activity of the **creative power of the individual**, the process by which we each make original conceptions of ourselves and our world as we develop a style of life for solving the three great problems of life (Adler, 1932). Thus, each of us is the sculptor of our personality. Childhood beliefs, typically developed between the ages of three and five, are particularly influential in the process that nurtures the developing style of life. Once these beliefs have been held for a short time, experiences out of tune with them have little influence. Behavior, thoughts, and feelings spring from a person's ideas about self and life.

Future Goals versus Past Events

It is also during childhood that each person establishes a **prototype**, the "complete goal" of the style of life that is a fiction conceived as a means of adapting to life and includes a strategy for its achievement (Rychlak, 1981, p. 128). Development of this concept was suggested by Hans Vaihinger's (1925) philosophy that people create fictional ideas for themselves "as if" they were objectively true. Under Vaihinger's influence, Adler conceived of **fictional finalism**—a fictional goal toward which all psychological currents flow, thereby unifying the personality (Adler, 1933b). This notion later became virtually synonymous with "prototype," which took over the title of "fictional goal." In fact, Adler discarded fictional finalism, although some of his modern-day followers cling to it (Watts & Holden, 1994).

A goal orients the individual's personality toward future expectations, not the past. It provides direction for promised security, power, and perfection, and awakens feelings consistent with one's anticipations. Freudian instincts, mechanisms, impulses, and childhood traumas are far less important in this process than Adlerian teleology or purposiveness. One's prototypical goal appears

> in one's attitude toward others, toward one's vocation, toward the opposite sex. Thus we find concrete single purposes, such as: to operate as a member of the community or to dominate it, to attain security and triumph in one's chosen career, to approach the other sex or to avoid it. We may always trace in these special purposes what sort of meaning the individual has found in his existence, *and how he proposes to realize that meaning* (Adler, 1930, p. 400).

The attitude we adopt toward solving the three great problems is necessarily reflected in our personality. Because personality is a unity, the nature of our capacity for living life in common with others is manifested even in the slightest of our expressive movements. Our beliefs, misconceptions, social interest—or failure to achieve it—characterize all forms of personal expression, including our memories, dreams, bodily postures, and physical ailments. This framework underlies Adler's personality-assessment technique of collecting and interpreting early recollections dating to our toddlerhood.

Further, an individual's style of life is best seen in new situations, especially those that confront the person with difficulties. This is because one's stylistic "gait"—whether it is best characterized as a trot, a canter, or a gallop—is more clearly displayed during crises than during untroubled times. Problems result when the individual's fictions clash with reality, thereby "disclosing his wrong meaning—the mistaken significance he has foisted on life" (Adler, 1964, pp. 40–41). A type of psychological **shock** may be experienced when a person's fiction runs head-on into reality. It results in a narrowing of the person's field of action or path of advance, an exclusion of threatening tasks, and a retreat from problems for which the person is not prepared. Disillusionment, disappointment, and isolation may occur. In fact, Adler defines **neurosis** as an extreme form of reaction to shock, "a person's automatic, unknowing exploitation of the symptoms resulting from the effects of a shock" (1964, p. 180). The general level of social feeling is not high among neurotics, who likely have been pampered as children. At the lowest level, negative personality traits such as shyness, anxiety, and pessimism indicate a "defective inclination and preparation of the whole personality" in all its relations with other people (p. 112). The essence of Adlerian therapy is to increase the neurotic's awareness of this lack of manifested social feeling. A technique he found helpful in working with neurotics is to bring out the "courage" and "optimism" aspects of social feeling still existing within the neurotic personality.

Overcoming Inferiority

Adler believed in the thesis that to be human means to feel inferior, insufficient, and helpless. As mentioned earlier, this orientation became de-emphasized in his later writing, but if one considers his writings as a whole, it is quite central. The universal human experience of inferiority generates a struggle for perfection. Individuals are "always possessed and spurred on by a feeling of inferiority," brought about by their perpetual comparisons of themselves with unattainable ideals of perfection (Adler, 1964, p. 37). As in evolution, there is a "great upward drive" toward perfection or a "compulsion" to carry out a better adaptation. In essence, all personality develops from **inferiority**, the persistent feeling that one does not measure up to society's ideals or to one's own fictional standards (1964). The individual's movement in life is from a minus to a plus condition.

Inferiority complex is Adler's term for the consequences of an exaggerated, persistent form of inadequacy that is partly explained by a deficiency in social interest (Adler, 1964). Adler discussed three childhood handicaps contributing to inferior feelings and a resultant lack of social feeling: inferior organs, neglect, and overindulgence (Adler, 1933a).

Inferior Physical Organs
To Adler, an "organ" could be any physical attribute. His study of organ inferiority led him to conclude that feelings of psychological inferiority might be due to a person's physical

limitations (Adler, 1907/1917). This is because children born with organ weaknesses are necessarily required to **compensate**, to overcome their weaknesses by striving to become superior in some way (Adler, 1971). They may even **overcompensate**, bend over backwards to do or become whatever their weaknesses have denied them. The ancient Greek Demosthenes had weak lungs and a weak voice, yet he became a famous orator. Pianist Klara Schumann overcame childhood hearing problems. In this context, I am reminded of a colleague's blind student who ended a classroom talk about personal career plans by reciting all the possibilities open to him, including becoming an astronomer. Adler saw human development as "blessed with inferior organs" (1930, p. 395) because of the achievements that can be traced to the efforts aimed at overcoming physical inferiorities.

Parental Neglect: The Unwanted or Hated Child

The neglected child does not experience love, cooperation, or friendship, and seldom finds a trustworthy other person. Throughout life, problems are overrated as "too difficult" and personal resources for problem-solving are underrated as being too limited. Neglected children may be described as cold, suspicious, untrusting, hard, envious, and hateful.

Parental Overindulgence: A Harmful Practice That Often Produces a Pampered or Spoiled Child

Adler proposed overindulgence as an alternative to Freud's "misinterpretation" of observations that led him to the Oedipus complex (Adler, 1964). To Adler the Oedipus complex is not a universal fact but something that occurs infrequently. It is an abnormality, the unnatural outcome of overindulgence by the child's opposite-sex parent. The basic pattern is one in which the pampered child is allowed contact mainly with the person doing the spoiling, thereby excluding others. The result of this pattern is a child who feels superficially superior and expects homage from others.

Striving for Superiority and the Superiority Complex

During the transition from emphasizing inferiority to stressing service to society, Adler wrote of **striving for superiority**, a universal psychological phenomenon that parallels physical growth and involves the goal of bringing about perfection, security, and strength. It is represented by the dictates "Achieve! Arise! Conquer!" Specific paths to perfection differ in a multitude of ways, just as do the chosen goals. **Superiority complex** is Adler's term for an exaggerated, abnormal form of striving for superiority that involves overcompensation for personal weakness. Like other severe psychological problems, this one is partly explained by a deficiency in social interest development. The neurotic person may present a false front of superiority as a method of escaping from social difficulties. Normal people do not have superiority complexes. Their strivings for superiority are aimed at common ambitions for success, expressed through work, love, and cooperation in society. In this light, striving for superiority is a positive pursuit akin to "self-actualization" as discussed in the Rogers and Maslow chapters. By contrast, a superiority complex "invariably" stands in opposition to social cooperation.

As the concept "superiority complex" implies, Adler's theory has something to say about *braggarts*, people who may irritate us with their constant claims of superiority. Many of us probably assume that braggarts believe themselves to be superior. However, Adlerians would be inclined to a different interpretation. The more people brag about themselves, the more an Adlerian might see them as just compensating for unresolved feelings of inferiority. That is, braggarts may actually be people who feel inferior and are boasting to compensate.

Whether or not it is to cover up inferiority, braggarts' behavior may reflect on us, making us look inferior by contrast to them. When people make very positive statements about themselves in our presence, they may make us look bad by comparison. Dismissing braggarts' exaggerated claims and assuming they are just trying to cover up their inadequacies would seem to save us from feeling inferior relative to them. If, in fact, people adopt this logic they should describe braggarts in negative terms. Tucibat (1986) did a study to see how people respond to a braggart. Surprisingly, he found that subjects in his experiment tended to use favorable terms to describe a braggart who boasted about doing very well *in the future*.

If Adler had known of these results he might have asserted that our acceptance of other's boastfulness may be an indication that we assume our own inferiority relative to them. However, final conclusions await additional research. Future studies may show that when braggarts boast about past accomplishments we tend to reject their attempts to exalt themselves over us. Only when people stick their necks out by boasting about future accomplishments do we admire them (for example, Mike Tyson boasting that he will knock out his opponent in the first round).

Family Influences on Personality Development

Of the several family influences on personality development discussed by Adler, the most important is the mother (Adler, 1964). Contact with her probably makes the largest contribution to the social interest of the child. Two tasks are involved. One is encouraging social feeling by providing the deepest and most genuine love and fellowship the child will ever experience. Another is spreading this connectedness, trust, and friendship to others in the form of displaying a cooperative attitude when interacting with them. Adlerian therapists perform these tasks for patients who are deficient in social interest.

Second in importance for personality development is experience with the father. Adler offered a number of specific suggestions concerning how fathers may contribute to their children's development: allow freedom to speak and ask questions; encourage the pursuit of personal interests; do not ridicule or belittle; do not seek to supplant the mother; make mealtimes pleasant; be supportive.

Third in importance is **birth order**, the child's birth position relative to other siblings (Adler, 1964; see Table 4.1). In addition to birth order in and of itself, Adler's theory addresses the impact of family size and sex of siblings on personality. He deemed it a "superstition" to believe that a given family situation is the same for each individual child. This qualification helps to account for cases where circumstances may be psychologically similar for children in seemingly inconsistent birth order positions. Thus, it is not birth order itself that accounts for differences among siblings, but the psychological situation resulting from it.

The "birth order" factor has been heavily researched in the decades after it was posed by Adler (Falbo & Polit, 1986). For example, reviews of the literature indicate a total of

TABLE 4.1   Some Adlerian Hypotheses about Birth Order

Birth Order	% of Population*	Hypotheses
Only child	5	The center of attention, dominant, often spoiled because of excessive parental timidity and anxiety
First-born	28	Dethroned from a central position, has negative attitudes and feelings toward the second child and a passion for domination, but protective and helpful toward others
Second-born	28	Actively struggling to surpass others, with success related to competition with the first-born, restless
Last-born	18	The most pampered (the smallest and weakest), not unhappy, able to excel over others by being different, often a problem child
Only girl/boy		Extreme feminine or masculine orientation

*From Simpson, Bloom, Newlon, & Arminio (1994); percentages do not add up to 100 because a "middle-born" category used by Simpson et al. is not included.

391 studies on birth order between 1963 and 1971 alone (Miley, 1969; Vockell, Felker, & Miley, 1973). Birth order was also the sole topic of the May 1977 issue of *Individual Psychology*. After all these investigations, it is now clear that most of the differences, insofar as they exist, are between firstborn (or only) and laterborn individuals. Research suggests that firstborns and only children are higher in achievement motivation and actual success than laterborns. Such may be the case, because their environment contains only adults, mature people who are capable of creating an achievement-oriented atmosphere. On the other hand, laterborns have an atmosphere that is less mature, because it is composed of children as well as adults (Zajonc & Markus, 1975). Thus, one is more likely to find firstborns rather than laterborns in the U.S. Senate or the executive boardroom. However, firstborns are not better in every way. For example, laterborns are less self-centered (Falbo, 1981).

Robert Zajonc and his colleagues have focused on the dilution of the home intellectual atmosphere by mixing laterborn children with firstborns and the adults who constitute the firstborn's mature environment. Zajonc and Markus (1975) have related family size to intellectual development. Using data on nearly 400,000 Dutch nineteen-year-old males, they found larger family size detrimental to intellectual development. They explained this result by reasoning that each laterborn child added to a family of increasing size dilutes the intellectual atmosphere for all children. Further, the larger the family, the more compressed the spacing between children, which leads to a decline in average age of family members, and, in turn, a more immature intellectual atmosphere for each child. In sum, large families immerse children in a laterborn intellectual atmosphere, one created by cognitively primitive people, a sharp contrast to the adult atmosphere that exists for firstborns. Table 4.2 illustrates the effects of spacing on intellectual atmosphere. Note that "I.Q." for children is relative to adults rather than to children the same age (see Table footnotes).

TABLE 4.2   The Effect of Spacing on Intellectual Atmosphere

	Ideal Spacing	Close Spacing
1st Born	Father I.Q. = 100* Mother I.Q. = 100 Atmospheric Average = 100	Father I.Q. = 100 Mother I.Q. = 100 Atmospheric Average = 100
2nd Born	When 1st born is 8 years Father I.Q. = 100 Mother I.Q. = 100 1st Born I.Q. = 60 Atmospheric Average = 86.6**	When 1st born is 1 year Father I.Q. = 100 Mother I.Q. = 100 1st Born I.Q. = 10 Atmospheric Average = 70
3rd Born	When 1st Born is 16 and 2nd Born is 8 Father I.Q. = 100 Mother I.Q. = 100 1st Born I.Q. = 95 2nd Born I.Q. = 60 Atmospheric Average = 88.7	When 1st Born is 2 and 2nd born is 1 Father I.Q. = 100 Mother I.Q. = 100 1st Born I.Q. = 20 2nd Born I.Q. = 10 Atmospheric Average = 57.5

*Adult I.Q. points (children's scores are equivalent adult I.Q. points; that is, children's scores represent their intellectual ability relative to adults, not other children their age).

**This figure is the sum of father's, mother's, and existing children's I.Q.s at the time of a new child's birth, divided by the number of preexisting family members ([100+100+60])/3 = 86.6).

Some more contemporary studies also appear to support Adler's notions about birth order. For example, Parrish (1990) investigated teachers' evaluations of ninety-four students' support systems (a support system is composed of friends and relatives who provide aid and comfort in times of distress). He found that firstborns experienced fewer dysfunctional support systems than laterborns. Parish also reported that firstborns experienced fewer support system failures than laterborns when both were from divorced and remarried families. The two birth order positions did not differ if both were from intact families or from divorced-nonremarried families.

In line with earlier results, Cherian (1990) found that among 1021 South African school children, the later children were born into their families, the lower was their academic achievement. An additional study by Ishiyama, Munson, and Chabassol (1990) produced logically related results. Among 194 Canadian high school students, compared to laterborns, firstborns showed less fear of the possible negative consequences of academic success (an example of negative consequence would be facing higher expectations after scoring a success).

Evaluation

Contributions

Early Recollections: A Prediction of the Present
Adler employed a simple method to assess aspects of people's lifestyles (Lyer, Woods, & Boudewyns, 1989). **Early recollections (ERs)** indicate how a person views her or himself

BOX 4.1   Frankenstein and His Monster Reconsidered: An Adlerian Analysis

When R. John Huber, Joan Widdifiel, and Charles Johnson (1989) recently took another look at Mary Shelley's (1965) classic novel about a brilliant scientist who creates life in the laboratory, they noted remarkably clear illustrations of Adler's major principles and conceptions. Huber and colleagues contend that Frankenstein was not a scientist interested in advancing his discipline and benefiting humanity who was victimized by laboratory manipulations gone wrong. Rather he was a man overwhelmed with compensatory strivings for godlike superiority because of inferior feelings dating to his pampered childhood. Further, his "monster" began life with human qualities, including the desire to be a loved member of the community, and might have developed his natural propensity to social feeling had it not been for the neglect of his "father," Frankenstein. An examination of the two main characters in Shelley's misunderstood novel provides helpful illustrations of Adler's most critical concepts.

Victor Frankenstein: The pampered child becomes the adult seeker of grandiosity. The first five years of his life, Victor Frankenstein was an only child, the recipient of his parents' "inexhaustible stores of affection from a very mine of love" (Shelley, 1965, p. 32). He was his parents' "innocent and helpless creature bestowed on them by heaven" their "plaything and idol" and their "only care" (p. 32). When his parents adopted a daughter, Frankenstein was not threatened. His new sister was presented to him as his "pretty present." He came to regard her as a possession. During what was for him an idyllic childhood, Frankenstein had only his family and one friend, all of whom regarded him as the center of the universe. However, at maturity, having ventured forth from his privileged realm and arrived at the university, he felt immediately alienated from the other students, a sure sign of deficient social interest. Neither did he seek the help and cooperation of his professors. Frankenstein earned his own way into the halls of science. Throughout his early adult years, he yearned only for those who had pampered him during childhood. Finally, the longing became so strong that he

partially transferred his childhood universe to his new galaxy by marrying his adopted sister!

You may wonder how a pampered child harbors feelings of inferiority and resultant strivings for superiority as Adler has claimed and as Huber and colleagues extrapolated to Frankenstein. Pampering may promote inferiority because coddled children do not recognize their feelings of inferiority, much less feel the need to struggle with those basic emotions. Rather they respond to exaggerated attention by assuming their superiority and letting close relatives grapple with their problems. Consistent with these ideas, Frankenstein grew to adulthood laboring under the delusion that he was a superior being.

Then, suddenly, he was at the university, facing the shock of being surrounded by people who, by their inattention, challenged the fiction of his genius. [To Adler (1931) a true genius is one who creates a timeless contribution to all of humanity, not a memorial to her or his presumed superiority.] His response to shock was withdrawal into plans to rise above all students, all people. Through the creation of life, Frankenstein expected to transcend mere mortals. Instead he suffered the fate of all those who are dominated by the superiority complex, self-destruction.

Frankenstein's creation: Unsupported attempts to develop social feeling yield monstrous results. In complete contradiction to movie depictions, Frankenstein's "monster" began life with clear signs of social interest. His "life" is a profound testimony to the truth of Adler's belief that social feeling is a potential common to us all that may or may not become actual. The "monster," whose strength and intelligence were extraordinary, showed the need for upward striving by immediately displaying an intense desire to learn. In particular, he strove to learn language, a definite sign of emerging social feeling. A still clearer mark of social interest was his need for companionship and desire to relate to others. He peered from his miserable hovel at the villagers as they passed by and longed to become one of them. When they were joyful so was he; when they were unhappy he was depressed. "The creation wept with sensitivity when he

Continued

BOX 4.1   *Continued*

observed displays of affection, heard of injustices to mankind, or heard beautiful music" (Huber et al., 1989, p. 275).

Despite this evidence that social feeling was blooming in the "monster," events began to remind him of his inferiority. When he visited a blind priest from whom he expected sympathy, all went well until others arrived on the scene and recoiled in horror at his appearance. It was the first time that others' abhorrence of his organ inferiority fully registered on him. When he saw his own image in a pool of water for the first time, he was able to understand their revulsion at the mere sight of him.

The final blow was struck when "The Creation" read an abandoned copy of *Paradise Lost* and contrasted his own existence with that of Adam. Adam was loved; Adam had a mate; he did not. When he revealed the agony of his loneliness to his creator and pleaded for a mate, Frankenstein at first expressed intentions to sculpt a wife for him. But when the scientist began what was to be his second creation, he was overcome with guilt and concern. If the monster had a mate, they would have offspring that might terrorize the world. Was this concern a vestige of social interest? Huber and colleagues think so. Was his guilt a sign of his genuine affinity for people and love of

community? The authors thought not. His display of guilt was merely an attempt to appear more sensitive and thoughtful than others.

Extreme strivings for superiority end in self-destruction. When guilt led Frankenstein to destroy his laboratory, and thereby end the possibility of a female creation, the monster realized that his "father" had abandoned him. At the same time the scientist's rash act made him apperceive that the life he had created in his lab had visited catastrophe on the world rather than heaped glory on himself. His creation, upon accepting that his desire for companionship and membership in the community had been dashed forever, declared ". . . if I cannot inspire love, I will cause fear" (Shelley, 1965, p. 147). Truly there is no hatred so intense as that born of unrequited love. The enraged monster went on an unmerciful rampage. He stalked Frankenstein, leaving the mangled bodies of the scientist's loved ones in his wake. Finally, they adopted a mutual goal: destroy the other. In the end, Frankenstein's desperate striving to overcome inferiority due to a pampered childhood, and the monster's struggle to compensate for the repulsive appearance that constituted his organ defect, led to the demise of both. Each was a victim of failure to develop social feeling.

---

and other people and reveal what the person strives for in life, what he or she anticipates, and, more generally, his or her conception of life itself. ERs also index present attitudes, beliefs, and motives. That is, ERs are more important for what they say about a person as she or he is now, than for what the person was like as a child.

The best way to appreciate an ER is to do one. Read the instructions in Box 4.2 concerning how to do an ER. Do one, then read on to find out how to interpret your ER.

The technique of asking people to state their earliest recollection (ER) was dear to Adler. He would "never" investigate a personality without asking for the first memory, which he considered one of the most trustworthy ways of exploring personality. In essence, ERs are summary statements about personality, closely tied to the person's style of life.

Adler's reliance on ERs reflects his special brand of determinism: *the present determines the past*, exactly the opposite of Freud's determinism. According to Adler, the individual's *current style of life* forces him or her to select precisely those events from the past that best represent its contemporary condition. One has little choice in the matter. Also, it makes no difference whether the events appearing in our ER really occurred. It is only important that we believe such events happened, in the particular way we remember them.

BOX 4.2   Doing and Interpreting ERs

To do an ER, simply think back to the earliest time in your life that you can remember. Write down this earliest recollection as completely as you can. After you are finished, return to the next paragraph.

You can interpret your ER by answering some questions concerning it (Manaster & Perryman, 1979). Answer each question fully.

1. Who is present? Mother, father, siblings, grandparents, friends?
2. Who is not present?
3. How are different people portrayed? What are the basic thoughts, feelings, words, and actions of all present?

4. What is the world like? Friendly? Hostile? Cooperative? Uncooperative? Unfamiliar?
5. What is your role or behavior? Active? Passive? Independent? Dependent? Sick?
6. What is the outcome of your behavior? Success? Failure? Uncertainty? Good? Bad? Right? Wrong?
7. What is your primary social attitude? "I" or "we"?
8. What is your dominant emotion? Happy? Sad? Fearful? Worried? Guilty? Proud?
9. What is your primary motive? To gain attention, power, revenge, or to be left alone?
10. What is the underlying "story" of your life?

Among all psychological expressions, some of the most revealing are the individual's memories. His memories are the reminders he carries about with him of his own limits and of the meaning of circumstances.

There are no "chance memories": out of the incalculable number of impressions which meet an individual, he chooses to remember only those which he feels, however darkly, to have a bearing on his situation. Thus memories represent his "Story of My Life"; a story he repeats to himself to warn him or comfort him, to keep him concentrated on his goal . . . A depressed individual could not remain depressed if he remembered his good moments and his successes. He must say to himself, "All my life I was unfortunate," and select only those events which he can interpret as instances of his unhappy fate. Memories can never run counter to the style of life (Adler, 1956, p. 351).

Sanitioso, Kunda, and Fong (1990) produced results consistent with Adler's belief that people's current conceptions of themselves influence their recollections of the past. These researchers first informed some subjects that it is better to be introverted. Others were told that being extraverted is better. It may be assumed that subjects in the first group would come to see themselves as introverted, and those in the second group would see themselves as extraverted. Then subjects read a message on a personal computer screen and pressed a key to signify "yes" as soon as they had a memory related to the message. Each message pertained to introversion or to extraversion. Subjects who were made to feel "introverted" were quicker to come up with a memory when cued by an introverted message than those who were led to feel "extraverted." The analogous results occurred for those led to feel extraverted. Thus, as Adler would have predicted, individuals whose current conception of themselves was "extravert" were relatively quick to retrieve extraverted memories and those whose conceptions were "introvert" were relatively quick to recollect introverted memories.

Two examples of ERs follow, accompanied by Adler's (1956) interpretations of them.

#1. When I was three years old, my father purchased for us a pair of ponies. He brought them by the halters to the house. My sister took one strap and led her pony triumphantly down the street. My own pony, hurrying after the other, went too fast for me and trailed me face downward in the dirt. It was an ignominious end to an experience which had been gloriously anticipated. The fact that I later surpassed my sister as a horsewoman has never mellowed this disappointment in the least (pp. 354–355).

Adler offered a "blind interpretation" of this memory, which means he knew nothing about the person who gave it. He assumed the person to be a girl who was more interested in her father than her mother, just as he had been. The older sister, who may have been the mother's favorite, experienced triumph. The girl is unable to keep up with her older sister. She believes she must be careful or her older sister will always win and she will always be left behind "in the dirt," defeated. The girl's attitude conveyed in the ER is "If anyone is ahead of me, I am endangered. I must always be first."

#2. When I was about four years old I sat at the window and watched some workmen building a house on the opposite side of the street, while my mother knitted stockings (p. 356).

This memory was provided by a thirty-two-year-old man, an eldest sibling whom Adler identified as the "spoiled son of a widow." His life was characterized by severe anxiety attacks, except when he was at home. Past school and professional pursuits had proved difficult for him. While good-natured, he had found it difficult to make social contact with others. Although his ER may seem rather insignificant, it is not. His recollection of a solicitous mother in the background probably knitting his stockings supports the possibility that he was a pampered child. More importantly, playing the role of the onlooker characterized his childhood preparation for life: "he looks on while other people work." Once his anxiety has been eliminated through therapy, planning for future work could be guided by his natural dispositions toward seeing and observing. Adler recommended a business dealing with art objects.

Adler's measure of ERs has received much attention and proven quite useful (Mosak, 1969). Olson (1979) estimated that 100 articles had been written about ERs prior to 1979. By 1992, Watkins counted another thirty written between 1981 and 1990. Using ERs, Burnell and Solomon (1964) were able to predict success or failure in basic military training of Air Force recruits. Jackson and Sechrest (1962) reported more ER themes of fear in anxiety neurotics, abandonment in depressed clients, and illness in psychosomatic patients. In a study by Hafner, Fakouri, and Labrentz (1982), more alcoholics than nonalcoholics remembered threatening situations and showed themes of being controlled externally rather than internally. Hyer, Woods, and Boudewyns (1989) report ER evidence that Vietnam veterans suffering from Post-traumatic Stress Disorder (PTSD) are low in social interest, pursue goals in a devious manner, are vigorously acted upon by others, and pursue more negative outcomes and themes.

Of the thirty studies reviewed by Watkins (1992), the great majority produced statistically significant and strong results. Watkins drew six conclusions. First, there was consistency between ERs and current interpersonal behavior. Second, psychiatric patients' ERs tended to be more negative in emotional tone, showed more fear/anxiety themes, and reflected greater external locus of control or passivity than normal controls (external locus of control refers to the belief that one's outcomes are determined by factors outside oneself; for details see the chapter on Julian Rotter). Third, psychiatric patients' ERs showed changes over the course of treatment: ER content became more positive as favorable life changes occurred. Fourth, male delinquents and criminals, in comparison with controls, showed memories that reflected more negative emotionality, injury or illness, rule breaking, victimization, and having been alone in an unpleasant situation. Fifth, although the nature of the differences were not entirely clear, ERs elicited while awake differed from those reported during hypnosis. Sixth, ERs of individuals having different college majors or occupations were different, but again, reasons were unclear.

Measures of Social Interest
In recent years measures of social interest have been developed and validated. Most prominent among them is the Social Interest Scale (SIS) developed by James E. Crandall (1980). In deriving the SIS, Crandall attempted to account for Adler's conceptions of healthy and unhealthy striving for superiority that involve social interest (Ansbacher & Ansbacher, 1964). Healthy striving involves a blending of superiority needs with social interest requirements such that the individual's development and accomplishments are integrated with concern for others. Unhealthy striving entails a decided lack of social interest.

Crandall found that the SIS is reliable: A typical subject's score tends to be similar from one occasion to the next. It was also valid: It related to measures that assess certain aspects of social interest. In particular, the SIS correlated well with several measures of psychological adjustment and well-being: Well-adjusted individuals and people with positive senses of well-being scored high on the SIS.

Leak and Williams (1989a) used three measures of social interest, finding their own measure and one by Greever, Tseng, and Friedland (1973) to correlate better with family environment than the SIS. For these two superior measures, the greater the social interest, the greater the family cohesion and expressiveness and the less the family conflict. Also, the greater the social interest, the greater the degree of interest in political, social, intellectual, and cultural activities and the greater the emphasis on ethical and religious issues and values. Finally, Leak and Williams found that the higher the social interest the more positive were perceptions of the family environment.

A second study by the same researchers related social interest to hardiness and alienation (Leak & Williams, 1989b). Hardiness consisted of three factors: commitment, challenge, and control. "Commitment involves an active approach to coping with life's challenges . . . because of a sense of courage and psychological tolerance" (p. 370). "Challenge entails a perception that novel events and changing circumstances offer an opportunity for development" (p. 370). Control "refers to a belief in personal, internal control over the events in one's life" (p. 370). Subjects received alienation scores on alienation from work, alienation from self, alienation from others, alienation from family, and total alienation. Across two studies, social interest was significantly and inversely related to all four alienation scales and total alienation: the greater the social interest, the less the alienation. Social interest was significantly and positively related to total hardiness (sum across the three scores): The greater the social interest the greater the hardiness. A breakdown of hardiness into its three scales revealed a more specific outcome: The greater the social interest the higher the commitment and control scores, but challenge was unrelated to social interest.

Leak and Gardner (1990) looked at social interest in relation to sexual and love attitudes. Scores of fifty-nine students on two measures of social interest were related to their responses to the Sexual Attitude Scale and the Love Attitude Scale. Subjects who scored high on social interest tended to possess nonpermissive sexual attitudes, endorsed a companionship style of love, and showed contempt for an egocentric "game playing" style of love.

Although research on social interest is just beginning, the outlook is quite hopeful. At present it appears that social interest is positively related to psychological adjustment and hardiness and inversely related to alienation. Social interest also is meaningfully related to a number of family environment factors. It may well be that social interest measures will one day take a place alongside such measures as introversion–extraversion on the list of primary psychological indexes.

Adlerian Therapy: A Going and Growing Concern

While the psychoanalytic brand of therapy developed by Freud may be fading in popularity, it appears that Adlerian therapy is gaining advocates. An entire journal devoted to Adlerian theory and therapy has been thriving for years. It is *Individual Psychology*, a major contributor to this chapter.

A survey of thirty-two Adlerian therapists, conducted by Kal (1972), contains many insights into the nature of Adler's therapeutic methods. He found that Adlerians are more likely to view people in terms of wishes, expectations, goals, convictions, and mistaken apperceptions, not in terms of needs, conflicts, drives, and pleasure. Their primary question in relation to patients is "What purpose does the symptom serve?" not "What caused the symptom?" Therapists' interest is forward-looking, not backward-looking. One of the questions in Kal's survey was "What in your practice do you consider most typically Adlerian, in contrast with other schools?" Respondents indicated the following beliefs, rank-ordered according to the frequency with which they were mentioned:

1. social nature of man
2. "soft determinism": freedom of choice
3. purposefulness of all behavior
4. therapist's optimism
5. therapist's effectiveness
6. holistic approach
7. emphasis on reason and understanding versus instincts and emotions
8. active role of the therapist
9. cooperative, egalitarian aspect of therapy
10. use of early recollections

More recently, counselors have adapted the Adlerian approach to their arena. Kern and Watts (1993) point to basic Adlerian assumptions that are important to success during counseling: (1) the social context in which a behavior occurs must be considered; (2) persons are best viewed as wholes rather than parts interacting with one another; and (3) behavior changes in relation to life situations and long-term goals. Primary targets of counseling include establishing and maintaining a good relationship, discovering clients' lifestyles and goals, making interpretations of these discoveries, and reorienting the client.

One practical problem with some therapies, such as psychoanalysis, is the large number of sessions assumed to be required. The greater the number of sessions, the more the time and money invested. In light of this problem, Adlerian therapy seems to have a definite advantage over some other therapies. It seems especially easy to adapt Adler's methods to the **brief therapy approach**, techniques that address and solve clients' problems in a specifiable and relatively small number of sessions.

Carlson (1989) illustrates brief therapy of the Adlerian type in the case of a patient, Jim, who wished to stop smoking. Jim's mother and stepfather were married when he was two years old. When he learned of his "real" father at age nine, his entire life changed. Up to that point he had been a rather typical child. Thereafter he became a "hellraiser," perhaps in response to feelings of inferiority born of the perception that being abandoned by the real father meant rejection by him.

Background information collected on Jim's first appearance for therapy indicated that he had smoked for some twenty years, consuming on the order of 150,000 cigarettes at an estimated cost of $15,000. His physical addiction to cigarettes may be viewed as similar to an organ defect. Despite drinking too much coffee—about ten cups a day—and having had past problems with alcohol, Jim's general health was good. To assess his lifestyle, Carlson gave Jim the Kern Life-style Scale (Kern, 1986). It revealed that Jim's two lifestyle priorities were perfectionism and being a victim. ER data was also collected and indicated that Jim was a thrill seeker and bent on oral gratification. More specifically, at six or seven years of age, he remembered running down a hill toward the ocean too enthralled by the roar of the water to heed his mother's terrified pleas for him to stop. At age seven Jim recalled being at a large family gathering during which someone pushed him off a tree stump, breaking his arm. He ran around howling in pain unable to stop even when others attempted to comfort him. In both cases an Adlerian point of focus, the social context, is evident in the presence of significant others.

Putting together the background information, the ERs, and the lifestyle data, Carlson indicated that Jim was "an excellent candidate to stop smoking" (p. 222). After all, he had managed to keep his weight down and beat his alcohol problems. Carlson went on to inform Jim that he would need to work on his *self-efficacy*, the perception of one's ability to perform a specific task, such as losing ten pounds. This useful notion is covered more fully in the chapter on the work of Albert Bandura that occurs later in the book. Its relation to striving for superiority is evident: to increase self-efficacy is to improve mastery over one's circumstances.

The discussion of self-efficacy was preliminary to the first step in therapy, the education phase which began with Carlson asking Jim why he wanted to stop smoking. Jim answered that he knew it was bad for his health—he was experiencing morning coughing and shortness of breath. He also indicated that smoking was offensive to his friends—their "kidding" caused him to hide in the bathroom when he needed to smoke, another manifestation of inferior feelings.

Carlson's first suggestion was that Jim write his reasons for not smoking on a card and refer to it when he had the urge to smoke. The therapist's second suggestion regarded diet. Jim was advised to eat sunflower seeds when he felt the need to smoke. These seeds are botanically related to the tobacco plant and curb the urge to smoke because they generate "a glandular reaction very similar to that caused from tobacco" (p. 223). Thus, sunflower seeds would ease his craving for cigarettes. Both of these pursuits are very goal-directed.

Carlson's third suggestion revolved around the observation that nicotine raises the alkaline level in the body, thus shifting the pH balance, which is the ratio of the alkaline level to the acidic level. When an individual stops smoking, the pH balance is shifted again. The problem of a changed pH balance after smoking cessation is minimized by the consumption of fruits and vegetables. Jim agreed to increase his consumption of apples and oranges. The principle of compensation is well illustrated here.

Carlson also suggested that Jim cut down on meat, eggs, sugar, and caffeine: consumption of these substances also makes smoking cessation difficult. To lower caffeine, intake, it was suggested that Jim use a smaller mug and mix in decaffeinated coffee. Because smokers are also deficient in vitamins C and B, Jim was asked to consider taking vitamins for a few weeks after quitting.

Next Jim was given some psychological techniques that are useful in combatting the stress associated with giving up cigarettes. Carlson outlined a simple, deep-breathing method: one hand is placed on the belly, one on the chest, and the patient is told to practice breathing such that the hand on the belly moves, not the one on the chest. This technique generates diaphragmatic breathing, a known stress reducer. Jim was also taught some simple stretching exercises and encouraged to continue his walking and recently initiated bicycling. Again striving for superiority, in the form of pursuing self-efficacy, is illustrated.

Carlson also equipped Jim to avoid situations that elicit smoking behavior. Jim was instructed to avoid the chair he typically sat in during smoking. He was also advised to discard ashtrays, clean his car thoroughly to eliminate smells and brush his teeth regularly, following professional teeth cleaning. Finally, Jim was given an audiotape containing a hypnosis routine and told to play it at least once a day. The tape was designed to reinforce the points made in the initial session. These are also self-efficacy endeavors.

True to Adler's orientation, Carlson focused on Jim's present problems, using ERs only to assess his current characteristics. In contrast to psychoanalysis, Jim was not just encouraged to "talk things out in order to gain insight"; in line with striving for superiority, he was given some tasks to do. Also, in line with the Adlerian assumption that people need to enhance self-esteem, Jim was encouraged to build his self-efficacy, a very specific kind of self-esteem. Finally, Jim was encouraged to fulfill his need to accommodate his friends at work, a community concern involving an opportunity to show social feeling.

Jim checked back with Carlson only on a few additional occasions in order to assess his progress. The brief therapeutic method had equipped him to handle his smoking problem on his own. To support the success of his practices, Carlson reported that 70 percent of research patients who adopted the suggested activity-changes were still not smoking one year after initial sessions. Other therapists report success in adapting Adlerian methods to brief therapy. In just ten sessions, Dinkmeyer and Sherman (1989) helped a disturbed family to become more functional and showed them how to support one another in coping with personal problems.

Limitations

Birth Order Research: A Big Boondoggle?

The vast number of studies concerning birth order are beginning to create more confusion than enlightenment. Contradictory findings are more the rule than the exception and often result from the absence of a coherent theoretical rationale, a disregard of family size, and inattention to the sex of siblings (MacDonald, 1971; Schooler, 1972). In one illustrative study, MacDonald (1971) explored relationships between birth order and six personality variables in 1,262 college students. The mean differences among birth-order groups were slight, and the relationships uncovered were complicated: firstborns appeared rigid, firstborns and only children appeared socially responsible, only females appeared high in need for approval, and laterborns appeared to be controlled more by external than by internal factors. Havassy–De Avila (1971) urged that greater attention be paid to psychological processes underlying birth-order differences, rather than looking at the simplistic fact of birth order itself. In support of this position, Jordan, Whiteside, and Manaster (1982) evaluated seven different schemas for measuring birth order effects among 467 business majors. The only schema that predicted academic achievement was the one that included information on sex of subject and sex of siblings rather than birth position alone. Competitive desire to succeed and career strivings were highest in only-child males. Relative indifference to negative interpersonal consequences of achievement was highest in only-child females.

Discouragement with the birth order effect has become epidemic, even spreading to the popular literature. Kohn (1990) interviewed some leading researchers on the topic and concluded that birth order probably does not matter unless parents take it seriously. Among the experts interviewed was Toni Falbo whose work was cited earlier. Falbo conceded that "Birth order doesn't really explain a whole lot . . . But people like it. It's much like astrology. It says, 'I'm not to blame for the way I am' " (Kohn, p. 34).

Much criticism has been aimed at the Zajonc and Markus (1975) assertion that large family size, which produces large numbers of laterborns, has a negative effect on intellectual development. The June, 1988 *American Psychologist* included several letters concerning Zajonc's (1986) article in which his earlier moderation in regard to the potency of the birth order factor was replaced by new claims for the power of "position in the family." Basically these letters, some of which contained original data, indicated that Zajonc had overstated his case. The writers, all researchers and theorists, felt that birth order was probably a weak determinant of intellectual development. Nevertheless, well into the 1990s, researchers are still promoting the pursuit of birth order (Newman, Higgins, & Vookles, 1992; Simpson, Bloom, Neulon, & Arminio, 1994).

ERs Revisited

While ERs are interesting, they are also open-ended and abstract, thus, subject to various interpretations (Carlson, 1990). Because of their nature, they are also difficult to quantify. As a case in point, Hyer and colleagues (1989) attempted to quantify some subjects' ERs and relate them to several personality measures. Their results were notable for displaying an almost complete lack of relationship between ER variables and many different personality factors. Watkins (1992) also found nil or weak ER/other-variable relationships in a few of the studies he reviewed.

Conclusions

In the chapters ahead you will find that Alfred Adler's influence on other theorists is very great, if not widely recognized. His effect on others was not just in terms of theory or the practice of psychotherapy. Adler was a model of the responsible, humanitarian professional. As a person who fervently sought world peace and fought for more humane treatment of people, especially children, he almost certainly had impact on the senses of moral responsibility of the psychologists who followed him.

There are several other ways in which he influenced psychological theorists of his time and of this time. He advocated a holistic approach, shunning the view that people could be thought of as a collection of pieces loosely connected and remotely interacting with one another. In so doing, he anticipated Rogers, Maslow, and Murray. He also was among the first to focus on the present and the future, rather than the past. Finally, his optimistic and brief therapeutic approaches are being mimicked today. Judging by the apparent increase in the number of research and commentary articles published between the writing of the first edition of this book and the present writing, Adler will probably overtake some of his contemporaries who now may be viewed as ahead of him (Watkins, 1992).

Summary Points

1. In 1870, Adler was born the second of six children. He was a "father's son" who overcame childhood weaknesses. At school he was average and at the University he failed to develop a close relationship with a professor. Adler met his wife, Raissa, among the rebellious company he kept at this time. During his early medical career, he favored poor patients. After his bitter break with Freud, Adler began to blossom as a theorist. During a minor political career, he established children's clinics. After these were closed by the Nazis, he fled to the United States and devoted his time to applied psychology.

2. Adler viewed the person as an indivisible whole. Over the years, he changed his view, at first emphasizing inferiority, and finally stressing contributions "to human welfare." His basic assumptions included: all behavior has social meaning; all behavior has a purpose and is goal-directed; all behavior has unity and pattern; behavior is designed to overcome feelings of inferiority and move toward feelings of superiority; behavior is a result of our subjective perceptions. A synthesis of self-interest and social interest assumes that what one does for oneself is also done for others. Adler set the stage for today's diversity driven attention to the needs of disadvantaged children, oppressed people—including women—and the necessity of eliminating war.

3. Adler's most useful concept, social interest, the development of social feeling, is directed to the solution of three life problems: society, work, and love. Individuals' unique movement toward self-created goals are their styles of life. Their "laws of movement" are the directions they take. The "creative power of the individual" is the process by which people make original conceptions of themselves as they develop their styles of life.

4. During childhood we develop prototypes, fictional goals. This point of view illustrates the teleological nature of Adler's theory. Shock occurs when the individual's fiction runs head-on into reality. Neurosis is an extreme reaction to shock. An extreme reaction to inferiority is the inferiority complex that may require overcompensation, rather than the more usual compensation. Inferiority and its aftermath take different forms depending on whether the person has been neglected or overindulged during childhood.

5. Striving for superiority is a reaction to inferiority and can lead to the superiority complex. People with this complex may brag to cover up inferiority. That we may sometimes give braggarts high marks may say something about our own feelings of inferiority. Mothers are most important in the development of their children, but fathers are important too.

6. Adler believed only children tend to be dominant and are often spoiled. Firstborns are disturbed by a new arrival and strive for domination. Secondborns struggle to surpass others and lastborns are pampered. Much research suggests that differences between firstborns or onlychildren and laterborns do exist, as does the tendency for many laterborns (large family size) to have a negative effect on intellectual development. Frankenstein and his misunderstood "monster" provide good illustrations of Adlerian principles. Their lack of social interest was their downfall.

7. An ER simply involves recalling an early childhood event. Adler believed that ERs are indexes of a person's present style of life. Sanitioso and colleagues did a memory study that confirmed Adler's view. Supportive studies show ERs' ability to predict the success of military training, the effects of posttraumatic stress syndrome, and alcoholism's affect on personality. Thirty recent studies point to additional ER/other-variable relationships.

8. A measure of social interest (SIS) by Crandall is based on the assumption that there are healthy and unhealthy ways to pursue superiority. Crandall found the SIS to be well related to psychological adjustment. Leak and Williams report that two additional measures of social interest are negatively related to alienation and positively related to favorable family environment and hardiness. They also report relationships between social interest and sexual as well as love measures. Adlerian therapists emphasize wishes and goals, purposiveness, freedom of choice, holism, social factors, ERs, and an active therapist. In an illustration of many Adlerian principles, Carlson led "Jim" to quit smoking by developing self-efficacy, changing his diet, using deep breathing, cleaning out traces of cigarettes from his life, and using hypnosis and exercise.

9. Limitations of Adlerian theory and practice include the fact that birth order studies sometimes show mixed results, no results, or results that are contradictory. Even the popular press has become suspicious of birth order. The prestigious *American Psychologist* contained several negative responses to Zajonc's claim that the birth order factor and family size (including spacing) affect intellectual development.

10. ER measures have also been questioned, but continue to be used. Despite these limitations, Adler will long be remembered, especially when psychologists reflect on the roots of their social activism and the source of many of their ideas, including holism, optimism, present/future orientation, and brief therapy.

Running Comparison

Theorist	Adler in Comparison
Freud	He rejected sexualism and the universality of Freud's Oedipus Complex. He focused on community (social) factors, rather than intrapsychic ones. Consciousness and the present were more emphasized than in psychoanalytic theory (PT). He believed that people are pulled by goals rather than pushed by instincts. Unlike PT, personality was viewed holistically and people have freedom of choice. To Adler, insight is not enough; people have to have the courage to act.
Abraham Maslow and Carl Rogers	Striving for superiority has the flavor of "self-actualization." Adler was holistic like these two.
Albert Bandura	Like Bandura, anticipations of the future rather than motivations rooted in the past determine behavior. Self-efficacy and striving for superiority have much in common.
Murray	Murray also endorsed holism.

Essay/Critical Thinking Questions

1. Knowing what you now know about Adler, and recalling what you learned about Freud a short time ago, contrast the two as people. How were they different as people?

2. What were the essential differences between Freud's view of people and Adler's view? Indicate the five most basic philosophical differences that separated Freud and Adler.

3. Adler believed that people have free will. What does his assumption predict about the kind of therapy that Adler would be expected to develop? Describe aspects of Adlerian therapy that are consistent with "free choice."

4. What is your style of life? Outline your style of life, being careful to include how your prototype has developed and how you have evolved since childhood.

5. What was the shock of your life? Using Adler's definition of the term, indicate the clearest instance of "shock" that has occurred to you.

6. How do healthy and unhealthy "striving for superiority" differ? Indicate examples of both kinds, being sure to clearly differentiate between them.

7. How do you spoil a child the Adlerian way? Map out the child-rearing techniques parents would use to develop a spoiled child. Remember to stick with Adler's theory, not your own.

8. What could Frankenstein have done to make a super good human being of his creation? Where did he go wrong as a "parent" and how would you correct his course? Use Adlerian terms in this discussion.

9. In what ways did Adler and Jung differ as people? Also, indicate a major philosophical difference between them that led to differences in their theories.

10. Could you come up with a measure of social interest? Try it. Write a ten item questionnaire that would be designed to assess people's social interest, or lack of it.

E-mail Interaction

(Write the author at mfbpa@wiu.edu)
Forward any of the following, or write your own.

1. Why do you paint a kinder, gentler picture of Adler than of Freud and Jung?
2. Are styles of life that people display related to the age that they happen to have attained?
3. How do I know if I was spoiled?
4. What is the most important piece of information I need to know about Adler's theory?
5. Was Adler ever a communist sympathizer?

5

MOVING TOWARD, AWAY FROM, AND AGAINST OTHERS: KAREN HORNEY

- How basic is anxiety? Does everyone suffer from it?
- What makes people jealous?
- If some women are "castrating," why are they?
- What is your orientation to others: toward them, away from them or against them?
- Is there any need for a psychology of women?

Karen Horney

Recall that Freud saw personality largely as a function of instinctive influences. Jung's "collective unconscious" was intimately tied to humans' ancestral past and Adler's point of view was anchored by present strivings for superiority. By contrast, Karen Horney's most central concepts emerge from explorations of parent–child relationships. Thus, her theory does refer to early childhood. But, interactions between parents and children are the critical consideration, not repressed attraction to the opposite-sexed parent, early experiences with remnants of humans' ancestral past, or strivings to overcome inferiority that date to early childhood. Nevertheless, Horney used Freud's theory as a reference point beyond which she ventured to build a new, more socially oriented theory that reconstructed Freud's conception of females and reformulated his hypotheses about parent–child relationships.

Horney, The Person

Karen Clementina Theordora Danielsen was born on September 15, 1885, in Eilbek, Germany, a community near Hamburg (Quinn, 1988). However, she was not really German. Her father, Berndt Henrik Wackels Danielsen, was a Norwegian sea captain working for a Hamburg-based shipping line. Her mother, Clothilde Marie Van Ronzelen, was born to a well-regarded Dutch–German family. Clothilde, called Sonni, was the beautiful and commanding daughter of Dutch architect Jacob Van Ronzelen, born during the second of his three marriages. Sonni's mother died giving birth to her and she was reared by Van Ronzelen's third wife.

Captain Danielsen was eighteen years older than Sonni and had four children by a previous marriage. Karen, the second child of his second marriage, had mixed feelings about him. She apparently admired her father, but he was stern, a man of religious fervor who attempted to control her life. There was a time when she felt attracted to men like her father, "brutal and . . . forceful men" (Quinn, 1988, p. 160). Perhaps to establish some bond with him, she even claimed that they made an extended sea voyage together, an assertion that Quinn doubts. However, she also expressed loathing for him and they had many conflicts, one of which involved the educational arena.

Because Karen was very bright, and early on expressed an interest in pursuing an advanced education, the Captain's conventional belief that education was for men predicted a clash. When the inevitable happened and he opposed her educational aspirations, Karen's mother stood by her. While Sonni's support was important, Karen's determination to be an educated person may have come from knowledge of her maternal step-grandmother's unusual childhood. Wilhelmine Lorentz–Mayer Van Ronzelen, or Minna, who reared Sonni as her own, was educated by her father along with her seven brothers, very unusual treatment at that time (Quinn, 1988). Fortunately, Captain Danielsen was at sea so often that he proved a paper barrier in Karen's path to academic success.

Having thus escaped from under the thumb of her father, she submitted to the protection of her mother. Consequently, her sense of security was undermined, a state that was enhanced by a self-perceived lack of physical beauty (Quinn, 1988). As a remedy, Horney immersed herself in her studies and seemed to assert that if she could not be beautiful, she would be smart.

At about this time Horney began to overtly display a concern for human relationships and the role of women. In her adolescent diaries, she displayed both of these orientations: "I think very highly of men who can bear to love a woman just as she is without demanding that she be in one certain uniform" (Horney, 1980, p. 177).

Horney's goal to study medicine was clear to her at age fourteen. Though encouraged by her intelligent and freethinking mother, the pursuit of a medical career was unconventional for a woman of her day. However, Karen proved to be in the right place at the right time. Social changes in Germany allowed her to move to the forefront of new circumstances favorable to women's rights: secondary education and medical training. At the age of twenty she became one of a very few women immersed in a sea of first-year, male, medical students at the University of Freiburg. During this first semester, she met Oscar Horney, with whom she maintained a lively correspondence after he left almost immediately to pursue a law degree (Quinn, 1988). Some four years later they were married. She had the first of their three daughters during the second part of her medical training. While Oscar was becoming a success as the rapidly promoted manager of an investment firm, Karen was trying to balance mother, homemaker, and medical student roles. She succeeded at this early attempt to be "superwoman" and completed her final requirements for the M.D. degree in 1915.

Possibly stresses involved with her protean life style partly explain the depression and an alleged suicide attempt that Horney experienced during her medical training. Her melancholy condition may have initiated her interest in Freudian therapy. In any case she began analysis with Dr. Karl Abraham in 1910. Eventually she attended weekly meetings on psychoanalysis at Abraham's house and he became her mentor, the same role he played for Erich Fromm. These excursions into psychoanalysis lead to the founding of the Berlin

Psychoanalytic Institute of which Horney was an active member from 1918 to 1932. They also planted the seeds of doubt in Horney's mind. Her criticisms of Freud's point of view began to blossom at this time.

Horney's early letters to Oscar reflected the personal questioning and deep inner exploration mentioned earlier. Alfred Adler's concepts of inferiority and striving for superiority, especially regarding women in social relationships, were prominent in Horney's thinking at this time. When her marriage began to dissolve in 1926, writing in search of the "truth" became her passion. She could think of nothing more unbearable than "disappearing quietly in the great mass of the average" or "of being told one is a nice, friendly, average person" (Horney, 1980, p. 245).

Horney emigrated to the United States in 1932, perhaps to escape the possibility that the Nazis would seize power and probably to escape the remnants of her marriage. Almost immediately she became associated with the Psychoanalytic Institute. However, after Institute members criticized her for questioning Freudian theory, she and her followers left the organization and founded the Association for the Advancement of Psychoanalysis (Frosch, 1991). They also started a training institution, the American Institute of Psychoanalysis. Horney was a founding editor of the Association's official organ, the *American Journal of Psychoanalysis*. While in the United States, she had the opportunity to associate with Fromm, Harry Stack Sullivan, Margaret Mead, and other luminaries of the time. Karen Horney died of cancer in 1952.

Horney's View of the Person

I realized . . . that my search for a better understanding had led me in directions that were at variance with Freud. If so many factors that Freud regarded as instinctual were culturally determined, if so much that Freud considered libidinal was a neurotic need for affection, provoked by anxiety and aimed at feeling safe with others, then the libido theory was no longer tenable. Childhood experiences remained important, but the influence they exerted on our lives appeared in a new light (Horney, 1945, p. 13).

As you can see, Horney parted company with Freud and his more pessimistic and instinctually based point of view. However, she did agree with him on the importance of anxiety-provoking childhood experiences in the development of psychological maladjustment. Anxiety became a central aspect of Horney's theory, accounting for the personality's various defensive and security operations. Along with Freud, Horney saw neuroses, which are anxiety-based, as the predominant form of maladjustment in the early twentieth century.

At the same time, there are irreconcilable differences with Freud. Horney discarded Freud's theory of instincts as the explanation of human behavior. She openly declared, ". . . the libido concept is unproved" (Horney, 1939, p. 52). In addition, she pointed out that oral, anal, genital, and aggressive drives do not exist in all human beings (1937). To her the aim of compulsive drives is not to satisfy sexual instincts but to provide safety from feelings of isolation, helplessness, fear, and hostility.

Horney declared that Freud's Oedipus complex was not universal or even central to understanding personality. In fact, she rejected his overemphasis on sexuality: "But the one-sided emphasis Freud has given sexual factors may tempt many people to single them out above others . . . To be straight in sexual questions is necessary; but to be straight only with them is not enough" (1942, p. 295). At best, psychosexuality is relevant to some cases of neurotic jealousy in parent–child relationships (Horney, 1937).

Horney also took issue with Freud's view of the differences between the sexes. She (1937) began her questioning in response to Freud's biased postulations about the psychology of women, especially his concept of "penis envy" (Erkardt, 1991). While she acknowledged that in some cultures women may be jealous of men's anatomy, in other cultures it is the other way around (1937). In this way she chastised Freud for generalizing from his perception of his own culture to all other cultures. In regard to the United States, that is, European–American culture, envy of male anatomy may be limited to neurotic women. Horney used this point to criticize Freud and other psychoanalysts for extrapolating from their biased samples of disturbed patients to all people.

Horney linked "penis envy" to women's alleged "castrating tendencies." This inclination to excise the male organ, often associated with Freud's point of view, supposedly derives from women's need to take from men what the feminine gender lacks. Horney's response was straightforward: "Much of what in psychoanalytic literature is regarded as castrative tendencies in women and is traced back to penis envy is in my opinion the result of a wish to humiliate men" and, one might add, not the desire to take the symbol of masculinity from men (Horney, 1937, p. 199).

Most importantly, Freud was seen as lacking a social orientation. Beyond ignoring other cultures, he showed a "total" disregard of cultural factors as influences on personality. As Horney (1937) remarked:

> *Freud sees a culture not as the result of a complex social process but primarily as the product of biological drives which are expressed or sublimated, with the result that reaction formations are built up against them. The more complete the suppression of these drives, the higher the cultural development . . . Historical and anthropological findings do not confirm such a direct relation between height of culture and the suppression of sexual or aggressive drives (pp. 282–283).*

Freud's view was contrary to social experience. For example, when Horney (1945) first came to the United States in 1932, she noted important differences between the behaviors of persons in this country and in some European countries that "only the difference in civilizations" could account for.

In response to these shortcomings, Horney developed alternative, socially-oriented concepts. The real forces motivating human attitudes and actions were believed to be social ones: dependency, cooperation, interpersonal anxiety, hostility, love, jealousy, greed, competitiveness, inferiority, and work. Even a newborn's first experience, feeding, is one of social cooperation. The collective emphasis is clearly on human interactions in cultural and interpersonal contexts: parents, siblings, peers, significant social figures, and one's total society.

In general, Horney placed greater emphasis on conscious processes. Thus, id influences recede into the background. The influence of superego (conscience aspect) remains important. However, it is tied to the process of *socialization*, learning one's particular culture, not

BOX 5.1   Horney on Adult Sexuality and Sexual Orientation

Although Horney largely bypassed or reconceived of Freud's psychosexuality, she had much to say about adult sexuality, an unusual propensity for a woman of her era.

Horney regarded masturbation as normal. However, individuals who masturbate compulsively—engaging in this activity frequently and without the ability to stop themselves—are attempting to release anxiety through a sexual "safety-value" (Horney, 1937, p. 52).

In the realm of sexual relations with other people, Horney saw four types of troubled individuals. All of these types primarily seek sex for reasons other than physical gratification. The first variety crave sexual interaction because it allows them to establish human contact. Unfortunately, malevolent motivation lies behind their desire to have relations with others: ". . . it is not so much a need for affection as a striving to conquer, or more accurately, to subdue others" (1937, p. 154).

The second type ". . . are prone to yield to sexual advances from either sex, [and] are driven by an unending need for affection, especially by a fear of losing another person through refusing a sexual request, or through daring to defend themselves against any requests made upon them, whether just or unjust" (p. 154). These people have interpersonal problems that go far beyond sexuality. They become the slaves of others because they cannot bear the thought of losing them. Horney is quick to point out that these people are not genuine bisexuals, people who have a real attraction to both sexes. Rather they will submit to anyone in order not to lose that person.

The third type experience increased sexual excitement because ". . . it is an outlet for anxiety and for pent-up psychic tensions" (p. 155). When these individuals find themselves in a context that provokes their anxiety, they become attracted to the most prominent individual present. It is among these people that patients who become infatuated with their psychotherapists are found. They either become passionately attracted to their psychotherapists or they are highly aloof, unconsciously preferring to transfer the need for sexual closeness to an "outside" person who resembles the therapist. Alternatively, individuals in this category may manifest their need to establish sexual contact with the therapist exclusively in dreams. Ironically they have a "deep disbelief in any kind of genuine affection" and feel that the analyst is interested in them only for "ulterior motives" (p. 156).

The fourth type, homosexuality of the neurotic variety, is due to fear of competitiveness. This type is composed of individuals who (1) withdraw from attempts to attract the opposite sex so that they may avoid competition with their own sex, and (2) deal with the anxiety that competitiveness with the same sex engenders by seeking the sense of reassurance that only affection from the same sex can provide. Apparently these individuals stand in contrast to genuine homosexuals who are as normal as heterosexuals (Bailey, Gaulin, Agyei, & Gladue, 1994; Friedman & Downey, 1994).

Horney's views on two other issues are worth brief consideration. Horney, in characteristic straightforward fashion, dismisses the Freudian allegation that women are masochistic—desire to be hurt, even physically—a probable source of the myth that women wish to be raped (Allen, 1990). In a major section on masochism, which goes well beyond sexuality, Horney used only masculine pronouns and examples. She closed this discussion with a general statement that makes no reference to gender: "Masochistic drives are neither an essentially sexual phenomenon nor the result of biologically determined processes, but originate in personality conflicts" (1937, p. 280). Other commentators cite Horney when they attribute masochistic behavior in women to culture (Shafter, 1992).

Finally, Horney addressed women's alleged sexual frigidity by first acknowledging that, with the close of the Victorian era, frigidity was no longer considered a "normal condition in women" (1937, p. 199). Still, it may occur as a "deficiency" for two reasons. First, women may display frigidity, not because they have no sexual desire, but because they wish to humiliate the men in their lives. This explanation is especially applicable if their men have a neurotic fear of

Continued

BOX 5.1   *Continued*

being humiliated by women. Second, women may display frigidity because of ". . . a feeling of being abused, degraded and humiliated by sexual relations." Sex was, and to some degree still is, something that is done to them, even against their wills, as in the popular male exclamation "I put the make on her"; that is, "I tried to make her do it." Marriage gave women license to have sex, but many still felt the obligation to be frigid in order to avoid the feeling that they were willingly submitting to humiliation.

Horney felt comfortable with her own sexuality.

To her sex was a normal, natural, and enjoyable experience. She was known to have had meaningful affairs before, during, and after her marriage to Oscar Horney (Quinn, 1988).

In sum, Horney reminds us that sex is rarely, if ever, just to achieve physical orgasm. Almost always there are psychological reasons behind sexual expression that are far more important than physical gratification. In turn, we are reminded that any sexual interaction is complex, a human relationship not to be taken lightly or to be engaged in thoughtlessly.

---

just the identification process. The primary vehicle of socialization is the family, which passes culture from generation to generation. The family's importance as a psychosexual unit—children lusting after parents—is of secondary importance.

There were also some differences in regard to the origin of human values. Horney believed there is no such thing as a universal trend in human nature or a "normal" psychology that holds true for all humankind. Nevertheless, she did endorse a view of healthy people as having the capacity to bestow genuine friendliness on other people (1937).

Basic Concepts: Horney

Basic Anxiety: Infantile Helplessness in a Parental World

According to Horney (1950), normal personality development occurs when factors in the social environment allow children to develop basic confidence in themselves and other people. This is most likely to result when parents convey genuine and predictable warmth, interest, and respect toward their children. Abnormal development occurs when environmental conditions obstruct a child's natural psychological growth. Instead of developing confidence in self and others, the child develops **basic anxiety**, "an insidiously increasing, all-pervading feeling of being lonely and helpless in a hostile world" (Horney, 1937, p. 89). The child feels "small, insignificant, helpless, deserted, endangered, in a world that is out to abuse, cheat, attack, humiliate, betray, envy" (Horney, 1937, p. 92). Basic anxiety is an irrational emotional experience involving a pervasive, unpleasant feeling of extreme discomfort.

A wide range of factors in the family environment contributes to this fundamental insecurity: parental domination, belittling attitudes, indifference, unkept promises, overprotection, a hostile home atmosphere, encouraging the child to take sides in parental disagreements, isolation from other children, and lack of respect for the child's individual needs (Horney, 1945). Perhaps Horney's sensitivity to these conditions comes from the observation that some of them existed in her own childhood home: her father was domineering, her mother somewhat overprotective, and her family divided, with Karen, Sonni, and beloved brother Berndt, taking sides against her father and his other children (Quinn, 1988). However, "the basic evil is invariably a lack of genuine warmth and affection" because of the parents' own incapacity to give it (Horney, 1937, p. 80). Horney saw neurotic people as requiring excessive amounts of reassurance, and as incapable of loving. In the final analysis, disturbances in human relationships are expressed in **neuroses**—"psychic disturbance[s] brought about by fears and defenses against these fears, and by attempts to find compromise solutions for conflicting tendencies" (1937, pp. 28–29).

Coping by Way of Ten Neurotic Needs

The child's methods of adjusting to basic anxiety form enduring motivational patterns which crystallize into important aspects of personality. These patterns are called **neurotic** *needs*, the coping techniques that are initiated in childhood and composed of excessive, insatiable, and unrealistic demands developed in response to the basic anxiety that dominates the person (Horney, 1950). Their aim is not instinctual satisfaction, as Freud believed, but social safety or security.

Needs are considered neurotic (1) when a person adheres to them more rigidly than do other people in the culture, and (2) when there is a discrepancy between the person's potentialities and actual accomplishments. Neurotic people lack flexibility in reacting to different situations. For example, most people are likely to react indecisively or suspiciously when there are appropriate reasons for doing so. It is reasonable to be somewhat indecisive in response to having to make a difficult choice or in reaction to evidence of insincerity from another person. However, neurotic individuals tend to be indecisive or suspicious most of the time, regardless of the circumstances and persons involved. They usually are unable to make up their minds, or repeatedly indicate how impossible it is to trust anyone because "everyone" is out to get whatever they can. They experience a discrepancy between their potential and their actual productivity or enjoyment. Even though they may seem to have everything going for them, their feelings point to an inappropriate sense of inferiority and an absence of happiness. They sense that they stand in their own way.

Moving Toward, Against, and Away from People

According to Horney, identifying the characteristics of an individual's dominant needs can reveal the direction the person is likely to take in relationships with other people. The overall pattern of needs also suggests the form intrapsychic conflict is likely to take. For Horney (1945), contradictory dispositions toward other people constitute a critically important form of conflict. She called attention to the dramatization of one such contradiction, the story of Dr. Jekyll and Mr. Hyde. One side of Dr. Jekyll is "delicate, sensitive, sympathetic, helpful," while a second side is "brutal, callous, and egotistical." Horney did not imply that the Jekyll–Hyde story is the precise form that intrapsychic conflict takes, only that the central character shows a basic incompatibility of interpersonal dispositions.

"Conflict" is an essential aspect of Horney's description of neurosis. All normal people experience conflict; however, conflict of neurotic proportions is an excessive deviation from the cultural norm. Eventually, neurotic conflict comes to involve contradictory orientations to the self that pervade the entire personality.

Horney (1945) discussed three generalized trends that individuals may show in regard to others and themselves. These trends may be thought of as a synthesis of the neurotic needs. Each trend is "a whole way of life," including thinking, feeling, and behaving. A given trend encompasses a subgroup of the group of ten needs summarized in Table 5.1.

Moving toward people reflects neurotic needs for a partner and for affection; it also involves compulsive modesty. This trend is associated with the first three needs listed in the table. The predominant direction is one of helplessness and compliance.

> *Such a person accepts his own helplessness, and in spite of his estrangement and fears tries to win the affection of others and to lean on them. Only in this way can he feel safe with them. If there are dissenting parties in the family, he will attach himself to the most powerful person or group. By complying with them, he gains a feeling of belonging and support which makes him feel less weak and less isolated (p. 42).*

A neurosis solution to anxiety often adopted by people extreme in this orientation is called **self-effacing**, a mode of responding to others in which the person will seek accom-

TABLE 5.1   Ten Neurotic Needs Identified by Horney

	Excessive Needs for	Shown in behaviors
T O W A R D	1. Affection and approval	Striving to be liked and pleasing to others, to live up to the expectations of others, dreading self-assertion and hostility
	2. Having a "partner"	Seeking to be taken over by another through "love"; dreading being left alone
	3. Narrowly restricting one's life	Trying to be inconspicuous, undemanding, and modest; contented with little
A G A I N S T	4. Power	Seeking domination and control over others; dreading weakness
	5. Exploiting others	Taking advantage of others, using others, dreading being "stupid"
	6. Social recognition or prestige	Seeking public acceptance; dreading "humiliation"
	7. Personal achievement	Striving to be best; defeating others; ambitious; dreading failure
A W A Y	8. Personal admiration	Self-inflating; not seeking social recognition, but admiration for an idealized self-image ("I'm a saint")
	9. Self-sufficiency and independence	Trying not to need others; maintaining distance; dreading closeness
	10. Perfection and unassailability	Being driven toward superiority; dreading flaws and criticism

modation at any price including backing down whenever there is an interpersonal conflict in order to avoid loss of friendship, support, or love of others (Muller, 1993). Individuals displaying this characterological profile will sabotage their own best interest, deny their own points of view, and derogate themselves publicly if it seems necessary in order to keep the affections and attentions of others.

Moving against people is associated with needs 4, 5, 6, and 7 in Table 5.1. This trend reflects compulsive, exaggerated cravings for power and prestige, as well as personal ambition. There is such an overemphasis on hostility that these people may be thought of as suffering from "basic hostility."

> *In this case, the person accepts and takes for granted the hostility around him, and determines, consciously or unconsciously, to fight. He implicitly distrusts the feelings and intentions of others toward himself. He rebels in whatever ways are open to him. He wants to be the stronger and defeat them, partly for his own protection, partly for revenge (p. 43).*

The neurotic solution to anxiety of people who exhibit this orientation to the extreme is called **expansive,** which is to be "in control," to not admit that one is incorrect (or another person is correct), and to never give an inch in a conflict (Muller, 1993). These people are invested in avoiding the "horror" of being the "controlled" rather than the "controller." They must always determine who does what in a setting, never letting others determine behavioral outcomes. They are also afflicted with **hyper-competitiveness**—the indiscriminate need by individuals to compete and win (and avoiding losing) at any cost as a means of maintaining or enhancing feelings of self-worth. To them, winning is everything; how the game is played is nothing.

Moving away from people reflects a person's concern with self, as seen in needs for admiration and perfectionism. This attitude is associated with needs 8, 9, and 10 in Table 5.1. The predominant direction is one of isolation. The individual in this category

> *wants neither to belong nor to fight, but keeps apart. He feels he has not much in common with them, they do not understand him anyhow. He builds up a world of his own—with nature, with his dolls, his books, his dreams (p. 43).*

The neurotic solution to anxiety displayed by people extreme in this orientation is termed **resignation,** which is to free oneself from the risks involved in approaching or attacking others by being an onlooker, a noncompetitor, an avoider, and a reactive person who is hypersensitive to influence attempts (Muller, 1993; Horney, 1950). When conflict arises, these people are inclined to say "What difference does it make? . . . Let's forget the whole thing" (Muller, 1993, p. 266). Muller (1993) has pointed out that persons showing this syndrome resemble the "borderline" personality type as classified in the American Psychiatric Association's manual of abnormal behaviors.

These orientations can exist within a single person. **Basic conflict** involves contradictory orientations to move toward, away from, and against others all existing within a neurotic. Likewise, a single person can show, at times, elements of self-effacement, expansiveness, and resignation.

BOX 5.2   Which Is Your Orientation?

Table 5.1 may be regarded as a rough test of whether people show one trend or another. Go back to the table and pick the four (4) entries that fit you best. It is "forced choice": even if it is difficult to make up your mind, force yourself to choose four entries. After making your choices, return here.

If three of your choices include the first three needs in the table, your dominant trend tends to be "moving toward people." Should your choices include any three of 4, 5, 6, and 7, your trend tends to be "moving against people." Finally, if you chose a foursome including 8, 9, and 10, your trend is "moving away from people."

For many, if not most of you, your choices failed to fit any of the patterns: choices did not include three entries fitting one of the trends. This outcome is a reminder that fitting one of these extreme trends is unusual. However, if it does turn out that your choices do fit one of the trends, interpret the outcome with caution. Do not regard yourself as "neurotic." To do so would be to assume the validity of Horney's trends, which still await empirical confirmation.

Developing an Idealized Versus a Real Image of Self

Once firmly established, basic anxiety gives rise to additional feelings of alienation toward one's self and growing self-hatred. Genuine realization of the self is sacrificed to an **idealized image of self**, an artificial pride system that the person creates to give the personality a sense of unity that does not exist. Horney (1945) refers to a cartoon she once saw in *The New Yorker*. A heavyset, middle-aged adult is depicted as looking in a mirror and seeing the image of a trim, young adult. Such an idealized image of self serves five functions: (1) It substitutes for the absence of realistic self-confidence and pride, through an inflated but ungrounded feeling of significance and power; (2) it counteracts the presence of actual inner weakness and self-contempt, by falsely allowing the person to feel better or more worthy than others; (3) it compensates for a lack of genuine ideals, the absence of which otherwise would lead the person to feel quite lost; (4) it represents an idealized, private mirror on which to rely so that one's most blatant faults and handicaps disappear or take on an attractive coloration; and (5) it offers the appearance of reconciled conflicts and inconsistencies within the individual, even though such is not the case. By contrast, the **real self** is the potential for growth beyond the artificial idealized image of self. It is the self one can become if all the potentialities that one has are fully developed.

Creation of an idealized self takes place unconsciously. It also may be accompanied by other forms of pretense, such as **externalization**, the tendency to experience internal processes as if they occurred outside oneself and to hold these "exterior" factors responsible for one's difficulties. Externalization serves to eliminate oneself as the cause of personal problems by projecting or shifting blame onto entities "outside" oneself, especially other people. Externalization is not just shifting responsibility. "Not only one's faults are experienced in others but to a greater or lesser degree all feelings" (1945, p. 116). One externalizes many aspects of oneself. Thus, externalization is much broader than Freud's defense mechanism, projection.

"Another inevitable product of externalization is a gnawing sense of emptiness and shallowness" (p. 117). Along with it comes an *externalization of self-contempt* in which one either despises others or feels "that it is others who look down upon oneself" (p. 118). Finally, *rage* results and is itself externalized in three ways. First, anger is "thrust outward" either as general irritability or as "specific irritation directed at the very faults in others that the person hates in himself" (p. 120). Second, rage is externalized in the form of an ever-present expectation that the faults "which are intolerable to oneself will infuriate others" (p. 121). As an illustration, Horney referred to a former patient whose idealized self-image was as saintly as the priest in Victor Hugo's *Les Miserables*. When she deviated from this angelic image and became angry, she was amazed to find that others liked her better. The patient had *expected* that others would have contempt for her as she was so she hid behind a "holier than thou" facade. The third way to externalize rage is to channel it into physical ills. Individuals who use this form of externalization are incessantly complaining of various vague maladies, from headaches to fatigue.

"The discrepancy between *a neurotic's actual behavior* and his *idealized picture of himself* can be so blatant that one wonders how he himself can help seeing it" (Horney, 1945, p. 132; emphasis added). Here Horney refers to the **actual self**, who one currently is, that stands in contrast to the idealized self, who one *should* be, and real self, who one *could* be. The inevitable trauma of the brutal collision between the idealized and actual selves is akin to shock, the term Adler reserved for "fiction running head-on into reality." However, the individual can postpone the clash by resorting to one or more of seven defenses (Horney, 1945).

A **blind spot** is an area of contradiction about which the individual manages to remain unaware. As an example, Horney referred to a patient who never saw the contradiction between his "game" of figuratively killing colleagues at a meeting by "gunning them down" with an index finger and the "Christlike" idealized image he maintained. In **compartmentalization**, individuals separate key aspects of themselves and their life situations into "logic-tight" compartments. "There is a section for friends and one for enemies, one for the family and one for outsiders, one for professional and one for personal life, one for social equals and one for inferiors. Hence what happens in one compartment does not appear to the neurotic to contradict what happens in another" (p. 133).

Rationalization "may be defined as self-deception by reasoning" (p. 135). Here the individual attempts to excuse socially unacceptable actions by passing them off as laudable behavior (Allen, 1990). By mental gymnastics the individual makes despicable behavior into benevolent deportment. Horney refers to someone who sees himself as helping another, when, in fact, "strong tendencies to dominate are present" (p. 135).

Excessive self-control arises in reaction to a flood of contradictory emotions and involves holding feelings and behavior in a vise-grip. "Persons who exert such control will not allow themselves to be carried away, whether by enthusiasm, sexual excitement, self-pity, or rage" (p. 136). **Arbitrary rightness** is the strategy of people who see life as a merciless battle and, therefore, feel they must be definite and "right" about everything lest "foreign influence" control them. For these people, doubt is a dangerous weakness. In the event of a conflict, they can feel "in control" only if they can declare themselves "in the right."

Elusiveness, the ability to slither away from conflicts by refusing to ever take an identifiable stand. People "inclined to this kind of defense often resemble those characters in fairy tales who when pursued turn into fish; if not safe in this guise, they turn into deer; if the hunter catches up with them they fly away as birds. You can never pin them down to any statement" (p. 138). If one of their pronouncements is challenged, people who use this defense deny having said whatever they said, say they did not really mean it, or reinterpret it.

Cynicism is "the denying or deriding of moral values" because of a deep-seated uncertainty with regard to morality (p. 139). These people's response to moral uncertainty is skepticism about morality. To them, wrong can be twisted into right and right can be transformed into wrong. All that matters is doing what they please and looking good in the process. Those who reason and behave otherwise are thought to be either hypocrites or stupid.

A Basic Diversity Issue: The Psychology of Women

Women lived for centuries under conditions in which they were kept away from great economic and political responsibilities and restricted to a private emotional sphere of life. This does not mean that they did not carry responsibility and did not have to work. But their work was done within the confines of the family circle and therefore was based only on emotionalism, in contradistinction to more impersonal, matter-of-fact relations. Another aspect of the same situation is that love and devotion came to be regarded as specifically feminine ideals and virtues. Still another aspect is that to women—since their relations to men and children were their only gateway to happiness, security, and prestige—love represented a realistic value, which in man's sphere can be compared with his activities relating to earning capacities. Thus, not only were pursuits outside the emotional sphere factually discouraged, but in women's own minds extrafamilial activities assumed only secondary importance (Horney, 1939, pp. 114–115).

Horney made significant contributions to the psychology of women by questioning Freudian assumptions about them. She was an influential critic of Freud and his "boy's eye" view of physical anatomy as the basis of psychological differences between men and women. Horney challenged Freud's theoretical speculations that lacking male anatomy led women to (1) envy men for their penises (Symonds, 1991); (2) feel shame over biological "deficiency"; (3) resent their mothers, who were to blame for their anatomical deficiency; (4) overvalue relationships with men, including having male babies as a way of possessing male anatomy; (5) become jealous of other women as competitors for men and the anatomical superiority they supposedly represent; (6) seek sexual stimulation through the clitoris because it is penis-like; and (7) pursue desires for submissiveness, dependency, and masochistic abuse that are allegedly unique to women (Eldredge, 1989).

There were several reasons why Horney viewed Freud's underlying assumptions about gender as suspect. First, Horney considered it illogical that persons built for specific biological functions should be obsessed with obtaining the biological attributes of the other sex. "It would require tremendous evidence to make it plausible" (1939, p. 104). Second, Horney saw no evidence of universal support for Freud's conjectures. As mentioned earlier, cross-cultural investigations failed to demonstrate the universality of the supposed female wish for male anatomy. In fact, there are societies whose males show "womb envy."

Third, Horney (1926) asserted that a psychological theory "written" by men may not be wholly relevant to women. Psychoanalysis was created by "a male genius," almost all of whose followers were men. In fact, the masculine point of view pervades all science and most of European-American thought. "Like all sciences and all valuations, the psychology of women has hitherto been considered only from the point of view of men" (Horney, 1967, p. 56).

Horney endorsed philosopher Georg Simmel's view that European (and one could add, European American) culture is dominated by masculine ideology. For centuries, women have been enmeshed in social systems that have promoted a "too exclusive" concentration on, and "overvaluation" of men. Women's lives have been structured around political, economic, and psychological dependency on men (Eldredge, 1989). The specific social vehicle contributing to female dependency is the development of "love" relationships, based on the belief "I must have a man" that is foisted on women (1942). Horney saw this belief as motivating women to unconsciously conform to the wishes and demands of men and then assume, erroneously, that the behavior and feelings they adopt at the behest of men represent true feminine nature.

From a social perspective, Horney saw women's submission to the control of men as "cultivated" through a process of systematic selection by men. Male selectivity fosters the development of relationships with certain types of conforming women. Women are selected whose willingness to please would compensate for specific male deficiencies such as vulnerable self-esteem. The selection process instills in women the dispositions of dependency, inconspicuousness, frailty, suffering, emotionality, and jealousy of other women, traits that serve men well. In sum, systematic selection promotes a self-fulfilling prophecy in which women became what men want them to be.

Psychologically speaking, Horney felt that society's "masculine tendency" conveys demeaning attitudes toward women. Women are then led to compensate for the consequent heightened sense of inferiority by further increasing their overvaluation of relationships with "superior" men. The net result is, once again, a strengthening of male dominance. More generally, Horney's reconceptualization of Freudian theory redirects attention away from the instinctive position that favors the masculine gender to a trend that is more sociocultural in nature.

Horney's impact was important in her day as well as now. Then, it was great enough to elicit Freud's (1925/1959) direct opposition—and that of American psychoanalysts—as well as the support of Adler and Fromm. Adler, for example, addressed the myth of women's inferiority when he asserted that decisions about birth control and abortion are best left entirely to women (1982, p. 63). Recall that he also regarded macho, warmongering nations as most likely to oppress women. Nowadays, there is renewed interest in the work of Horney, associated with the ongoing development of the women's movement and specific interest in the psychology of women (Rohrbaugh, 1979; Williams, 1983). She continues to be cited as an important figure on the issue of culture and sex roles.

Evaluation

Contributions

Help With Everyday Problems

Horney was noted for working with neurotics, but there was another side to her. She had much concern for the everyday problems of normal people. Horney promoted self-exploration by presenting her ideas in popular books. She wrote expressly for interested laypeople "who want to know themselves and have not given up struggling for their own growth" (1945, p. 8). Her purpose was not to offer clear-cut answers or cures for neurotic conflicts, which would be unrealistic as well as unprofessional, but to offer information useful for self-examination. Her books include *The Neurotic Personality of Our Time* (1937), *Self-Analysis* (1942), *Our Inner Conflicts* (1945), and *Are You Considering Psychoanalysis?* (1946).

Consistent with her interest in helping normal people with normal problems, Horney wrote extensively about issues that concern the typical person. Her books are filled with discussions of ambition, depression, self-confidence, dependency, greed, and other concepts from the everyday language of everyday people. Her consideration of these common concerns is illustrated by her treatment of "jealousy."

Horney defines **jealousy** as the fear of losing a relationship that is seen as the best available means of satisfying an insatiable concern for affection and incessant demands for unconditional love (Horney, 1937). She recognized that jealousy is fully in evidence even in early childhood. A child can be jealous of siblings. She or he can also be jealous of a parent who seems to be receiving more attention from the other parent than is the child. Furthermore, Horney acknowledged that jealousy of the Oedipal type may also exist: a child may be jealous of the parent of the same sex for monopolizing the physical (sexual) and emotional attention of the opposite-sex parent. However, here she reiterates that Oedipal jealousy is not found in all cultures and may be confined to neurotic people in this culture.

Some degree of jealousy is true of all of us and may be a quite reasonable reaction to the real but generally remote possibility that an important love relationship may end. However, the kind of jealousy considered here—the sort that Horney concentrated on in her writings—is exaggerated beyond the bounds of reason. Morbidly jealous people show fear of losing someone's love that is way out of proportion to the actual danger. The fear of these people is so great that any interest on the part of a loved one that does not revolve around themselves is a threat to them. "This kind of jealousy may appear in every human relation—on the part of parents toward their children who want to make friends or to marry; on the part of children toward their parents; between marriage partners; in any love relationship" (p. 129).

According to Horney, morbid adult jealousy can be a carryover from childhood neurosis in that both spring from the same source: an insatiable appetite for love arising from unresolved basic anxiety. In recognizing a possible tie between jealousy involving childhood relationships and jealousy in adult relationships Horney was ahead of her time. Philip Shaver and his colleagues have established a link between the way children relate to their parents and how they later relate to important people in their adult lives, most especially lovers (see Shaver and Hazan, 1987). Certain insecure people whose childhood needs were not consistently met by their parents show, as adults, the same kind of insatiable need for unconditional love that Horney alluded to. Because they cannot get enough assurance of love, they are morbidly jealous of anyone who is a rival for the attentions of their loved ones. Box 5.3 contains information relevant to Shaver's attachment theory and also a jealousy scale. Read and follow the instructions in the box before returning here.

There has been additional recent work on Shaver's attachment trichotomy. DeAngelis (1994) reported on work by Shaver and his colleagues. They collected data suggesting that secure adults, Shaver's first category, are high on interpersonal sensitivity, but low on compulsive, obligatory caregiving. Anxious adults, the second category, showed exactly the opposite pattern. In other work, Shaver and a colleague showed that avoidant individuals, the third category, tend toward "one-night stands" and find pleasure in sex without love. Another study by the Shaver team found that secure adults experiment sexually, but only in the

BOX 5.3 Attachment Styles and Jealousy

First read the three descriptions of attachment styles and choose the one that fits you best. Then respond to Mathes's Interpersonal Jealousy Scale. Finally, refer to the information at the end of the box to learn of the relationship between the two exercises.

Part 1: Attachment Styles

An attachment style is the mode of relating to important people in your life that you developed through your relationships with your parents. Now follow the instructions.

Shaver's Attachment Styles

Read the statements below and simply check the one that is most applicable to you. If you are not sure, check the statement that is more applicable than the others.

1. I find it relatively easy to get close to others and am comfortable depending on them and having them depend on me. I don't often worry about being abandoned or about someone getting too close to me.
2. I find that others are reluctant to get as close as I would like. I often worry that my partner doesn't really love me or won't want to stay with me. I want to merge completely with another person, and this desire sometimes scares people away.
3. I am somewhat uncomfortable being close to others; I find it difficult to trust them completely, difficult to allow myself to depend on them. I am nervous when anyone gets too close, and often, love partners want me to be more intimate than I feel comfortable being.

Quoted from Shaver (1986, p. 31), with permission.

Part 2: The Interpersonal Jealousy Scale

In responding to each item, place the name of your boyfriend or girlfriend in the blank for each item. If you have no boyfriend or girlfriend at present, use the name of a person from a past relationship. If you are married use your spouse's name. Then use the

scale below to express your feelings concerning the truth of the item. For example, if you feel the item is "absolutely true" of you, place a 9 in the blank before the item. If it is only definitely true place an 8 in the blank, and so on.

9 = absolutely true; agree completely
8 = definitely true
7 = true
6 = slightly true
5 = neither true or false
4 = slightly false
3 = false
2 = definitely false
1 = absolutely false; disagree completely

[Gay/Lesbian individuals, please forgive and ignore the references to "opposite sex"; place your current or past partner's name in the blanks.]

1. If _____ were to see an old friend of the opposite sex and respond with a great deal of happiness, I would be annoyed.
2. If _____ went out with same-sex friends, I would feel compelled to know what he/she did.
3. If _____ admired someone of the opposite sex I would feel irritated.
4. If _____ were to help someone of the opposite sex with his/her homework, I would feel suspicious.
5. When _____ likes one of my friends I am pleased.
6. If _____ were to go away for the weekend without me, my only concern would be with whether he/she had a good time.
7. If _____ were helpful to someone of the opposite sex, I would feel jealous.
8. When _____ talks of happy experiences of his/her past, I feel sad that I wasn't part of it.
9. If _____ were to become displeased about the time I spend with others, I would be flattered.
10. If _____ and I went to a party and I lost sight of him/her, I would become uncomfortable.
11. I want _____ to remain good friends with the people he/she used to date.
12. If _____ were to date others I would feel unhappy.

Continued

BOX 5.3 *Continued*

13. When I notice that _____ and a person of the opposite sex have something in common, I am envious.
14. If _____ were to become very close to someone of the opposite sex, I would feel very unhappy and/or angry.
15. I would like _____ to be faithful to me.
16. I don't think it would bother me if _____ flirted with someone of the opposite sex.
17. If someone of the opposite sex were to compliment _____, I would feel that the person was trying to take _____ away from me.
18. I feel good when _____ makes a new friend.
19. If _____ were to spend the night comforting a friend of the opposite sex who had just had a tragic experience, _____'s compassion would please me.
20. If someone of the opposite sex were to pay attention to _____, I would become possessive of him/her.
21. If _____ was to become exuberant and hug someone of the opposite sex, it would make me feel good that he/she was expressing his/her feelings openly.
22. The thought of _____ kissing someone else drives me up the wall.
23. If someone of the opposite sex lit up at the sight of _____, I would become uneasy.
24. I like to find fault with _____'s old dates.
25. I feel possessive toward _____.
26. If _____ had previously been married, I would feel resentment towards the ex-wife/husband.
27. If I saw a picture of _____ and an old date I would feel unhappy.
28. If _____ were to accidentally call me by the wrong name, I would become furious.

Note: To calculate your score, put minuses in front of the scale numbers you assigned to items 5, 6, 11, 16, 18, 19, and 21, then add these numbers. Next add the numbers for the other items. Your score is this total minus the negative total. The higher it is, the more the jealousy. Reprinted with permission of Eugene Mathes.

Part 3: Relationship between the Exercises

About 55 percent of the respondents surveyed by Shaver checked the first statement in Part 1, indicating *secure* style. Twenty per cent endorsed the second statement, *anxious style*, and 25 percent checked the third statement, *avoidant style*. The last two statements indicate insecure attachment styles. People with these two styles, especially the anxious style, would be expected to be unusually jealous. Notice that Shaver's second statement indicates high need for assurance of love. It could have been made by one of Horney's patients with "an insatiable need for affection."

Assume that scores on the Interpersonal Jealousy Scale of 100 or above indicate high jealousy, and scores of 25 or below indicate low jealousy. If Horney and Shaver are correct, those of you who checked the last two statements, especially the second, would be expected to score relatively close to 100, while those who endorsed the first statement would be expected to score close to 25. More realistically, those of you who checked the last two statements should score relatively higher on the Interpersonal Jealousy Scale than those of you who checked the first statement.

There are a couple of points to remember in evaluating your responses to the two exercises and the relationship between them. First, both the research associated with Shaver's statements and Mathes's scale are oriented to romantic involvements, but Horney's point of view relates to a broader range of relationships (see Mathes, Adams, & Davies, 1985). Thus, whether or not your attachment style choice matched your jealousy score reflects only partially on Horney's theory. Second, as always, do not take a single score or outcome on any psychological instrument very seriously. Much more information about you would be needed before solid conclusions could be drawn concerning whether or not you are a particularly jealous person and concerning what your attachment style might be.

Before leaving this box, go back to the Interpersonal Jealousy Scale one more time and look for items that fit Horney's conception of jealousy well. For example, items 7 and 17 are clear examples of what Horney meant by "morbid jealousy."

context of a continuing relationship. They tend to enjoy all kinds of physical contact, from hugs to oral sex. By contrast, avoidant types liked only sexual forms of physical contact. Anxious types liked the more nurturing kinds of physical contact, but were not overly enthralled with sexual contact. Shaver wondered whether the 40,000 people who wrote Ann Landers proclaiming a preference for hugs over intercourse were predominantly anxious types. Recent research continues to support Shaver's trichotomy (Griffin & Bartholomew, 1994).

Anticipating Research on Concepts of Interest to the Public

"Jealousy" was not the only idea conceived by Horney that was ahead of its time. As will be apparent, she anticipated many beliefs of the humanists whose theories are considered in later chapters. Like Adler, Horney's therapy was not just for gaining what Freud called "insight." It was for growth.

Another of Horney's notions anticipated a popular idea of psychotherapist Albert Ellis, the psychologist who is known for his assumption that people are basically irrational. As reflected in Ellis's concept "musturbation," Horney believed that some people are subject to the **tyranny of the shoulds**, the belief that one should do this and that, whatever a good person *should do*, whatever is expected by others, rather than whatever one feels it is his or her nature to do. People afflicted with this malady think of themselves as miserable worms who must forever wriggle forth in pursuit of the ethereal perfection that eludes them. Horney wrote: "Forget about the disgraceful creature you actually *are*; this is how you *should* be; and to be this idealized self is all that matters. You should be able to endure everything, to understand everything, to like everybody, to be always productive . . ." (Horney, 1950, pp. 64–65). The shoulds dominate the individual, so that not to do what one "should" generates anxiety and guilt. "He should be the utmost of honesty, generosity, considerateness, justice, dignity, courage, unselfishness. He should be the perfect lover, husband, teacher . . . he should love his parents, his wife, his country . . . he should never feel hurt, and he should always be serene and unruffled" (p. 65). He should be whatever others deem to be the "right kind of person," never himself. Needless to say, many of us are bound by the chains of the "shoulds." Horney believed that the first step in working free of this bondage is to recognize the tyrant who has tied us up. Then we may begin to acknowledge that the ideal of perfection we pursue is impossible to obtain, and in fact, detracts us from being who we really are and who we could become.

Developing New Clinical Techniques: Self-Analysis

One of Horney's contributions was the development of clinical and therapeutic techniques. Martin (1975) has characterized Horney's therapeutic approach as one of trust, confidence, respect for each person's individual uniqueness and inner constructive resources, and adherence to the principle that exploration always precedes explanation. The goal is to seek the real self, not to discover some awful problem and correct it somehow.

One of her contributions that has been relatively ignored is **self-analysis**, a process whereby people come to understand themselves better through their own efforts, often outside the context of psychotherapy (Horney, 1942). You may recall that Jung allowed patients to do self-analysis, although it was not a main weapon in his therapeutic arsenal. It is apparently rare that theorist/therapists trust people under their care to probe their own psyches in the hope of useful self-discovery without their psychologist, psychiatrist, or counselor being present. But Horney was a rare theorist/therapist.

In Horney's view, self-analysis apparently is not analogous to self-hypnosis, a process that a person takes over after training, and continues to use without any further professional assistance. It certainly is not the same as "self-help," which is typically done by people with no assistance, except possibly that provided by a popular book. Rather it is a step that a person takes in the direction of **self-recognition**, coming to know one's neuroses, idealized self-image, and real self, including positive and negative attributes. It is also a step taken under supervision. The patients on whom Horney concentrates in her 1942 book may have tried "self-analysis" (the book title) while not in therapy, but they likely had received therapy and would have it again. As you will see, there are problems with self-analysis that make it risky without supervision.

To illustrate self-analysis, I have chosen the case of Clare, because, of the several case histories covered in the book *Self Analysis*, it is the most detailed. Reading the summary of it will not only tell you something about self-analysis, it will partially reiterate Horney's theory.

Clare was unwanted by her mother who unsuccessfully attempted to abort her. Her father simply was uninterested in any of the children. However, Clare was intelligent and received a good education. By the time she entered therapy at age thirty she had been married—her husband died—and had become an apparently successful magazine editor. During analysis she was involved with Peter, a businessman and the focus of her problems. Clare was morbidly dependent, lacking in self-confidence, and in the grip of an insatiable need for reassurances of love. This account concentrates on instances of self-recognition that occurred to Clare.

Clare's whole life was wrapped up in Peter. She wanted to be with him all the time. When he failed to keep a promised date with her, which happened often, she was devastated. A lightbulb went on for Clare and illuminated both herself and her relationship with Peter when she awoke on a Sunday morning intensely irritated at an author who broke his promise to submit an article for her magazine. While reflecting on this puzzling incident, it occurred to Clare that she was not really angry with the author, nor at people who fail to keep promises. Rather, she was angry because Peter had frustrated her desire to be with him by failing to show up on that weekend as promised. This realization caused her to remember the heroine of a novel who lost her feelings for her husband while he was away at war. In turn, she wondered whether she wanted to sever her emotional ties with Peter, but dismissed the thought "because I love him so much" (p. 194). Thus, despite the correct recognition that she was really angry with Peter, an important opportunity to break Peter's hold on her was lost.

Clare "managed to shake off the whole problem," fell back to sleep and dreamed she was lost in a foreign city where people spoke an unknown language and had left her luggage and money at the train station (p. 196). Then she was at a fair where there was gambling and a freak show. Reflecting on this dream she realized that counting on the unreliable Peter was a "crap shoot," and that he was something of a freak. This shallow analysis was, however, as far as she was able to go. She missed the symbolism of being lost without luggage and money: she had "invested" everything in Peter, and it all had been lost.

One morning a notice of a shipwreck brought back a dream in which she was adrift on the waves. Being in danger of drowning, a "strong man put his arms around her and saved her" (p. 202). She had the feeling of belonging and of endless protection. "He would always hold her in his arms and never leave her" (p. 202). In turn this dream reminded Clare of another nocturnal revelation in which she was hand in hand with Bruce, an older writer who had promised to be her mentor. He was a "hero" whose interest in her was described as a "blessing." These experiences moved Clare closer to recognizing that she wanted everlasting love and protection. She also realized that Bruce was not as brilliant as her dream implied. Unfortunately, she did not generalize her revelation about Bruce to the "superior" man in her life, Peter. It was to be some time before she fully acknowledged Peter's many deficiencies. Nevertheless, it was the first time she truly recognized that Peter was not giving her what she wanted and that she was dissatisfied with the relationship.

Clare's mood hinged on every nuance of Peter's behavior. An instance of his lateness plunged her into deep depression. The smallest favor granted to her generated disproportionate joy. When he gave her a scarf, she reacted as he had presented her with the Hope diamond. If he relented and said that he would go somewhere with her after all, her gratitude was that of a dying patient saved by the surgeon. She was like a robot controlled by a less than benevolent scientist.

Later Clare recalled a dream of a large bird flying away. It was glorious in color and grace, not unlike Peter who was handsome and a fine dancer. It meant that Peter, under whose "wing" she wanted to hide, had flown away, or was about to.

Reflecting on her tearfulness during a movie, Clare noticed that she had cried not when "the girl in the movie was badly off but when her situation took an unexpected turn for the better" (p. 211). She then coupled this recognition with two other recollections concerning friends' comments about love: (1) a confirmed bachelor asserted that "woman's love is merely a screen for exploiting men"; (2) another friend, Susan, had proclaimed that love was nothing more than an "honest deal" in which each partner did his or her share to create "good companionship" (p. 213). She wondered, was her love nothing more than "sponging on somebody else!" (p. 212). Was it merely a "deal"? She began to recognize that her need for Peter was based on something other than affection.

Eventually, Clare recognized that she desperately needed Peter for the protection and reassurance that she hoped he would provide, not because he was a great hero or because she had true affection for him. Fortunately she was in the process of weaning herself from him when the rumor mill told her he was having an affair. When his subsequent letter asking for a separation confirmed what others were telling her, she averted the emotional collapse that would have occurred earlier. Instead she got through the crisis and later came to recognize that her problem was broader than Peter: "Her picture of herself was determined entirely by the evaluation by others" (p. 245). The revelation almost made her faint. When Clare returned to therapy later, she executed the final incision to excise Peter from her psyche, but Horney acknowledged that she probably could have done it on her own in continued self-analysis.

While self-analysis is valuable, Horney acknowledged its several shortcomings. During self-analysis, patients: (1) may perceive something about themselves that is not true, but see it as accurate; (2) may come up with correct information about themselves, but misinterpret it; (3) may have a partial and accurate recognition regarding themselves, but fail to extend it to core personality dispositions; and (4) may analyze an incident correctly with regard to its implications for themselves, but not know what to do with the result. These are all reasons why self-analysis is better done under supervision. Clare made all four errors. Nevertheless, self-analysis is certainly a first bold step on the path to self-recognition.

Some Research Support

While research support for Horney's theory has been relatively meager, there is one concept that has been the object of significant research. Ryckman, Thornton, and Butler (1994) have collected data supporting Horney's hypercompetitiveness. This orientation is accompanied by a need to manipulate and denigrate others in a variety of situations. Recall that this notion is associated with Horney's "moving against others" pattern and expansiveness.

Ryckman and colleagues related their index of hypercompetitiveness to several measures related to Horney's writings about the constellation of characteristics that embody hypercompetitiveness. The first of these measures will be familiar. According to Ryckman and colleagues, Horney believed that hypercompetitive individuals are prone to be narcissistic. They are overtly self-laudatory, but beneath all the bravado they are beset with feelings of inferiority accompanied by apperceptions of powerlessness and insignificance.

A second measure Ryckman and colleagues expected to correlate with hypercompetitiveness revolved around Horney's contention that hypercompetitive individuals tend to be exhibitionistic and unconventional. These inclinations should cause them to score high on a Sensation Seeking instrument. A third measure related to Horney's description of hypercompetitive individuals as tending to be "everything to everybody" (p. 86), a disposition that is indexed by the Type E Scale. Type E's want to be the best at everything. Consequently they are habitually taking on multiple roles leading to overload and conflict. They are also, according to Horney, Machiavellians. This disposition and the scale named for it refer to Italian Prince Niccolo Machiavelli, a master of the fine arts of manipulation and exploitation. Machiavellians attempt to have their way with others by any means at their disposal. They lie and cheat, whatever it takes to beat their enemies, who are numerous, as they dislike almost everyone.

The best predictors of hypercompetitiveness were, first, narcissism, followed by Type E orientation and some measures of sensation seeking. Although Machiavellianism was not a strong predictor of hypercompetitiveness, it was significantly correlated with the tendency to be overcompetitive. All in all, Ryckman and colleagues were able to show that the validity of Horney's conception "hypercompetitiveness" looms large under the scientific microscope.

Limitations

Horney's theory shares two major limitation with classical psychoanalysis: a relative absence of research testing its concepts. The lack of research effort to support her theory is quite unprecedented; few other prominent theories are so neglected. Also, few theorists have had so few followers. The scarcity of scientific literature can be traced to the observation that a number of Horney's concepts related to personality are difficult to measure. Neurotic needs, externalization, and the real self are examples.

Horney's basic deficit as a theorist was shared by all the theorists covered so far and also the two to be considered in the next couple of chapters: she, like the others, was trained as a physician and psychiatrist, not a psychological scientist. She and the others were simply not equipped to conduct the scientific research that might have confirmed or disconfirmed their points of view. Further, none of these theorists seemed able to recognize contradictions to their theories found in their own writings. For example, according to Horney's notion of "need for assurance of love" and "jealousy," Clare ought to have been an especially jealous person. In fact, there are few, if any, lines in the description of her case that can be clearly interpreted as references to jealousy.

Conclusions

Despite the observation that some of Horney's concepts are too broad and general "to get a handle on," some of them are not too global to deal with scientifically. Among these are many concepts that are defined in crystal clear fashion. While other theorists are evasive, Horney is refreshingly straightforward.

To take these credits a step further, Horney is an outstanding writer, probably the best among the theorists covered in this book. Unlike those of some other theorists, I can recommend her books as both an enjoyable read and a useful source of information. Further, she, more than some others, addressed the considerations that are of interest to normal people and are embedded in their language. Also, her intuitively optimistic "growth approach" is a refreshing contrast to the gloomy view of the psychoanalysts (Rubin, 1991).

The alleged untestability of her concepts may also be overstated. If it is true that she defined her concepts clearly, many should be testable. In fact, her ideas about jealousy in relation to need for reassurances of love are quite testable. Actually, in the jealousy/attachment styles exercises you considered earlier, you tested her views. So also did Shaver in some of his research.

Given that Horney's ideas are more testable than the lack of research on them would have one believe, one may ask why they have not often been subjected to scientific scrutiny. The answer may well be that the only woman theorist taken seriously by modern personality psychologists is taken less seriously than male theorists. A reconsideration of Horney's writings seems in order.

Finally, Karen Horney was a fascinating person. Even as an adolescent she wrote literate, often poetic lines about herself that were extraordinarily candid. If she seemed to be more troubled during her early life than other theorists, it may be because she was more honest and self-disclosing than the others. Reading her adolescent diaries (1980) and her life story (Quinn, 1988) is more than the act of perusing biographies of a famous figure. It will allow you to get under the skin of an interesting human being and also follow the development of a significant contributor to understanding the human condition.

Summary Points

1. Karen Clementina Theordora Danielsen was born to Norwegian and Dutch/German parents in a community near Hamburg, Germany. Her father, a sea captain, was often gone, but attempted to dominate her life when he could. In response she clung to her mother. De-

spite paternal resistance, Karen received a good education and entered medical school at age twenty. There she met Oscar Horney, her eventual husband. Balancing school with typical homemaker "obligations" was stressful. Depression led to therapy and she gained exposure to psychoanalysis. Overcoming these early hardships, Horney grew to be a forceful and well-known figure in the area of personality.

2. Freud and Horney both oriented to childhood experiences. However, Horney questioned the sexual instincts, Oedipal theory, Freud's view of gender differences, and the psychosexual stages. Penis envy was deemed not generally true and, in this culture, is confined to neurotic women. "Castrating tendencies" were also snubbed and Freud's inattention to social matters criticized.

3. Horney regarded masturbation as normal when not compulsive and identified four sexually troubled types, some of them related to sexual orientation. She also dismissed the Freudian allegation of female masochism and frigidity. Basic anxiety, an all-pervading feeling of being lonely and helpless in a hostile world, was due to a number of family background factors. Horney's neurotic needs include affection and approval, having a "partner," narrowly restricting one's life; power; exploiting others; social recognition or prestige; personal admiration; personal achievement; self-sufficiency and independence; and perfection and unassailability.

4. Neurotic conflict stems from contradictory attitudes the person holds toward other people. The three orientations are moving toward others (self-effacing); moving against people (expansive, hypercompetitive); and moving away from people (resignation). The idealized image of self is an artificial pride system that substitutes for realistic confidence and counteracts real inner weakness and self-contempt. It stands in contrast to the actual self, who one currently is, and the real self, who one could become. Along with the idealized self comes externalization. People can postpone the inevitable clash between actual behavior and idealized self by resorting to blind spots, compartmentalization, rationalization, excessive self-control, arbitrary rightness, elusiveness, and cynicism.

5. Horney anticipated diversity concerns when she threw out the Freudian assumption that women long for male anatomy and the several implications of that alleged need. She noted the illogical nature of women's alleged desire for male anatomy, the lack of evidence for the universality of Freud's assumptions about the sexes, the irrelevance to women of a theory written by men for men, and the false belief "I must have a man." Finally, Horney condemned male selection processes that create a self-fulfilling prophecy and the socially conveyed attitudes that demean women.

6. Horney wrote plain language books for everybody. She also showed an unusual interest in concepts that are important to rank-and-file people. For example, jealousy begins in childhood, can include Oedipal jealousy, and, in adults, can be reasonable and normal. However, morbidly jealous people show fear of losing someone's love that is way out of proportion to the actual danger. Their excessive jealousy, which may be a hold-over from childhood, is due to an insatiable need for love caused by unresolved basic anxiety.

7. Horney's views of jealousy anticipated the work of Philip Shaver, who proposed three attachment styles dating back to parent–child interactions, two of which predict inordinate jealousy. Recent work by Shaver and colleagues showed differences among secure, anxious, and avoidant people on interpersonal sensitivity, caregiving, and sexual attitudes–behavior. The interpersonal Jealousy Scale has the flavor of Horney's views and may relate to the at-

tachment styles. Horney's idea—the tyranny of the shoulds—clearly conveys the currently important picture of people who feel they should do this and that, whatever is demanded by the idealized self.

8. She also revamped psychoanalysis, making it more concerned with "being a better person," rather than discovering something awful in the psyche. She uniquely recommended self-analysis, during which one can begin to gain self-recognition. Clare, a self-analysis case, was unwanted by her parents and grew to be a dependent, assurance-seeking adult. She was morbidly dependent on her lover, unreliable Peter, whose every mood determined her own.

9. Several dreams, fantasies, and other revelations showed approximations to self-recognition: Clare realized that anger at an author's lateness was really directed to Peter; she had dream images, including symbols of a "crap shoot" and a "freak"; being "cast adrift" and rescued; a bird dream about Peter "flying the coop," and love as "sponging." Peter left and Clare survived, coming to realize that her picture of herself was determined by others. Work by Ryckman and colleagues showed that Horney's concept, hypercompetitiveness, is related, as she would have predicted, to narcissism, Type E orientation, and Sensation Seeking.

10. Horney's theory has received little scientific support. A lack of scientific training limited her ability to test her theory or even to recognize contradictions in her writings. But she often defined her concepts with such clarity that they could be adequately tested by others. Thus, it appears that lack of scientific attention to her ideas by others may be due to their lack of respect for her gender. Horney was a fascinating person whose writings should be reconsidered and who is well worth reading.

Running Comparison

Theorist	*Horney in Comparison*
Freud	She agreed with Freud on the importance of anxiety-provoking childhood experiences on adult personality, neurosis, gaining insight, dynamic view of motivation, conscience, instincts, and case histories versus scientific research. But they disagreed on libido (she said "unproven"), sexual motivation ("over-emphasized"), Oedipus Complex ("not true of all people"), penis envy ("rare worldwide"), culture ("Freud ignored"), consciousness ("Freud neglected"), and women (rejected his treatment of them).
Adler	She agreed with him on the importance of social cooperation and her discovery of conflict between the idealized and real self is akin to his "shock." Also, she acknowledged his conception of "striving for superiority."
Rogers and Maslow	Her "real self" matches their recognition of people's endless potential for positive growth.
Jung	She also encouraged patients to do self-analysis, but more formally than Jung.

Essay/Critical Thinking Questions

1. What was it about Horney's childhood that made her a different person as a child and adolescent than as a adult?

2. What was it that so upset American psychoanalysts with Horney's criticisms of Freud? Was it the criticisms themselves? Her gender? The particular "soft spots" she picked on? All of these? Explain your answer.

3. What are some reasonable criticisms of Horney's hypotheses concerning the sexual types who are (1) ". . . prone to yield to sexual advances from either sex" and (2) those who avoid competition within their own gender?

4. What is a parent to do in order to be a good parent in Horney's eyes? [Try to respond to the criticism that it is difficult or impossible to be an effective parent from Horney's point of view.]

5. Horney makes it "bad" to show any of her three trends. How could you transform one of them so that it would be adaptive rather than maladaptive?

6. Could you write a paragraph describing a person who would likely be the jealous type according to Horney's point of view?

7. Look at yourself. Can you isolate some instances in which you have been victimized by the "tyranny of the shoulds"? Describe a couple of them.

8. Describe a person you have known who fits one of Shaver's and colleagues' findings regarding his attachment trichotomy and attitudes toward love and sex.

9. You have probably done self-analysis, even if you are not aware of it. There have been times when something unusual that happened to you has caught your attention and you have used the occurrence to better your understanding of yourself. Can you provide an example?

10. Horney's theory has been unjustifiably neglected. Can you find among her concepts one that can be easily tested (excluding jealousy)? Tell how it could be tested.

E-mail Interaction

(Write the author at mfbpa@wiu.edu)
Forward one of the following or phrase your own.

1. Tell me which of Horney's contributions is her most important.
2. How would you fit a sexually disinterested type into Horney's theory?
3. What is wrong with doing what you *should* do?
4. Was Horney a real feminist?
5. If my mate is insanely jealous, does that mean she or he really loves me?

6

PERSONALITY FROM THE INTERPERSONAL PERSPECTIVE: HARRY STACK SULLIVAN

- Can a person with severe psychological problems give useful advice to others?
- Was your mother or father a "good parent" or a "bad parent" (or neither one)?
- Was there a time during your early infancy when you had no sensations or feeling or any thoughts?
- Are there just four ways to classify the sexual orientations of people?
- How important is physical contact with other human beings in the development of the infant?

Harry Stack Sullivan

The chapters in the first half of this book may be thought of as starting with Freud and withdrawing from him gradually. Jung was more closely tied to Freud and maintained a relationship with him longer than any of "The Master's" other notable followers. Adler quarreled with Freud, but composed a different theory that was, nevertheless, in part a response to Freudian thought. Horney never had personal contact with Freud, but she began her theorizing from the psychoanalytic perspective. Harry Stack Sullivan also had no personal relationship with Freud. One of his mentors even warned him against Freud and encouraged him to be critical of psychoanalysis (Perry, 1982). Yet Sullivan was influenced by Freud, and, like Horney, used the framework of psychoanalytic theory to build his own point of view. Nevertheless, he joined the others in deserting the sexual emphasis. To Sullivan, the critical consideration in attempts to understand personality is **interpersonal relations**, the relationships between a person and each other important person in his or her life. These crucial twosomes or dyads were behind much of what Sullivan wrote and theorized about. His emphasis on them distinguishes his theory.

Sullivan, The Person

Harry Stack Sullivan is sometimes considered "America's psychiatrist" (Perry, 1982). Born in 1892 to recent Irish immigrant parents in the rural New York town of Norwich and raised on a nearby farm, Sullivan was traditionally American through and through. The people in the area where he grew up were "farm folk." They were advocates of the Protestant work ethic who came to America to better themselves, but in some ways led lives that did not fit the idyllic image of rural America. The surrounding region was known for its high suicide rate, with isolated farm wives most often taking their own lives, and sometimes taking their children with them.

Sullivan was an only child, worshiped by his mother, Ella Stack, but considered by his father "no good to work, for he has his nose stuck in a book all the time" (Perry, 1982, p. 85). Although Harry was prone to greatly overstate their accomplishments, the Stack family was well regarded in the community. The same could not be said for the Sullivans. This comparison is an example of the "social law of relativity"—the Stacks had relatively high status in a very humble community, compared to the Sullivans. In fact, Sullivan's family background is among the most ordinary and pedestrian of the theorists covered in this book. Horney's name on her mother's side, Ronzelen, began with Van, a mark of nobility. By contrast, the Sullivans were pretty much "fresh off the boat" and "working class." One of the factors that may have spurred Sullivan to fame may have been his desire to rise above his background. Alternatively, his delusions about the accomplishments of Mother Ella Stack's family may have driven him to "live up to her standards." The vacillations of name change that he displayed support the contention that Ella's influence was behind his drive to achieve. When he entered medical school, he was Harry Francis Sullivan, or H. F. Sullivan (Francis was given to him at age thirteen, on his confirmation). Later he used a variety of combinations, for example, Harry F. Sullivan and just plain Harry Sullivan. But eventually, Francis dropped out in favor of the maternal surname, Stack. This indecisiveness regarding his name may also be interpreted as indicative of identity confusion, a trait he shared with Erik Erikson.

As a person, Sullivan was lonely, somewhat reserved, rather fatalistic about his health, and a user of alcohol "to combat anxiety" (Perry, 1982, p. 175). He had the vulnerable, haunted look of movie actor James Dean. During childhood and preadolescence, Sullivan was a loner at school who conveyed a sense of ambiguous sexuality that lingered into adulthood. Supposedly he was involved in a homosexual relationship during preadolescence. As an adult, he wrote that he entered puberty late, possible as late as age seventeen.

In college he did report "lust" for a girl in one of his classes, but Perry (1982) indicates that people close to the adult Sullivan were never quite sure about his sexual orientation. Friends indicated that they thought Sullivan had sexual contact with both men and women during his adulthood. Whether these speculations were true or not Sullivan was known to long for marriage and to lament his bachelorhood. Perry even suggests that Sullivan may have sent proposals of marriage to astounded women with whom he was merely acquainted. At one point, he was reported to be "attentive" to Karen Horney (Perry, 1982, p. 335). Nevertheless, sustained love for women was probably directed exclusively to his mother and his Aunt Maggie. Contrary to rumors, Clara Thompson, a beloved colleague, apparently was not sexually involved with Sullivan. Whether Sullivan was gay, bisexual, or heterosexual probably will never be known. His were not the times in which people who were other than "straight" admitted as much in public.

Traces of conflict and psychological turmoil were present throughout Sullivan's life. While a student at Cornell University, allegedly he was involved in "mail fraud," supposedly as a part of a "criminal gang" (Perry, 1982). Scant detail of the relevant incidents led Perry to speculate that Sullivan and "the gang" were using the mail to obtain "chemicals" from a drugstore (1982). Yet the penalty meted out to Sullivan was slight: he was suspended from Cornell for a year and could have returned to school (but he never did).

Between his suspension in 1909 and his arrival at medical school in 1911, Sullivan disappeared. It is remotely possible that he was in jail—maybe he was "sprung" by his uncle, a judge. More likely, Sullivan suffered a psychotic break during this period and was receiving treatment. In any case, the youthful Sullivan was known to have had bouts of *schizophrenia*, withdrawal from reality and disturbances in thoughts, feelings, and behaviors. These episodes probably explain his burning interest in the disorder.

Sullivan was admitted to the Chicago College of Medicine and Surgery (CCMS) despite the absence of credits from Cornell where he did poorly as a physics student (Chapman, 1976; Perry, 1982). In effect, he went directly from high school to medical school without the benefit of a full college education. Though valedictorian honors in high school implied significant academic abilities, his record in medical school was dismal. While living in poverty and working as an elementary physics teacher and a Chicago Elevated Railway conductor, Sullivan received only one "A" at CCMS, but accumulated several "Ds" (Perry, 1982). This undistinguished performance was recorded at a school that may have been suspect in its time. Although Perry (1982) regarded CCMS as most likely average for its day, Chapman (1976) described it as one of many fly-by-night physician factories that sprang up during the late 1890s and early 1900s. Sullivan called it a "diploma mill" (Chapman, 1976). It was defunct by 1917, leaving behind no record of Sullivan's graduation (his diploma was later found among his personal effects).

These aspersions cast upon CCMS and Sullivan's performance there may seem to mean that he was mediocre as a scholar and intellect. To the contrary, he was a brilliant, original thinker who may well have "gone through the motions" during medical school to make himself eligible for what he really wanted to do, become a psychiatrist.

Rather than receiving formal psychiatric training, Sullivan trained himself while a staff physician at St. Elizabeth's Hospital in Washington, D.C. (Chapman, 1976). The lack of formal training in psychiatry led him to make numerous erroneous statements about psychiatry and abnormal behavior, some of them in print (Chapman, 1976). Yet having learned about psychiatry from the patients, rather than from the dogmatic psychiatric professors of the day, may have permitted the creative ideas that made him famous. Of the ironies that surround Sullivan's training, none is more profound than the implication of the observation that he is a central figure in the development of psychiatric training (Conci, 1993).

Sullivan's most significant clinical work involved schizophrenic men, for whom he established a successful residential treatment program grounded in experiences of interpersonal trust (Sullivan, 1994/1927). He believed in the principle "like cures like," which guided his selection of "sensitive, shy" ward staff.

The aura of instability that permeated Sullivan's life and work survived his death. In 1957 two people, one a graduate of the White Foundation and the other claiming to be a former Sullivan patient, established a colony bearing Sullivan's name (Hoban, 1989). They call themselves the "Sullivanians" and claim to practice Sullivan's brand of therapy on each other. In fact, the White Foundation has dissociated itself from them and has asserted that

BOX 6.1   Sullivan: Diversity Incarnate

When we think of diversity we often dwell on issues of race. There are, however, many more dimensions to diversity. Religion, for example, is an important dimension. Although neither Freud nor Adler were devout Jews, being Jewish was an apparent source of insecurity for Freud. Sullivan's investment in religion was apparently rarely considered, but whether his family was Catholic or Protestant may have had something to do with their immigration to the United States. In any case, that Sullivan was Irish almost certainly affected him. His was an era of prejudice against recent immigrants, including those from Ireland. It was the same time in which the Kennedy family battled anti-Irish bigotry.

That Sullivan was possibly gay or bisexual placed him on another dimension of diversity. Ambiguities surrounding his sexual orientation probably greatly affected his interpersonal relations. Finally, still another dimension, mental health status, probably shaped Sullivan's life to a degree. He may have suffered from the "schizophrenia" stigma most of his life.

what they do is not in the Sullivanian tradition. The "cult" has been accused of breaking up families, promoting sexual interchanges across family lines, farming out children to boarding schools, and holding parents as virtual hostages both financially and physically. While Sullivan would never have approved of such behavior, it is conceivable that his disordered life may have been partly the inspiration for it.

Harry Stack Sullivan died under mysterious circumstances on January 14, 1949 (Perry, 1982). He was found in a Paris hotel room, sprawled on the floor, his heart medication scattered about him. Rumors of self-destruction circulated immediately, especially in the suicide-ridden rural community where he was reared. Perry dismissed speculations that Sullivan directly committed suicide. She was well acquainted with Sullivan's heart ailment and knew that the official cause of death, "meningeal hemorrhage," was entirely plausible in view of his medical condition. However, she wondered whether certain thoughts that may have occurred to him on the day of his death had not contributed to his demise, or even caused it.

When he arose on the day of the fatal attack, the fact that it was his deceased mother Ella's birthday must have been on his mind. It was also close to the anniversary of a dear friend's death, and he may have remembered that relative Leo Stack had died of a similar attack in a hotel room on a day in January. Finally, Sullivan's prediction, made in 1931, that he would die of a "rupture of the middle meningeal artery at the age of 57 . . ." was astoundingly accurate. Perhaps memories of these four events came together to hasten what was already inevitable. The mystery will likely never be solved, but, had he lived on, personality psychology certainly would have benefited.

Sullivan's View of the Person

Significant Others and the Self

Sullivan's theory revolves around the idea that a person's needs and developmental tasks are met in a series of two-person relationships, beginning with "a mothering one" and culminating in the selection of a sexual partner. While Sullivan believed we have as many personalities as we have interpersonal relationships, he formally defined *personality* as "the relatively enduring pattern of recurrent interpersonal situations which characterize a human life" (1953, pp. 110–111).

This orientation is certainly different from that of Freud, who emphasized biologically based instincts. Sullivan did see himself as a psychoanalyst. Further, he used many of Freud's methods. Nevertheless, he backed away from Freud's underlying assumptions revolving around instincts and psychosexuality. Sullivan's point of view is, however, in the spirit of Adler's "social interest." It also bears some similarity to Horney's inclination: she considered anxiety dating to infancy to be critically important and she also was very concerned about relationships. Little wonder they developed a friendly and cooperative relationship.

Significant others are those people who are most meaningful to us in our lives. In essence, personality does not exist in the absence of important other people. Without them, there can be no development of a **self-system**, "that part of personality which is born entirely out of the influences of significant others upon one's feeling of well-being" (Sullivan 1954, p. 101). As most people know, our sense of self-esteem depends largely on the positive and negative evaluations we receive from other people. Interestingly, our relationships with them may be fantasized as well as real, including imaginary playmates, literary characters, and idealized public figures with whom we have never had face-to-face contact. An example is John Hinckley's fantasized relationship with movie actress Jodie Foster, whom he tried to impress by attempting to assassinate Ronald Reagan.

A Need for Tenderness

For Sullivan, personality is derived from human experiences, all of which involve the reduction of tensions. Tensions are of two kinds: in common with Freud, physical needs, and, in contrast with Freud, interpersonal anxiety. *Needs* seek *satisfactions*: ". . . all those end states which are rather closely connected with the bodily organization" such as relief of deprivation of oxygen, water, food, body warmth, and so forth (Sullivan, 1947, p. 6). **Interpersonal anxiety** is a tension that is alleviated in relationships with significant others or in feelings of well-being.

Like Horney, Sullivan saw infants as being totally powerless and at the mercy of other people for their security. However, Sullivan further theorized that the infant's nearly absolute dependency revolves around a **mothering one**—a ". . . significant, relatively adult personality whose cooperation is necessary to keep the infant alive" (1953, p. 54). This critically important individual addresses the infant's **need for tenderness**; which, different from "love," refers to relief from various tensions (1953).

Sullivan effectively captures the essence of the almost umbilical connection between the infant and the mothering one in one of his "theorems": "The observed activity of the infant arising from the tension of needs induces tension in the mothering one, which . . . is experienced as tenderness and [leads] to activities [that provide] relief of the infant's needs" (1953, p. 39). The externally oriented, social implications of this statement set Sullivan apart from Freud and his emphasis on intrapsychic events.

Basic Concepts: Sullivan

Empathy, Anxiety, and Security

Another of Sullivan's theorems is: "The tension of anxiety, when present in the mothering one, induces anxiety in the infant" (1953, p. 41). Anxiety may be transferred to the infant when it is subjected to certain unsympathetic behaviors by the mothering one that communicate something is "bad," "disapproved of," or "wrong." This occurs even though the origin of tension in the mothering one has no direct connection with the infant. It may be due to the caregiver's personality, uncertainty about the parenting role, or circumstances unrelated to the infant, such as parental illness, fatigue, or upset due to bad news. However, the infant has no way of knowing about these possibilities. She or he simply participates in the caregiver's tension or discomfort, through **empathy**, "the term that we use to refer to the peculiar emotional linkage [that exists between the] infant [and] other significant people—the mother or the nurse" (1947, p. 8). It involves the reciprocal role-taking seen in the infant's expression of need for tenderness and the mother's motivation to provide tenderness (Hayes, 1994). Anxiety acquired by this and other means can interfere with the satisfaction of physical and tenderness needs. For example, the infant may cry or regurgitate, thereby disrupting critical behaviors such as feeding, which further increases both its own and the mothering one's anxiety. Since it has no effective means to remove, reduce, or escape from the anxiety, the infant is totally dependent on a cooperative other person for relief. Because of the infant's helpless condition, only the mothering one can provide relief in the form of **interpersonal security**—"relaxation of the tension of anxiety" which is experienced as a return to a tranquil, untroubled state (1953, p. 42). This unique experience is different from the satisfaction that occurs when physical needs are met.

Three Modes of Experience and Six Stages of Development

Sullivan (1953) conceptualized personality development as consisting of six stages or developmental epochs, spanning infancy through late adolescence. Each stage centers on a unique kind of interpersonal relationship. Three of the stages revolve around his rather abstract and complex "modes of experience." Because they are critical to Sullivan's thinking about the stages and are difficult to "put a finger on," it is best to consider them first.

Modes of Experience

The **prototaxic** mode is the earliest (infancy), most primitive type of experience, a state of generalized sensation or feeling, in the absence of thought (Sullivan, 1953). The infant knows only what William James called a "big, blooming, buzzing confusion"—vague perceptions of momentary states having no "before" or "after." There is no awareness of self as separate from the world. Sullivan, who often avoided formal definitions, is helped by sympathetic colleague Patrick Mullahy, who characterized the prototaxic mode as follows:

> The infant vaguely feels or "prehends" earlier and later states without realizing any serial connection between them . . . He has no awareness of himself as an entity separate

from the rest of the world. In other words, his felt experience is all of a piece, undifferentiated, without definite limits. It is as if his experiences were "cosmic" (Mullahy, 1948; as quoted by the editors of Sullivan, 1953 p. 28).

The **parataxic** mode is experienced as the infant becomes a child who begins to use speech, but still makes few logical connections within the sequence of its experiences (approximately the pre-school years; Sullivan, 1947; 1953). Thinking and speech are disorganized and disjunctive as in a dream, and understanding remains minimal. There is a sense of "magic" in which things "just happen," as in seeing colorful Christmas lights suddenly appear with the simple flip of a switch. In adults, parataxic experience may serve as a rough basis for memories related to habits. Examples include routine activities that often occur without conscious decision-making, such as dressing, walking to class, eating, or doing repetitive arithmetic calculations. Again, Mullahy comes to Sullivan's aid:

As the infant develops and maturation proceeds, the original undifferentiated wholeness of experience is broken. However, the "parts," the diverse aspects, the various kinds of experience are not related or connected in a logical fashion. . . . The child cannot yet relate them to one another or make logical distinctions among them. . . . Since no connections or relations are established, there is no logical movement of "thought" from one idea to the next. The parataxic mode is not a step by step process. Experience is undergone as momentary, unconnected states of being (Mullahy, 1948; as quoted by the editors of Sullivan, 1953 p. 28).

In other words, the unbroken mass—like a glob of jelly—that was feeling and perception is now segmented into parts, like separate cubes of jelly. Nevertheless, the parts are disconnected and not logically related to one another.

The **syntaxic** mode becomes important when the meaning of words becomes shared with most other people so that experience, judgments, and observations can be shared (approximately the early elementary school years; Sullivan, 1953). An individual becomes able to communicate syntaxic experiences with another person because both parties define language symbols alike. This is the stage of "consensual validation" in which children learn to separate experiences they share with others from experiences peculiar to them, to make their thoughts and feelings clear to others, and to appreciate what others are thinking and feeling (Sullivan, 1953). Again, Mullahy is helpful:

The child gradually learns the . . . meaning of language—in the widest sense of language. These meanings have been acquired from group activities, interpersonal activities, social experience. Consensually validated symbol activity involves an appeal to principles which are accepted as true by the hearer (Mullahy, 1948; as quoted by the editors of Sullivan, 1953, p. 28).

When children acquire the syntaxic mode, others have taught them the shared rules of organizing thoughts so that thoughts and speech are no longer disconnected and disjunctive. The undifferentiated mass that became the unsystematically linked assortment of pieces has now become an assemblage of separate parts, each bearing some relationship to some of the others.

As you can see, the direction of development as reflected by the three modes is toward increased socialization. Over time, the "social majority" rules over personal interpretations.

Infancy: Prototaxic Feelings about "Good" and "Bad" Caregivers

The **infancy** stage starts at birth and continues until the appearance of speech (Sullivan, 1953). The development of personality begins with feeding. This is because the infant's initial interpersonal situation is the "nipple-in-lips" experience, which revolves around the infant's mouth and the mother's breast. Should the bottle replace the breast, the same principles of interpersonal contact still hold. The experience integrates the infant's need for water, food, and contact, and the caregiver's need to show tenderness. Notice that this period is much like the "oral stage" as conceived by Freud, but departs from the psychoanalytic view by including the interpersonal notion of "caretaker tenderness." The infant's accompanying hand and foot movements, touching, grasping, pulling, pushing, rubbing, patting, and cuddling, become an increasingly important part of this first interpersonal situation.

As the infant begins to accumulate experiences, it forms **personifications**, investments of human attributes in persons or objects that do not actually possess the assigned traits, at least not in the degree to which they are applied. For example, if the infant's need for nourishment is accommodated by the willing presentation of a satisfying nipple, it forms the early personification "good nipple." When the infant's interactions with mothering ones are experienced as satisfying, warm, and comforting, it forms the personification "good mother." This empathic sensory image is not of the real mother, but of the infant's vague, prototaxic sense that feeding experiences are "good" because they result in relaxations of tensions. If the same caregiver, or a substitute, interacts with the infant in ways that are "rough, sound unpleasant, hurt the baby, and generally discompose him," the infant will be led to form a second rudimentary personification, that of the "bad mother" who has the "nipple of anxiety" (Sullivan, 1953, p. 116 & 87). Sullivan summarized these personifications: ". . . all relations with . . . people . . . [who] are a part of . . . satisfying . . . the infant's needs blend into a single personification which I call the good mother . . . all experience . . . which results in severe anxiety blends into a single personification which I call . . . the bad mother" (Sullivan, 1953, p. 120).

These personifications may endure in memory as "eidetic people"—"illusory people," "imaginary people," or "past people" who are sometimes dredged up and matched to people in adult life (boss as "bad mother"). Personal personifications develop as well. The individual comes to know "me," "good me," "bad me," and "not me." Interestingly, Blechner (1994) has proposed a fifth category. "Maybe me" is a me under consideration. It is a potential me that involves some dissociated aspect of personality that the individual has yet to muster the courage to accept. The threatening, aggressive side of the infant is an example. Later the sexual facet of the child would fit the "maybe me."

Despite understanding the difference between "rough" behavior and "tender" behavior, you may still wonder how the rather primitive prototaxic skills of the infant allow it to differentiate between "bad mother" and "good mother." The infant cannot understand what the mothering one says, nor can it interpret "appearances" (Sullivan, 1953). "Good" and "bad" mothers may look the same in basic physical appearance, including clothing. The "good nipple" and the "bad nipple" may be identical in appearance. The signs the infant must read to tell "good" from "bad" are subtle. In the case of the "bad mother" they are **forbidding gestures**, negative, covert cues such as a wrinkled brow, a cold tone of voice, a too tight grasp, a hesitancy, reluctance, or even revulsion at having to interact with the infant. Sullivan put it this way:

> *The discrimination of heard differences in the mother's vocalization and seen differences in the postural tensions of the mother's face, and perhaps later of differences in speed and rhythm of her gross bodily movements in coming toward the infant, presenting the bottle, changing the diapers, or what not—all these rather refined discriminations [made] by the . . . receptors of vision and hearing . . . are frequently associated with the unpleasant experience of anxiety, including the nipple of anxiety instead of the good nipple (Sullivan, 1953, pp. 86–87).*

At this and later stages Sullivan wrote of a process having the flavor of Freud's and Jung's "complex" but called **dynamisms**—"the relatively enduring energy [units] which [periodically] characterize the organism in its duration as a living organism" (Sullivan, 1953, p. 103). These energy systems are self-contained, intact entities that can operate on their own, but may function in relationship to other such systems. Think of them as packages of energy that wax and wane in their power and in their impact on the individual. They may de-

---

BOX 6.2 What Were (and Are) Your Personifications?

Sullivan would argue that you have had many personal personifications as an infant, as a child, and on through the other stages into adulthood. Think back to your childhood and forward in time in an attempt to identify your personifications. It will help if you recall the "early experience" exercise from the Adler chapter. Also search your memory for incidents that reflected on you as a person. To help in this process some possible personifications are listed to stimulate your thinking or, if they apply, to be selected by you.

"good me"	"bad me"	"not me"
"clever me"	"mischievous me"	"worthless me"
"brilliant me"	"kind me"	"awkward me"
"helpless me"	"ingenious me"	"devious me"
"shy me"	"bold me"	"manipulative me"
"self-sacrificing me"	"altruistic me"	"martyred me"
"sensitive me"	"faithful me"	"uncertain me"
"beautiful me"	"shameful me"	"maybe me"

You may wish to share the choices you made with those of other members of the class. Note choices that are shared with other people and exchange recollections of what events inspired the coincidental personifications.

velop at one stage or another, but can continue to crop up throughout life. Like tensions, dynamisms are of two kinds: (1) integrating, organizing, isolating tendencies; and (2) energy packages that involve certain "zones" or arenas of interaction. The self-system is a dynamism of the first kind. An example of the second kind that has its origins in the infancy stage is the *oral dynamism*, an energy system that encompasses interactions focusing on feeding or nourishment. Because dynamisms organize and channel physical energy, they have the power to dominate personality and cause it to follow one developmental direction rather than another.

It is from early experiences with others that the infant begins to differentiate its own self-system from the world around it. Experiences of positive satisfactions, in which the mothering one is pleased, are organized around a personification of "good me." In this case, interpersonal security prevails. On the other hand, experiences of anxiety in the parent/infant relationship are organized around a personification of "bad me." Insecurity is the prevailing tendency. In this way, the undifferentiated nature of early experience begins to break down into parts. The infant has learned to make some distinctions between itself and the world.

Sullivan (1947) was very concerned with child-rearing practices. He identified the early parental attitudes that contribute to psychological maladjustment later in childhood: believing the infant must be clean and dry (achieve bowel and bladder control by fifteen months), becoming upset when the infant tinkers with its genitals, treating an infant as if it were being willfully troublesome, and fancying that the infant "takes after" some other person in the family.

Childhood: Parataxic Learning Applicable to Social Habits and Self

The **childhood stage** emerges with articulate speech and ends with the appearance of the need for peers (pre-school years). A number of important developmental tasks are begun during this stage. First, there is rapid social acculturation in what is "proper." Children come to accept their parents' lessons in cleanliness, feeding habits, toilet training, obedience, oughts, and musts. Second, language is acquired as a communication tool for manipulating the outside social world into alleviating the child's tensions. Third, there is continuing development of the self-system, the function of which becomes to avoid or minimize incidents of anxiety.

Through a maturing ability to learn, the child becomes more skillful at reading the forbidding gestures of significant others. In this sense, the self-system is somewhat parallel to Freud's concept of ego in seeking to secure necessary satisfactions without incurring much anxiety. The self-system maintains normal functioning by minimizing anxiety through *selective inattention* to threatening events and by anticipating, and thereby avoiding, experiences that are incompatible with its past development. It sinks into maladjustment when it resorts to *dissociation*, completely severing any connection of the threatening events or experiences to the self. More generally, it is through our self-systems that we psychologically carry our parents around with us throughout our lives, as a continuing frame of reference regarding what is "approved" and "disapproved." In this sense, the self-system is partly analogous to what Freud called "superego."

Fourth, there is learning of such negative emotions as disgust, shame, anger, and resentment. "Willie, I told you not to do that. Now say you are sorry" (Sullivan, 1953, p. 200).

There also is learning of such negative forms of social interaction as malevolence, hatred, and isolation. Sullivan considers the learning of malevolence as "perhaps the greatest disaster" to happen during the childhood phase of personality development. Ironically the child may develop malevolence while seeking tenderness.

> *. . . many children have the experience that when they need tenderness, when they do that which once brought tender cooperation, they are not only denied tenderness, but they are treated in a fashion to provoke anxiety or even, in some cases pain. A child may discover that manifesting the need for tenderness toward the potent figures around him leads frequently to his being disadvantaged, being made anxious, being made fun of, and so on . . . Under those circumstances, the developmental course changes to the point that the perceived need for tenderness brings a foresight of anxiety or pain. The child learns . . . that it is highly disadvantageous to show any need for tender cooperation from the authoritative figures around him, in which case he shows something else . . . the basic malevolent attitude, the attitude that one really lives among enemies . . . (Sullivan, 1953, p. 214)*

Sullivan had a strong interest in the processes by which children learn. He proposed five main avenues to acquiring new, useful information. Three of these are straightforward, commonsensical, and rather self-evident: (1) *trial and success* (behaviors that succeed are stamped into memory as habits); (2) *rewards and punishments*; and (3) *trial and error* (noting errors in order to avoid them). However, two of them are unique and innovative, thus, worth more extended consideration. Children may **learn by anxiety**—when anxiety is not severe, individuals may become acquainted with the situations in which it is present so that those circumstances may be avoided. Even early in life children can learn that some situation or object is not desirable, thus to be avoided. Later, with the arrival of language ability, such circumstances can be labeled as anxiety-provoking, thereby making them easier to shun. A still higher plane of learning by anxiety involves the **anxiety gradient**, "learning to discriminate increasing from diminishing anxiety and to alter activity in the direction of the latter" (Sullivan, 1953, p. 452). Here the children must be able to monitor sometimes subtle changes in their feelings and become aware of the situations in which the changes occur. Then when anxiety rises, they can move themselves to circumstances that will likely lower anxiety. For example, the child might learn that playing with the genitals when the mothering one is present causes steadily rising anxiety. To change the gradient, in the presence of the mothering one, the child must withdraw its hands from the genitals and apply them to a task that is associated with lowered anxiety. An example task would be drawing pictures that please the mothering one. "Acting like an artist" is an example of **sublimation**, avoiding anxiety by engaging in activities that meet some need, such as deriving pleasure from use of the hands, but are socially acceptable.

The second type of learning that is unique to Sullivan is **eductive**—learning relationships by "pulling them out" of the entities that contain them (this term is more related to induction/deduction than "education"; Sullivan, 1953, p. 156). This process of extracting a relationship from the concrete or abstract parts involved in it *does* imply the ability to appreciate "mechanical-geometric relations" that appears for some people at intellectual maturity (p. 156). However, it may be displayed earlier, in more primitive form. For example, very early in life the child learns to appreciate the relationship between the parts of its body.

By reference to three broad considerations, Sullivan wrote of the socialization of the child—becoming a functional citizen of society. First, the *frequency* with which the child behaves in specifiable ways can cue her or him, and those who train the child, as to which behaviors are being acquired. Attention to frequency may allow children and their parents to cultivate behaviors that are socially desirable and cull those that are undesirable. Second, and closely aligned with frequency, is *consistency*, the "repetition of particular patterns of events." In contrast, inconsistency is represented by a "reduced frequency of a pattern of events or a greater variety of patterns of events" (p. 172). If the child behaves consistently, it can be assumed that he or she is learning or has learned the behaviors being performed. Consistency cues the child and his or her trainers that a certain course of behavioral acquisition is underway. Third, the parental contribution to socialization is emphasized in the notion of *sanity*, "parental modification of [training] efforts in accordance with the [child's] capacity for observation, analysis, and elaboration of experience at a given time" (p. 173). Sanity is shown by parents who fully understand the capabilities and deficiencies of their children so that educational demands are reasonable and appropriate to their children. Without sanity children may never discover what they are good at, and thus, they may arrive at later stages with uncertainty as to their worth (Bromberg, 1993). Box 6.3 will help you explore your childhood training.

Juvenile Era: Syntaxic Experiences of Finding Playmates and Questioning Parents

The **juvenile era** is ushered in with the child's need for peer companions, or "playmates rather like oneself." It coincides with the early elementary school years, during which the child has many opportunities to learn the ways of other children and show social subordination to new authority figures such as teachers, coaches, and club leaders. During this time children gain *compeers*, playmates who teach them more about their social capabilities and shield them from loneliness.

The juvenile develops an appreciation of certain variations in living never conceived of before, some "right" and some "wrong." Ideas and social operations learned at home may be found not to apply at school or with friends, and are reformulated. Authorities, including one's parents, are reduced from godlike figures to people. Along with cooperation are experiences of competition, stereotyping, ostracism, and compromise. References are made to "our team" and "our teacher." Social accommodation is partly motivated by peer pressure. A personally meaningful orientation to living begins to take form, based on a growing understanding of one's needs and future goals.

Preadolescence: Collaborating with a Chum

The period of **preadolescence** is brief, beginning with the need for interpersonal intimacy in the form of a close relationship with another person "of comparable status." Somewhere between the ages of 8-1/2 and 10, the child "begins to develop a real sensitivity to what matters to another person" (Sullivan, 1953, p. 245). One's predominant interest is in establishing a relationship with a *chum*, a particular member of the same sex who becomes a close friend. Preadolescents contribute to the happiness of their friends through collaboration: making personal adjustments aimed at providing mutual satisfactions. When two young

---

BOX 6.3 What Learning Processes Were Involved in Your Childhood Training?

Four of Sullivan's learning processes are arranged into two categories and each is briefly defined for you (the eductive process is excluded as it emerges spontaneously and, therefore, is not highly trainable). For each of the four, pick a number between 0 and 100 to represent the percentage of your train-ing—instituted by you or your parents—that employed the process in question.

Your four numbers should add up to one hundred. For example you might assign 10 to "learning by anxiety," 20 to "rewards and punishments," 40 to "trial and success," and 30 to "trial and error."

Positively Oriented Processes

Process	Number out of 100
Trial and success—attempting a behavior until it succeeds.	
Trial and error—observing own and others' behavior to profit by knowledge of mistakes.	

Negatively Oriented Processes

Process	Number out of 100
Learn by anxiety—individuals become acquainted with the anxiety-provoking situations so that these may be avoided.	
Rewards and punishments—arranging for pleasure to encourage a behavior and punishment to discourage its undesirable counterpart.	

Note which process you assigned the largest number. If its assigned number is 40 or greater, you are indicating that it was clearly the primary training procedure in your learning history. Tally by category: Add the two numbers in the positive category and the two in the negative category. If one of these two subtotals is 60 or more you are indicating that you were primarily subjected to positively or negatively oriented processes, depending on the category to which the larger number applies.

---

people become mutually important to each other, the personal worth of both is supported by the process of consensual validation, in this case, sharing attitudes. Preadolescents may spend hours with one another in mutual daydreaming. Participation in cliques or gangs may be traced to interlocking, two-person relationships in which pair members A and B also have individual relationships with pair members C and D, respectively. Loneliness resulting from the absence of close peer relationships may be overcome by acting on an irresistible need for cooperative companionship. This need is so powerful that people seek relations with others despite the fear of being rebuffed.

Early Adolescence: Experiencing Lust toward a Sexual Partner

Early adolescence erupts at puberty when the need for intimacy evolves toward lustful feelings of closeness and tenderness with a sexual partner. Interest in a member of one's own sex is replaced by interest in a member of the opposite sex. The object of interest is no longer a person quite like oneself, but one who is "very different." During this time patterns of behavior emerge that satisfy **lust**, Sullivan's term for "certain tensions of or pertaining to the genitals," culminating in orgasm (1953, p. 109). A "lust" dynamism along with *intimacy* needs now becomes important.

Sullivan classified the lust dynamism and intimacy needs into three categories: (1) orientation to others on the basis of intimacy needs; (2) orientation to others on the basis of partner's status (self or other, same or different gender, human or not, alive or dead); and (3) orientation to others on the basis of how the genitals are used during sexual interaction. As should be apparent, (1) refers to intimacy needs, while (2) and (3) refer to the lust dynamism.

Sullivan used the Greek root word *philos*, meaning "loving" as the foundation for terms referring to expressions of intimacy needs (1). He postulated modes of *intimacy expression* that correspond to three kinds of people: each mode is chosen by a different type of person. First there is the **autophilic person**, one who manifests no preadolescent development, because it has not occurred or was attempted without success, causing the continuation of self-directed love. This kind of person's intimacy expressions have the flavor of "narcissism. "An **isophilic person** has been unable to progress past preadolescence, and continues to regard as suitable for intimacy only people who are as like himself as possible . . . that is, members of his own sex" (Sullivan, 1953, p. 192). Finally, "A **heterophilic person** has gone through the preadolescent period and made the early adolescent change in which he has become intensely interested in achieving intimacy with members of. . . the other sex" (Sullivan, 1953, p. 192; emphasis added).

The "orientation to others according to status" category (2), related to the lust dynamism, contains mostly familiar entries. *Homosexuals* orient to the same sex, *heterosexuals* orient to the opposite sex, and *autosexuals* orient to themselves. Less familiar is *katasexual*, which refers to a preference for nonhumans such as animals or dead people.

The lust dynamism regarding use of the genitals (3) has six varieties. **Orthogenital** involves the integration of one's own genitals with the "natural receptor genitals" of the opposite sex, that is, heterosexual use of the genitals (p. 293). In **paragenital** use of the sex organs one acts to seek contact with genitals opposite one's own, but in such a way that impregnation will not occur. Rubbing one's own genitals against those of an opposite sexed person is an obvious example. **Metagenital** use does not involve one's own genitals, but another person's genitals are involved. Masturbating someone else or performing oral sex on another person are examples. **Amphigenital** refers to the case where one or both members of a pair, who both may be homosexual or heterosexual, take on a role that is different from their usual role. For example, a woman straps on a penis-like device and uses it in sex with her partner. The other two entries in this category are more straightforward: *mutual masturbation*, which is self-explanatory, or *onanism*, which refers to heterosexual intercourse that is terminated before orgasm occurs.

In sum, Sullivan thought that one's sexual expressions exist on three planes: with regard to intimacy needs (heterophilic and so forth), with regard to sexual orientation to others (homosexual and so forth), and with regard to use of the genitals (paragenital and so forth), where the last two involve the lust dynamism. In this way Sullivan argued that sexuality has implications for both intimacy and physical gratification.

In terms of sexual attitudes, Sullivan saw Americans as the most "sex-ridden" people on earth. He related this unfortunate inclination to two cultural conventions: discouraging early marriage and discouraging premarital sex. The effect of the sexual twilight zone we erect between the beginning of adolescence and adulthood is to widen the gap between the awakening of adolescent lust and the "proper" time in life for "appropriate" sexual expression (marriage). Obviously Sullivan anticipated the present era in which puberty is reached earlier, marriage is put off longer, and adults view young people's sexuality from either the "just say no" or the contraceptive perspective.

Late Adolescence: Establishing Love Relationships

What separates early and late adolescence is not so much biological as interpersonal maturation. Here partially developed aspects of personality fall into place. People are able to tolerate some previously avoided anxiety, which allows favorable changes to be made in the self-system. **Late adolescence** begins with the acknowledgment of an orientation to genital behavior and how to fit that revelation into the rest of life, then ends with "the establishment of a fully human or mature repertory of interpersonal relations" (Sullivan, 1953, p. 297). Being able to take first steps on adult legs, one can "establish relationships of love for some other person, in which relationship the other person is as significant, or nearly as significant, as one's self" (p. 34).

Table 6.1 summarizes the six stages along with the corresponding bench marks.

TABLE 6.1 Sullivan's Six Developmental Epochs

Epochs	Characteristics	Capacities for
Infancy:	Need for contact with caregiver Prototaxic experience	Beginning speech
Childhood:	Need for adult participation in activities; Parataxic experience	Language
Juvenile Era:	Need for acceptance by peers; Syntaxic experience	Compeer or playmate relationships
Preadolescence:	Need for intimate exchange with a loved one.	Close, same-sex relationship; chum
Early Adolescence		Close, opposite-sex relationship; patterning of lustful or genital behavior
Late Adolescence		Mature and independent development of love relationships in which another person is as important as oneself.

Evaluation

Contributions

Physical Contact and Peer Relationships

Sullivan's theory of personality development emphasizes the importance of physical contact between the infant and "a mothering one," as well as progressive involvement in peer relationships over time. His point of view stresses the role of empathic, nonverbal communication in close, child–maternal relationships. These emphases are supported by independent lines of research.

Human infants do show a need to have intimate physical contact with a parental figure, termed "primary object-clinging" by John Bowlby (1969). In a 1951 report to the World Health Organization, Bowlby concluded that mental health in infants requires the experiencing of a warm, intimate, and continuous relationship with a maternal figure, not necessarily the biological mother. He indicated that infants placed in institutional settings, such as hospitals and orphanages, who do not receive physical contact from a nurturing figure soon show developmental and survival difficulties attributable to interpersonal deprivation.

To illustrate, Spitz (1946) observed symptoms of depression in 45 of 123 infants who had been placed in nursery homes following separation from their parents. Symptoms included loss of appetite, trouble sleeping, crying, slow motor movements, apathy, physical withdrawal such as turning toward a wall, vulnerability to infection, and slowed development. An extreme form of this reaction is *marasmus*, a hospitalization syndrome in infants who self-destructively "waste away" in the absence of any demonstrable physical cause (Bosselman, 1958). Fortunately, such symptoms in an infant can be counteracted by daily physical contact with a particular adult who consistently cares for the infant, such as a nurse. This important finding has been translated into international prevention programs involving routine, daily "cuddling" of all babies in institutions. As you may recall, after the fall of the Communist regime in Rumania, many institutionalized infants and children were found to be suffering from a condition similar to that described by Spitz. During the early to mid-1990s, many U.S. citizens traveled to Rumania and brought children back with them, or stayed and provided the kind of close and warm interaction that they needed for survival.

Researchers have also differentiated two patterns of infant behaviors in experiments involving limited separation and reunion with mothers. On the one hand, separation may elicit *attachment* behaviors, through which infants try to find the missing caregiver and reestablish physical contact. On the other hand, infants, especially those subjected to more prolonged separation, may show *detachment* behaviors of indifference, protest, or despair (Bowlby, 1969; Suomi, Collins, Harlow, & Ruppenthal, 1976). Ainsworth (1979) has linked personality adjustment at ages 4–6 to the type of attachment characteristic of infant/mothering one interactions during infancy. In follow-up studies, infants who were "*securely attached*" at age 1 were not only socially more cooperative and emotionally positive in later years, but also less angry, aggressive, and avoidant, compared with "*anxiously attached infants.*" Ainsworth noted that secure attachment is fostered more by how the caregiver holds the infant, close to the body and face-to-face, rather than how long the infant is held. As you have likely surmised, Philip Shaver's research built on this earlier work and extended infant attachment styles to adult relationships.

The research of Harry Harlow (1959) and his co-workers is also relevant to Sullivan's theory. Harlow placed infant rhesus monkeys in individual cages containing two substitute or surrogate mothers (also see Harlow, 1958). One cage was constructed of wire mesh containing a milk-supplying nipple. The other was made of terry cloth and in some cases also contained a nipple. Observations revealed that infant monkeys spent far more time climbing and clinging on the cloth-covered surrogates, regardless of whether they were the source of milk or not. When frightening stimuli were introduced into the cages, such as a mechanical teddy bear beating a drum, the infants immediately sought security by running to the cloth mothers. Results showed that bodily contact and the comfort it supplies to infants is overwhelmingly important compared to the "oral sensations" of psychoanalysis.

Harlow and Harlow (1974) have stated that "the importance of peer relationships . . . cannot be overemphasized" (p. 199). Such social interactions provide critical opportunities for learning affection toward peers, control of fear and aggression, sex roles through play, sexual competence, and parental behavior. Many of these social functions are the same as may be served by Sullivan's "compeer" or "chum." There even may be an evolutionary advantage in having independent sources of affection, with parents and peers compensating for potential deficiencies in one another.

Suomi and Harlow (1972) reported fascinating use of younger age peers as "therapists" in successfully rehabilitating monkeys who had been socially isolated for six months. Isolates were permitted to interact with socially normal monkeys. The nonthreatening and supportive behaviors of the young monkey "therapists" may be analogous to the "trust" and the gradual "reeducation" dimensions characteristic of Sullivan's approaches to therapy with humans. It certainly is analogous to the benefits peers offer one another.

The "Psychiatric Interview": A Contribution to Helping People Achieve Psychological Adjustment

Sullivan's (1954) posthumous book, *The Psychiatric Interview*, is a classic text on the most widely used assessment technique, the interview of individuals with psychological problems. Sullivan saw the interview as an alternative to Freud's methods, because it appears to work better with a wider range of patients, from the mildly to the seriously disturbed. Sullivan's three contributions to understanding people through interviewing encompass: (1) assumptions about the nature of interview data; (2) structural outlines for obtaining and organizing information; and (3) guidelines for interpreting the interview process and defining the roles of the participants.

Sullivan (1954) believed that two factors determine that "there are no purely objective data in psychiatry" (p. 3). First, a large degree of inference is required before the information people provide about themselves begins to make sense. Second, the interviewer directly influences the information people provide. In brief, data about the patient passes through the interviewer who operates as a *participant observer:*

> *the psychiatrist cannot stand off to one side and apply his sense organs . . . to noticing what someone else does, without becoming personally implicated in the operation. His principal instrument of observation is his self—his personality, him as a person. The processes and the changes in processes that make up the data which can be subjected to sci-*

entific study occur, not in the subject person nor in the observer, but in the situation which is created between the observer and his subject (Sullivan, 1954, p. 3).

This statement indicates an ironic circumstance, not fully recognized by Freud but clearly acknowledged by Sullivan. Attempts to assess the personality of another individual inevitably involve the intrusion of the assessor's personality. Once the assessor's personality intervenes, it contaminates the data bearing on the interviewee's personality. Then one is stuck with a dilemma: To what degree do the data tell us about the interviewee's personality and to what degree does it inform us about the interviewer's personality?

Sullivan makes several points concerning the organization of personality as it is revealed in the psychiatric interview. The heart and soul of the interview is:

a situation of primarily vocal *communication in a* two-person *group . . . [which involves] a progressively unfolding expert–client . . . [relationship that illuminates]* characteristic patterns of living *[and offers the] . . . benefit[s] [that derive from learning about] . . . patterns he experiences as particularly troublesome or especially valuable (Sullivan, 1954, p. 4).*

Sullivan identified four stages of the interview. First, the *inception* of the interview is the formal reception of the client and inquiry about why he or she has come to the interviewer. Second, the *reconnaissance* stage "consists in obtaining a rough outline of the social or personal history of the patient" (p. 40). In the critically important third phase, *detailed inquiry*, in-depth exploration occurs that involves many "subtleties and complexities" of technique all employed in the interest of examining "another person's life" (p. 410). In the fourth phase, *interruption* signals that a particular interview session has come to an end, but other sessions are expected to occur, and *termination* means no further sessions are expected.

The detailed inquiry is the core of the psychiatric interview. It begins with an attempt on the part of the therapist to gain an accurate impression of the patient. This pursuit is hindered by the patient's understandable concern about what the "doctor" thinks of him or her. Initially the patient attempts to avoid a bad impression if not create a good one. At this point the job of the therapist is to gain the patient's confidence so that honest disclosures about her or him will be made. This task may be accomplished by showing irritation-free tolerance for the patient's circuitous answers to questions, "walking around the obvious," as Sullivan put it (p. 98). Eventually, the patient will see that direct and forthright answers will be favorably received.

Beyond the initial game of cat and mouse played by interviewer and patient, there are two substantive issues addressed during the detailed inquiry phase. The interviewee may signal anxiety, the first issue, by abrupt changes or transitions in the course of the interview. The interviewer may take advantage of these changes to either lessen anxiety, for the comfort of the patient, or raise it, for the purpose of exploring it. Episodes of anxiety may be especially intense when the patient is concerned about the therapist's view of her or him. In any case, these episodes are uniformly unwanted. Unlike fear, which may sometimes attract us—we may attend a scary movie or ride a roller coaster—anxiety is never wanted, according to Sullivan. Thus, in therapy, as in everyday life, when anxiety is on the rise, patients do whatever is necessary to lower it. They may even sometimes "act . . . like asses" (Sullivan,

1954, p. 101). As you might surmise, episodes of anxiety during therapeutic interviews cue interviewers that they have "hit a nerve" of the interpersonal kind.

The second substantive issue involves the self-system. During the later part of childhood, the individual refines **security operations**, skills that allow avoidance of forbidding gestures. When these skills are properly and successfully applied, the child can maintain a state of relative euphoria. Should these abilities fail—the self-system is unable to protect the person's feeling of well-being—a drop in euphoria occurs and is experienced as anxiety. Thus, protecting well-being or relative euphoria is a basic task of everyone from infant to adult and certainly is a major goal of the patient during the interview. The exercise of security operations gives the person better **foresight**, the capacity to look ahead in search of good experiences and in the interest of avoiding bad ones. Foresight is facilitated by looking constantly for signs of approval and disapproval in others.

What the patient needs from the interviewer are signals indicating that he or she is doing fine and is "approved." Absent or ambiguous signals from the therapist generate anxiety. Under these circumstances, the game of cat and mouse may begin again: "You are reading me and I look good . . . No! I'm coming across badly . . . I'll try to communicate another impression." All these signals, communications and miscommunications, are evidence that the self-system is "up and running." The job of the interviewer is then to help the patient tune the self-system, make it run right so that she or he can receive euphoria-maintaining signals.

These are the therapeutic tasks of the psychological professional during the psychiatric interview, but what can patients do for themselves? Believing, like Adler, that troubled people must take action in their own behalf, Sullivan outlined three jobs to be done by patients (Sullivan, 1947). First, the patient, and everyone else, can learn to **notice changes in the body** that signal decreases or increases in the tension signifying anxiety. By monitoring their bodies, patients can recognize when anxiety is rising or falling and the situations in which these events occur. Being aware of the situations associated with increases or decreases of anxiety is a kind of insight that precedes coping with anxiety.

Second, the patient—and the rest of us—can learn to **notice marginal thoughts**, thoughts that monitor, critique, and alter speech in terms of formation and grammar, and in terms of errors that may cause incomplete or misunderstood communications to others. There are two kinds of "critics." The first is called I_1 and is merely concerned with the mechanics of speech. We are often aware of this "rather unfriendly critic" (Sullivan, 1954, p. 99). It is an irritant that chastises us for our failures to speak correctly. By contrast, I_2, a "rather intelligent creature," is concerned with more central matters: how well we are presenting ourselves to other people. I_2 is a mirror that reflects the impression we are making on others back to us. We may pay attention to I_1 and, based on its feedback, correct ourselves as we go. However, I_2, because it deals with more threatening interpersonal matters, is likely to be beyond our conscious awareness and show up only in increased tensions. Should we be able to tune in to I_2, we would be taking the first step toward dealing with the interpersonal issues that face us, and, at the same time, moving toward lowering tension.

The third action that all of us can take, patients or not, is to **make prompt statements of all that comes to mind**, a process that is enabled by trusting the "situation to the extent of expressing the thoughts that it provokes" (p. 100). Performing this feat is easier said than done, however, because of inhibitory factors. People are likely to be plagued with thoughts of past behavioral disasters. They may wonder whether they are currently creating a bad impression in the mind of the interviewer and, therefore, may be reluctant to "speak their minds" about the current circumstances. Instead they may provide "a circumstantial account of some insignificant current event, or an extravagant report of the marvelous good results that have . . . been achieved by exposure to the . . ." therapist (p. 100). Only when they learn to speak straightforwardly about the current situation will they be able to provide the information that the interviewer needs to help them.

The tasks of the interviewer, revolving around anxiety and the self-system, and the three actions by the patient jointly constitute the therapeutic benefits that are associated with the psychiatric interview. The psychiatric interview is a productive "two-person group" partnership that exists for the benefit of the patient.

Limitations

Formal science was not well understood nor highly valued by Sullivan, who was marginally trained as a physician and psychiatrist. Like Freud, Horney, and Jung, and to a lesser degree Adler, he was a clinician and theorist rather than a scientist. In fact, as noted earlier, Sullivan declared the virtual impossibility of "doing science" with regard to personality. He placed greatest reliance on informal methods of study: His ideas were developed in offices, hospitals, and libraries, not in scientific laboratories. More generally, unlike psychologists of Sullivan's day, psychiatrists of his time did not make "doing science" a major priority. They were strictly therapists who were more apt to be guided by nonscience concerns, such as addressing the psychological problems of persons who are struggling with their lives and in need of help. In view of these circumstances, it is little wonder that, to this day, there is a virtual absence of direct scientific support for Sullivan's theory. The computer search, mentioned in the Freud chapter, that covered the early to mid-1990s revealed few cites of Sullivan's work. In examining those citations, I found only nine that seemed substantive and only one not-very-relevant study that reported scientific research relating to Sullivan's theory. Although consistent with Sullivan's ideas, even the results of the "monkey" studies by Harlow that are cited earlier were not directly inspired by Sullivanian theory. In fact, these studies support the ideas of Bowlby, as well as those of many other theorists including Horney, not just Sullivan. It seems that Sullivanians must look to other people for support of their ideas, as they have generated precious little of their own.

If Horney is the best writer among the theorists covered in this book, Sullivan is probably the worst. By any criteria, his written communications were poor, and he knew it (Chapman, 1976). After being frustrated in attempts to interpret writings concerning some of his major concepts, readers may wonder whether he was being purposefully evasive, or whether his alleged schizophrenic condition interfered with his ability to communicate. In any case, his writings were so obscure in places that his editors had to insert footnotes containing others' interpretations in order to alleviate reader frustration (see, for example, Sullivan, 1953, pp. 28–29). I was so stumped by certain passages regarding some of his central notions that I had to rummage through many adjacent pages before coming up with an interpretation. At these times, a haunting question came to my mind, "Does anyone fully understand Sullivan?"

While many of Sullivan's concepts approached profundity, others bordered on the trivial and still others appeared to be borrowed from someone else. For example, "rewards and punishments" is a commonsense notion familiar to everybody's grandmother, and "trial and success" appears to be borrowed from E. L. Thorndike, without credit. Sullivan seemed to theorize about everything, but it mattered little to him whether others had already thoroughly "covered the subject."

Sullivan used virtually all of Freud's concepts, for example, free association, repression, and insight. This observation could make one wonder whether he was really a Freudian who developed a language that made him "sound" different. While he may not have simply co-opted Freud, he may have gotten major ideas from other theorists. For example, did he originate the emphasis on anxiety, or did he get it from Horney, a theorist with whom he was personally familiar?

Conclusions

Sullivan may have borrowed from Freud and others. It has been argued, however, that some of what readers of Sullivan attribute to Freud is actually original Sullivanian thought that was not even inspired by Freud (Robbins, 1989). In any case, as you have seen, his theory and therapy bear only superficial resemblance to Freud's. He may also have sometimes written about trivia, but he certainly introduced some highly original and useful ideas, including some that anticipated certain modern theorists. For example, "prototaxic, parataxic, and syntaxic" are ideas that originated with Sullivan and will always be associated with his name. These and others of his ideas anticipated modern cognitive theories. Also, one may wonder, who "stole" from whom? Maybe Horney was heavily influenced by Sullivan. Finally, some of his ideas laid a solid foundation for future theory and research. "Foresight"—being pulled by the future rather than being pushed by the past—was one of his creative ideas that has several modern advocates. Perhaps he did not originate "looking ahead," but he certainly cast some new light on it. Forbidding gestures, subtle signs often communicated without words, was an early consideration of what has become the currently fascinating field of "nonverbal communication."

Some individuals question the credibility of a disturbed psychiatrist who tried to offer the rest of us advice concerning our problems. However, one must remember that many creative contributors to the human condition, scientists, artists, and entertainers, were individuals who had "brilliant lights in the attic that sometimes blinked erratically." The revered artist Van Gogh was considerably off-center. Relativity theorist Albert Einstein and "the father of the atomic bomb" Robert Oppenheimer were at least eccentric. Even extraordinary comedians, such as Lenny Bruce and Richard Pryor, led troubled lives (the Woody Allen you see on the screen and who stands accused of seducing his stepdaughter could well be the real Woody). In fact, even profoundly disturbed people, such as schizophrenics, can be unusually creative (Carson & Butcher, 1992). Perhaps what some of us may view as "obscurity in Sullivan's writings" is creative thinking that is too unique and complex to be penetrated by less than deeply reflective contemplation. It may be time to reconsider Sullivan's works, this time with attention to what is "written between the lines."

Summary Points

1. Harry Stack Sullivan's family lived in a rural New York community. His achievements may have been spurred by a desire to rise above his background. The child and adolescent Sullivan was a loner. His life reflects the diversity he represented: Irish, recent immigrant family, possibly gay or bisexual, and probably schizophrenic. As his time at Cornell was troubled, he soon left the university and disappeared, possibly because he suffered a psychotic episode. When he surfaced, it was to enter a medical school of uncertain reputation where he performed poorly. Without benefit of a formal residency, he became a psychiatrist interested in schizophrenia. In the middle of a distinguished career, Sullivan died under mysterious circumstances.

2. Sullivan's definition of personality highlighted his "two persons at a time" approach to personality. In fact, the core part of personality, the self-system, "is born entirely out of the influences of significant others upon one's feeling of well-being." Sullivan postulated that people experience two kinds of tensions: (1) physical needs and (2) interpersonal anxiety. He believed that tension in the infant induced tension in the mothering one, which is experienced as tenderness and leads to meeting the infant's needs.

3. "Empathy" is the mode through which the infant participates in the other person's tension or discomfort. Anxiety aroused through the empathy mechanism can lead to disruptive behavior. Relief is provided by interpersonal security. Sullivan postulated three modes of experience: the "booming, blooming, buzzing confusion" of infant prototaxic reality, the parataxic mode involving speech but little logical connectiveness, and the syntaxic mode entailing the advent of shared meanings.

4. In infancy "nipple-to-lips" contact with a mothering one becomes central. Personifications and the ability to read "forbidding gestures" occur at this time. Dynamisms, self-contained energy packages, first develop during this period. The self-system is an example of the organizing, integrating kind of dynamism.

5. During the childhood stage, speech and the need for peers emerge. The self-system continues to develop greater facility at avoiding anxiety. Manifestations of the need for tenderness become more complex: what once brought tenderness may now bring pain; since seeking tenderness may be disadvantageous, the child may develop a malevolent attitude. Sullivan posed five learning processes of which two are highly unique: (1) learn by anxiety: the child appreciates the anxiety gradient and may resort to sublimation; and (2) eductive: learning relationships by pulling them out of entities. Sullivan also pointed out the importance of frequency, consistency, and sanity in the training of the child.

6. During the juvenile era peers become central. Here what the child has learned at home about living may not apply to life among peers. Parents lose their godlike aura and children begin to see themselves as members of groups and connected to nonfamily. During preadolescence, the child becomes genuinely sensitive to the needs of others and seeks a comparable status person for a close relationship. During early adolescence, lustful feelings arise and tenderness with a sexual partner is sought. Both intimacy needs and the lust dynamism become central.

7. Expression of the intimacy need takes several different forms: (1) autophilic, intimacy need directed to self; (2) isophilic, directed to people like oneself; (3) heterophilic, directed to opposite sex. The sexual orientations are autosexual, homosexual, or heterosexual (they may also be katasexual). Genital use forms are: (1) orthogenital, integration with opposite sex person; (2) paragenital, sex without the risk of pregnancy; (3) metagenital, one's

own genitals are not involved; (4) amphigenital, pair members switch roles; (5) mutual masturbation; and (6) onanism, termination of intercourse before orgasm.

8. Harlow's work with wire and cloth "monkey mothers" confirms the critical importance of close physical intimacy with a mothering one: infant monkeys prefer the cloth to the wire "mother" with a milk-supplying nipple. Spitz showed that infants without a mothering one develop severe depression. Other work indicates that separation from a mothering one may elicit attachment seeking in some infants and detachment in others. "Monkey therapists" improved the condition of young monkeys that had suffered the despair of social isolation.

9. Sullivan noted two limitations of his psychiatric interview: (1) inference is required to interpret the information that people provide; (2) the interviewer may influence what the interviewee provides. The interview has four stages: (1) inception; (2) reconnaissance; (3) detailed inquiry; and (4) interruption or termination. Stage 3 begins with a game, in which patients are concerned with the impression they make. The self-system institutes security operations to maintain a state of relative euphoria. If these operations work well, the person gains better foresight. The patient can make three contributions to the success of her or his therapy: (1) notice changes in the body that herald tension changes; (2) notice marginal thoughts, especially I_2; and (3) make prompt statements of all that comes to mind.

10. Sullivan was a clinician, not a scientist. Not surprisingly, there has been very little scientific research in direct support of his theory. Readers may have to scramble for additional information to interpret a given passage of Sullivan's. Sullivan was known to theorize about everything, even the trivial. He used so many of Freud's concepts that one wonders whether Sullivanian theory is actually Freudian. Nevertheless, many of Sullivan's ideas are highly original and extremely useful. Others, such as foresight and forbidding gestures, anticipated much modern theory and research. If he was a troubled person, disturbed individuals are often creative.

Running Comparison

Theorist	Sullivan in Comparison
Freud	He questioned Freud's sexual instincts and psychosexuality, but agreed on physical needs. He also talked about "oral gratification," but with emphasis on tenderness, not physical tension reduction. He used Freudian terms: free association, repression, and insight. "Dynamisms" were something like complexes, the self-system somewhat ego-like and a little superego-like. The juvenile era was somewhat equivalent to the latency period and the autophilic are somewhat narcissistic.
Adler	Some of his ideas had the flavor of social interest (preadolescent need for companionship) and he, like Adler, believed people must do for themselves. He supported Adler's complexes like his dynamisms.
Horney	They both showed interest in anxiety dating to infancy and in human relationships.
Fromm	The "katasexual" was somewhat like the necrophilous character of Fromm.

Carl Rogers   Both sought to make patients feel approved and both thought that patients could do much for themselves.

Essay/Critical Thinking Questions

1. Sullivan had a life-long sexual identity problem. What factors led to this problem? What factors might lead to the problem in anyone?

2. Can a person's fears or perceptions that it is time to die hasten her or his death? Answer by using Sullivan as the case in point.

3. Sullivan thought that a person's world is made up of twosomes: the person coupled with each significant other in his or her life. Can you develop an argument against this central assumption?

4. What are the critical traits of a "mothering one"? Is gender an important factor? Why or why not?

5. Prototaxic, parataxic, and syntaxic are probably the best known of Sullivan's concepts. Are they really that central or does something else account for their familiarity? [If you argue that they are not really that central, tell what is. If you do see them as central, defend your position and forget the second half of the question.]

6. Examine Sullivan's eleven lust and intimacy orientations. Can you distribute these into the "normal" and "abnormal" categories. If you can, do it. If you cannot, detail why you cannot.

7. Why is physical contact between infant and mothering one so important to primates, monkey and humans alike? What is the essential reason it is so important? An example answer is that the infant, being recently removed from fetal status, is accustomed to being physically close to a mother.

8. Sullivan's detailed stage of the psychiatric interview is complex. Can you break it up into at least three parts?

9. Sullivan outlines three actions that patients can take to contribute to the therapeutic aspect of the interview. Can you add two more that are consistent with his theory?

10. The text states that disturbed people, even schizophrenics, can be quite creative. How could that be? What is it about a disturbed person that may generate or promote creativity?

E-mail Interaction

(Write the author at mfbpa@wiu.edu)
Forward any of the following, or write your own.

1. Tell me what is the central idea that distinguishes Sullivan from the other theorists covered so far.
2. What is the real truth about Sullivan's sexual orientation?
3. If you had to choose a therapist from among the theorists covered so far, would you choose Sullivan over the others?
4. Who was the most "significant other" in Sullivan's life?
5. Why are researchers ignoring Sullivan's ideas?

7

THE SEASONS OF OUR LIVES: ERIK ERIKSON

- Does everyone have an identity crisis?
- Does the development of human personality end with adolescence?
- At each stage of our lives, are we caught on the horns of a new dilemma?
- Does adolescent rebellion and civil unrest among young adults have any redeeming social value?
- Are the major tasks of life over by retirement age?

Erik Erikson

Erik Erikson is quite different from the other theorists covered in this book. He is the only one who has no advanced degree. In fact, Erikson never went beyond high school (Woodward, 1994). Yet he made it all the way up the academic ladder to a professorship at Harvard. Because he lacked formal training, he was not so devoted to the usual academic traditions in psychology. His point of view is quite cross-disciplinary, mixing Freudian with anthropological language, but being mostly unique. Some observers may regard his orientation as more philosophy than science. But unlike others who have wandered away from psychological science toward philosophy, such as Erich Fromm, some of Erikson's concepts have received significant scientific support.

Despite his devotion to Freud as a person, his basic concepts are highly original and drawn from the common language rather than psychological jargon, Freudian or otherwise. This inclination makes his ideas not well related to most of the other theorists' concepts. His most creative idea, one for which he will always be known, is the "identity crisis." It is the vehicle upon which he rode into a personality territory that was virtually unexplored by other theorists. Gordon Allport did write about the "mature personality," but it was Erikson more than anyone else who popularized the idea that personality development does not end with adolescence. It was also Erikson, in contrast to other theorists, who detailed personality development during the adult years. While Allport wrote of adult life without reference to stages, Erikson elaborated three stages of adult development. Just as he has expanded the horizons of personality psychology, he will broaden the scope through which you view the rest of your life.

Erikson, the Person

Erik Homburger Erikson was born, 1902, of Danish parents in the German town of Frankfurt (Stevens, 1983). His name, sans Homburger, meant "Erik son of Erik," an appellation taken from his father whose only other legacy was a genetic gift contributed during a brief affair with his mother ("Erik Erikson," 1970; Woodward, 1994). Abandoned by the senior Erik even before his birth, Erikson was reared and nurtured by the Jewish pediatrician who married his mother when he was only a few years old (Stevens, 1983).

A look at Erikson's childhood makes it easy to see where his interest in "identity crises" originated. He was a child with an identity dilemma. As most boys are, he was pressured to pin his identity to his biological father, but it is almost impossible to tack anything onto a virtual void. Thus, he turned to his adopted father, who loved him and treated him well (Hall, 1983). As a reflection of his esteem for his adopted father Erikson initially chose "Homburger" as his surname. Even early in his career, including the period when he worked with Henry Murray, he went by Erik Homburger. Yet his ambivalence showed when later he relegated Homburger to a middle initial. This display of confusion about his stepfather was only a rare outward sign of the identity crises that occurred to him repeatedly. An ideal Aryan in appearance—he was tall and blond—Erikson faced taunts served up by the children at his father's synagogue. At the same time he was shunned by some of his German schoolmates because of his stepfather's religion. Later he toyed with the idea of following in his stepfather's professional footsteps, but threw it aside, along with other aspirations for an advanced education. The lack of an advanced degree was itself a source of identity conflict. Was he a full-fledged academic or not? A former colleague thought that the lack of the academic "union card"—the Ph.D.—haunted Erikson when he joined the faculty at Harvard (Keniston, 1983). Later in life Erikson aptly expressed how vacillation between one kind of identity and another affected him during his youth, "I was," he recalled, "morbidly sensitive" ("Erik Erikson," 1970, p. 87).

In lieu of college, young Erikson took up painting (Roazen, 1976). This career move paid off in 1927 when an old friend and director of a progressive school in Vienna invited Erikson to ply his trade in the Austrian capital. Sponsors of the friend's school included American Dorothy Burlingham, scion of the immensely rich and famous Tiffany family, who could well afford to commission portraits of her four children. It turned out that she also was undergoing psychoanalysis at the hands of the Master himself, Freud. Through this connection Burlingham became a friend of Freud's daughter Anna, who counted the four Tiffany heirs among her first child patients. Erikson experienced only brief interaction with the four children before Burlingham and Anna Freud began persuading him to become a child analyst. Though he was unfamiliar with this new specialty, Erikson was intrigued and agreed to undergo training analysis with Anna Freud. Soon he was drawn into the inner circle of the Vienna psychoanalytic society.

Owing to Erikson's shyness and the oral cancer that already plagued Freud, the two seldom conversed. Nevertheless, he became a follower of Freud who reveled in the excitement of a secretive psychoanalytic movement that was forced underground by the disdain of the medical establishment. In the six years that Erikson remained in Vienna, he delivered his first paper before the Vienna Psychoanalytic society, pursued an education in the Montessori method of schooling, and met his bride-to-be, a Canadian-born American student, Joan Serson.

A number of factors made Erikson view his time among the Vienna analysts as somewhat uncomfortable. Roazen (1976) thought that Erikson was "dissatisfied as one of Freud's younger disciples" (p. 4). As a newcomer, Erikson felt called upon to be a "servant for the master" (p. 4). He was even known to drive Freud around in Burlingham's car. Also, his status as a "lay" analyst may have bothered him. The lack of a medical degree probably was another source of status reduction, but there were two reasons why he was at least reasonably well-respected, despite his deficiency. First, Freud was upset with the medical establishment for not openly accepting his point of view. Therefore, he could readily overlook Erikson's and others' lack of "proper credentials." Second, it was deemed less essential for child analysts to have medical qualifications. In fact, Freud welcomed lay analysts in the hope of attracting a variety of people with broad backgrounds. Erikson was also attractive because he was one of the few men willing to pursue the fledgling profession of child analysis. Thus, the highly sensitive Erikson may have had status concerns, but they appear to have been largely unfounded.

Another source of discomfort was the constitution of the Vienna group, especially the child analysts. Freud had lost some of his most able male analysts and had surrounded himself with women, mostly recruited by daughter Anna. "Erikson felt stifled by what he described as the maternalistic overprotection of the women analysts" (p. 6). Further, he, like the males who had abandoned Freud, felt the pressure to conform. He wrote about "a growing conservatism and especially a subtle yet pervasive interdiction of certain trends of thought. This concerned primarily any idea which might be reminiscent of the deviations perpetrated by those earliest and most brilliant of Freud's co-workers . . ." (quoted in Roazen, 1976. pp. 6–7).

Perhaps his disaffection with Freudian thought, which he never openly admitted, accounted for his quick response to Hitler's assumption of power in Germany during 1933. Erikson and his new wife first tried to establish citizenship in Denmark. When that effort failed, they migrated to the United States, where Erikson became the first child analyst in Boston (Stevens 1983). There he was immediately accepted as a member of the American Association of Psychoanalysis, despite his lack of medical qualifications. Although lay analysts were rarely admitted, the American Association so revered the International Psychoanalytic Association to which Erikson belonged and was so in awe of anyone who had been close to Freud that they easily sidestepped the matter of credentials.

Erikson did try to do something about his deficient qualifications. He attempted a graduate course in the psychology program at nearby Harvard, but failed (Roazen, 1976). That apparently was his last effort at a formal, advanced education. His alliance with Harvard, however, did not end. Soon he was working on research leading to the book that made Murray famous. During this period he had the opportunity to work with children of both the wealthy and the poor (Stevens, 1983).

After a stint at Yale's Institute of Human Relations, during which he made a side trip to a Sioux Indian Reservation, the Eriksons moved to California where, in 1939, Erik took a position at Cal Berkeley. His observations of the Sioux and the Yurok, a Northern California tribe who preserved many of their ancient traditions, changed his orientation profoundly. These experiences convinced him that Freud's sexual ideas were not universal.

Rather, it was passing through stages of identity acquisition that was generalizable across cultures (Evans, 1967).

After ten years on the West Coast working on a longitudinal child development program, analyzing Hitler's speeches during the war, and studying life aboard submarines, he took a teaching post at the University of California. Unfortunately it was short-lived. When confronted with the demand that he sign an anti-Communist loyalty oath, Erikson, who was not Communist, refused and resigned (Woodward, 1994). Returning to the East Coast, he received an appointment to a psychoanalytic center specializing in child psychiatry.

The appearance of *Childhood and Society* in 1950 was destined to bring him fame. This seminal work was followed by other popular successes: *Young Man Luther*, a psychobiography of religious rebel Martin Luther, the Pulitzer prizewinning *Gandhi's Truth*, and, finally, *Life Cycle Completed*.

By 1960, he was so well-known and respected that he was appointed Professor of Human Development and lecturer in psychiatry at Harvard, an extraordinary development in view of his nonexistent academic credentials. After his retirement, he and his wife returned to the San Francisco area. Until his death on May 12, 1994, he remained active advocating rights for children as well as for the elderly and campaigning for an emphasis on people rather than nations. A colleague summed up the respect that she and others have for this prophet who preached that personality development never ends: "As they used to say of Gandhi, he was a mahatama, a great soul, very wise, [a] very wide-ranging humanist" (Diana Eck quoted in *Peoria Journal Star*, 1994, C8).

Erikson's View of the Person

Freudian?

Erikson has been counted among the Freudians (or neo-Freudians). Roazen (1976) asserted that he was a self-proclaimed Freudian. There is no question that he was devoted to Freud as a person. Having read everything Freud wrote, including his correspondence, Erikson could not resist citing Freud at every possible opportunity.

His dedication to Freud seems to stem from his beliefs about "great leaders." During his study of Gandhi, his reflections on the Indian practitioner of nonviolent protest revealed his conception of the dilemma that followers of giants must resolve: ". . . who is the true representative of revolutionary advance—he who modestly continues the work of a giant and adapts it to less heroic circumstances, or he who continues to flex his muscles to see whether he may prove to have gigantic measurements himself" (Erikson, quoted in Roazen, 1976). It seems that Erikson came down on both sides, one explicitly and the other implicitly. Explicitly he pronounced himself a Freudian, often excusing the Master's personal weaknesses—his railroad phobia—and his theoretical vulnerabilities—his conception of women. Erikson waved his hand at Freud's bizarre middle-aged abandonment of sexual relations and overlooked his nearly neurotic correspondence with Wilhelm Fliess. He felt obligated to dig for a seemingly appropriate citation of Freud with each mention of his own original ideas. In fact, he was in the habit of giving Freud credit for some of his personal ideas that can be traced to Freud only with a considerable stretch of the imagination. Even Erikson's most original and important idea was laid at Freud's door. "Erikson's many citations of Freud's single mention of the concept of inner identity is an instance of a disciple trying to foist off an original idea onto the founder of psychoanalysis" (p. 12). As late as 1967 he would declare, "I am primarily a psychoanalyst . . ." (quoted in Roazen, 1976, p. 3). In terms of his explicit pronouncements, there is little question that Erikson was Freudian.

Accepting credit for one's own ideas is to abandon humility. Taking credit is also accepting blame. Erikson tacitly acknowledged that it is difficult for creative people to achieve "the courage of their own originality" (Erikson, quoted in Roazen, 1976, p. 12). "When I started to write extensively about twenty-five years ago, I really thought I was merely providing new illustrations for what I had learned from Sigmund and Anna Freud. I realized only gradually that any original observation already implies a change in theory. The scientific climate has changed so much that older and new theories cannot really be compared" (quoted in Evans, 1976, p. 292). Thus, Erikson implicitly acknowledges that his ideas are more his own than Freud's.

As you will see, though he often resorts to Freudian jargon when elaborating his ideas, his concepts are unique, common language notions, not reducible to Freudian conceptions. He de-emphasizes sexual motivation in favor of the quest for identity. The unconscious takes a backseat to the ego, which, in Erikson's hands, becomes molded into a form of the self. The superego becomes more the conventional conscience. At times he seems more like Jung than Freud, as his interest in anthropological issues and ancient cultures appears to exceed his

---

BOX 7.1   Acknowledging Diversity: Erikson's Evolving View of Women

Erikson not only used masculine pronouns in writing, which was common in his time, he also frequently couched his pronouncements in masculine terms: "Evolution has made man . . .," "mature man," "Whatever chance man has to transcend the limitations of his self . . ." (Erikson, 1968a, p. 291).In writing about the sexuality of male and female children, he proclaimed, "In the boy, the sexual orientation is dominated by phallic-intrusion; in the girl, by inclusive modes of attractiveness and 'motherliness'" (p. 289). In Vienna, he felt "stifled" by the women with whom he worked (Roazen, 1976, p. 6).

Yet, he was an open person who appears to have changed as he matured during the early stages of the women's movement. In almost no other area did he so closely approximate declaring that Freud was "wrong." In an interview he indicated,

Obviously [Freud and I] would not agree today with all the generalizations which have been made with regard to the Oedipus complex, least of

all the female Oedipus complex (Evans, 1976, p. 294). My feeling is that Freud's general judgment of the identity of women was probably the weakest part of his theory. Exactly what is to blame for that I don't know, except that he was a Victorian man, a patriarchal man (p. 299). Freud's perception might also have been colored by the sexual mores of his time, which could not admit at first that an upper-class woman could have passionate and active sexual wishes and yet be refined and intelligent (pp. 299–300). At any rate, psychoanalytic literature tends to describe woman as an essentially passive and masochistic creature, who not only accepts the roles or identity assigned to her submissively, but needs all the masochism she can muster to appreciate the phallic male (p. 299).

Erikson was flexible and changed. In altering his view of women, he moved away from Freud in yet another important way.

concern for the obsessions of current, Western society. His experiences with the Sioux and Yurok made him more an anthropologist–sociologist than a psychoanalyst. At the same time it made him see that Freud's ideas were culture-bound: founded on European culture and thus not applicable to many other cultures.

He was more concerned with people's mission in life as it evolves through the life span than their struggles with unresolved traumas of childhood. In fact, he openly expressed his reservations about Freud's emphasis on cataclysmic events of early life: "If everything 'goes back' into childhood, then everything is somebody else's fault, and trust in one's own power of taking responsibility for oneself may be undermined" (Erikson, quoted in Woodward, 1994, p. 56).

In sum, Erikson was certainly not a Freudian and probably not even a Neo-Freudian, despite his protests to the contrary. His theory was too much a mix of psychology, anthropology, and sociology to be called "psychoanalytic."

On the Tasks and Polarities of Life

The "tasks of life" theme is at the heart of Erikson's theory. At each succeeding stage of human development the person has new tasks to master. Thus, to Erikson, life and its challenges are constantly evolving. Contrary to the way Freud thought of it, or even the way Allport conceived of it, maturity to Erikson is not something most people achieve or not. Instead it is something that people approximate well or not so well.

How well people conquer the tasks of a given stage determines toward which of two poles they migrate, one representing positive development and the other negative development. The poles symbolize the horns of a dilemma. Parents, the society in which the individual is immersed, interactions with peers and the individual's own skills and talents determine how well the dilemma is resolved. In turn, resolution promotes the development of a new **strength**, a virtue arising from dominant movement toward the positive pole. With resolution comes the ability to face the challenges of the next stage.

Basic Concepts: Erikson

Erikson believes that people go through eight stages of psychosocial evolution that is termed **psychosocial development**—a union of physical yearnings and the cultural forces that act on the individual ("Erik Erikson," 1970). These phases include four childhood stages, one adolescent stage, and three adult stages. They are characterized by **epigenesis**—*epi* means "upon" and *genesis* means "emergence": the stages literally emerge "one on top of another in space and time" (quoted in Evans, 1976, p. 294). Each is built on the other like each upper-level math course is built on lower-level courses. His most basic concepts are tied to the eight stages.

Apparently, Erikson was strongly influenced by German philosopher Georg Hegel, who advocated a reality in which thesis and antithesis, the conflict of opposites, yielded synthesis, the resolution of conflict. Maturity and contentment result from synthesis; stagnation and maladjustment follow failure to resolve conflicts. The conflict at each stage is termed a "crisis." In effect, at each stage, the crisis that the individual experiences entails be-

---

BOX 7.2 What are Your Own Sources of Identity?

Exploring your own feelings of "identity" should help you get the flavor of Erikson's ideas on the subject. First, examine all of the "sources of identity" listed below. Then try to decide which are most important to you. It is a difficult task. Once the late Barbara Jordan, the famous former Congresswoman turned professor, was asked to choose between two prominent sources of identity, being African American and being a woman. This eloquent devotee of the U.S. Constitution paused to reflect for a moment. She did make a decision, but, fortunately, I do not recall what it was: it would not be proper to hold her to it in any case.

After examining the sources, rank them in order, giving the most important source a rank of one ("1"), the second most important a two ("2") and so forth until all sources are ranked. Force yourself to make choices; the result of the ranking will tell you much about yourself. The choices are listed alphabetically.

career (specify present or anticipated career)
child of my parents
ethnic group (specify African American, "white,"
or whatever applies)
friend to several people
gender (male or female)
hobbyist (specify sports, exercise,
or whatever applies)
human being
parent
sibling (brother or sister)
[others of your own choosing]

---

ing stretched between the opposing positive and negative poles associated with the stage. Successful resolution of a crisis prepares the person for the next step in the struggle for identity. As you may have already surmised, the popular phrase "identity crisis" originates in Erikson's conception of the eight psychosocial crises.

Erikson makes it clear that resolution of the crisis is never absolute. To approximate resolution the person must experience a **favorable ratio**, the greater the magnitude of the pull to the positive pole relative to the pull of the negative pole the better (Erikson, 1968a). In turn, the more favorable the ratio, the more the individual manifests the strength or virtue available at a given stage.

Lest the reader think that Erikson's repeated references to "crises" make a pessimist of him, it is important to note that resolution of conflicts is normal and expected, and "crises" are welcomed turning points, not threats of catastrophe (Erikson, 1968a). Each resolution of a crisis brings with it progress toward a full and rich identity.

Infancy

Infants (first year) arrive with basic physiological needs that parents must be willing and able to meet. Nearly always, parents satisfy those needs, at least to some degree. The opposite condition, the one that generates the first crisis, is the inevitable delay or neglect of satisfaction and the occurrence of weaning. **Basic trust** results from the infant's sense that it can count on satisfaction of its needs (Erikson, 1968a); the world takes on the aura of a "trustworthy realm." Its opposite is basic mistrust, the feeling of abandonment and helpless rage that accompanies uncertainty of satisfaction. Trust is injected into the infant in different ways by different mothers. Each mother is unique and, thus, conveys trust in a unique way. "Moreover, mothers in different cultures and classes and races must teach this trusting in different ways, so it will fit their cultural version of the universe" (Erikson, quoted in Evans, 1976, p. 293).

Erikson makes a point of the observation that both trust and mistrust are learned. We all must learn trust if we are to be fully functional humans, "But to learn to mistrust is just as important" (Erikson, quoted in Evans, 1976, p. 293). Mistrust is part of life also, and we must become familiar with it. We can hope, however, that trust will outweigh mistrust in the ratio of the two orientations.

Basic trust lays the foundation for the first of the strengths or virtues, **hope,** the enduring belief in the attainability of basic satisfactions. "You see, hope is a very basic human strength without which we couldn't stay alive" (Erikson, quoted in Evans, 1976, p. 293). It is the foundation of faith, often manifested in adult religious practices (E. Hall, 1983). In fact, faith is protected by religion, its **institutional safeguard,** a cultural unit that protects and promotes products of crisis resolution. Failure to develop basic trust yields mistrust and hopelessness, conditions that can lead in adulthood to severe addiction or psychotic states.

Early Childhood

During this second stage (age 2–3), the child develops motor skills that open up the first possibilities of independence (Erikson, 1968a). Part of the trauma the child experiences at this time is in the transition from the first to this more mature second stage. Just when the child has learned to trust his mother and the world, he must become self-willed. He must change from being the one-sided trusting soul to being also worthy of others' trust. Only by calling on others to trust him, rather than just trusting in others, can he exercise his will.

Children can now move to desired objects and thereby possess them without the aid of parents. The dawning of grasping ability allows children to experience the power of imprisoning an object within fingers, hands, and arms. Power also comes from letting go, but so does conflict. To hold can be destructive, as in restraining, or it can be positive, as in cuddling. Letting go can have two additional meanings: giving up something desirable, or casually "letting it be." Here Erikson hints at the "dilemma of freedom" attributed to Fromm, to let go of something is to be free of it, but it is also to be without it.

With the newly acquired muscular skills, the child experiences doing for herself. Unfortunately, she also knows the frustration generated by needing the help of others who can do more for her than she can do for herself. For Erikson as well as Allport, self-esteem derives from doing for oneself.

Consistent with this orientation, the two poles of the crisis involve the themes of independence and the self-esteem that comes with it versus the self-estrangement that accompanies dependency. **Autonomy** is independence stemming from the reasonable self-control that allows children to hold rather than restrain, to let be rather than lose. **Shame and doubt** is the estrangement that results from the feeling of being controlled and of losing self-control. It is the precursor of neurosis, a desperate struggle for control of one's environment, and paranoia, a manifestation of feeling controlled by others. A child who is tentative and self-effacing is reflecting shame and doubt.

The strength that emerges from resolution during early childhood is **will power,** "the unbroken determination to exercise free choice as well as self-restraint in spite of the unavoidable experience of shame, doubt, and a certain rage over being controlled by others" (Erikson, 1968a, p. 288). The exercise of free choice has its institutional safeguard—the principles of law and order and of justice. However, Erikson argues that "law and order" gone awry can rob people of the very choice it is supposed to protect.

Erikson acknowledges that infants go through a Freudian "anal stage," but "we have to consider that the anal musculature is part of musculature in general" (Erikson, quoted in Evans, 1976, p. 293). The task of the infant is to learn management of all his musculature, including his sphincters. In contrast to Freud, culture is more emphasized than universal physiology in accomplishing the task of sphincter control. Erikson asserts: "It would, of course, only be in cultures in which cleanliness and punctuality are overemphasized for technological and sanitary reasons that the problem of anal control might develop into a major issue in childhood" (quoted in Evans, 1976, p. 293).

Play Age

In the third or fourth year, children become aware of the differences between the sexes. During this third stage, sex-role playing and sexual feelings occur for the boy. But to Erikson the girl plays the feminine role, trying to look attractive and to be nurturing, rather than being sexual. Conscience appears at this stage and forever places a restraint on actions, thoughts, and fantasies. One of the poles at this stage is **initiative,** acting on one's desires, urges, and potentials. The other is **guilt,** the harness that restrains pursuit of desires, urges, and potentials; the exercise of an overzealous conscience. The boy learns that competition for a favored position with his mother leads to the inevitable fear of damage to his genitals. The result is guilt at having taken the initiative well beyond that which is permissible (Evans, 1967). Erikson turns further from Freud when he suggests that it is only natural for the boy to fall in love with his mother, because she is everything to him. She is the center of his life and his caretaker. Any fantasies a person may have will tend to focus on what is crucial to her or his survival and prosperity. Therefore, any fantasies the boy has will likely center on his mother, including fantasies arising from his emerging genital urges. Presumably, the girl has analogous problems associated with pursuit of her father's attentions. For both genders, guilt can arise from a failure to demonstrate capability when the initiative is taken (Evans, 1967).

At first children's play involves only wish fulfillment and fantasy, rather than real purpose, but gradually it changes. "The child begins to envisage goals for which his locomotion and cognition have prepared him. The child also begins to think of being big and to identify with people whose work or whose personality he can understand and appreciate" (Erikson, quoted in Evans, 1967, p. 25). That is, children begin to display realistic, practical **purpose,** "the courage to envisage and pursue valued and tangible goals guided by conscience but not paralyzed by guilt and by fear of punishment" (Erikson, 1968a, p. 289). It is the strength that comes from resolution of the play-age crisis. Failure at resolution leads to general repression or inhibition and to adult pathology such as sexual impotence, overcompensation, exhibitionism, and psychopathic acting out. All of these are attempts to regain the lost initiative.

School Age

According to Erikson, at each stage (ages 6 through 12), the child becomes a somewhat different person. At the school age, the fourth stage, children evolve into intellectually curious people. They want to know, to learn. During this time, children begin to lay the groundwork for becoming parents. They play at the parental role to prepare themselves for the real thing. For the first time, they relate to the larger society and one of its core elements, work. They learn to apply themselves to tasks that have practical outcomes, like salary for work. These tasks may be schoolwork for grades or housework for a monetary allowance.

Erikson sometimes referred to the school age as the latency period. In so doing he acknowledges that Freudian sexual interest and activity is repressed during this phase. He is quick to add, however, that Freud missed all the cognitive development that blossoms during the school age "because he was only concerned with what happens to sexual energy during that time" (Erikson, quoted in Evans, 1976, 295). This apology, issued on Freud's behalf, is a charitable way of saying that an overly narrow focus on sexuality caused his former mentor to miss the most important developments.

One of the poles of school age is **industry**, children's absorption in the "tool world" of their culture—the workaday world—thereby preparing them "for a hierarchy of learning experiences which [they] will undergo with the help of cooperative peers and instructive adults" (Erikson, 1968a, p. 289). Of course, school is the first productive situation that provides an inkling of the "tool culture." Here "work" is school performance. In other settings it may be athletic performance or organization of group-play activities. In each case the child is learning adults' rules of work, as directly seen in playing "house" or "doctor." The other pole of the crisis, **inferiority**, occurs if children perceive their skills or status among peers to be inadequate. This perception arises because of failures at establishing competence in some specialized way, such as playing a game or spelling well. Race or ethnic background may become barriers that prevent children from experiencing success and the accompanying actualization of the will to learn. Inferiority can yield regression to the hopelessness of over-concern about the opposite-sexed parent that characterized the previous stage. The triumph of inferiority may lead to an obsession with work so that it becomes the sole source of identity. A workaholic orientation may result. "If the overly conforming child accepts work as the only criterion of worthwhileness, sacrificing too readily his imagination and playfulness, he may [as an adult] submit to 'crafty-idiocy' . . . [becoming] a slave of his technology . . ." (Erikson, 1968a, p. 289).

Resolution of the crisis at the school age gives children critical experiences, including working beside and with others and "division of labor." From this resolution emerges the strength of **competence**, "the free exercise (unimpaired by an infantile sense of inferiority) of dexterity and intelligence in the completion of serious tasks" (Erikson, 1968a, pp. 289–290). With competence, children are ready to become cooperative participants in some segment of the culture.

Adolescence

As Allport indicated and most theorists agree, the adolescent search for self represents the fulcrum on which the lifelong struggle for identity is balanced. For Erikson, adolescence (the teen years), the fifth stage, allows a synthesis of previous stages, but it is more than the mere sum of what developed earlier. It is also an extension into the future.

One pole of the adolescent crisis is **identity**, accumulated confidence that the sameness and continuity one has previously cultivated are now appreciated by others, allowing, in turn, the promise of careers and lifestyles to come. "Continuity" is an important term in the conception of identity. "Identity means an integration of all previous identifications and self-images, including the negative ones" (Erikson, quoted in Evans, 1976, p. 297). Continuity ensures that one is all that one was, but also something new and something yet to be. The opposite of identity is **identity confusion**, the failure of previous identity developments to coalesce in such a way that it is clear what roles one is expected to play in the future. While all teens may change superficial identity periodically—punk one month, preppy the next—repeated changes at short intervals may signal abnormal identity confusion. The victory of confusion predicts acute maladjustments due to a feeling of meaninglessness. These symptoms can lapse into psychotic episodes.

Adolescent identity is not merely obtaining genital maturity in the Freudian sense. It is an ability to be concerned about others, because one's own problems relating to previous periods have been largely solved (Evans, 1976). Identity problems for teens are in part related to their personal histories and in part arise from identity pitfalls peculiar to their historical era. For example, today's teenage boys may be torn between the macho orientation that so heavily influenced their father's identity and the more gender-neutral identity that seems appropriate today.

In their struggle to answer the question "Who am I?" adolescents often form cliques. These clans bolster self-images and provide a mutual defense against "enemies" whose different characteristics challenge the "truth" of their own developing identities (E. Hall, 1983). If teens turn this condemnation of the "different" against society, delinquency can result. In fact, modern teen gangs can be viewed as Eriksonian clans formed to foster identity development. Antisocial behavior may also occur in "A person whose potentialities as a person have no place in the historical trends of his time . . ." (Erikson, quoted in Evans, 1976, p. 297). However, adolescent rebellion is not seen by Erikson as a necessarily negative force, at least when the larger culture is considered (Erikson, 1968a). Societies must be flexible, and Erikson sees adolescent challenges as a source of cultural rejuvenation. Youth, in their quest for identity, question the norms of their society, vigorously supporting those that meet the challenge and contributing to the demise of rules that cannot bear close scrutiny. Times of unrest among the young attest to the sickness of a society failing to meet the promise of youth—that the best will rule and the rulers will bring out the best in people. The unrest of the 1960s can be interpreted as a response to a society whose leaders were not "bringing out the best." During periods of upheaval, the mind of youth and that of society become one in the pursuit of ideological unification and return to coherent purpose.

The strength that comes from the adolescent period is **fidelity**, "the opportunity to fulfill personal potentialities . . . in a context which permits the young person to be true to himself and true to significant others . . . [and to] sustain loyalties . . . in spite of inevitable contradictions of value systems" (Erikson, 1968a, p. 290). For Erikson, fidelity is the cornerstone of identity. It is, however, not devotion to a particular ideology, but loyalty to ideologies that are appropriate to the individual. As Erikson put it, "I would go further and claim that we have almost an instinct for fidelity—meaning that when you reach a certain age you can and must learn to be faithful to some ideological view. Speaking psychiatrically, without the development of a capacity for fidelity the individual will either have what we call a weak ego, or look for a deviant group to be faithful to" (Erikson, quoted in Evans, 1976, p. 296).

BOX 7.3   Erikson on Cultural Diversity

Except for Jung, no other theorist covered in this book has left her or his theoretical door more wide open to cultural diversity than did Erikson. He recognized that mothers from different cultures must teach trusting in ways that are consistent with their traditions. You can well imagine that compared to North America, trust is imparted differently in South American and Asian societies where babies are strapped for hours on the mother's back facing away from her. It is also taught differently in African societies where "it takes a whole village to rear a child." Erikson recognized as well that during the school age avoidance of inferiority was more difficult for the children of oppressed social and ethnic groups than for others. As for the adolescent period, Erikson observed that youth are both the architects of the cultural evolution that occurs during times of upheaval and the victims of it. His popularity among youth during the 1960s arose from his recognition that U.S. society needed changing and that youth would be the catalysts for change. In effect his writings predicted that youth would be in the forefront of the civil rights movement and of the campaign to end the U.S. role as police officer for the world.

The need to adopt ideologies, particularly a focal ideology, can be a trap that ensnares the impulsive teen. Erikson believes that "Adolescents are easily seduced by totalitarian regimes and all kinds of totalistic fads" (Erikson, quoted in Evans, 1976, p. 297). Like Allport, he is especially concerned because youth are prone to succumb to the siren song of "nationalism." The allure of nationalism is in its ideological simplicity and resultant promise to answer all questions and solve all problems. As far back as 1942 Erikson recognized the effect of the nationalistic narcotic on the "Hitler Youth" (Hoffman, 1993). Youth must somehow avoid impulsivity in responding to the almost instinctual demand of fidelity that one quickly adopt the most obvious ideology available. Only with restraint will the magnetic force of simplistic ideologies like nationalism be resisted until broader ideologies are considered.

Another danger posed by ideology is that it may become the basis of identity. An ideological framework, such as tribal norms, may be forced on youth in such a way as to become the foundation of identity. In so-called "primitive" societies, youth go through puberty rites that concretely and immediately define for them their place in their society. In such cases, the option to exercise choice in adopting identity is precluded. Of course, whether an identity so obtained is benevolent or malevolent depends on the nature of the society. In most such societies puberty rites are centuries old. Obviously they could not have enjoyed such exceptional longevity had they been dysfunctional in the sense of having malevolent effects.

It is important to note that the imposition of "tribal norms" is not peculiar to "primitive" societies but can occur in "advanced" technological societies as well. When we thoughtlessly become what our parents are and what our grandparents were, an identity has been imposed on us and we have passively accepted it.

Young Adulthood

During previous stages, strengths allowed the genders to merge in cooperation and fruitful communication. When "falling in love," teenagers attach themselves to another person in an attempt to arrive at self-definition. Teens "in love" see themselves reflected in an "idealized other," but do not actively attempt to differentiate themselves from the other. Now, during the sixth stage (early to mid-twenties), the biological differences come to the fore, so that the genders, similar in consciousness and language, become different in the mature quest for love and procreation. The two poles of this sixth stage are tied to the themes of attachment to and alienation from others. **Intimacy** "is really the ability to fuse your identity with somebody else's without fear that you're going to lose something yourself" (Erikson, quoted in Evans, 1967, p. 48). It is more than the mere physical intimacy that occurs in sexual exchanges (E. Hall, 1983). "Of course, I mean something more—I mean intimate relationships, such as friendship, love, sexual intimacy, even intimacy with oneself, one's inner resources, the range of one's excitements and commitments" (Erikson, quoted in Evans, 1976, p. 300). With this broader definition of intimacy in mind, Erikson anticipated modern theories of marital success (Allen, 1990). He asserted that intimacy is what makes marriage possible; without it marriage is meaningless.

The other pole in the crisis for this stage is **isolation**, the failure to secure close and cooperative relationships with the same and especially the opposite gender such that partners' identities are important to, but distinct from, one's own. The triumph of isolation dooms the individual to infantile fixations and lasting immaturities that interfere with love and work. On the other hand, intimacy brings the strength of this period. **Love** "is the guardian of that elusive and yet all-pervasive power of cultural and personal style which binds . . . the affiliations of competition and cooperation, procreation and production" into a "way of life" (Erikson, quoted in Evans, 1976, p. 291). Love is also the shared devotion that overcomes antagonisms caused by differences in the functions assigned to partners in a relationship. "Love, then, is a mutuality of devotion greater than the antagonisms inherent in divided function" (p. 291).

Adulthood

"At this stage one begins to take one's place in society, and to help in the development and perfection of whatever [society] produces" (Erikson, quoted in Evans, 1976, pp. 301–302). Humans are not only "learning animals," they are teachers as well. It is at the maturity of adulthood (mid-twenties to mid-sixties) that the need to be needed and the accumulation of wisdom lead to assumption of the "teacher" role. Thus, during the seventh stage, people strive for **generativity**, "the concern with establishing and guiding the next generation" (Erikson, 1968a, p. 291). It is manifested in the advice that middle-aged people are inclined to offer younger individuals. Erikson admitted that *generativity* is "not an elegant word" (Evans, 1976, p. 301). He indicated that he might have used *creativity* instead of *generativity*, but the substitution would put "too much emphasis on the particular creativity which we ascribe to particular people" (Evans, 1976, p. 301). *Generativity* has a broader meaning that is applicable to people in general: "everything that is generated from generation to generation: children, products, ideas, and works of art" (p. 301).

The failure of generativity leads to **stagnation**—the arrest of the ripening process that comes with inability to funnel previous development into the formation of the next generation. Boredom is the constant companion of stagnation, as is false intimacy and adult self-indulgence. Inevitably, the failure of generativity shows up in the next generation as the aggravation of estrangements in childhood, adolescence, and early adulthood.

Care, the strength of maturity, is "the broadening concern for what has been generated by love, necessity, or accident—a concern which must consistently overcome the ambivalence adhering to irreversible obligation and the narrowness of self-concern" (Erikson, 1968a, p. 291). Care is a major force behind utilization of "proven methods with which each generation meets the needs of the next" (Erikson, 1968a, 291).

Erikson was at first concerned about the selection of "care" because of its multitude of connotations, including "anxious solicitude" (Evans, 1976). However, he was able to conclude that the word has evolved and now means " 'to care to do' something, to 'care for' somebody or something, to 'take care of' that which needs protection and attention, and 'to take care not to' do something destructive" (Erikson, quoted in Evans, 1976, 301).

Old Age

Power in old age is wit in full bloom—a storehouse of knowledge, an inclusive understanding, and a maturity of judgment. These intellectual contributions provide a bridge to the next generation by reminding all that the knowledge of a given generation is not "truth," but a cog in the infinitely large and ever-turning wheel of human experience. Crisis at this time (mid-sixties until death) involves contributing to the continuity of the human condition versus distraction from that noble purpose by an obsession with death. The poles for this eighth stage revolve around wholeness and completeness versus disintegration and defeat. **Integrity** is "an emotional integration faithful to the image bearers of the past and ready to take (and eventually renounce) leadership in the present" (Erikson, 1968a, p. 291). Integrity is the continuity that comes from being solidly founded on a past that contributes to the present and projects into the future. My grandmother had it.

Lack of resolution leads to **despair,** a feeling that time is too short for the achievement of integrity and the accompanying contribution to the connection between generations. Despair can result in bitterness at not being able to extend oneself into the future, a losing

---

BOX 7.4   Assessing Crisis Resolution

"Epigenesis" characterizes Erikson's stages: one builds on the other. Resolving crises at one stage can affect how well one does at subsequent stages. However, unlike Freud, Erikson felt that failure of resolution of a crisis at a given stage means neither failure at subsequent stages nor permanent failure at the stage in question (Ochse & Plug, 1986). Erikson was optimistic, believing that later crisis resolution might retroactively resolve earlier crises.

In view of Erikson's position, it should be interesting and encouraging for you to examine how well you did in resolving earlier crises. Look at Table 7.1 closely, starting at the top. Assess how well you have done at each succeeding stage by whether or not you show the presence of the characteristics under "Resolution," the absence of the traits under "Poor Resolution" and at least some evidence for the strength that is associated with the stage. Remember not to despair should you fail to show resolution at some early stage. At some later point you may experience resolution that retroactively resolves earlier crises.

battle with death, rather than a calm acceptance of it. Despair yields psychological death before the physical counterpart. The symptoms of despair often include depression, hypochondria, and paranoia.

The strength that comes from resolution of the eighth crisis is **wisdom**, a "detached and yet active concern with life in the face of death," not magical access to "higher knowledge" (Erikson, 1968a p. 292; E. Hall, 1983). With wisdom, death is accepted, and one's role in the human drama is assured.

Erikson was not entirely satisfied with the word *wisdom* "because to some people it seems to mean a too strenuous achievement for each and every old person" (Erikson, quoted in Evans, 1976, p. 301). In fact, during old age people may show a renewal of infantile traits, even including senile childishness. Wisdom in any sense of the word is not a necessity during old age. "The main point is again a developmental one: Only in old age can true wisdom develop in those who are thus gifted. And in old age, some wisdom must mature, if only in a sense that the old person comes to appreciate and to represent something of the wisdom of the ages, or plain old wit" (p. 301). Though he was not old when he died, wisdom is what Malcolm X had at the end of his life.

Table 7.1 summarizes Erikson's eight stages and the crisis of identity associated with each.

TABLE 7.1   Erikson's Eight Stages

Stage	Crisis	Resolution	Poor Resolution	Strength
Infancy	Basic trust vs. mistrust	Confidence in satisfaction of needs	Rage due to uncertainty of satisfaction	Hope
Early childhood	Autonomy vs. shame and doubt	Independence stemming from self-control	Estrangement due to being controlled	Willpower
Play age	Initiative vs. guilt	Acting on desires, urges, potentials	Conscience restrains pursuits	Purpose
School age	Industry vs. inferiority	Absorbed in "tool world"	Skills and status inadequate	Competence
Adolescence	Identity vs. identity confusion	Confident that sameness seen by others	Pervious identity developments fail	Fidelity
Young adulthood	Intimacy vs. isolation	Fusing identity with another	No close relationships	Love
Adulthood	Generativity vs. stagnation	Guiding the next generation	Arrest of the ripening process	Care
Old age	Integrity vs. despair	Emotional integration	"Time is short"	Wisdom

Theoretical and Empirical Support for Erikson's Point of View

Daniel Levinson (1978) and Gail Sheehy (1977) developed theories about adult crises. Although their postulations are more elaborate than Erikson's, they were probably heavily influenced by the Danish psychologist's point of view. Erikson's theory predates their points of view and he pioneered the idea of the "crisis of identity." He also was their predecessor in writing about adulthood crises. In view of these circumstances, the widespread attention and acceptance of their theories can be considered support for Erikson's orientation regarding adult life.

Levinson: The Midlife Crisis

Daniel Levinson was in his mid-forties when he conceived of a research project on mid-life (Levinson, 1978). He was in his late forties when the project began with a sample of adult men. Like Erikson, Levinson had been inspired by his own life experiences. His struggle for meaning at the mid-point of life resulted in a landmark study.

The *mid-life transition* is a bridge between young adulthood and middle age, a time at which individuals look back at their previous successes and failures and make assessments concerning their future prospects (Levinson, 1978). Part and parcel of this soul-searching is reappraising the past. Because of a heightened awareness of mortality at about forty, people begin to reevaluate the past in order to use the future more wisely. They raise questions about their contributions to spouses, children, and careers and the contributions of family and career to themselves. The consequence of this reassessment is almost always *de-illusionment*, a reduction of illusions, a recognition that assumptions and beliefs about self and the world are not true. Illusions have worked well in earlier life as fuel to drive ambitions and ideals. At mid-life it is time to cast them aside in favor of objective assessment.

With reappraisal comes restructuring, a change in the organization of one's life. It may take the form of major upheaval, the mid-life crisis, during which family and career may be replaced and an entirely new lifestyle adopted, or appear as a simple reordering of priorities. In any case the process of *individuation* begins, a procedure by which a person's relationship between self and the external world is changed so that there is a clearer separation between self and the world (the influence of Jung is clearly seen here). It is a reintroduction of the method for achieving maturity that operated during childhood. As an infant, as a child, and as an adolescent, people progressively see themselves as distinct from their parents, their home life, and their peers. At mid-life, the distinction becomes sharper and includes differentiation from family, career, friends, and the expectations that restrict the behavior and thought of all adults. Levinson acknowledges that along with individuation comes Erikson's generativity (versus stagnation).

Some people sail through the mid-life transition with little questioning and searching. Their lives may be sufficiently stable and satisfying that they need not experience severe crisis. Others come to terms with the loss of some dreams and are able to contemplate the future without much pain. However, Levinson contends that most people's struggles with the self and the external world reach crisis proportions (80 percent in his sample). They display anguish, show guilt and upset, and explore, even try, new lifestyles. Their impulsivity approaches that of adolescents. They may astound friends and family with changes in personality affected by variations in clothing, hairstyle and use of language.

To realize that one has reached middle age is to realize that life is partly over, and, in turn, that death must be considered. According to Levinson, we all cling to the illusion of our own immortality. When certain declines in function occur at age forty or so, such as a relative lack of vigor and intellectual quickness, people can no longer avoid thinking about the unthinkable. The possibility of death runs head on into the cherished assumption of immortality. The contradiction thus generated is not eliminated by giving up the illusion of immortality. Rather, in those who successfully pass through the transition of mid-life, immortality is seen in a new light. If one leaves behind a *legacy*, material goods, wisdom for others to use, and examples for others to follow, one lives on despite the demise of the body.

Levinson has been criticized for excluding women from his famous study. That problem should be solved with the appearance of *The Seasons of Woman's Life* (1996). Levinson had no illusions; he was comfortable with his mortality. Nor did he falter in his quest for growth in himself and in others. "He could be impatient with those who could not see the continual capacity for development through life" (Astrachan, 1994). When his time came in 1994, he gave up life as gracefully as he lived it.

Sheehy: Women Are Different

Gail Sheehy (1977) was heavily influenced by exposure to an advanced copy of Levinson's manuscript on his study. She became even more concerned about the "mid-life" crisis, its variations and the paths out of it than Levinson.

Unlike Levinson, Sheehy does not neglect women's crises. For Sheehy, age thirty-five begins a dangerous period for women. Thirty-five is usually the age at which the last child is sent off to school, ending the period of intense childcare. Now a woman has time to think and her thoughts may turn to her attractiveness. She may reason that she will lose her looks soon so she had better use them while she can. Alternatively, she may seek reassurances that she is still attractive. In either case, an affair may result.

The end of the intense childcare period is also a time when women enter the work force. Economic necessity as well as filling the childcare void is a reason for working outside the home. Whatever the reason, when a woman enters the work force, she is likely to stay. This highly significant event can be good or bad or a mixture of both. She may be well-educated and thereby equipped to enter the professional ranks. If so, she will be frustrated to find that competitors for advancement, often men, are way ahead of her by virtue of their greater experience. Yet, she may eventually obtain acceptance and the status that comes with it. If she is poorly educated, she will soon come to realize that advancement is unlikely for her. Frustration caused by being behind or despair due to being stuck at a low-level job may cause a crisis.

Age thirty-five may herald the onset of other events that could precipitate a crisis. If she is divorced, she may take a new husband. If she is distraught for any of the reasons just covered, she is at an age where running away is most probable. In addition, at this time she is likely to contemplate physical changes that hit at the heart of her identity: physiologically she will be able to bear children for only a few more years. To lead a productive mid-life and old age, she must come to grips with the changes in her social roles, such as those involved in work and childcare. She must also learn to accept the physical changes that will be more abrupt and visible than those associated with men's mid-life.

Empirical Support: Research Confirming Erikson's View

Ochse and Plug (1986) looked at the status of trust, autonomy, initiative, industry, intimacy, and generativity among white and black South Africans aged 15 to 50 (integrity was omitted due to the lack of elderly subjects). These researchers generally accepted Erikson's "epigenesis" and, therefore, expected that "one stage would build on another."

The seven positive poles of the first seven stages were represented by questionnaire items, along with a measure of well-being. As expected, subjects' responses to the questionnaire indicated that the more the positive poles were manifested in their responses, the higher their senses of well-being. Also, as would be expected from adult subjects, a factor analysis of results revealed factors corresponding only to adult poles: intimacy versus isolation and generativity versus stagnation.

In addition, it was expected that intercorrelations among the poles relating to crises that had already been passed—those of childhood—would be relatively strong. Such was the case for white women and to some degree for white men, but not for blacks. In fact, the intercorrelations among the poles tended to be high regardless of whether subjects had yet passed crises. This result was taken to mean that "Erikson's personality components to some extent develop in parallel and are interdependent even before the relevant crises are resolved" (p. 1246). This outcome seems to contradict the "epigenesis" notion that earlier crises are resolved before later ones. However, Erikson "does suggest that all the components develop to some degree throughout life, even before their critical stages" (p. 1246).

It was predicted that "intimacy" would be generally higher for women than for men. This prediction was confirmed, but only for whites. For blacks it was reversed: intimacy was higher for men than for women. This outcome was one of several cases in which results of blacks were different from those of whites, and, in some cases, less consistent with Erikson's point of view. Once again we are reminded that theories derived by Western World psychologists may not apply to people from other places. You may recall, however, that Erikson knew his theory would have to be stretched to accommodate different cultural settings.

One would also expect that identity would become more highly related to intimacy in the early twenties than in the teens. Further identity would become most highly related to generativity in middle age, when generativity becomes salient. This prediction was borne out for white women. For white and black men, only the prediction regarding generativity was supported.

Other results showed that scores associated with poles of already-passed childhood stages showed declines with increases in age, but those associated with adult poles increased with age. Also men showed stronger autonomy, initiative, and industry, as sex-role adoption would predict. Finally, and very importantly, factor analysis revealed a strong and overriding factor. The researchers felt that it might be labeled "identity" in the global sense. This interpretation suggests that the various crises at the several stages are indeed "identity crises."

Kowaz and Marcia (1991) showed impressive support for Erikson's "industry" concept. First they developed a measure of industry that focused on three components: (1) cognitive (skills and knowledge); (2) behavioral (applications of skills and knowledge); and (3) affective (attitudes and experiences relating to the acquisition and application of skills and knowledge). Example items were the following: for component 1 (cognitive), "Some kids at my grade level really know the basics of spelling, arithmetic, reading, and science. BUT other kids don't really know the basics"; for component 2 (behavioral), "Some kids finish doing everything they start to do. BUT other kids don't get things finished"; for component 3 (affective), "Some kids feel there is at least one kind of thing they do really well. BUT other kids are average in everything they do" (p. 392). These components were developed into rating questionnaires for elementary school children, their parents, and their teachers.

Results showed that the children's self-ratings of industry were highly correlated with teachers' industry ratings of children and parents' ratings of children. That is, all three groups agreed on industry ratings of the children. Further, there was a general tendency toward high interrelations among the components of measures of industry. These results mean that industry can be measured reliably and shows high coherence.

Evidence for the validity of the concept "industry" was also strong. Component 1 industry scores were positively correlated with achievement scores, whether measured by children's subjective judgments of school achievement or grades. An overall score on industry was also related to achievement test scores. For teachers' judgments, being on- versus off-task was positively related to industry scores. "Level of reasoning" was also positively related to the overall measure of industry.

The researchers developed a measure of concern for the process involved in a task, as opposed to interest only in the task outcome. This measure was positively related to the overall measure of industry: the more the industry, the more the interest in the process versus the outcome. Finally, overall contentment was positively related to industry. The results showed that the concept "industry" strongly applies to the age-group that should orient to this pole, according to Erikson.

McAdams, Ruetzel, and Foley (1986) looked at a measure of generativity in relation to indexes of power and intimacy motivation as measured with use of the Thematic Apperception Test (TAT) developed by Murray. Subjects were adults between the ages of 35 and 49. The index of generativity was taken from an interview in which subjects explored plans for the future. Two independent scorers looked for evidence indicating concern for guiding the next generation either directly—caregiving, teaching, leading, mentoring—or indirectly—contributing in a literary, scientific, artistic, or altruistic sense.

Results showed that TAT scores indexing power and intimacy motivation were positively associated with the measure of generativity: the greater the generativity, the greater those motives. The researchers interpreted this result to mean "that generativity calls on an adult's fundamental needs to feel close and to feel strong vis-à-vis others" (p. 806).

More recently, McAdams and Mansfield looked at the relationship between generativity and communion—being self-sacrificing and "one with" others (Mansfield & McAdams, 1996). They found that the higher the level of communion shown by subjects, the higher was their level of generativity.

Peterson and Steward (1993) derived TAT scores on achievement, affiliation–intimacy, and power. Generativity was separately indexed by scores on parenting involvement, personal productivity, and societal concern. Results showed a gender difference. For women, power motive related to parenting and achievement motive related to forms of generativity expression outside the home. Men showed the opposite tendency: power motive related to generativity outside the home and achievement motive related to parenting. Peterson and Stewart concluded that difference in opportunities and expectations for men and women accounted for the gender difference. As subjects were, on average, age 27.7, results also showed that people begin to develop generativity well before middle age.

Franz, McClelland, and Weinberger (1991) followed up research beginning in the early 1950s. Participants, now aged about forty-one, were ninety-four men and women who completed a questionnaire and submitted to an interview. The measure of generativity was taken from written details of "hopes and dreams for the future" submitted by subjects (p. 589). These plans were scored by two students using a method developed by McAdams. Results showed that psychosocial maturity—indexed by having close friends at mid-life, a long, happy marriage, and children—was positively related to generativity: the higher the generativity score the higher the psychosocial maturity score.

Evaluation

Contributions

Erikson's is a remarkable story. With only a high school education, he made it to the lofty status of Harvard professor. More importantly, he has written a theory that has heavily influenced not only academics, but also the public. Erikson was a hero during the 1960s because of his views regarding youth and rebellion. His assertion that people continue to grow and change in specifiable ways not only opened new vistas to millions of older people, it also revolutionized the study of personality. Prior to Erikson it was becoming a dogma that personality is set in stone by the end of the teens at the latest. Erikson's unique and creative thoughts opened the eyes of other theorists, such as Levinson and Sheehy, to the possibility of personality growth after youth has ripened into middle age. Never again will psychologists neglect older people or believe everything currently happening in their lives was predetermined by events in their youth.

Like a few other theorists covered in this book, such as Adler, Horney, Fromm, Rogers, and Allport, Erikson is important because of the person he is. Making it as an academic without academic credentials is somewhat akin to making it as a politician without the backing of the political power brokers. Similarly to Adler and Murray, Erikson turned psychological deficiencies into ideas that not only helped him but are now valuable to countless others as well. If we adopt his respect for the goals and aspirations of people of all ages, we will take an enormous stride in the direction of respecting all people everywhere.

While researchers have found little of interest in the concepts of certain theorists with the "right credentials," they have paid considerable attention to some of Erikson's notions. There is now up-to-date evidence that people pass through something at least akin to Erikson's epigenic stages. Further, at least some of the ideas that he apparently took right off the top of his head have been supported by research. In particular, the concepts of "industry" and "generativity" have received appreciable support. Noting that these concepts cut across the lifespan, one can bet that others of Erikson's ideas will eventually receive empirical support.

An overriding message in Erikson's writings is that identity is dynamic, not static. "Who a person is" changes and evolves over time. Although stages are built on top of stages, what a person will become is not necessarily "better" than what that person currently is, just different. Neither is it the case that we abandon what we currently are when we seek to be something else. Rather mastery of current pursuits signals the development of new capabilities that can be used to foster further accomplishments. According to Erikson, we are able to continually expand and broaden our horizons with much benefit to ourselves and to others.

Limitations

While it is admirable that someone could gain the respect of academics without obtaining the academic union card, a doctorate, Erikson's lack of advanced training showed up in his thinking. There is a certain lack of logical consistency in his ideas. For example, it is not entirely clear why he chose the labels "autonomy versus shame and doubt" to characterize developments at early childhood. Likewise, why was "initiative versus guilt" chosen for the play age? While "autonomy" makes some logical sense, why is "shame and doubt" the other side of the coin representing the early childhood crisis? "Guilt" or "inferiority" or another label might fit just as well. The opposite of "autonomy" is "dependence" and the counterpart of "initiative" could be "dependence" as well, or it could be "passivity." "Competence" seems to fit as well at early childhood as "willpower," which may be regarded as a cliché that has been adopted by everyone from frustrated dieters to Adolf Hitler. Erikson was openly dissatisfied with *wisdom*. Aside from the multiple meanings attached to the word, which he does mention, he might have added the fact that the word is so overused it has become trite. One could add, why eight stages? It has been suggested that eleven stages, including one for very old age, may better fit current demographics and related factors of the contemporary human condition (Kishton, 1994). A stage for very old age makes sense as more and more people live beyond 100 years. Relatedly, other stages may need to be realigned. The Adulthood Stage subsumes too much: it extends from young adulthood and, with no consideration of middle age, ends in the sixties. Perhaps Young Adulthood should be stretched through age thirty-five, with a new stage, "Middle age," going from thirty-six to sixty, Old Age from sixty-one to eighty, and new stage, "Very Old Age," eighty-one and beyond.

"Fidelity" seems to be a particularly murky concept. The way Erikson defines it and the way he talks about it do not match well. If it is related to adoption of ideologies as Erikson indicates, one could wonder whether adolescence is the appropriate place for it. Perhaps the seeds of ideological flowering are planted during the teens, but the blossoming may well occur during young adulthood or even later.

Research on Erikson's point of view, while generally supportive, turned up some weaknesses. Ochse and Plug (1986) found some evidence that Erikson's poles of crises develop in parallel, as opposed to building one on another. These researchers try to save epigenesis by pointing out that Erikson had suggested that all poles develop to some degree throughout life. But can he have it both ways? From a scientific point of view, the answer is "no." It must be shown that various poles are obvious in their manifestations at the time when they are supposed to appear, but exist only in "trace amounts" at other stages.

These same researchers found that Erikson's theory worked much better for white than for black South Africans. This outcome raises the possibility that the theory is limited to people of European descent (white South Africans are mostly of Dutch and English stock). Further, there were gender differences that seem not to be predicted by Erikson's theory.

Because Ochse and Plug (1986) showed men display stronger autonomy, initiative, and industry, the theory may be more applicable to them than to women.

The lack of factors relating to childhood poles reported by these same researchers indicates that those poles may not be distinct, one from the other. As the researchers put it, the concepts relating to these poles may overlap. Had they been nonoverlapping, they would been reflected in distinct factors. Ochse and Plug note that other researchers have also alluded to the overlap of Erikson's concepts. These interpretations certainly are consistent with my earlier suggestion that some of Erikson's concepts could fit stages other than the ones to which he assigned them.

While Erikson has inspired several researchers as well as many ordinary citizens, he has apparently failed to recruit notable followers to take up his cause. There are few if any Eriksonians around, at least among well-known psychologists. Perhaps it is because his theory has relatively little practical import compared to others. It has no therapy associated with it, and unlike other theories, such as that of Bandura, Erikson's theory has been relatively little used to solve real world problems.

Conclusions

While Erikson's lack of academic training may be a fault that places limits on his theory, it may also be regarded as a virtue. One wonders whether he would have seen that personality development does not end at age twenty if he had been trained in the typical psychology department. As it is, his vision is characterized by greater acuity than most. He anticipated the "mid-life" crisis and reminded us all that elderly people can be productive. Not only does he provide us with the possibility of productivity during old age, he points out creative tasks appropriate to the golden years.

Erikson's example reminds us that creative thoughts applicable to the lives of people are not the sole province of the highly educated. Not being encumbered by academic dogmas and methodologies, he was able to focus on what others had neglected. He brought an end to the overemphasis on youth just at the right time. As we enter the era of the "graying of the population" the thoughts of Erik Erikson will become more and more relevant.

Summary Points

1. Erikson was born the son of Danish parents, but he was reared by a Jewish physician whose surname he adopted for a while. As a young man a job as a children's portrait painter proved to be his passport into Vienna's secretive psychoanalytic society. There he developed an undying loyalty to Freud. On arriving in the United States, he made an abortive attempt to do graduate work and was employed by Murray for a time. After jobs at Yale and the University of California, he became a professor at Harvard.

2. Erikson was a Freudian in the sense that he felt he owed allegiance to Freud and he couched explanations of his own concepts in Freudian jargon. Most of his important concepts, however, are distinct from and independent of Freud's ideas. While he showed a rather stereotyped conception of women early in his career, later he began to reject Freud's

unflattering view of women. He believed that life and its challenges were constantly evolving. At each successive phase of life, people find themselves on the horns of a new dilemma and confronted with new tasks.

3. Erikson believed that we pass through a series of eight psychosocial stages, each building on the earlier ones (epigenesis). Each stage brings with it a new crisis: people are caught between two new conflicting poles. The crisis thus represented is never fully resolved, but, hopefully, the ratio of orientation to the positive pole, relative to the negative pole, is favorable.

4. In the first stage, infancy, the poles are basic trust and basic mistrust. The strength of this period is hope. It is the foundation of faith that is protected by the institutional safeguard, religion. Early childhood presents the poles autonomy versus shame and doubt. Its strength is willpower, the determination to exercise free choice, which is protected institutionally by law and justice.

5. The third stage involves initiative versus guilt. The boy does fantasize about his mother, even in a sexual way, but it is because she is central to his life, not solely because of his genital urges. The strength of this period is purpose. At the school age, the horns of the dilemma are industry and inferiority. The child at this stage prepares for the workaday world and the "tool culture." The strength of this period is competence.

6. During adolescence identity itself comes into focus: the poles are identity versus identity confusion. At this stage previous identity developments either come together or not. It is a time of rebellion against the rules and norms of society. Fidelity is the strength: loyalty to self, others, and to personal ideologies. Ideologies must be adopted, but the dangers are seduction of youth by totalitarian ideology and subordination of identity to ideology.

7. Erikson's theory accommodates diversity because he acknowledged that his stages and their dilemmas would manifest themselves differently in different cultures. He also understood the mark of oppression and that youth are both the authors of and the victims of cultural change. In young adulthood, intimacy is fusion of one's identity with another's without loss to self. Love binds together competition and cooperation, procreation and production. It overcomes the antagonisms of differences in function between relationship partners. In adulthood, generativity is concern for guiding the next generation. Care, the strength of this period, is "to take care of," "to do for," and "to care for" others.

8. In old age, integrity opposes despair: passing on the power and leadership to the next generation versus failure to establish a connection between generations. The strength is wisdom in the sense of "wisdom of the ages." Levinson's mid-life transition entails a show of de-illusionment and individuation. To prosper, we must give up our illusion of immortality and contemplate a legacy. To Sheehy, women's crisis begins at thirty-five: children leave and attractiveness declines. At work women face competition with men of greater seniority. Divorce and concern that their biological clocks are ticking also confront women.

9. The poles for young adulthood and adulthood were extracted from factor analysis, but the lack of appearance of the other poles suggests overlap among them. An overriding factor that may be labelled "identity" was also extracted. Several predictions from Erikson's theory were supported, but usually for whites, not blacks. There were also some troublesome gender differences. In another study teacher, parent and child ratings of children's industry were closely related and measures of industry predicted achievement, grades, and being on- versus off-task. Two other studies showed the viability of the concept "generativity." A recent study, however, showed gender differences on power and achievement related to generativity and revealed generativity striving in young adult subjects.

10. Erikson's theoretical and career accomplishments are remarkable considering that he had no advanced education. He became a hero to youth during the 1960s and a champion of the elderly later in life. He turned psychological difficulties into benefits for us all. Research support for his view has been mostly positive and he has taught us that "identity" is a dynamic process. Unfortunately his theory is in part illogical. Some concepts seem exchangeable across stages, some are trite in meaning, some, like "fidelity," are murky, and some have too many meanings. Research has turned up other problems and raised questions, such as "are eight stages enough?"

Running Comparison

Theorist	*Erikson in Comparison*
Freud	He de-emphasized the unconscious in favor of psychosocial factors. Although he mentioned oral, anal, and phallic factors and the latency period, he played down their physical-sexual side in favor of psychosocial aspects. He came close to calling Freud "wrong" about women and disagreed with him that a stage's "problems" must be resolved before a more advanced stage can be approached.
Gordon Allport	He agreed with Allport that self-esteem derives from doing for oneself. Like Allport he wrote about maturity, but with subdivisions and in more detail. They both deplored nationalism.
Erich Fromm	He also considered the dilemma of freedom and was somewhat philosophical.
Sullivan and Horney	Like them, he was concerned about lasting effects of early, faulty parent–child relationships.
Jung	Like Jung he emphasized the polarities (opposites).

Essay/Critical Thinking Questions

1. Tell how Erikson's life and theory might have been different had he been reared by his natural father and mother under nonaffluent conditions.

2. Had Erikson, like Jung and Adler, completed a doctorate, but worked with Freud, would he have clung so tenaciously to giving "the Master" credit for his own ideas?

3. What are the tasks of your life now and what do you expect them to be in ten years?

4. For Eriksonian strengths other than hope and willpower, can you conjure up at least two other possible institutional safeguards?

5. Besides "guilt," what could you come up with that might be a better opposite to "initiative" for the play age, but still be true to Erikson's theory?

6. Of Erikson's concepts, why have "industry" and "generativity" been singled out for special research attention?

7. Why do "identity developments . . . coalesce" during adolescence? Why not at some other stage?

8. In young adulthood, how are you able to "fuse your identity with somebody else's without losing" it?

9. Erikson's "care," the strength at adulthood, is very much like the common notion of "being a caring person." Why is "being a caring person" so "in focus" during adulthood? Why not earlier or later?

10. Drawing on Erikson, Levinson, and Sheehy, summarize the differences between the mid-life crises of men and women.

E-mail Interaction

(Write the author at mfbpa@wiu.edu)
Forward any of the following questions/comments, or write your own.

1. What kind of professional was Erikson: psychiatrist, sociologist, or psychologist?
2. Was Erikson a person with deep-seated inferior feelings?
3. Indicate Erikson's single most important contribution.
4. In view of his lack of degrees, would Erikson have been given a break by academics if he had not been close to Freud?
5. Was Erikson really sexist?

8

THE SOCIOPSYCHOLOGICAL APPROACH TO PERSONALITY: ERICH FROMM

- Does sociology have anything to say about personality?
- Are there basic needs rooted in the very essence of humans?
- Is it reasonable to assume that most people in a given society share a generalized "character"?
- Do some people love death?
- What can study of life in a Mexican village tell us about personality?

Erich Fromm stood at the crossroads of modern personality psychology. Similarly to Erikson, some say that he came from the Freudian branch of the psychological tree. If so, he retreated to the tree trunk and from there nurtured a new limb supporting a broadly based personality theory. Fromm, compared to theorists covered earlier, described Freud's scientific contributions in glowing words: "He is founder of a truly scientific psychology, and his discovery of unconscious processes of the dynamic nature of character traits is a unique contribution to the science of man which has altered the picture of man for all time" (Fromm, 1962, p. 12). Yet Fromm's lengthy criticisms of Freud center on the claim that psychoanalysis "can define man scientifically" (Funk, 1982, p. 13). Indeed, Fromm believed that Freud's most basic notions are not amenable to scientific consideration, because most of his critical ideas cannot be converted to forms that can be observed scientifically. As if to take back the words of praise just quoted, when he compared Freud with social theorist Karl Marx, as he often did, Marx was the clear winner. "I consider Marx, the thinker, as being of much greater depth and scope than Freud" (p. 12).

Another reason that Fromm is pivotal in the history of personality theory resides in his academic training and background. He is the first of the theorists covered in this book who was trained in a university graduate school. Like Erikson, he had no medical school training, opting instead to study psychology, philosophy, and sociology. He received his Ph.D. from Heidelberg in 1922 following completion of "a dissertation on the sociopsychological structure of three Jewish Diaspora communities . . ." (Funk, 1982, pp. 2–3). Quite naturally his orientation would be away from biological/medical matters toward a **sociopsychological orientation,** the sociological study of people that sheds light on their psychological nature. During his long career, Fromm held professorships in several departments of psychology, including those at Michigan, Michigan State, Yale, New York University and the University of Mexico. Because his background was a mixture of sociology, political philosophy, and psychology, he was the prophet of things to come: personality research and theory was to be taken away from psychiatry/psychoanalysis and given over to psychology and allied sciences.

Fromm, the Person

Erich Fromm was born in Frankfurt, Germany, March 23, 1900, the only child of Orthodox Jewish parents. As a Jewish boy in a Christian community, he experienced feelings of "clannishness" on both sides, along with occasional episodes of anti-Semitism. He characterized his father, the owner of an independent business, and his mother, a homemaker, as "highly neurotic" and himself as an "unbearable, neurotic child" (Funk, 1982, p. 1). Fromm wrote that "an anxious and moody father and a depression-prone mother was enough to arouse my interest in the strange and mysterious reasons for human reactions" (Fromm, 1962, pp. 3–4).

Spurred by a deeply religious family, young Fromm became engrossed in the teachings of the Old Testament "which touched me and exhilarated me more than anything else I was exposed to" (Fromm, 1962, p. 5). While he was bored by the biblical account of Canaan's conquest, the stories of Mordecai and Esther and the Song of Songs, he was enthralled by the tale of Adam's and Eve's disobedience, by Abraham's plea for the deliverance of Sodom and Gomorrah's inhabitants, and by Jonah's mission to Nineveh. Isaiah, Amos, and Hosea were Fromm's favorite biblical characters. They moved him not so much by their prophesies of disaster as by their visions of the "end of days" when nations "shall beat their swords into plowshares and their spears into pruning hooks: nation shall not lift sword against nation, neither shall they learn war any more" (p. 5). These words were adopted by the international peace movement to which the adult Fromm was to contribute substantially.

Fromm developed his concepts in large part by reflecting on the thoughts of Freud and Marx, whose ideas he tried to synthesize (Fromm, 1962). His interest in psychoanalysis was triggered by an incident that occurred during his adolescence. A twenty-five-year-old friend of the family, an artist, killed herself following the death of her widowed father, with whom she had spent nearly all of her time.

> *I had never heard of an Oedipus complex or of incestuous fixations between daughter and father. But I was deeply touched. I had been quite attracted to the young woman; I had loathed the unattractive father; never before had I known anyone to commit suicide. I was hit by the thought 'How is it possible?' How is it possible that a beautiful young woman should be so in love with her father, that she prefers to be buried with him to being alive to the pleasures of life and of painting (Fromm, 1962, p. 4).*

In 1929 Fromm began a psychoanalytic apprenticeship under the tutelage of Hans Sachs and Theodor Reik at the Berlin Institute, which was also the site of Karen Horney's training (Funk, 1982; Hausdorff, 1972). Like Horney, he had no direct exposure to Freud. Because he lacked medical training, Fromm was suspect in some corners of the Freudian world. Although Freud's notions were rather simplistic from a biological perspective, even for the time, somehow many Freudians thought that one needed medical training to fully comprehend psychoanalytic concepts. They probably believed that Fromm de-emphasized Freud's biological notions because, with no medical training, he had difficulty understanding them.

For a short time after his psychoanalytic training, Fromm appeared to be a devout Freudian (Hausdorff, 1972). *The Development of the Dogma of Christ*, published in 1931, supported Freud's idea that religion is an illusion adopted in the interest of infantile gratification. But appearances can be deceiving. Although Fromm's Freudian period continued past his move to the United States in 1934, later he was to call himself at best ". . . a very unorthodox Freudian" (Hausdorff, 1972, p. 3). Fromm's retreat from Freudianism may have begun during the writing of his highly successful book, *Escape from Freedom*, published in 1941. This widely read declaration of independence from Freud advanced Fromm's unique ideas concerning how a totalitarian society and its ideology (e.g., Nazi Germany) can shape the thinking of its citizens. Needless to say, *Escape* was the right book at the right time: the United States was entering World War II against Japan and Germany, models of the authoritarian societies.

Fromm declared that World War I was "the event that determined more than anything else my development" (Fromm, 1962, p. 6). In this pronouncement, he joined Jung and Adler. Fromm was fourteen when the war began and, at first, was confused by people's reactions to armed conflict. Prior to the outbreak of hostilities, his Latin teacher, who seemed peace-loving, proclaimed his favorite "law" to be "if you want peace, prepare for war" (p. 6). In a show of true colors, when the war began, the Latin instructor showed obvious delight. "How was it possible that a man who always seemed to have been so concerned with the preservation of peace should now be so jubilant about the war?" (p. 6).

Experiences in his English class helped him deal with the "armament preserves peace" paradox. He and other students were told to learn the British national anthem over the summer. However, by the time they returned to school, the British had become "the enemy." The students proudly announced that they would not learn the anthem. Fromm's teacher answered their defiance with a calm, prophetic reminder, "Don't kid yourself; so far England has never lost a war" (p. 7). "Here was the voice of . . . realism in the midst of insane hatred—and it was the voice of a respected and admired teacher!" (p. 7). Never again would Fromm think it merely odd that "arms bring peace"; he would view it as insane.

Amidst Orwellian doubletalk of "strategic retreats" and "victorious defenses," he found that a number of uncles, cousins, and schoolmates had been killed. He again asked himself "How is it possible?" Fromm puzzled over the bugles of war-justification blaring from the headlines of German newspapers: "was Germany not fighting against the very embodiment of slavery and oppression—the Russian Czar?" (p. 7). When he read convincing evidence that Germanic nations were, in fact, responsible for the war, his consternation deepened. But confusion became mixed with horror when he realized that young men were buying their country's propaganda and paying dearly for it. They were *not* sacrificing life and limb for peace, freedom, and justice. They were being maimed and killed because their governments had declared the other side "evil," just as the other side had denounced them as "evil." This projected-image view of mutually antagonistic groups persists today in places like Bosnia: when one looks at the other, one sees what the other sees when looking to oneself, evil. He became "deeply suspicious of all official ideologies and declarations" (1962, p. 9).

Fromm was truly a citizen of the world. He received his academic training at the Universities of Heidelberg, Frankfurt, and Munich, Germany. While in the United States he lived in many different locations. His last professorship was at the National Autonomous University of Mexico in Mexico City. Retirement in 1965 was followed by a blitz of professional activity: 20 percent of his books were completed, including the report on his monumental study of Mexican villagers. The area surrounding beautiful Lake Maggiore, straddling the Swiss–Italian border, became the setting for Fromm's last years. He took up residence there in 1976, the year his last book appeared. Fromm died in the Swiss town of Muralto on March 18, 1980 (Funk, 1982).

Fromm's View of the Person

It was Fromm's continued search for answers to perplexing questions regarding the ills of society that led him to Marx and Freud. Yet in studying the theories of these twentieth century giants he began to see flaws, defects in their attempts to be scientific and deficiencies in science itself. Eventually, he began "believing in the superior value of blending empirical observation with speculation (much of the trouble with modern social science is that it often contains empirical observations without speculations) . . . I have always tried to let my thinking be guided by the observation of facts and have striven to revise my theories when the observation seemed to warrant it" (pp. 9–10). With these words, he adopted the scientific principle of empirical observation and also assigned heavy weight to speculation.

Fromm's socialist inclinations began in childhood when he talked politics with a socialist who worked with his father (Fromm, 1962). Although he considered himself at the time "not suited for political activity," after he settled in New York City he became a member of the American Socialist Party (p. 10). During the Vietnam era, he was active in the peace movement and supported peace candidate Eugene McCarthy (Funk, 1982). Fromm was a co-founder of SANE (the Organization for a Sane Nuclear Policy).

Though Fromm was a lifetime socialist, like Adler, he had serious reservations about the Soviet brand of socialism (Funk, 1982). When Fromm was in his seventies, Hausdorff (1972) asked him to define himself. Fromm replied, "[I am] a socialist who is in opposition to most Socialist and Communist parties . . ." (p. 3). He saw socialism from a humanitarian perspective and was repelled by what he regarded as Communist attempts at subjugation of the human spirit in the interest of perpetuating the power of party officials. That he thought of Soviet Communism as a failed attempt at instituting the Marxist form of socialism is seen in his derisive reference to the "perversion of the Russian revolution" (Fromm, 1962, p. 11).

Despite these reservations, Fromm's continued devotion to socialism, even in its communist form, is seen in his solution to the confused social order that existed in his time. To solve social ills he offered **humanistic communitarian socialism**, a political system embracing economic, social, and moral functions wherein ordinary citizens interact cooperatively and are actively involved in the various functions (Fromm, 1955; 1976). With this process of governing, the governed would participate in all facets of society. In so doing each person would help to ensure that all people equally enjoy the products of society, and no one is exploited. The object would be "serve the people" not "make a profit."

Fromm was also influenced by *existentialism*, the pursuit of meaningfulness in human existence, a philosophy that is considered in more detail later. He, like Horney, was concerned about the existential matter of self-realization—in Horney's terms, knowing the real self (Eckardt, 1992). Both believed that the pursuit of self-realization is innate, but only Fromm contended that people cannot find it through their own devices, even if they are free of neurosis. They require the psychological understanding that an appreciation of humans needs can offer them. Thus, a major goal of Fromm's theoretical efforts was detailing the needs that constitute striving for meaning in the sense of finding one's self, what one could become.

The sociologist and psychologist in Fromm coalesced in his attempt to assess the personality of whole societies. He believed that each society has its own unique personality. In profiling those personalities he made profound comments about the state of modern societies.

Basic Concepts: Fromm

Fromm considered a broad spectrum of social factors. He discussed such cultural influences on personality as the feudal system of the Medieval Age, the Protestant Reformation, nineteenth-century industrialization, and twentieth-century Nazism, fascism, Communism, and capitalism. Despite the diversity of his writings on social matters, his terminology remained at least somewhat psychoanalytic. Nevertheless, he was a **humanistic psychoanalyst**, one who believes in the essential worth and dignity of each person, and in the importance of helping each person to do the most with what she or he has. Speaking from this perspective, he was quite comfortable talking about human values, ethics, and meaning. In his willingness to deal with these abstractions, he followed in the steps of Jung. Fromm was convinced that psychology cannot be divorced from philosophy, ethics, sociology, or economics. He saw psychology as having the potential to debunk false ethical judgments and build objective and valid rules of conduct.

Existential Needs

According to Fromm, people are alike in that they all experience the same dilemmas and contradictions that are heart and soul of human existence. These worrisome paradoxes and conundrums are grounded in opposites that are rooted in the very essence of humans—for example, freedom–subjugation (Fromm, 1973). Thus, all persons find themselves joined with others, yet alone; living, yet dying; free, yet responsible; conscious of their potentialities, yet powerless over their limitations. People also are alike in sharing **existential needs**, needs that must be met if one's *existence is to be meaningful*, one's inner being is to be developed, one's talents are to be fully exploited, and abnormality is to be avoided. Fromm emphasized eight such needs.

Frame of Orientation and Object of Devotion.
People need a **frame of orientation,** a cognitive "map" of their natural and social worlds that enables them to organize and make sense of puzzling matters and allows them to operate in the arena of rational understanding. A frame of orientation is an important factor in a person's life whether or not it is "true" or "false." Thus, although they are falsehoods from an

objective point of view, beliefs "in the power of a totem animal, in a rain god," or in the "superiority and destiny of [my] race" may function as frames of orientation (Fromm, 1959, p. 160). In fact, false or irrational ideologies may be particularly seductive when adopted as frames of orientation. Unlike rational or scientifically based frames of orientation, political and religious doctrines may seem to offer solutions to every important problem. "The more an ideology pretends to give answers to all questions, the more attractive it is" (Fromm, 1973, p. 231).

In addition, people need some **object of devotion**, a *goal* that gives meaning to their existence and position in the world. Such an "ultimate concern" provides direction in life, reduces isolation, and permits transcendence beyond one's immediate self. Fromm wrote:

> *The objects of man's devotion vary. He can be devoted to an idol which requires him to kill his children or to an ideal that makes him protect children; he can be devoted to growth of life or to its destruction. He can be devoted to the goal of amassing a fortune, of acquiring power, of destruction, or to that of loving and of being productive and courageous. He can be devoted to the most diverse goals . . . yet . . . the need for devotion itself is a primary, existential need demanding fulfillment regardless of how this need is fulfilled (Fromm, 1973, pp. 231–232).*

These two motivational forces together provide a synthesis of one's self and one's life circumstances (Grey, 1993). A way to deal with life's puzzles and a goal to pursue in life weld the self to life circumstances.

Relatedness

Humans have an intense need for **relatedness**, "the necessity to unite with other living beings . . . [constitutes] an imperative need on the fulfillment of which man's sanity depends" (Fromm, 1955, p. 30). Among the ways that one can fulfill the relatedness need is by joining another person in a **symbiotic union**, a coupling of beings in which each meets the needs of the other while they "live 'together' " as "two, and yet one" (Fromm, 1956, p. 15). As birds feed on the pests that infest the crocodile and the rhinoceros, each member of a symbiotic pair serves the other.

There are two forms of the symbiotic union, both destructive. In the *passive* union, the person submits to the control of another person, institution, or substance that "directs him, guides him, protects him; . . . is his life and his oxygen . . ." (Fromm, 1956, p. 16). Submission takes the form of masochism in that the person is used and abused by the power to which he or she has submitted. If one becomes subservient to another person, the other becomes an idol. Subjugation can involve the whole body, as in sexual submission. Horney's moving toward others is similar. Submission can be "to fate, to sickness, to rhythmic music, to the orgiastic state produced by drugs or under hypnotic trance—in all these instances, the person renounced his integrity, makes himself the instrument of somebody or something outside of himself . . ." (p. 16). If submission is to a country or society, the subservient person may show **automaton conformity**, the condition that occurs when the person, out of fear of aloneness, gives up freedom for union with society, and she or he bends over backwards to maintain the union by strict adherence to social norms and conventions (Fromm, 1956). Constricting cultural values can lock us into a stranglehold until we do what they dictate, never what our inner voices demand (Lesser, 1992).

In the *active* symbiotic fusion, the theme of the union is domination "or to use the psychological term corresponding to masochism, sadism" (p. 16). The dominating individual seeks to escape from aloneness by making another person a part of him or her. People of this sort sadistically achieve self-inflation by incorporating another person who, in turn, masochistically worships them. Each is so dependent on the other that neither can live without the other. "The difference is only that the sadistic person commands, exploits, hurts, humiliates, and that the masochistic person is commanded, exploited, hurt, humiliated" (p. 17). While the sadist and the masochist are different, they also are the same: they have fused with another at the sacrifice of their personal integrity. Not surprisingly, a given person can react both sadistically and masochistically, usually toward different objects. Hitler, for example, was sadistic toward the German people, who worshiped him as a god. But he was masochistic in regard to fate: He rode destiny wherever it carried him, from the glory of conquest to the ignominy of suicide.

In contrast to the tragedy of symbiotic union, **mature love** "is union under the condition of preserving one's integrity, one's individuality . . . [it] is an active power of man" (p. 17). The power of love demolishes the barriers that separate people. It overcomes isolation and separateness, yet it maintains personal integrity. Love is "becoming one and yet remaining two" (p. 17). In the case of love, there is no need to inflate either one's own or the other person's image. The need for illusions regarding the other person and oneself vanishes. Fromm believed that "In the act of loving, I am one with All, and yet I am myself, a unique, separate, limited, mortal human being" (Fromm, 1955, p. 32). When one truly loves another person, one loves all of humanity, and therefore, oneself. These ideas, as you probably recognize, are reminiscent of Erikson's identity resolution at the young adult stage.

Rootedness

Rootedness is a deep craving to maintain one's natural ties and not be "separated" (Fromm, 1973). Without roots we would have to stand alone, in isolation and helplessness, not knowing who we are or where we are. Most people show progress in life by substituting new roots for old. When biological separation occurs, through birth and maturation, substitute attachments are sought, both symbolically (God, country) and emotionally (love, community). The more complete the original separation, the greater the need to form new roots that approximate the paradise of security represented by envelopment in the womb. The intensity of the craving for roots as deep and secure as the original ones can be so overwhelming that the individual may regress to a near infantile state in which dependence on some symbolic substitute for mother occurs. Such substitutes include "the soil," "nature," or "God." The healthy opposite to this regression toward a primitive state is finding new roots in "the brotherhood of man, and by freeing [oneself] from the power of the past" (Fromm, 1973, p. 233). A destructive "symbiotic" regression was illustrated by the young woman who committed suicide after her father's death. She was unable to separate herself from her father. An example of mature love is provided by Fromm himself in his marriage to Annis Freeman in 1953 (Hausdorff, 1982). He was truly one with her, but he clearly maintained his integrity as reflected in the enormous productivity he showed during the years of their marriage. In sum, one can respond to the need for roots through love, or one can take the destructive route by seeking a symbiotic relationship.

We can become detached from our roots, if, for example, we are identified as Latino, Asian, or Native American, and do not know the language or traditions of our culture. Reattachment can be a powerful experience.

Identity

Identity is the need to be aware of oneself as a separate entity, and to sense oneself as the subject of one's own actions (Fromm, 1955). The person is able to say and feel "I am I." This need also applies to seeing others as separate persons.

Members of ancient clans sometimes are unable to see themselves as existing separately from the group, expressing their identity as "I am we." Throughout history, individuals have identified themselves with social roles. Medieval roles included" I am a peasant" or "I am a lord." You may recognize these ideas as akin to "persona," the mask concept Jung developed. When the feudal system broke down, major uncertainties were created. Peasants and lords were unable to answer the questions "Who am I?" or "How do I know who I am?" They then turned to nation, class, religion, and occupation as substitutes for unique identity. People have sought to obtain a false sense of personal identity, security, or status by adhering to such social roles as "I am an American . . . a Protestant . . . an executive." Citizens living in the twentieth century also have sought to *Escape from Freedom* (Fromm, 1941) by giving up their individuality to totalitarian governments.

Fromm maintained that we must discontinue these tragic and fruitless strivings for identity. We must abandon "being" the roles that we play or "being" as others desire us. Instead we must devote ourselves to "being" separate entities who can relate to others without dissolving into them.

Unity

Unity is a sense of oneness within one's self and with the "natural and human world outside" (Fromm, 1973, p. 233). Unity can be attempted through dressing in animal skins, in efforts to unite with the animal portion of nature. It can also be attempted by subordinating one's energies to an all-consuming passion for power, fame, or property. Failures to achieve unity can evade consciousness if one anesthetizes oneself through alcohol, drugs, sexual orgies, trances, or cultist rituals. These tricks played on consciousness are attempts to restore unity within oneself. Indeed, when one is drugged or drunk one achieves a sense of unitary experience that is a kind of oneness. However, Fromm believed that this method has only temporary positive effects and is counterproductive in the long run. It cripples those who use it, estranges them from others, twists their judgment, and makes them dependent on the substance or passion in which they have chosen to invest themselves.

The true and certain path to unity lies in developing human reason and love. Religion can be the light to illuminate that path, but only if one participates in it, rather than passively submits to it. All the great religions of the world have a common goal: "to arrive at the experience of oneness, not by regressing to animal existence but by becoming fully human—oneness with man, oneness between man and nature, and oneness between man and other men" (Fromm, 1973, p. 234).

Transcendence

Transcendence is the act of transforming one's accidental and passive role of "creature" into that of an active and purposeful "creator" (Fromm, 1955). As you will soon see, this idea is much like the humanistic notions of Carl Rogers and Abraham Maslow. It can be accomplished through various means, in as simple a process as planting seeds and producing material goods or in as complicated a manner as creating art and ideas, and loving others. By creative acts humans can rise above the "creature" in them and ascend to new heights where purposefulness and freedom dwell. But "How . . . does man solve the problem of transcending himself, if he is not capable of creating, if he cannot love? There is another answer to this need for transcendence: if I cannot create life, I can destroy it. To destroy life makes me transcend it" (Fromm, 1955, p. 37). Because humans must transcend themselves, they are compelled to create or to destroy, to love or to hate. Both the destructive and the creative paths lead to transcendence. "However, the satisfaction of the need to create leads to happiness; destructiveness to suffering, most of all, for the destroyer himself" (Fromm, 1955, p. 38). It follows from this position that we must do all we can to foster creativity, a potential that exists in all of us, so that happiness prevails rather than destructiveness. Later you will read about programs suggested by Carl Rogers and B. F. Skinner that are designed to promote creativity.

Effectiveness

Effectiveness is the need to compensate for "being in a strange and overpowering world" by developing a sense of being able to do something that will "make a dent" in life (Fromm, 1973, p. 235). To be effective is to "get things done," "to accomplish," and to be a person "who has the capacity to do . . . something" (p. 235). It also offers some proof of one's existence and identity, based on the realization "I am, because I effect." People may experience joy by producing effects that are either positive or negative—making a noisy clatter, eliciting a smile from a loved one, doing what is forbidden, destroying property, or even causing terror in a victim. We first manifest effectiveness in child's play when we experience the "joy of being a cause" (p. 235). One of the earliest expressions of effectiveness is the child utterance "I do . . . I do." As you will see later in a consideration of Gordon Allport's ideas, seeking to be effective, to do for oneself, is a landmark developmental event. According to Fromm, it arises in part from being overwhelmed by parental power: ". . . to rule when one had to obey; to beat when one was beaten; to do what one was *forced to suffer*, or to do what was forbidden to do" become principle goals of the child (p. 236). As adults we are preoccupied with effects and are compelled to be the producer of those effects. We must "elicit an expression of satisfaction from the baby being nursed, a smile from the loved person, sexual response from the lover, interest from the partner in conversation" in order to feel "I am because I effect" (pp. 235–236). As with other concepts of Fromm, this one has its down side. If we cannot by our actions elicit loving feelings in others, we can, like Shelley's Frankenstein monster, cause them fear and suffering. The choice between construction and destruction is, as always, ours to make.

Excitation and Stimulation

Excitation and stimulation is the need for the nervous system to be "exercised," that is, to experience a certain amount of excitation (Fromm, 1973). The importance of this need is supported by research showing brain-generated dream activity during sleep, by the abnor-

mal reactions of infants and monkeys reared in environments lacking varied sensory stimulation, and by studies of normal young adults exposed to environments lacking in sensory
variation.

Consistent with Fromm's view, hundreds of studies on sleeping and dreaming demonstrate that the brain most be continuously stimulated, even during some phases of sleep
(see Anch, Browman, Mitler, & Walsh, 1988). Because sensory stimulation is shut off during sleep, the brain, in effect, self-stimulates. During rapid eye movements (REM) associated with dreaming, the senses act as if they are functioning, even though they are
receiving no information. Behind the eyes, ears, and other sense organs, the brain, even in
terms of its electrical activity, operates almost as if it is awake and receiving sensory input.
Thus, we can experience vivid, full color dreams that are so real we may awake perspiring
and in a state of terror (or ecstasy). When experimental subjects are deprived of dreams, by,
for example, being awakened whenever their eyes move under their lids (REM), they appear to suffer difficulties in problem-solving and may show at least short-term emotional
disturbances (see Anch, et al., 1988, for a cautionary note). Stimulation and excitation are
ever present needs.

The work of Canadian psychologist D. O. Hebb (1949) established that proper functioning of the brain requires continuously varied sensory stimulation. Primates, experimental monkeys or children in institutions were reared in stale environments where there was
little variation in what was seen or heard or felt. Compared to monkeys and children reared
amid everchanging sights and sounds, the deprived primates' brains were undernourished.
Thus their intellects and perceptual capabilities were blunted.

Hebb's collaborators placed normal college students in an environment designed to
eliminate variation in visual, auditory, and tactile stimulation (Heron, 1957). They wore dif-
fusing goggles that let in light, but no pattern or form. Also, they had their hands covered
and were exposed to a fan that generated "white noise" (all the auditory frequencies humans
can hear scrambled together). Living two to four days under these circumstances was
enough to cause the students' brains to malfunction. Not only were their electrical brain
waves abnormal, they showed bizarre hallucinations ("A tiny spaceship is firing pellets at my
arm"), emotional disturbances ("The experimenter is out to get me"), and intellectual deficiencies (poor problem-solving). Subjects were so starved for stimulation they would have
cherished a phonebook to read. Environmental conditions like these were a part of the
"brainwashing" methods used on U.S. prisoners of war by the Chinese Armed Forces during the Korean War.

According to Fromm, the need for varied sensory input can be satisfied by two kinds of
stimuli: simple or activating. **Simple stimuli** generate reflexes that call for reactions more
than actions, particularly *surface reactions* that are immediate and passive in nature. Simple
stimuli are often associated with "thrills": accidents, fires, crimes, wars, arguments, sex-re-
lated movies and advertisements, and television violence. These stimuli cause knee-jerk, automatic, gut reactions. Repeated presentation of them destroys their power.

Activating stimuli are more complicated than simple stimuli in that they cause the person to become engaged in productive activity for longer periods of time. Examples include
stimulation from generating ideas, reading novels, painting landscapes, enjoying musical
works, and being with loved ones. Unlike simple stimuli, activating stimuli engage the
"stimulee" to be a participate in the stimulation, not a passive pawn manipulated by it
(Fromm, 1973, p. 240). Rather than losing their power with repetition, truly activating

BOX 8.1 Which Needs are Most Prominent in Your Life?

Fromm believed that all of his existential needs must be met by all people. Nevertheless, he certainly wrote or spoke nothing to contradict the possibility that some needs may be more prominent in some people than in others. In fact, part of the uniqueness associated with a person's individual character may be associated with paying more attention to some needs as opposed to others. This exercise will help you appreciate this point with regard to yourself in comparison to other members of the class. Below each brief statement of the several needs you will find a scale. By placing an "X" nearer one end of the scale than the other you can indicate the degree of time and attention you devote to each need (for a given need, you can place your mark above any scale point that you deem appropriate). When you finish making the marks, you will have one more task to do before comparing your responses to those of other students.

Frame of orientation and object of devotion is a cognitive map to guide us in making sense of puzzling matters and a goal that gives meaning to our existence, respectively.

__:__:__:__:__:__:__:__:__

spend much time and   spend little time and
attention to this need   attention to this need

Relatedness is the necessity of uniting with other living beings, to relate to them; it is an imperative need on the fulfillment of which rests our sanity.

__:__:__:__:__:__:__:__:__

spend much time and   spend little time and
attention to this need   attention to this need

Rootedness is a deep craving to maintain one's natural ties and not be "separated."

__:__:__:__:__:__:__:__:__

spend much time and   spend little time and
attention to this need   attention to this need

Identity is the need to be aware of oneself as a separate entity, and to sense oneself as the subject of one's own actions.

__:__:__:__:__:__:__:__:__

spend much time and   spend little time and
attention to this need   attention to this need

Unity a sense of oneness within one's self and with the "natural and human world outside."

__:__:__:__:__:__:__:__:__

spend much time and   spend little time and
attention to this need   attention to this need

Transcendence is the act of transforming one's accidental and passive role of "creature" into that of an active and purposeful "creator."

__:__:__:__:__:__:__:__:__

spend much time and   spend little time and
attention to this need   attention to this need

Effectiveness is the need to compensate for "being in a strange and overpowering world" by developing a sense of being able to do something that will "make a dent" in life.

__:__:__:__:__:__:__:__:__

spend much time and   spend little time and
attention to this need   attention to this need

Excitation and stimulation is the need for the nervous system to be "exercised," that is, to experience a certain amount of excitation.

__:__:__:__:__:__:__:__:__

spend much time and   spend little time and
attention to this need   attention to this need

Now, draw a line from the mark on the first scale to the one on the second scale and so forth all the way down to the mark on the last scale. You have drawn your "need profile." If all students simply hold up their books so they can see each other's profiles, all can appreciate the uniqueness of individual profiles. Even though the number of need scales is small, it is likely that each student's profile line will be different from that of each other student (individual differences). That observation will confirm that people and their need patterns are unique; each person is an original, unduplicated by any other person in the world.

You will come across further considerations of "needs" later in this book. The theory of Henry Murray revolves around needs to a great extent, as does that of Abraham Maslow.

stimuli continue to be potent with repeated presentation. To Fromm, activating stimuli are healthier but require greater maturity because they do not lead as quickly to excitement. Activating stimuli require great effort, patience, discipline, concentration, tolerance, and critical thinking. Rather than reacting, the person must bring these stimuli to life.

Individual And Social Character

Individual Differences among People

Although they share common existential problems and needs, people are also different from each other. This is seen in Fromm's definition of **personality**—"the totality of inherited and acquired psychic qualities which are characteristic of one individual and which make the individual unique" (1947, p. 50). Inherited differences, and differences among people in their developmental histories, lead them to experience the same environment in different ways. People also show uniqueness "in the specific way they solve their human problem" (1947, p. 50).

Fromm actually devotes much greater attention to the concept of character than to personality. *Character*, which is based on the individual's relatedness to the world, develops at two levels: individual and social.

Individual character is the pattern of behavior characteristic of a given person—"the relatively permanent system of all noninstinctual strivings through which man relates himself to the human and natural world" (Fromm, 1973, p. 226). Because character involves deeply rooted habits and opinions, it serves a decision-making function. It is a semiautomatic process of action and thought that saves an individual from having to make deliberate, conscious decisions every time choices must be made. Character is analogous to reflexes in that it becomes activated as soon as appropriate stimuli are present, without the intervention of thoughtfulness. Once energy is channeled in a certain way, action takes place "true to character."

Individual Differences among Societies

Thus far in this book, differences among people have been emphasized. A contribution unique to Fromm is his interest in identifying character differences among entire societies.

Social character represents "the core of a character structure common to most people of a given culture . . . [and] shows the degree to which character is formed by social and cultural patterns" (1947, p. 60). Social character is clearly the product of one's society. In a sense, individual character becomes partly "lost" as it is subsumed by social character. Fromm put it this way: "the whole personality of the average individual is molded by the way people relate to each other, and it is determined by the socioeconomic and political structure of society to such an extent that . . . one can infer from the analysis of one individual the totality of the social structure in which he lives" (Fromm, 1947, p. 79).

Fromm (1947) has identified six types of social character: receptive, exploitative, hoarding, marketing, necrophilous, and productive. These social character types express themselves in how individuals relate to things and to people (including themselves). Fromm classifies the first five as *nonproductive*, those that yield at best pseudo-connection to others and, at worse, destructive relations with others. They are distorted, incomplete, or ultimately unfulfilling. In contrast, the *productive* orientation is based on *love*, the mutual intimacy that preserves individual integrity. Although the types are "ideals," one type is likely to be dominant depending on cultural values. Also, because of the interaction between individual and culture, it is always possible for individuals to affect their society.

Fromm cast each type in terms of **assimilation,** how people acquire things, and **socialization,** how people relate to others (see Table 8.1). Also, four of the five nonproductive types were divided into two pairs. One pair was labeled *symbiotic* because persons partaking of these types were involved in relations where one member submits to the exploitation of the other. The second pair is dubbed *withdrawal,* as people of these types view other people as threats who are to be treated destructively or kept at considerable distance. A fifth nonproductive type is considered separately. The only productive type is covered last. Again, symbiosis and withdrawal remind us of Horney's moving toward and moving away from others.

Persons of a **receptive** orientation experience the source of all good as being outside themselves (Fromm, 1947). According to Fromm, the receptive person ". . . believes that the only way to get what he wants—be it something material, be it affection, love, knowledge, pleasure—is to receive it from that outside source" (p. 62). People of this type receive from others, and they show their oral nature by being fond of food and drink. Receptive people are dependent, favor saying "yes" rather than "no," listening to others rather than talking, and seeking to be loved and helped rather than giving love and help. They show "gratitude for the hand that feeds them and fear of ever losing it" (p. 62).

If they are religious, they want and expect everything from God and nothing from their own efforts. If they are not religious, they may wish for a "magic helper," someone who will

TABLE 8.1   Fromm's Social Character Types

Assimilation	Socialization	
Nonproductive Orientation		
Receiving (accepting)	Masochistic (loyalty)	
		symbiosis
Exploiting (taking)	Sadistic (authority)	
Hoarding (preserving)	Destructive (assertiveness)	
		withdrawal
Marketing (exchanging)	Indifferent (fairness)	
Necrophilous	Murderous	
		unhumanize
(life into death)	(war-like)	
Productive Orientation		
Working	Loving & Reason	
		humanize
(creating)	(integrity)	

meet their every need and solve their every problem. Should they look to many people as sources of life's benefits, they will show loyalty to many people. As a result they will stretch themselves thin and frequently get caught between conflicting loyalties and promises. More generally, they tend to be optimistic and friendly. They exude confidence in life and what it has to offer, but they show extreme anxiety when they sense that a "source of supply" may be withdrawn. In terms of *assimilation*, people of this type passively receive (accepting). On the *socialization* side, they masochistically submit (loyalty).

The receptive orientation is found in societies that are stratified such that the lower classes depend on the upper classes. The "unfortunate members" are led to assume that through "sacrifice, duty, and love" they will be "taken care of" by the "fortunate" (powerful) members of society (p. 108). They rationalize their masochism by arguing that it is their "lot in life" to submit to the care of others. Peasants in a feudal society may fit this model.

People of an **exploitative** orientation also experience the source of all good as outside themselves, but rather than expecting to receive from others, they take things through force or cunning. Their orientation is to grab, steal, and manipulate, while being suspicious, cynical, jealous, and hostile. They underrate what they have and overrate what others have. Their mottos are "I take what I need" and "Stolen fruits are sweetest." Therefore, in the realm of love, stolen affection is a jewel, love freely offered by an unattached other is a lump of coal. Not surprisingly, they find married or otherwise attached people very attractive. Expressions of love are reserved for "marks": people who are "promising objects of exploitation" (Fromm, 1947, p. 65). Obviously, Fromm joined Horney in pioneering concern for the exploitive potential of humans.

Like the receptive type, exploitive individuals cannot do for themselves. They must take the fruits of others' labors, including their mental efforts. People of this type are intellectual bandits. Having no useful ideas of their own, they literally pick others' brains. More generally, they get no thrill from creating their own "goods," but they get a rush from taking others'.

In terms of traits, exploitive types are hostile and cynical. To them there are two kinds of people, those who get in the way and must be removed, and those who are useful for some selfish purpose. Instead of the optimistic, accepting attitude of the receptive type, these individuals are suspicious of others—what are they withholding? are they trying to do to me what I want to do to them? Instead of a friendly orientation to others, they are jealous—"whatever others have is better than what I have." As you might guess, they are masters of the cutting remark and the subtle putdown. In terms of assimilation, people of this type are exploiting (taking). As to socialization, they relate to others in a sadistic fashion (authority). Like the receptive type, they relate to others in a symbiotic manner, but they are the takers, not the receivers.

This orientation is represented in societies dominated by feudal lords and nineteenth-century barons, who exploited human and natural resources through power, wealth, ruthless competition, authoritarianism, and the "right of might." In more modern times, it seems well illustrated by the Soviet Union during the Stalinist era (1920s to the 1950s). Peasants were required to give what they produced to the "state" (actually Stalin and party members close to him). If they refused, they were allowed to starve; after all, they were useless. If they protested, they were "removed": sent to the infamous Soviet prisons, the gulags, or killed. Stalin was a true exploitive sadist who enjoyed sending warped communications to his victims. He would greet people warmly . . . just before having them killed (Fromm, 1973). He would assure representatives of a Soviet ethnic group that their favorite poets would not be arrested . . . they would be seized shortly thereafter.

Persons of a **hoarding** orientation differ from the two preceding types: they believe the "goods" come from the inside not the outside, from themselves not others, so security is based on an attitude of saving, of letting out as little as possible (Fromm, 1947). Rather than seeking symbiotic relations with others, they withdraw from others. They set up "a protective wall, and their main aim is to bring as much as possible into this fortified position and to let as little as possible out of it" (p. 65). Their motto is "Mine is mine, and yours is yours."

People of this type are misers about everything: money, material things, the past, love. They do not give love, they get it by owning the "beloved." Everything they had in the past which is now only a memory is still cherished. They would keep everything they have grabbed since they were old enough to grasp if they could. Thus, they are "sentimental": they ruminate endlessly about bygone feelings and experiences.

These people are sterile, "tight-lipped," even grim. Being prone to withdrawal, they are unpleasant to be around: They regard others as candidates for possession, not potential companions in a human relationship. Hoarding applies to information as well as everything else. They know much, but can do little with it, because they are rigid, bound by the extreme orderliness that is peculiar to them. Hoarding types are compulsively clean, obsessively punctual, and irritatingly obstinate. "No!" is their favorite exclamation. To say "yes" threatens them with the possibility of giving up something. They peer through the gates of their fortresses, beckoning to those who would enter and be counted among their possessions, but never venturing forth into others' world. In terms of assimilation, they are hoarding (preserving). As to socialization, they are destructive (assertiveness).

This orientation is represented by societies adopting a Puritan ethic of hard work and success, in which middle-class stability is provided through family and possession of property. North America during the late 1600s and the 1700s through the early 1800s may illustrate this kind of society. The Puritan religion was thriving during a great part of that period. Self-sufficient family farms were the basic social units of that time. Farms produced almost all that a family needed and hard work in the family interest was necessary for survival. Insofar as people had specialized professions, such as blacksmith and candlemaker, they were even more literally defined by their jobs than we are today. The European tradition of naming people for their professions came to the "new world" with the first settlers. Thus, surnames such as "Butcher" and "Goldsmith" still exist today. Nevertheless, American society of this period did not wholly fit Fromm's "hoarding" notion: The spirit of cooperation among and within family units appears to have been much greater than Fromm would have expected.

The **marketing** orientation is unique to the modern historical era in which exchanging goods for money, other goods, or services became the backbone of a "supply and demand" economy (Fromm, 1947). In this contemporary economy, supply of a commodity determined its value, not its inherent usefulness. For example, fuel is essential for running industry and automobiles and for heating homes, but its value is determined by whether it is in short supply or there is plenty of it. Thus, although the usefulness of gasoline remains constant, it is relatively inexpensive when much is available, but expensive when some world crisis makes it in short supply.

By analogy, people of this orientation experience themselves as saleable commodities whose "exchange value" depends on whether they are in short supply or not. They seek to package and sell themselves so that they seem unusual or rare and, thus, "in demand." Here is where "personality" enters the picture. While a minimum level of competence is necessary to be marketable at all, in a given profession, a great many people will possess that degree of skill. Further, in almost every profession, there will be many people with much more than minimum competence. With so many people being relatively indistinguishable in terms of skills, whether a given person stands out enough "to get hired" depends on such personality traits as " 'cheerful,' 'sound,' 'aggressive,' 'reliable,' 'ambitious' . . ." (Fromm, 1947, p. 70). People battle to distinguish themselves so that they will look like "one of a kind" and thereby appear to be in short supply. Ironically, "since success depends largely on how one sells one's personality, one experiences oneself as . . . simultaneously . . . the seller and the commodity to be sold" (p. 70).

Under these circumstances, people are not concerned with their lives or happiness, but with being saleable. They begin to feel so much like commodities that Fromm analogized them to "handbags." Each handbag must make itself more attractive than its rivals if it is going to be sold. To demand a higher price, it must look more expensive than its rivals. If it "sells" it can "feel" elated because it has been proven more "valuable" than its rivals. Conversely, if it fails to sell it will "feel" dejected, worthless.

"Like the handbag, one has to be in fashion on the personality market, and in order to be in fashion one has to know what kind of personality is most in demand" (p. 71). Helpfully, the media supplies the raw materials one needs to construct a marketable personality. Personality traits that have sold are depicted on the TV, in the movies, and in popular magazines. "The young girl tries to emulate the facial expression, coiffure, [and] gestures of a high-priced star as the most promising way to success. The young man tries to look and be like a model he sees on the screen" (p. 71). Some people do well at this game, but, in a sense, all fail in the end. One can manipulate one's traits to form a hopefully marketable commodity, but one can never be sure whether the finished product will sell. Therefore, one's self-esteem is at the mercy of the market: It is high if, on occasion, one "sells," low if one does not, and one can never predict the sales outcome for sure. Assimilation is represented here in "marketing" (exchanging) and socialization in "indifference" (fairness). Because Fromm believed that the modern capitalistic society of which you are a member clearly generates the marketing type, no further example is needed.

The **necrophilous character** is engrossed by death, dwells on it, and glories in it (Fromm, 1973). Fromm added this social character after the others. Contrary to the well-known clinical use of the term, desire to have sexual relations with corpses, in Fromm's use, *necrophilous* is *generalized* to mean a preoccupation with death. The origin of the term dates to an incident during a speech by a General Millan Astray, delivered at the onset of the Spanish Civil War (1936). When one of the General's followers shouted his favorite motto from the back of the room—"Viva la muerte!" ("Long live death!")—Spanish philosopher Miguel de Unamuno arose from the audience to express his disgust. In so doing he described "Long live death!" as a "necrophilous and senseless cry . . ." (p. 331). When Fromm reflected on this incident during the early 1960s he conceived of the new "death-loving" character.

The necrophilous type gains meaning and identity by transforming life into death. Fromm wrote: "Necrophilia in the characterological sense can be described as the passionate *attraction* to all that is dead, decayed, putrid, sickly; it is the passion to transform that which is *alive* into something *unalive*; to destroy for the sake of destruction; the exclusive interest in all that is purely mechanical. It is the passion 'to tear apart living structures' " (p. 332; emphasis eliminated). The necrophilous person extracts a feeling of power and elation from vicariously or directly participating in the transformation of life into death. Although Fromm did not explicitly refer to assimilation and socialization for this type, it is possible to extrapolate from his writings: The assimilation term would be "necrophilous" (life to death) and the corresponding socialization concept could be "murderous" (war-like). Analogous to "symbiosis" and "withdrawal," individuals of the necrophilous type might be labeled "unhumanizing" in testimony to their fascination with lifeless people.

Fromm saw the necrophilous inclination emerge for dreams and the subtle actions of people. Albert Speer, Adolf Hitler's personal architect, later his armaments minister, and possibly his only friend, had a dream that symbolically illustrated the Nazi leader's necrophilous tendencies (Fromm, 1973). In it Speer finds himself in Hitler's car. "Our drive ends at a large square surrounded by government buildings. On one side is a war memorial. Hitler approaches it and lays down a wreath" (Fromm, 1973, p. 333). And Hitler lays another wreath, and another, and another. All the while he is chanting "Jesus Maria," possibly a remnant from his Catholic upbringing. By laying the wreaths on the memorials, Hitler pays homage to death, but does so in the typical mechanical, unfeeling fashion of the necrophilous person. The chant may also be seen in symbolic terms: Hitler's religion had become death.

Other dreams of death on a grand scale are provided by Fromm to illustrate the destructive nature of the warlike, necrophilous person. One dreamer reported: "I have made a great invention, the 'superdestroyer.' It is a machine which, if one secret button is pushed that I alone know, can destroy all life in North America within the first hour, and within the next hour, all life on earth" (p. 334). Referring to another scene, the dreamer said, "I have pushed the button; I notice no more life, I am alone, I feel exuberant." This report could describe the dream of a twisted computer-game player or perhaps a deranged devotee of Dungeons & Dragons or Puppet Master.

In another dream, the mechanization of everything that so thrills the necrophilous person is well illustrated. The dreamer is at a party where young people are dancing, but their rhythm becomes slower and slower until everyone is immobile. At this moment two very large people enter the room carrying some equipment. One of them approaches a boy and bloodlessly cuts a hole in his back into which a box is inserted. The same is done to a girl by the other oversized person. Keys are inserted into the boxes and, when switched on, the boy and girl dance vigorously. The same "operation" is performed on all the other people present. They became machines whose aliveness can be switched on or off.

Illustrations of societies that spawn the necrophilous type are numerous and familiar. Some societies of this century include those that revolved around Hitler, Italian dictator Mussolini, Stalin, and the bloodthirsty Cambodian despot Pol Pot, who slaughtered two million of his people. Unfortunately, certain leaders continue to set a necrophilous tone for

BOX 8.2   Social Character Types Applied
to Societies

Now that you have considered Fromm's "social character types" it will be interesting to see how they fit your own society. Go back to Table 8.1 and give a rank of "1" to the type that you feel fits your society best. Give a rank of "2" to the type that fits next best and so forth for all six types. If everyone in your class does this exercise, your professor might be willing to poll the class to see which type was ranked highest. Each student could announce the rank given to a particular type and the professor could determine the modal rank for each type (the most frequently used rank). This could be done for all types, thereby revealing which is ranked highest on average. It would be interesting to repeat this process for some other society, such as that represented by the former Soviet Union or India. Then your society could be compared with others as to which type fits best.

their people even in the 1990s. Witness the works of Saddam Hussein and certain military leaders involved in "ethnic cleansing" during the Bosnia war.

Table 8.1 summarizes Fromm's social character types, including the only positive one, **productive orientation**—an attitude of relatedness to the world and oneself that encompasses all realms of human experience: reasoning, loving, and working (Fromm, 1947). Productive people "comprehend the world, mentally and emotionally, through love and through reason" (p. 97). The productive orientation is not concerned with practical results or "success."

The human capacity for *productive reasoning* can be used to penetrate the surface of ideas, actions and emotions, get into them, and, thereby, gain understanding of their essence. The power of *productive love* can break through walls that separate people, allowing each of us genuine understanding of other people's mental and emotional cores. Productive love is characterized by care, responsibility, respect, and knowledge (note the resemblance to Erikson's "care" at the adulthood stage). *Productive work* allows people to transform materials into other forms, using reason and imagination to visualize things not yet existing. It also promotes creativity and fruitful planning. These three orientations point to the opposite of necrophilia, **biophilia**, which is love of life (Eckardt, 1992).

In essence, the productive orientation provides an answer to the basic contradictions of human existence. It suggests that a person's main task in life is to give birth to oneself, to become what one potentially is, a theme that is elaborated by the humanists covered next. The most important product of this effort is one's own "mature and integrated" personality. This is because Fromm, like Jung, believed that every person is more than "a blank sheet of paper on which culture can write its text" (1947, p. 23). A human nature exists (Biancoli, 1992). Therefore, what is ethically good in Fromm's humanistic framework is the unfolding of personal powers according to the laws of human nature. This view led Fromm (1959) to propose a positive concept of mental health that is not just the absence of sickness but the presence of "well-being." To manifest well-being one must be aware, responsive, independent, fully active, united with the world, and able to understand that only living creatively gives meaning to life. One must be joyful in the act of living—expressing joy throughout one's whole body—and concerned with being rather than having (Fromm, 1976). Failure to make use of one's innate, human powers results in unhappiness, psychological disturbance, and neurosis. It appears that Fromm saw no former or present major society able to reliably generate productive types.

Evaluation

Contributions

Many of Fromm's important contributions revolve around reinterpretations of institutions and Freudian theory, his groundbreaking social character research in an actual society, and his influential books.

The Family Reconceived as the Agent of Society

Fromm (1973) saw the family as the psychological agency through which a child acquires the core of social character shared by most other children partaking of the same culture. Parents are the representatives of a society's atmosphere and spirit, which they transmit just by being the persons they are. An important developmental aim is for parents to help the child "desire to act" as it "has to act." This is best seen when social and individual character coincide. An example is a person of the hoarding orientation who saves money, purchasing necessities only, and gains psychological and social satisfactions by doing business in a society that values economic efficiency and thrift. An authoritarian, exploitative person who listens attentively and frequently to ideological speeches about political forces so powerful that human submission is the only alternative, also achieves dual satisfactions. Thus, individual psychological traits cement the social structure.

The Sociocultural Reinterpretation of Freud

Fromm (1941) suggested that Freud, in proposing his psychosexual stages, got the causal relationship between erogenous zones and personality traits backwards. "Oral" personality is not due to physiologically pleasant oral sensations. Rather, personality, in the form of a receptive character, feeds back on physiology to create the "oral language of the body."

Contrary to Freud, the personality originates as a reaction to social experiences with other people. Recognizing that parental care or affection is given only under conditions of surrender, the child becomes fearful and experiences a weakening of its strength and self-confidence. The child then gives up its natural self-initiative and learns to direct its energies toward "an outside source from which the fulfillment of all wishes will eventually come" (Fromm, 1941, p. 292).

Fromm (1947) also reinterpreted Freud's concept of the Oedipus complex. In Fromm's view, it represents the child's struggle for individual freedom from parental authority rather than an awakening of genital sensations. The child's fight is to minimize the effects of guilt or submission, which threaten to weaken the self, by seeking to become a full-fledged human being rather than a cultural robot.

Fromm maintained a lively interest in the Freudian therapeutic concepts of "free association," "transference," and "insight" (Bacciagaluppi, 1989). Nevertheless, he had reservations about the strict Freudian interpretations of these concepts. In fact, there was almost nothing about Freud's theory that Fromm accepted without raising major questions.

Social Character in Mexican Villagers: Implications for Diversity

Fromm and Maccoby (1970) undertook a field study of social character in a Mexican village as a test of Fromm's (1947) theory. They wanted to demonstrate that the social character common to a group could be assessed and related to socioeconomic variables. In so doing, perhaps unwittingly, they showed diversity *within* a culture.

An open-ended "interpretative questionnaire" of about ninety items was given to 406 adults (95 percent of all residents) of a Mexican farming village. Social character among the villagers was found to be high in receptive orientation (44 percent) and low in exploitative orientation (11 percent). Men were more receptive than women, who were more hoarding. Sociopolitically, villagers were most often submissive (49 percent) rather than democratic (7 percent) or rebellious (7 percent). Fixations involving parents were almost entirely directed toward the mother (96 percent). Fourteen percent of adult male villagers were alcoholic. Of them, 80 percent were receptive in character, compared with only 37 percent of abstainers.

The results pointed to three main categories of social character mixtures: productive–hoarding, nonproductive–receptive, and productive–exploitative. These social adaptations corresponded to three distinct socioeconomic conditions: free landowner, landless day laborer, and a kind of business entrepreneur, respectively. The hoarding orientation was the one "best adapted" to the economic demands of peasant farming in the village. By contrast, the receptive peasant, who was seen as being "out of tune" with the world was poorly adapted. It follows that women were better adapted than men. Interestingly, even the type of crop landholders chose to plant was related to social character. Productive–hoarding landowners tended to plant rice, a crop requiring harder work but promising higher profit. Receptive landholders tended to plant sugarcane, a crop requiring less work but twice the time to grow, and promising less profit. Overall, support was provided for the general hypothesis that "social character is the result of the adaptation of human nature to given socioeconomic conditions" (p. 230).

Interesting Books on Popular Issues

Fromm dealt directly with sweeping societal, ethical, and political issues and related them to the great twentieth-century socioeconomic systems. Countless people have been influenced by his best-selling books. *Escape from Freedom* (1941) introduced a novel idea that was alien to democratic people at the time. Contrary to the "universal human desire to be free," all people at some times, and some people all the time, may desire to relinquish their freedom to "the state" or to another person. *The Sane Society* (1955) discusses the insanity of many societies and offers some alternatives. *The Art of Loving* (1956), entitled like current self-help books, taught people that to be in love is not merely to desire another person. It is becoming one with another but remaining oneself. His 1973 book, *The Anatomy of Human Destructiveness*, is a cogent and provocative commentary on the forces promoting life and death in contemporary culture. It is a chronicle of the evil and sickness that characterized such necrophilous figures as Nazi leaders Hitler and Himmler, the architects of the holocaust. His 1976 book, *To Have or to Be?*, discusses humankind's critical need to control irrational social forces and proposes guidelines for a new society.

Limitations

Fromm may be regarded as more of a philosopher than a scientist. His theory consists of rather isolated categories of concepts that are not systematically related to one another. For example, those under the category labels "needs" and "character types." In fact, there appears to be no conceptual glue capable of sticking these distinct categories of concepts together. They deal with different domains, in the one case the psychological realm, in the other, the social arena. At best, Fromm writes about "needs" in the context of "social character." Even here he does not make a direct conceptual link between categories in the manner that Freud ties id, ego, and superego to the psychosexual stages.

Also troublesome is the apparent abandonment or redefinition of major concepts somewhere between 1955 (*The Sane Society*) and 1973 (*The Anatomy of Human Destructiveness*). The perfectly meaningful needs "relatedness," "identity," and "transcendence" are displaced by the equally important "unity," "effectiveness," and "excitation–stimulation." Fromm may have intended "unity" as a replacement for "identity" and "effectiveness" as a substitute for "transcendence," which, in 1973, he dismissed in a footnote. The newer concepts are unique and worthwhile, but they do seem to overlap with the earlier notions that they may have been intended to replace. While "excitation–stimulation" seems a reasonable addition in view of developments in neuroscience, the apparent abandonment of the useful notion "relatedness" is difficult to understand—and Fromm does not explain it. A theory that changes for reasons other than in response to hard evidence belongs more in the realm of philosophical speculation than science.

Fromm's social character types, as interesting as they are, nevertheless involve serious shortcomings. To confirm that a person has a trait, a component of personality, one must be able to look at the person's behavior in a given situation and assume that it will *generalize* to many other different situations. Only then, it is widely assumed, can one say the person has a trait corresponding to the behavior. Unfortunately, personality psychologists have had major difficulties demonstrating that such generalization is warranted (Allen, 1988a, 1988b; Allen & Potkay, 1981, 1983a; Mischel, 1968, 1977, 1984). People show a tendency to vary in their behavioral performances from one situation to the next and from one occasion to the next. If making the critical generalization at the individual level involves considerable risk, how much more cautious must we be in generalizing a social character type to many if not most members of a society? Given that people vary within themselves from occasion to occasion, as total persons they certainly must differ one from the other to a large degree. In view of the great variability within and among individuals, it is tenuous to assume that many, much less most, members of a society are "marketing types," or "receptive types," or any other type. Without much firm evidence—and there is little available—it simply is unreasonable to believe that even a simple majority of any large society's population share the same type. Thus, *The Handbook of Social Psychology* through its first two editions alluded to this problem of generalization in its chapter on "national character," which was acknowledged to be equivalent to "social character" (Lindzey, 1954; Lindzey & Aronson, 1969). Apparently the problem became insurmountable. By the third edition, the chapter on "national character" was deleted (Lindzey & Aronson, 1985). Perhaps the social character types should be recast as personality types.

While Fromm was an open person, he still had Western biases. In his theorizing he virtually condemned melting into the collective, thereby losing oneself. From the Western *individualistic* perspective, his point is well taken. However, from the standpoint of many *collectivistic* Asian cultures, "melting into the collective" has been a tried and true survival technique for millennia.

In regard to scientific backing for Fromm's theory, a computer search failed to turn up current, scientific research done to support his theory. Either Fromm's concepts are difficult to transform into concrete terms so they can be studied scientifically, or they are too alien to modern scientific thinking to be of interest to contemporary sociopsychological scientists. Even Fromm's own research on the Mexican village failed to support the existence of a single, core character that fit most villagers. A diversity of character orientations was supported instead. Only when and if Fromm's theory generates scientific data can it be legitimately called "scientific."

Fromm's overemphasis on the negative side of human nature and culture was determined, in part, by factors associated with the German militarism and anti-Semitism present during his formative years. Other social and individual influences may have contributed as well, for example, the childhood experiences of isolation and disturbances noted in his biography. Whatever the reasons for this pessimistic outlook, one could certainly argue that it is not an accurate picture of reality. Perhaps Fromm was wrong in depicting humans as struggling to overcome the evil, misery, and conformity that, he thought, constitutes their basic nature.

Finally, one might think that Fromm, with his emphasis on "culture," would have anticipated modern diversity concerns. While such an argument can be advanced—witness the Mexican village study—another seems easier to make. Instead of proposing diversity within a society, Fromm's theory collapses across sources of variation, such as gender, ethnicity, and religion. As a result, diversity is swallowed up by "the core of a characteristic structure common to most people of a given culture . . ." (Fromm, 1947, p. 60).

Conclusions

Maybe Fromm was more of a philosopher than a scientific theorist. Then so be it; science is not the only legitimate approach to personality. Whatever label applies, he was an original thinker and one of our most helpful commentators on modern life. Perhaps his concepts have received relatively little attention because they are complex and thus difficult to study. Also, maybe he was realistic rather than pessimistic. In fact, it is possible to see optimism emerging from many of his ideas (Biancoli, 1992; Eckardt, 1992).

While his Mexican village study may not have supported his point of view very strongly, it does have important implications for diversity: Even in a small village, people differ along several diversity dimensions. Another indirect contribution relating to diversity is found in his notion of human nature, a general human inclination that rides roughshod over notions of racial differences (Biancoli, 1992). Diversity has many legitimate dimensions, but, as will be argued forcefully later, racial variation is not among them.

Fromm had a talent for selecting the very topics that interest people the most. Further, he could get right to the heart of problems with modern societies and with contemporary humans. As a person, Fromm inspired love and admiration from his friends and colleagues. "I can see his piercing blue eyes full of understanding, of love, expressive of his being. . . . They could cry with the pain of others or Fromm's own pain, but they also knew how to laugh to tears at some funny or jocular event. His tears or his laughter touched the heart of the other" (Silva–Garcia, 1989, p. 245).

He was also a pioneer. As an early psychological humanist he did much to shape current humanistic thought, the topic of the next two chapters. His conceptions of love, productivity, and union with other people and nature were nutrients added to the fertile soil out of which psychological humanism grew. Unfortunately, the humanistic theorists have made little effort to remind us of Fromm's contributions. Therefore, in beginning to read the chapters on humanism, you will need to actively recall his groundbreaking ideas.

Summary Points

1. Fromm praised Freud, but took a sociopsychological stance, a natural position for one whose training was academic rather than medical. Fromm was born into a "neurotic" German family of Jewish descent. The suicide of a young woman following the death of her father led Fromm to Freud. He was also greatly influenced by Marxism and by existential philosophy. The massive destruction and governmental doubletalk associated with World War I shaped his humanistic and antiwar orientations.

2. Each of us has a "frame of orientation," a cognitive map of our worlds that helps us make sense of puzzling matters. We all also have "objects of devotion": goals that give meaning to our existence. Relatedness is the need to unite with other living beings that can take on two symbiotic forms: (1) one person masochistically submits to another and (2) one person sadistically dominates another. The positive alternative is mature love in which there is union with another, but maintenance of one's personal integrity.

3. In rootedness, the alternatives are destructive pursuit of substitutes for that secure, dependent state represented by the womb or finding new roots in the brotherhood of man. The recovery of lost roots has major benefits. Identity is the need to be aware of oneself as a separate entity. Tragically we tend to use nations, races, or religions as sources of identity. Unity is a sense of inner oneness. We can seek it through the quest for power, fame, and property. Having failed to achieve unity, we may turn to some drug or passion. The productive alternative is love and reason.

4. Transcendence is the act of transforming one's accidental and passive role of creature into that of an active and purposeful creator. The alternative to creativity is destruction. Effectiveness is the need to compensate for "being in a strange and overpowering world." To be effective is to accomplish and to resist parental domination. If we cannot be effective through love of others, we can affect others by causing them to suffer.

5. Excitation and stimulation is the nervous system's need to be "exercised." The brain must be stimulated even during sleep. Needed sensory input is of two kinds: (1) simple and (2) activating. People differ among themselves: the essence of "personality." However, character, based on the individual's relatedness to the world, was more emphasized by Fromm. Individual character is a personal pattern of behavior that is deeply rooted in habits and opinions.

6. Fromm postulated six social character types, five nonproductive and one productive. Each is cast in terms of assimilation and socialization. The nonproductive types are divided into two pairs and one isolated type. One of two symbiotic nonproductive types is receptive—oriented to experience the source of all good as being outside oneself. People of this type take from and depend on others, they do not give. They show unusual loyalty to their providers and may display sacrifice, duty, and love regarding the powerful people who care for them.

7. A second symbiotic type is exploitive. This type grabs, steals, and manipulates and is cynical, suspicious, and jealous. One of two "withdrawal" types are hoarding. People of this type build a fortress, take inside what is theirs, and allow others to enter only if they will become possessions. A second withdrawal type is marketing—oriented to an exchange of goods for objects of value or services. These people are overwhelmed by the supply and demand economies in which they are immersed. They seek to take on personality traits that will "sell."

8. The last nonproductive type is necrophilous—engrossed by death. The necrophilous person extracts a feeling of power and elation from vicariously or directly participating in the transformation of life into death. Necrophilous themes show up in dreams in the form of mechanically paying homage to the dead, envisioning oneself in possession of the power to destroy the world, and seeing people as robots whose aliveness can be turned off or on. Societies ruled by the despots of World War II and present nations ruled by war lovers provide fertile ground for this type.

9. People of the productive orientation have an attitude of relatedness to the world, and themselves, that encompasses reasoning, loving, and working. Productive people are biophilic, lovers of life. They break down walls between people and relate to others in terms of care, responsibility, respect, and knowledge. Out of thoughts about the productive type came Fromm's ideas about well-being. Fromm saw the family as an institution headed by parents who transmit their society's atmosphere and spirit to children.

10. Contrary to Freud, oral personality feeds back on physiology to create an "oral language of the body." The Oedipus complex arises from a struggle for freedom from parental authority. Fromm's research in a Mexican village produced evidence of three character mixtures. It is an example of diversity, even in a small village. His books dealt with sweeping issues that were of interest to many people. However, his theory was more philosophical than scientific and lacked coherence. Further, concepts tended to drop out of his theory and new ones entered with little explanation. Fromm's social character types entail difficulties and his theory has received little scientific support. Also, he showed Western biases. Further, his conceptions may be seen as smothering diversity. Yet his Mexican village study results and his notions relevant to "race" relate well to diversity. He was a warm person, an original thinker, and a pioneer humanist.

Running Comparison

Theorist	*Fromm in Comparison*
Freud	He was ambivalent about Freud's scientific contributions, de-emphasized biological causation, thought the Oedipal complex was due to a struggle for freedom from parents, but talked about free association, transference, and insight, and partially agreed that religion is an illusion. His social character types bore some resemblance to Freud's adult, fixated types.
Jung	Like Jung (and Adler) he was heavily influenced by WWI, and willing to talk about abstractions such as value, ethics, and meaning. Identifying self with social roles was akin to Jung's personas. He also believed that people are not like blank tablets at birth (e.g., human nature may be innate).
Erikson	His productive love is similar to Erikson's care of the adulthood stage. His mature love is similar to resolution at Erikson's young adult stage.
Carl Rogers	Transcendence was akin to some of Rogers' humanistic ideas (and Maslow's). Like Rogers (and Skinner), he was concerned about creativity.
Abraham Maslow and Henry A. Murray	Like these two theorists, he was concerned about needs.
Horney	They both embraced the pursuit of self-realization. Her "moving toward others" is similar to passive symbiosis. They both recognized the exploitive potential of humans.

Essay/Critical Thinking Questions

1. How might Fromm have been affected by war in contrast to the way he was, in fact, affected? In answering, retrace Fromm's experiences, during his school days and at other times.

2. Fromm was a socialist like Adler. Out of that tradition, did he come up with a concept comparable in importance to social interest? Defend why he did or did not.

3. Select one of Fromm's needs, the one that you think fits reality the best. Can you illustrate how it has been manifested in your own experience, direct or indirect?

4. Can you describe a symbiotic relationship from your experience? Select a couple from your experience who have such a relationship and describe the way they interact.

5. Which social character type fits a modern society of your selection (but not your own or others covered in the text)? Defend your decision with examples.

6. Could you argue that a certain historical figure was a necrophilous type? Select a figure—other than the ones listed in the text—and give examples that show this individual to be necrophilous.

7. Could you do number 6 over again, but this time select a figure who is a productive type? Be sure to use examples.

8. Look at your own community, the one you grew up in. What social character fits it best? If more than one type fits, what are the types? Give examples.

9. Can you defend the application of a social character type to an entire society? Argue that a type might be reasonably seen as fitting a whole society, or suggest why it will never fit everyone.

10. Can you explain why Fromm's concepts have been so lightly researched?

E-mail Interaction

(Write the author at mfbpa@wiu.edu)
Forward any of the following or phrase your own.

1. Why were socialist leanings relatively common among the theorists covered so far?
2. Explain why Fromm was so popular among the public.
3. Are many societies of today slipping into a more exploitive, necrophilous direction?
4. Why did Fromm emphasize the personalities of societies as much or more than the personalities of people?
5. Was Fromm really a humanist?

9

EVERY PERSON IS TO BE PRIZED: CARL ROGERS

- If it were possible to regard everyone you encounter in an unconditionally positive manner, would it be the right thing to do?
- When what you experience is out of tune with your self-concept, what becomes of you?
- Is there anything psychologists can do to make world peace more likely?
- Are therapists doing their jobs if they refuse to offer the people they serve any advice?
- Should therapists and the people they serve be equal partners in the therapeutic process?

Carl Rogers

Psychologists often classify personality theories into categories: the psychoanalytic tradition begun by Freud, the humanistic tradition represented by Carl Rogers and Abraham Maslow, the behavioral tradition popularized by B. F. Skinner, the cognitive tradition represented by George Kelly, and the trait tradition championed by Raymond Cattell, Hans Eysenck, and Gordon Allport. Rogers is one of the leading figures in modern psychology because of the impact he has had on so many psychologists, professionals from other disciplines, and laypeople. His ideas have also received more systematic research, study, and validation than those of any other humanistic psychologist, and also more than some other theorists covered in this book.

Rogers, the Person

Carl Ransom Rogers was born on January 8, 1902, in Oak Park, Illinois. The fourth of six children, he was "tender and easily hurt, yet feisty and even sarcastic in his own way," since this was necessary to survive in family give-and-take (Kirschenbaum, 1979, p. 5). His home atmosphere was marked by fundamentalist religious practices, little social mixing, and a firm belief in the virtue of hard work. Carl even recalled experiencing a slight feeling of "wickedness" while drinking his first bottle of soda pop.

Carl was a lonely, "solitary boy, who read incessantly, and went all through high school with only two dates" (Rogers, 1961, p. 6). An outstanding student, he was nicknamed "Mr. Absent-Minded Professor" by his practical family. He loved reading the Bible and adventure stories, as well as creating stories of his own. During adolescence, he became fascinated with night-flying moths, which he observed and bred year-round, and he enjoyed reading advanced, scientific books on agriculture.

> *There was no one to tell me that Morison's Feeds and Feeding was not a book for a fourteen-year-old, so I ploughed through its hundreds of pages learning how experiments were conducted—how control groups were matched with experimental groups, how conditions were held constant by randomizing procedures, so that the influence of a given food on meat production or milk production could be established. I learned how difficult it is to test a hypothesis. I acquired a knowledge of and a respect for the methods of science in a field of practical endeavor (Rogers, 1961, p. 6).*

As you will see, Rogers fruitfully applied his knowledge of scientific procedure learned at this early date and later in graduate school. However, he used it more to show that his therapy was effective, to acknowledge the biological side of humans, and to render his concepts testable, than as a comprehensive approach to understanding people.

As an undergraduate at the University of Wisconsin, Rogers majored in agriculture and history. Later he dropped these initial majors, became quite religious, and began a curriculum aimed at the ministry. He was one of twelve American students selected to travel to China for a World Student Christian Federation Conference. It proved "a most important experience" in stretching his thinking and teaching him that sincere and honest people could have very different beliefs. Much later in life he was to lose his religious zeal because of his objection to "original sin" (Thorne, 1990). He just was not able to accept that humans are inherently flawed by the mark of sin. Still later he reconsidered the Christianity preached by those who see humans as partakers of a divine nature.

The trip to China was an intellectually liberating experience, but, because it was, he found himself withdrawing from family traditions. His newfound independence of thought caused "great pain and stress" in his relationship with his parents, but "looking back on it I believe that here, more than at any other one time, I became an independent person" (Rogers, 1961, p. 7).

In 1924, Rogers married Helen Elliott, a classmate of his in second grade and his first date in college. Helen, an art major, was a gentle, straightforward person whose good sense and willingness to think openly about real issues appealed to Rogers. Her "steady and sustaining love and companionship during all the years since has been a most important and enriching factor in my life" (Rogers, 1961, p. 7). Carl credits their two children, David and Natalie, with "teaching me far more about individuals, their development, and their relationships than I could ever have learned professionally" (Rogers, 1961, p. 12). David later became an administrator in a medical setting, and Natalie worked with her father as a cotherapist in encounter groups.

Rogers studied religion at Union Theological Seminary, which had the most liberal such program in the country. However, Teachers College, Columbia University was right across the street. Perhaps partly because his disaffection with religion was beginning to emerge, he enrolled at Columbia and soon drifted into child psychology, "just following the activities which interested me" (Rogers, 1961, p. 9). After receiving his Ph.D. in 1928, he worked for several years at a child guidance center in Rochester, N.Y. During these early professional years, Rogers soaked up the views of Freud. He found these ideas to be in great conflict with the rigorous, experimental aspects of his academic training. Relying on his own clinical experiences with people, he began formulating a person-centered point of view: The person seeking guidance should choose the direction of personality change. Unlike Freudian psychoanalysts, he would not adopt the role of authoritarian doctor vis-à-vis a passive, subservient patient, because "it is the [person] who knows what hurts, what directions to go, what problems are crucial, what experiences have been deeply buried" (Rogers, 1961, pp. 11–12). In fact, he rejected the **medical model**, the idea that people with psychological problems are sick and need some sort of treatment, at least analogous to medication, that will make them normal again (Rogers, 1987a). Consistent with this orientation, he used the term *client* instead of *patient*. He did not want to bring clients back to normal, that is, back to average. Instead he endorsed the **growth model**: he wanted to help people "remove whatever blocks to growth exist" so they could move beyond being normal or average (p. 40).

In subsequent years, Rogers held teaching, therapy, and administrative positions at Ohio State University, the University of Chicago, and the University of Wisconsin. In 1947, he served as president of the American Psychological Association. He was the first psychologist in the association's history to receive both the Scientific Contribution Award and the Distinguished Professional Contribution Award.

Rogers, in the years before he died, continued to work very actively in La Jolla, California, at the Center for Studies of the Person, which he co-founded: "The days are not long enough to accomplish my purposes" (communication to Charles R. Potkay, May 9, 1985). Rosalind Cartwright, one of his former colleagues, has spoken of him as a living example of his own theory, "a man who has continued to grow, to discover himself, to test himself, to be genuine, to review his experiences, to learn from it, . . . to live honestly, fully, in the best human sense" (Kirschenbaum, 1979, p. 394).

> *So, who am I? I am a psychologist whose primary interest, for many years, has been in psychotherapy . . . I rejoice at the privilege of being a midwife to a new personality—as I stand by with awe at the emergence of a self, a person, as I see a birth process in which I have had an important and facilitating part (Rogers, 1961, pp. 4–5).*

Carl Rogers died unexpectedly on February 4, 1987 following surgery for a broken hip (Gendlin, 1988). At the time he had been particularly energetic and effective. In his last years he traveled the world, from South Africa to the Soviet Union with a stop-off in Northern Ireland, in order to promote world peace and an end to conflict between warring groups (see Rogers & Ryback, 1984; Rogers & Malcolm, 1987; Rogers & Sanford, 1987; Rogers, 1987b). Fortunately, he published a number of articles during these final years. Many of them are used in the pages that follow to help me help you better understand this extraordinary individual and his contributions to people everywhere.

BOX 9.1   The Real Rogers: Not So Emotionally Neutral,
Not So "Equal," Not Really a Counselor,
but a Pioneer Clinical Contributor to
Understanding Diversity Issues

Being a world-famous person, a figure larger than life, Rogers came to be regarded in stereotypic fashion. Textbook writers and some teachers have come to view him as someone who (1) never became angry, much less directed verbal aggression to someone during therapy; (2) who believed in the absolute equality of therapist and client; (3) who never showed strong emotion during therapy; (4) who believed that empathy was a passive process in which the therapist merely listens to clients and becomes a mirror in which they can see their own emotions; and (5) who regarded himself as a counselor and was heavily identified with that area. None of these perceptions of Rogers were true, at least not in the absolute terms they sometimes have been stated.

While conducting conflict resolution groups composed of black and white South Africans, Rogers became enraged when a white psychologist claimed that one of the young black revolutionaries was just trying to "get attention" (Hill–Hain & Rogers, 1988). "That was just grossly untrue . . . one white guy got up and going hit [the white psychologist] and I exploded at him too" (p. 62). In the same interview Rogers said, "I draw the line when I feel that one person is hurting another person in the group" (p. 65). He also referred to this event when making the point that no one is always able to step into another person's emotional shoes, not even himself. "That's why I offered no apology for exploding at [the white psychologist]" (p. 65).

During one of his South African group sessions, Rogers was strongly affected when a key black participant left the group (Hill–Hain & Rogers, 1988). As he sat on the floor, in the middle of the group, absorbing the agony of South African blacks, he began to cry. It was not because others were in tears. It was because he felt like "one of the group in every sense" (p. 68). This kind of reaction was rare for him—"I've been in enough groups that it takes quite a lot to really touch me personally" (p. 68)—but again, he had no apologies.

Rogers agreed with a critic's condemnation of person-centered therapists who show absolute commitment to acting as nothing more than a sounding board, misunderstandings of empathy, and thoughtless commitment to equality between the therapist and client. "I totally agree with her . . . in deploring the inauthentic, mechanical, wooden, dogmatic, client-centered therapist. In fact, I probably feel worse about such therapists than they do, because I feel personally offended" (Rogers, 1987c). In a similar vein, Rogers wrote of empathy: "It is regarded superficially; it is regarded as passive when you just sit back and listen. To be really empathic is one of the most active experiences I know. You have to really understand what it feels like to this person in this situation. . . . To really let oneself go into the inner world of this other person is one of the most active, difficult, and demanding things that I know" (Rogers, 1987a; p. 45).

To address the issue of client–therapist equality, Rogers considered the questions he would pose for himself before each therapy session: " 'Can I be totally present to this client? Can I be with him or her?' . . . It would never occur to me to ask myself, 'Can I make this relationship an equal one?' " (p. 38). In fact, relationships in Rogerian therapy sometimes are not equal; they are tilted in the direction of the client or person. If Rogers and an African-American person were in therapy, as was sometimes the case when he was at the University of Chicago, he would give himself over to being a student undergoing instruction in the African American experience. Only when an African American client communicated that Rogers was adequately schooled would he attempt to feel as one with him or her. This procedure would be profitably adopted by all therapists who have clients of a different ethnicity than their own. Another of Rogers's diversity contributions is seen in his recollections of forty-six years as a psychologist. Rogers (1974) counted among his accomplishments evidence that his theory was having influence on those who deal with interracial and intercultural relationships.

Rogers is often identified with counseling, a multidisciplinary pursuit often practiced by nonpsychologists and people without doctorates. Even the longtime colleague who wrote Rogers's obituary regarded Rogers as a founder of counseling as a disci-

BOX 9.1 *Continued*

pline, and considered him highly identified with counseling (Gendlin, 1988). In response to Gendlin's "fine memorial," Donald E. Super (1989), who had known Rogers since 1935, acknowledged counseling's debt to Rogers. He also pointed to the fact that Rogers's therapy section was called the Chicago Counseling Center and that his 1942 book was entitled *Counseling and Psychotherapy*. Then he wrote, "But Carl remained a psychotherapist, out of the mainstream of counseling psychology, a member of the Clinical but not of the Counseling Division [of the American Psychological Association]" (p. 1161).

In view of these facts, why include *counseling* in the title? Ray Bixler (1990), a Rogers student, indicated that he and other students in Rogers's graduate seminar were consulted by their professor concerning an appropriate book title. Professor and students decided on *counseling* because they thought it might recruit counselors to client centered therapy and on *psychotherapy* because the term was at the heart of their professional identities. Thus, it seems, Rogers was primarily identified as a psychotherapist, but he was open to sharing his methods with others.

Rogers's View of the Person

Rogers's point of view revolves around a subdiscipline of psychology he helped to found. **Humanistic psychology** emphasizes the present experience and essential worth of the whole person, promotes creativity, intentionalism, free choice, and spontaneity, and fosters the belief that people can solve their own psychological problems. It gained momentum during the 1950s and early 1960s with the publication of several important books (Maslow, 1954, 1959, 1962; Buhler, 1962; Rogers, 1961, 1970) and a flagship journal, the *Journal of Humanistic Psychology*, founded in 1961. Proponents of humanistic psychology proclaimed their movement a "major breakthrough," because of the primary importance it placed on understanding the entire person, "the functioning and experience of a whole human being" (Bugental, 1964, p. 25). This emphasis also characterizes psychology's holistic (Angyal, 1965), organismic (Goldstein, 1939), and Gestalt (Perls, 1969) points of view, in which every person is understood in a comprehensive and integrative manner as being more than the simple sum of his or her parts (Kohler, 1947).

Humanistic psychology emerged from two other philosophical orientations. **Existentialism** is an approach to understanding each person's most immediate experience, the conditions of his or her existence, and the necessity of exercising freedom of choice in a chaotic world (Binswanger, 1963; Boss, 1963; Kierkegaard, 1954; May, Angel, & Ellenberger, 1958; Merleau–Ponty, 1963; van Kaam, 1963, 1965, 1969). The origin of humanistic psychology was closely tied to developments in the application of existentialism to psychology. Existentialists encourage psychologists to get inside each person's world, to understand how that person lives, moves, and experiences his or her "being-in-the-world" (Heidegger, 1949). The critical existential concept *being* refers to a condition that is unique to each entity, whether it is a person or a grain of sand, and that transcends the particular qualities of the entity (size, weight, color). Being cannot be assessed by the usual scientific or psychoanalytic methods. It can only be intuitively grasped.

Existentialists also encourage psychologists to value consciousness and personal responsibility (Frankl, 1963). Human freedom is defined not as freedom *from* responsibility but freedom *to accept* responsibility. Thus, one cannot rely on upbringing, early experience, heredity, or present environment to shape oneself. One must make oneself. This rather total responsibility for oneself can be burdensome and even frightening (Sartre, 1957). For this reason, existentialists often write about nothingness, alienation, despair, absurdity, and anxiety.

Although humanistic psychologists have been influenced by the existential concept of personal responsibility, their outlook is typically more positive. Humanists stress the unique capacities of each individual for self-realization and personal growth, not his or her despair, alienation, and anxiety. They assign greater importance than other personality theories to the study of choice, joy, love, creativity, and authenticity. In contrast to proponents of classic or methodological behaviorism (Watson, 1930/1959), humanistic psychologists do not believe that humans begin their lives as blank sheets of paper on which the environment writes its text. Instead, like Fromm, they see the aim of each person's life as an unfolding of inherent powers present in human nature. They stress the uniquely human aspects of experience, including personal choice, interpersonal relationships, intentions, purposes, and transcendental or spiritual experiences (Bugental, 1964).

The second orientation contributing to humanistic psychology is a method of addressing reality that is a strong companion to existentialism. **Phenomenology** involves an attitude of discovery that encompasses a search for essential issues, an emphasis on consciousness, the necessity of describing experience, and a desire to grasp reality as each individual uniquely perceives it. This subjective approach to knowledge and understanding is a major characteristic of humanistic psychology (Husserl, 1961; Heidegger, 1949). "The only reality I can possibly know is the world as I perceive and experience it at this moment. The only reality you can possibly know is the world as YOU perceive and experience it at this moment. And the only certainty is that those perceived realities are different. There are as many 'real worlds' as there are people!" (Rogers, 1980, p. 102). An experience is real for the experiencer at the time it is experienced. That an experience is unique to whoever has it was acknowledged by Rogers when he used such qualifiers as "real for me" and "based on my experience" in his writings and conversation. This is not to say that there is no objective world, one we can all agree on. Rather it acknowledges the subjective world and gives it at least equal status with the objective world.

On the one hand, it is up to each person to decide what he or she is to do or to be, based on an individualized vantage point of perception and experience. On the other hand, a person should leave how other persons behave and how they lead their lives up to them. Thus, each person must assume personal responsibility for his or her own decisions and for no one else's. Some psychologists believe that Rogers is wrong to refuse the role of expert therapist and answer clients' questions, such as "What do you think I should do?" Right up to the last year of his life, Rogers refused to accede to critics' wishes that he tell others how to live their lives (Hill–Hain & Rogers, 1988).

Apart from questions of scientific truth, the phenomenological approach has particular implications for studying persons. If we wish to understand a person, we need to get inside his or her individual world of meaning. We do so by showing **empathy**, sensing and participating in the emotions of others. Thus, humanistic psychologists are less interested in studying behavior as an empirical or neurophysical event than they are in investigating the meaning that each person attaches to what she or he does.

As theorists and therapists, therefore, humanistic psychologists seek to avoid "the sort of scientific detachment pretended to or achieved at great cost by other orientations"

(Bugental, 1964, p. 24). They seek to validate their findings through subjective experience rather than relying solely on impersonal, objective criteria such as statistical methods and experimental tests. This approach has made it necessary to discover new methods for studying human experience. Like Gordon Allport, humanistic psychologists typically emphasize the *idiographic* approach: the belief that meaningful and generally applicable discoveries will come from understanding one case at time. As Rogers writes, "What is most personal is most general" (1961, p. 26).

For Rogers, as well as other humanistic theorists, the most important matter in the consideration of personality is the person as a whole, including the individual's conscious awareness, freedom to choose, self-determination, and quality of experiences. His is an **organismic approach**: The human organism is viewed as a total being whose physical, psychological, and spiritual aspects cannot be separated except by artificial means. In brief, it is the *person* who is placed first. This is why Rogers's theory of therapy is now usually called the *person-centered* approach (formerly it was "client-centered," a phrase still used by some therapists and Rogers, even in his last articles; Rogers, 1987c; Super, 1989). The central hypothesis of the person-centered orientation is that "Individuals have within themselves vast resources for self-understanding and for altering their self-concepts, basic attitudes, and self-directed behavior" (Rogers, 1980, p. 115). Further, these resources can be tapped by providing "a definable climate of facilitative psychological attitudes" (p. 115).

Rogers thus differs from Freud in assuming that humans have positive potentialities that they can develop themselves. The natural development of human beings is toward the "constructive fulfillment" of their inherent possibilities.

> *I am inclined to believe that fully to be a human being is to enter into the complex process of being one of the most widely sensitive, responsive, creative, and adaptive creatures on this planet. So when a Freudian such as Karl Menninger tells me (as he has, in a discussion of this issue) that he perceives man as "innately evil" or more precisely, "innately destructive," I can only shake my head in wonderment (quoted in Kirschenbaum, 1979, p. 250).*

Rogers rejected the conception of learning he attributed to most universities. "A . . . unique element is that [my theory] is based on a learning that is experiential as well as cognitive. That is something that seems very hard for universities to accept. Most of the universities I know think that education goes on [only] from the neck up . . . That is not so! Education may be limited to that, but learning is something else" (Rogers, 1987a, p. 39). This statement is another expression of the organismic approach. It is also an endorsement of pedagogical procedures that entail active student participation in college classroom activities. Such methods are gaining popularity among professors so rapidly they threaten to supplant the traditional fifty to seventy-five minutes of straight lecture (DeCarvalho, 1991). As a teacher, Rogers "distributed an optional reading list, gave a few assignments (e.g., come to class, keep a journal, write a final paper on a subject of your choice) and indicated a willingness to lecture occasionally or do a demonstration if the students requested it" (Kirschenbaum, 1991, p. 412).

Rogers recognized that his ideas have been heavily influenced by his relationships with clients in therapy. However, he believed that these experiences are representative of all human relationships. Psychotherapy relationships are only a special instance of interpersonal relationships in general, and "the same lawfulness" governs all such relationships (Rogers, 1961, p. 39). He has supported this belief by writing a number of popular books on such topics as freedom to learn in education (1969), encounter groups (1970), becoming marriage partners (1972), and the revolutionary impact of personal power (1977). Sullivan generally shared this point of view.

Basic Concepts: Rogers

Actualization

Actualization is both a general and a specific tendency. These inclinations are closely linked and central to Rogers's thinking.

The General Actualizing Tendency

All living things display the **general actualizing tendency,** an "inherent tendency of the organism to develop all its capacities in ways which serve to maintain or enhance the organism" (Rogers, 1959, p. 196). This constructive biological tendency is the "one central source of energy in the human organism," giving rise to all other motivations (Rogers, 1980, p. 123).

The actualizing tendency expresses itself through a wide range of behaviors, in response to a wide variety of needs. It has four significant characteristics:

1. It is *organismic*—a natural, biological, inborn predisposition reflected in the total functioning of every living being.
2. It is an *active* process. It accounts for the observation that organisms are always up to something, whether seeking food or sexual satisfaction, initiating, exploring, producing change in the environment, playing, or even creating.
3. It is *directional* rather than random; it inclines every form of life toward growth, self-regulation, fulfillment, reproduction, and independence from external control.
4. It is *selective*, meaning that not all of an organism's potentialities are necessarily developed (for example, the ability to bear pain).

Rogers illustrated the operation of the actualizing tendency using a boyhood observation. Recalling that his family stored its supply of winter potatoes in the basement, several feet below a window, he noted:

> *The conditions were unfavorable, but the potatoes would begin to sprout—pale white sprouts . . . these sad, spindly sprouts would grow . . . toward the distant light of the window. They were in . . . futile growth, a sort of desperate expression of the directional tendency . . . They would . . . never mature, never fulfill their real potentiality. But under the most adverse circumstances they were striving to become. Life would not give up, even if it could not flourish (Rogers, 1979/1983, p. 228).*

The organismic propensity for actualization is true of beings from potatoes, through protozoa, to rabbits, all the way to humans.

Self-Actualization

In addition to the general actualizing tendency, Rogers postulated a specifically human tendency, **self-actualization**—a person's lifelong process of realizing his or her potentialities to become a fully functioning person. The goal of self-actualization is "to be that self which one truly is" (Rogers, 1961, p. 166). The direction of self-actualization is toward "the good life," defined as whatever is *organismically* valued by the total person who is inwardly free to move in any direction.

Rogers (1961) associated the process of self-actualization with enhanced functioning in three areas. First, self-actualization involves an increased openness to **experience**, which is all the emotions, cognitions, and perceptions occurring to the organism at any given moment that potentially can be consciously considered. Experience is comprehended through **awareness**, the conscious apprehension of experience.

Second, the self-actualizing person lives existentially, going with the flow of each moment in life and participating fully in it. She or he is *time competent*, experiencing life in the "here and now," without rigid preconceptions that things must be the way they have been in the past and without needing to control how things should be in the future.

Third, the self-actualizing person places full trust in his or her organismic intuitions, doing what feels right after weighing all available information. She or he relies little on the past or on social conventions. The self-actualizing person also displays genuine appreciation of free choice, creativity, the trustworthiness of human nature, and the richness of life.

The Importance of the Self

Obviously, self-actualization implies a central role for the "self" in Rogers's theory. "Self" is clearly reflected in our everyday language: "I am in love"; "Walking in the rain makes me feel good"; "This is what I like." Belief in the importance of *self* is one of the distinguishing marks of humanistic psychologists. For Rogers (1947), the person's experience of self is a basic aspect of life. It forms and determines behavior, cognition, and feeling.

"Self" was not always central to Rogers's theory. He started with a notion of the self that was "a vague, ambiguous, scientifically meaningless term" (1959, p. 200). Clearer ideas about the self emerged from his observations of therapy clients, who regularly expressed such ideas as "I wonder *who I am*," "I don't want anyone to know the *real me*," "It feels good to let myself go and *just be me*."

Self as Self-Perceptions

Although Rogers has never formally defined personality, he did define **self**, the organized, consistent, conceptual whole composed of perceptions of the characteristics of the "I" or "me," the values attached to these perceptions, and the relationships of the "I" or "me" to various aspects of life (Rogers, 1959, p. 200). The definition reflects Rogers's basic commitment to the phenomenological approach. One can see how it emerged from expressions of clients. Its emphasis is clearly on the perceptual origins of self: a person's self is a set of perceptions that have the perceiver as its target. Further, because "values are attached to these perceptions," the self is functionally equivalent to self-concept. It includes all of the individual's evaluations of his organismic functions and human relationships, which he uses "to order and interpret his . . . experiences" (Shlien, 1970, p. 95). Also relevant to self is how self-perceptions relate to other perceptions and to objects in the external world (Evans,

1975). To illustrate, a person may have the self-perception, "I am six feet tall." She may relate this to her perceptions of other people, as in "I am tall," and place a value on her perception, as in "I am too tall."

For Rogers, the **ideal self** is the self a person most values and desires to be. It is "the self-concept which the individual would most like to possess, upon which he places the highest value for himself" (Rogers, 1959, p. 100). Therefore, successfully pursuing the ideal self is a major precondition for feelings of worth. Rogerians often have a person describe actual and ideal selves and then ask her or him to compare the two descriptions. That is the purpose of Box 9.2.

BOX 9.2   Adjective Descriptions of Your Actual and Ideal Self

Instructions: On the left side of a sheet of paper, write down adjectives that best describe the self you are at the present time in your life (actual self). On the right side, write down adjectives that best describe the self you would like to be (ideal self). Work quickly, and be sure to write down single words that are found in the dictionary, not sentences, paragraphs, or words that you invent. Attempt to write down between ten and fifteen self-descriptive adjectives under each heading, but not less than five under each. Do not worry if some of your words seem contradictory; just write whatever adjectives best describe your actual and ideal self.

Your Actual Self   *Your Ideal Self*

Students in past research studies by Allen and Potkay typically write down about ten adjectives when allowed to record as many as they want (see our 1983a book). How do you compare with them and how do your words compare with those of other students in class? In what ways are your descriptions of self *as you are* and self as *you would like to be* the same or different? What do you make of words that do and do not appear on both lists? Consider how you would go about transforming yourself from present self into ideal self.

Consistent with the implication that you are now a certain self (actual self) and may become another self (ideal self), Rogers believes that the self is best understood as a continuing process, not a fixed endpoint. Thus the self, yours or anyone else's, is very likely to be undergoing change. This is why a person may organize self-views in different ways at different points in time. You probably do not view yourself the same way today as you did five years ago, and you likely have had the experience, "I used to think of myself that way, but now I think of myself in the opposite way."

Other people may not see you the same way you see yourself. A student at my university was quite surprised to learn of this discrepancy while doing a self-study as a term project. She had been asked to describe her true self with adjectives and then obtain adjective descriptions of her true self from her mother, father, boyfriend, and best girlfriend. The words she used to describe her own self—insecure, stubborn, impatient—were much more negative than those used by other persons in her life—intelligent, friendly, lovable. Her explanation was that "I failed to update my . . . self to match my true self of today" (Allen & Potkay, 1983a).

The closer the correspondence between a person's actual and ideal self, the greater the person's sense of self-acceptance and adjustment. You may regard the correspondence between your actual and ideal selves as indicating degree of self-acceptance and adjustment, but be cautious. Unless you know the typical degree of correspondence shown by many other people like yourself, you lack a good standard of comparison to use in evaluating your level of correspondence.

Congruence with Experience

Our self-concepts may be more or less in agreement with experiences related to self. When a person is in a state of **congruence** his or her self-concept and experiences relating to self are consistent. The actualizing tendency is then relatively whole and unified, and the person shows maturity as well as psychological adjustment. By contrast, **incongruence** reflects

---

BOX 9.3   Rogers Related to Adler, Freud, and Jung

People who knew the works of Rogers and Adler could see a similarity. Rogers wrote of an encounter with Adler:

> *I had the privilege of meeting, listening to, and observing Dr. Alfred Adler. This was the winter of 1927–28, when I was an intern . . . Accustomed as I was to the rather rigid Freudian approach of the Institute [where he was interning]—seventy-five-page case histories, and exhaustive batteries of tests before even thinking of 'treating' a child—I was shocked by Dr. Adler's very direct and deceptively simple manner of relating to the child and the parent. It took me some time to realize how much I learned from him (Rogers, quoted in Ansbacher, 1990, p. 47).*

Rogers apparently received two important lessons from Adler. First, exhaustive case histories may be regarded as mechanical, cold, and unnecessary methods for getting to know a person. More warm and informal techniques will work as well or better. Second, a therapist need not spend many sessions indirectly probing the past of a client in order to understand him or her. One can jump right in and relate to the person during her or his *here and now*.

The passage referring to Adler also makes a "backdoor" reference to Freud. Obviously, Freud was thrust down Rogers's throat during the internship, a period of neophyte status when thoughtless acceptance is likely. Before he could begin to think of the person-centered approach he eventually adopted, Rogers had to rid himself of Freudian notions. That he did in the 1940s. During this time he was accused of "destroying the unity of psychoanalysis" by founding his client-centered approach to therapy and of "violating the sanctity of the analytic rela-

tionship" when he used an early electronic device to record therapy sessions (Gendlin, 1988, p. 127). Reactions to these "heresies" helped Rogers make a clean and total break with Freudianism.

Campbell Purton, a Jungian enthusiast as a teen, began to become aware of common ground between Jung and Rogers when he later became a therapist and studied Rogers's ideas (Purton, 1989). Purton makes a reference to a particular aspect of Jungian therapy that is quite Rogerian, one that you may recall from the chapter on Jung. Jung anticipated Rogers by rejecting the authoritarian relationship between therapist and "patient" that was popularized by Freud. He worked with clients on a one-on-one basis and regarded them as partners. Often Jung participated in whatever he had asked clients to do. As a therapist, Rogers is known to have rejected the authoritarian posture with at least equal vigor (Zhurbin, 1991).

There are other coincidences between Jung and Rogers (Purton, 1989). Both believed that the techniques used in therapy were of secondary importance. Helping the client was the primary concern. Jung had his "persona," Rogers his "facade": a front behind which people suffering from incongruence would frequently hide. Jung wrote of "individuation," a process somewhat similar to Rogers's "self-actualization." Both concepts involve "wholeness," "uniqueness," and "becoming one's own self."

Although there is little evidence that Rogers was aware of a debt to Jung, a pioneer who predated him, it is still interesting to note that their ideas overlap a great deal. Both showed a deep and abiding belief in the worth of people. By contrast, Rogers was very aware of his debt to Adler and his disagreement with Freud.

an inconsistency between self-concept and experiences relating to self. Self-perceptions may be inaccurate because of beliefs that are rigid, distorted, unrealistic, or overgeneralized. Inaccuracy may also result from the defensive tactic **denial**, which involves the inability to recognize or accept the existence of an experience that has occurred. It is reflected in the reaction "No! It can't be!" to a rumor circulating among office workers that one has failed to receive a desperately sought-after promotion. **Distortion** involves a reinterpretation of an experience so as to make it consistent with how one wants things to be, as in the reaction "You are all wrong. Yesterday the boss was very friendly to me." You can see that Rogers, like Freud and Horney, believed that people have defenses against threatening experiences.

Inaccurate self-perceptions can contribute to experiences of inner confusion, tension, and maladaptive behavior. Rogers cites the example of a boy who had been observed lifting girls' skirts. When questioned, the boy denied what he had done, stating that it "couldn't" have been he, a disclaimer which confirmed that he was in a state of incongruence. His perceptions led him to maintain a self-concept inconsistent with his actual experience. Because his self-concept did not include sexual feelings or desires, his organismic experiences of sexual curiosity and desire were in conflict with his self-concept. He closed his awareness to behaviors, feelings, or attitudes inconsistent with his self-concept. The boy's denial reflected *defensiveness* aimed at maintaining the current structure of the self in the face of contradictory information (Rogers, 1959). It is a typical response when one's self-concept is threatened. "In the strictly technical sense, his self-picture couldn't do it, and didn't do it" (Rogers, quoted in Evans, 1975, p. 17). This condition is somewhere between what George Kelly called *fear* and what he referred to as *threat*.

Movement toward growth and improved adjustment in this boy would require him to revise his self-concept toward congruence. The process undoubtedly would be accompanied by anxiety as the boy became aware of the incongruence between his self-concept and his experiences. The reason for the discomfort is that "each of us seeks to preserve the concept or picture that he has of himself and that a sharp change in that picture is quite threatening. Any change destroys some of the security that we feel we need" (Rogers, quoted in Evans, 1975, p. 17). If the boy were able to lower his defenses, the new information about himself could then be incorporated as part of his self-concept. If not, *maladjustment* could occur with the boy remaining unaware of what is going on in himself. His growth and self-actualization would stagnate.

Personality Development: Some Favorable Conditions

What determines whether a person's self-concept becomes congruent or incongruent with experience? Rogers points to external circumstances, particularly of an interpersonal nature, under which personal growth is facilitated or blocked. His boyhood observation of his family's potatoes highlights the importance of environmental conditions as influences on the actualizing tendency of living things. The potatoes failed to realize their fullest potentials because of unfavorable conditions outside themselves.

Similarly, the interactions between persons and interpersonal environments represent an important aspect of human development. The actualization tendency points all people in the direction of becoming the persons they truly are, regardless of the social environment. However, certain interpersonal conditions facilitate actualization strivings, whereas others do not. Rogers's work with clients in therapy led him to identify some necessary and sufficient conditions for growth and change in personality (Orlov, 1992). These three conditions are interrelated and may be best understood as general attitudes toward a person that are held by other people. When these conditions are present, persons may become fully functioning, showing optimal maturity and adjustment. The conditions are: being a recipient of unconditional positive regard, developing accurate empathy, achieving congruence in personal relations, and developing positive self-regard.

Unconditional Positive Regard

All people have needs that can be fulfilled only in human relationships. Chief among these is a universally learned need for **positive regard**, the experiencing of oneself as making a positive difference in the lives of other people and as receiving warmth, liking, respect, sympathy, acceptance, caring, and trust from others (Rogers, 1959; Standal, 1954). This need is met when other people in a person's life provide **unconditional positive regard**: they communicate, with no strings attached, that one is accepted, valued, worthwhile, and trusted, simply for being who one is. The person experiences others' acceptance without feeling that it depends on his or her doing some "right" thing or having to be the way others think the person "should" be. When we release people from Horney's "tyranny of the shoulds" we help them along the road to self-actualization. Further, no aspect of the person is judged "more or less worthy of positive regard than any other" (Rogers, 1959, p. 208). There is no generalized labeling of the person as "bad" or "good." Rather, the person feels unconditionally "prized," valued, and accepted, simply for being whoever he or she is.

However, there is an unproductive way for a person to feel valued. Under this circumstance, positive regard is received only when the person meets certain conditions of worth set up by significant others. Here the individual feels prized in some respects, but not in others. She or he then avoids certain experiences judged by other people to be relatively "unworthy" and seeks out certain other experiences judged relatively "worthy." This occurs even if the person was once attracted to the "unworthy" experiences and repelled by the "worthy" experiences. The unproductive way is "conditional" because it involves contingencies stated in if–then terms. Significant others say, in effect, "If you say or do the things I like or want, then I will value you and consider you important. If you don't, then I won't."

When conditional acceptance characterizes the social environment, a child learns to behave and think mainly in ways approved by others, especially parents. The child learns, "If I do what my parents want, then I will be loved. If I don't, I won't be loved." This lesson generates incongruence between one's self-perception and "who one is." Under these circumstances one's actualizing tendency is likely to become blocked. Then denials and distortions of personal experiences that are disapproved by others are likely to occur. Also, acceptance of experiences that are incongruent with "who one is" becomes probable.

A common misconception about unconditional positive regard is that people who provide it to a person must always approve of everything the person says or does. To combat this misinterpretation, Rogers carefully distinguishes between the individual as a person and the individual's freely chosen values and behaviors. For example, while thoughtful and caring parents may always prize their child, they do so without valuing all of the child's behaviors equally. They may express pride when their child shares a candy bar with a friend, or displeasure when their child bites a friend. However, the child's specific behaviors are approved or disapproved, not the child as a person. It is the sharing that is approved and the biting that is disapproved, not the child. Although the parents undoubtedly wish the child would not bite, biting does not lead to rejection of the child as a person. The child continues to be prized, regardless of his or her behavior.

Accurate Empathy

If a person is to achieve congruence of self-concept with his or her experience, therapists and other people must correctly "hear" what the individual is experiencing and refrain from judging it. Rogers believed the ability to understand another person is of "enormous" value. He found it "enriching to open channels whereby others can communicate their feelings, their private perceptual worlds, to me" (1961, p. 19). **Accurate empathy** is Rogers's term for the ability to accurately perceive the client's internal world in a nonevaluative way. Such empathic understanding goes beneath the surface of another person's words and actions, to inner feelings, attitudes, meanings, values and motives.

Congruence in Relations with a Therapist and Others

In order for a person to grow, significant other people, including a therapist, must naturally and openly demonstrate their willingness and ability to be themselves in relationships with that person. This state of genuineness on the part of one person toward another can be regarded as a kind of congruence: The two people feel the same level of comfort or emotional involvement with the issue they are considering. In therapy, the therapist must exhibit an openness to inner experiences in such a way that it conveys congruence with the client. Even an experienced therapist might admit to the client, "I find myself frightened because you are touching on feelings I have never been able to resolve myself" (Rogers, 1959). A therapist uncomfortable with some aspect of the relationship with the client would be considered incongruent if she or he remained unaware of the discomfort, avoided dealing with it, or communicated reactions opposite to what is real for him or her. Incongruence on the part of the therapist retards progress in therapy, because the therapist's wholeness is not present in the relationship.

Developing Positive Self-Regard

When individuals receive unconditional positive regard from others, particularly during the formative years, they will develop **positive self-regard**, a favorable attitude toward themselves. This, in turn, allows them to develop their own values in accordance with their real experiences, independently of "approving" others. Although they will be aware of expectations concerning what they "should" do, they will trust their own judgments instead of being bound by those of others. Positive self-regard unlocks actualizing tendencies and allows individuals to become fully functioning humans.

By contrast, when others impose conditions of worth on an individual, her or his chances of developing positive self-regard become less. In this case, people's **locus of evaluation**, source of evidence about themselves, does not lie within them but outside, in others. The judgments of others form the standard for evaluating an experience. A young woman's letter to Rogers (1980) illustrates locus of evaluation in others, rather than in oneself:

> *I think that I began to lose me when I was in high school. I always wanted to go into work that would be of help to people but my family resisted, and I thought they must be right . . . about two years ago . . . I met a guy that I thought was ideal. Then nearly a year ago I took a good look at us, and realized that I was everything that he wanted me to be and nothing that I was. I have always been emotional . . . My fiancé would tell me that I was just mad or just happy and I would say okay . . . Then when I took this good look at us I realized that I was angry because I wasn't following my true emotions.*

Procedures for Changing Personality: Client-Centered Therapy

Rogers's ideas about personality development, when applied to person-centered therapy, involve the assumption that, if certain conditions exist, then a characteristic process of personality change will occur (Rogers, 1959). These conditions are positive regard, accurate empathic understanding, and congruence (Bozarth & Brodley, 1991). Also important are the client's anxiety level and motivation to change. The specific techniques of person-centered therapy are designed to reflect these basic premises.

Research has shown that the direction of change for clients in Rogerian therapy is from a personality that is fixed, separated, and tied to the past to one that is spontaneous, integrated, and flowing with experiences occurring in the present. Seven characteristic stages of this process unfold during therapy according to Rogers (1961). It is impossible to capture all aspects of these complex and comprehensive stages as experienced by the client, but the following observations are representative:

Stage 1. The client's communications are mostly about externals, not about self.
Stage 2. The client describes feelings but does not recognize or "own" them personally.
Stage 3. The client talks about self as an object, often in terms of past experiences.
Stage 4. The client experiences feelings in the present, but mainly just describes them, with distrust and fear, rather than expressing them directly.
Stage 5. The client experiences and expresses feelings freely in the present; feelings "bubble up" into awareness with a display of desire to experience them.
Stage 6. The client accepts his or her feelings in all their immediacy and richness.
Stage 7. The client trusts new experience and relates to others openly and freely.

If this process occurs, then certain cognitive, emotional, and behavioral changes will occur. These changes, wrought in therapy, lead the person closer to self-actualization. They reflect increases in congruence, openness to experience, adjustment, correspondence between actual and ideal self, positive self-regard, and acceptance of self and others.

An example of a therapeutic session illustrates the course of person-centered therapy. Imagine a successful lawyer who works 60–70 hours a week but is unsatisfied with his life. In an early session, the client begins by talking about trivia not really related to his concerns. "I can't understand why my kids are so materialistic. They just want more junk . . . everything they see on TV. I'm just the 'horn of plenty,' satisfying their every whim."

The therapist replies, "So you feel that your kids just use you to satisfy their needs." The remark reflects the client's feeling and emotions back to him so they may be affirmed, a process that makes them more available for reconsideration.

The client continues in this vein for a time and then, in a later session, he begins to express his more central emotions, but acts as if they are not his own. "It's funny, today, how people end up with careers that are unrelated to what they want to do or are capable of doing. I know this guy who is selling insurance and making a fortune, but living for a camping trip on the weekend. He's an outdoor type . . . wanted to be a forest ranger." The therapist nods, indicating that the client is understood.

On a later date the client begins to talk about himself, really for the first time. However, he talks about the past as if to analyze another person rather than his present self. "I can remember trying to copy the Mona Lisa when I was a kid. How naive can you get! Here was this little kid trying to act like a great artist. I did some pretty good drawings on my own . . . my teachers said so, but they weren't good enough to satisfy me." The therapist listens intently and utters "uh huh" to communicate that the client's feelings are appreciated.

After several sessions, the client gets around to himself in the present, but he is merely descriptive rather than analytical. "I still paint, you know. Sometimes late at night . . . sometimes on weekends. Did you know that I have an arrangement with an art gallery? I've sold some of my paintings, but didn't get much . . . can't make a living that way. They want me to come in with them . . . invest, you know, in the gallery and help manage it. Small change that would be . . . but you know I'm really happy when I'm there among those paintings . . . get a bigger kick out of selling a painting for a hundred bucks than settling a case for a hundred thousand."

The therapist indicates, "You feel that painting is very enjoyable and that you have had some success at it." The client begins to recognize how important art is to him.

In subsequent sessions, the client comes back to art more and more and talks about his current feelings to a greater and greater extent. "Well today was something else. I took off from work early and went to the gallery . . . I have a corner in a back room where I can paint. I'm working on something right now that really excites me. I'll have to show it to you. I know now that art is a part of me . . . heart and soul."

In the last sessions before termination of therapy the lawyer hardly mentions law. All he can talk about is his latest work of art and his plans to slowly substitute hours at the gallery for hours at the office. Here he shows awareness of courses of action that are more in tune with his actualizing self. "I have enough money saved to help make a go of the gallery. I find that my younger colleagues take care of the law practice quite nicely. You know I've never been happier. My kids don't seem so greedy anymore. Let them have what they want . . . I'll give them all I can. They'll eventually find themselves."

Evaluation

General Contributions

Rogers has had great impact on personality psychology and psychotherapy. In particular, he has contributed to an understanding of people as whole beings, to an appreciation of interpersonal relationships characterized by caring, to understanding personality growth processes, and to scientific openness and theoretical flexibility.

Rogers's phenomenological approach has had major influences on understanding personality. It has allowed individual human beings to speak for themselves about the nature of their own personal experiences. Rogers has guided psychological professionals in suspending views as to what a person *should be*, so they can understand how a person actually *is*. He suggested that important information is likely to come less from authorities with professional training than from common people during a genuine interpersonal exchange.

Rogers's phenomenological approach has questioned scientific psychology's so-called objective frameworks which have sought to understand people from the outside: behaviorally, mechanistically, and impersonally. Rogers has doubted the existence of an absolute way of interpreting reality and the desirability of even seeking such a narrow "truth" (Rogers, 1980). He paved the way for multiple interpretations of human experience, even at the highest, most complete levels of self-actualization.

Rogers has also tried to enhance our understanding of people by emphasizing trust in them. Given sufficiently supportive psychological conditions, individuals can be trusted to actualize their biologically based resources and move in directions that are ultimately good for them and other people. This basic assumption is an outgrowth of Rogers's belief that all organisms have inherent, natural capacities for growth, understanding, change, and purposeful direction.

Rogers has promoted the responsible use of personal freedom. This is why he was so perplexed by psychoanalytic conclusions about human destructiveness and irrationality (Freud, 1930/1961) and by behavioristic conclusions that human beings are under the control of highly structured external environments (Skinner, 1948). Rogers believed that rational solutions to human problems are possible without recourse to strict environmental controls.

Caring about the Person in Human Relationships

Rogers has stressed the role of caring interpersonal relationships in the process of developing, maintaining, and changing personality. In person-centered therapy the therapist is not a blank screen or expert technician, but a person, "a viable human being engaged in a terribly human endeavor" (Truax & Mitchell, 1971, p. 344). Under the influence of Rogers, even behavioral therapists, often criticized for ignoring interpersonal relationships, have modified procedures "which used to seem less than human to their critics" (Gendlin & Rychlak, 1970).

In fact, one could argue that Rogers has done more to revise the concepts and practices relating to personality change than any single psychologist. He did so by demonstrating caring for others, even when such demonstrations violated traditional psychoanalytic "rules." For instance, early in his career he showed human responsiveness by departing from routine child-guidance procedures and answering "yes" to a despairing mother's question, "Do you ever take adults for counseling here?" (Rogers, 1961). Later, in a filmed therapy session, Rogers departed from traditional psychoanalytic taboos against communicating "countertransference" feelings to patients by saying to the client, Gloria, "I care about you right now, in this moment" (Shostrom, 1965). He even indicated he could see himself as a father to Gloria, who would make a fine daughter. Gloria continued to keep in occasional touch with Rogers because of the closeness achieved during this half-hour interview.

Rogers's Scientific Contributions

Rogers has changed the field of psychotherapy through the value placed on subjecting his clinical observations to independent research investigation (Rogers, 1989a). His (1942) case of Herbert Bryan was the first complete series of therapy sessions to be electronically recorded and transcribed (800 78-rpm record sides and 170 book pages). Never before had such a wealth of information been made available to psychologists, word for word, complete with "U-hms" and pauses. Standard procedure, beginning with Freud, was for therapists to rely entirely on memory when summarizing sessions, often at the end of a full day's contact with six or eight patients. By exposing their practice to the scrutiny of other professionals and the public, Rogers and his students showed how psychotherapy could be demystified (Wexler & Rice, 1974). Their work "turned the field . . . upside down" and "made possible the empirical study of highly subjective phenomena" (Rogers, 1974, p. 116).

Rogers has also changed professionals' ideas about scientific procedures and theory by modeling flexible attitudes toward theoretical formulations and methods. His own theorizing began with full recognition that every theory is fallible. Each theory is a "changing attempt" to construct a network of fragile threads containing an unknown amount of error and mistaken inference (1959). Rogers believed that science may begin anywhere, even away from the laboratory. He has always been stimulated and excited by the new ideas of younger colleagues who seem "less stuffy, less defensive, more open in their criticism and more creative in their suggestions" than his older colleagues (1974, p. 121). Following his example, Rogers's students and colleagues have shown a responsiveness to new ideas rather than orthodox, blind devotion (Wexler & Rice, 1974).

Unlike some theorists covered so far, a number of Rogers's concepts can be translated into a form that can be quantified or expressed in numbers. An outstanding example of how readily certain of Rogers's ideas can be translated so that they become scientifically testable entities is provided by Harrington, Block, and Block (1987).

These researchers were interested in Rogers's theory about the process by which child-rearing practices determine level of creativity at adolescence. Their subject sample was composed of individuals who had been followed and periodically tested beginning at approximately age three and continuing to approximately age fourteen. Subjects' parents were also involved in the testing.

Harrington, Block, and Block studied Rogers's writings about child-rearing and creativity. Then they translated his notions about that relationship into items on some instruments designed to measure child-rearing practices. One of these measures involved having parents report the practices they typically used. Some items that were judged most typical of Rogers's "creativity fostering environment" (CFE) included, "I respect my child's opinions and encourage him to express them"; "I let my child make many decisions for himself"; and "I encourage my child to be curious, to explore and question things" (p. 852). Some items judged least typical of Rogers's CFE included, "I do not allow my child to get angry with me"; "I believe that children should be seen and not heard"; and "I do not allow my child to question my decisions" (p. 852).

Other measures assessed parental teaching behavior during parent–child, task-completion sessions that were observed by raters. Resultant ratings were then transformed into items related to Rogers's CFE. Items judged to be most typical of CFE included, "Parent was warm and supportive"; "Child appeared to enjoy the situation"; and "Parent was sup-

---

BOX 9.4   Carl Rogers: Globe-Trotting Peacemaker

Not all of Rogers's contributions were related to "psychotherapy" and "personality theory." Rogers the person had great influence on individuals involved in some of the most disturbing and serious conflicts occurring in the world today.

His efforts to end disastrous conflicts took him to every quarter of the globe. On a trip to Northern Ireland he attempted to induce Protestants and Catholics to regard each other as humans beings rather than mortal enemies (Rogers & Ryback, 1984). Using his client-centered method adapted to a group context, Rogers brought religious rivals together in close proximity. As you might expect, initial reactions were explosive. For example, Gilda, a Protestant, who Rogers described as young and pretty, said, "If I seen an IRA man lying on the ground . . . I would step on him, because to me he has just went out and taken the lives of innocent people" (p. 5). Yet, under Rogers's skillful guidance, individuals revealed themselves and, thereby, came to appreciate one another's humanity. After considerable interaction in the context of Rogers's group, Dennis, a Protestant, and Becky, a Catholic, spoke warmly of one another:

> Dennis: *The general impression back in Belfast is, if [Becky] is a Catholic . . . you just put her in a wee box and that is the end of it. But you just can't do that. She has communicated to me that she is in a worse position than what I am . . . I feel that she feels the absolute despair that I would feel. I don't know how I would react if I were one of her lads. I would probably go out and get a gun . . . and end up dead.*
>
> Becky: *Words couldn't describe what I feel towards Dennis from the discussion we had at dinner time. We spoke quietly for about ten minutes*

and I felt that here I have got a friend and that was it.

> Dennis: *We sat at dinner time and had a wee bit of yarn [storytelling] quietly when you were all away for your dinner . . .*
>
> Becky: *I think he fully understands me as a person.*
>
> Dennis: *I do, there is no question about that . . .*
>
> Becky: *And for that reason I am very grateful and I think I have found a friend (p. 5)*

These same techniques were used in the encounter between black and white South Africans that reduced Rogers to tears (Hill–Hain & Rogers, 1988). Similar methods produced similar results in the former Soviet Union (Rogers, 1987b). This last adventure in group interaction, played out in Moscow and Tbilisi, was responsive to Rogers's larger concerns. He had in mind more than just settlement of local conflicts. For the last several years of his life, Rogers wrote passionately about the need to eliminate nuclear weapons, a concern that I share with him (Allen, 1985). He believed that social scientists could contribute much toward the end of the nuclear threat (Rogers & Malcolm, 1987). In fact, it was his fervent wish that his group interaction methods, used so successfully to alleviate local tensions, might be applied to international conflicts that have the potential to produce nuclear holocaust (Rogers, 1989b; Rogers, 1987c; Rogers & Ryback, 1984). I can picture a group composed of the United States and Russian presidents and their underlings interacting under Rogers's guidance. If only he could be here to lead such a group. Because he cannot, the best we can do is to apply his wisdom and sensitivity, and we had better hurry.

---

portive and encouraging of the child." Items judged to be least typical of CFE included, "Parent tended to control the tasks"; "The parent was hostile in the situation"; and "Parent appeared ashamed of child, lacked pride in child" (p. 852).

Creativity items were developed in an analogous fashion and used to assess creativity when subjects were teens. Items that were judged applicable to creative individuals included, "Tends to be proud of own accomplishments"; "Is curious, exploring, eager for new experiences"; "Has a wide range of interests"; and "Values own independence and autonomy." Items that were judged applicable to noncreative individuals included, "Is uncomfortable with uncertainty and complexities"; "Gives up and withdraws where possible in the face of adversity"; and "Is self-defeating" (p. 853).

Harrington, Block, and Block (1987) found statistically significant, positive relationships between instruments with items that measured Rogers's CFE and instruments with items that measured creativity. These results convinced them that Rogers's ideas about creativity, and the environmental circumstances that foster it, are scientifically valid. Just looking at the items they used gives one a relatively clear impression concerning what creativity is and what parental practices promote it.

Although this kind of high-level empirical work has been relatively rare, the future of research on Rogers's point of view looks bright. Cartwright, DeBruin, and Berg (1991) have developed the Feelings Reactions and Beliefs Survey (FRBS) to measure nine concepts gleaned from Rogers's writings: focusing conscious attention, openness to feelings in relationships, trust in self as an organism, functioning fully as person, feeling uncomfortable with people, struggling with feelings of inferiority, feeling ambivalent in relationships, openness to transcendent experiences, and religio-spiritual beliefs. With the FRBS available, researchers will have a wide spectrum of potential research projects from which to choose.

Limitations

Although emphasis on subjective experience is a major contribution, it creates limitations in regard to the scientific status of Rogers's personality theory and therapy. The major weaknesses thus generated are: (1) difficulty in translating some concepts into testable form; (2) problems involved in accepting self-reports; and (3) the inadequacy of nondirective therapy for some individuals. Also discussed are concerns about Rogers's basic assumptions, some allegations that Rogers's "genuineness" in therapy was limited and that, before he died, he repudiated, if not his entire point of view, at least his views on humanistic education.

Problems of Translating Concepts

Despite the ease with which some of Rogers's concepts can be translated into measurable terms, many others defy straightforward translation. For example, some scales have been developed for measuring Rogerian concepts of empathy, warmth, and genuineness. The natural difficulty in measuring these notions is reflected in the fact that scales developed by Truax and Carkhuff (1967) differ somewhat from those developed later by Carkhuff (1969). In appraising the predictive effectiveness of these scales, Mitchell, Bozarth, and Krauft (1977) judged results to be inconclusive, and explained this unsatisfying outcome by reference to the possible low relevance of the measurement scales to the concepts. Efforts have also been made to develop measures of other Rogerian concepts. The Experiencing Scale, developed by Gendlin and Tomlinson (1967), is a refinement of Rogers's (1959) earlier Psychotherapy Process Scale (PPS). The PPS is aimed at evaluating the degree to which a client is in touch with or avoids important emotions. Although this measure does not rely on client self-reports, thus avoiding some problems, it does rely on therapists' ratings, thereby introducing biases related to therapists' personal or professional expectations.

Acceptance of Conscious, Self-Reported Experience

In his classic text on personality, Gordon Allport (1937) alluded to the inclination of behaviorists and psychoanalysts "to distrust the evidence of immediate experience" and dismiss the self, ego, or "person" in psychology. While scientific evidence has shown that "self-concept" is amenable to measurement, these critics of self-notions make some telling points. First, self-perceptions may be incomplete or inaccurate representations of the self, because of people's limited ability to see themselves realistically. Second, even accurate self-perceptions may not be reflected in self-statements if the individual is unwilling to communicate them. Third, both self-perceptions and self-statements may not correspond to what the person is doing, thinking, and feeling. While inability to measure concepts does not make them useless, it does put them beyond the realm of science.

The Nondirective Approach

Unlike most other psychotherapists, Rogers has accumulated considerable evidence supporting the effectiveness of his therapeutic procedures (see Kirschenbaum & Henderson, 1989). Nevertheless, these methods are apparently not for everyone. In the filmed psychotherapy session mentioned earlier, the client, Gloria, was rather obviously frustrated with Rogers's unwillingness to offer expert advice. Despite her continued contact with Rogers later, at the time of the session, it seemed that Gloria preferred the other two therapists to Rogers. Not long ago I overheard some counselors expressing similar frustration. They were describing an observation of a Rogerian session in which the client was seeking advice and not getting any. It seemed obvious to them not only that the client needed advice but what advice he needed. Despite their observations, the therapist persisted in merely nodding and saying "Uh huh." Perhaps Rogers's predominantly intelligent and not-so-severely disturbed clients were better off left to their own devices. However, other clients, who may be more disturbed and less well-equipped, may need some suggestions as to how they might deal with their problems.

Some Problems with Basic Assumptions

I have attempted to acquaint you with the basic assumptions underlying theorists' notions about personality. With Rogers that is difficult because he did not define personality. Without a formal definition of personality, statements about Rogers's underlying assumptions regarding personality must be indirect at best: Reading between the lines of Rogers's statements about "self" is as close to underlying assumptions about personality as one can get.

One of Rogers's most basic assumptions is that people are inherently "good." As classroom discussions on the topic always show, just as it is philosophically difficult to declare that humans are essentially "bad," it is hard to defend a judgment that people are basically "good."

One can more easily argue that people are neither "good" nor "bad"; rather, they are exceedingly complex and fully capable of both goodness and badness. An alternative perspective is seen in the question, "How do we maximize the goodness and minimize the badness?"

Allegations Regarding Rogers's Genuineness and Repudiation of Views

No matter who a theorist might be, no matter how benevolent, reasonable, and honest he or she may seem, no matter how solid her or his point of view may appear, it will be criticized, given only that fame finds the theorist. This fact is important to keep in mind when one considers any criticisms and allegations. Two charges have been lodged against Rogers. Quinn, (1993) alleges that recordings of Rogers in therapy, including the Gloria case, show that Rogers's genuineness is limited, because he adamantly refused to be confrontational. Supposedly, to be truly genuine, all that the therapist encounters, feels, and thinks must be fair game for placement on the therapeutic table, including feelings that the client has behaved in ways that the therapist wishes to confront. Graf (1994) countered by arguing that (1) all the recordings Quinn refers to are of short-term therapy demonstrations, too preliminary to include most of Rogers's typical reactions, and (2) including confrontation when the therapist may feel the need of it is something other than genuineness; namely it is likely to be a case of giving the therapist's issues priority over the client's. Graf concludes that viewing Rogers in more extended sessions confirms his complete genuineness.

The second allegation is that, before he died, Rogers repudiated his humanistic educational philosophy and even his entire point of view. This astounding charge was leveled by William Coulson, who, according to Kirschenbaum (1991), made the allegation in other than professional journals (for example, on the radio). Coulson claimed to have co-developed humanistic education with Rogers and Maslow, then, along with them, abandoned it in the light of research results that failed to support it. Kirschenbaum makes it clear, by use of numerous quotes of Rogers, that Rogers never abandoned humanistic education, much less the general humanistic, person-centered point of view. In fact, Kirschenbaum shows that Rogers became an even more radical humanistic educator as time went on. Further, Coulson was never able to point out any published statements by Rogers that clearly renounce humanistic education.

While Rogers was, as always, flexible and backed away from some elements of humanistic instruction, he consistently supported it. In fact, once he developed a point of view or practice he stuck with it (Bozarth, 1990).

While these two allegations seem weak at this point, they are unlikely to go away. Such is the case because "lack of genuineness" and "unstructured schools run by the students" are the kinds of issues that will be on the public mind into the indefinite future.

Conclusions

Carl Rogers was many things to many people, but disliked was hardly ever one of them. He was a person who practiced what he preached. As a result, Rogers was the warm, accepting person that he hoped we would all become. In reading the various interviews with Rogers and tributes to him offered by his many disciples, it is evident that his followers were not just interested in his point of view. They were sincerely devoted to Rogers the person. These loving colleagues and friends comforted, protected, and nourished him, just as he did them.

Rogers exemplified the best of the human spirit. He could truly melt into another person so that he became one with her or him. In so doing, he surrendered himself in the interest of someone else, perhaps the most noble act a human can perform.

Summary Points

1. Rogers was a farm boy from Illinois who learned principles of science and growth from an agricultural book. He cut his teeth on Freud, but later abandoned psychoanalysis and the medical model in favor of the growth model. As an adult, Rogers became a warm person who backed away from religion temporarily, but was somewhat different from his image. He could become angry and agitated, he thought equality in therapy was not an issue, he was sometimes overcome with emotion during therapy, he deplored the rigid use of the client-centered method, and he was not heavily identified with counseling. At the same time, he contributed to understanding diversity as it applies to interracial relations and therapist–client ethnic mismatches.

2. Humanistic psychology emphasizes the present experience of the whole person. It has close ties to existential psychology. The more positive humanistic approach focuses on joy, love, and authenticity. The phenomenological approach, central to Rogers's view, assumes the reality that one knows is subjective and personal. However, we can participate in the private world of others through empathy. He applied these notions to create humanistic education at the college and earlier educational levels.

3. "The person" is literally the center of Rogers's theory and therapy. People are viewed in a positive light and are seen as capable of solving their own problems. Relationships with people in therapy are only instances of those that occur everyday. People have an inherent "general actualizing tendency" that is organismic, active, directional, and selective. Self-actualization is a lifelong process of realizing one's potentialities that involves openness to experience, awareness, living existentially, and trust in one's organismic functions.

4. The existence of the self is verified by statements like "Who am I?" and "This is what I like." The self is perceptions of the characteristics of "I" and is functionally equivalent to "self-concept." It can be related to an "ideal self." Congruence occurs when our self-concepts are in agreement with the selves we actually experience. Incongruence occurs when the opposite is the case, which entails denial and distortion.

5. Adler taught Rogers the error of rigid adherence to Freud's psychoanalysis and of dwelling on clients' pasts. Rogers came to oppose psychoanalytic principles, but his ideas sometimes coincided with Jung's: Both rejected authoritarian relationships with clients, both believed using specific therapy techniques to be of secondary importance, both talked of a "facade," and both wrote of "wholeness," "uniqueness," and the self.

6. External factors, particularly interpersonal ones, often determine whether personal growth occurs: (1) unconditional positive regard, (2) accurate empathy, and (3) congruence. (1) concerns being regarded with acceptance and trust just for who one is. Unconditional positive regard means accepting the person, no matter what, but not necessarily the person's behavior. (2) means correctly perceiving the client's world in a nonevaluative way. (3) is applicable to therapist–client relationships.

7. Unconditional positive regard can lead to positive self-regard, but not if the locus of evaluation is in other people. Personality change flows from fixed, separated, and tied-to-the-past to spontaneous, integrated, and "in-the-present." Progress in therapy proceeds from talk about externals, to disowned descriptions of feelings, to self in the past, to feelings in the present that are merely described, to feelings freely expressed in the present, to full acceptance of feelings, to relating to others openly and freely and trusting in new experiences.

8. Rogers's self-description reflected the open, creative, accepting, tolerant, effective, and gentle person that he was. Rogers's contributions include allowing people to speak for themselves with regard to the nature of their feelings. His methods have led to questioning the attempt to understand people from the outside. He has been the great promoter of trusting people. He attributes positive motivations to people and honors their natural actualizing tendencies, while recognizing they do not always behave well.

9. Rogers, while humanizing other approaches, adopted the motto "do whatever is necessary to enhance the person." As a scientist he has demystified psychotherapy, opened it to the public eye, and revised mechanized approaches to therapy. Many of his concepts have been translated into measurable form as evidenced by Harrington, Block, and Block's verification of his proposed relationship between child-rearing practices and creativity. New measures of his concepts bode well for the future of research on his theory. As a person, Rogers has attempted to do something about serious conflicts in various parts of the world. Further, he has suggested that his group method may be used to help lower the probability of nuclear conflict.

10. Limitations of Rogers's point of view include problems of translation of some concepts, problems with the self-report method he used, and inadequacy of the nondirective therapy method for some people. Allegations of lack of genuineness and abandonment of humanistic education have been lodged against him. Despite these shortcomings, Rogers the person stands as an example of human warmth and concern for the well-being of each person.

Running Comparison

Theorist	Rogers in Comparison
Freud	Rogers was optimistic and positive compared to Freud, rejected his involved probing into the past, but shared his belief in defenses.
Jung	He shared Jung's nonauthoritarian, mutual participant orientation to therapy, belief that method was less important than helping clients, "facade" (persona), individuation (self-actualization), interest in the self, and belief in wholeness and uniqueness of each person.
Adler	He learned to be direct and straightforward from Adler. Also he agreed with Adler on eschewing lengthy case histories and multiple tests to discover past problems.
Abraham Maslow	Shared many ideas with fellow humanistic psychologist Maslow, especially self-actualization.
Gordon Allport	Shared Allport's idiographic approach, humanism, and concern for the self-concept.
Harry S. Sullivan	Shared Sullivan's interest in significant others.
Karen Horney	Her real self was akin to his self-actualization. Both posed defenses against the clash of actual and ideal selves.

Essay/Critical Thinking Questions

1. Beyond the religious perspective, what is the meaning of death?

2. What was it about Rogers's early history—childhood through young adulthood—that led to his scientific, anti-psychoanalytic, yet humanistic orientation?

3. Aside from a moral or philosophical point of view, what are the disadvantages of Rogers's assumption that people are basically good and worthy?

4. Picture yourself as a self-actualized person. How would you describe yourself?

5. Indicate the ways your self-concept is incongruent with your actual experience of yourself. How is self and self-ideal involved in this discrepancy?

6. Explain how a religious Rogerian could reconcile "original sin" with "humans are inherently good."

7. Unconditional positive regard should apply to the person, not her or his every behavior. Despite this assumption, in practice, what problems might be encountered in applying unconditional positive regard to a person?

8. What does it take to be truly genuine? Must one express whatever one feels?

9. It seems reasonable to "operationalize" concepts in order to study them scientifically (define concepts in terms of how they are measured). Nevertheless, what happens to concepts such as warmth, empathy, and positive self-regard when these notions are operationalized?

10. When someone begins to tell you about a minor or major problem that she or he has, begin to react to this person in good Rogerian fashion. How does the person react to your "uh-huhs," nods, and rephrasing instead of advice?

E-mail Interaction

(Contact the author at mfbpa@wiu.edu)
Forward one of the following or phrase your own.

1. Was Rogers an atheist?
2. Since Rogers did not change his view much over the years, was he dogmatic?
3. Was Dr. Rogers much like Mr. Rogers of TV child-show fame?
4. Tell me what central notion was at the heart and soul of Rogers's theory.
5. Will Rogers be remembered as more important than Freud at some time in the future?

10

BECOMING ALL THAT ONE CAN BE: ABRAHAM MASLOW

- Can a psychologist who despised his mother turn out right?
- Must we meet our basic physiological needs before we can address other kinds?
- Is it enough to attain high self-esteem or should one expect to rise above society's demands and thus be free to reach all of one's potential?
- How admirable is it to be devoted to creativity, the pursuit of beauty, and fully accepting of oneself, but relatively unconcerned about what others think and feel?
- If one achieves the highest level of personality attainment, is there still more to seek?

Abraham Maslow

The two brightest stars in the humanistic firmament are certainly Carl Rogers and Abraham Maslow. Not surprisingly, they share much in common. Both are more concerned with the here and now and being all one can be, rather than with the past or even the future. Both flirted with the ideas of Sigmund Freud briefly, and both were influenced by Alfred Adler. Both also emphasized the importance of self-actualization in personality functioning and development, but here the similarities fade. For Rogers, self-actualization was one of several central concepts. By contrast, Maslow emphasized it above all other concepts. According to Rogers, self-actualization was within the grasp of most people, but to Maslow it was reserved for a special few.

As people they were quite different. Rogers came from a traditional family. Maslow considered himself an abused and neglected child and a victim of prejudice. Rogers was totally warm and accepting and assumed the basic goodness of humans. Maslow could show the same traits, but he seethed with suppressed anger and was more than willing to acknowledge the sinister side of human nature. Yet in their own separate ways, both humanists sought to help people lay aside others' expectations and become what they were destined to be.

Maslow, The Person

When Samuel Maslow arrived in the United States from the Ukrainian city of Kiev, he brought little with him, except the ability to speak Russian and Yiddish, a language common among European Jews (Hoffman, 1988). After a brief sojourn in Philadelphia, he moved in with relatives residing in New York City. There he met and married his first cousin, Rose, a woman who would prove more devoted to religion than to her family. Abraham, the first of their seven children—one died in infancy—was born on April Fool's Day, 1908. Fate played a trick on him, giving him parents who were part of a master plan to ensure his eternal torment.

Maslow claimed that his mother was cold, vicious, superstitiously religious, and dedicated to making him miserable (Hoffman, 1988). Even the most trivial of his youthful transgressions inspired her to declare that God would strike him down. Continual threats of divine retribution affected Maslow profoundly. For one thing, it nurtured the scientist in him: "I tested . . . that if you do such and such, God will strike you down. If I climbed through the window, [I was told that] I wouldn't grow. Well, I climbed through the window and then checked my growth" (p. 2). Finding his growth rate unchanged, Maslow concluded that religion was a virulent form of superstition, a position he clung to with great tenacity.

The experiments saved his sanity, but they did not deliver him from continued religious harassment at the hands of his mother. While undergoing religious instruction forced on him by her, he was required to proclaim his love for Mother Rose. When he choked on the words, dropped materials from which he was reading, and fled in tears, his ever "insightful" mother exclaimed, "You see! He loves me so much he can't even express the words!" (p. 11).

His mother's alleged cruelties were numerous and varied. She would see to it that he received less food than his siblings, an affront to his status as eldest son, and a not too subtle message: insofar as food means "love" he was unloved (Hoffman, 1988). One day young Maslow brought home some prized 78 rpm recordings, laid them and the rest of his collection on the living room floor for inspection, and absent-mindedly left the room without honoring Rose's command to "pick up your mess." When he returned she was screaming "What did I tell you?" and grinding her heels into his treasured recordings (p. 8). On another occasion he brought home two kittens and spirited them away to the basement, but Rose heard the meowing and confronted him. He had dared to bring stray cats into her house and feed them from her dishes. While Maslow watched in horror, she picked up each kitten in turn and smashed its head against the brick basement wall until it was dead. To the dismay of his siblings, Maslow publicly expressed his antagonism toward Mother Rose several times during his life. When she died, he refused even to attend her funeral.

In contrast to Mother Rose's cruelty, Maslow's father Samuel was merely absent. Probably owing to the sad state of his marriage, he left early in the morning for the long trek to his job and made a point of staying late at work to chat with his cronies. When he finally arrived at home, his children were often already in bed. During childhood, Maslow basically had no relationship with Samuel. When Maslow grew to young adulthood, however, the elder Maslow's business failed, a victim of the Depression, and the father became a ward of the son. They lived together for some time and became friends. Thus, like Adler, and unlike Freud or Sullivan, Maslow was something of a father's son, rather than a mother's boy.

Like Julian Rotter, whose ideas will be covered soon, Maslow's fledgling intellect was nourished by the Brooklyn libraries. But life in Brooklyn for Jewish boys was harsh, and access to the libraries difficult. He learned to stay on Jewish turf lest he fall prey to ethnic youth gangs that controlled surrounding areas. When he ventured forth to visit the local library branch, he had to use special paths, ones with handy escape routes. In self-defense, Maslow tried to join a Jewish gang, but they wanted him to kill cats and throw stones at girls, acts that were against his nature. Instead he skillfully sneaked from home to the library with such high frequency that he soon finished the children's books and was awarded an adult's card.

At school, anti-Semitism was also an everyday problem. Once, when he won the class spelling bee, his bigoted teacher refused to accept the outcome. The "horrible bitch" pitched words at Abraham until he fumbled one: *parallel* (p. 4). Then she announced to the class that she knew all along he was just a fake. Still Maslow did well at school, so well he was dubbed "that smart Jew."

Added to these miseries was the problem of Maslow's appearance. Like Horney, he felt unattractive. Gangly and afflicted with a prominent proboscis, he was sometimes subjected to ridicule. His own father declared before the whole family, "Isn't he the ugliest kid you've ever seen?" (p. 6). Occasions like these gave Maslow a serious inferiority complex and led him to describe his childhood as "miserably unhappy" (p. 6).

After attending a select boy's high school where he performed reasonably well in all but a few key courses, Maslow began a career as an itinerant college student. He wanted to attend revered Cornell at Ithaca, N.Y., one of the few universities in the Eastern United States that did not have strict quotas limiting the number of Jews admitted. His best friend, cousin Will, was accepted there, but Maslow lacked the confidence to apply.

Having given up on Cornell, Maslow enrolled at City College in the winter of 1925. There he found some joys and some sorrows. Trigonometry proved to be a major source of grief. Maslow hated it so much that he could not bear to attend class. Thus, he failed owing to poor attendance, despite having passed the tests. Unlike most of us, he could not grind through life's drudgeries. If Maslow could not bear to do something, he refused to do it, even if doing it was a practical necessity.

After working briefly as a busboy—he felt mistreated and walked off the job—and following a semester on academic probation, Maslow decided to try law. He enrolled in a less than prestigious school and immediately became bored. True to character he quit, disappointing his father at whose behest he had tried law.

During this period Maslow flirted with socialism, but never became the activist that Adler and Fromm had been. Perhaps he was preoccupied with other matters, most especially his attraction to first cousin Bertha. Probably his fear of approaching Bertha "who I couldn't get close to . . . anyhow" and his desire to join Will led to Maslow's transfer to Cornell in 1927 (p. 24).

Just as had been the case for Sullivan, Cornell was mainly a bad experience for Maslow. Despite its relative lack of exclusionary policies regarding Jews, anti-Semitism was alive and well in Ithaca and on university grounds as well. Accordingly, Maslow located in College-town, a community that contained housing for "lesser-status . . . Bohemians and those neither interested in nor acceptable to the Greek letter societies" (p. 25). Not only did the Greeks exclude Jews, many Ithaca landlords refused to rent to them and the *Cornell Sun*, a university-sanctioned student newspaper, barred Jews from its staff.

Cornell also provided Maslow with his first exposure to psychology. As was true for George Kelly, the beginning psychology class made the discipline look anything but inviting. Maslow had the bad luck to enroll in a class assigned to a pretentious dinosaur among professors by the name of Edward B. Titchener. A disciple of Wilhelm Wundt, psychology's founder, Titchener had come to Cornell in 1892 as the chief American proponent of Wundt's "structuralism." Some thirty-five years later Maslow witnessed the spectacle of Titchener, adorned in academic robes, parading to the lectern followed obediently by an entourage of his graduate students. There he espoused a point of view considered long dead by nearly everyone but himself. Structuralism was dull stuff indeed. Such lame academic fare was one of two important reasons why Maslow transferred back to City College after only one semester.

The other reason was Bertha. But when they met, inherent shyness prevented him from expressing his tender feelings for her. One day he was sitting beside his sweetheart longing to touch her when Bertha's assertive sister Anna witnessed his reticence. Growing impatient with the timidity of Maslow and the passivity of Bertha, Anna pushed the reluctant lovers together and exclaimed, "For the love of Pete, kiss her will ya!" Then "life began" (p. 29).

By the spring of 1928, Maslow was restless again. He had learned of the liberal atmosphere at the University of Wisconsin and of the school's esteemed professors whose ranks included Kurt Koffka, one of the original Gestalt psychologists. So once again, he transferred.

The summer before moving to Wisconsin, he visited a former City College professor who recommended *The Psychologies of 1925*, a book containing an essay by John B. Watson, the leading behaviorist of the time. Maslow later wrote, "The thing that really turned me on was Watson's chapter . . . In the highest excitement, I suddenly saw unrolling before me into the future the possibility of a *science of psychology* . . ." (p. 33). How ironic it was that a future humanist would be beckoned to his academic destiny by a psychologist devoted to simple stimulus–response relationships. But Maslow was stuck on psychology, despite the discovery that Koffka, actually only a visiting professor, had departed by the time he arrived on the Wisconsin campus.

While his career had been launched, his personal life was still on the beach. Bertha was in his every thought. Finally, he could stand it no more. He proposed via telegram and she accepted. On the last day of 1928, they were married.

His disappointment at Koffka's departure was soon quelled. Wisconsin's small and not-yet-esteemed psychology department contained faculty and students who would eventually become famous. Professors were also congenial: Students were treated more like colleagues than underlings. By 1930, when he had finished his B. A. degree, he had already taken many graduate courses. During his subsequent graduate school years, he was exposed to likes of Clark Hull, soon to become the foremost learning theorist of the 1930s. However, he eventually migrated to the laboratory of Harry Harlow, whose influential research with monkeys was considered in the Sullivan chapter.

As time passed and Maslow achieved fame, the anger left over from childhood mistreatment and the resentment he felt toward anti-Semites faded. He began to develop the warmth and trust that early experiences had disallowed. However, there was still an undercurrent of bitterness that seemed to obstruct his best efforts on occasion. Alderfer (1989) noted that Maslow had trouble leading *sensitivity training groups*—an assemblage of people who come together to reveal their inner feelings and to achieve intimacy with others. "The man whose intellectual work played such an important role in the then rapidly growing humanistic psychology movement was unable to act in ways . . . consistent with his own theory" (p. 359). When the protest era of the 1960s emerged, Maslow was a natural for the role of guru, the wise leader of soul-searching youth. However, Alderfer suggests that Maslow was uncomfortable with young people's propensity for questioning authority. It can be said that Maslow courageously overcame a tragic childhood, but it left its indelible mark on him.

Maslow spent some time as an academic vagabond. He continued working at Wisconsin while leisurely finishing his dissertation—completed in 1934—then he took a temporary position at Teachers College, Columbia University, Rogers's doorway to academe. Finally Maslow landed a permanent position on the faculty of the brand new Brooklyn College (1937–1951). The rest of his academic career was spent at Brandeis University (1951–1969), where he chaired the psychology department for ten years. In 1968, he served as president of the American Psychological Association. After several bouts with poor health dating back to early mid-life, Maslow died of a heart attack in 1970.

Maslow's View of the Person

The Evolution of a Theorist

Maslow's love of music and his attraction to free-thinking politicians and academicians rested uneasily with his initial devotion to the study of neurologically programmed behaviors in animals (Hoffman, 1988). Yet success is a magnet that has pulled many researchers along, even against their wills. After early publications with Harlow, Maslow gained his own fame. He showed that what looked like sexual behavior in monkeys—the constant mounting of one monkey by another—was actually a display of dominance. "The higher a monkey's dominance position, the more likely it is to mount its subordinates; the lower its position, the more likely it is to be mounted by others" (p. 61). Although he helped to establish interest in primate "dominance hierarchies," Maslow eventually abandoned the study of mechanistic animal behavior.

During the period following completion of his Ph.D. requirements, Maslow searched desperately for a stable means of livelihood. Because the Depression was going on, he opted for future security and entered medical school. But, as always when he did something for reasons other than intrinsic interest, he became bored and dropped out. Earlier attempts to work at the famous Yerkes primate facilities also fell through. Facing a poor job market and an "old gentile boy" network—he had already been denied a research grant because of anti-Semitism—Maslow was ready to take anything. Much to his joy, famed learning psychologist Edward L. Thorndike became interested in his work. Thorndike, of Columbia University Teachers College, had been the author of the "law of effect," a basic principle of learning. By this time, however, he had become a generalist. Instead of watching cats learn to escape from boxes, he had grand plans for applying psychology and was awarded the unheard of amount of $100,000 to carry them out. Maslow could return to New York City, continue his research, and make a living while doing so.

Even as he was immersed in his animal studies at Wisconsin, Maslow had become interested in the Freud–Adler quarrel. Now he found himself in the middle of the most exciting place at the most fascinating time during the early history of personality psychology.

New York City was sparkling with the brilliance of Horney, Fromm, Adler, and others, including Gestalt psychologist Koffka. Among these luminaries, Adler was singled out by Maslow as having special impact on him. When Maslow showed up for a series of lectures by the renegade ex-Freudian, he was pleasantly surprised to find a nearly empty classroom. Having few competitors for Adler's attention, the two became well-acquainted. Undoubtedly, Adler's notions of social interest, law of movement (directed free choice), striving for superiority, and the prehumanistic idea "creative power of the individual" influenced Maslow heavily.

The Gestalt Influence

However, it was the Gestalt psychologists who probably contributed the most to Maslow's intellectual evolution. The New School for Social Research in New York City had become the "University in Exile" for European scholars fleeing Hitler. Among them was the founder of Gestalt psychology, Max Wertheimer, an inspiring teacher, but not a prolific writer. Thus, it was left to Koffka to lay some important planks in the flooring of Maslow's theory.

Gestalt psychology—initially concerned only with perception—held that simple perceptions were "wholes" made up of integrated parts (Matlin & Foley, 1992). One could consider the parts or the whole, but not both at once. Thus, a mosaic, the tiny tiles that form faces and figures in works of art (and in institutional flooring), could be appreciated as a whole, or its parts could be considered. More importantly, the parts and the whole were not separate entities, but were inextricably tied up together: A whole is an integration of parts such that the parts and the whole cannot exist separately from one another. Gestalt theory was largely composed of "laws of organization" that explained how parts are formed into wholes. Among these laws are: (1) grouping similar objects together to form a whole; (2) grouping proximal (near) objects; and (3) the law of closure, incomplete objects such as a circle with a section out are completed by "the mind's eye." Another is the familiar *figure–ground* rule: scenes are divided into a *figure* in the foreground displayed against a *background*. This principle is illustrated by the "vase and the face" reversing picture that has portions alternating as figure or ground. True to general Gestalt theory, one may see a white vase against a black background, or black faces against a white background, but not both at once.

The idea of wholeness and of parts that are inextricably tied to the whole became fundamental to Maslow's thinking. In Maslow's words, "Our first proposition states that the individual is an integrated, organized whole" (1954, p. 63). To elucidate this point, he drew an analogy to the study of the stomach. This top end of the intestines can be investigated by extracting a specimen from a cadaver and examining it as if it normally functioned independently of the body from which it was taken. Alternatively, the stomach can be studied in living, breathing organisms. To Maslow, the latter is much preferred, because the stomach cannot be fully understood apart from the living body into which it is integrated. It is not the stomach that "is hungry," it is the individual. "Furthermore, satisfaction of hunger comes to the whole individual, not just to a part of him" (p. 63).

Motivation

Motivation comes from the same word root as the term *motion* and refers to the process by which organisms are propelled toward goals. To Maslow, motivational factors underlie personality. However, *drive*, a simple tension that demands to be satisfied—hunger is an example—is not an entirely satisfactory motivational concept. While drive is a traditional psychological concept and seems easily understood, Maslow (1954) considered it to be inherently ambiguous. Looking at behavior that appears associated with a certain drive may mislead us. People apparently behaving at the behest of the hunger drive may find food and eat it. However, their ultimate goal may be security, not reduction of the hunger drive. Likewise, people engaging in sexual behavior may actually be seeking increased self-esteem. It is these end-goals—security and self-esteem in the examples—that hold the key to understanding people. Such goals transcend the particular life circumstances of the given person. Goal-seeking can be cast as **needs** for certain satisfactions that are sought by all humans, regardless of their culture, environment, or generation.

Maslow took the unique point of view, overlooked by most theorists, that a given behavior, thought, or feeling may occur at the behest of multiple motivations (Maslow, 1954). Henry Murray adopted a similar position. We are in the habit of attempting to find *the* reason for every significant action displayed by either ourselves or others. Actually, human behavior is extraordinarily complex. Anything a person does is likely to be traced to many motivations, not just one. Not only do we perform sexually for physical gratification, we

---

BOX 10.1   Why Do We Do What We Do? Let Us Count the Reasons . . .

Nonprofessionals and psychological professionals alike can sometimes be quite simple-minded about human thought, behavior, and feeling. Even obviously complex actions like proposing marriage, committing suicide, and changing careers may be discussed as if only one motive is involved. "He proposed because he is in love"; "People commit suicide because they hate themselves"; "She changed careers to make more money." Rarely are single motives sufficient to explain such complex actions.

Below are several ordinary decisions, activities, or psychological conditions. Contemplate each and for each imagine that you are the person involved. Then write down as many reasons why you "did what you did" as you can conjure up. An example precedes the exercise items.

I spent the afternoon cleaning out my cabinets and closets. I wanted to get organized. I couldn't
find anything. I wanted to be neat like my sister.
I felt the need to expend some energy. I wanted to take something apart and put it back together again. I was depressed and needed a distraction. I was bored and needed to fill some time.

"I went shopping all afternoon and didn't find a thing."

"I ate everything I could find in the house."

"I wrote my Mom a nasty letter."

"I told my best friend, 'I care for you more than anyone else.' "

"I took the afternoon off, started a novel, and read until 3 A.M."

may also be seeking closeness, friendship, safety, love, and, yes, self-esteem, among other important satisfactions. A person suffering from paralysis of the arm for which no physical basis can be found may experience many motivational benefits: pity, love, and attention, to name a few. Only the rarest of thoughts, behaviors, or feelings are likely to stem from just one motivational source.

According to Maslow, while the needs a person experiences are universal, the methods used to satisfy them may be specific to the person's culture. Everyone has a need to bolster and maintain self-esteem. Self-esteem may be boosted by being a good hunter, a superb athlete, an outstanding pottery maker, or a feared "witch doctor," depending on the culture. Likewise, environment may determine the particular form of need satisfaction, but Maslow was quick to point out that the role of environment is often overemphasized. Exactly how the urge to eat is satisfied will depend in some degree on whether we find ourselves in L.A., Chicago, New York, or Houston. It may also depend on whether we are on a camping trip, in a shopping mall, or stuck at Aunt Sue's house. However, an environmental circumstance does not force certain satisfactions on us. Rather our perceptions of that circumstance and operations on it shape need fulfillment. By making reference to "environmental barriers," Maslow explained that environments are what we make of them: "a child who is trying to attain a certain object of value to him, but who is restrained by a barrier of some sort, determines not only that the object has value, but that the barrier is a barrier. Psychologically there is no such thing as a barrier; there is only a barrier for a particular person who is trying to get something that he wants" (p. 74).

Finally, a motivation cannot be considered in isolation from other motivations. The satisfaction of a given need may depend on the prior, simultaneous, or subsequent satisfactions of other needs. Again, Henry Murray advocated a similar position. We can hardly be creative if our stomachs have been empty for days. During the process of supporting and comforting other people, we can expect to receive self-esteem bolstering comments from them. Only after we have secured a safe apartment in a big city can we expect to enjoy interactions with family at home. Motivations relate to other motivations in a multidimensional matrix of almost infinite complexity.

Basic Concepts: Maslow

Not by Bread Alone: Five Basic Human Needs

Maslow (1954, 1970) offers two answers to the question "Do people live by bread alone?" When people have no bread, the answer is "yes." But, when bread is plentiful, the answer is "no." Consider the example of desperately hungry people who constantly think about food, dream about food, and have recollections only about food. All other interests are unimportant. Life itself is defined in terms of eating. To them, Utopia is a place where there is plenty of food. Ex-POWs and concentration camp inmates can testify, once a person has been severely deprived of food, food becomes all that matters.

However, the picture is quite different when bread is available and the person's belly is continuously filled. Gratification of hunger frees the person to pursue higher-order needs. When these additional needs emerge, they begin to dominate the individual, taking the place of hunger. After second level needs are satisfied, still higher-order needs emerge. Maslow places all needs in a hierarchy ranging from the most fundamental biologically based needs to the most abstract, uniquely human needs.

Physiological needs encompass specific biological requirements for water, oxygen, proteins, vitamins, proper body temperature, sleep, sex, exercise, and so on (Maslow, 1954). At this primitive level of the hierarchy, biological urges may be thought of as "needs" rather than "drives," because the satisfactions in question are the ultimate goals. For example, when food is scarce, seeking food is not a means to some other end. Homeless people are often reduced to the physiological level: they may go days without food and without adequate shelter from the elements.

Safety needs include security, protection, stability, structure, law and order, and freedom from fear and chaos. These needs are readily inferred from negative reactions of children to sudden disruption and unpredictability in their lives. In fact, if children or adults are observed to feel endangered and threatened, this need can be assumed to have been activated by some currently prominent stimulus. Veterans home from Vietnam had plenty in their stomachs. However, many spontaneously recoiled when a car backfired nearby or when the peculiar whirring, whipping sound of a helicopter occurred within hearing range.

Belongingness and love needs orient the person toward affectionate relations with people, and a sense of place in family and groups. During the course of his career, Maslow witnessed the rapidly expanding acceptance of participation in sensitivity groups. He viewed this trend as an index of the widespread hunger for interpersonal contact, intimacy, and togetherness. Maslow noted that most theorists have stressed the "thwarting of love needs" as a fundamental cause of human maladjustment (Maslow, 1970). The growing number of children in foster homes and the numerous children of divorce often operate from this level.

Esteem needs are of two kinds: (1) There are personal desires for adequacy, mastery, competence, achievement, confidence, independence, and freedom; and (2) there are desires for respect from other people, including attention, recognition, appreciation, status, prestige, fame, dominance, importance, and dignity (Maslow, 1954). Satisfaction of esteem needs results in feelings of personal worth, self-confidence, psychological strength, capability, and a sense of being useful and necessary. "But thwarting of these needs produces feelings of inferiority, of weakness, and of helplessness" (p. 91). In turn, these feelings produce either discouragement, compensation, or neurosis. Children who succeed in school, in sports, and in the interpersonal arena have esteem. Those who are denied opportunities to succeed do not.

The quintessential longing is the **need for self-actualization**, "the desire for self-fulfillment . . . the tendency for [one] to become actualized in what [one] is potentially" (Maslow, 1954, pp. 91–92). This powerful force can be cast as the desire to become more of what one presently is, to become everything that one is capable of being. What a person *can* be, that person feels compelled to *become*, whether athlete, parent, or community leader. Musicians experience a powerful need to make music, artists to paint, poets to write. Each person hears a voice from within that whispers "Be true to your nature." It is in the manifestations of self-actualization that people differ the most. Because each person is different from each other person, that which each person feels the need to become is unique. "At this level, individual differences are greatest" (Maslow, 1970, p. 46).

Maslow characterized the first four basic needs as **deficiency needs or D-needs**, the satisfaction of which allows the person to avoid physical sickness and psychological maladjustment (Goble, 1970; Maslow, 1968). Citing evidence from research, Maslow concluded that an individual's food preferences are a fairly clear indication of actual physiological needs or deficiencies of the body (P. T. Young, 1941/1948). If the body is lacking a particular biochemical substance, the individual will attempt to satisfy the deficiency by developing a hunger for the missing nutritional element. Maslow (1970) also saw support for his concept of basic needs in Walter Cannon's (1932) theory of *homeostasis*, processes through which the body automatically attempts to maintain physiological equilibrium. The acid/alkaline balance is an example. D-needs meet the following criteria: (1) people yearn persistently for their gratification; (2) deprivation sickens people or stunts their growth; (3) gratification cures the deficiency illness; (4) steady supplies prevent these illnesses; and (5) healthy people do not demonstrate the deficiencies. Impoverished people tend to experience D-needs continually.

Although self-actualization does not clearly emerge until there has been some prior satisfaction of the physiological, safety, love, and esteem needs, gratification of basic needs is not sufficient to guarantee self-actualization. Self-actualizing people *do* enjoy sufficient gratification of their basic needs. In addition, they demonstrate freedom from illness. More importantly, however, they show positive use of their capacities, and motivations that are linked to a set of personal values. Further, while self-actualization implies the prior fulfillment of all lower-order needs, it is different from them. In contrast to the four other needs, its direction is positive or growth-motivated rather than negative or deficiency-motivated. Self-actualization is a *growth need*, not a D-need.

Maslow has arranged the basic needs into a hierarchy, in a first-things-first manner. Lower-order needs are *prepotent*, more immediately and urgently demanding than higher-order needs. They occur earlier in the developmental process and require gratification prior to higher-order needs. A deficiency in a lower-order need dominates personality functioning until it is satisfied. Only then is the person freed to begin addressing the need that is a step up in the hierarchy. Safety is a "stronger, more pressing, earlier appearing, more vital need" than belongingness, and the need for food is prepotent to both (Maslow, 1959, p. 123). Figure 10.1 shows the hierarchical order of needs proposed by Maslow, with physiological needs prepotent to safety needs which, in turn, are prepotent to belongingness and love needs, and so on, up the steps.

Hierarchical needs are not met in an all-or-none fashion, but are overlapping. The most common pattern is for people to experience some degree of need satisfaction that is below the maximum degree. Using arbitrary figures, Maslow (1970) speculated that, in this society, the satisfactions of an average person's five needs might be 85 percent physiological, 70 percent safety, 50 percent love, 40 percent self-esteem, and 10 percent self-actualization. Also, needs at a certain level do not have to be fully met before the person's attention turns to a higher level. People need not experience 100 percent satisfaction of a lower-order need before they can begin to pursue the next highest need on the hierarchy. The emergence of a new need occurs gradually as a lower need is satisfied. If belongingness and love needs are satisfied only 10 percent, esteem needs may not be visible at all. However, with 25 percent love satisfaction, the esteem need may arise to the 5 percent degree.

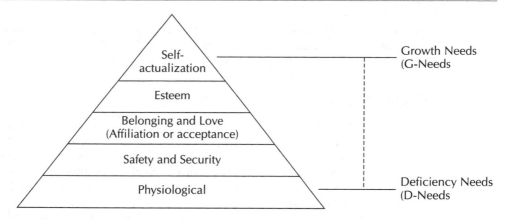

FIGURE 10.1   Maslow's Hierarchy of Needs

There are, of course, exceptions to the order of needs appearing in the hierarchy. Romeo and Juliet were willing to die for love. India's Mohandas Gandhi was willing to deny his own safety and physiological needs for self-actualization and higher-order values, including personal dignity, social equality, and political freedom. However, just as people do not realize complete satisfaction of lower order needs and then *suddenly* experience the next highest need in full bloom, they cannot *suddenly* deny lower order needs while continuing to pursue high order needs. Gandhi was able to gradually deny lower-order needs as he focused on higher-order needs. Had he been abruptly placed in a Nazi concentration camp and *suddenly* reduced to an animalistic level via torture, starvation, and exhaustion, he might have been scratching for food and clinging to survival like other inmates (Allen, 1990). Abruptly take away the satisfaction of basic physiological needs and most people would slide down Maslow's hierarchy. The comfortable and secure can choose not to eat, sleep, or even breathe. People precipitously reduced to a basic survival level are usually compelled to eat if they can.

In the most typical reversal of needs, the relatively higher-order need for belongingness and love is subordinated to esteem. The person who believes that satisfaction of the esteem need carries with it satisfaction of the love need may adopt the assumption that love comes to those who are powerful, respected, and feared. For this person, the need to be an object of affection is met by adopting the belief that a self-confident, aggressively assertive persona will elicit "love."

It is also possible to experience permanent loss of a need, as in the case of an antisocial (psychopathic) individual whose cravings for love during infancy were never met. By adulthood, the desire and ability to give and receive affection has been lost. A critical period in this person's development was probably bypassed, similar to animals who lose their sucking or pecking reflexes when these are not exercised soon enough after birth. An individual's level of aspiration may also be permanently lowered. For example, someone who has experienced chronic poverty or unemployment may continue to seek only minimal satisfactions in life, such as obtaining just adequate food or shelter. As homeless people experience both poverty and unemployment, many may never get beyond seeking satisfaction of physiolog-ical needs and safety needs. Little wonder they may not be motivated to form relations with others (belongingness) and to "take pride in themselves" (esteem).

Human Nature Is Born, Not Made

Although Maslow recognizes that external environments may be helpful to people in actu-alizing their inherent characteristics, he did not believe environments can teach people to be human or that environments shape humanness. Although culture, family, and parents may function as sun, food, and water to human actualization, they are not its seed. For Maslow (1970), human nature is inborn, not made. It has an essential, built-in structure comprised of potentialities and values that are intrinsic and common to all members of the species. Maslow considers all human needs and values **instinctoid**, or instinct-like, because of their biological, genetic, and universal characteristics. Thus, all basic and higher-order needs are, "in the strictest sense," biological needs, "related to the fundamental structure of the human organism itself," with "some genetic basis" involved, however weak (Maslow, 1969, p. 734). Maslow used the term *instinctoid*, because the term *instinct* is fraught with problems. *Instinct*, when applied to humans, has traditionally placed them on the same plane with lower animals. Although his career was launched by animal research and he sometimes drew analogies to animal study results, Maslow rejected the assumed strict con-tinuity of humans and other creatures. In Maslow's thinking, "sexual," when applied to hu-man beings, was analogous to but not the same thing as "sexual" in other beings. Further, the idea of instincts seems to imply that we are born only with lower-order needs. From this perspective, higher-order needs, such as love, are developed after birth by associative learn-ing. For example, while the infant is being fed, the mother "expresses love." Thus, according to the associative account, love gains its power and, in fact, its very existence as a motivat-ing force, through its association with feeding. Maslow clearly rejected this association ac-count of higher-order needs, and asserted that these needs do not depend on lower-order needs for their existence. The only essential link of higher-order needs to lower-order needs is that humans' longing for esteem and self-actualization arises only after physiological, safety, and belongingness needs are addressed.

Self-Actualizing Persons: Superior Personalities

Maslow did not believe that all choices or choosers are equal. Consider an analogy to ani-mal choosers. Chickens allowed to select their own diet showed great individual differences in their ability to choose beneficial foods (P. T. Young, 1941/1948). Some were "good choosers," and some were "bad choosers." Good choosers became stronger, larger, and more dominant than bad choosers, allowing them to get the best of everything. Later, when di-ets selected by good choosers were forced on bad choosers, the latter did get stronger, big-ger, healthier, and more dominant, although they never reached the level of good choosers. Thus, organisms who were good choosers could select what was good for the bad choosers better than the bad choosers actually chose for themselves.

Maslow believed human choosers operate similarly. He attempted to understand the values embedded in human nature by observing the cream of the human crop. "Only the choices and tastes and judgments of healthy human beings will tell us much about what is good for the [entire] human species in the long run" (Maslow, 1959, p. 121). Maslow studied the "best" of human personalities, defined as those he viewed as being the most psychologically healthy, mature, highly evolved, and fully human. He designated a few of these superior persons **self-actualizers**, people who fulfill themselves by making complete use of their potentialities, capacities, and talents, who do the best they are capable of doing, and who develop themselves to the most complete stature possible for them. Self-actualizers live Nietzsche's exhortation, "Become what thou art!"

One may wonder who these "best personalities" are and what they are like. A list of likely self-actualizers would include Abraham Lincoln, Thomas Jefferson, Sojourner Truth, Albert Einstein, Eleanor Roosevelt, Harriet Tubman, Cesar Chavez, Albert Schweitzer, Jane Addams, Frederick Douglass, Kahlil Gibran, Paul Robeson, Harry Wu, Sitting Bull, Susan B. Anthony, Adlai Stevenson, William James, Mildred "Babe" Didrikson, Martin Luther King, Malcolm X, and Mother Teresa. A number of the common characteristics of super-personalities are summarized in Table 10.1.

Do not feel too disappointed to learn that you probably are not a self-actualizer or that self-actualizers are not likely to be present among your college classmates. Maslow's (1970) initial screening of 3,000 students yielded only one usable subject, partly because typical students are too young to have had the experiences necessary for a good approximation to self-actualization.

Even superior psychological health was defined by Maslow as applying to less than 1% of college students, those evaluated as "growing well." Any such disappointment you may feel should be tempered by learning that self-actualizers are extremely rare. Maslow identified

---

TABLE 10.1   Characteristics of Self-Actualizing Persons

Clear, efficient perceptions of reality and comfortable relations with it

Acceptance of self, others, and nature

Spontaneity, simplicity, and naturalness

Problem centering (having something outside themselves they "must" do as a mission)

Detachment and need for privacy

A forceful will and relative independence from environment

Continued freshness of appreciation

Mystic experience, peak experience

Gemeinschaftsgefuhl, feeling of kinship and identification with the human race (the same German word used by Adler and later translated as social interest)

Personal relations with others (deep but limited in number)

Democratic character structure

Ethical discrimination between means and ends, between good and evil

Philosophical, unhostile sense of humor

Creativeness

Transcendence of any particular culture, resisting cultural molding

Imperfections: sometimes thoughtless, socially impolite, cold, boring, irritating, stubborn, ruthless, forgetful, humorless, silly, angered, superficially prideful, naively kind, anxious, guilty, and conflicted (without maladjustment)

BOX 10.2   **Where Are You on Maslow's Hierarchy Right Now?**

Now that you have a preliminary understanding of the hierarchical needs, go back to Figure 10.1. Think of yourself as you are at this point in your development. Assuming that you are well fed and feel safe and secure, what need is in focus at this time? Is it belongingness and love? Esteem? (If Maslow is correct about the rareness of self-actualizers, it is probably not self-actualization.) Choose one and write a paragraph to verify your choice (list the kinds of experience you seek right now).

---

only a tiny fraction of the general population as meeting his criteria for self-actualization. Further, being self-actualized is not all good. Note the self-centered, self-absorbed imperfections of self-actualized people (bottom of Table 10.1).

Needs and Values beyond the Pale and Experiences from the Mountaintop

Accompanying self-actualization are certain special needs. These include **cognitive needs**, motivations to know, to understand, to explain, and to satisfy curiosity, and a variety of **aesthetic needs** related to beauty, structure, and symmetry. Such needs have been identified collectively by Maslow (1967) as **meta-needs or growth needs (G-needs)**, terms that "describe the motivations of self-actualizing people" (Maslow, 1970, p. 134). All of these meta-needs are closely enmeshed with the overriding need for self-actualization and are not, in the strictest sense, "motivated" but meta- or beyond motivation.

Maslow (1967) has also identified **B-Values**, ultimate or end-goals of meta-need fulfillment. They include truth, goodness, beauty, unity and wholeness, transcendence, aliveness, uniqueness, perfection, completion, justice, order, simplicity, richness, totality, effortlessness, playfulness, self-sufficiency, and meaningfulness. These values are more likely to be possessed by self-actualizers than by others.

Maslow believed that self-actualizers are more likely than others to have **peak experiences**, intense, mystical experiences associated with simultaneous feelings of limitless horizons, powerfulness, and helplessness, a lost sense of time and place, and great ecstasy, wonder, and awe (Maslow, 1970). These experiences have a high degree of personal importance, strengthening or transforming the person. They come from love and sex, bursts of creativity, moments of insight and discovery, and times of fusion with nature. Peak experiences are natural phenomena, not supernatural, and were described by William James many years ago (1902/1958).

Evaluation

Contributions

Maslow's contributions are many and diverse. The emphasis here is on his beliefs that human values and needs are inherent and that humans are self-directing, his insightful criticisms of psychological science, his speculations about a psychological Utopia, and his contributions to diverse fields and disciplines.

Humans Have Inherent Needs and Values and Are Self-Directing

Unique among psychologists is Maslow's (1959, 1967, 1969) insistence that needs are as much a part of the human constitution as voice boxes and symbolic thought. He places emphasis on (1) the existence of universal human needs and values and (2) their biological origin. Like Rogers, Maslow believed that "the organism is more trustworthy, more self-protecting, self-directing, and self-governing than it is usually given credit for" (1970, p. 78). Also like Rogers, he believed strongly in a universal, inborn *organismic valuing process*, or "bodily wisdom." Maslow (1959) analogized to hundreds of free-choice experiments in which animals of all kinds behaved in ways that were "good" or "right" for them. Recall that animals were able to select adequate diets when offered alternatives (P. T. Young, 1941, 1948). As for human infants, Maslow observed the evolution of psychologists toward increased confidence in "the internal wisdom of our babies" (Maslow, 1959, pp. 120–121). Infants can make good choices with regard to diet, time of weaning, amount of sleep, time of toilet training, need for activity, and so on. This point of view contrasts with that of behaviorists like B. F. Skinner, who emphasize environmental control over infant behavior.

Insightful Criticisms of Psychological Science

Maslow has been especially critical of traditional approaches to determining standards for optimal personality functioning. Scientific approaches too readily assume that people are so similar to animals that results of animal studies can be generalized to humans. While useful analogies between humans and animals may be drawn, their essential natures differ.

Clinical approaches rely too heavily on samples of maladjusted people, thereby offering a warped view of human nature based on observations of disturbed and miserable lives. Other approaches adopt a statistical-averaging procedure in which findings from all people are thrown into a single hopper. With this methodology, individual differences are lost. More specifically, Maslow considers this technique of little use, because it mixes information from healthy and sick people equally, resulting in a concoction that is neither vintage champagne nor cheap wine.

Psychological Utopia: Eupsychia

Maslow, like Sullivan, believed that most basic human needs could be satisfied only through interpersonal relations. Although he developed no method of psychotherapy, he often saw therapeutic interactions as exemplifying "good human relationships." Quality relationships facilitate fulfillment of human needs for security, belongingness, and self-esteem, the fulfillment of which eliminates obstructions to the pursuit of self-actualization (Maslow, 1970). Psychotherapy relationships dispense "psychological medicines" needed by all human beings: mutual frankness, trust, honesty, lack of defensiveness, emotional release, healthy passivity, relaxation, affection, playfulness, and love. Effective, democratic psychotherapists can do much to help individuals identify their inner needs and compensate for earlier deficiencies. These benefits then transfer to relationships outside the therapy setting.

Maslow (1970) firmly believed that self-actualization could be promoted by the presence of good people who would be part of a *good environment* that would (1) offer the individual all necessary raw materials needed for creative and spiritual endeavors, as well as basic need fulfillment; (2) allow the individual to pursue her or his own wishes, demands, and choices; (3) accept delays and abandonment of choices; (4) respect the wishes, demands, and choices of individuals; and (5) "get out of the way" whenever appropriate.

To make the criteria for the ideal environment more concrete, Maslow speculated about a future *Eupsychia* (Yew-sigh-key-ah), a utopian society characterized by psychological health among all its members. Its philosophical base would be anarchistic, meaning there would be no governmental imposition on individual liberty. Basic and meta-needs would be respected, much more than usual. There would be more free choice as well as less control, violence, and contempt. It also would be Taoistic in its philosophy, valuing what is simple, loving, and unselfish. Overall, the good environment would stress spiritual and psychological forces as well as material and economic ones. Eupsychia would not work for all, however. "When we speak of free *choice* in human beings, we refer to sound adults or children who are not yet twisted and distorted" (Maslow, 1970, p. 278). You may find it interesting to compare Maslow's conceptions of the Utopian society with those of B. F. Skinner, whose ideas have formed the basis of a real, functioning community.

Contributions to Many Fields and Concerns

Maslow's ideas, especially his hierarchy of needs, have been adapted to many different professional areas. The hierarchy has been especially useful to people concerned with personnel management, marketing, and organizational operations (Alderfer, 1989; Buttle, 1989). In organizational settings, relations among employees within and between management levels will not be smooth and efficient unless each employee recognizes the need satisfactions being sought by other employees. Only with such understanding will employees be able to facilitate one another's need satisfactions and integrate the pursuit of satisfactions with company goals. Creativity will be locked out of the executive board room unless high-level management personnel are encouraged and aided in attempts to approximate self-actualization. Finally, the marketing of products will be less than optimally effective if the needs that products address are not considered when decisions about product "packaging" are made. Maslow's book *Eupsychian Management* (1965) is in large part devoted to these issues.

The enormous variety of fields to which Maslow's ideas have been applied is illustrated by two additional examples. First, Maslow's hierarchy has been useful in speech–language pathologist training (Houle, 1990). Prior to a conference between a pathologist and his or her advisor one of Maslow's needs is selected to be a conference focus. Second, self-actualization in athletes has been recently examined. A group of researchers compared blind and sighted athletes on scores derived from responses to Shostrom's Personality Orientation Inventory (POI) measure of self-actualization (Sherrill et al., 1990; Shostrom, 1966). The POI is a paper-and-pencil personality questionnaire made up of 150 pairs of items, presented in a forced-choice format. People respond to each item–pair by selecting the pair member that best applies to them. An example similar to a POI item is "(a) I enjoy my life" or "(b) I do not enjoy my life."

Blind and sighted athletes were identical in self-actualization profiles, except that blind athletes scored lower on Existentiality and Self-Acceptance. Athletes as a group scored lower than the general population on two major POI scales: Time Competency and Inner-Directedness. However, they were average or strong in Self-Actualizing Value, feeling Reactivity, Spontaneity, Self-Regard, and Acceptance of Aggression.

Supporting Evidence

Some fundamental concepts of Maslow's theory have received at least partial support. Confirmation of the tendency toward self-actualization, evidence of a need hierarchy, and support for the existence of peak experiences has been reported in the psychological literature over the last four decades.

Self-Actualization

Maslow emphasized the idea of an inborn tendency toward actualization. Support for this emphasis comes from a number of other humanistic theories. Maslow credits a follower of Gestalt tradition, Kurt Goldstein (1939), with originating the concept "self-actualization." Goldstein saw "the drive of self-actualization" as the only human motive (Maslow, 1954). Although Maslow's position was broader than Goldstein's, they both believed that organisms strive toward growth and utilization of available resources.

Shostrom's POI provides scores on a variety of humanistic dimensions and he has reported evidence for the validity of self-actualization. In a study cited by Shostrom (1966), the POI scores of two therapy–patient groups were compared. One group of patients was predicted to be relatively high in self-actualizing tendency, because members had received twenty-seven months of therapy on average. The other group, patients just beginning therapy, was expected to be less self-actualizing. The differences between group scores were statistically significant on all dimensions. The two groups also differed on seven of nine maladjustment scales of another measure, the Minnesota Multiphasic Personality Inventory (MMPI).

Hierarchy of Needs

Graham and Balloun (1973) first had participants freely describe the most important aspects of their lives and, second, rate their present *degree of satisfaction* at the physiological, security, social (acceptance by others), and self-actualization levels. Graduate students rated the descriptions as to *desire expressed for satisfaction* of the four needs. Results supported the hypothesis that there would be greater satisfaction of lower-order needs than higher-order needs. Analysis of the relationship between the first and second measures confirmed the hypothesis that the *degree of satisfaction* of any given need would be negatively correlated with *desire for satisfaction* of that need: the less the satisfaction, the more the desire for satisfaction.

As just illustrated, until recently there has been a tendency for researchers to consider the hierarchy as a whole or concentrate on measurement of self-actualization. Williams and Page (1989) corrected that shortcoming by developing measures relevant to the safety, belonging, and esteem levels of the hierarchy. For each of these levels they assessed: (1) need gratification (perceptions of the degree to which a need is being gratified; (2) need importance; (3) need salience (the degree to which a need is "on one's mind and demands one's attention"); and (4) self-concept (as related to a given need level; for example, one could have a positive or negative self-concept regarding how much others are seen as caring for oneself).

Williams and Page made a number of predictions that clarify how their measures would pinpoint the level at which a person is functioning and whether the person is preparing to move to a higher level. A person's degree of need gratification at a given level should be negatively correlated with the salience of the need at that level. That is, the more a need has been gratified, the less it should be on one's mind (salience). As one is entering a new, higher level, one's self-concept should become attuned to the new level. For example, if one has accommodated belongingness needs and is moving to esteem needs, one's self-concept should be based more on feelings of adequacy, competence, achievement, and status in others' eyes (esteem) than on affectionate relations with others (belongingness).

Further, the self-concept should be in tune with need gratification for the level at which one currently dwells, but negatively related to need gratification for the level one has just transcended. Finally, it should be possible to ascertain at which level a person dwells and predict whether the person is primed to move up. Suppose a person indicates that all needs up to and including those relating to esteem are important, and the person's highest self-concept score is at the esteem level. Then it can be concluded that person is operating at the esteem level. In addition, suppose the person is somewhat unsatisfied in terms of esteem, but all lower-order needs are satisfied. Under these conditions it is possible to predict that the person is not likely to move from esteem to self-actualization.

Williams and Page used undergraduate psychology students in three studies designed to test their hypotheses. Generally, the students were found to be functioning at the esteem level. Evidence supporting this conclusion included: (1) "importance" scores were highest for esteem needs and self-concept was most in tune with that level; (2) the needs at the two lower levels were rated as important, but not particularly "on the mind" (salient); and (3) need gratification was high for all levels, but of the three under investigation, it was lowest for esteem. In all, the researchers made sixteen predictions. One such prediction was that the higher the safety need gratification, the lower the safety self-concept, because, having met safety needs, the individual would be pursuing needs at higher levels. Fourteen of the sixteen predictions were confirmed. This outcome lends credence to the researchers' contention that their measure shows the level at which a person dwells and predicts where the person will go next in the pursuit of need satisfactions.

As you will see, a number of psychologists have failed to support Maslow's hierarchy of needs. To address some of these negative outcomes, Wicker, Brown, Wiehe, Hagan, and Reed (1993) examined failures to support the hierarchy and found that nonsupporting research often measured "importance" of need satisfaction. These studies frequently found that lower-order needs were not less important than higher-order needs being currently addressed, an apparent contradiction of hierarchy assumptions. But Wicker and colleagues suspected that "importance" was ambiguous. For example, imagine a person who finds creative gardening very "important." On a hot and humid day, while working in her garden, a point of discomfort is reached at which she stops gardening and flees to her air-conditioned house. Gardening still reigns supreme in "importance," but another need has become more pressing. "Importance" may be a poor measure, because it confounds the value of a need with its pressing nature. Wicker and colleagues felt "intention" ("I intend to get out of this heat") would provide a better measure of needs' pressing nature. In fact, when they used both an "importance" and an "intention" measure, only the intention measure confirmed hierarchy assumptions: The more subjects felt they had attained satisfaction of a need, the less they *intended* to address the need. An additional study by the same group (Wicker, Wiehe, Hagan, & Brown, 1994) found additional support for the hierarchy using "intention" and another measure rather than "importance."

Peak Experiences

Research findings have contributed some support to Maslow's concept of "peak experience." Ravizza (1977) interviewed twenty athletes in twelve different sports who reported expanded views of themselves as fully functioning individuals. Their "greatest moment" in sports showed many similarities to Maslow's description of the peak experience: loss of fear (100 percent of sample), full attention or immersion (95 percent), perfect experience (95 percent), godlike feeling of control (95 percent), self-validation (95 percent), universe as integrated and unified (90 percent), and effortlessness (90 percent). Nevertheless, some aspects of Maslow's description were not met: the athletes' experiences were more narrow in focus than broad, more oriented to the body than to cognitive or spiritual reflection, and more important to immediate circumstances than to bringing about major changes in their lives. Thus, athletes' "greatest moments" were only partially equivalent to Maslow's peak experiences.

Mathes, Zevon, Roter, and Joerger (1982) reviewed the research literature on peak experiences and then developed a 70-item scale to measure peak-experience tendencies, the Peak Scale. An "empirical picture" of individuals reporting peak experiences that was consistent with Maslow's theorizing emerged after five studies using the scale. Individuals who scored high on the Peak Scale evidenced cognitive experiences of a transcendent and mystical nature, as well as feelings of intense happiness. High scorers reported living in terms of B-values such as truth, beauty, and justice. Women, but not men, tended to show slightly higher self-actualization scores on the POI compared with persons not reporting peak experiences.

Limitations

It will come as no surprise to you that criticisms of Maslow's work are most frequently lodged against ideas relating to self-actualization, and against the hierarchy of needs. "Peak experience" has received a measure of criticism as well. By and large, Maslow has been charged with arbitrariness and failure to consider alternatives. In addition, research relating to his ideas has generated contradictions.

Self-Actualization

Maslow supported his ideas about self-actualization by observing "super-personalities." Unfortunately, he used a small, arbitrarily selected sample that was not objectively observed, rather than using systematic assessment and a representative sample. Maslow's identifications of "self-actualizers" were based on his personal selections, resulted from inferential reviews of a variety of materials not publicly available, and were biased toward Western culture. While he recognized some of these shortcomings (1959), other commentators have emphasized the shaky nature of his methods for identifying self-actualizers and the traits they are supposed to possess. Dismissing his own approval of Maslow's values as "beside the point," M. Brewster Smith (1973) declared that Maslow's values are too one-sided.

Phillips, Watkins, and Noll (1974) compared a measure of Maslow's "self-actualization" with a measure of existentialist Viktor Frankl's "self-realization": the POI (self-actualization; Shostrom, 1966) and the Purpose in Life Test (PIL) (self-realization; Crumbaugh & Maholick, 1969). Although the two measures should have been closely related, which would have cross-validated both, Phillips and colleagues found them related in some ways and not in others. Tosi and Hoffman (1972) could only validate the POI as an index of the more specific concept "healthy personality," not of the general concept "self-actualization."

After Mittelman (1991) cited several articles that criticized Maslow's theory and its hallmark concept "self-actualization," he posed the question "which aspects of Maslow's thought, if any, can be salvaged, and retained [?]" (p. 114). He concluded that "self-actualization" can be rescued only if it is reduced to "openness," defined as being open to information, including that provided by the environment and by other people. The remainder of self-actualization he deemed difficult to defend.

Heylighen (1992) found "self-actualization" inherently ambiguous. In his opinion, Maslow was not consistent in his treatment of the concept. For example, self-actualization expressed in Maslow's theory is not the same as self-actualization as manifested by the super-personalities he observed. Consistent with this observation, the theory does not predict that self-actualizers would turn out to be so self-centered. To save the day for Maslow, Heylighen redefined self-actualization as perceived competence to satisfy basic needs in due time. Heylighen and Mittelman show that self-actualization is a rather nebulous concept that must be clarified if it is to be useful.

More than any other criticism of Maslow's central concept, the most damning has to be the charge that his conception of "self-actualization" is neither universal nor the "best" rendition of "human fulfillment." Ajit K. Das (1989), in a paper entitled "Beyond

---

BOX 10.3   Diversity: An Asian Religion's Alternative to Self-Actualization

According to Buddha, the way to Nirvana, the ultimate state characterized by oblivion of care, pain, and external reality, is to first grasp the Four Noble Truths and then follow the Eightfold Path (see Das, 1989).

The Four Noble Truths

1. Dissatisfaction and suffering are inherent in the lives of humans.
2. Dissatisfaction and disappointment arise from people's desires and cravings. Most people are not able to accept life as it is. Instead they deny that craving creates tension and attempt to prolong pleasant experiences even as they try to shorten unpleasant experiences.
3. Suffering is abolished only by eliminating cravings. One need not deny all desires, but only the most demanding desires that dominate one's life.
4. The way to eliminate craving and dissatisfaction is to follow the Noble Eightfold Path.

The Eightfold Path
(broken down into three categories of behaviors)

1. Adhere to moral conduct—right speech, right action, right livelihood—which requires that no act harmful to self or others be committed and that one actively help others. The mind must also be kept free of evil thoughts.
2. Maintain mental discipline—right effort, right alertness, and right concentrations—which requires control of one's mind. After a rigorous period of training, one will be able to control one's thoughts and feelings and also empty one's mind of all contents so that perfect tranquility can be achieved.
3. Develop intuitive wisdom—right understanding and right purpose—which requires correct understanding of the Four Noble Truths and the tendency to abide by them.

Self-Actualization," has suggested that other notions of "fulfillment" exist in nonwestern societies and may, in some respects, be more attractive than "self-actualization." In contrast to self-actualization, Das offers "self-realization" extracted primarily from Buddhism. Compared to self-actualization, self-realization is a more active process. It does not just happen after lower needs are satisfied, with the only given being that one is free to develop potentialities; one must actively work at self-realization. Further, the self-absorption that characterizes self-actualization is relatively de-emphasized in the case of self-realization in favor of concern for others. Box 10.3 contains some information about self-realization that, when compared with Table 10.1, will allow you to see the difference between it and self-actualization. Then you can draw your own conclusions about which is "best."

Buddha

The selfishness that taints the otherwise benevolent self-actualization, but not self-realization, is a problem for many individuals inside and outside of psychology (Das, 1989; see the bottom of Table 10.1). For example, had Maslow applied his criteria for self-actualization to candidates for the annual *Mother Jones* magazine humanitarian awards, he would have rejected most of the actual recipients. The focus of recipients' lives is selfless concern for others, not "self-knowledge," "creative expression," or "having peak experiences."

Peak Experiences

As already emphasized, scientific criteria usually demand that it be possible to translate important concepts into measurable terms. However, many of Maslow's concepts are difficult or impossible to translate. Concepts such as "truth," "joy," and "beauty" are examples. "Peak experiences" provide another illustration. Different researchers and theorists have used the phrase differently, lending a flavor of arbitrariness to it (Mathes, Zevon, Roter, & Joerger, 1982).

There are contradictions regarding peak experiences as well. Such experiences are supposed to be the province of high "self-actualizers" who are supposedly very rare people. Yet, while Sherrill and colleagues (1990) found that athletes tended to be relatively low on self-actualization, Ravizza (1977) found that athletes are prone to having peak experiences, albeit limited ones.

The Hierarchy

The needs hierarchy itself has not escaped criticism. Alderfer (1989) saw enough deficiencies in the hierarchy that are relevant to business and industry to warrant replacing it with his own. With obvious disapproval, Buttle (1989) indicated that Maslow's hierarchy "is reified, if not deified, in the marketing literature" (p. 201). He went on to declare that "Maslow never explained why he selected the five basic needs, why they were ranked as they were, or why others were not included" (p. 202). Buttle concluded his criticism of Maslow's hierarchy by suggesting alternative conceptions of needs for use in marketing.

Neher (1991) goes a step further, criticizing the hierarchy in general, not just its specific applications. Among his complaints is that Maslow stubbornly downplayed influences of culture, which he saw as only creating some variation in the *methods* by which needs are fulfilled. Maslow even saw culture as opposing organismic need fulfillment. How could a culture survive if it opposed the fulfillment of physiologically based needs? Neher goes on to imply that the hierarchy itself, rather than just the methods of need satisfaction, would have to be different for different cultures. For example, cultural norms peculiar to a society, such as those governing child-rearing, would have to exert strong influence on which needs have priority.

Neher also notes that Maslow viewed self-actualization as somehow different from the other needs in that only lower order needs are quelled by satisfactions. How can self-actualization be a "need" if it acts differently from the other needs in being the only one not quelled by satisfactions? Neher points out that, in fact, *any* need may be stimulated rather than quelled by satisfactions (a boost in self-esteem may whet the appetite for more inflation of self-esteem; the more security you have the more you want). These many contradictions and questions must be resolved if Maslow's popularity is to grow in the future.

Conclusions

Many of the criticisms lodged against Maslow's work seem less telling in view of research evidence produced relatively recently. Witness the validating work by Wicker and colleagues (1993; 1994) and Williams and Page (1989). The allegation that he relied on arbitrarily obtained "simple observations and descriptions" in conceiving of "self-actualization" will grow irrelevant if scientific evidence increasingly supports his assumptions about the concept. The growth in the application of his hierarchy to various professional areas may some day obliterate the charge that the needs are not universal and are misapplied to some areas.

Maslow considered his most important educational experiences to be those that taught him what kind of a person he was: psychoanalysis, his marriage to Bertha, and the "thunderclap" of having a child. World War II also had a dramatic impact on him, making him want "to prove that human beings are capable of something grander than war and prejudice and hatred" (in M. Hall, 1968, p. 54). He advised his two daughters, "Learn to hate meanness." Thus, Maslow became a caring and wise person, if not the warm and relatively untroubled individual that Carl Rogers was. While one could dote on Rogers because of the fine person that his benign upbringing allowed him to become, one could be filled with admiration for Maslow, because he became an exemplary human being despite cruel treatment at the hands of his mother and the anti-Semites who abused him at every turn.

Maslow's unique approach to understanding human experience was to find "the best" humankind has to offer—that fraction of the population who display superior self-actualization, peak experiences, understanding, and creativity. Having discovered "the best," he used them to show us how to become better than we are. Although these superior personalities tell us much, none can better inform us about how to be than the example set by Maslow himself.

Summary Points

1. Abraham Maslow was the first of seven children born in 1908 to a neglectful father and an allegedly cruel mother. During childhood, Maslow's first love were the books of the Brooklyn Library, access to which was perilous due to neighboring anti-Semitic gangs. After undistinguished performance at a prestigious high school, Maslow enrolled in City College, Cornell, law school, and finally the University of Wisconsin. There he became a "monkey psychologist," a kind of fame that led to his first job.

2. After temporarily rejecting psychology because of exposure to the archaic Edward Titchener, and contemplating the Adler–Freud quarrel, Maslow landed a research position under Edward L. Thorndike. Thus, he returned to New York City where he fell under the influence of Adler and the Gestalt psychologists. Armed with Gestalt holism, Maslow turned his attention to motivation, the process by which people are propelled toward goals. These goals can be cast as "needs" for certain satisfactions that are sought by all humans, regardless of culture, environment, or generation.

3. While needs are universal, methods of satisfying them can be culturally or environmentally determined. Maslow believed that needs are formed into a hierarchy, with more primitive, lower-order needs demanding satisfaction before more complex and uniquely human needs are addressed. Physiological needs demand satisfaction first, second, safety needs, third, belongingness and love needs, and fourth, esteem needs. These are the Deficiency needs (D-needs).

4. "Self-actualization" is "the tendency for [one] to become actualized in what [one] is potentially." D-needs are prepotent: stronger and demanding prior satisfaction before other needs can be addressed. Needs are not met in an all-or-none fashion, but higher-order needs cannot be met until lower-order needs are largely satisfied. In exceptional cases, people may deny lower-order needs and still pursue higher-order needs as Gandhi did.

5. Although culture, family, and parents may function as sun, food, and water to human actualization, they are not its seed. Human nature is inborn, not made. Thus, even self-actualization needs are instinctoid, because of their biological, genetic, and universal characteristics. Genuine self-actualizers, however, are quite rare. Self-actualizers are the good choosers who show the rest of us what is good for the human species. They are people who fulfill themselves by making complete use of their potentialities.

6. Although self-actualizers possess such positive traits as spontaneity, autonomy, ethicality, and creativity, they may also be thoughtless, prideful, and socially impolite. Self-actualizers have their own sources of motivation, meta-needs and B-values. They also have peak experiences: intense, mystical feelings of powerfulness and helplessness.

7. Maslow believed that humans have universal, positive needs and values and are self-directing. In fact, organisms, whether they be lower-animals or human babies, if left to their own devices, can do well choosing what is best for them. His optimistic view of people led him to propose a psychological Utopia, called Eupsychia. This proposal assumes that environments can be contrived that will foster the satisfaction of higher-order needs.

8. The enormous variety of fields to which Maslow's ideas have been applied include business and speech pathology. Researchers have shown that blind athletes, and athletes in general, show a unique pattern of responses to the POI. In support of "self-actualization," Shostrom has confirmed that people who would be expected to make a better approximation

to self-actualization scored higher on all POI dimensions than others. Graham and Balloun showed that individuals display greater satisfaction of lower- than of higher-order needs.

9. Williams and Page confirmed this result and demonstrated that self-concept is most in tune with the level of the hierarchy at which a person is currently operating. Further, needs gratification at a given level is negatively correlated with salience of needs at that level. Wicker and colleagues showed that failures to support the hierarchy are reversed if intention rather than importance is investigated. While there is some evidence for peak experiences, they may be realized only partially, and people not expected to have such experiences report them.

10. The needs hierarchy has been revised in some fields and Maslow's failure to explain its origins has been noted. Self-actualization deficiencies include Maslow's arbitrary selection of self-actualizers to study, the nonuniversality of self-actualization, the selfishness of self-actualizers, and the existence of an attractive alternative, self-realization. Mittelman and Heylighen have redefined self-actualization. Neher claims that the hierarchy may be different for different cultures and self-actualization is unreasonably different from other needs. Nevertheless, current research is erasing many of these criticisms. Maslow himself is an exemplary human being, despite a troubled upbringing.

Running Comparison

Theorist	Maslow in Comparison
Adler	Like Adler, he was a father's boy. Adler's concepts, social interest (*Gemeinshaftsgefuhl*), law of movement, striving for superiority, and creative power of the individual probably influenced him.
Horney	Like her, he felt unattractive. Her "basic anxiety" is similar to his safety needs.
George Kelly	Like Kelly, his first experience with psychology was not positive.
Henry A. Murray	He agreed with Murray that a behavior is a function of many needs and the satisfaction of any need may be tied to the satisfaction of other needs.
Sullivan	They both believed that needs may be satisfied through interpersonal relations.

Essay/Critical Thinking Questions

1. We often think of child abuse as physical. In fact, it can be verbal and "psychological." Could you put yourself in Maslow's shoes when he was a child? His mother apparently did not abuse him physically, but did mistreat him verbally. Write a short piece indicating other forms of such abuse that Maslow might have suffered.

2. There is much to-do about quotas these days. In fact, as Maslow's case illustrates, quotas have always been with us: They have been used to exclude Jews and people of color. Until the 1960s, the quota for African Americans at most major universities was zero. Nowadays, quotas still mean that members of the present majority are most likely to be hired or otherwise selected ("12 percent of new hires must be black; thus, 88 percent can be white"). But can you imagine yourself in a situation similar to young Maslow's? Sometime during the next century people of color will be the majority. Imagine that you are European American, it's 2080, and the quotas seem designed to exclude you. Write a paragraph telling how you would feel.

3. Are there other meaningful hierarchies? How about a hierarchy of feelings, of rewards? Construct your own psychological hierarchy.

4. Has Maslow missed some meaningful needs? Write a brief argument supporting an addition to Maslow's hierarchy.

5. Does Maslow have needs in the right order? Write a brief argument for another order. For example, could you argue that esteem really belongs before belongingness and love?

6. Maslow assumes that self-actualization is a better, more worthy need. Can you argue that the lower-order needs are in some sense at least as worthy? Hint: Imagine telling a person who is near starvation that it is better to be creative than to eat.

7. Could you elaborate on Maslow's Eupsychian society? Write a paragraph describing a society that would foster self-actualization.

8. Is Maslow's claim that he chose "super-personalities," observed them, and then conceived of "self-actualization" legitimate? Indicate how his preconceptions about "self-actualization" may have led him to choose certain "super personalities" rather than others. Hint: Did his preconceptions cause him to exclude self-denying people (people more concerned about others rather than themselves)?

9. Could you compare at least two products and show how each appeals to a different need on Maslow's hierarchy?

10. Maslow would say it is highly unlikely that you and I are self-actualizers. Yet, we probably have had some peak experiences. Can you describe some peak experiences that you have had?

E-mail Interaction

(Contact the author at mfbpa@wiu.edu)
Forward one of the following or phrase your own.

1. Do you really believe Maslow was an abused child, or was he just paranoid?
2. Which is better, a self-actualizer or a self-realizer?
3. What is the basic difference between Maslow's conception of self-actualization and Rogers's?
4. Tell me how I can raise my self-esteem to a high level and keep it there.
5. If I have learned Maslow's hierarchy thoroughly, do I know his theory?

11

MARCHING TO A DIFFERENT DRUMMER: GEORGE KELLY

- What psychological dimensions do you use to conceive of your world and its people: good–bad? ambiguous–clear? sane–insane? other?
- Can you apply the principles of science to the solution of your own problems?
- Can people be divided up into those whose thinking processes are complex and those whose thinking processes are simple?
- Can you imagine you are a child again, relating to your mother?
- Who is the most pitied person in your life?

George Kelly

One of the issues running through most previous (and subsequent) chapters has been whether the "inside" or the "outside" of people is stressed by theorists. As you will see, the behaviorists generally look only outside. As you already know, the psychoanalysts are rather exclusively concerned with the inside. Other theorists to be covered later consider both perspectives. This chapter focuses on a theory of personality that emphasizes an internal aspect, cognition, while not neglecting the external world. It introduces an important figure in yet another break with the Freudians, a break as profound as the rift created by the humanists. George Kelly is aptly described as in the vanguard of the "cognitive" revolution.

Kelly, The Person

George Kelly was the maverick son of a preacher, born in a small Kansas town (1905). A rugged individualist, quite literally of pioneer stock, he was skeptical concerning psychological principles from day one of his first psychology class. Sitting in the back row of the introductory psychology classroom, Kelly tilted his chair against the wall and waited for something interesting (Kelly, 1969). After two to three weeks he could state only one clear impression, his professor seemed nice. Then one day he was inspired to sit up and take notice. A capital "S" and a capital "R" were prominently displayed on the blackboard, connected by an arrow pointing from the former to the latter. Here, thought Kelly is the meat of the matter. Unfortunately, further lectures only disappointed him. Many years later he wrote of the experience,

> *Although I listened intently for several sessions, after that the most I could make of it was that the 'S' was what you had to have in order to account for the 'R' and the 'R' was put there so the 'S' would have something to account for. I never did find out what that arrow stood for—not to this day—and I have pretty well given up trying to figure it out (1969, p. 47).*

And he pretty well gave up on psychology, for the time being, choosing instead to pursue a career in engineering. Three years later he was out of engineering and back in school, forced by the Great Depression to learn something more practical. Being interested in sociology and labor relations, he thought it high time to have a look at Freud. "I don't remember which one of Freud's books I was trying to read," wrote Kelly (1969, p. 47), "but I do remember the mounting feeling of incredulity that anyone could write such nonsense, much less publish it."

Skepticism, ironically, may explain why he eventually became a psychologist. Kelly needed to practice his considerable gift for healthy skepticism and psychology provided the perfect forum: One can argue that all psychological principles can be questioned.

Skepticism was sometimes accompanied by sarcasm. When prompted to consider Russian physiologist I. P. Pavlov's famous conditioning research (dogs salivating to a bell), he spoke with tongue not so deeply buried in cheek: "Salivation . . . takes place in a manner that suggests the anticipation of food, or perhaps hunger—I am not sure which. Perhaps what is anticipated is an activity we call eating. Whatever it indicates, Pavlov seems to have demonstrated it and there is no reason we should not be grateful even through we are not quite sure what it was he demonstrated" (Kelly, 1980, p. 29). When inspired to cite examples of people who fail to benefit from experience, he recalled a naval officer with "a vast and versatile ignorance," and a school administrator who "had one year of experience—repeated thirteen times" (Kelly, 1963, p. 171). He even took a verbal swing at all of his colleagues. In observing that his fundamental assumptions apply to everyone, he wrote, "The same goes for psychologists, who are known to have human characteristics too" (p. 25).

Sometimes, however, he was more motivated to generate laughter than to engage in mild ridicule. In making the point that people orient to the future, not the past, he described a friend's peculiar approach to driving: "A friend of mine, while driving her car, customarily closes her eyes when she gets caught in a tight spot. This is an anticipatory act; she suspects something may happen that she would prefer not to see. So far, it hasn't happened, though it is hard to understand why" (Kelly, 1980, p. 26).

If sarcasm was a characteristic of Kelly, it certainly was overridden by a more central feature of his personality, warmth. He practiced therapy to help people and to learn from them. In thirty years as a psychotherapist, he never collected a penny for his services. George Thompson, a former colleague, wrote:

> *At the 1963 Convention of the American Psychological Association, some 40 former students of George Kelly attended a dinner to pay tribute to their good teacher and warm*

friend. These professors, scientists, and therapists came from all parts of the United States. All of them knew that here was a man who had helped them find their ways to more productive lives. Many others who could not attend wrote letters of appreciation for his wise counsel and guidance (1968, pp. 22–23).

Similarly, in the summer of 1965, Kelly's associates at Ohio State gathered to salute their colleague and friend who had just been granted an endowed chair at Brandeis University. Papers were read by three of Kelly's former doctoral students and by a visiting professor from England, who had spread Kelly's ideas through several of Britain's universities. At the end of these presentations, Kelly rose to invite the entire assembly to his house for dinner. Nearly 100 accepted the gracious offer. Thompson wrote of the occasion:

There was good food for all and a characteristic abundance of warm fellowship. The dinner [was] only a token to a man who had contributed so much, but [it] did reflect in modest measure the affectionate humanity of George Alexander Kelly—scholar, teacher, and warm friend (1968, pp. 22–23).

Above all, Kelly was open-minded. Perhaps this aspect of his personality stemmed from his extreme versatility (or perhaps his openmindedness was the cause and his versatility the effect). That versatility is clearly reflected in Kelly's own words:

I had taught soap-box oratory in a labor college for labor organizers, government in an . . . institute for prospective citizens, public speaking for the American Bankers Association, and dramatics in a junior college . . . I had taken a Master's degree with a study of workers' use of leisure time, and an advanced professional degree in education at the University of Edinburgh, and . . . I had dabbled . . . in education, sociology, economics, labor relations, biometrics, speech pathology, and cultural anthropology, and had majored in psychology . . . for a grand total of nine months (Kelly, 1969, p. 48).

Kelly's training in psychology yielded a Ph.D. from Iowa State University in 1931. While his early career was spent at Fort Hays State College in Kansas, Ohio State University claimed him for more years than any other academic institution.

His extraordinary versatility led Kelly to a dozen or so universities, each for an appreciable period of time, and around the globe for the purpose of applying his theory to the problems of the world. Little wonder that he embraced the assumption, adopted by many philosophers of science and dismissed out of hand by few, that in the realm of science there are no truths (Hempel and Oppenheim, 1960). In psychology, as in other sciences, there are theories which are supported by evidence to varying degrees, but no truth. For a personality theorist, this was an unusual assumption, but then Kelly was an unusual theorist.

Unfortunately, Kelly died in his early sixties (1967), having produced relatively few writings. Fortunately he has had such great impact on his students that his writings, as well as numerous speeches and lectures, have been thoroughly mined. The psychological "gold" produced by several posthumous publications edited or written by his students contributed greatly to this chapter.

Kelly's View of the Person

As you recall, Freud thought of humans as helpless particles blown about by the hidden winds of hedonic impulse. Each human was seen as an effect of inaccessible and uncontrollable causes. Jung viewed humans from a broader perspective, but one might argue that he regarded them as captives of their ancestral past. Adler, Sullivan, Fromm, and Horney saw people as the products of their social environments. By contrast, Rogers and Maslow assumed that humans are capable of determining their own fates.

True to character, Kelly did not even approximate the orientation of any of his predecessors or contemporaries. Rather, he declared that people are governed by an internal process: the way they construe events in their worlds. While this process is internal, it results from consequences of an external factor, social relations (Kelly, 1955). Kelly also thought that people had free will in that they could choose from many alternative constructs that emerged from their relations with others.

Kelly's conception of time was different from that of the theorists covered so far, except possibly Adler. While he did not neglect the distant past, the recent past, or the present, he declared humans to be basically future-oriented (Kelly, 1980). He thought that the behavior of people was determined largely by their predictions of future events.

It is interesting to speculate about how Kelly came to adopt such an intellectual, pragmatic, and "hard-nosed" point of view. He was an engineer and a person made practical by the Great Depression. It was natural for him to orient to thinking rather than other psychological modes. As a victim of the Depression, little wonder that he looked more to the future than to the dismal present. As a person who was constantly changing not only physical location, but himself as well, he had little inclination to the past.

Perhaps Kelly's most important departure from the precepts of traditional, psychoanalytic psychology was that he saw himself as no different from those he studied and attempted to help in therapy (Kelly, 1969; for more about the inconsistency between researchers' views of themselves and of the people they study, see Allen, 1973 and Allen and Smith, 1980). Most psychologists, he charged, viewed themselves as objective, rational scientists who determine the causes of people's actions and suggest corrections for maladaptive behavior. On the other hand, their clients in therapy and their research subjects are seen as incapable of objective observation, unable to sort out the causes of their behavior and inept at developing a systematic program for positive behavioral change. By contrast, Kelly saw himself as a scientist in his roles as research psychologist, psychotherapist, and just plain person. Thus, because he was no different from others, clients, research subjects, and people in general were viewed as scientists. The best way to understand Kelly's belief that all of us operate like scientists on a day-to-day basis is to consider Kelly's recollection of how he discovered "people as scientists."

> *A typical afternoon might find me talking to a graduate student at one o'clock, doing all those familiar things that thesis directors have to do: encouraging the student to pinpoint the issues, to observe, to become intimate with the problem, to form hypotheses . . . to make some preliminary test runs, to relate his data to his predictions, to control his experiments so that he will know what led to what, to generalize cautiously, and to revise his thinking in the light of experience. At two o'clock I might have an appointment with*

a client. During this interview I would . . . be . . . helping the distressed person work out some solutions to his life's problems. So what would I do? Why, I would try to get him to pinpoint the issues, to observe, to become intimate with the problem, to form hypotheses, to make test runs, to relate outcomes to anticipations, to control his ventures so that he will know what led to what, to generalize cautiously, and to revise his dogma in the light of experience. At three o'clock I would see [the] student again. Likely as not he was either dragging his feet, hoping to design some worldshaking experiment before looking at his first subject to see firsthand what he was dealing with, or plunging into some massive ill-considered data-chasing expedition. So I would try to get him to . . . [do] . . . all the things that I had [tried to get him] to do at one o'clock. At four o'clock another client! Guess what! He would be dragging his feet, hoping to design a completely new personality before venturing his first change in behavior, or plunging into some ill-considered acting-out escapade, etc., etc. (Kelly, 1969, pp. 60–61).

Kelly had what the Freudians would call insight. Of course, he was acting as a scientist, and so was the student, when they were discussing the student's research. However, he was also a scientist when he was getting his distressed client to become a better scientist. Thus, students doing research, their advisors, clients in psychotherapy, their psychotherapists, and "people on the street" behave like scientists daily. Sometimes they do well at it and sometimes badly. Each tries to pinpoint the relevant issues related to his or her problem, make observations of the people involved in the problem, become intimate with the problem, form hypotheses, run "experiments," relate outcomes to predictions of the future, control pursuits so that it is clear what led to what, generalize cautiously, and revise strongly held beliefs in the light of experience. For Kelly, people are scientists, all of them, every day (Hermans, Kempen, & van Loon, 1992).

Basic Concepts: Kelly

Personality as a System of Constructs

Underlying all of Kelly's thinking are the cognitive structures known as **constructs**, ways of construing events or "seeing the world" so that the future is anticipated (Kelly, 1980). Thus, his theory was called "Personal Construct Theory" (PCT). The individual's **personality** consists of an organized system of constructs that may be ranked as to importance. "Construct" became the foundation on which Kelly built his most basic theoretical framework or postulate. A *postulate* is a basic assumption which is the starting point for a theory. It is a broad statement that is just accepted; it cannot be directly tested. Kelly's **fundamental postulate** is the assumption that a person's psychological processes are routed through various channels or pathways by the ways in which she or he anticipates events (Kelly, 1963). In a sense, ways of "seeing the world" form the channels that are directed toward the future. Predictions *pull* the person along through life, as opposed to being *pushed* by unconscious impulses and drives or pricked into action by stimuli in the environment.

To set the stage for Kelly's other theoretical concepts, it is helpful to build on the notion of constructs by looking at how two individuals, Jim and Joan, go about a day in their lives. As you read, pay special attention to the words in boldface.

Jim's Problem

"What's wrong now?" Joan inquired as she approached a figure who was slumped against the wall outside a classroom. Jim's reply was inaudible, partly because his hands covered his face and partly because he was too depressed to speak up.

Undeterred by the lack of a response to her question, Joan continued, "Let me guess . . . It's Professor Martinson again."

Jim's head sprang upright. Though his hair cascaded over his eyes, it failed to hide the fierce look that distorted his face. "Damn it," he was nearly screaming, "I've tried everything. I give up."

Joan looked around self-consciously, hoping that, somehow, students passing them in the hall had not noticed the outburst. Then she eased down next to her friend. Softly she entreated, "Tell me about it."

"It's the same thing . . . same old thing," he muttered.

Joan leaned back against the wall and exclaimed with a sigh, "Ok then, tell me about your latest clash with Martinson."

"He hates me, I'm sure of it. The jerk said we could turn our papers in late, if we had a good excuse. Well, I had a good excuse . . . it was spring break . . . I was stuck in Florida . . . we were in somebody else's car. I mean, how could I get home . . ."

Joan's chin drew back and down. A familiar frown curled her lips. Martinson had looked much the same when Jim had first related the "stuck in Florida" story. It was that incredulous look.

Jim's Constructs

"See there, see there," rasped Jim. "you're no different. I thought I could expect some sympathy from you . . . you're supposed to be a **good friend**, someone with a little **intelligence**. Go away . . . just get lost."

Joan moved closer and slipped her arm around Jim's shoulders, but he elbowed her away. "Jim, you know you can **trust** me . . . I am your **good friend**, but gimme a break. I know you believe that your excuse is ok . . . let me just put it this way . . . try it on some other people; I'll bet you that you'll get the same reaction."

There was silence for a minute, then Joan continued. "Look, let me make a suggestion. Why don't you . . ."

"That's not all . . ." Jim broke in. This time he was shouting. Joan was looking for a place to hide. "He laughed at me! . . . said he was just kidding about the excuse. 'I don't take excuses. The other students know that . . . it was just my way of making a joke . . . a little irony, you know.' Does he ever think I'm **stupid**! He probably thinks he couldn't **trust** me farther than he could throw me. And I thought **educated** people were my kind of people. Well, you live and learn. I'll know better next time."

Joan's Suggestions for Change

"That's what you said the last time you had it out with him," Joan could sense the taste of foot-in-the mouth the minute she uttered the words. Jim climbed to his feet. He'd had enough of her, but before he could get away, Joan grabbed his shirt sleeve and dragged him back down. "Look, I'm sorry," she pleaded, "but it's just that ... sometimes it seems like you don't learn from **experience**. I mean you just stick with an old idea, no matter what. Why is it so important that Martinson like you? I don't care whether he likes me or not."

After a time Jim settled down and he began to chatter amiably with his friend, which was usual for them. They talked about Jim's relationship with Martinson. "Ok, you win," asserted Joan, "so you have some kind of fixation for Martinson—father figure is what my psych teacher would say—ok, I accept that. Now let me give you a suggestion . . . try this out. I mean you have had plenty of time to **evaluate** *him. You think he's one of the* 'good guys,' *right?" Jim shook his head in a vigorous "no" sign, but Joan ignored him. "What you have to do is let him know you think he belongs in select company. I mean, as I see it, you expect him to think you're a 'good guy,' but you won't put him in that same category. I know how you are. Surely you can understand that people like those who like them—it's sort of a law—but they can't read your mind. You have to communicate your feelings to people. If I know you, you've been very stiff and formal with Martinson. Am I right?"*

Jim's head was hanging down, "Yeah," he mumbled, "you do know me."

"Actually, what it amounts to," Joan was talking rapidly now, "you think he's a 'good guy,' *you* **admire** *him and you want him to* **admire** *you. I know, because, if I like someone, I want that somebody to throw a little admiration my way."*

"Admire?" Jim was puzzled. "Trust maybe, but **admire?** *I don't resort to hero worship."*

"Well you had better consider 'admiration.' If you like someone, admiration is a way to communicate it without saying anything . . . I mean, without using words . . . the sound of your voice will do."

"All right," said Jim, almost in a whisper, "I'll try it."

Joan's Constructs

Now Jim hopped up and offered Joan a hand. They left the building and strolled along leisurely toward their dorms. Silence prevailed for a while, then Jim casually remarked, "You know, sometimes I wonder who I am. Who am I anyway?" he was smiling as he posed the question.

"Good ole Jim, that's who you are," came the reply. "A little weird, but fun to be around."

He shoved her playfully. "Ok, who are you, smarty?"

"Is that a serious question?"

"Yeah," he mocked, "who are you?"

"Well I don't stay up at night thinking about it, but I guess I'd answer in terms of who I'm **like** *. . . you know, similar to."*

"And who is that?" said Jim in a sober voice adopted to match her own suddenly serious tone.

"I guess I'm an **athlete** *at heart," mused Joan, a member of the varsity track team. "Steffi Graf, that's who I'm like . . . or uh . . . who I'd like to be."*

"Tough break," kidded Jim. "You don't have her killer instinct."

Joan went along with the teasing and added, "Nor do I have the ability . . . but who knows, maybe I'll get better and maybe track will be as big as tennis some day."

They reached the crossing that split the paths to their dorms and paused for a moment. "Big bash at the 'Gin Mill' this Saturday, need a ride?"

"No thanks," responded Joan as she backed down the path to her dorm. "I'm going home . . . back to God's country . . . down on the farm . . . with the **good** *neighbors and the wide open spaces . . ."*

"And the horse manure," interjected Jim in a loud voice, as they were now many yards apart.

She lobbed a rock at him, "You can have your stinking old city, full of dopers and muggers. You love it . . . I'm going back where everything is small and people are concerned . . ." her voice trailed off.

Jim's and Joan's Personalities

It is instructive to analyze Jim's and Joan's conversation from Kelly's point of view. A look at Figure 11.1 will allow you to examine some concrete examples of constructs (Kelly disliked the concrete, but could not avoid it). The figure displays Jim's and Joan's construction systems. A **construction system** is an organization of many constructs with the more important, and often more abstract, at the top and the less important constructs at the bottom. The constructs at the top are called **superordinate** while the ones at the bottom are called **subordinate**.

The Construction System Is the Individual's Personality

Jim's most superordinate construct is represented by "trust–distrust," while Joan's most superordinate construct is "evaluative–descriptive." To evaluate is to pass judgment on, to describe is to label someone or something. As Kelly (1963) readily acknowledged, a construct can be thought of as a special kind of concept. Constructs have two opposite poles,

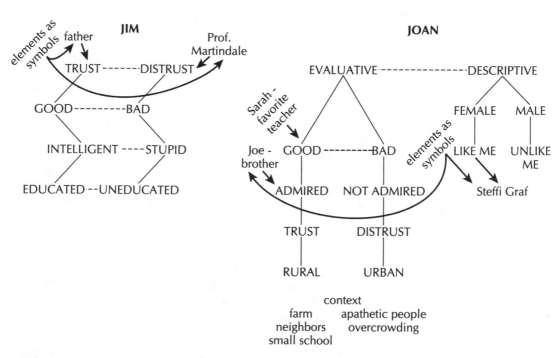

FIGURE 11.1   Joan's and Jim's Construction Systems

like an automobile battery. The **emergent pole** is the primary and principle end, like "good" in good–bad and "intelligent" in intelligent–stupid (Kelly, 1955). The **implicit pole** is the contrasting end, like uneducated in educated–uneducated and not admired in admired–not admired. Normally, the emergent pole is formed first, but as soon as it develops, the implicit pole usually comes into existence. According to Kelly, people see the world in terms of contrasts; every thing or being has an opposite. This point of view is reminiscent of Jung's position. The contrasts exist even if a person adopts a construct such as tolerant–intolerant and has never expressed or is unaware of the implicit pole, intolerant. Adopting *tolerant* almost always brings *intolerant* with it.

Armed with these concepts, you can begin the analysis of Jim and Joan. It is easy to see that Jim is highly dependent on the construct "trust–distrust," his superordinate construct. Like other constructs, it has what Kelly called **a range of convenience**, the extent and breadth of the event category to which a construct applies. For example, trust–distrust is applicable to events involving people, such as the episodes of Jim's conflict with Professor Martinson. Because it is reasonable to assume that Jim experiences many events involving many different people, trust–distrust may be said to have a wide range of convenience. Nevertheless, it has its limits. Trust–distrust is scarcely applicable to solving mathematical problems or to viewing unique architecture. A superordinate construct's range of convenience may be thought of as including its subordinate constructs.

By contrast, a construct's **range of focus** refers to the events to which it is most readily applied. Trust–distrust is more readily applied to relations with people to whom Jim feels close, rather than to relations with more casual acquaintances.

Jim's construct, trust–distrust, can be characterized in yet another way. It is relatively **impermeable**, a reference to certain constructs that tend not to change in terms of range of convenience or place in the construction system. In fact, Joan noted that Jim's constructs are impermeable in general. Trust–distrust is also part of Joan's system, but it is much more subordinate. Thus, the construction systems of Jim and Joan display **commonality**, a reference to the sharing of constructs by two or more people whose experiences are similar. Jim and Joan are both students, thus, as you might expect, Figure 11.1 reveals that they do share constructs.

In comparison to commonality, **individuality** refers to differences among construction systems both in terms of the constructs comprising the systems and in terms of how the constructs are organized. Such differences are due to differences in experiences. Joan is an athlete, Jim is not. Jim's problem, as Joan pointed out, is that he, unlike her, has failed to learn from **experience,** what one learns from the events of the past. Jim continues to try the same old strategies with Professor Martinson, and they are not getting him what he wants, mutual trust. Thus, Joan suggests a change in Jim's construction system. She thinks that Jim should embrace a new construct, "admire–not admire," and reorganize his construction system to be more like hers, with "trust–distrust" subordinated to "admire–not admire." Joan is trying to save Jim from **anxiety**, what a person experiences when his or her construction system does not apply to critical events, as Jim's fails to apply to events in his relationship with Professor Martinson. Joan should be cautious. In suggesting the new construct "admire–not admire" she may subject her friend to **fear,**—the experience one has when a new construct appears to be entering the system, and may become dominant. On the other hand, she need not worry too much about subjecting Jim to **threat,** the realization of the possibility that a person's entire construction system will be overhauled. Joan is suggesting a new construct and some reorganization, not a major upheaval.

Joan as Scientific Psychotherapist

Joan the psychotherapist acts like a scientist in attempting to make a better scientist of Jim. She pleads with him to make his constructs more permeable. More importantly, she suggests a hypothesis for Jim to test. She feels that expressing admiration will allow Jim to obtain the mutual trust that he wants to exist in his relationship with Professor Martinson. To test the hypothesis, Jim is told to try admiration out on Martinson. He then can observe how it works. If admiration has the intended effect, he should **replicate**, repeat a test in the hope that the results will be the same as before. Replication provides the basis for anticipating future events. If one can repeat an observation of the successful application of a construct, one can be confident that the construct will apply again in the future, under similar circumstances. The greater the number of replications, the greater the confidence.

If Jim carries out Joan's suggestions, he will be acting according to one of Kelly's most basic principles, **constructive alternativism,** the assumption that a person's present interpretations of her or his life situation are subject to revision and replacement (Kelly, 1963). It is assumed that a construction system cannot remain the same, but must change with changes in the person's life situation.

Relations among Constructs

Looking back at Figure 11.1, the different organizations of Jim's and Joan's construction systems can be appreciated. Jim's system is organized by **extension of the cleavage line,** a reference to the observation that the poles of Jim's subordinate constructs fall directly under the corresponding emergent and implicit poles of his superordinate constructs. Thus, "good" falls under "trust," "bad" under "distrust" (Kelly, 1963). However, Joan's system begins at the top by **abstracting across the cleavage line,** whole constructs fall under superordinate emergent and under superordinate implicit poles. In Joan's case, all of her constructs fall under her most superordinate construct, "evaluative–descriptive." The whole construct "good–bad" falls under the emergent pole, "evaluative," while the whole construct, "female–male" falls under the implicit pole, "descriptive." This feature of Joan's system makes it more complex and flexible than Jim's. She can approach her life situations from an evaluative stance (there are good people and bad people) or from a purely descriptive stance (there are North Americans and Europeans).

Elements are objects, beings, or events. The **context** of a construct is composed of all those elements to which the construct applies. The context of Joan's construct, "urban–rural", includes the elements farm, neighbors, apathetic people, and overcrowding. Whereas "range of convenience" and "focus of convenience" refer to rather gross and abstract event categories such as "relations with authority figures" and "leisure activities," context and elements refer to the actual, concrete objects or people that exist in a person's life circumstance.

A **symbol** is one of the elements to which a construct applies that may be used as the name of the construct. Figure 11.1 indicates that, for Jim, "father" symbolizes the trust–

BOX 11.1   Similarities of Kelly's Ideas to Those of Other Theorists

As a theorist, Kelly's relationship to other theorists warrants special attention, because he did not closely resemble any of them, but shares assumptions with some of them. While Kelly chastised the behaviorists for their alleged obsession with minutiae, such as "Ss and Rs," he shared some assumptions with them. For example, like B. F. Skinner, who advocated the arrangement of environments to maximize positive reinforcements, Kelly believed that constructs could be changed by human intervention.

Similar to Albert Bandura and other social learning theorists, Kelly believed that anticipation of the future, rather than the accumulation of past events, governs human thought, feeling, and behavior. "I believe that everything [people do] follows lines laid down in [their] effort[s] to anticipate what will happen . . . [People] never wait to see what will happen; [they] look to see what will happen. Even my motorist friend is looking for something, though she shuts her eyes to do it" (Kelly, 1980, pp. 26 & 27).

Kelly wrote, "The phenomenological psychologists, of whom I certainly am not one, usually take the view that it is only the experience of the passing instant that is of essential psychological significance" (Kelly, 1980, p. 22). Nevertheless, he shared some assumptions with the humanists and phenomenologists (Benesch & Page 1989). In fact, his position has been viewed as essentially phenomenological (Tyler, 1994). Like Rogers, Kelly did not believe that one and only one set of procedures is effective in therapy: "Unlike most personality theories, the psychology of personal constructs does not limit itself to any pet psychotherapeutic technique" (Kelly, 1980, p. 35). Recall that Jung had a similar point of view. Like Rogers and Jung, Kelly also held that therapy is an *experience* in which both therapist and client participate and contribute as partners: "Psychotherapy needs to be understood as an experience. . . . Psychotherapy takes place when one person makes constructive use of another who has offered himself for that purpose. The professional skills of the therapist, as well as much of his repertory as an experienced human being, are brought into the transaction" (p. 21). Further, like Rogers, Kelly thought of therapy as an opportunity to become one's own self, relatively free of the constraints imposed by society and other people: "Psychotherapeutic effort, . . . as well as any other worthwhile human undertaking, is not to conform to oneself, whole or fragment; or to society, lay or ordained . . . [The] objective is for man continually to determine for himself what is worth the price he is going to end up paying . . . to keep moving toward what he is not . . ." (Kelly, 1980, p. 20).

Like Skinner and Rogers, creativity was one of Kelly's concerns: "The creativity cycle we envision is one that employs both loosening and tightening in a coordinated fashion. The cycle starts with a loosened phase in which construction is vague, elastic, and wavering. Out of this fertile chaos shapes begin to emerge and one seeks patiently to give them definite form until they are tight enough to talk about and to test" (Kelly, 1980, p. 34). Because creative people are flexible, and Kelly was a creative person, there was not much he dismissed out of hand. Even though his orientation was to conscious thought, Kelly acknowledged the psychoanalytic view that people have an unconscious (Jankowicz, 1987).

---

distrust construct. For Joan "Steffi Graf" symbolizes the construct, like me–unlike me. Of course, the picture of Jim and Joan as indicated in their conversation and in Figure 11.1 is oversimplified. Kelly would argue that no one's personality could be neatly represented in a figure. For one thing, the figure would have to be as large as a house, and for another, many constructs are too abstract to be represented as concretely as in Figure 11.1. Also, people normally do not blurt out their constructs as cooperatively as did Joan and Jim. More sophisticated methods of getting at constructs are needed, such as those considered below.

Personality Development

You may have wondered how Jim and Joan acquired their construction systems. That is, how did Jim and Joan develop their personalities? Kelly's comments about the transition from childhood to adulthood supplemented his theory nicely.

Predictability

Because "anticipation of future events" is a cornerstone of Kelly's PCT, it is not surprising that "forecasting the future" has a prominent place in his discussion of construct development in children. **Predictability** refers to the ability to predict the future. A construct is as useful as the degree of predictability it provides (Hermans et al., 1992). Thus, parents, the major components of every child's environment, are well advised to provide predictability. If they fail to do so, their child's need for anticipation of the future may be reflected in some rather extreme behavior (Kelly, 1955).

For example, if "predictability" is a scarce commodity in certain children's lives, they may cling to instances of it, even if their resultant behavior has negative consequences. As an illustration, assume a child, Johnny, has parents who treat him in a consistent manner only with regard to a few issues, all involving punishment. Johnny cleans his room; sometimes it is noticed, sometimes not. Johnny helps fold clothes and sometimes he is praised. However, Johnny has noticed that should he stop up the bathroom sink while playing "laundry" the consequent overflow, brings a highly reliable reaction from his parents. They apply the palm of a hand to his bottom. So, a naive behaviorist might assert that Johnny will avoid stopping up the sink. Not so, according to Kelly. Stopping up the sink is the best way to acquire the precious predictability that Johnny so badly needs.

In a recent book on PCT, Dalton and Dunnett (1992) consider Kelly's construct types that relate to predictability. **Tight** constructs yield unvarying predictability while **loose constructs** yield varying predictability (Kelly, 1955). Dunnett and Dalton indicated that the perspective on life held by people who tend to have tight constructs, called tight construers, "is organized rigidly, full of regular habits, and fast held views of the world" (p. 56). By contrast, loose construers "seem to make different predictions at the drop of a hat. Other people find them difficult to predict . . . because their constructs do lead to varying predictions" (p. 56).

Dependency Constructs

Even given a reasonable amount of predictability in a child's social environment, early construction systems will still be characterized by impermeability of the few simple constructs that compose them. Children are small, weak, and vulnerable. They must depend on others for survival. Thus, the bulk of a child's early construction system is constituted by **dependency constructs**, special constructs that revolve around the child's survival needs. A "mother" construct would be an example. For a young child the "mother" construct might have a context containing elements such as warmth, safety from frightening sounds, nourishment, and so forth. Notice the similarity to Jung's mother archetype and mother complex and to Sullivan's conception of mother–child relations.

At first the child might see the world in terms of "like mother–not like mother." The construct is very global and mother is seen in a very restricted manner. The university classes she teaches and the Chamber of Commerce committees she chairs play no role in the child's conception of her. She is warmth, comfort, and food. However, with growth and development, the construct will become more permeable and she will be more than warmth and kindred elements. In time, the entire construct will likely disappear altogether and "mother" will become a symbol for some other construct or an element of several constructs. The general disposition to impermeability of constructs dissolves in the tide of ever increasing maturation.

Role Playing

The relationship with the mother is but the beginning of a long line of relationships that will extend throughout life. The extent to which one can appreciate the construction system of another person is the extent to which one can play a role in a relationship with that other person (Kelly, 1963). Playing a **role** involves behaving in ways that meet the expectations of important other people in one's life.

In turn, such behavior provides the predictability that one requires. Thus a six-year-old may assume that her role relative to her parents is that of the passive, compliant "seen but not heard" child. If she behaves in a passive, compliant, quiet manner, she predicts that she will be fed, cuddled, provided with toys, and so forth. At least during childhood, the hypothetical child's assumed role might work out fine, provided she correctly perceives that her predictions are confirmed.

However, assume that all does not go so well. Assume that her observations are faulty and she is seeing confirmation of her predictions that, in fact, does not exist. Eventually, she will have to stop deluding herself. Sooner or later she will have to face up to the fact that her parents do not really want a passive, compliant, quiet child. Perhaps in "reality" they expect her to play the role of the assertive, active, independent child. The outcome of such a revelation would be **guilt**, the result of the person's perception that he or she is being dislodged from some critical role, one that was thought to be very important in relating to important people. In more common terms, guilt in this case comes from not measuring up, not being one's parent's child, not fitting the mold that important others have sculpted for oneself.

Choices: The C-P-C Cycle

Whenever individuals face significant or dramatic change in their life situations, whether it is a short-term variation or a long-term upheaval, they must search their systems of constructs for dimensions that will best accommodate the change. They must make an **elaborative choice**, a selection of an "alternative, aligned to one . . . construct dimension, which appears to provide the greater opportunity for the further elaboration of [one's] . . . system" (Kelly, 1980, p. 32). "At a certain stage in one's development it may be more promising to choose to do something that will help . . . define [one's] position more clearly and thus consolidate ... gains. . . . But at other times one will choose to extend his [or her] system so it will embrace more of the unknown and bring more of the future within [one's] grasp" (p. 32).

No matter which of the two directions we take in confronting life change, the process is the same. We go through the C-P-C choice cycle. First we construe. "To do this we go through a **circumspection phase** . . . a period of 'trying on for size' the various constructs available in our personal repertory" (Kelly, 1980, p. 32; emphasis added). To illustrate the process, suppose, on short notice, a person receives a promotion. Now, for the first time, she is boss to several employees and must decide how to relate to them. If she does not have many relevant constructs, this phase will not take long and she may look like "a person of action." If circumstances are changing too rapidly for her to keep up, she may race through this phase of the cycle and appear to be impulsive. Of course, she may take her time.

In any case, she next moves to the **preemption phase**, a period during which "one construct is allowed to preempt the situation and define the pair of alternatives between which the person must make his [or her] choice" (Kelly, 1980, p. 33). Henceforth, unless she backtracks, she will stick with the construct that has surfaced. Suppose that construct is "authoritarian–egalitarian." Finally, commitment occurs, the principle of elaborative choice takes over, and she makes a **choice**, a decision between the alternatives provided by the construct that has preempted the situation. She chooses to be authoritarian in her relations with her new subordinates. Thus, she completes the C-P-C cycle: circumspection, preemption, and choice.

Evaluation

Contributions: Supporting Evidence and Practical Applications

There have been some problems in supporting Kelly's PCT. One reason is the nature of the theory: it is a tight logical system incorporating numerous abstract concepts, few of which are easy to translate into testable terms. Also, the fact that each person's construct system is different from that of each other person creates a paradox. Researchers must resolve the dilemma of employing a sample of persons to make generalizations about construct systems that are different for different people. Nevertheless, there are some studies that seem to support Kelly's theory, both in terms of verifying some of his concepts and in terms of supporting his assumptions.

Poles
Kelly (1963) indicates that a critical testable aspect of his theory is the assumption that people cast their worlds in terms of opposites. Kelly's theoretical structure is built on the supposition that each construct has two poles. If that supposition proved false, the structure might tumble. Predictions of the future would fail if a construct, for example, was represented by "all people are good," rather than "some people are good" and "some people are bad." In fact, if each construct had only one pole, there would be nothing to predict: All people would be treated in an equally positive manner. Life would be one certainty after another.

Accordingly, Kelly (1963) made special reference to some work by William H. Lyle, a former student. Lyle first selected some words that appeared to belong to four categories:

"cheerful–sad," "broad-minded–narrow-minded," "refined–vulgar" and "sincere–insincere." A pilot sample of subjects then were told to place the words into the eight different classes represented by the eight words just listed. This procedure provided a basis for accuracy scores in the main study. Main study subjects were given the same words and told to place them into the eight classes (plus a ninth, "don't know" class). They were given a point for a "correct response" each time they placed a word in the same class as did the pilot subjects. Thus, each main study subject had eight accuracy scores, one for each of the eight word classes. Then a method to be considered later, factor analysis, was used on the accuracy scores to see what word classes clustered together and distinguished themselves from other clusters. Results revealed five collections of words or factors, one for "general intelligence" and four others exactly matching the four categories "cheerful–sad," "sincere–insincere," and so forth. Subjects tended to lump together "cheerful" with "sad" words and "sincere" with "insincere" words. If, for example, they made classification mistakes with "refined" words, they made mistakes with "vulgar" words as well. In short, they classed or organized the words into sets of opposites, just as Kelly believed constructs are organized.

Extension of Kelly's Theory

Kevin Benesch and Monte Page (1988) investigated the circumstances under which individuals are able to appreciate the important constructs of other people. To pursue that interest, subjects were recruited in triads, each consisting of three people who were close acquaintances. One triad member was designated the "target." The other two members, called "peers," reacted to the target in various ways that amounted to attempting to specify the target's critical constructs. Targets also indicated their own critical constructs. Results revealed good correspondence between targets' and peers' perceptions of targets' constructs. Peers tended to accurately perceive targets' critical constructs—they matched targets' self-perceived critical constructs—when those constructs reflected high meaningfulness and high stability (consistent use of constructs across people and objects). Commonality among the contents of these friends' construction systems may have helped them appreciate each other's critical constructs. These results extend Kelly's theory by indicating the circumstances under which individuals are able to "read" others' constructs.

Kelly's PCT was originally used as a way to conceptualize personality and as a basis for helping people in therapy. In more recent years it has been used with greater specificity. PCT is now employed to account for specific circumstances faced by a restricted category of people, for example, elderly people who have lost a spouse. Viney, Benjamin, and Preston (1989) found that elderly people who had suffered the loss of a spouse displayed "guilt" in Kelly's sense of the word: They felt dislodged from important roles. As an illustration, a woman whose husband had died felt dislodged from the roles of wife and homemaker, roles that involved core constructs. Viney and colleagues suggested that elderly persons who have lost spouses lack the means of validating their core constructs and need help in locating new sources of validation.

Cognitive Complexity

An additional source of supporting evidence was provided by another of Kelly's former students, James Bieri. One of Kelly's basic beliefs was that an effective construct system is well differentiated (Tyler, 1994). Probably inspired by this belief, Bieri (1955) defined a new dimension, cognitive complexity–cognitive simplicity. A **cognitively complex** person has a construction system containing constructs that are clearly differentiated, that is, sharply distinguished one from the other. Complex people, having a differentiated construction system, cast other people into many categories and thus see much variety in people. On the other hand, a **cognitively simple** person has a construction system for which distinctions among constructs are blurred—a poorly differentiated system. They cast other people into a few categories. Hypothetically, an extremely cognitively simple person would use mainly one construct such as good–bad, lumping half of humanity into the "good" class, and the other into the "bad" class. Bieri (1955) showed that cognitively simple people have difficulty seeing the differences between themselves and others (they tend to assume that others are pretty much like themselves). By contrast, complex people can draw sharp distinctions between themselves and others.

Kelly (1955) believed that the more constructs one uses the better she or he will be at predicting future events, including the behavior of other persons. Bieri (1955) confirmed this assumption: Complex subjects were better at predicting the behavior of others. If people use mainly one construct, say "good–bad," they are likely to put themselves in the "good" class. Given little information about other people—the circumstance of Bieri's subjects—they will predict that others are good, like themselves. Complex persons use many constructs, some for application to themselves and some for application to the many other people in their lives. Table 11.1 summarizes the characteristics of cognitively complex and simple people.

Other researchers have over the years used the complex–simple dimension to provide strong support for Kelly's theory. For example, Signell (1966) reported that children tend to increase in cognitive complexity during the period 9–16 years of age. Also, Sechrest and Jackson (1961) found that social intelligence—an index of social effectiveness—was strongly related to cognitive complexity. In a more recent study, Linville (1982) reported the following results: (1) students who were relatively simple in their representations of older males were extreme in their evaluation of older males; (2) individuals who were induced to adopt a simple orientation toward food used in a study of taste gave more extreme evaluations than did those induced to adopt a more complex orientation; (3) young males gave older males more extreme evaluations than they gave to members of their own age group; and (4) these young college students had more constructs available for use in description of their own age group than of an older age group.

Interest in the observation that people are more complex in their construal of the "in-group," (their own group) than they are of the "out-group" (another group) has been grow-

TABLE 11.1   Comparison of Cognitively Complex and Simple People

Cognitively Complex Person	Cognitively Simple Person
Maintains a clear distinction among constructs	Distinction among constructs blurred
Casts others into many categories	Casts others into few categories
Can easily see differences between self and others	Has difficulty in seeing differences between self and others
Skilled at predicting behaviors of others	Inept at predicting behaviors of others

ing. Bernadette Park and her colleagues, Carey Ryan and Charles Judd (1992), reported that subjects produced more constructs in describing the in-group compared to the out-group. Subjects also saw more subgroups within the in-group compared to the out-group. While both of these outcomes confirm that people are more complex in viewing the in-group, other results were complicated, indicating that original conceptions of cognitive complexity were too neat and straightforward in differentiating complexity from simplicity.

In a similar vein, Philip Tetlock and his colleagues are showing, contrary to original assumptions, that it is not necessarily "better" to be complex than simple. Examining historical records of pre-civil war politicians, Tetlock, Armor, and Peterson (1993) found that a category of politicians who showed partial tolerance for slavery were more complex than either extreme slavery supporters or abolitionists. Given that slavery is morally indefensible, even partial support of it by complex people is contrary to arguments for their moral superiority.

In a study with a similar theme, Tetlock, Peterson, and Berry (1994) looked at the personality profiles of business administration master's degree candidates. Their results draw a complicated picture that does not readily fit the "complex is better" original portrait. Complex candidates' self-reports reflected higher openness and creativity, but they were lower on the valued trait "conscientious" and also lower on the sometimes valued trait "social compliance." On other measures they were higher on initiative and self-objectivity, but on still other measures they were high on narcissism, antagonism, and power motivation. As is usually the case, a closer look at useful but all-too-straightforward personality dichotomies like complexity–simplicity reveals that originally sharp distinctions between extremes give way to more blurred distinctions eventually.

Complexity–simplicity also sheds some light on nonverbal communication processes. Uhlemann, Lee, and Hasse (1989) asked subjects to rate the expertness of a counselor depicted conducting a therapy session on videotape. The expertness measure assessed subjects' sensitivity to nonverbal cues that were systematically displayed by the counselor. Subjects were categorized into four levels of cognitive complexity based on a test of complexity. They were also subjected to one of three levels of arousals: (1) low—they were alone while viewing the video; (2) moderate—others were present; and (3) high—the others present were supposedly "observers" who would evaluate the subjects. Complexity theory would predict that a complex person would be more sensitive to the nonverbal cues: She or he would have higher social intelligence and would be more sensitive to the behaviors of other people that might allow discrimination among them. Results showed the expected effects, but were qualified by level of arousal. When arousal was moderate or high, high-complex subjects were more discriminating of nonverbal behaviors than low-complex subjects.

The REP Test

Among Kelly's most enduring contributions is the **Role Construct Repertory (REP) Test,** an assessment device designed to reveal an individual's construct system. It has not only been useful as a method for the assessment and study of personality, but has also been a helpful companion to the therapy process. As you will see, it is being even more broadly applied at present and promises to be applicable to an expanding variety of problems in the future.

BOX 11.2   Joan's Responses to the REP Test

The best way to understand the REP test is to experience an example of its use: Consider Joan's completion of the REP. Read the instructions, beginning in the next paragraph, and then follow the responses Joan "wrote" into List A and Figure 11.2.

List A provides fifteen role definitions. Read each definition carefully. In each blank, write the first name of the person who best fits that role in your life. It is essential to use the role definitions as given in List A. If you cannot remember the name of the person, put down a word or brief phrase that will bring the person to mind. Do not repeat any names; if some person has already been listed, simply make a second choice. Thus, next to the word "Self" write your own name. Then next to the word "Mother" put your mother's name (or the person who has played the part of a mother in your life), and so on, until all fifteen roles have been designated with a specific individual.

List A: Definition of Roles for the Demonstration

1. *Self*: Yourself *Joan*
2. *Mother*: Your mother or the person who has played the part of mother in your life. *Sandra*
3. *Father*: Your father or the person who has played the part of a father in your life. *Michael*
4. *Brother*: Your brother who is nearest your own age, or, if you do not have a brother, a boy near your own age who has been most like a brother to you. *Joe*
5. *Sister*: Your sister who is nearest your own age, or, if you do not have a sister, a girl near your own age who has been most like a sister to you. *Sue*
6. *Spouse*: Your wife (or husband), or, if you are not married, your closest present girl (boy) friend or partner. *Ed*
7. *Pal*: Your closest present friend of the same sex as yourself. *Rowda*
8. *Ex-Pal*: A person of the same sex as yourself whom you once thought was a close friend of yours but in whom you were badly disappointed later. *Sharon*
9. *Rejecting Person*: A person with whom you have been associated, who, for some unexplained reason, appears to dislike you. *Howard*

10. *Pitied Person*: A person whom you would most like to help or for whom you feel most sorry. *Ronald*
11. *Threatening Person*: The person who threatens you the most or the person who makes you feel the most uncomfortable. *Sally*
12. *Attractive Person*: A person you have recently met whom you would like to know better. *Paula*
13. *Accepted Teacher*: The teacher who influenced you most. *Sarah*
14. *Rejected Teacher*: The teacher whose point of view you have found most objectionable. *Donald*
15. *Happy Person*: The happiest person whom you know personally. *Al*

Now look at the first row of the matrix in Figure 11.2. Note that there are circles in the squares under Columns 9, 10, and 12. These circles designate the three people whom you are to consider in sort number 1 (Rejecting Person, Pitied Person, and Attractive Person). Think about these three people. In particular, how are *two of them alike* in some way that *differentiates them from the third person*? When you have decided the most important way that two of them are alike but different from the third person, put an X in the two circles that correspond to the two people who are alike. Do not write anything in the third circle; leave it blank. Next, write a word or short phrase in the column marked "Emergent Pole" that tells how the two people are alike. Then, in the column marked "Implicit Pole," write a word or short phrase that explains the way the third person is different from the other two. Finally, consider the remaining twelve people and think about which of these, in addition to the ones you have already marked with an X, also have the characteristics you have designated under "Emergent Pole." Place an X in the square corresponding to the name of each of the other persons who has this characteristic. When you have finished this procedure for the first row, go to the second row (sort number 2). The process should be repeated until the procedure has been carried out for each of the rows. In summary, the steps to be followed for each row (sort) are:

BOX 11.2   *Continued*

Sort Number	1 (Self)	2 (Mother)	3 (Father)	4 (Brother)	5 (Sister)	6 (Spouse)	7 (Pal)	8 (Ex-Pal)	9 (Rejecting Person)	10 (Pitied Person)	11 (Threatened Person)	12 (Attractive Person)	13 (Accepted Teacher)	14 (Rejected Teacher)	15 (Happy Person)	EMERGENT POLE	IMPLICIT POLE
1									×	O		×				Admired	Not Admired
2		O	×	×												Trust	Distrust
3				O									×		×	Like Me	Not Like Me
4	O						×						×			Strong	Weak
5	×							O		×						Rural	Urban
6				O			×						×			Capable	Incapable
7				O			×		×							Female	Male
8					×			O						×		Cheerful	Sad
9						×	O			×						Interesting	Uninteresting
10	×			×	O											Good	Bad
11		×	O							×						Talkative	Quiet
12						×	O			×						Athletic	Unathletic
13	×				×	O										Calm	Anxious
14	×	O	×													Invulnerable	Vulnerable
15			×					O					×			Ambitious	Unambitious

FIGURE 11.2   Joan's Responses to the REP Test

1. Consider the three people who are designated by circles under their names. Decide how two of them are alike in some important way, and different from the third.

2. Put an X in the circles corresponding to the two people who are alike; leave the remaining circle blank.

3. In the "Emergent Pole" column, write a brief description of the way the two people are *alike*.

4. In the "Implicit Pole" column, write a brief description of the way the third person is *different* from the two who are alike.

5. Consider the remaining twelve people, and place an X in the squares corresponding to those who can also be characterized by the description in the "Emergent Pole" column.

6. Repeat steps 1 through 5 for each row of the matrix.

Briefly consider Joan's responses. First she completed Figure A. There Joan listed important persons in her life who fit such categories as Father, Pal, Rejecting Person, Attractive Person and Accepting Teacher. Next, she completed the sorts indicated in the matrix shown in Figure 11.2. She used the circles marked in each row to compare the different individuals. In sort 1, Joan compared Rejecting Person, Pitied Person, and Attractive Person and indicated which two were most alike. Her "X's" show that she sees her Rejecting Person (Howard) and her

Continued

BOX 11.2 *Continued*

Attractive Person (Paula) as more alike than other possible combinations of the three people. For each sort, Joan was asked to write a word or phrase under "emergent pole" that describes how the two similar people are alike. Then she was to place a word or phrase under "implicit pole" to represent how the third person is different from the two similar individuals. Joan's entries for sort 1 demonstrate that, for her, Howard and Paula are alike in being admired, while Pitied Person (Ronald) is different from the other two in being "not admired." Similarly, in sort 4, Joan found that her Ex-pal (Sharon) and her Accepted Teacher (Sarah) were alike in being strong,

while Mother was seen as weak. Any additional "X's" Joan might have put on a given row would have indicated other persons who fit the label under the "emergent pole" for that row. Taken together, Joan's responses for all the sorts reveal her construction system.

Now that you've run through Joan's responses, you may wish to complete the test yourself. You will find a blank form for your use in Box 11.3, which is located just after the conclusion section near the end of the chapter. You may wish to read the remainder of the chapter first, as it will prime you for the task of generating your own construction system.

The Rep Test and PCT in Business and Industry

According to A. D. Jankowicz (1987), "A major stimulus for the broad application of personal construct psychology came with the early abandonment of the fixed set of role titles used as elements in Kelly's original [REP test]" (p. 484). In the place of Kelly's traditional titles, self, mother, father, brother, sister, and so forth, applied researchers have inserted a variety of labels that are relevant to various situations in business and industry. For example, through the use of products' names in place of the usual role titles, researchers discovered the constructs applied by home testers to cosmetics and perfumes. They could then use the dimensions represented by the constructs, for example, poignant–bland, to rate the products. This method allowed the researchers to get at the heart of consumers' conception of the products, an achievement that might have eluded them had they tried to use dimensions *they* thought were relevant. In an analogous fashion, researchers discovered the beliefs, values, and items of knowledge used by senior managers so that this information could be used by new managerial employees to smooth the way into their novel positions of authority.

Jankowicz, who works in the banking industry, has concentrated on identifying the "constructs the effective loan agent used and to examine whether they are different in kind and extent from the constructs used by less effective loan agents, effectiveness being defined objectively in terms of the relative size of loan defaults" (p. 485). Researchers have also used the REP technique to reveal the constructs that quality control inspectors use to separate defective from acceptable products. Other business/industry applications of the REP are outlined in Dalton and Dunnett (1992).

The REP grid, as contemporary researchers and clinicians often call it (see Figures 11.2 and 11.3), has often been used in work with people displaying a variety of psychological problems. Examples include response to psychotherapy by people who suffer from nervous tics (O'Connor, Gareau, & Bowers, 1993); differentiation between successful and unsuccessful psychotherapy clients (Catina, & Tschuschke, 1993); assessment of "quality of life" among medication-therapy, anxiety disordered patients (Thunedborg, Allerup, Bech, & Joyce, 1993); detecting increases in construed similarity of self and others following psychotherapy (Winter, 1992); and identification of disordered thinking characteristic of schizophrenia (Pierce, Sewell, & Cromwell, 1992). Other REP grid uses include measurement of construct change as a result of a teacher education workshop (Fischl & Hoz, 1993); indexing educational psychologists' competencies (McClatchey, 1994); assessment of cognitive and social representations of body parts and byproducts among potential organ donors (Oliviero, 1993); and evaluation of a master's degree student's changed perceptions of the school psychologist's role as "consultant in the school," following mentoring by a professional school psychologist (Salmon & Fenning, 1993).

Fixed-Role Therapy

Though Kelly was not tied to a particular kind of therapy, he did develop a unique therapeutic method. In **fixed-role therapy** a client plays the role of an imaginary character who possesses certain constructs that are in contrast to his or her actual constructs (Kelly, 1955). The therapist would use the client's actual constructs as a basis for creating the construct or constructs of the imaginary character.

The process would go something like this: (1) the client would describe himself in terms of central and troublesome constructs; (2) the therapist would, in the simplest case, write a fixed role for the imaginary character, requiring the client to assume a construct that demands very different behavior than is usual for him (his verbally aggressive tendency to cut in when others are talking and talking over them is replaced with an orientation to "biting the tongue" and "letting others speak their piece"); (3) the client tries the role, then he and the therapist discuss reactions of others to the new character; and (4) the client does not necessarily adopt the new role, but gains some insight into what it is like to be on the other side of the role he normally plays.

PCT and Diversity

Kelly's PCT does not directly deal with diversity. Nor have Kelly's students or followers pursued diversity issues. Nevertheless, because of PCT's one-person-at-a-time, open-ended, flexible, and content-free nature, including its REP Test and fixed role therapy, it has great potential for use in many and varied cultures and subcultures. Because it is a way of viewing the world, rather than an internal entity with specific content like "extrovert" (content: out-going, talkative, social), a construct is not restricted to any culture. People partaking of any culture associated with a language can state their constructs. That their constructs may be different from those of Westerners is not a problem. Contrast this open-ended, content-free essence with the nature of typical trait theories. A trait like "assertiveness" may have no meaning in some non-Western cultures, because there are minimal individual differences with regard to it (in some cultures, most people are nonassertive; in other cultures, most are highly assertive). Likewise the REP test can be easily recast to fit any culture. For example, role-persons who have mostly Western relevance (attractive person) can be replaced by culturally relevant role-persons (pious person). In a similar fashion, the fixed role therapy method can be adapted to different cultures. A fixed role written for the imaginary character could be peculiar to any culture. The only requirement is that a construct is assigned that demands very different behavior than what is usual for the assignee. Applications of PCT to different cultures would highlight both differences and similarities among the cultures. In so doing, it could increase intercultural understanding.

Limitations

Like those of other theorists, Kelly's basic assumptions can be attacked. In addition, Kelly may be seen as concentrating too much on cognition and too little on other aspects of people. Also like other theorists, some of Kelly's ideas have not been strongly verified by research. Finally, despite its usefulness for many purposes, the REP test has some limitations.

The Notion of Opposites

As indicated earlier, Kelly's theory is based on the notion of opposites as manifested in constructs. The most obvious attack on this central idea is that some candidates for "construct" do not involve opposites. Either the opposite is missing altogether, or it is not a true opposite. To illustrate the lack of a true opposite, for some candidates the only specifiable opposite to the emergent pole is the negation of that pole. For example, "admire–not admire" was purposely used in the Jim and Joan illustration (see Figure 11.1). "Admire–not admire" would certainly qualify as a construct (so would just about any set of two words which are apparent opposites). However, the implicit pole is the negation of the emergent pole; it is not something, but the absence of something. One can admire a person, but not to admire a person lacks specifiable content. It implies no definite relationship or action. Similarly, an examination of a list of words that were all generated during the process of self-description (that is, disclosure of constructs) reveals a large number of emergent poles the opposites of which are negations (Allen and Potkay, 1983a). For example, "awful" and "bizarre" seem to have no opposites except "not awful" and "not bizarre."

While, in some cases, implicit poles are merely negations of emergent poles, in others, they may be absent entirely. Kelly himself acknowledged that his clients sometimes cannot articulate an implicit pole for a construct. He assumed that, in such cases, the implicit pole is submerged. A **submerged pole** has either never been put into word form, perhaps because the construct is new, or is being suppressed (a client insists "all people are good" in order to escape the perception that people are bad and out to get him; Kelly, 1963). Perhaps some people do submerge implicit poles, or it may be that they did not express an implicit pole because none exists for them.

One may say, "all well and good, but what about Lyle's support of Kelly's conception of constructs?" Examination of the word list mentioned previously reveals that all of the eight labels for the eight classes of words used in Lyle's study have extreme favorability values. For each of the four sets of words, one member of the pair refers to a characteristic that is highly valued and desired by people in our society, while the other word refers to a highly undesirable characteristic. Table 11.2 presents these words and accompanying values falling along a scale where "600" represents highest favorability and "0" lowest favorability. Also, all eight emergent poles do have rather obvious opposites that are not just negations. However, one might question whether these words are representative of construct labels that are used by real people. Do the emergent poles of real people's constructs all have such clear opposites? Do the constructs of real people have poles that are so extremely different in favorability? It seems intuitively obvious that some real people would

TABLE 11.2 Lyle's Word Categories and Associated Favorability Values*

Cheerful	475	Sad	213
Broad-minded	425	Narrow-minded	142
Refined	342	Vulgar	77
Sincere	504	Insincere	107
Average (mean)	437		135

* From Allen and Potkay (1983a)

have constructs with no opposites to emergent poles and constructs with poles that are not extremely different in favorability. Thus, Lyle's study should be replicated with a more representative sample of potential constructs.

Where Are the Emotions?

You may have noticed that reference to emotions (roughly "feelings") is largely absent from Kelly's list of concepts. Anxiety, fear, threat, and guilt are mentioned but defined in rather unconventional and emotionally bland cognitive terms. People are not just "thinkers"; they also have emotions. While Kelly did acknowledge "feelings," he was unable to say much about the constructs that would apply to them. He did indicate that "feeling" constructs would mainly be preverbal—constructs that have no words associated with the emergent and implicit poles. If "feeling" constructs are preverbal, they are forever relegated to the unconscious. Being in some sense unconscious, feelings or emotions are not substantially considered in Kelly's conception of personality, which is so clearly dominated by consciousness.

Some Concepts Not Verified

Like those of several other theorists, some of Kelly's concepts are too vague to verify empirically. Among these are some of Kelly's attempts to include emotionality in his theorizing. Excellent illustrations include the concepts: (1) threat that the system of constructs may be overhauled; (2) anxiety that the system does not apply to critical events; and (3) fear that new constructs may be dominating. Aside from these being strange definitions for words commonly used by other theorists, a recent attempt to verify them has failed. Beck (1988) investigated these concepts and found little support for hypotheses based on them. In fact, in some instances results were the opposite of predictions.

Shortcomings of the REP

One of the REP test's virtues is also a major limitation. It involves an idiographic approach, one person at a time. Each REP outcome is unique to the person who produced it. A given person's constructs, as revealed by her or his REP responses, may not be meaningfully compared with those of other persons, much less generalized to all other people. Such is the case even in industry and business applications. The REP outcomes produced by successful loan officers or product quality-control inspectors cannot be readily generalized to other loan officers or inspectors, whether successful or not. Just as a radiologist's method for reading an X ray is unique to her or him, one's REP outcome is specific to oneself (Matlin & Foley, 1992). In fact, the REP reflects the highly idiographic PCT from which it is drawn.

That the PCT is highly idiographic makes it alien to the most popular orientation in the United States: nomothetic—identifying universal characteristics and broad principles that can be generalized across all humans. Parity in popularity with other major theories will probably have to await a change in the orientation of most U.S. personologists.

Conclusions

George A. Kelly is certainly one of psychology's most original thinkers. In fact, research support for his theory may not be optimally great, because it is so original that researchers may not know how to approach it. Although some of his ideas resemble those of some other theorists, Kelly did not directly borrow from anybody. His theory is composed mainly of fresh, new ideas. Nothing resembling ids, archetypes, or needs exist in the theory. Little wonder that some U.S. psychologists have had trouble relating to PCT. In Britain it is a different story: his popularity is great and growing. However, the state of Kelly's popularity in the United States seems to be changing. Examination of current personality texts and journals reveals that Kelly is resurgent. While a computer search turned up rather few references to Kelly himself, references to PCT, constructs, and the REP test were in triple digits. Because his theory was made public some forty years ago, people have had time to get used to his very different and highly novel ideas.

If Kelly is to be criticized for having little to say about feelings, he is to be congratulated for emphasizing what others have ignored. Kelly, more than any other psychologist, has made cognition the primary basis for the study of personality. Also, Kelly's "one subject

---

BOX 11.3 Your Own Construction System

List A lists fifteen role definitions. Read each definition carefully. In each blank, write the first name of the person who best fits that role in your life. It is essential to use the role definitions as given in List A. If you cannot remember the name of the person, put down a word or brief phrase that will bring the person to mind. Do not repeat any names; if some person has already been listed, simply make a second choice. Thus, next to the word "Self" write your own name. Then next to the word "Mother" put your mother's name (or the person who has played the part of a mother in your life), and so on, until all fifteen roles have been designated with a specific individual.

List A: Definition of Roles for the Demonstration
1. *Self*: Yourself _____
2. *Mother*: Your mother or the person who has played the part of mother in your life. _____
3. *Father*: Your father or the person who has played the part of a father in your life. _____
4. *Brother*: Your brother who is nearest your own age, or, if you do not have a brother, a boy near your own age who has been most like a brother to you. _____
5. *Sister*: Your sister who is nearest your own age, or, if you do not have a sister, a girl near your own age who has been most like a sister to you.
_____

BOX 11.3   *Continued*

6. *Spouse*: Your wife (or husband), or, if you are not married, your closest present girl (boy) friend. _____

7. *Pal*: Your closest present friend of the same sex as yourself. _____

8. *Ex-Pal*: A person of the same sex as yourself whom you once thought was a close friend of yours but in whom you were badly disappointed later. _____

9. Rejecting Person: A person with whom you have been associated, who, for some unexplained reason, appears to dislike you. _____

10. *Pitied Person*: A person whom you would most like to help or for whom you feel most sorry. _____

11. *Threatening Person*: The person who threatens you the most or the person who makes you feel the most uncomfortable. _____

12. *Attractive Person*: A person you have recently met whom you would like to know better. _____

13. *Accepted Teacher*: The teacher who influenced you most. _____

14. *Rejected Teacher*: The teacher whose point of view you have found most objectionable. _____

15. *Happy Person*: The happiest person whom you know personally. _____

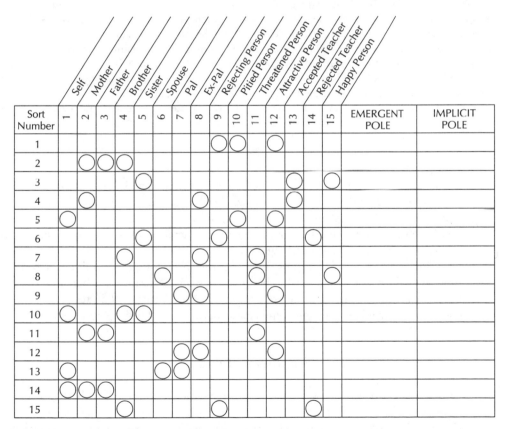

FIGURE 11.3   Your Construction System

Continued

BOX 11.3   *Continued*

Now look at the first row of the matrix in Figure 11.3. Note that there are circles in the squares under Columns 9, 10, and 12. These circles designate the three people whom you are to consider in sort number 1 (Rejecting Person, Pitied Person, and Attractive Person). Think about these three people. In particular, how are *two of them alike* in some way that *differentiates them from the third person*? When you have decided the most important way that two of them are alike but different from the third person, put an X in the two circles that correspond to the two people who are alike. Do not write anything in the third circle; leave it blank. Next, write a word or short phrase in the column marked "Emergent Pole" that tells how the two people are alike. Then, in the column marked "Implicit Pole," write a word or short phrase that explains the way the third person is different from the other two. Finally, consider the remaining twelve persons and think about which of these, in addition to the ones you have already marked with an X, also have the characteristics you have designated under "Emergent Pole." Place an X in the square corresponding to the name of each of the other persons who has this character-

istic. When you have finished this procedure for the first row, go to the second row (sort number 2). The process should be repeated until the procedure has been carried out for each of the rows. In summary, the steps to be followed for each row (sort) are:

1. Consider the three people who are designated by circles under their names. Decide how two of them are alike in some important way, and different from the third.
2. Put an X in the circles corresponding to the two people who are alike; leave the remaining circle blank.
3. In the "Emergent Pole" column, write a brief description of the way the two people are *alike*.
4. In the "Implicit Pole" column, write a brief description of the way the third person is *different* from the two who are alike.
5. Consider the remaining twelve persons, and place an X in the squares corresponding to those who can also be characterized by the description in the "Emergent Pole" column.
6. Repeat steps 1 through 5 for each row of the matrix.

or client at a time" approach is not lacking in merit just because it is not often embraced, especially in the United States. My colleague, Charles Potkay, and I personally favor the idiographic approach (see Allen & Potkay, 1983a and Potkay & Allen, 1988). Humans are just too complicated and each is too unique to readily generalize from what one displays to most others (also see Allen, 1988a and 1988b).

Finally, because Kelly has provided a cognitive basis for understanding personality at a time when the cognitive approach is burgeoning, many of his ideas are here to stay. The notion of "constructs," the dimension of complexity–simplicity, the REP test, and many other contributions will likely cement Kelly's name in the halls of psychology, evermore.

Summary Points

1. George Kelly was an individualistic, unconventional person whose background ranged from engineering to labor relations. He made a point of rejecting "stimulus–response" and Freudian psychology. Yet with all of his sarcasm and skepticism he was a warm friend and mentor to colleagues and students. He believed that thought processes were the key to understanding people and that people, as well as therapists and researchers, act like scientists in their pursuits.

2. Constructs, ways of construing events, were basic to Kelly. His fundamental postulate was that people's processes are routed by the ways they anticipate events. Jim's and Joan's conversation illustrates two different construction systems, each having superordinate and subordinate constructs that have emergent or primary poles and implicit or contrasting poles. A construct's range of convenience is the extent of the event category to which it applies and its range of focus is the events to which it most readily applies.

3. Some constructs are impermeable, while some are characterized by commonality and others by individuality traceable to differences in experience. Anxiety occurs when a construction system does not apply to critical events, fear when a new construct enters a system and may be dominant, and threat when a system appears to be facing overhaul.

4. When Joan tried to get Jim to change his system, she recommended that he adopt "admired–not admired," try it out, and then try it again (replicate). Joan was assuming constructive alternativism: that people's present interpretations of their life situations are subject to change. Though Kelly mimicked no other theorist, he shared assumptions with some. He believed in people's ability to change what controls them (Skinner), was future-oriented (Bandura), was in agreement with the humanists on some issues. He was not an advocate of a particular therapy (Rogers and Jung) and he was also interested in creativity (Skinner and Rogers).

5. Jim's construction system was organized by extension of the cleavage line, poles of subordinate constructs fall under emergent and implicit poles of superordinate constructs. Joan's system reflected abstracting across the cleavage line, whole constructs fell under superordinate emergent and under superordinate implicit poles. The context of a construct is all the elements, objects, beings, or events to which it applies. A symbol is an element to which a construct applies that may serve as its name.

6. Children will do whatever is necessary to achieve predictability—including "misbehavior." Tight and loose constructs vary on the predictability they yield. Dependency constructs tend to dominate early systems ("mother construct"), but eventually they give way to more permeable constructs. Playing a role involves behaving in ways that meet expectations of important other people. However, if we misread others' expectations guilt results. The need for elaborative choice starts the C–P–C cycle: circumspection (trying constructs on for size), preemption (a construct preempts the situation and defines alternatives), and choice (decision between alternatives).

7. Lyle provided some evidence that words referring to constructs are organized into pairs of opposites. Banesch and Page showed that friends are able to appreciate the critical constructs of one another. PCT helps in understanding the plight of elderly people who have lost a spouse. Bieri demonstrated that cognitively complex people have constructs that are clearly differentiated, while the opposite is true of cognitively simple people. Signell showed that complexity increases with age and Linville reported that simple college males described older males in less complex terms and gave them more extreme evaluations.

8. Park and Judd showed that people apply more constructs to the in-group and see more subgroups among in-group members. Tetlock and colleagues have shown that being cognitively complex is not necessarily "good." Uhlemann, Lee, and Hasse reported that complex subjects were more discriminating of nonverbal behavior when moderately or highly aroused. Kelly's increasingly popular REP test involves having individuals indicate the important people in their lives and, while considering them in threes, pick two who are alike in some way and different from the third.

9. Jankowicz found that the REP procedure is useful in business and industry, when role titles are replaced by product names. The REP test grid has many applications both for assessment of people with psychological problems and for numerous other purposes. In fixed role therapy, a client adopts the role of an imaginary person having a construct(s) that contrasts with the client's. Kelly's PCT is ripe for use in investigating similarities and differences among cultures, because it is basically content-free and involves methods that are easily adapted to any culture.

10. Limitations of PCT include the fact that some constructs have no real opposites to their emergent poles (perhaps they are submerged?), just the negation of that pole. Lyle's work in support of PCT suffers for nonrepresentativeness of the words he used. Kelly has also been criticized for ignoring emotions which were written off as "preverbal." Some of his concepts have not been clearly verified by research, such as threat, anxiety, and fear. Finally the REP test suffers from being too "idiographic": It is applicable to only the particular people who complete it. Yet Kelly's novel ideas and idiographic approach are catching on, especially in Britain.

Running Comparison

Theorist	Kelly in Comparison
B. F. Skinner	Unlike Skinner, he was oriented to the future, but both believed that people could be changed by planned human interventions, and both were interested in creativity.
Rogers	Like Rogers, Kelly held that individuals have choices. They also agreed that one should not limit oneself in therapy to traditional methods. Both were concerned with creativity and both felt that clients were more like partners.
Maslow	"Becoming oneself" was a major goal in therapy for both, but Kelly was less concerned with the present moment.
Jung	The Mother construct resembles Jung's Mother Archetype and mother complex. They both cast psychological reality in terms of opposites.
Sullivan	His view of mother–child relations was similar to Kelly's.

Essay/Critical Thinking Questions

1. Think of a problem that you have right now, one that is of a psychological or interpersonal nature. How would you go about solving it—locating the source of it and taking steps to eliminate it? (Hint: use the scientific approach.)

2. Based on your presumed earlier completion of the REP test, draw your construction system as in Figure 11.1 (if you have not completed the REP test, do so first).

3. Indicate the constructs of a close friend (could be a romantic partner). Then write a fixed-role script for that friend.

4. Imagine that you suffered "threat" as Kelly defines it. How would you cope with the possible overhaul of your entire construct system?

5. Based on your answers to questions 2 and 3, how would you conceive of the commonality between your construction system and that of your friend?

6. Think back to your childhood. What dependency constructs characterized your immature construction system?

7. Think of a change in your life situation that occurred at some time in the past (a change in one or more of your interpersonal relationships would be a good example). What was the form of the resultant guilt—in Kelly's sense of the word—and what did you do about it?

8. Think of another past change in your life (high school to college change in friendships?). Use the C-P-C cycle to indicate how you arrived at an alternative provided by a construct that allowed you to deal with your new situation.

9. Concentrate on the complex–simple dichotomy. What evidence can you provide to support the argument that you are a complex individual?

10. How does the "they all look alike" phenomenon as it applies to perceptions of the out-group relate to cognitive complexity–simplicity?

E-mail Interaction

(Contact the author at mfbpa@wiu.edu)
Forward one of the following or phrase your own.

1. Was Kelly really a maverick or was he more Horney's expansive type?
2. Are you a tight construer or a loose construer?
3. How would I benefit from taking the REP test?
4. Tell me what is good about being cognitively simple.
5. Do you really support studying one person at a time?

12

THE SOCIAL–COGNITIVE APPROACH TO PERSONALITY: JULIAN ROTTER AND WALTER MISCHEL

- Does it make any sense to talk about "personality" outside the social settings in which it unfolds?
- What determines your outcomes—your traits, values, and efforts or fate, luck, chance, and powerful others?
- Do people tend to size up a situation before deciding how to behave in it?
- Do your abilities have anything to do with your personality?
- Do you lay plans to regulate your behavior in advance of behaving in a social situation?

Julian Rotter

George Kelly's cognitive approach laid good groundwork for this chapter. The theorists covered here, Walter Mischel and Julian Rotter, emphasize our cognitions about the *social situations* that we encounter. Their theories are relatively closely connected—Mischel was a student of Rotter. Mischel follows Rotter's lead in emphasizing *expectancies*, what people expect will happen when they perform certain behaviors in a certain situation. That personality cannot be considered apart from the social situations in which it unfolds is a basic tenet of Rotter's theory that is adopted by Mischel. Skepticism about the basic assumption underlying *traits*—that behavior is quite stable across social situations—was initiated by Rotter and made a major issue by Mischel. Consequently, neither apply the label "trait" to any of their basic components of personality. However, Mischel's theory goes well beyond his mentor's and, as a result, has more scientific if not practical applications. Nevertheless, their general orientations are so similar that they may be placed in the same overriding theoretical category: **social learning**—acquiring useful information through interacting (relating) to people and other elements of the environment (Phares, 1976).

Rotter, The Person

Like Maslow, Julian B. Rotter traces his roots to Brooklyn, New York, where he was born to Jewish parents in 1916. Noting the obligation to acknowledge the "teacher who most contributed to my intellect," Rotter (1982, p. 343) takes a page out of Maslow's book by citing the Avenue J Library in Brooklyn. As a high school student, he spent so much time with his "teacher" that he soon exhausted its wisdom, at least in the category of fictional works. Then he searched the stacks for something new and stumbled onto books by Adler and Freud. By the time he was a senior in high school, he was interpreting other people's dreams. His senior thesis was entitled, "Why We Make Mistakes."

Rotter pursued psychology while an undergraduate at Brooklyn College, but not as a major. Like George Kelly, the background of the Great Depression caused Rotter to choose a practical major, namely chemistry. Nevertheless, he took more psychology than chemistry. This combination of a hard science and a psychology emphasis paid big dividends when Rotter later entered graduate school in psychology.

While pursuing his studies, Rotter was inspired by the lectures of social psychologist Solomon Asch, a student of Gestalt psychology famous for his conformity research. In turn, Asch got Rotter interested in the ideas of Kurt Lewin, a pioneer in the study of group dynamics who was strongly influenced by the Gestalt movement. These more socially oriented individuals must have had a great impact on Rotter, because, relative to other personality psychologists, he emphasized the importance of social situations over traits.

Part of Alfred Adler's importance was his influence on many young theorists of his day. Already you have seen that Rogers and Maslow acknowledged Adler's contribution to their thinking. During Rotter's college years, Adler resided in Brooklyn. His almost evangelistic lectures further convinced young Julian that psychology was his destiny.

After Brooklyn College, Rotter arrived at the University of Iowa with empty pockets. Thanks to the chair of the psychology department, Lee Travis, he was able to earn enough to survive and pursue a master's degree. Soon he was enrolled in a seminar run by Kurt Lewin, who convinced him that interactions between people and the social situations in which they find themselves are of central importance.

From there it was on to Worcester State Hospital where he met his wife to be, Clara Barnes. At Worcester, Rotter participated in one of the first-ever clinical psychology internships. Determined to be among the first clinical psychologists, he then entered Indiana University to pursue a Ph.D. in clinical psychology. Having finished his work in 1941, Rotter looked at job prospects with some trepidation. Like Maslow, he had learned that many academic doors were closed to Jewish people. Fortunately, he was able to land a clinical position in a state hospital where, for practical purposes, he taught for the first time. Unfortunately, World War II intervened and Rotter joined the Army, serving as a psychologist and personnel consultant. There, among other contributions, he devised a method for reducing the incidence of "absence without leave."

After World War II, Rotter found that a strong demand for still scarce clinical psychologists was more than enough to overcome anti-Semitism. He had his choice of universities and he selected Ohio State where George Kelly was to be counted among his colleagues. After Kelly gave up the clinical directorship in 1951, Rotter took it over.

It was in the army and at Ohio State that Rotter begin work on his social learning theory. While he was happy and productive at Ohio State, the fascist spirit of Communist-baiting Senator Joe McCarthy was all too alive and well in the Midwest. Accordingly, in 1963, Rotter moved East, taking his current position at the University of Connecticut. There his thinking on social learning fully crystalized.

Rotter's View of the Person

To this point theorists have tended to place heavy reliance on explanations of behavior, thought, and feeling in terms of internal factors. Here the focus is on a point of view that considers the interplay between internal and external factors. Rotter (1966) believes that people gripped by the forces of a powerful situation show a general trend in behavior not characteristically displayed in other circumstances. However, within such situations, people still exhibit individual differences in behavior.

Consider an example. Rotter (1966) writes of several studies in which some subjects were exposed to a *chance* or *skill* situation. In the chance situations, subjects were told that luck would determine how well they would do, but in the skill situations their own abilities would determine their performance. As an illustration, Phares (1962) presented subjects with a list of twelve nonsense syllables (such as ilo, pmn, rfv). First, he determined how long each subject had to view each syllable before she or he could correctly call out its letters (exposures were for fractions of a second). Then, the entire list of syllables was presented ten times, with the same six syllables always accompanied by the delivery of shock to a given subject and the other six never associated with shock. During the ten presentations, the shock could be terminated if subjects learned which of several buttons was the one that shut it off. Subjects in a "chance" condition were told that sometimes a certain button would stop the shock accompanying a particular syllable and sometimes a different button would work, depending on chance. Skill condition subjects were informed they could terminate the shock by determining which of the buttons *always* stopped the shock associated with a particular syllable.

After these ten presentations, it was again determined how long each subject had to view each syllable before being able to correctly name its letters. If a subject required less viewing time to identify a shocked syllable after the presentations than before, it was assumed that the subject had learned the syllable during the presentations. A comparison of the exposure times before and after the ten presentations revealed that subjects in the skill condition *reduced* the exposure times needed to identify the nonsense syllables followed by shock more than did subjects in the chance condition. Because skill allows people to experience control over circumstances, they do better in skill than in chance situations. However, individual differences in behavior among people assigned to the chance situation can be considerable. The same is true for the skill situation. For example, before each attempt at the chance or skill task, subjects were asked to indicate how well they expected to do. Regardless of whether they had been in the chance or skill conditions, some subjects tended to show the **Gambler's Fallacy**, the expectation that a failure on one attempt means that success on a subsequent attempt becomes more likely, whereas success means a greater likelihood of failure in the future. People who are prone to the gambler's fallacy think that a string of losses means they will surely soon be winners. They reason that luck determines their outcomes and luck is supposed to change. Other individuals show the opposite of the gambler's fallacy. They believe that skills determine outcomes. A string of successes means to them that they have mastered the situation and will continue to experience success.

In sum, Rotter believes that environments can control behavior: "Behavior in different situations will be different . . ." (Rotter, 1990, p. 491). People in the chance condition, as a group, behaved differently than those in the skill condition. However, even within powerful situations, people may show individual differences in behavior. Some people are prone to the gambler's fallacy, others are not, and they show these trends across many different situations: ". . . there may be a gradient of generalization from one situation to another" (Rotter, 1990, p. 491).

Unlike some theorists, Rotter has laid out his basic assumptions in plain sight.

1. "The unit of investigation for the study of personality is the interaction between the individual and his or her environment" (Rotter, 1982, p. 5).

2. "Personality constructs are not dependent for explanation on constructs in any other field" (p. 6). Simply put, personality constructs can stand on their own without being specified in terms of physiology or neurology.

3. "Behavior as described by personality constructs takes place in space and time" (p. 6). This assumption admits that personality constructs can also be specified in the terms of physics, chemistry, or neurology. Nevertheless, Rotter cautions against such dual specification, because it can lead to fruitless attempts at reducing constructs to the lowest common denominator (for example, events at the connection between two nerve cells).

4. "Not all behavior of an organism may be usefully described with personality constructs. . . . This postulate simply recognizes that each construction system has a particular range of convenience" (p. 7). Notice that Rotter borrows language developed by George Kelly, his former colleague. Rotter continues, "Not all events can be usefully described in personality terms. Just as some events are not amenable to description in chemical terms, so too do some events resist psychological interpretation" (p. 7). Simple reflexes are examples as they are better described in physiological terms.

5. "A person's experiences (or a person's interactions with his or her meaningful environment) influence each other. In other words, personality has unity" (p. 8). Rotter believed that, with experience, the individual's personality begins to develop relative stability: There is some generalization of behavior across situations.

6. "Behavior as described by personality constructs has a directional aspect" (p. 8). It may be said to be goal-directed. Here Rotter's position coincides somewhat with that of Maslow, but he is relatively more behavioristic, even showing some agreement with B. F. Skinner: "The preceding principle is based on the empirical law of effect" (p. 8). Thus, goals are achieved by behaviors that have been rewarded (reinforced) in the past for leading to goal attainment. The circularity inherent in this account is avoided by assuming, with good reason, that goals can be specified *before* behavior has been rewarded by goal attainment.

7. Finally, "The occurrences of a behavior of a person are determined not only by the nature or importance of goals or reinforcement, but also by the person's anticipation or ex-

pectancy that these goals will occur. Such expectations are determined by previous experience and can be quantified" (p. 10). According to Rotter, people are not merely pushed by past rewards, they are pulled by the anticipation of future goal attainment.

Basic Concepts: Rotter

Reinforcement Value, Psychological Situations, and Expectancy

For our purposes, Rotter's social learning theory is based on three main concepts (Rotter, 1975, 1982, 1990). These are reinforcement value, psychological situation, and expectancy. **Reinforcement** refers to anything that has an influence on the occurrence, direction, or kind of behavior (Phares, 1976). You will find this view in sharp contrast with that of B. F. Skinner.

Reinforcement value is the degree of preference for any reinforcement to occur if the possibilities of many different reinforcements are all equal (Rotter, 1954). The value of a reinforcement depends on how much it is preferred by an individual, compared to other reinforcements that are equally available. Imagine a woman named Martha who sometimes dates a man named Fred. For Martha, going out with Fred has low reinforcement value, because, given a choice among several other dates, Fred would be just about the last selected.

A **psychological situation** is characterized in a way peculiar to a person, allowing the person to categorize it with certain other situations, as well as differentiate it from still others (Phares, 1976). Situations are in the "eye of the beholder." If a given situation is seen in a certain way by a particular individual, that is the way it is for that person, no matter how strange the categorization might seem to others. For some individuals an exhibition of classical music is "entertainment," for others it is "a scholarly endeavor," and for still others it is a waste of time. Further, a given person will see classical music as belonging in the same category as other forms of entertainment, such as baseball and movies. Others would place it in the same category as reading or researching library files, forms of scholarly pursuits. In terms of our dating example, Martha plans to attend a rock concert, which she considers to be a social gathering. She believes one should take a companion to a concert, but it should be a person one would not be afraid to ignore when opportunities to mingle with others arise.

Expectancy is "the probability held by the individual that a particular reinforcement will occur as a function of a specific behavior on his part in a specific situation or situations" (Rotter, 1954, p. 107). Our hypothetical Martha has every reason to expect that, should she pick up the phone and dial Fred's number, he will be right over. Fred is madly in love with her, a feeling she does not reciprocate. That is, Martha has the specific expectancy that calling Fred will be reinforced by his presence with her at the concert—an outcome of high likelihood and, in and of itself, low reinforcement value. But she has another important expectancy as well. She expects opportunities to mingle with her friends at the concert, an outcome of high reinforcement value.

In addition, Martha has a relevant **generalized expectancy**, an expectancy that holds for a number of situations that are similar to one another to some degree (Rotter, 1966,

1992). The operation of generalized expectancies becomes more probable when individuals are faced with *new or ambiguous situations* that they characterize as bearing some resemblance to known situations (Rotter, 1966). Martha has been to relatively few rock concerts, but she expects that these will be like other social occasions. Her generalized expectancy is that whether she impresses her friends will depend on chance rather than her social skills (whether her friends are "in a good mood," the concert goes well, and so forth). On the basis of these assumptions about Martha, we can predict that she will call Fred who will escort her to the concert where she will encounter friends whom she will impress or not, depending on "what fate has in store."

Locus of Control: Internals and Externals

Rotter (1966, 1967) has identified two important generalized expectancies. One is the basis for as famous a personality measure as exists in psychology.

Locus of control refers to "the degree to which persons expect that . . . reinforcement [and other outcomes] of their behavior is [dependent on their] behavior or personal characteristics versus the degree to which [they expect it is due to] chance, luck, or fate, . . . powerful others, or is simply unpredictable" (Rotter, 1990, p. 489). That is, the control of outcomes can be perceived as located in one's own behaviors and skills, or as residing in luck and chance. According to Rotter, locus of control is "currently one of the most studied variables in psychology and the other social sciences" (1990, p. 489).

People who believe in **external locus of control** perceive that reinforcement of their behaviors is due more to luck, chance, fate, powerful others, or complex and unpredictable environmental forces, rather than determined by their own behaviors or characteristics (Rotter, 1966). Individuals believing in **internal control** perceive that reinforcement is dependent on their own behavior or characteristics—not fate, luck or chance. People who believe in internal locus of control are often called *internals*, while those who believe in external control are called *externals*.

Beliefs in external control or in internal control are certainly individual difference factors. However, Rotter (1975) is extremely careful to point out that calling a person an "external" or an "internal" is not a reference to a "trait" or a "type" (Rotter, 1990). In fact, he chastises researchers who apply factor analysis to his measure of locus of control and conclude that the method has little generality across circumstances (Rotter, 1990). He never indicated that external or internal loci of control would generalize strongly across situations. As illustrated in the gambler's fallacy study, situations can determine locus of control, just as people's beliefs about control can determine their behavior in a situation. Being a generalized expectancy, locus of control may determine outcomes if a situation is ambiguous. But, if a situation by its nature is associated with outcomes determined by chance or outcomes dependent on personal skills, the situation, not the locus of control, will determine outcomes.

Although there are several measures of locus of control, the one most in use has been the Internal–External (I–E) Scale, developed by Rotter (1966). Rather than presenting it here verbatim, I have designed a measure that mimics the I–E Scale, but has items composed of common beliefs. By completing my version of the I–E Scale, you should easily get a flavor of what is involved with being an external or internal. The measure is presented in Box 12.1 for your use. Remember, the scale is for educational purposes. Do not use it in an attempt to classify yourself as an external or as an internal.

BOX 12.1   An I–E Scale

Instructions. For each item, select the alternative that you more strongly believe to be true. You must select one and only one alternative for each item. Be sure that the alternative you select for a given item is the one you actually believe to be most clearly true, not the one you think that you should choose or the one you wish were true. Remember that this is a measure of your personal beliefs. There are no correct or incorrect answers and no high or low, good or bad scores.

Do not spend much time on each item, but do make a choice for each item. In some cases, you will find that you believe both statements or neither one. Please make a decision anyway.

1. a. I often find myself saying something to the effect of "What will be will be."
   b. I believe that what happens to me is my own doing.
2. a. I deserve credit for most of my accomplishments.
   b. I've been fortunate to have done well on a number of occasions.
3. a. When your time comes, you pass away; that's just the way it is.
   b. I plan to live a long time, and I wouldn't be surprised if I made it to 100.
4. a. I'm a pretty confident person. I can make things happen.
   b. Sometimes I'm amazed at how things seem to happen to me all by themselves.
5. a. I feel like a Ping-Pong ball. Life just bounces me back and forth between happy and sad.
   b. If I want to be happy, I just choose a fun thing to do and go to it.
6. a. You get what you deserve and deserve what you get.
   b. I don't feel guilty about the good things that happen to me or moan about the bad things. It could just as well have happened to someone else.
7. a. I wish the world wasn't full of so many bullies.
   b. If people start to coerce me, I just stand up and look them in the eye.
8. a. People are good to me because I treat them right.

   b. I don't know when to expect that people are going to be nasty to me or nice.
9. a. I plan things, and they turn out as I expect.
   b. "Come what may," that's my motto. I'm a tumbleweed, caught in the wind.
10. a. I live my life one day at a time.
    b. I plan my day, my week, my month, and my year. I look ahead.
11. a. I'm not afraid to risk life and limb. What the heck, you could fall in the shower and break your back.
    b. I'm pretty careful at driving, sports, and so forth. I expect to keep this body a long, long time.
12. a. I feel pretty helpless when I'm with friends. I usually end up doing what they want.
    b. My friends and I are democratic about deciding what we'll do together, but my voice is always heard.
13. a. My voice is heard above the crowd.
    b. People just seem to drown me out.
14. a. When it comes to making love, if my partner wants to, fine; if not, that's OK too.
    b. I tend to decide when, where, and what my partner and I do in the love category.
15. a. I enter many lotteries, drawings, and things like that. I keep hoping I'll strike it rich.
    b. I steer clear of everything from bingo to poker. The odds are too long.
16. a. I'm always rooting for the underdog.
    b. Me, I stick with the winners.
17. a. In this country, anyone with some talent and some sweat is going to make it.
    b. If you're lucky, you're rich; if not, join the crowd.
18. a. Minorities are doing better, because they are getting more education and working harder.
    b. Minorities are doing better, because they are finally getting a few breaks.
19. a. Some people wander around under a black cloud, while the sun shines on others.
    b. Let's face it, some people have ability and use it; some have it and waste it; and some just don't have it.
20. a. Life is a great glob of complexity. It would take an Einstein to win at it.

Continued

BOX 12.1   *Continued*

b. It's really quite simple: if you're good and work hard, you succeed.

21. a. I like to compete because if I win it's great, and if I lose I can say "the gods frowned on me."

b. I like to compete because if I win, I can say "I did it."

22. a. I think we should help each other, because misfortune could strike any of us.

b. I think people should help themselves. If something bad happens to them, they caused it, and they can fix it.

23. a. Sometimes I feel powerful, able to do whatever I want.

b. Sometimes I feel powerless, the victim of mysterious forces.

24. a. Things happen that puzzle me. I just can't make sense of them.

b. Give me enough time and enough information, and I can usually make sense of anything.

25. a. We are likely to be swept up in the ebb and flow of events.

b. If we can get to the moon, we can change the course of mighty rivers and make the weather do our bidding.

Give yourself a point if you chose each of the following alternatives: 1.a.; 2.b.; 3.a.; 4.b.; 5.a.; 6.b.; 7.a.; 8.b.; 9.b.; 10.a.; 11.a.; 12.a.; 13.b.; 14.a.; 15.a.; 16.a.; 17.b.; 18.b.; 19.a.; 20.a.; 21.a.; 22.a.; 23.b.; 24.a.; 25.a. The higher the score, the more external you are.

If you scored 20–25 on the I–E scale, you are in the *high external* range. A score of 0–5 makes you *high internal*. Most people fall between those extremes (whatever your score, remember the cautions mentioned above). If you are inclined toward one end of the scale or the other you are probably curious as to whether it is better to be an internal or an external. Originally Rotter (1966) thought that neither was "better" than the other in a practical sense. More recent evidence has caused him to reconsider.

Characteristics of Internals and Externals

Conformity and Maladjustment

Because externals believe that they are hapless victims of their environments, one would expect that they would be more conformist. Indeed, Phares (1976) reports that externals are more likely to conform in the standard conformity experiment. More generally, they tend to be more compliant (Blau, 1993). By the same token, internals react against attempts to influence them, even sometimes moving in a direction opposite to the influence attempt.

Rotter (1966) originally recognized a greater likelihood of *maladjustment* among externals. At the same time, he also hypothesized that there would be a curvilinear relationship between locus of control and psychological adjustment, with both extreme internals and extreme externals being maladjusted. However, more recently, he has conceded that such is probably not the case (Rotter, 1975). It seems that externals are considerably more likely to be maladjusted, relative to internals. Current research also finds externals to be more "worn out" and "uptight" (Ferguson, 1993).

Phares (1976) reported that externals are higher in anxiety and lower in self-esteem than internals. In terms of more serious maladjustment, schizophrenia may be related to externality. There is also preliminary and tentative evidence that it is associated with depression. More recent work supports the possibility that psychological problems are related to externality (Hermann, Whitman, Wyler, Anton, and others, 1990; Ormel & Schaufeli, 1991).

Substance Abuse

Perhaps surprisingly, internals may be more likely to abuse substances such as alcohol and heroin. It may be that high internality scores among substance abusers can be explained by the fact that recovering abusers are continually told "your cure is up to you." Alcoholics may therefore be using their I–E responses to reflect what they think is expected of them. If so, they may not be real internals. Alternatively, they may be internals who "self-medicate" to avoid externally imposed medications. Further, some research found no relationship between locus of control and parental alcoholism, a result contrary to the intuition that children of alcoholics would be relatively external (Churchill, Broida, & Nicholson, 1990). A clearer understanding of drinking behavior and internal orientation may be achieved with use of a new I–E measure with items specifically referring to alcohol-use situations (Johnson, Nora, & Bustos, 1992).

Achievement and "Race"

A literature review of academic achievement and locus of control indicates the higher the internality the higher the achievement and raises an interesting question about the nature of locus of control (Findley & Cooper, 1983). From the very beginning (Rotter, 1966), it has been reported that externality was greater among African Americans than European Americans. This result seems to make intuitive sense, as relatively powerless people should believe that they are at the mercy of their environments. However, the result seems to be due to culture rather than to "race," a suspect concept (see Allen & Adams, 1992; Hirsch, 1981; and Yee, Fairchild, Weizmann, & Wyatt, 1993, for questions about the validity of "race"). Support for this contention comes from studies that find it is African Americans of lower socioeconomic class who are highly external, not their middle-class counterparts (Rotter, 1966).

Findley's and Cooper's (1983) failure to support the greater externality in African Americans reported by Rotter (1966) may be due to the small number of studies they reviewed. Alternatively, perhaps African Americans have changed in more recent years or it may be that middle-class subjects were used in most studies reviewed by Cooper. The change-over-time proposition would be consistent with the hypothesis that how well one is doing in life determines one's level of internality–externality. If African Americans are doing better, they should become less external.

Divorce and Marital Adjustment

Although a person may be generally characterized by internality or externality, a study of divorce illustrates how internality–externality changes with the ebb and flow of life's fortunes. Doherty (1983) reported that women increased in externality following divorce, and then dropped back toward internality with the passage of time. Nevertheless, more recent work shows that externals and internals react to divorce differently. Via mailed questionnaire, Helen Barnet (1990) asked 107 divorced men and women about how long it took them to decide on a divorce, their locus of control, stress due to divorce, and adjustment to divorce. Internals showed more pre-divorce decision distress and less post-decision distress than externals. They were also less distressed overall than externals. Because internals believe that they have control, they tend to display more distress-inducing lengthy deliberation over divorce, relative to externals. For the same reason they adjust better to divorce, once a decision is made. Contrary to previous results, men were more external and experienced more post-divorce maladjustment.

Other work suggests that internals may be less likely to experience a divorce, because they are better at resolution of marital conflicts. Miller, Lefcourt, Holmes, Ware, and Saleh (1986) had married couples complete a special Marital Locus of Control (MLC) questionnaire and then resolve some conflicts. In an example of conflict resolution, husbands and wives were instructed in private. One was told to assume "you are resigned to visit in-laws" while the other was to assume "you have reservations about visiting in-laws and plans are not finalized." Then they got together in front of a video camera and resolved this and two other conflicts. Analyses of the MLC responses and the videotapes revealed that individuals who were internal for marital satisfaction were more active and direct in problem-solving than externals. Also internals were more effective in communicating and achieving their desired goals and showed higher levels of marital satisfaction than externals. Regarding marriage in general, Johnson and colleagues (1992) reported tentative results suggesting that married people are more internal than either single or divorced people.

Child-Rearing Practices and Personality Development

Researchers have studied how the processes of personality development differ for internals and externals. After reviewing the literature on locus of control and child-rearing practices, Phares (1976) concluded that internality is linked to parental warmth, protectiveness, positivity, and nurturance. On the other side, externals tend to have cold, rejecting, and negative parents. Evidence also exists that parents may actually tutor their children to be internals or externals. Davis and Phares (1969) found that parents whose children's locus of control was similar to their own tended to be more indulgent and less disciplinarian than parents whose children's locus of control was dissimilar.

A child who believes in external locus of control may be produced by a capricious, unpredictable world in which a given behavior is one day punished, the next rewarded, and the next ignored altogether. The degree to which the outcome of a behavior is stable is the degree to which one has the possibility of claiming credit for that outcome. Following this logic, the literature reflects a definite connection between inconsistency of reinforcement within the family and tendency toward externality.

Changing Externals

Because extreme externality, not extreme internality, is apparently a serious psychological handicap, changing externals has occupied a number of researchers and psychotherapists. Change appears possible because externality is not a trait and thus not assumed to be entirely stable. Examples of interventions into natural settings and psychotherapeutic interventions illustrate attempts to change externals.

DeCharms (1972) sought to change African American teachers and students from "pawns" to "origins." **Pawns** are instruments of outside forces, while **origins** are the locus of their own intentions and behaviors. Obviously pawns are essentially externals and origins are internals. DeCharms required the teachers to attend a week-long motivational training session and designed exercises for teachers to use throughout the school year. The training included (1) encouragement of self-study; (2) becoming familiar with affiliative, achievement, power, and other motives; (3) learning to appreciate planning and setting realistic goals; and (4) general training to promote "origin" behavior. Results included greater professional advancement among trained compared to untrained teachers. Questionnaire results suggested that students of trained teachers saw them as encouraging the behavior of origins. Academic achievement by students of trained teachers also showed improvement.

Ryan and Grolnick (1986) investigated whether a classroom environment perceived to be more "origin" than "pawn" would promote academic success. These researchers assessed children's perceptions of the degree to which their teachers and classroom climates were "origin." They found that the more "origin" the classroom the higher the children's perceived self-worth, cognitive competence, internal control, and mastery motivation, and the lower their perceived control by unknown sources or powerful others. Child subjects also wrote projective stories about an ambiguous classroom scene. Ratings of these stories revealed that origin-like behavior of students was related to autonomy-oriented teachers and to low aggression. These results indicate that making classroom environments more "origin" would help children both personally and academically.

Phares (1976) reports greater decreases in externality by clients who seek psychotherapy because of acute problems as compared to those who enter therapy to treat more chronic difficulties. He also describes an adolescent who moved toward internality by adopting an active, success-oriented means of controlling his parents, rather than the shrinking, meek, and submissive techniques he had been using. In other work, students became more internal after four half-hour therapy sessions centering on "personal growth experiences."

Certain questions raised by I/E research remain unanswered. Are internals more likely to be depressed because they would be expected to attribute failure to their own internal processes, an orientation related to depression by other researchers? Are Asians, who tend to be more *collectivistic* than *individualistic* North Americans, more external because of their dependence on the esteem accorded them by members of groups to which they belong? Answers to these and other intriguing questions await further activity by I/E researchers

Other Generalized Expectancies

Internality and externality are not the only possibly generalized expectancies that might be specified. In fact, Rotter's theory allows for an indefinite number of expectations that show a gradient of generalization across situations. Interpersonal trust and negative mood regulation provide examples.

Interpersonal Trust

A great deal of what one communicates to others and what others communicate to oneself is done without words. Facial expressions and posture tell other people about a person, just as those factors tell the person about them (Ekman & Friesen, 1974). Obviously the better one is at "reading" others' nonverbal signals, the better one is able to ascertain whether whatever behavior she or he is directing to another person is working to yield reinforcement. If a person is trying to fish for a compliment from someone, it is like casting a line into muddy waters if he or she cannot read from the face and body of the target whether the hook is close to sinking in.

The ability to intercept and correctly interpret nonverbal communications may be related to **interpersonal trust**, a generalized expectancy that people's verbal promises are reliable. That is, people who possess the generalized expectancy that they can rely on the word of other people are said to be high on interpersonal trust. Especially in view of the connection between successful detection of deception and ability to read nonverbal communications (DePaulo & Rosenthal, 1979), it seems reasonable to expect that people who trust others are people who have the ability to tell when others are being truthful. Conversely, people who are low in interpersonal trust are likely to be people who cannot tell when others are being straight with them. Applying this logic leads to the prediction that people who are high in interpersonal trust will be skilled at deciphering nonverbal communications. In fact, Sabatelli, Buck, and Dreyer (1983) found interpersonal trust higher in married people who were skilled at decoding nonverbal communications.

Generalized Expectancy for Negative Mood Regulation

Catanzaro and Mearns (1990) suggested that some people may develop a generalized expectancy for **negative mood regulation** (NMR), a belief that one can muster the cognitive and behavioral means to alleviate a negative-affective state or bring it under control. They reasoned that a measure of generalized expectancy for NMR should predict success at attempts to cope with negative moods. They found that the higher were subjects' scores on a measure of NMR the lower were their depression scores and their self-reports of sadness. Mearns (1991) also found that high NMR yielded more active coping and NMR scores predicted level of depression in the first week after a romantic relationship ended.

Evaluation

Contributions to Controlling Our Lives

There seems to be little question that locus of control is here to stay. If anything, interest in it is increasing (Rotter, 1990, 1992). As long ago as 1975, Rotter was able to count at least 600 studies dealing with the I-E measure. Inspection of journals during the late 1980s and the first half of the 1990s indicates that the number has greatly increased and is going up at an accelerating rate. Interest is likely to continue increasing because locus of control is in tune with the current trend to focus on the interaction between personality factors and situations.

Rotter (1954, 1966, 1990) was a pioneer in recognizing that one can account for human behavior only by considering multiple determinants, including situational effects. He has always maintained that mindless use of just a personality measure is a fruitless approach to understanding people. In addition to expectancies like locus of control and factors like the situation, one must also consider values of reinforcements (Rotter, 1975). Further, internality-externality resembles a trait dimension only in that people can be distributed along the continuum. However, rather than being discrete, positions on the internality–externality dimension blend one into the other, more so than is alleged in the case of traits. Also, a person will vary her or his position at different points in time and under differing circumstances. This "sliding scale perspective" suggests that the meaning of internality-externality must be considered in the context of many other factors, and, relative to traits, cannot be interpreted meaningfully apart from that context. This kind of flexibility and openness characterizes Rotter and guarantees that his notions will contribute to psychology indefinitely.

The concept of "control" over one's circumstances has become very important to personnel in the behavioral medicine field (Shapiro et al., 1993). If individuals can gain an appreciable degree of mastery over their environments, as is implied by internal locus of control, various psychological problems can be mastered (for example, depression, anxiety, and panic attacks). While others are jumping on the "control" bandwagon, Rotter is busily steering the horses, just as he has been, dating from the time when the wagon was empty, save for himself.

Limitations

Locus of control is the centerpiece of Rotter's point of view. Evidence for and against this crucial notion in large part determines the validity of his theory. Rotter himself has noted some problems with "locus of control." In 1966 he presented evidence that it overlaps with **social desirability,** the need to please others by displaying the characteristics that are valued in our society (for example, goodness, honesty, sincerity, and so forth). The implication of this association is obvious. In completing the I-E Scale, subjects and clients may be trying to favorably impress researchers or psychotherapists, rather than accurately reporting their actual characteristics. One could argue that the extent to which social desirability is manifested in I-E responses is the extent to which locus of control scores reflect response distortion rather than being an index of an actual personality factor. Davis and Cowles (1989) showed that social desirability continues to be a problem for locus of control measures.

Another, perhaps more severe problem, is the apparent existence of two kinds of externals, one of which contradicts very basic assumptions about externality (Rotter, 1975). **Defensive externals** are people who are highly competitive and do well on tests, but endorse external items for the apparent purpose of blaming others for their failures. **Passive externals** (also called "congruent") believe they are controlled by fate or chance. Whereas passive externals are consistent with Rotter's theory, defensive externals are not. According to Rotter's social learning theory, people who indicate that they are controlled by outside forces are not supposed to be competitive.

Rotter (1975) tried to skirt the problem by indicating that the theory and scale are still valid, but I-E scores simply identify two kinds of externals. Such an explanation does not explain the puzzling nature of defensive externals. Defensive externals may well be people who are using locus of control to provide an excuse for their failures, but the problem is that many other equally plausible explanations of their behavior are possible. For example, "defensive externals" may be subject to the widely known social condition of *alienation* as well as its accompanying feeling of powerlessness and estrangement from others, but fight it by being highly competitive. Adequately explaining how two types of externals can coexist in a theoretical domain that is constructed to account for only one remains to future researchers and theoreticians. Unfortunately, defensive tendencies on the part of some externals continue to be a problem in the 1990s (Holmstrom, Karp, & Silber, 1991).

An additional problem is the possibility that Rotter's I-E scale is not unitary: two rather than just one kind of control are being measured. Ferguson (1993) reports that "a consensus is emerging in the literature in favour of a two factor structure (personal and political control) . . ." (p. 1268). Political control is illustrated by the item "This world is run by a few people in power, and there is not much the little guy can do about it" (p. 1273). Personal control is illustrated by the item "Sometimes I feel I don't have enough control over the direction my life has taken" (p. 1273). Consistent with this observation, he found the same two factors. Harper, Oei, Mendalgio, and Evans (1990) also found two factors which they labeled "political control" and "general control" (similar to personal control). Other researchers have found the I-E scale to be a relatively weak predictor (Johnson et al., 1992; Sharpiro et al., 1993). There appears to be a need for a more unitary and accurate measure of I-E.

Conclusions

The key to being a personality theorist with lasting impact is to have a few continually useful concepts associated with one's name. Freud has his "psychosexual stages," Jung his "archetypes," Adler his "style of life," Rogers his "unconditional positive regard," and Maslow his "hierarchy of needs." Rotter has his "internals and externals." A hundred years from now when some theorists covered in this book are forgotten, "Rotter" probably will still be a name known to most psychologists. Aside from locus of control, Rotter should also be remembered for two other reasons: (1) his recognition that stability of personal attributes across social situations is limited, and (2) his belief that the consideration of the interplay between personal and environment factors is essential to understanding people.

MISCHEL: A CHALLENGE TO TRAITS

Walter Mischel

Rotter (1982) acknowledged the contributions of his many students and elected not to list them, lest some seem more prominent than others. Nevertheless, it is clear that his most accomplished student is Walter Mischel, who may some day come to be regarded as the founder of *modern* personality theory. Mischel expanded on Rotter's social learning ideas in two important ways. First, he went far beyond Rotter in questioning *traits*—permanent, invariable, internal entities that determine stable behavior across many social situations (Mischel & Shoda, 1994). Beginning with his famous 1968 book, Mischel started a revolution that caused psychologists to rethink their assumptions about traits. Although the "fire-bombing" of basic assumptions about traits has subsided, some of those assumptions lie smoldering in the ruins. Trait psychology will never be quite the same.

Second, in the place of *traits* Mischel inserted cognitive facilities as the controllers of behavior. In so doing he originated some productive thinking about personality and, at the same time, opened up whole new research vistas. Mischel's work is living proof that personality may be conceptualized solely in terms of cognitive capacities, without reference to "traits" in the traditional sense.

As you recall, social learning theory emphasizes how people learn from other people. It addresses personality and, in some of its forms, amounts to an **interaction point of view**, the interplay between *internal entities* or person factors and *social situations* is emphasized, rather than either in isolation from the other (Mischel. & Shoda, 1995; Shoda & Mischel, 1993). For Mischel, certain personal cognitive factors interact with situations to produce behavior. However, his point of view, called **cognitive social learning theory** proposes that the important factors are cognitive facilities rather than traits. Specifically, Mischel's **personal cognitive factors** are memories of previous experiences, from the past history of an individual, that determine strategies and skills the person employs for producing behavior at the present time. In interaction terms, Mischel's theory predicts that the history of rewards and punishments experienced in a given situation and skills and strategies developed in that situation will determine present behaviors.

Mischel, The Person

Like Adler—and Freud, in terms of his principal residence—Walter Mischel is Austrian (*American Psychologist*, (*AP*) 1983). He was born February 22, 1930 near Freud's office in Vienna. Also like Adler and Freud, Mischel and his family fled Vienna when the Nazis overran Austria in 1938. Following two years as refugees, Mischel's family settled in Brooklyn, the childhood home of Maslow and Rotter. Mischel attended primary and secondary school there and was the recipient of a college scholarship. Unfortunately, his father's illness required that he temporarily forgo postsecondary education in favor of employment. Later, while working as a stock boy, elevator operator, and assistant in a garment factory, young Mischel attended New York University where he pursued interests in painting, sculpture, and psychology. His passion for art was fueled in part by exposure to life in Greenwich Village, where a youthful B. F. Skinner also spent some time.

Just as Kelly had been turned off by S-R psychology studies in rat laboratories, so was Mischel. He much preferred reading Freud, the existentialists, and poetry. By 1951, Mischel had made a professional choice in favor of clinical psychology and entered the master of arts program at City College. There he studied with Gestalt-oriented Kurt Goldstein, who had been one of Maslow's mentors. During this period he became a social worker, helping impoverished teens and elderly people. It was these real-life experiences that soured him on the usefulness of Freudian notions and projective testing as avenues to understanding people. Thus, he resolved to pursue a more research-oriented clinical program, leading to the pursuit of a doctorate at Ohio State during the Rotter-Kelly era.

From 1953 to 1956, Mischel soaked up the wisdom of Rotter and Kelly. Although Mischel may be considered a Rotter student—his theory is more like Rotter's than any other—he also relies considerably on Kelly's thinking (Mischel & Shoda, 1995; Shoda, & Mischel, 1993). Kelly's cognitive "constructs" and his belief that research subjects and clinical clients can be "scientists" had much impact on Mischel.

Armed with a solid cognitive background, Mischel spent 1956–1958 in a Trinidad village studying religious cult groups that practiced spirit possession. He assessed cult members' fantasies, cognitions, and actions both during possession and while in a normal state. Out of this work grew his interests in "choice preferences for delayed, more-valued outcomes versus immediate, but less-valued outcomes" (*AP*, 1983, p. 10). These experiences led to his studies of delay of gratification and his determination to investigate people in their natural environments, not the laboratory.

Following two years at the University of Colorado, Mischel became an assistant professor at Harvard where he came under the influence of Gordon Allport and Henry A. Murray, among others. There he met and married Harriet Nerlove, a graduate student in cognitive development. In 1962, Walter, Harriet, and their three children moved to Stanford where he chaired the department 1977–1978 and again beginning in 1982. He is presently at Columbia University in New York City.

Mischel's View of the Person

Mischel's 1960s work in developing methods for identifying potentially successful Peace Corps volunteers led directly to the foundation of perhaps his most important thesis: "under appropriate conditions people may be able to predict their own behavior as well as the best available indirect tests and inference methods" (*AP*, 1983, p. 10). That is, he came to believe that people know themselves better than psychologists can come to know them by use of their best personality assessment techniques (1973). Mischel's almost phenomenological attitude, "if you want to know about people, ask them about themselves," greatly influenced Charles Potkay and me in our own investigations of people's self-descriptions (Allen & Potkay, 1983a; Potkay & Allen, 1988).

Mischel stated this position even more clearly in his classic book *Personality and Assessment* (1968) where he challenged the basic assumption underlying notions of "traits": cross-situational consistency. He declared that objective observations indicate that people tend to discriminate between one situation and the next, leading to change in behavior from situation to situation. Such cross-situational inconsistency would predict that measures of traits would be poor predictors of corresponding behaviors. Indeed, Mischel showed that the correlations between measures of behaviors in various situations and measures of traits hover around .30, thus, accounting for only about 9 percent of behavioral variation. When trait testers responded with attempts to improve their measures, Mischel suggested that they had missed the point: ". . . much of the personality assessment practiced at that time stereotyped individuals into categories that grossly oversimplified their complexity and that had limited predictive value for the individual case" (*AP*, 1983, p. 10).

These proclamations left Mischel with a dilemma: People perceive cross-situational consistency in their own and other people's behavior, but scientific observations offer little confirmation of those perceptions. To account for the discrepancy between perceived and actual consistency, Mischel and his colleagues showed that certain *prototypical behaviors* do have *temporal stability* that is often mistaken for cross-situational consistency. For example, a prototype of aggressiveness is objecting to, arguing with, disputing, and "putting down" other people (verbal aggression). A student may see displays of this prototypical behavior by a classmate as stable, because the classmate may show it in the *same situation* (class) across many points in time (during most class sessions). The student's temporally stable aggressiveness may be mistaken for cross-situational consistency, because the observer fails to recognize that the aggressive behavior is occurring repeatedly in the *same* situation across time, not across *different* situations.

You may wonder how we may expect accurate reports from people about their own behavior when they mistake temporal consistency for cross-situational consistency. In fact, we should not expect accuracy unless we ask people the right questions. If one asks people, in effect, "are you consistent" or "is your friend consistent," they will say "yes, of course." In our society we value being consistent, which often means "reliable" (Cialdini, 1985). However, instead of this or other leading questions, one can ask people to describe themselves, in effect, describe what they have been doing, and also ask them to describe the situations in which they behaved. With this kind of questioning, people reveal that they vary from situation to situation (Allen & Potkay, 1983a; Potkay & Allen, 1988).

In a similar vein, if we ask a person what some other person "is like," the response may be some global trait label (Shoda & Mischel, 1993, p. 579). But if we instead ask that one person understand, empathize with, or remember something about another person, the response will be richer and include situational information.

Instead of defining "personality," Mischel refers to a **personality system** which "is characterized by . . . available cognitive and affective [or feeling] units" such that "When certain configurations of situation features are experienced by the individual a . . . subset of cognitions and affects become activated" (Mischel & Shoda, 1995, p. 254). Obviously Mischel is an interactionist: a situation by its unique nature activates cognitive/affective units appropriate to that nature and these units then determine behavior.

BOX 12.2   How Consistent Are You?

To demonstrate that you may vary more than you realize, you could repeat the "actual self / ideal self" exercise from the Rogers chapter, but with a twist. This time, on scratch paper, write down five self-descriptive adjectives each day for a week. Also, briefly record in long hand what happened to you each day. Do this in a spontaneous and uncritical manner, without any thoughts about being "consistent." After accumulating seven such self-descriptions, give them to a friend who is open and honest with you and have her or him place a plus (+) by each adjective that seems "favorable" when used to describe a person and a minus (−) next to "unfavorable" adjectives (tell the friend to put a zero next to adjectives that cannot be classified, but to use the zero very rarely). If you are a typical person, you will notice two characteristics of your descriptions. First, you will tend to mix favorable and unfavorable adjectives in a single day's descriptions and you will tend to record different adjectives on different days. This result occurs because you encounter many different situations during a day and different situations on different days. Second, notice the correspondence between what happens to you and the words you use to describe yourself. The words you use in self-descriptions may be thought of as labels for the behaviors you performed (Allen & Potkay, 1983a). They should correspond rather well with "what happened to you"—the situations you were in. For example, if you whispered tender sentiments to the love interest in your life (situation), you may have recorded "romantic" (behavioral label) to describe yourself.

Basic Concepts: Mischel

Competency

Chief among cognitive facilities that are activated by certain situations are abilities that allow effective performance in those situations. **Competency** embraces both the cognitive ability to size up a situation so that one understands how to operate effectively in it and the ability to perform behaviors that will lead to success in the situation. It involves "knowing what to do" in a situation and being able to do it. Some people may not know that the ability to engage in "small talk" is critical to success at parties. Others may know the importance of small talk, but just cannot do it. Still others recognize the significance of small talk and do it well. Only this last set of people would have the competencies leading to success at parties.

Of course, people vary in how many competencies they possess. Some people have a large "bag full of tricks" they can use in a wide variety of situations. Others, unfortunately, have rather few competencies and can operate efficiently in a relatively small number of situations. Shoda, Mischel, and Wright (1993) have shown that different situations demand different competencies of those who operate in them. Further, individuals who have much competence can vary their behaviors appropriately across situations to meet the varying situational demands for competency.

Characterizing Event

"Sizing up" a situation is a more intricate and demanding process than it may appear to be, because each situation tends to be complex: constituted by many components. A **component of a situation** is some part of the total situation, such as its physical characteristics, or, more important, factors associated with people who are present when the situation is unfolding. Components generate events. **Events** are simply occurrences that are produced by components of a situation. "Stuffiness" is an example of an event produced by a component of a possible college-class situation, a small poorly ventilated room. More potent events are the behaviors that are performed by people who operate in a situation.

Characterizing events associated with a situation is placing them into meaningful categories. It is an early and critical step in sizing up a situation. A person may characterize events associated with an entire situation, or with individual components of it. For example, a student may place verbal events associated with the college class situation into the "silence is golden" category, one signifying that speaking out is inappropriate. Another student may decide that the college class is the appropriate place for voicing any opinion that is relevant to the topic at hand. Obviously, these two people will behave quite differently in class. Which person is most successful will depend on which "reads" the dominant component of the situation—the professor—most accurately. Does the professor prefer "silence is golden" to "free expression of opinions"?

In addition to such global characterization, or instead of it, a person may place specific events associated with a situation into several separate categories. These specific events are often behaviors of critical persons who are found in the situation. For example, a student may characterize instances of rapid and enthusiastic professorial speech as attempts to "impart important information," the stuff tests are made of. Such a characterization could lead to some frantic notetaking. The same student may interpret a dramatic pause following the presentation of a "main point" as a signal that it is time for students wishing to express their vital interest in the professor's lecture to pose questions.

Shoda and Mischel (1993) have concocted a similar example to show that individuals with different goals categorize situations differently, such that the same situation may call forth different behaviors from the individuals: one person sees the approach of a homeless individual as an opportunity to promote a justice goal through an offer of money, while another person who does not share that goal sees the approach as an irritation.

Special note should be taken of the observation, made from the point of view of a given individual, that others' actions are not the only important behavioral events in a situation (Mischel, 1973). A particular person who is trying to size up a situation is also one of its components. That person's own behaviors are important events associated with the situation. One of the most valuable cognitive competencies that a person can possess is the realization there are certain behaviors the person can perform that will change a situation, making it one in which he or she can operate more effectively (Mischel & Shoda, 1995). According to Mischel, people do not just passively respond to situations, they actively shape them. For example, suppose hypothetical person Sue finds herself at a business meeting during which the participants are all talking loudly and in unison. In this setting, she is not able to "do her thing," which is to apply precise logic to practical problems. Being somewhat soft-spoken, Sue feels the need to change the situation to better suit her capabilities. Thus, she makes her way to the front row, waves her hand so that the presiding official cannot miss it, and raises a "point of information." This action causes the official to pound her gavel until there is silence in the room and then to turn the floor over to Sue. Now Sue has transformed the situation into one in which she has a long history of effective operation.

Expectancies

An extensive past history in a situation is likely to give a person a good grasp of what to expect when certain stimuli are present and when certain behaviors are performed. For Mischel, a **stimulus** is a very definite, well-defined component or event associated with a situation and can be either physical or behavioral (Mischel & Shoda, 1995). Anybody who has spent years as a lawyer will likely believe that certain stimuli lead to predictable outcomes in the courtroom. When the person dressed in black robes emerges from an adjoining room and steps behind the bench, lawyers have the expectancy that everyone will rise. For Mischel, an **expectancy** is a belief based on past experience that provides a prediction of future outcomes (Mischel & Shoda, 1995). In our courtroom example, the stimulus can be a component of the situation—the judge—or a behavior—the bailiff's verbalization "all rise." In either case, the stimulus gives rise to the expectancy of certain outcomes, often behaviors.

People have beliefs with regard to what will occur should they or others behave in a certain way in a given situation. That is, people have expectancies concerning the outcome of particular behavioral performances. Knowing the rules of the court, lawyers can easily predict what will happen if they continually interrupt the proceedings by shouting at each other (as Johnny Cochran and Marcia Clark found out in Judge Lance Ito's court).

In sum, knowing a situation is, in part, knowing what will result from the performance of a given behavior in the situation. It is also knowing what will happen when a certain stimulus is present.

Values of Outcomes

In sizing up a situation so that successful behaviors can be performed, it is not enough to know what to do and to be capable of doing it. If ones fails to accurately characterize the situation, its components and its events, one will not know *when* to do whatever will lead to success. However, accurate characterization is still not enough. One must know what to expect when specific stimuli emerge from the situation and when specific behaviors are performed in the situation. Additionally, success in the situation may depend on **values of outcomes**—how much one prizes results of behavioral or stimulus occurrences in the ongoing situation. In fact, **success** itself may be defined as effectively performing the behaviors that yield the outcomes that are valued by the performer.

To take an example from Mischel (1973), people familiar with a particular form of psychotherapy will know that clients who make favorable references to themselves experience a definite outcome, approval from the therapist. Among those people are some who, when acting as clients, will greatly value the approval that results from favorable self-reference. Other clients, however will not value approval or will value it less. It is a good bet that the frequency of favorable self-reference will be very different for the two groups of knowledgeable clients. The value of an outcome, be it a behavioral outcome or the outcome of some stimulus, is a powerful part of "sizing up" a situation. Knowing the outcomes that are typical of a situation, a person will adopt strategies and perform behaviors that will increase the likelihood of valued outcomes.

Self-Regulatory Plans

A final aspect of sizing up a situation is one's own **self-regulatory plans**, rules, established in advance of opportunity for behavioral performance, that act as guides for determining what behavior would be appropriate under particular conditions. Self-regulatory plans involve more than rules covering a kind of situation, such as being at a party (Mischel & Shoda, 1995). People are aware that situations do not stay the same from one point in time to the next. A given situation will tend to vary even on a single occasion during which it is in effect. Have you attended a party where everyone engaged in the same activities throughout the duration of the affair? Probably not. Parties often start with "feeling each other out," figuratively speaking, until people are acquainted or reacquainted, and thus, feel comfortable with one another. Then the merrymakers loosen up, and the fun really begins. Although one may have plans for parties in general, such as how to dress, whether to approach others or wait for them to approach oneself, and so forth, one must also have plans concerning what to do at different phases of the party. For example, what to do if somebody has too much to drink; what to do when "things are dragging a little." People generally have answers to these and other questions worked out in advance, in the form of plans.

Supporting Evidence

Delay of Gratification

Self-regulatory plans tend to be different for different people, because each person has a unique past history. Furthermore, plans are flexible. They may change permanently due to experience or may be altered temporarily due to the demands of the situation in which one finds oneself (Mischel & Shoda, 1995). Much of Mischel's and colleagues' research efforts have gone into determining how children accomplish the self-regulatory task of **delaying gratification**—postponing some pleasure so that it can be enjoyed to the maximum degree or in its most optimal form. In a review of their work, Mischel, Shoda, and Rodriguez (1989) report that enduring individual differences in this variety of self-control have been found as early as the preschool years. Further, children of preschool age who, in certain laboratory situations, delayed gratification longer than others, developed into adolescents who were more competent, showed higher scholastic performance, and coped better with frustration/stress. In addition, inability to delay gratification is related to antisocial behaviors such as aggression and delinquency (Krueger, Caspi, Moffitt, White, & Stouthamer-Loeber, 1996).

Shoda, Mischel, and Peake (1990) described the procedures they have used in several studies to demonstrate that preschool delay-ability is positively related to adolescent competence. They revealed what personality factors are associated with the ability to delay. In these studies, an experimenter first asked children to identify which of several objects they found most desirable (for example, marshmallows or pretzels). Then they are placed in a room stripped of distracters and asked whether they would *prefer* a little or much of the desired object (for example one versus two marshmallows). Then the experimenter announces she must leave and indicates, "if you wait until I come back . . . then you can have this one [points to two marshmallows]. If you don't want to wait you can ring the bell and bring me back any time you want to. But if you ring the bell then you can't have this one [points to two marshmallows], but you can have that one [points to one marshmallow]" (p. 980).

Children use different strategies to accomplish delay: (1) covering up the preference (for example, M&Ms) or leaving them in the open; (2) thinking of the preference abstractly or concretely (M&Ms are "round buttons" rather than "yummy and chewy"); and (3) thinking of the task or the enjoyability of the preference ("I'm waiting for the M&Ms" or "The M&Ms taste yummy and chewy"; p. 360). Overall Shoda, Mischel, and Peake (1990) found positive correlations between preschool seconds-of-delay-time and adolescent cognitive/academic competence as well as the ability to cope with stress/frustration. They also found that particular coping strategies used in preschool (covering or not covering preferred items such as M & Ms) were related to certain adolescent personality factors such as the degree to which the child is sidetracked by minor setbacks, yields to temptation, is distractible, has self-control, and copes with important problems.

People Are Interactionists, Not Trait Theorists

A number of years ago, Gene Smith and I showed that, contrary to popular belief among many psychologists, when asked the "right" questions, ordinary people reveal themselves to be interactionists, not trait theorists (Allen & Smith, 1980). Usually people are asked to "observe" someone's behavior and then to indicate whether the other person's behavior was caused by her or his "traits" or the situation he or she was operating in. If, instead, people are asked to choose the most plausible explanation of behavior from definitions of several such explanations, including a definition of *trait*, a definition of *situation*, and one of *interaction*, they choose interaction. Mischel and his colleagues have gone beyond this beginning effort by showing that specifying the situation in which a behavior occurs or qualifying a trait explanation of behavior improves people's predictions of behavior. Shoda, Mischel, and Wright, (1989) investigated adults' impressions of children's aggressive behavior. When sit-

---

BOX 12.3   Uncovering Natural Interactionism

You can discover for yourself that people are natural interactionists, rather than trait theorists, if you ask the right questions. Ask a friend to describe someone he or she knows well by using the method employed in Box 12.2 ("Write down five adjectives to describe [so-and-so]"). Pick one of the words generated by your friend and probe deeper. "You say that so-and-so is [for example] kind. Is that always true?"

When the answer almost inevitably comes back "no," ask "how often?" The answer is practically certain to be words to the effect of *sometimes*. Then ask, "*When* is so-and-so kind?" Repeat this process with another target (a new "so-and-so") and, perhaps, with another friend. You will likely become convinced that people are fully aware that behavior varies across situations in *if . . . then* fashion.

---

uations were specified ("child hits when provoked") rather than unspecified ("child hits") impressions (for example, "is an odd child") were more accurate in predicting differences among children in overall, actual aggression. Other work by Wright and Mischel (1988) took a closer look at the "trait" statements children and adults used to explain behavior. This more careful observation revealed the use of qualifiers (the target person *sometimes* is aggressive), and conditional statements (the target person is aggressive *when* teased by others). These outcomes indicate ordinary people recognize that behavior is not altogether cross-situationally consistent (*sometimes*) and its performance often depends on the existence of certain situations (*when*).

More recently Mischel and his colleagues have come to use *if . . . then* language to describe the behavior-situation relations that are peculiar to particular individuals (Mischel & Shoda, 1995; Shoda & Mischel, 1993). For example, if Kwanda, a school teacher, is confronted with an aggressive child, she tends to implement calming procedures. On the other hand, Marty, another teacher, tends to respond with his own aggressiveness. Further, people who associate with Marty and Kwanda, and thus must understand them, are capable of appreciating the *if . . . then* relations peculiar to each of them (Shoda & Mischel, 1993). These people may sometimes be heard to make utterances such as "Marty is very aggressive," but they often preface such sweeping, trait-like attributions with qualifications or probability statements like "If someone gets in Marty's face, he gets aggressive" or "Marty is *likely* to be hostile only when someone gets in his face."

Mischel Summed Up: Consistency of Cross-Situation Behavioral Patterns

Mischel and his colleagues have recently published a study of 84 children in a summer camp that quite literally graphically depicts Mischel's point of view (Shoda, Mischel, & Wright, 1994). These children's behavior was recorded and scored on verbal aggression (teased, provoked, or threatened), as well as physical aggression, compliant behavior, and pro-social behavior. The recordings were made in different *nominal* situations, such as woodworking and cabin meetings, where the children were confronted with five different *interpersonal* situations: when a peer initiated positive contact, when a peer teased, provoked or threatened, when praised by an adult, when warned by an adult, and when punished by an adult. Indexing behavioral variation across these five interpersonal situations was the goal of the research.

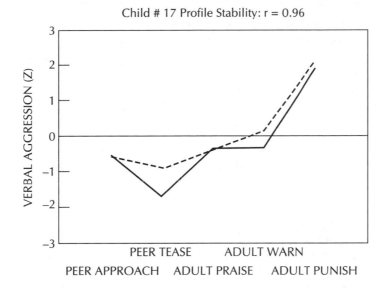

**FIGURE 12.1   A child's behavior-situation profile at a time
1 and at a time 2.**

Results are well illustrated by Figure 12.1. As you can see, child number 17 showed low cross-situation consistency in verbal aggression: the child's behavior is below the norm (zero line) for "peer approaches," but well above the norm for "adult punishes." Notice, however, there are two lines: the solid line represents responses to the interpersonal situations at time 1, while the dotted line is the verbal aggression behavioral-profile at time 2. While cross-situational consistency is low at both times, the cross-situational *behavioral profiles* are highly consistent across times 1 and 2: when confronted with the set of situations at a second time, the child shows very much the same pattern of behaviors across the situations as she or he displayed on the first encounter with the situations. While subjects as a group showed low cross-situational behavioral consistency, as a group they tended to display much the same patterns of behaviors at the two different times (solid and dotted lines much alike). These results nicely illustrate Mischel's theory. Although people do not show cross-situational consistency, each can be characterized by a unique behavioral pattern or profile across situations that she or he displays repeatedly and that is different from other people's patterns. These real-life results define interactionism in new, more meaningful terms: Each person shows a unique relationship between a set of situations and his or her particular personal cognitive/emotional characteristics that is consistent across time.

Evaluation

Mischel's Contributions

Walter Mischel started an intellectual revolution in personality psychology. He opened up minds with his declaration that the notion of trait, and the assumption of behavioral stability that lies behind it, is of limited utility for understanding and predicting behavior.

BOX 12.4   Mischel Actively Takes Diversity
into Account

Mischel's position vis-à-vis diversity is similar to Kelly's. Neither embraces content-laden traits, thereby avoiding the embarrassment of theoretically important traits failing to have meaning in cultures and subcultures different from European-American culture. But Mischel's position also avoids the problem posed by cultures whose participants often fail to use trait labels when describing themselves or others. Shoda and Mischel (1993) cite evidence that when Easterners (Japanese) are asked to describe themselves they tend to refer to social roles ("I am a college student"). By contrast, Westerners (Americans) resort to trait labels ("I am honest"). When asked to explain others' behaviors, Indian Hindus mention the context of others' behavior ("It was dark") while, again, Westerners (Americans) tend to apply trait labels ("He's a coward"). Morris and Peng (1994) report similar evidence in a comparison of Americans and Chinese.

Culture is embedded in language and language can shape the cognitive processes that Mischel emphasizes (Shoda & Mischel, 1993). Thus, characterizations of situations can vary across cultures and subcultures, because, even where the language is the same for two or more cultures or subcultures, usage can differ by culture or subculture.

Take, for example, the European American culture and African American subculture. The African American subculture is an amalgamation of African and American traditions. To illustrate the impact of this fact, consider an old African adage: "If you throw a stone into a pack of dogs, the one that yelps is the one that was hit." Now suppose an African American tells a group of European Americans "Whites are racists!" European Americans, because of their unique cognitive devices, are likely to see the remark as an attribution to all "whites" and be offended. But the African American, having at least slightly different cognitive devices, may have intended something quite different. The African American person may have been casting a stone into a crowd of European Americans to see who yelps. The one(s) who yelps when the "racist" stone lands may be viewed as racist(s), not "all whites."

Personologists who had previously just accepted "trait" were forced to dredge up the assumptions underlying the concept and support them. The result was more incisive thinking and greater caution in using the concept. Trait theorists sharpened their definitions and honed their research techniques.

Further, the intuitively reasonable position "interactionism" that was unsuccessfully championed by Rotter suddenly became the "position of choice." Faced with undeniable evidence that behavior varies considerably across situations, rather than remaining stable, most trait theorists found it expedient to call themselves "interactionists." Unfortunately, many of them continued to operate as if behavior is rigidly stable across situations. The net result was mainly lip service to the observation that certain behaviors occur mostly in particular situations that call them forth, not in all situations. The fact that "lip service" very often is followed by real change virtually ensures that interactionism will actually catch on in the future. Then the point of view of personologists will be more in tune with that of the people they study. A big boost for this needed change comes from Mischel's and colleagues' recent demonstrations of the "if . . . then" principle.

In addition, Mischel's work on delay of gratification has numerous important implications (Mischel, Shoda, & Rodriguez, 1989). Early ability to delay gratification has been solidly related to later academic achievement and emotional stability. It follows that techniques useful in enhancing delay should be developed and taught to children. Examination of the procedures used by Mischel and colleagues and the results they have obtained indicates that such techniques could be readily developed. These methods for enhancing delay may be especially beneficial to "children at risk," a growing constituency of our public schools.

Limitations

While Mischel's new expanded point of view (Mischel & Shoda, 1995) is even more convincing than the old, it does contain a serious ambiguity. "Affect" is now being emphasized, but its role is unclear. Does "affect" stand alone or is it part of a "cognitive/affective package"? Until this question is answered, "affect" seems an afterthought.

The rejection of traits and the complete absence of them from his theory has not been well received in some quarters. Certain theorists and researchers think that Mischel has overstated his case (for example, Bem & Allen, 1974). Others reject his position outright (for example, Epstein, 1977). In fact, the debate over traits has become so acrimonious that Mischel has been in danger of isolation from his colleagues. This circumstance may explain why Mischel has considerably softened his earlier rejection of traits (Mischel, 1984).

Conclusions

Mischel's challenge to "traits" is one of the most important events in the modern history of personality research. However, a contribution of possibly greater importance has been largely ignored. Personologists should take another look at his theory with an eye to what it tells them about alternatives to understanding personality. For too long it has been assumed that personality cannot exist without the behavioral consistency assumed by trait theorists (Allen, 1988a, 1988b). To the contrary, Mischel's work has shown there are other ways to cast personality that are not burdened by trait assumptions. In fact, Mischel has quietly demonstrated that personality can be constructed in nontrait terms. His cognitive approach that eschews traits accounts for personality development and functioning without making tenuous and limiting assumptions about behavioral consistency. Instead, there is consistency in the pattern of behaviors a person displays across situations: The same pattern of behaviors across a set of situations is shown each time the set is encountered. If Walter Mischel has taught us nothing more than to consider alternative conceptions of personality free from trait assumptions of behavioral consistency, we have learned a profound lesson indeed.

Summary Points

1. Rotter was born in Brooklyn and was nurtured by the Brooklyn Library. As a high school student he read Freud and Adler. When he entered Brooklyn College during the Depression, he chose chemistry as a major, but took more psychology. After training at the University of Iowa, and an internship in clinical psychology, he completed a clinical Ph.D. at Indiana University. Following service in World War II, he chose Ohio State. Rotter focused on situations, but acknowledged individual differences in behavior. He showed that subjects in a "skill" condition performed better than subjects in a "chance" condition, but there were individual differences within the chance and skill conditions.

2. Rotter emphasizes the interaction between the person and the environment. He asserts that personality has unity and its constructs are not always the best way to describe behavior and he holds that behavior is directional and is guided by expectancies. Reinforcement value is the degree of preference for any reinforcement to occur if the possibilities of different reinforcements are equal. In turn, an expectancy is the probability held by the individual that a particular reinforcement will occur.

3. By contrast, a generalized expectancy is one that holds for a number of similar situations. Rotter's most emphasized generalized expectancy is locus of control. It led to the development of the internal-external dichotomy and the I-E Scale. Research has shown that externals are more conformist and more maladjusted, but less prone to substance abuse than internals, who are higher in academic achievement. "Race" may also be related to locus of control. Also, internality/externality may change during the divorce process, but individual differences in I-E explain diverse reactions to different stages of the divorce process. Also, married people may be more internal.

4. Research on I-E and child-rearing practices indicates that only internals' parents are warm, protective, positive, and nurturing. Teachers trained to be "origins" did better at teaching "origin behavior" and their students showed improved academic performance. Creating an "origin" climate in the classroom promotes self-worth, cognitive competence, and internal control in students. Whether externals change may depend partly on the beliefs they bring to therapy.

5. Other generalized expectancies that have emerged through research include interpersonal trust. Another is negative mood regulation. Locus of control is such a solid concept that Rotter's name is sure to be known many years from now. Internality/externality is on a "sliding scale" in that a person will vary her or his position on the I-E continuum at different points in time. Rotter was a pioneer in the now hot research area, "control." Unfortunately, social desirability contamination of the I-E dimension and the existence of "passive externals" raise unresolved dilemmas about locus of control. Also problematic is the possibility that the I-E scale may measure not one factor but two and the scale may not yield accurate predictions.

6. Born in Austria, Mischel was reared in Brooklyn. His undergraduate days were spent at New York University where he studied art and psychology. Turned off by S-R psychology, he embraced clinical psychology at City College and eventually earned a Ph.D. in that area at Ohio State University. There he was influenced by Rotter and Kelly. His studies in Trinidad launched his interest in delay of gratification.

7. Mischel asserts "if you want to know about people, ask them about themselves." He found little relationship between measures of traits and behavior. This position created a dilemma: People perceive stronger cross-situational consistency than exists, which is resolved by recognizing that prototypical behavior displays temporal stability that is mistaken for cross-situational stability. Mischel defines a personality system as available cognitive and affective units that are activated by situations. Competency is the cognitive ability to size up a situation and to perform behaviors that will lead to success. Different situations demand different competencies and people with much competency can vary behavior appropriately across situations. Situations have components including physical ones and people. In turn, events are occurrences that are produced by components.

8. Characterizing events associated with a situation is placing them into meaningful categories. People with different goals characterize situations differently. From the person's point of view, one of the most important components of a situation is her or himself. A stimulus is a definite component or event associated with a situation. An expectancy is a belief based on past experience that provides a prediction of future outcomes. Sizing up situations also involves establishing values for outcomes. Success is effectively performing the behaviors that yield the outcomes valued by the performer.

9. Self-regulatory plans are rules that act as guides for determining what behavior would be appropriate under particular conditions. One kind of self-regulatory plan involves methods used to delay gratification. In experiments, children used various methods for delaying, such as covering the preferred object. Covering the desired objects or not was related to a number of personality factors. People prove to be interactionists, not trait theorists, when they are asked the "right" questions.

10. Mischel has shown that adults are more accurate in predicting aggression in children if the setting of aggression is specified. Also, prediction is better when "qualifiers" and "conditional statements" are used. Each person displays her or his own repertoire of "if . . . then" situation-behavior relations and others who know them accurately perceive these relations. The Mischel group, in a summer camp study, showed that children's cross-situational behavior patterns are repeated each time they encounter the same set of situations. Mischel has addressed diversity directly by noting that not all cultures have participants who use trait labels to describe themselves or others. Further, different cultures use language differently and even subcultures sharing the same language may use different cognitive devices.

Running Comparison

Theorist	*Rotter in Comparison*
Maslow	Like Maslow, he was a "student" of the Brooklyn library and like Maslow, he thought behavior to be "goal-directed."
Adler	Adler turned him on to psychology.
Kelly	He took over Kelly's clinical directorship and used some of his language.
Albert Bandura	Like Bandura, he believed that people are pulled by the future.
B. F. Skinner	They both talked about "reinforcement," but Rotter had a broader definition.

Theorist	*Mischel in Comparison*
Kelly	Like Kelly, he rejected S-R psychology. He was impacted by Kelly's cognitive constructs and "people can be scientists."
Bandura	Like Bandura, Mischel emphasized expectancies and cognitive control of behavior.

Essay/Critical Thinking Questions

1. Does the gambler's fallacy occur in reality with reasonable likelihood? Attempt to come up with a scenario in which someone is guilty of the gambler's fallacy though not actually gambling (investing in the market rather than visiting Las Vegas).

2. What we call "reinforcing" or "rewarding" is somewhat in the eye of the beholder. Can you provide three examples of outcomes that are reinforcing to you, but not to one of your friends?

3. What are you, an internal or an external? Decide which and give examples verifying that you are what you claim to be.

4. How were you reared? You should be able to describe your upbringing so that the way your parents reared you fits the choice you made in question number 3.

5. Try this: Look at what an acquaintance does, attribute a trait to him or her as an explanation of what s/he did, then ask for a description of the circumstances surrounding the observed person's behavior. Would you stick with your trait attribution or withdraw it?

6. Can you provide two examples of what looks like "cross-situational consistency," but is actually cross-time (temporal) consistency.

7. Briefly describe a situation (for example, a fraternity party) giving its critical components, including events, and characterize those events. What expectancies would you have for that situation and what self-regulatory plans might be successful in the situation?

8. How good were you at delaying gratification as a child? Think back on your ability to resist temptation. Give a couple of examples to show it was strong or weak. Now relate your ability to delay in childhood to your characteristics now.

9. Do the "if . . . then" analysis on your own behavior. If you find yourself in a certain situation, what behaviors would you show? Now imagine yourself in a different situation and indicate the behaviors you would show.

10. Do the "if . . . then" analysis again, but this time do it for a close friend.

E-mail Interaction

(Contact the author at mfbpa@wiu.edu)
Forward one of the following or phrase your own.

1. You "sound" Mischelian. Are you?
2. Tell me how it could be good to be an external.
3. How could I find out about the situation-behavior relations in my life?
4. When are traits any good anyway?
5. What else besides traits and behavior-situation relations may play a role in personality?

13

THINKING AHEAD AND LEARNING MASTERY OF ONE'S CIRCUMSTANCES: ALBERT BANDURA

- People learn from imitating others, but are these lessons powerful or trivial, compared to learning through rewards?
- Are we pushed by our past histories or pulled by our anticipation of future rewards?
- Do biology, cognition, and other internal events, *or* the environment drive behavior?
- Is it possible to be totally "self-confident" or is it more reasonable and possible to be confident concerning specific pursuits in life?
- Can a personality theory have anything meaningful to say about the cognitive processes that allow humans to do evil to other humans?

Albert Bandura

Albert Bandura's account of how we acquire new behaviors, thoughts, and feelings is in the "social learning" category, but it is broader than the theories of Rotter and Mischel. In fact, you are about to consider perhaps the most comprehensive theory covered in this book, and a point of view that may well be more applicable to the full range of human functioning than any other. Bandura's ideas help explain how we acquire everything from motor behaviors—how to swing a tennis racket properly—to how we overcome irrational emotions, such as fear of snakes. In addition, his concepts not only explain how we have gained mastery over critical aspects of our environments, they also lay out procedures for achieving and maintaining new competencies. Bandura and his colleagues have studied and elucidated human pursuits ranging from aggression to the cognitive processes that allow humans to oppress other humans. Here is an opportunity for you to acquire knowledge that will be truly useful to you in your life.

Bandura, The Person

Albert Bandura, possibly the most generally admired of living psychologists, was born on the fourth day of December, 1925, in the Canadian village, Mundare, Alberta (*American Psychologist (AP)*, 1981). After experiencing the climate in the area, his answer to the common question "Where do cold fronts come from?" is sure and certain: his birthplace. Bandura attended the typical small town school of the day, with elementary through high school in one facility. It was, however, not devoid of virtues. Due to a shortage of teachers and resources, pupils were forced to learn on their own initiative. Sometimes that included group initiative. Because only two high school teachers were responsible for the entire curriculum, and were not competent in some areas, Bandura and his peers formed study groups to educate themselves (*APA Monitor*, 1992). Perhaps his school days were at least partly the source of Bandura's faith in the power of self-directiveness.

The path to a more hospitable environment, and a college degree, lay through the forbidding Yukon. Young Bandura took a job patching the Alaskan Highway, which was slowing sinking into its muskeg foundation. There he encountered a variety of individuals, ranging from parole violators and debtors to divorced men avoiding alimony payments. While his co-workers were less than model citizens, they were enterprising. Running a concoction of potatoes and sugar through a homemade still produced an ample supply of raw vodka, enough for an entire month (Stokes, 1986a). Unfortunately, this source of periodic bliss was interrupted one month when the grizzly bears that inhabited the area beat the men to the still. For some time thereafter Bandura witnessed considerable human misery and some very frisky bears. These observations may have been the origin of his interest in innovation and the psychological problems of everyday life.

While an undergraduate at the University of British Columbia, Bandura first experienced the enormous impact of chance. In order to share transportation with a group of engineers and pre-med students, he had to arrive at school early. As chance would have it, the only early class available was introductory psychology. He took it, loved it, and the rest is history (Stokes, 1986b).

After obtaining an undergraduate degree at the U. of B. C., he enrolled at the University of Iowa where Kenneth Spence, a famous learning psychologist of the day, had the psychology department under his spell. Because of Spence's prominence, and Iowa's ties to Yale and Neal Miller, the furor over learning theories that raged at the time consumed Bandura and his classmates.

While at Iowa, chance struck Bandura again, this time delivering a gentle blow to the heart. During a golf outing with a male friend, his eyes fell on one of two women playing one green ahead (Stokes, 1986a). The twosome became a foursome and a few months later, Bandura was wed to Virginia Varns, a teacher in the College of Nursing. Her career brought another chance encounter of significance. "The Great Imposter," Ferdinand Waldo Demara, showed up as a resident in obstetrics at her hospital, once again posing as a physician. Bandura probably marveled at the ability of some people to sell others on competencies they do not possess.

Having received his doctorate in 1952, and finished an internship at the Wichita Guidance Center, Bandura was appointed instructor at Stanford University. Working his way up through the ranks, he became a full professor in 1964 and occupied an endowed chair in 1974. Because he loves the area, in particular San Francisco's fine restaurants and Napa Valley's quaint wineries, it seems that he is unlikely to leave.

In 1980 he received the American Psychological Association's award for Distinguished Scientific Contributions. He was cited "For masterful modeling as researcher, teacher, and theoretician" and for "innovative experiments on a host of topics including moral development, observational learning, fear acquisition, treatment strategies, self-control . . . and cognitive regulation of behavior . . . His vigor, warmth, and humane example have inspired his many students . . ." (*AP*, 1981).

Bandura's View of the Person

Observational Learning and Reciprocal Determination

Observational Learning

On coming to Stanford, Bandura fell under the benevolent influence of Robert Sears, who was studying familial antecedents of social behavior and identification learning. Branching off from this work, he and his first doctoral student, Richard Walters, launched a series of studies on aggression in children that are still being cited today (for example, the famous Bobo doll studies). Their investigations into **observational learning**, learning by observing models as they perform useful behavior, demonstrated that "Modeling is not merely a process of behavioral mimicry" (Bandura, 1989a, p. 18). People who observe a model learn the value of a behavioral performance in terms of what it will achieve.

Inside/Outside and Reciprocal Causation

A major issue in the area of personality has been whether forces inside or outside of individuals control their behavior. Bandura's theory relates behavioral consistency to the inside/outside question. Advocates of determination by factors outside of individuals emphasize the variability of behavior, due to the dynamic action of the environment. Those who believe that control of behavior comes from within assert that stable processes from inside individuals give rise to stable behavior. By contrast, Bandura is concerned with the interplay of inside and outside factors and, thus, social cognitive theory focuses on both the variability and consistency of behavior (Bandura, 1977, 1989a). It is concerned with the interplay of factors inside and outside of people. "In *social cognitive theory* people . . . function as contributors to their own motivation, behavior, and development within a network of reciprocally interacting influences" (Bandura, 1989a, p. 6, emphasis added). To Bandura, *behavior, person factors*—such as cognition, biological variables, other internal events—and the *external environment* have reciprocal influences on one another: Each influences the other and is influenced by the other. Figure 13.1 displays these reciprocal relationships.

Person Factors, Behavior, and the External Environment

Behavior Can Affect Cognition, Feelings, and Even Neurobiology

Figure 13.1 implies some rather remarkable and even surprising assumptions. It is not so amazing that behavior could affect certain person factors, such as those in the cognitive category. If you do a thing well the first time you attempt it, you may change your thinking about your ability to do it. Should an individual attempt to approach a porpoise on a visit to a marina and succeed in repeatedly touching it on the first try, he may come to view

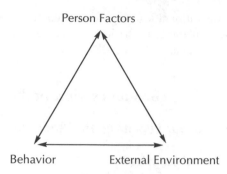

Person Factors

Behavior   External Environment

**FIGURE 13.1   Reciprocity in the
Relationship between
Person Factors,
Behavior, and the
External Environment**

"making friends with seagoing mammals" as a thing "I can do." Likewise, success on a first attempt may change certain internal events, such as feelings about the circumstances involved with the success. The individual may develop positive feelings about being in the water with ocean-dwelling relatives. However, that his behavior may affect his neurobiological functions may come as a surprise. If, over several years, he repeatedly reads, talks about, and writes about sea-dwelling mammals, he will develop a "neurological network" for processing information about such mammals. In turn, it will make learning more about whales and porpoises easier in the future.

Environments May Also Affect Neurobiology

A woman who moves in with other women—takes up residence in a suite occupied by several women—adopts a new environment that may affect hormonal cycling. In time, the onset and ending of her menstrual cycle may come to match that of her suitemates (Matlin & Foley, 1992). Cognitions, such as beliefs and expectations, can also impact on hormonal cycling and its accompaniments. If the woman, because of religious indoctrination, believes that "the curse" will strike her every 28 days, she will more regularly experience depression and physical discomfort premenstrually than other women (Paige, 1973). Regardless of her religious beliefs, if she comes to expect that she is about to start her "period," whether or not she really is, she may experience certain physiological changes, such as increased water retention (Ruble, 1977).

Behavior Affects Environment and Vice Versa

It is obvious that humans' behaviors can affect their physical environment: witness the tragic increase in pollution due to thoughtless human behavior in the service of immediate gratification (Bandura, 1995). Influence in the other direction is equally obvious: Because of pollution-driven ozone depletion, people may avoid sunny beaches in the future.

Cognition and Feeling Affect Behavior and Environments.

According to Bandura's model in Figure 13.1, cognitions and internal events, such as feelings, influence both behavior and environments (Bandura, 1989a). If certain people believe that their behavior will not succeed in a given setting, the odds are great that it will fail (Bandura, 1995). If they feel frightened when entering a given situation, they will avoid it. If their feelings and beliefs about forested lands are indifferent or negative—"turn them into commercial properties"—they will allow the forests to vanish.

Free Will, Personal Agency, and the Power of Forethought

In recent years, Bandura has turned his attention to what people can contribute to their own fruitful motivation and effective action (Bandura, 1995). Unlike B. F. Skinner, who admonishes us to abandon the "false" assumption of free will, Bandura (1989b) believes that people can, through their own cognitive mechanisms, gain a significant measure of control over their environments. People can develop a sense of **personal agency,** a condition in which they come to believe that they can make things happen that will be of benefit to themselves and to others.

Consistent with the contention that people have "free will" to a meaningful degree, Bandura believes that people not only select the situations in which they will operate, they create many of those situations. One may feel forced to go to class or work, but one may choose to attend a concert or drop in on a friend. People may insert themselves into ready-made situations, or they may create their own: "throw a party" or start a debate.

Learning

In contradiction to some others who theorize about learning, Bandura believes that learning occurs because people are aware of the consequences of their responses. They can and do think about what these consequences will be. In support of these assumptions, Bandura (1977) reports considerable evidence that learning is difficult for humans, if there is little or no awareness of the link between behavior and consequences. Further, it is nearly certain that learning is *facilitated* by awareness. Being aware makes people capable of **forethought**—anticipation of "likely consequences of . . . [future] actions" (Bandura, 1989a, p. 27; Bandura, 1994a). Forethought frees people from the tyranny of past rewards or reinforcements. People behave in anticipation of future consequences. Their current behavior is not necessarily explained by the fact that present circumstances resemble those associated with reinforcement in the past. "The eye to the future," as opposed to "eyes in the back of the head," is a philosophical position that Bandura shares with Kelly.

Behaviorists prefer animal research subjects; Bandura prefers humans. Animals do not have symbolic thought; people do. People can record consequences of actions as sentence structures or sets of symbols and thereby form hypotheses concerning what will happen in the future (Bandura, 1995). If one observes that smiling at waiters yields efficient and prompt service, she or he will store that observation in words and construct the hypothesis that smiling works with waiters. This hypothesis operates as a motivator for smiling behavior in the presence of waiters and will, therefore, increase the likelihood of smiling at waiters on subsequent occasions.

"Social" and "Cognitive" in "Social Cognitive Theory"

Another principle underlying social cognitive theory is tied up in the term *social*. People learn as much vicariously, through observing the behavior of others, as they learn through direct experience. Further, the terms *cognition* and *social* are close associates, because cognition is the vehicle by which people learn from people. If an individual watches another person receive a reward as a consequence of a behavioral performance, the observer will likely think (cognition), "If I behave in the same way, I'll receive the same reward." Observing another person model some behavior that results in reward is enough for learning to occur; rewards need not be directly received. In fact, individuals may learn even if their observations in no way include rewards.

Basic Concepts: Bandura

Models and Modeling

Learning by Others' Example
There are two fundamental concepts associated with observational learning. A **model** is a person who performs some behavior for an audience, showing how it is done and what benefits accrue from it. **Modeling** refers to the act of performing a behavior before one or more observers.

When people learn from observing others, they do not simply soak up whatever models have to offer. They begin observations of others with certain predispositions that determine what they learn from what they see. People want to master aspects of their own particular environments. Thus they look for those behaviors, among the many displayed by available models, that will allow mastery.

Symbolic Representation
People do not passively adopt a model's behavior (Bandura, 1989a). They "turn it over" in their minds, relating it to information they already have, rehearsing it, criticizing it, and thereby remembering it, if it is useful. In addition, people may transform information learned from a model into symbolic form so that it may be quickly and easily turned into action in the future. For example, one may ask, "Which way to the psychology building?" and hear in reply, "Follow me." If the questioner is a psychology major, and thus will frequently use the directions, the model's movements might at first be visualized as a series of right and left turns, then as "right(r), left(l), r,l,l,r." In this way information provided by the model may be represented symbolically, after it has been initially accepted in more concrete form.

Models need not be actual persons performing "live" (Bandura, 1994a). In **symbolic modeling** verbal and pictorial means are used to convey information necessary for adoption of behaviors associated with rewards. Media presentations, especially advertisements, provide good examples of symbolic modeling. Notice that TV ads do not always involve people. A well-set table containing food items for sale may create anticipations of future rewards.

Turning Observations into Behavior

Of course, people do not stop with accepting models' behavior and transforming it into symbolic form. They will attempt to turn their observations into behaviors. The extent to which they are successful will depend in part on whether they have the skills to execute the modeled behaviors. Success will also depend on whether people have gleaned all the relevant elements of the modeled behavior from observations before they try to behave. Given these conditions are met, observers create an *internal representation* of the behavior and then hone and refine it, along with the behavior, to suit their particular needs. This "polishing" is accomplished by an interplay between behavioral performances and the internal representation. For example, a baseball player who has watched an expert hitter will have a mental representation of the hitter's swing. When she practices the swing, she will compare her attempt to her mental image and change the swing to coincide with the image. At the same time, as the swing evolves so that it becomes successful, the mental representation will change to accommodate peculiarities of the newly effective swing.

Attractive Models

Characteristics of models and observers are also important in determining what is learned, or even whether anything is learned. People do not observe whoever happens to be present. Attractive, successful models, those who have done well both generally and on specific tasks are the ones whose behaviors are adopted. Why are they attractive?: Partly because they have characteristics that are interesting to us (e.g., appearance, skills, and confidence) and partly because of their success. On the other hand, what people learn from models or other sources is in part determined by their own capabilities that existed prior to observations (Zimmerman, Bandura, & Martinez-Pons, 1992). If observers are unschooled in chemistry, they are unlikely to benefit from a laboratory demonstration in that field, no matter how effective the model.

Incentives

Reinforcements or rewards for the performance of behaviors enter the learning sequence in three different ways. First, a person may observe a model being rewarded for performing a behavior. Such an observation would produce an **incentive**, any circumstance, concrete or abstract, that creates an anticipation of positive outcome following the performance of a behavior (Bandura, 1989a). For example, a child observes another child receive lavish praise for preventing an altercation between some younger children. In the future the development of another conflict situation between younger children will act as an incentive for the observer to intervene in anticipation of praise. Second, the model, for example, a parent trying to teach an observing child to pronounce a word, may reward the child's efforts to reproduce the verbal behaviors being modeled. Third, and perhaps most importantly, the observer may reward himself or herself for a good approximation to correct performance of a response (Bandura, 1994b). So if some children are trying to learn the utterance *arithmetic*, they may "pat themselves on the back" when they come close to the proper pronunciation.

What constitutes an incentive depends on the person. Box 13.1 contains some example incentives.

BOX 13.1   What Is an Incentive to You?

Different circumstances are incentives to different people. Check off all the following which would be incentives for your behavioral performances. Add any incentives you deem appropriate.

An offer of money
A chance to interact with children
An opportunity to confront someone you do not like
An encounter with a person in need
An occasion to be alone
A chance to talk to friends

A gathering of strangers
A chance to impress an important person
An offer of vacation time
An encounter with a person who has psychological problems
An opportunity for advancement on the job

Now for each incentive you checked, list the behaviors you would perform and the outcomes you would expect. If you have the opportunity, compare lists and outcomes with other students.

Goals and Self-Regulation

Goals are anticipated achievements that are in line with current personal standards. Goals in and of themselves are immensely important determinants of performance. Bandura (1991a) shows that the more challenging the goals people set the more effort they put into task performance. A goal, however, is pursued vigorously only if the goal-setter receives feedback indicating progress toward the goal. Thus, Bandura (1991a) reported that experimental subjects who set goals and received feedback regarding progress-to-goals exhibited highly effortful performance. Their effort was high in an absolute sense and also in comparison to subjects who (1) only set goals, (2) only got feedback, or (3) neither set goals nor got feedback. Subjects in the last three conditions showed equally low effort.

Even with effort, goal attainment remains uncertain without the institution of **self-regulatory processes**—internal, cognitive/affective functions that guide and govern efforts toward goal attainment (Bandura, 1991a). These processes include self-persuasion, self-praise (and criticism), valuation of personal standards, readjustment of standards, acceptance of challenges, and reactions to performances (Bandura, 1990a, 1991a, 1994b). All of these may be regarded as attempts at self-influence. Bandura (1990a) indicated that the greater the number of self-influence factors brought to bear on a task the greater the increase in performance motivation.

Self-Efficacy: Avenue to the Correction of Harmful Behavior

One of the most powerful self-regulatory processes is **self-efficacy**, a belief concerning one's ability to perform behaviors yielding an expected outcome that is desirable (Bandura, 1989a, 1989b, 1994b). When self-efficacy is high, one has confidence that she or he can perform behaviors allowing control of a difficult circumstance. Self-efficacy may be thought of as a specific form of confidence. While no one can be confident about everything he or she does, every person can develop beliefs in abilities to perform certain specific behaviors, each of which will yield a desirable outcome in a particular context.

BOX 13.2   Self-Efficacy Maintained in the Face of Defeat: Resilience

If people did not have ways to maintain self-efficacy in the face of defeat and humiliation, the world of science and art would be impoverished. Have you ever heard of James Clerk Maxwell? Probably not. Even the people of his day, the last century, were pretty much ignorant of him as well (Sagan, 1995). Yet his discoveries regarding the electromagnetic spectrum showed that light is related to electricity and led to the discovery of radio and TV. But he was "odd." As a young man he was called "dafty," which to his British peers meant "not quite right in the head" (p. 10).

Robert Goddard, considered by many the "father" of the modern rocket, "was bitterly rejected by his scientific peers on the grounds that rocket propulsion would not work in the rarefied atmosphere of outer space" (Bandura, 1994b, p. 76). Still he never lost faith in his innovative ideas about rockets. His persistence should have been better remembered on that fateful day in 1969 when ". . . one step for mankind . . ." was heard around the world.

Successful authors typically suffer many rejections before finally being blessed with a bestseller. Willian Saroyan received literally thousands of rejection letters before he finally got published. James Joyce's classic *Dubliners* was rejected by twenty-two publishers. It took Gertrude Stein twenty years of frustration before she finally got published. When e. e. cummings finally got published, his dedication read "With no thanks . . ." to the sixteen publishers who had previously rejected his work (Bandura, 1990a, p. 145).

In the world of art, Van Gogh sold only one painting during his life and died a pauper. But he left hundreds of paintings now worth many millions. Auguste Rodin could not get his art into the best museums and Frank Lloyd Wright's unique architectural works were initially shunned.

How did they manage to persist in the face of multiple rejections and humiliations? They showed unbelievably effective and hardy self-regulatory processes. Apparently e. e. cummings maintained his self-efficacy as a writer by anticipating the time when he could chastise his detractors. Maxwell persisted with little attention because his ability to satisfy his own curiosity kept his scientific self-efficacy high. Van Gogh and Frank Lloyd Wright may have persisted because their art was its own reward. Goddard enjoyed solving problems so much that a problem in need of solution was a stronger incentive than others' lack of faith was a disincentive. All of them undoubtedly called on friends to bolster their self-efficacy when it was flagging, praised themselves for meeting their own standards, and looked on defeat as a challenge. Whatever their particular reactions to defeat and frustration, each one of them showed remarkable **resilience**, the ability to absorb the slings and arrows of outrageous fortune and still believe that one can accomplish what one desires to do. Self-efficacy that can take the hard knocks will survive to be justified by success. No matter what one might think of Bill Clinton he certainly has admirable resilience. Whenever you witness the success of an African American (Colin Powell) or Latino(a) (Anthony Quinn) or Native American (Senator Ben Lighthorse Campbell), you are seeing resilience. It is the stuff that overcomes adversity.

As an illustration of the relationship between self-efficacy level and outcome expectancy, consider a contrast between Sarah and Sam on the matter of public speaking. Both individuals expect that making an effective public speech will be met with applause and other positive social outcomes. However, Sarah has strong feelings of self-efficacy with regard to critical behaviors involved in public speaking. She feels that she can obtain the relevant information that will go into her speech, organize it properly, memorize it, and present it in a clear and articulate manner. On the other hand, Sam has a different conviction with respect to self-efficacy. He feels that he cannot adequately perform any of the behaviors that will lead to the desired outcome.

Self-efficacy influences not only whether a person will attempt a behavior, but also determines the quality of performance once an attempt is made. High efficacy, entailing expectations of success, will generate persistence in the face of obstacles and frustrations. Persistence eventually leading to success will yield further bolstering of self-efficacy. Low efficacy will lower effort, thereby increasing the probability of failure and the likelihood of further decreases in efficacy (Bandura, 1991a).

The single most efficient method for boosting self-efficacy is *performance accomplishment*. Doing is believing. If a person with low self-efficacy can somehow be induced to perform a feared or repugnant behavior, self-efficacy may be dramatically bolstered. However, vicarious experience can also be effective, especially if people with low self-efficacy can view persons who share their fears performing the inhibited behaviors (Bandura, 1994b). **Participant modeling,** in which the person with low self-efficacy imitates a model's efficacious behavior, can be very beneficial, even where persuasion and other influence attempts have failed. Because people read their state of efficacy by reference to their level of emotional arousal in the face of a threatening situation, any methods that will lower arousal will increase feelings of efficacy (1994b). Successful actual performance or positive vicarious experience are methods of lowering arousal.

Other Things We Learn from Models, besides Behavior

Expectancies

Behavior is not all that is learned from models. In **vicarious expectancy learning** people adopt other people's expectancies concerning future events, especially expectancies of those with whom they share relevant experiences (Bandura, 1977, 1989a, 1994a). For example, people who have lived through a hurricane, but suffered little from its devastating winds, still have witnessed the suffering of people like themselves who were victims. Accordingly they adopt the victims' expectations. Thus, their vicarious expectancy of disaster may be almost as strong as that of actual victims, as reflected in their willingness to join with others in preparing for future storms. In general, vicarious expectancy learning is most likely to be transmitted to people from models with whom they share many experiences.

Creativity, Facilitation, and Innovation

An individual first accepts the behaviors of a model and then may creatively branch out from there. Thus, Beethoven adopted the forms of Haydn and Mozart, later going well beyond those artistic styles into his own greater emotional expressiveness (Bandura, 1977).

By contrast, in **response facilitation** nothing new is learned, but some old responses may be disinhibited as a result of watching a model's performance (Bandura, 1977, 1989a). In this case, the model's behavior acts like a social prompt, communicating that it is "OK" to perform the behavior which was inhibited. For example, a person who is fearful of dancing, because religious training made the practice seem "evil," may experience disinhibition of dancing by watching a "good" person dance, with no ill effects. Students at Baylor University, a Baptist school, may have experienced response facilitation when their president recently performed the first sanctioned on-campus dance steps in the school's history.

Diffusion of innovation occurs when models try something new and thereby display its benefits and advantages to others. Once people have accepted an innovative behavior, its longevity will be partially determined by the permanence of the incentives associated with its adoption. The more permanent the incentives for adopting something new, the longer the innovation will stay around. Fads are short-lived, because adoption results only in fleeting social recognition. Hula hoops are an example. By comparison, the automobile illustrates a novelty that has become permanent. People who drive desirable cars are afforded continuous social recognition and also needed transportation.

There are some definite restraints on the adoption of novelties, however. These include lack of the skills needed to perform behaviors associated with the novelty (Bandura, 1993). Soccer is finally catching on in this country, thanks to the super model, Pele, but adoption has been limited to those with adequate athletic skills. Likewise, computers are pervading most of life's spheres, but at least minimum "computer literacy" is needed to "surf the Net" or create a spread sheet.

Given at least minimal skills, self-efficacy regarding performance of a to-be-adopted innovation is critical (Bandura, 1994a). Anything that models of innovations can do to boost self-efficacy will increase the likelihood of adoption. Likewise, when modeling is symbolic, its ability to bolster self-efficacy largely determines its effectiveness. For example, communications promoting preventive health practices work insofar as they elevate self-efficacy regarding practices.

Rewards

While behavior is often acquired vicariously, it is primarily maintained by rewards. There has been much debate concerning the relative importance of **extrinsic rewards**—rewards originating outside the individual—money, and **intrinsic rewards**—rewards from within the individual—self-satisfaction (Bandura, 1977). Extrinsically rewarded behaviors appear to be done for tangible payoffs. By contrast, intrinsically rewarded behaviors seem to be "done for their own sake." From Bandura's vantage point, both are necessary for a full account of human action. External rewards are needed to direct a person's attention to a behavior and to institute initial performance. Nevertheless, long-term maintenance of the behavior depends largely on development of intrinsic rewards. For instance, in order to begin the task of teaching a child to write, tangible rewards, privileges or even money, will likely be needed to generate beginning attempts. Such rewards may have to be presented even on a sentence by sentence basis. The child may then progress to performing for less tangible rewards, such as praise from parents for a job well done, though the payoff is still external. Finally, if writing behavior is to be maintained, the child must learn what constitutes good writing behavior so that she can praise herself "under her breath" for writing a grammatically correct sentence. If she does so, intrinsic rewards have come into play.

Intrinsic motivation refers to the desire for intrinsic rewards, leading to the pursuit of the same. One of the problems with the notion of intrinsic motivation is that its presence is often inferred from the persistence of a behavior in the absence of any obvious external rewards. As Bandura (1977) notes, such an inference is unwarranted. To support his skepticism by example, if a person watches TV for many hours a day, one would be hard-pressed to invoke "intrinsic motivation." More than likely, the lack of behavioral alternatives explains persistent gazing at the tube. To be sure that intrinsic motivation is at work, more information is needed. One must observe the persistence of behavior in the absence of appropriate external rewards, but in the presence of other behavioral alternatives. Alternatives would include some that could lead to external rewards.

Problems with support for the operation of intrinsic motivation can be avoided by recording observations focused on a kind of self-regulation, **self-evaluation**—a process that involves assessing one's performance at various points along the way to task completion and issuing a vocal or "under the breath" judgment of its value. Thus, a clarinetist who repeatedly sounds a note, sometimes pausing to frown and shake her head, is engaging in self-evaluation. When a smile follows an attempt at the note, observers can conclude that the clarinetist has positively reinforced herself. Most forms of "practice" are intrinsically motivated, and, therefore, under the control of intrinsic reward.

Some people nurture the belief that extrinsic rewards are somehow antagonistic to intrinsic motivation. Supposedly, "being paid" for performance of behaviors implies external rather than self-control of behavior, with accompanying feelings of lost self-determination and competence. Although support for the notion that external reward destroys intrinsic motivation is mixed at best, belief in the idea persists (Bandura, 1977). Such is the case, despite numerous contradictions existing in everyday reality. Artists, professors, athletes, and many others are more than happy to receive money for what they love to do.

Intrinsic reward is not the only way that one's behavior may be maintained in the absence of immediate, external rewards available to oneself. **Vicarious reinforcement** occurs when one observes another person being rewarded for performing a behavior. An observation that helping others settle a dispute is followed by many warm "thank yous" is likely to transform cases of interpersonal conflict into approachable circumstances.

Vicarious reinforcement can increase the impact of modeling even where the modeled behavior is aversive. If a model exhibits a behavior that is frightening or repugnant to an observer and is rewarded for the performance, the observer may be induced to try the formerly shunned behavior (Bandura, 1989a). According to Bandura, vicarious reward can induce people to try an undesired food, give up a valued object, and disclose personal matters, any of which could be beneficial (Bandura, 1977). In addition, vicarious punishment can be efficient. Bandura (1977) cites a study in which observers of models who were punished for performance of a prohibited behavior, later were just as unlikely to perform the behavior as were the models.

External rewards, of course, do not have any inherent absolute value. Value of rewards is relative, established by the process of **social comparison**, determining how well one is doing in life by comparing oneself to those who share one's life situation (Festinger, 1954). A factory worker does not determine how well he is doing in life by comparing himself with the plant manager. Instead he compares himself to people doing the same job. If, for example, he is earning as much, or a little more, than people who share the same job, he can conclude that he is doing fine. "X" number of dollars earned per month is valued or not valued, depending on its standing, relative to what comparable others are earning.

Social comparison can yield welcomed or unwelcomed results, depending on whether one starts ahead then falls behind comparable others, performs consistently better than others, or starts behind comparable others but eventually surpasses them. Bandura (1991a) describes work in which managerial performance, self-efficacy for decision-making, goal-setting, and satisfaction were observed in a simulated business environment under varying feedback conditions. Some subjects received feedback indicating their performance was consistently superior to that of others, some were led to believe they started behind others but eventually surpassed them, and some additional subjects fell behind others, after initially being ahead. Relative to those who caught up with and surpassed others, subjects who progressively fell behind showed deficient self-efficacy, satisfaction, and performance. Catching up with and then surpassing comparable others was also better than consistently surpassing comparable others: Subjects who were consistently ahead of others showed complacency as reflected in mediocre performance and unambitious goal-setting.

Defensive Behaviors

Defensive behaviors are adopted in order to cope with unpleasant events that are anticipated on future occasions (Bandura, 1977). If "sitting in the front row" becomes associated with embarrassment because of failure to answer the professor's questions, the defensive behavior "sitting in the back" may be adopted. The adoption occurs and persists, because it allows anticipation of comfort, not because it is motivated by anxiety. If the latter were the case, people would always show anxiety when they perform defensive behavior. Instead, they show relief once they become confident that their defensive strategy is effective.

Thus, anxiety is an associate of early defensive behavior, not the cause of it (Leventhal, 1970). Initially the unpleasant event is accompanied by both anxiety and defensive behavior. An anxious child takes a big stuffed bear to bed "to scare the wolves away." But after the defensive behavior is seen as a way to avoid the unpleasant event, it is performed in the absence of anxiety. Because defensive behavior is due to anticipating the avoidance of unpleasant events in the future, rather than for the purpose of coping with present anxiety, it is very difficult to eliminate. The absence of the unpleasant event is "proof" to the performer that his or her defensive behavior is "working." Therefore, if a child is asked, "Why do you take that huge stuffed bear to bed?" The now calm child replies, "Because it keeps the wolves away." When the response is, "But there are no wolves around here," the retort is, "See how well it works." "The way out" may be through modeling. If a trusted model can be observed operating in the context of the unpleasant event without performing the defensive behavior, and the unpleasant event fails to occur, the defensive behavior may be discarded. "See me in bed? No bear, but no wolves ever get me."

Evaluation

Supporting Evidence

Self-Efficacy

Self-efficacy is the most researched of the self-regulatory mechanisms proposed by Bandura. In fact, it is one of the hottest research topics of the 1980s and 1990s. In view of the enormous number of studies on this self-regulatory mechanism—many more than could be reviewed here—a few research projects have been selected for detailed presentation because they aptly demonstrate the power of self-efficacy.

Bandura, Reese, and Adams (1982) conducted research in which subjects were recruited through a newspaper advertisement aimed at people with severe spider phobias. A *phobia* is an intense, irrational fear of an object that is not particularly dangerous. In one of their studies, subjects were 16 spider phobics, ranging in age from 16 to 61 years. Their fear of spiders was extreme, to say the least. One had difficulty taking a bath, because she had once encountered a spider in the tub. Another leaped from an auto she was driving, on noticing a spider inside the car. One had difficulty reading or watching TV, because she was fearful that a spider would happen by and catch her unawares. At the mere sight of a spider, even a picture of the insect, she would react with compulsive shivers, pounding of the heart, shortness of breath, and, on occasion, vomiting for hours.

Another subject indicated that whenever she even thought of a spider, she would picture herself being eaten by the creature. She had trouble sleeping at night, because she would wake up to inspect the ceiling for the presence of a spider. If she did detect one, she would stand on a stool, and kill it with insect spray. But sleep was still not forthcoming. Wide-eyed, she would lie awake staring at the ceiling lest the spider revive and climb back to its previous perch. Obviously these people had an incapacitating problem and sorely needed help.

Subjects first were administered a behavioral avoidance test, consisting of 18 items, each progressively more threatening than its predecessor. The test involved interactions with a large wolf spider, previously shown to be especially frightening to spider phobics. Table 13.1 provides examples of the behaviors included on the test.

As you can see, interaction with the spider ranged from remote, viewing it from a distance, to intimate, allowing the spider to crawl on subjects' laps. At the beginning of the experiment, the best a subject could do was to view the spider at a considerable and safe distance, a near zero level of efficacy.

Self-efficacy judgments were made quite simply. Subjects were presented with the 18 performances listed on the behavioral test, and for each were asked to indicate on a 100-point scale the degree to which they felt confident that they could perform the behavior; that is, the degree of efficacy that they felt with regard to performing the behavior. A "1" indicated no efficacy for a given behavior, and "100" meant a belief in complete mastery of the behavior in question. A subject's efficacy score was the number of behaviors for which the efficacy rating was at least 20 on the 100 point scale. Next subjects were randomly assigned to a low or medium efficacy-treatment condition. The induction of either a high or a low level of efficacy was administered by a female experimenter who employed two large wolf

TABLE 13.1   Example Items for the Behavioral Avoidance Test

Approach plastic bowl containing spider
Look down at the spider
Place bare hands in the bowl
Let spider crawl freely in a chair placed in front of [yourself]
Let spider crawl over gloved hands
Let spider crawl over bare forearm
Handle spider with bare hands
Allow spider to crawl on lap

spiders, different in color and shape from the one that had been used in the initial behavioral test.

As a warm-up, a spider was placed in a vial and subjects, each of whom was alone with the experimenter, were merely asked to inspect it. The experimenter then modeled several threatening behaviors as subjects watched. First, the experimenter placed the spider in a plastic bowl and poked it with her finger as it scurried about. Next she removed the spider from the container and handled the creature as it crawled over her arms, hands, and upper body. The model indicated how to control a freely moving spider by placing it on a towel draped over a chair and herding it about on the piece of furniture.

At regular intervals during the treatment each subject took the 100-point scale efficacy test. These administrations of the test were repeated until each subject reached the level of efficacy corresponding to her assigned treatment condition (low or medium efficacy). Low efficacy was defined as being able to allow the spider to roam over a chair placed near the subject and being able to place a hand in the bowl containing the spider, near the creature. Subjects in the medium efficacy condition continued in treatment until they could endure physical contact with the spider by holding it in a gloved or bare hand. After subjects had reached the assigned level of efficacy, the behavioral test, performed earlier, was repeated.

At the completion of major procedures, subjects in the low efficacy condition were raised to the medium level by further modeling, then their behavior and efficacy were again measured. Finally, at the end of the experiment, all subjects worked until they had achieved maximum efficacy.

As Figure 13.2 indicates, there was a very direct relationship between subjects' assigned level of self-efficacy and their behavioral performance after the treatment. Subjects assigned

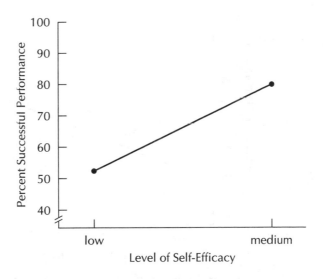

FIGURE 13.2 **Relationship between self-efficacy and behavioral performance after treatment for low- compared to medium-efficacy.**

to the low efficacy condition achieved low performance on the behavioral test, after treatment, while those in the medium efficacy condition achieved medium behavioral performance, after treatment. Also low-efficacy subjects' behavioral performance was measured when they were at low efficacy and when their efficacy was raised to a medium level. As Figure 13.3 indicates, there was again a direct relationship between efficacy level and performance. If a subject indicated that she felt she could at most place her hands on the inverted bowl with the spider inside, she was unable to go beyond that performance. Self-efficacy predicted performance almost perfectly.

This remarkable study showed that in the time it takes to run a single experimental session, lifelong spider phobics acquired the ability to touch a creature previously so frightening that the mere thought of its presence had provoked spasms of anxiety. Although permanency of their newly developed self-efficacy is in question, there is no doubt that a few additional sessions would have completely eliminated their irrational fears. Social cognitive theory is so powerful in a practical sense that it can transform lives.

In a similar study, Wiedenfeld, O'Leary, Bandura, Brown, Levine, and Raska (1990) again attempted to show that phobics' performance in the presence of a threatening creature corresponds directly to their perceived self-efficacy. In addition they wanted to measure effects on the immune system during self-efficacy acquisition and the relationship of those effects to certain physiological responses and endocrine (hormone) secretions. Subjects were snake phobics who had agreed to participate in a training session designed to help them overcome their fears.

The Behavior Avoidance test used by the researchers was virtually identical to that employed by Bandura, Reese, and Adams (1982), but a harmless corn snake was substituted for

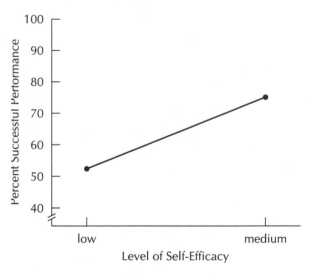

FIGURE 13.3   Relationship between self-efficacy and behavioral performance for subjects when at the low-efficacy level and when at the medium-efficacy level.

the spider (see Table 13.1). The procedure was also similar to that of Bandura, Reese, and Adams, except that all subjects went through all phases of self-efficacy enhancement, from a pre-test/baseline phase, through an efficacy-growth phase, finishing with a maximal efficacy phase. During the pre-test/baseline phase, subjects' perceived self-efficacy was measured (it uniformly was found to be very low) and indexes of endocrine, physiological, and immunological functioning were obtained. During the efficacy growth phase, subjects were exposed to the corn snake in much the same way that Bandura, Reese, and Adams exposed subjects to spiders. An experimenter modeled progressively more threatening interactions with the snake, and invited subjects to emulate her behavior. This two-hour session was later followed by an additional two-hour treatment during which subjects were brought up to and maintained at maximal self-efficacy and performance attainment.

Self-efficacy showed the same course of development reported by Bandura, Reese, and Adams—it stayed at rock bottom levels during pre-test assessments, rose dramatically during efficacy-growth phase assessments, and stayed near the maximal strength "100" level during maximal-efficacy phase assessments. Levels of immune system components, such as blood lymphocytes, helper T cells, and suppressor T cells, were assessed during the three phases. Indexes of these components showed dramatic changes from the baseline in the direction of immune system enhancement during the efficacy-growth phase, and a slight drop-off in immune system functioning during the maximal efficacy phase.

Cortisol elevations are often associated with immune system suppression and heart rate acceleration typically accompanies stress enhancement. "In accordance with prediction, the findings generally showed that slow growth of perceived self-efficacy, high cortisol activation, and heart rate acceleration were associated with lower immunological status during the efficacy acquisition phase" (p. 1089). The slower was acquisition of self-efficacy, the greater were cortisol levels and heart rate accelerations and the more sluggish was immune system functioning. By contrast, rapid acquisition of self-efficacy was associated with relatively high immunological status.

Wiedenfeld and colleagues' extraordinary study goes a step beyond Bandura, Reese, and Adams. Not only was self-efficacy enhanced, resulting in close contact with a previously feared creature, for most subjects immune system functioning was enhanced during such exposure. These results lay open the exciting possibility that social cognitive theory will yield methods for eliminating the multiple suppressions of phobics' immune systems that may accompany periodic thoughts of and real life exposures to feared objects.

It follows from Bandura's (1995, 1994b) theory that one kind of self-influence process associated with goal pursuits, self-evaluation, will have beneficial effects only if self-efficacy is high. When self-efficacy is low, people find themselves failing, see themselves as incapable, and, as a result, show emotional reactions that are debilitating. Under these conditions, performance will suffer. Lawrence Sanna and Paul Pusecker (1994) investigated self-evaluation in the context of high versus low self-efficacy. Subjects were all given the Remote Associates Test (RAT) in which, for example, they had to respond to "elephant," "lapse," and "vivid" with the correct associate, "memory." During a "practice" session, efficacy was manipulated by giving some subjects an easy version of the RAT (high efficacy condition) and other subjects a difficult version (low efficacy condition). In a self-evaluation condition, subjects were told they would be provided with the average RAT performance level of subjects in "previous research." In the "no-evaluation" condition subjects were told that they would not receive average performance information, though it was available. In the actual test phase all subjects were given a moderately difficult RAT. As expected, high-efficacy subjects performed better in the "evaluation" than in the "no-evaluation" condition, but for low-efficacy subjects it was the other way around. Self-evaluation has positive effects if self-efficacy is high, but in the context of low self-efficacy self-evaluation is debilitating.

Other Self-Regulatory Factors: Social Cognitive Theory in the Business Sector

Bandura and his colleague Robert Wood have applied social cognitive theory to problems regarding management of employees, decision-making, and productivity. In one of their studies, 24 business graduate students participated in a managerial decision-making project (Wood & Bandura, 1989). Their job was to fill 18 orders for furniture which constituted 18 trials in this production-simulation game (the trials were grouped into three blocks of six). The critical task in filling the orders was to allocate five employees optimally so that production was fast and efficient. To aid in their allocation decisions, grad-student subjects received a personnel file on each employee containing information about level of effort and skill, as well as experience, motivational level, and preference for routine versus challenging job assignments. Subjects also received information concerning the effort and skill required for each production sub-function (milling the wood, assembling the furniture, finishing the surface of each unit).

The manipulated factor in this experiment was whether or not decision-making skill was presented to subjects as a *stable entity* or an *acquirable skill*. Subjects assigned to the stable entity condition were told that decision-making ability is a "cognitive-processing capacity" revealed by performance. That is, it is something that one has or does not have. Subjects in the acquirable skill condition were informed that decision-making is developed during practice. Here, the more one works at developing decision-making skills, the better one becomes. Social cognitive theory predicts that self-regulatory mechanisms and productivity will be enhanced by the acquirable skill condition, because it promotes personal agency in decision-making.

Factors indexing several self-regulatory mechanisms were measured. Strength of self-efficacy was assessed in a manner similar to methods described earlier. *Assessing self-goals* was measured by the level of goals subjects set with each succeeding trial. Subjects could set production goals that ranged from 40 percent below to 30 percent above an established standard. *Analytic strategies* were assessed in terms of whether subjects changed *only one or several* motivational arrangement-factors in arriving at decisions—examples of these factors included instructive feedback to employees and social rewards meted out to employees. The more decisions a subject could make in a block of trials while changing just one factor, the better were his or her analytic strategies. Such was the case because genuine "hypothesis testing" requires the change of only one factor at a time. Changing more than one factor at a time makes it uncertain which changed factor yielded any changed outcome. Performance was measured in terms of the number of simulated hours required to fill each order. "The fewer the production hours, the better the subject's managerial decision-making" (p. 410).

Results showed that self-efficacy was very high in the acquirable skills condition, relative to the stable entity condition, and increased over blocks of trials. By contrast, self-efficacy declined over blocks of trials in the stable entity condition. Exactly the same trend was found for self-set goals, analytic strategies, and performance productivity. These factors were at a generally high level in the "acquirable skills" condition and increasing across blocks of trials, but were at a generally low level in the "stable entity" condition and decreasing across blocks of trials. Telling acquirable skills subjects that "practice makes perfect" in regard to decision-making skills enhanced their feeling of agency, and in turn, boosted three self-regulatory mechanisms. The result was increased productivity.

"Acquirable Skills" in the Athletic Arena
In a similar study, Jourden, Bandura, and Banfield (1991) had subjects perform a pursuit rotor task: They tracked a light moving in a circular path by trying to keep a stylus or pointer exactly on top of the light as it moved. Some subjects were told that skill at this hand-eye coordination task was "inherited" (like the "stable" case there is nothing one can do to improve performance). Others were told that the task "is an acquirable skill." As predicted, subjects in the "acquirable skill" condition showed increasing self-efficacy during task performance, positive self-reactions to their performance, widespread interest in the activity, and a high level of skill acquisition. "Inherited skill" condition subjects were low on all of these factors. Even on this basic motor skill, which was meant to be analogous to athletic activity, subjects who believed they could do well, in fact, did well and enjoyed themselves while they excelled.

Self-Regulation Out in the Open
Bussey and Bandura (1992) investigated the open and overt expression of self-regulatory processes in an area where self-influence is typically very strong, gender roles. Child subjects, 2 1/2 to 7 1/2 years of age, played with toys that were gender-specific (truck or baby doll) or neutral (xylophone). First, children were told to register how they would feel about playing with a particular toy by pressing a switch to activate one of five lights: One switch was to be pressed if they anticipated feeling "real great" about playing with a toy, and there were four other switches for other reactions ("kinda great," "nothing special," "kinda awful," and "real awful"). That is, the children could register reactions ranging from a high level of self-approval to a high level of self-criticism for playing with toys. Children later had an opportunity to actually play with the toys. They also watched and used the lights for registering reactions to a boy and a girl playing with toys "inappropriately": The boy played with a feminine toy and the girl played with a masculine toy.

Older children displayed self-approval of anticipatory gender "appropriate" behavior (boys in anticipation of playing with a masculine toy and girls expecting to play with a feminine toy) and self-criticism of "inappropriate" behavior. Further, these reactions accurately predicted how they actually behaved when given the opportunity to play with the toys. Younger children strongly showed conformity to the expectations of gender roles only with regard to their reactions to the boy and girl they watched. In general children felt "great" about their own and others' behavior only if it conformed to the expectations of gender roles assigned to themselves and to others. Some boys went so far as to refuse even to be in the same room with feminine toys.

Implications of Social Cognitive Theory for Moral Functioning

Crime
Beyond these many and varied contributions, social cognitive theory has implications for the well-being and prosperity of humans in the future. For example, social cognitive theory has something important to say about a common concern in our society—crime.

Why do people steal and commit other crimes despite the threat of arrest and imprisonment? A look inside the prisons suggests an answer. Poor people and people of color are greatly overrepresented in our penal institutions. People will survive, and in so doing, they will choose methods of survival from whatever is available to them. Two factors govern selection of criminal behavior as a means of survival. First, it is one of the few behavioral alternatives open to those relegated to the bottom of the social ladder. Second, compared to other available alternatives, the incentives are great, relative to the likelihood of negative future outcomes (that is, being caught and imprisoned). One could work at a dead-end job, for low pay—"flipping burgers at Mickey D's"—and suffer certain humiliation, and failure to prosper, or one could resort to crime. (Perhaps you will be able to imagine that making thousands weekly selling crack cocaine is more alluring than working for minimum wage at a fast food outlet, if these are among the few alternatives available to you.) In the case of many crimes, effort is minimal, likelihood of being caught and imprisoned minimal, and the outcome highly positive, relative to investment. It follows from these conjectures that public pronouncements to the effect that "people are imprisoned for criminal behavior" will fail to deter crime.

The middle class and above have more numerous and better behavioral alternatives available, relative to the poor and victims of social discrimination. The solution to many social ills, most especially crime, lies in making the full range of behavioral alternatives available to all the people, not just the relatively privileged.

Doing Evil and Avoiding the Cognitive and Emotional Consequences

Social cognitive theory has implications for the understanding of other troubling behaviors (Bandura, 1989a, 1990b, 1991b, 1995). As Bandura observes, "Over the years, much cruelty has been perpetrated by decent, moral people in the name of religious principles, righteous ideology, and social order" (1977, p. 156). Yet, "character flaws" do not adequately explain humans' inhumanity to humans. Instead the culprit is an intricate game of mental gymnastics. "People do not ordinarily engage in reprehensible conduct until they have justified to themselves the morality of their actions" (Bandura, 1990).

Social cognitive theory helps to explain how individuals perform inhumane behaviors without suffering severe psychological consequences. **Self-exonerative processes** is the general name given to cognitive activities that allow people to dissociate themselves from the consequences of their actions. Religion, ideology, and "order," all noble in concept, are abused in practice when they are invoked to justify doing evil. In social-cognitive terms, "noble causes" such as those mentioned above can be invoked to break the connection between behaviors and actual outcomes. Actual outcomes of behaviors that would otherwise be considered immoral and unforgivable are covered up, shoved aside and, thereby, effectively replaced by acceptable outcomes. For example, Klansmen/militiamen adopt a religious facade, including the cross symbol, to cloak their vicious behavior in an aura of purity (see *Klanwatch*, a publication of Southern Poverty Law, 1001 South Hull St., Montgomery, Alabama 36101).

However, Klan/militia behavior is sometimes so savage it is difficult to justify, even "with God on our side." In order to support murder and torture, it also becomes necessary for such people to dehumanize their victims. **Dehumanization** is a cognitive process that involves lowering the status of certain people from "human being" to "lesser being." It is difficult to perform, much less justify, torture of human beings, but it can be done to beings that are declared "not human" (Bandura, 1990b). Thus, labeling people "gooks," "hymies," "spicks," "spooks," "queers" or "injuns" makes them fair targets for cruelty. At Oklahoma City, labeling people "government officials" was enough to take away their humanity and, thereby, render them legitimate targets of a devastating militia bomb.

Other cognitive activities are helpful in setting the stage for the performance of reprehensible behavior. **Advantageous comparison** is a cognitive mechanism by which ". . . deplored acts can be made to appear righteous by contrasting them with flagrant inhumanities" (Bandura, 1990b, p. 171). When confronted with accusations that the Nazis mistreated the Jews, Hitler was in the habit of citing the subjugation of Native Americans and the oppression of Indians and other "colonials" by the British (Speer, 1970).

Euphemistic labeling is the cognitive process of assigning a name to deplorable behavior that makes it seem innocuous or even laudable (Bandura, 1990b, 1991b, 1995). The "Vietnam experience" included many such labels. Destroying crops and jungle habitats was called "defoliation." Disenfranchising and physically relocating whole villages of people was called "pacification." Killing as many as possible and collecting their bodies like trophies was called "body count." These labels, produced by the military hierarchy, were responsible for the atrocities in Vietnam, not the soldiers to whom labels were supplied. If one could replace the entire set of soldiers who served in Vietnam with another group, the result would be the same (Allen, 1978).

The Nazis, of course, were masters of euphemistic labeling. "Euthanasia Program" was the fancy name given to gassing retarded and physically handicapped people (Dawidowicz, 1975). "The Final Solution of the Jewish Question" was the official title of the human tragedy now known as the Holocaust.

Blaming victims for their own fate is all too common a cognitive exercise (Bandura, 1990b, 1991b, 1995). The Irish Republican Army (IRA) seems to specialize in this mental mechanism. When, during a war memorial ceremony, many innocent British sympathizers fell victim to a large IRA bomb exploded prematurely by a British scanning device, the IRA blamed the British. One must remember, though, the IRA does what it does partly because, historically, the British have done it to them.

Displacement and diffusion of responsibility involves placing the blame for one's deplorable acts onto others, and spreading the responsibility for reprehensible behavior to others who are present, respectively. Terrorists are prone to displacement. These mass murderers "warn officials of targeted nations that if they take retaliatory action they will be held accountable for the lives of the hostages" (Bandura, 1990b, p. 175). Diffusion of responsibility allows one to walk right by a person who is suffering a calamity and hardly notice, so long as there are many others present to whom the person may spread the responsibility for helping (Latane and Darley, 1970).

In **moral justification**, individuals invoke religious or other moral bases to support their inhuman behavior (Bandura, 1990b, 1991b). Hitler constructed a peculiar moral code to which he referred whenever his savage acts seemed to require justification: The "destiny of the German people" justified any and every act in its own interest. Famed World War I marksman Sergeant York never could have done his many heroic deeds had he not been able to reconcile his behavior with his religious beliefs. He registered as a conscientious objector, but that status was denied. Unconvinced by his battalion commander's Bible citations of conditions under which Christians are permitted to kill, York retired to a mountainside for marathon prayers. He emerged dedicated to killing "the enemy."

Gradualistic moral disengagement, a process during which people slowly slip unawares into what was normally unacceptable behavior, has made monsters of everyday people. Terrorists are trained in a step-by-step process taking many months. With each step a mental wave swells and pounds against the belief that taking human life is wrong. By the end of training, abhorrence of killing is fully eroded. "Development of the capability to kill usually evolves through a process in which recruits may not fully recognize the transformation they are undergoing" (Bandura, 1990, p. 186). In the famous "obedience to authority" studies by Stanley Milgram (1974), subjects were gradually sucked into ostensibly harming another human by the graduated procedure of escalating electric-shock punishments with each error on a learning task.

While certain immoral behaviors can be predicted and explained by social cognitive theory, so can some forms of self-sacrifice and altruism. *Self-evaluation* can be so dominant that it becomes more important than external rewards and punishments. Sister Teresa, win-

Martin Luther King, Jr.

ner of the 1979 Nobel Peace Prize, has such strong convictions concerning the elimination of human suffering that she worked for years in obscurity and deprivation to bring comfort to the poor, ill, and lame of Calcutta, India. During the early 1980s a young man rushed to the aid of a woman who was being raped on a public street, thereby totally ignoring the punishments for such behavior that were implied by the inaction of many bystanders. Similarly, Lenny Skutnik stood among several people as he watched a woman flounder in the Potomac following the crash of her plane. Seeing the helpless victim slowly disappear into the icy water, Skutnik dove in and hauled her to shore. His efforts received national acclaim, including introduction to the Congress by the President of the United States (*Life*, January, 1983). During the early 1980s, a crowd formed beneath a ninth-floor window where a man was poised to jump (Mann, 1981). It happened in Los Angeles, city of notables, one of whom was on the scene. Muhammad Ali talked the man from his perch. The crowd cheered. Altruism well-modeled is well appreciated.

Other models of noble behavior include Martin Luther King and Susan B. Anthony, a pioneer warrior in the battle for women's rights. King "had a dream" the fulfillment of which was more important to him than life itself. Assassination haunted him wherever he went, but he refused to be silent or to cease his travels. Dr. King faithfully continued his mission until the end. Anthony was a respected educator whose life could be described as very comfortable and secure. She readily jeopardized these advantages because she could not abide the absurdity and insensitivity of beliefs and practices to which the women of her day were subjected. Nor could she tolerate slavery. The humane exploits of these and many other individuals remind us that people are capable of compassion and kindness, attributes that will more strongly dominate cruelty and indifference when more is known about social learning processes.

Susan B. Anthony

BOX 13.3   Diversity: The "Battle of the Sexes" Is a War with Millions of Women Victims

Men beating the women in their lives, sometimes seriously injuring or even killing them, is a sad but familiar facet of life around the world. One of the favorite justifications for assault on women is "blaming the victim" (Adams, 1994). "She made me do it because she just wouldn't keep the house clean"; "She drove me to it because of her constant complaints every time I come home late"; or "I had no choice. She wouldn't stop looking at other men." Some men who abuse women also use other justifi-cations. "I know men who would kill their wives for less" (advantageous comparison). "It was a shoving match. I just pushed her around a little" (euphemistic labeling). "I only do it for her own good. She needs it; she behaves better after it happens" (moral justification). "The bitch got what she deserves" (dehumanization). Until this web of cognitive delusions is no longer spun in the heads of some men, women will suffer and the perpetrators will experience an erosion of their own humanity.

Limitations

With all its virtues, a serious fault of social cognitive theory appears to be that it attempts to explain too much of human behavior. It is too broad. Many of the all-encompassing theories that seem to explain everything, may actually explain very little. Such is the case because these universal theories mainly provide explanations after observations of behavior are made. Although social cognitive theory does make legitimate predictions, it is open to providing explanation after-the-fact (explaining immoral behavior after it has occurred is an example). A scientific theory explains behavior before it occurs, rather than after-the-fact (Allen, 1978).

As once was the case with cognitive dissonance theory in social psychology, social cognitive theory has no clear boundaries (Collins & Hoyt, 1972; Linder, Cooper, & Jones, 1967). It is incumbent on psychological theories without limits to explain such varied psychological problems as chronic anxiety, severe depression, and schizophrenia. It must also explain socially destructive behaviors like prejudice and deindividuation (harmful behavior that results from losing one's sense of self, as when "lost in a crowd"). Yet the theory provides no concrete explanations of these behaviors. Sadness and shyness, joy and jealousy are not addressed meaningfully by social cognitive theory. Perhaps social cognitive theory was not intended to provide explanations of these diverse behaviors. If such is the case, it should be publicly stated. In the meantime the theory awaits the construction of borders about it. Like cognitive dissonance theory, which now has definite boundaries, social cognitive theory would benefit from a proclamation concerning when it applies and when it does not apply (Wheeler et al., 1978). If it is known when a theory can predict and when it cannot, its percentage of accurate predictions will go up. Also, given boundaries, there will be no attempts to explain after-the-fact what the theory cannot predict.

Bandura's conception of "intrinsic motivation" as little more than "self-praise" seems empty compared to the fullness of Deci's and Ryan's (1985) view of the same concept. They see "intrinsic motivation" in terms of self-determination and striving for competence. In so doing they provide a link to an extra-social-learning area, humanism, which is absent from Bandura's notions.

Tudge and Winterhoff (1993) charge Bandura with not doing justice to his theory: They claim that the full range of the theory, in all of its complexity, has not been investigated. But these critics do not defend their allegations well. Nevertheless, there is an aspect of social cognitive theory that has been relatively neglected, moral functioning. An article by Bandura (1991b) on "moral thought and acts" reveals that he and his colleagues have done relatively little by way of research on this important segment of social cognitive theory. Researchers outside Bandura's camp have done even less. Most of the self-exonerative processes have not been investigated and those that have were studied years ago (Bandura, 1991b). Because literally millions and millions of people have died this century alone through justifications allowed by self-exonerative processes, much more research attention to moral thinking is needed.

Conclusions

The breadth of social cognitive theory is certainly not entirely illusory. The theory makes powerful predictions and generates useful applications in a large number of arenas for human behavior. You have already seen how the theory suggested techniques that, in a matter of hours, eliminated phobias that had plagued individuals for years. Further, it is reasonable to argue that social cognitive theory has more research support and greater practical applicability than most, or possibly all, theories covered in this book.

Social cognitive theory also has filled a void in other learning theories. It alone systematically accounts for the fact that humans can learn simply by observing. More generally, the theory can explain many differences between humans and lower animals, especially in the area of learning, differences that other theories have ignored or failed to explain.

Social cognitive theory is on the cutting edge of the cognitive movement in psychology. As such it represents an orientation that will guarantee continued growth in psychology's scientific prominence. Decades from now, when the contributions of cognitive psychology are reviewed, the name Albert Bandura will be spoken and written many times. By then Bandura's cognitive social theory may make some of the theories reviewed in this and other books seem like historical curiosities.

Summary Points

1. Bandura, Canadian-born and bred, was educated in the best tradition of the country school: few teachers and facilities led to much individual initiative. After graduation, he worked in the forbidding Yukon where he encountered fellow workers so unusual as to stimulate an interest in psychology. Following undergraduate work, he enrolled at the University of Iowa where he came under the spell of learning psychologist Kenneth Spence. On completion of his doctorate he was hired at Stanford, where he remains today.
2. At Stanford, Bandura was influenced by Robert Sears, but his unique contributions began with his and Walters' work on observational learning showing that "modeling is not merely a process of behavioral mimicry." His cognitive social theory acknowledges both the variability and the stability of behavior. It holds that person factors—including biological

ones—behavior, and the external environment reciprocally influence one another. To Bandura, learning is difficult or impossible without awareness, especially in the form of "forethought." A model performs some behavior for an audience. "Modeling" refers to the act of performing a behavior before an audience. People learn vicariously from a model.

3. People take information from models, "turn it over" in their minds, and put it into symbolic form. Symbolic modeling can also occur. Then they hone and sharpen what they have learned, translate it into behavior, and compare their performance with an internal representation. Rewards play a role in defining incentives for future performance learned from models and as benefits bestowed by models for good performance. Self-reward is also a factor. Goals are vitally important to productive human behavior. However, their attainment is uncertain without the institution of self-regulatory processes. Defensive behaviors are adopted in order to cope with anticipated unpleasant events. Self-efficacy may be thought of as a specific form of confidence that influences not only whether a person will attempt a behavior, but also the quality of eventual performance. Doing is believing: Managing to perform a feared or repugnant behavior will likely boost self-efficacy.

4. In participant modeling a person performs some behavior in imitation of an efficacious model. In vicarious expectancy learning other people's expectancies concerning future events are adopted. In response facilitation old responses may be disinhibited. Diffusion of innovation occurs when prestigious models try something new and thereby display its benefits. Diffusion of an innovation is not likely to occur if self-efficacy regarding the innovation is not bolstered. Extrinsic rewards originate outside the person and intrinsic rewards come from within. Intrinsic motivation involves self-evaluation. Vicarious reinforcement occurs when one person observes another being rewarded for performing a behavior. Reward value is established by social comparison.

5. In a spider phobic study, after observation of a model, subjects in a medium efficacy condition exceeded the performance of low efficacy subjects. Low efficacy subjects were then raised to medium efficacy. Other research showed that self-evaluation produces positive effects only when self-efficacy is high. Another study dealt with snake phobics whose self-efficacy was enhanced through modeling, resulting in close contact with a snake and enhancement of the immune system.

6. In a study of other self-regulatory factors, subjects in a decision-making simulation managed five "employees." Those in an "acquirable skill" condition showed relatively enhanced self-efficacy, self-goals, and analytic strategies. In a similar study using the pursuit rotor task, only acquirable skills subjects did well. In a study of the open expression of self-regulatory processes, boys and girls tended to adhere to their assigned gender roles and used self-approval and self-criticism to do so.

7. Crime is generated in part by limited behavioral alternatives available to the poor and oppressed. When the incentives for crime are great, the effort required small, and the likelihood of negative outcomes small, individuals with few other alternatives will adopt criminal behavior. Most people cannot do evil to other humans unless they engage in self-exonerative processes in order to dissociate themselves from the consequences of their actions. Dehumanization is one of the mechanisms they can use. Others include advantageous comparison and euphemistic labeling.

8. Blaming victims for their own fate is also a common self-exonerative process as is displacement and diffusion of responsibility. Moral justification involves invoking religious or

other moral bases to support one's inhuman behavior. In gradualistic moral disengagement people slowly slip unawares into what was normally unacceptable behavior. However, cognitive processes may also allow self-sacrifice and altruism. Through the process of self-evaluation, people like Mother Teresa, Martin Luther King, and Susan B. Anthony risk life and security for the sake of human rights.

9. Unfortunately self-exonerative processes are being used to justify violence against women. Men who assault women resort to blaming them for their own victimization, advantageous comparison, euphemistic labeling, moral justification, and dehumanization. Life for women, and men too, will not be fully human until these cognitive delusions are abandoned.

10. With all of its virtues, cognitive social theory can be faulted for having no clearly defined boundaries. So long as it remains without boundaries, it must explain an extraordinary diversity of phenomena and is open to providing explanations after the fact. Neglect of moral functioning is another problem. Still, the breadth of the theory is not entirely illusory. Further, it is reasonable to argue that social cognitive theory has greatest research support and greatest practical applicability. Decades from now social cognitive theory will make many other current theories seem like historical curiosities.

Running Comparison

Theorist	Bandura in Comparison
Mischel	Both deal with self-regulatory mechanisms, but neither is concerned with traits.
Rotter	Like Rotter, he is concerned with expectancies.
B. F. Skinner	He differs from Skinner in emphasizing anticipation of reward, rather than past history of reward.

Essay/Critical Thinking Questions

1. Can you cite an example, experienced by you directly or indirectly, in which a child learned aggressive acts without reinforcement or practice entering the learning sequence?

2. How might environmental conditions affect your neurobiology differently than illustrated by examples in the text?

3. If reinforcement or reward does enter the learning sequence at some point, at which two points in the sequence involving a model and an observer might it have the greatest facilitative impact on observers' likelihood of adopting modeled behavior?

4. The notion of "social comparison" has many implications. How does it play a role in friendship? Do you compare with friends? If so, how do you hope to come out in the comparison? What do the answers to these questions have to say about friendship and rivalry?

5. What examples of resilience can you cite from your own experience with people?

6. Can you cite examples of children's expressions of self-regulatory processes regarding gender-driven behavior?

7. Could you briefly design an experiment in which the self-efficacy and other relevant self-regulatory mechanisms of workers in a child mental health facility would be raised resulting in better care for the children? Hint: You could manipulate acquirability and attempt to raise self-goal setting along with self-efficacy.

8. How could you raise your self-efficacy with regard to performing exercise behaviors that have the potential of making you a healthier person?

9. Could you pick one of the self-exonerative processes and illustrate how it has led to undesirable social behavior on your part or on the part of someone you know well?

10. Supposedly, social cognitive theory has no boundaries and, thus, is too broad. In turn, its lack of boundaries forces it to address all kinds of phenomena. To counter this argument, could you use the theory to explain chronic anxiety or severe depression?

E-mail Interaction

(Contact the author at mfbpa@wiu.edu)
Forward one of the following or phrase your own.

1. Why do men beat women?
2. Tell me what to concentrate on in studying Bandura.
3. What is Bandura's status among psychologists today?
4. Who is the most resilient current public figure?
5. Should male and female gender roles be so different?

14

IT'S ALL A MATTER OF CONSEQUENCES: B. F. SKINNER

- Are the principles used to train animals relevant to understanding personality?
- Does environment determine behavior? Language? Creativity?
- Would you be willing to rear a baby in a box?
- Is it necessary to consider thoughts and feelings in attempts to understand people?
- Is one point of view sufficient to explain completely the psychological side of humans?

B. F. Skinner

The theories reviewed so far all have been concerned with "what is "inside," or a combination of "what is inside" and "what is outside." By contrast, **behaviorism** is a school of psychology for which the basic subject matter is "outside"; it is overt (observable) behavior. Consistent with the view of other scientists, behaviorists believe that the science of psychology should deal only with phenomena that can be verified by the senses. They eschew entities that are buried away in the "mind," such as private thoughts, feelings, expectations or motivations (Baum & Heath, 1992).

There are two types of behaviorists who differ from B. F. Skinner. They are the classic (before Skinner) and the methodological behaviorists (those who use behaviorists' methods but may depart from their assumptions). These two kinds of behaviorists have confined themselves to events that are currently observable—they focus on the here and now. Skinner developed a broader point of view, called **radical behaviorism**, which considers currently observable events and also potential, future events that can be observed and measured (Salzinger, 1990). Therefore, Skinner contemplated future environments that are arranged so that desirable behaviors are promoted. He believed we can design environments that select behaviors—pick some behaviors to be strengthened rather than others. In turn, selected behaviors are likely to be good for the people who behave as well as for others. This point of view may sound utopian. In fact it is. Skinner designed a utopian society when he wrote *Walden Two* (1948), a book about a community in which punishment is shunned and rewards guide people in the full exploitation of all their natural skills and characteristics. Skinner wished to make this a better world.

Skinner, The Person

Burrhus Frederic Skinner, born in 1904, spent his formative years in Susquehanna, Pennsylvania. Late in life, he remembered not being close to his parents and not being interested in pursuing the Protestant traditions of his family (Liptzin, 1994). He also remembered becoming intrigued with psychology at a very early age. As with most people, his first interest was in the more mystical psychological phenomena. While a third grader, he had an "extrasensory experience": He excitedly raised his hand to report that he had read a word just at the same moment his teacher spoke it. As an older child, he was fascinated by performing pigeons at a country fair, and during his college years he wrote a play on "glands that change personality" and a term paper analyzing Hamlet's madness. As a young man, Skinner recalled thinking about thinking while paddling a canoe. However, he later regretted his sojourn into "mentalism" (see Baum & Heath, 1992).

After having received his undergraduate degree in English from a small New York school, Hamilton College (1926), Skinner drifted for a while. He very much wanted to be a writer, even receiving encouragement from Robert Frost, but he settled for an ordinary job and ordinary daydreams. Then, as if he had stumbled onto the "truth," he discovered behaviorism from books by Bertrand Russell, a begrudging fan of early behaviorist John B. Watson, and H. G. Wells. Wells pondered what to do with a single life jacket if he were standing alone on a pier, with George Bernard Shaw floundering in the water on one side and Pavlov slowly disappearing from sight on the other (the reference was to I. P. Pavlov [1927] the famous Russian who taught dogs to salivate at the sound of a bell). The jacket was awarded to Pavlov—by implication, behaviorism—and so were Skinner's intellectual loyalties.

Soon thereafter, Skinner enrolled in the psychology graduate program at Harvard. During this period he spent some time in Greenwich Village, sampling the Bohemian lifestyle. There, in a nightclub, he noticed an attractive young woman, and, as was often the case when he found a woman interesting, he boldly introduced himself. When it was discovered that he was to be a psychology student, hypnotism became the topic. She professed a desire to be hypnotized and he accommodated her. It was an important experience for two reasons. It cemented his identity as a psychologist and it was the beginning of an affair.

Skinner took up residence with the woman and thereby revealed a willingness to defy danger: The woman was married and often received visits from her husband, who was away on military duty. This unsettling arrangement eventually led Skinner to decide that the lifestyle of Greenwich Village was not for him.

Other aspects of Skinner's personality are revealed in *Walden Two* (1948). It is no accident that a main character and obvious alter ego, "Professor Burris," is a straightforward, typical academic who resorts to his intellect rather than his emotions when trying to make sense of life. However, paradoxically, Skinner was capable of being frivolous and, on occasion, could even be the prankster. At his graduation ceremony, he delivered an oration in Latin that was designed to satirize the school administration. When a school official loudly queried "Why don't they bow when given a diploma?" Skinner made a point of bowing grandly upon receiving his diploma. The "cheap joke," as he put it, inspired laughter from the audience.

If one takes seriously what Skinner (1976b) says about Skinner, he has a personality that is difficult to pin down (Skinner, 1983a). Skinner himself has offered little help. In preparation for an earlier personality text by Charles Potkay and me, Potkay asked Skinner to complete a personality questionnaire. Skinner replied that he hated to be "crotchety," but he did not believe in such measures.

In addition, Skinner often played the iconoclast (Dinsmoor, 1992). He seized every opportunity to tweak the nose of the psychological establishment. For example, he was often accused by humanitarian and libertarian critics of devising fascist methods for the *control* of human behavior. Noticing that his critics blanched at the mention of the word "control," he used it often. This tactic also served to bait his adversaries. By going out of his way to *seem* to represent what they hated most, he "goaded" them into "ill-considered responses" to his sometimes inflammatory writings (Dinsmoor, 1992, p. 1458).

At the same time Skinner could be the breathlessly naive "discoverer" of nature's truths, similar to one of the child characters in a Steven Spielberg movie. Recounting his first observation of "extinction" (the disappearance of a learned response), Skinner (1979; also see Iversen, 1992) described how he, like other great scientists, made his momentous "discovery" by accident (for example, Marie and her husband, Pierre Curie, discovered nuclear radiation by accident). Once he left his lab after placing an animal in an apparatus that automatically delivered food when the animal pressed a lever. On returning, he found that an equipment failure had prevented food delivery. This fortunate mishap provided him with "the first" extinction graph. Gripped by scientific fervor, Skinner gushed, "All that weekend I crossed streets with particular care and avoided all unnecessary risks to protect my discovery from loss through my death" (Skinner, 1979, p. 95; also see Iversen, 1992).

Still, Skinner did not show a well-defined personality. That is, for every trait that can be inferred from his self-reports of behavior, he has also indicated behavior associated with the opposite trait. As a young man, Skinner was shy but outgoing, cautious but adventurous, intellectual yet sometimes quite silly. His personal life was rather conservative, but he occasionally violated sexual conventions. Perhaps it is all by design. It would not do for a person to have a clearly evident personality if he wishes to deny the existence of personality (Skinner, 1989). Despite these disclaimers, one can read a great deal about personality between the lines of Skinner's writings. Comparing his autobiography with his early scientific writings, one can see in both the "objectivity," concreteness, and emotional detachment that characterized him (Demorest & Siegel, 1996). In any case, Skinner has proven that a person can be interesting, even if he does not clearly manifest a large number of consistent traits.

Skinner was perhaps the most decorated of modern psychologists. He was one of the few psychologists elected to the scientists' "hall of fame," the National Academy of Sciences. He also received the Warren Medal from the Society of Experimental Psychologists (1942), the Gold Medal for Distinguished Scientific Contributions from the American Psychological Association (1958), and the National Medal of Science. In 1990 he received both the American Psychological Society's William James Fellow Award and the American Psychological Association's Presidential Citation for Lifetime Contributions to Psychology (Salzinger, 1990). After a long bout with illness, Skinner died on August 18, 1990 near the Harvard facilities where he did much of his research and writing.

Skinner's View of the Person

Environmentalism: The Importance of Consequences

Skinner (1972g) rejects the repeated accusation that he is an "S-R," or stimulus-response, psychologist (Iversen, 1992; Salzinger, 1990). According to the S-R conception, a stimulus in the environment, such as "the door within the door" that constitutes the dog's entrance into the house, absolutely demands a response from the dog—namely, entering the house. Not so, says Skinner. The dog's door sets the occasion for the response "enter," but it does so with some probability, not absolutely (Moxley, 1992). Further, to understand behavior, a dog's or a person's, one needs a concept that is missing from the S-R account. A **consequence** is an event that occurs after a response has been performed and changes the probability that the response will occur again. For the dog, gaining entrance to the house is the consequence that will increase the likelihood it will poke its nose through its door in the future. "Consequences" are so central to Skinner's point of view that it is in the title of one autobiographical volume (Skinner, 1983b).

While not an S-R psychologist, Skinner stands "guilty" of the charge of being an environmentalist (Skinner, 1983a). For him (1971), the environment controls everything, but, as you will see, is itself subject to control. He often referred to parallels between the environment–behavior relationship and "natural selection," the process developed by Charles Darwin to explain how humans and other animals evolved to their present state (Salzinger, 1990).

Natural selection can be illustrated by example. In Costa Rica, on a mountain top near the Poas volcano, there exists a certain flower with a curved stem and a deep recess formed at the base of its petals and extending into its stem. When a species of hummingbird took up residence on the mountaintop, only a few mutants among them had beaks that were sufficiently long and curved to dip into the flowers' stems far enough to reach its valuable contents. These oddities were the birds that survived, propagated, and prospered on the mountaintop. The environment, specifically the flower type, selected for survival those birds with the "right" shaped beaks allowing them to successfully perform the flower–stem insertion-response.

Likewise, humans over thousands of generations have become able to effectively perform certain behaviors. The environment has selected certain human physical characteristics, such as agile fingers and hands, because these traits permit the performance of critical behaviors that have survival value. Certain European people have among them men with very stout thighs and calves. These characteristics may have been selected for pushing a primitive plow in early agricultural times. Thus, the environment selects physical traits that permit behaviors having survival-promoting consequences, such as the provision of food. Survival, in turn, allows reproduction and, thereby, propagation of the genes controlling the traits.

Further, Skinner points to individual differences in the kinds of consequences that are likely to generate behavior (Skinner, 1948). Only some people are genetically disposed to effectively build novel objects from available materials. These people are likely to emit many responses that involve construction. Because typical environments provide numerous important consequences of such responses (provision of a house for escaping the weather), chances are that "building" behavior will often be selected and will increase in likelihood.

However, Skinner emphasizes that genetic input, determined by the environment through natural selection, predisposes individuals to certain behaviors rather than others, but it only defines the potential for behavioral development. The particular environment into which each of us is born determines our own peculiar repertoire of behaviors. An individual born with artistic potential will show artistic behaviors only if the opportunities relating to artistic acts are available in her or his particular environment (Skinner, 1972c). An environment cannot select artistic behaviors if it does not provide important consequences for such behavior. In sum, the actual behaviors a person develops depend on the characteristics of his or her environment.

"Beyond Freedom and Dignity"

If a stimulus has some probability of giving rise to a response, if genetic disposition defines the potential for behavioral development, and if our particular environments determine the actual behaviors we will develop, we are all slaves to our environments. That is, we lack freedom (Skinner, 1948, 1971, 1983a; Dinsmoor, 1992). According to Skinner, **freedom** refers to our belief that we can choose from various behaviors, rather than having our actions controlled by the environment (Skinner, 1972f). Obviously, Skinner does not accept the belief that he attributes to us. To him, it is a fact that we are controlled by the environment (1983a, 1983b, 1989). To deny environmental control is to risk being controlled by subtle and malignant circumstances and by malicious people (Dinsmoor, 1992). Governments and particular people sometimes control human beings for the benefit of the controller, not those controlled (Skinner, 1987a). Often we do not detect the harm done to us by this control, because there may be immediate positive consequences, while negative consequences are deferred until a later time. For example, we may stand aside while our government is lax in regulating the level of pollutants that are allowed to escape into our waterways and air. We fail to react because "jobs are preserved" and "the economy is stimulated"—immediate, positive benefits for us all. However, we should realize that this leniency in regulating pollutants has negative consequences in the long run (Skinner, 1983a).

Skinner (1971) asked, why not decide for ourselves what will determine our behaviors? The alternative is to leave the control of behavior up to chance, or worse, leave it up to people who would control us for their own gains. Radical behaviorism is well illustrated by the belief that we can create control of our behavior by manipulating our environments to increase the likelihood of beneficial consequences (Salzinger, 1990). We are not autonomous, but we can gain a measure of autonomy by changing aspects of our environments that relate to desired consequences. When we demand freedom, what we really mean is freedom from negative or aversive consequences and access to positive consequences (Dinsmoor, 1992). We can have that freedom only by arranging our own consequences, not by assuming we can control our behavior directly or by leaving consequences to "government" or "fate." Thus, Skinner does concede that we have freedom, but in a highly qualified sense. We can arrange our environment so that the consequences we desire become likely, but having done so, we are under the control of our creation (Skinner, 1983).

This conception of "freedom" and the qualifications of it make critics of radical behaviorism wrong when they charge that Skinner wanted to impose coercive control over human behavior (Dinsmoor, 1992). Skinner wished to eliminate the aversive techniques of control

BOX 14.1   Descriptive Words Once Referred to Behavior, but No More

Among the threats to his position that have bedev-iled Skinner throughout his career is **mentalism**, the belief that thoughts and feelings determine behav-ior, not external consequences (Skinner, 1983b; Baum & Heath, 1992). More recently he has lamented the birth and development of the "cogni-tive revolution," a movement that stresses the im-portance of thinking processes in determining behavior (Skinner, 1989).

Many of the words that we use seem to support the cognitive orientation in that they refer to inter-nal conditions. Our language is replete with words that refer to thoughts or states of mind: *experience, attitude, comprehension, need, will, worry,* and *inten-tion.* Nevertheless, Skinner (1989) believed that these terms originally referred to behavior, not inter-nal conditions. In earlier times, people were more behavioristic, but something happened between then and now to change that orientation. Partly be-cause people like to take credit for what they do and partly because people are unable to see the often subtle consequences of their behaviors, the meanings of words changed. One of the mechanisms by which these terms became converted into mentalistic words relates to the observation that feelings and thoughts occur after or at about the same time as be-haviors. However, rather than cause behaviors, these clearly evident thoughts and feelings are mistaken for causes because of their close proximity to behav-ior. The real "causes," consequences of behavior, are less often evident and frequently less proximal.

"*Experience* is a good example. . . . the word was not used to refer to anything felt or introspectively observed until the nineteenth century. Before that time, it meant, quite literally, something a person had 'gone through' (from the Latin *expiriri*). . . ." (Skinner, 1989, p.13). Skinner provides many other examples. *Intention* came from the Latin word *ten-dere* and originally meant to physically stretch or ex-tend, a reference to behavior. *Image*, which we now take to mean an internal copy of something, origi-nally meant a colored sculpture of a head and shoul-ders—from the Latin word *imago*. Later it meant "ghost" but in neither case was it something inside the head. The words *anxious* and *worry* originally meant choke as in "the dog worries the rat that it caught" (p. 15). *Aware* once meant to be cautious, to *comprehend* meant to seize or to grasp and to *solve* used to mean to dissolve, as sugar is dissolved in water.

Consistent with his beliefs, the terms he used when he wrote or spoke in public referred to behav-ior. Even when caught "off stage" Skinner could be the behaviorist he recommended that everyone should be. When my wife and I encountered him outside the site of a psychological convention, we could not resist introducing ourselves. Skinner re-sponded simply, "I'm waiting for friends." He made reference to what he was doing, not to anything he might have been thinking or feeling.

---

favored by despots. In the place of these totalitarian methods he would substitute control by positive consequences that may be arranged by those desiring benevolent control.

Aside from arranging for positive consequences, there is another sense in which we have freedom, one apparently not recognized by Skinner. In a sense, we choose the specific form of response that is followed by a given consequence (Rockwell, 1994). We can experi-ence the consequence "praise" by helping carry packages, donating to charity, or beating up a bully. If the counter is "we didn't choose; our reinforcement histories or genes made us do it the particular way we did it," the reply is "we arranged our environments to make us do it the particular way we did it."

While some measure of freedom can be achieved, dignity is unobtainable. "We recog-nize a person's **dignity** or worth when we give him *credit* for what he has done" (emphasis added; Skinner, 1971, p. 58). When, in our everyday lives, we cannot readily identify the consequences that control an individual's behavior, we attribute the behavior to the individual, rather than to the environment. Thus, when a person makes an anonymous donation to a worthy cause, we assume it was done because of something inside the person, called altruism. In so doing, we ignore the consequences in the person's early environment that have determined his or her behavior. For example, the person may have been exposed to a culture that "honors" (consequence) selfless giving. To credit people when they "do good" is to ignore the consequences that gave rise to "doing good" (Skinner, 1983a). Skinner (1971) suggests that we should identify those consequences and bring them under control so that more people can "do good" more often. To accept his suggestion is to give up taking credit for what we do, to give up "dignity." In return, he assures us that crediting the environment instead of ourselves will lead us to seek out some benevolent consequences that control behavior. The net result of that search will be a behavioral technology that will ensure "doing good" is a frequent occurrence and "doing bad" a rarity.

Attributing the "personality trait" altruism to another person when she or he behaves generously, while we ignore environmental determinants, is called the "fundamental attribution error" (Hineline, 1992). But we do not tend to make this error when attributing a cause to our own behavior. Typically we say our own behavior is "caused" by something in the environment. When we do, we show that we can appreciate environmental determinism (Allen, 1990).

Skinner practices what he preaches. In *Walden Two* (1948), his main character, Frazier, who designed the utopia described in the book, repeatedly denies that people are to be credited with what they do. Skinner himself once ended a speech with the following:

> *And now my labor is over. I have had my lecture. I have no sense of fatherhood. If my genetic and personal histories had been different, I should have come into possession of a different lecture. If I deserve any credit at all, it is simply for having served as a place in which certain processes could take place. I shall interpret your polite applause in that light (Skinner, 1972g).*

Basic Concepts: Skinner

Skinner claims not to have a theory (Skinner, 1983a), and is viewed by some people as antitheory (Kendler, 1988; Rockwell, 1994). Others felt he was only opposed to some theories, particularly those proposing mental entities (Schlinger, 1992) and that he actually looked forward to the emergence of a behavior theory based on careful observation (Chiesa, 1992). In any case, Skinner's point of view has all the trappings of a theory, including numerous concepts. Here only part of Skinner's position will be considered, the part that is most relevant to personality.

Operant Conditioning

Skinner's approach to psychology focuses on the kind of conditioning that many psychologists call "instrumental" (see Kimble, 1961). Skinner's term is **operant conditioning**, a process by which an organism operates on its environment with consequences that influence the likelihood that the operation, or behavior, will be repeated. The behavior that constitutes the operation on the environment is often called an *operant* (Lee, 1992). Because "respondent conditioning," Skinner's equivalent to the kind of conditioning done by Pavlov, is of less importance to the study of personality, it is not covered here.

Contingent is a close second to *consequence* as the key word in Skinnerian terminology. If event B is **contingent** on event A, the occurrence of B depends upon the prior occurrence of A (Holland & Skinner, 1961; Lee, 1992). If the singing of birds is contingent on the rising of the sun, the occurrence of singing depends on the prior appearance of the sun. In *operant conditioning*, consequences are contingent on the prior performance of some response, often a very discrete and concrete behavior, such as the "handshake" of a trained dog. Three kinds of consequences can be involved in operant conditioning: positive reinforcement, negative reinforcement, and punishment.

Positive Reinforcement

Reinforcement occurs when some event is contingent on the prior performance of some response and the response changes in likelihood of occurrence on future occasions. "Reinforcer" is a term often used in reference to a stimulus that is presented (event) as a consequence of a response. **Positive reinforcement** is a process whereby some event, usually a stimulus, *increases the likelihood* of a response on which its presentation is contingent. Food is a positive reinforcer. When a baby's crying responses produce its parent with food in hand, crying becomes more likely in the future. It is easy to see why the word *reinforcement* was chosen. *Reinforce* generally means "strengthen," and the occurrence of an event that *positively* reinforces a response strengthens it, in the sense of increasing its likelihood of being repeated.

Skinner (1983a) often placed a pigeon in a cage that bears the technical name "free-operant chamber," but has become popularly known as the *Skinner Box*. As Figure 14.1 reveals, it looks like any other cage for housing animals, except that it has a panel that the pigeon can peck (A). Pecking the panel activates a food magazine (B) that releases grain down a tube (C) into a cup (D) inside the cage. In the simplest case, every peck of the panel is followed by the presentation of some grain. That is, the response "panel peck" is followed by reinforcement in the form of grain. If the animal is a rat the device triggering the magazine is a lever. That different devices are used with different animals is consistent with the contention that Skinner acknowledged differences among species (Todd & Morris, 1992).

Notice the kind of response that occurs in operant conditioning. Unlike sweating or change of heart rate, operant responses are not automatic. The kind of response that occurs in operant conditioning is initiated by the animal, rather than occurring automatically. The pigeon can peck many times, or none at all. It can peck forcefully or softly. Further, it is the pigeon that gets things going in operant conditioning. Nothing happens until the pigeon starts pecking the panel, and it must perform the response itself.

Operant conditioning often begins when an animal starts responding more or less at random. A pigeon pecks quite a lot, for no apparent reason. Placed in a Skinner Box, it will peck all around, eventually peck the panel, and grain will come down the tube into the cup. The pigeon will eat the grain and then wander around some more. Sooner or later, it will peck the panel again, with the same result as before. If one watches closely, it is evident that

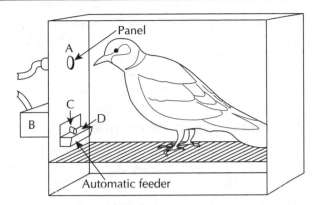

FIGURE 14.1   Skinner Box: pigeon pecks A, which activates food magazine at B, causing food to be delivered through tube C to cup D.

the time between pecks becomes less and less, until the pigeon is pecking at a fairly high rate. When the **rate of responding** becomes stable, conditioning is said to have been completed and a new response acquired. Rate of responding is also an index of *strength of conditioning*. In general, the higher the rate, the stronger the conditioning. **Extinction** occurs when a previously reinforced response is no longer followed by the same reinforcement and the response eventually decreases in frequency (Iversen, 1992).

Operantly conditioning more complex responses than panel pecks requires special procedures. Suppose one wishes to teach a dog to turn in a circle. It will be necessary to use **shaping**, a process by which natural variability in behavior is exploited so that a new behavior is acquired by reinforcing *successive approximations* to it (Epstein, 1991; Iversen, 1992). A *hungry* dog will often turn right and left in seemingly random fashion as it anxiously waits to be fed (note that animals are primed for operant conditioning if they have been deprived of a reinforcer). When it makes a pronounced turn to the right (or left), *give it a bit of food* (reinforcement). Wait for an even more pronounced turn in the same direction—a closer approximation—before providing more food. By reinforcing more and more complete turns—successive approximation—a full turn will soon be shaped. In shaping turning, it is usually best to allow the dog to initiate turns. However, some dogs may need *prompting:* They may have to be coaxed into performing at least an approximation of the desired response (Skinner, 1983b).

Positive reinforcement occurs every day in the life of every person, including a typical college student. Events occur during a student's day that include behaviors that have been reinforced many times in the past. At noon, the student makes his way to the cafeteria in his dorm, where he presents his student ID, picks up a tray, and fills it with food. These behaviors are positively reinforced by the food, although, admittedly, positive reinforcement may occur infrequently in some college cafeterias. The student proceeds to class, where his "class attendance" behavior is reinforced, as usual, by the stimulating lecture emanating from one of his several outstanding professors. Next, the student retires to the library for an afternoon of study, the reinforcement for which will be partially delayed until test day. For now, studying is followed by a rather abstract reinforcement, "the joy of learning." Leaving the library, the student reports to work where it happens to be payday. His work on that day, and several preceding it, is reinforced with a paycheck.

Negative Reinforcement and Punishment

Positive reinforcement is not the only means by which behaviors are learned. **Negative reinforcement** is a process whereby the likelihood of a response *increases* when it is followed by the *termination, reduction,* or *absence* of a stimulus (Holland & Skinner, 1961). Negative reinforcement involves aversive stimuli, such as electric shock. Such stimuli are called negative reinforcers. Behaviors that lead to success in escaping (terminating) or avoiding (ensuring the absence of) negative reinforcers will increase in probability of occurrence in the future.

Escape and avoidance behavior are illustrated by use of a shuttle box, as depicted in Figure 14.2. The box, actually a cage, has an electric grid floor and a partition down the middle. The animal is placed in the box on one side of the partition, and uncomfortable but not harmful electricity is activated on that side only. The animal *escapes* by simply jumping to the side without shock. The jump is reinforced by the termination of the shock.

Avoidance learning becomes possible when a light is placed at each end of the box (see Figure 14.2). First, the animal learns to escape. Then, the light on the side containing the animal is illuminated a short time before the shock is activated. At first, the light seems to have no influence on behavior. However, after a number of presentations of the light followed by the shock, the animal will begin to jump when the light is illuminated, before the shock is delivered, thereby avoiding it.

In the case of **punishment**, responses that are followed by the *presentation* of aversive stimuli *decrease* in likelihood of being performed in the future (Skinner, 1971). (This process

FIGURE 14.2   A top view of the shuttle box.

is technically known as *positive punishment*. *Negative punishment* is omission of a positive reinforcer following the performance of a response.) Punishment stands in sharp contrast to negative reinforcement, where responses *increase* in likelihood when followed by *the absence* (or *termination* or *reduction*) of aversive stimulation. If studying avoids housework, parents are using negative reinforcement to increase studying. If a child's hand is spanked for getting into the cookie jar, punishment is being used to decrease pilfering of cookies.

Skinner had long maintained that the aversive control technique "punishment" is not an efficient way to control behavior (Skinner, 1948). He (1971) argued that punishment may lead to only temporary suppression of a behavior that is not desired by the punishing agent. An organism may inhibit an undesirable behavior until the punishing agent is no longer present. Then the behavior may be performed at a high rate, making up for responses that were suppressed when the punishing agent was present. In addition, punishment may be accompanied by such unfortunate side effects as fear, anxiety, aggression, failure to perform beneficial responses, and, in humans, loss of self-esteem, confidence, and initiative.

As with positive reinforcement, it is easy to recognize many everyday examples of negative reinforcement and punishment. Some students avoid class the day after a test when grades are posted. Their behavior is reinforced by the absence of bad news about their test performance. Sometimes students fall asleep in class. Professors occasionally punish this behavior by a rude awakening.

Table 14.1 presents the various kinds of reinforcement so you can compare them at a glance.

Schedules of Reinforcement

To this point it has been assumed that every response an organism makes is reinforced. It is easy to recognize that such is often not the case in reality. Also it may be apparent that reinforcing every response, **continuous reinforcement**, is not even the most efficient way to proceed.

Suppose every time you make a comment in class, your behavior is reinforced by high praise from your professor. Your rate of responding would probably be rather low and not very persistent ("Ho hum, here comes another soft fuzzy from the professor"). However, assume that the professor praises only some of your comments. Your rate of making com-

TABLE 14.1   Varieties of Reinforcement

Reinforcement occurs when some event is contingent on the prior performance of some response and the response changes in likelihood of occurrence on future occasions.

Positive reinforcement is a process whereby some event, usually a stimulus, *increases the likelihood* of a response on which its presentation is contingent.

Extinction occurs when a previously reinforced response is no longer followed by the same reinforcement and the response eventually decreases in frequency (non-reinforcement).

Negative reinforcement is a process whereby the likelihood of a response *increases* when it is followed by the *termination, reduction,* or *absence* of a stimulus.

Punishment is a process whereby responses that are followed by the *presentation* of aversive stimuli show a *decrease* in likelihood of being performed in the future.

ments would likely become much greater than in the previous example, and would likely be highly persistent. You would persist at a high rate because, rather than being continuously reinforced, your behavior would be subject to **intermittent reinforcement**, where responses are reinforced every so often, or after some number of responses has occurred (Holland & Skinner, 1961).

As a general rule, intermittently reinforced responses are performed at a higher rate and are more resistant to extinction than continuously reinforced responses. Thus, intermittent reinforcement generates *stronger conditioning* or learning. For this reason it is of more practical importance than continuous reinforcement. (Note, however, that a response is more easily acquired with continuous reinforcement.)

A **schedule of reinforcement** determines whether reinforcement is to be delivered either every so often or after some number of responses has occurred (Holland & Skinner, 1961; Hayes & Hayes, 1992). Some schedules are based on the *amount of time* since the last reinforcement, while others are founded on the *number of responses* performed since the last reinforced response.

In the case of a **temporal schedule** there must be an elapse of some amount of time between one reinforced response and the next. With a **ratio schedule** some number of responses must be performed between one reinforced response and the next. These two kinds of schedules can each be fixed or variable.

Fixed Schedules of Reinforcement

In a **fixed schedule**, a response is reinforced after a constant amount of time has elapsed or after a constant number of responses have been performed. In the **fixed-interval (FI) schedule**, the amount of time between one reinforced response and the next is constant (Holland & Skinner, 1961). It may be 25 seconds or 5 seconds, but it is always the same, or fixed.

Figure 14.3 provides a record of behavior that is reinforced on a fixed-interval schedule. The graph in this figure and in Figures 14.4, 14.5, and 14.6 are called **cumulative records**, responses are accumulated and plotted against time (Holland & Skinner, 1961). The cumulative records shown here all assume that learning has already occurred.

Notice that the record for the fixed-interval schedule (Figure 14.3) looks a little like a bunch of scallops, all interconnected. The organism begins responding slowly at the point in time labeled 0. Because reinforcement does not occur until point in time P, the animal is in no hurry to produce responses. However, as the time for a response to be reinforced draws near, the rate of responding increases, as indicated by the steeper curve near the hatch mark at point P. When point P is reached, reinforcement occurs, and assuming it is food, the organism stops to eat. Then it begins responding slowly once again. This pattern of responding generates the scallops.

For some students, studying is on a fixed-interval schedule. Just after a test, the rate of studying is near zero. Then, as the time for another test approaches, studying is performed at a higher and higher rate, until a very steep curve occurs the night before the test, which is close to the time students are sometimes reinforced by high grades. After the test, these students pause (often over refreshment), savoring their reinforcement (assuming they are aware of having done well). Then the same old scallops begin again.

In a **fixed-ratio (FR) schedule** the number of responses occurring between one reinforced response and the next is constant. For example, on an FR(5) schedule, every fifth re-

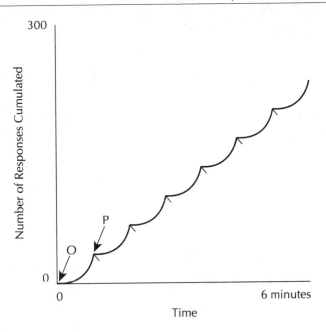

FIGURE 14.3   **Cumulative record for a fixed-interval schedule (hatch marks indicate reinforcement).**

sponse is reinforced. As Figure 14.4 indicates, an FR schedule generates a record that looks like stair steps. The organism responds at a high and steady rate until reinforcement occurs, then it pauses for a moment. The pay of farm workers is sometimes on an FR schedule. Every so many bags of vegetables collected yields some predetermined amount of money.

Variable Schedules of Reinforcement

Variable schedules are more frequently encountered in real life. In a **variable schedule** reinforcement is delivered after some X amount of time has elapsed, *on average*, or after some Y number of responses have been performed, *on average*. That is, instead of a response being reinforced after exactly X units of time have elapsed, or after exactly Y number of responses have been performed, it occurs after X units, on average, or after Y responses, on average.

A **variable-interval (VI) schedule** requires that a given amount of time elapses between one reinforced response and the next, on the average. On a VI(5 seconds) schedule, sometimes the organism waits only 1 second before a response is reinforced; at other times, it waits 9 seconds; occasionally, it waits exactly 5 seconds. Overall, the intervals average out to a 5-second wait.

Note that the record for the VI schedule, depicted in Figure 14.5, is more irregular than its fixed-interval counterpart, shown in Figure 14.3. Also, notice that the curve is steeper

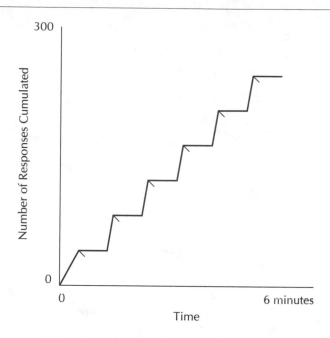

FIGURE 14.4   Cumulative record for a fixed-ratio schedule (hatch marks indicate reinforcement).

than for the fixed interval. That is, the curve goes up at an angle that is closer to 90 degrees than is the curve for a fixed-interval schedule. The steeper curve is indicative of a higher rate of responding. A moment of thought will reveal why variable schedules tend to generate higher rates of responding than fixed schedules. If a pigeon cannot anticipate exactly when a reinforcement is going to be delivered, it pecks away rapidly. After all, a response may be reinforced only a second after the last reinforcement. People act the same way. Not knowing when reinforcement will be delivered, people leave little time between responses, because only moments later a response might be reinforced. Contrast this situation with that of a fixed schedule. If one knows for sure that it is going to be 1 minute until a reinforcer is delivered, why work hard responding? Why not start responding in earnest about the time a response will be reinforced?

Variable schedules are also more resistant to extinction than fixed schedules. During extinction, reinforcement never occurs. However, organisms that have been on a variable schedule will continue to respond because past experience makes them used to long periods with no reinforcement. Higher rates of responding and greater resistance to extinction add up to stronger conditioning than fixed schedules.

Fishing seems to provide a real-life example of VI scheduling. As any person who fishes can tell you, there may be an hour between the initial cast and the one that lands the first fish, but, minutes later, a cast may land another fish. However, the next cast that lands a fish may come two hours later. It may average out so that a cast is reinforced after a forty-

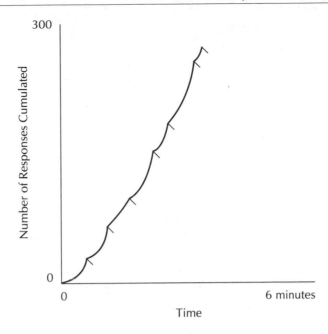

FIGURE 14.5 **Cumulative record for a variable-interval schedule (hatch marks indicate reinforcement).**

five minute wait. Consequently, fishing behavior may be quite resistant to extinction despite relatively long periods without reinforcement.

A **variable-ratio (VR) schedule** requires that, on the average, a given number of responses be performed before a response is reinforced. As a general rule, a variable-ratio schedule will generate the highest rate of responding and the strongest resistance to extinction (see Figure 14.6). A VR(10) schedule designates a procedure by which every 10th response is reinforced, on the average. Sometimes the organism must respond 19 times before the reinforcer is delivered; sometimes, 1 response is sufficient. The schedule averages out to reinforcement after 10 responses.

Shooting basketballs is on a VR schedule, as is selling merchandise, but the clearest example is gambling. A person diligently working at a slot machine does not experience reinforcement after a fixed number of coins are placed in the slot. Nor does reinforcement occur on a per-unit-of-time basis. Rather, on the average, every so many responses of placing a coin in the slot is followed by reinforcement—the machine yielding up some of its monetary contents. Casual observation in casinos confirms that gambling behavior is highly resistant to extinction. Interestingly, such schedules, for as yet unknown reasons, tend to be addictive for certain personalities.

To sum up, schedules of reinforcement determine delivery of reinforcement based on the amount of time that has lapsed since the last reinforced response, or on the number of responses since the last reinforced response. A fixed schedule requires that an exact amount

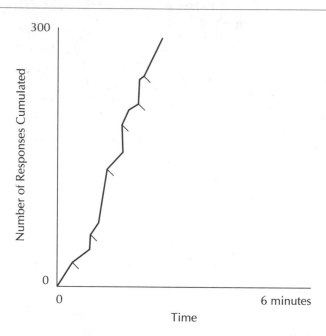

**FIGURE 14.6   Cumulative record for a variable-
ratio schedule (hatch marks
indicate reinforcement).**

of time must elapse or an exact number of responses must be performed before reinforcement is delivered. With variable schedules, the amount of time or the number of responses
required for reinforcement to occur is not exact, but variable. On the average, X elapse of
time or Y number of responses is required for reinforcement to occur. As a rule, variable
schedules generate higher rates of responding and greater resistance to extinction.

The Development of Humans: Language, Personality, and Child-Rearing

Although Skinner rejects "personality," his responses to questions about how behavior is acquired relate to the concept. In this section, Skinner's ideas for the design and construction
of personality are examined along with his explanation of language learning and some of his
notions about rearing children.

Development of Speech

A central part of child-rearing and child development is the role the family plays in language learning. Skinner (1957, 1972e) contends that learning to use words orally is a relatively simple matter. When a child of age two is confronted with the stimulus "red light"
and utters the word "red," he is reinforced by the "verbal community" (Mom, Dad, and sib-

lings) with everything from praise to candy. When the child puts two words together, for example, "That red," he is reinforced by the same verbal community. Correct insertion of a verb ("That is red") is reinforced in a similar way, leading to the use of complete sentences that are grammatically correct. To put it more technically, use of oral language is learned by a process involving the formation of contingencies between verbal responses and reinforcements delivered by the verbal community. So-called "rules of language" are learned by the same principles as single words are learned. If the child says "I am five years old" instead of "I are five years old," praise by Mom and Dad will follow (Skinner, 1976a). Thus, in Skinner's view, the acquisition of language in children can be explained by reference to operant conditioning.

As soon as Skinner's book on language learning appeared (Skinner, 1957) multiple critics raised objections to it. The most notable were offered by now famous linguistic scientist, Noam Chomsky (1959). Chomsky proposed the existence of an innate, genetically programmed "language faculty" able to account for the explosive rate at which young children learn language (Palmer & Donahoe, 1992). He reasoned that the abrupt and rapid verbal learning displayed by young children cannot be explained by plodding, step-by-step operant conditioning. Children are supposedly preset at birth to appreciate grammatical rules that allow them to acquire language in leaps and bounds. Evidence for this point of view comes not only from the exceedingly rapid language acquisition rate, but also from observations of children's speech errors. Suppose a child errs in saying "Look, the deers are running across the road." Her comment both indicates knowledge of the rule for forming the plural and, because an error has been made, that she could not have acquired the rule through reinforcement (parents do not reinforce incorrect speech).

While initially Skinnerians seemed unable to handle Chomsky's challenge, modern radical behaviorists are fighting back, partly by finding flaws in the "language faculty." They have suggested that the language faculty is like the little person (homunculus) in an individual's brain who interprets all inputs through the senses (and in that little person is another who interprets for the first, and so on). Further, Palmer and Donahoe, (1992) argue that language inputs have to "already be segmented into phrases, words and parts of speech" for the language faculty to make its interpretations (p. 1351). So what good is it?

Many questions have been raised about the language faculty. For example, if it is inherited, who can trace the evolutionary history of its development? If it is inherited, who has even a clue as to the location of the relevant genes on human chromosomes? It seems that behaviorism is not unique in having trouble accounting for language acquisition.

Rather than being content in finding fault with Chomsky's view, modern behaviorists have begun to slightly revise behaviorism so that it more readily accommodates language acquisition (Hayes & Hayes, 1992). They are beginning to discuss such seemingly mentalistic notions as "stimulus equivalences" (for example, two words that are equivalent: *push* and *shove*). These equivalences seem to emerge spontaneously in the course of using language, rather than through the operations of a language faculty. In turn, equivalences give rise to rules (if *push* is equivalent to *shove*, they both belong to a class of words that refer to actions [verbs]). These slight deviations from orthodox Skinnerianism bode well for the future survival and prosperity of radical behaviorism.

BOX 14.2   Baby in a Box

Skinner has been controversial at least since his wartime attempts to use pigeons to guide missiles (Skinner, 1972d). However, nothing he has done has caused more comment than rearing his infant daughter Deborah in a box. The apparatus used to house the child has been described by Skinner (1972a), along with the behaviorist's rationale for the unusual procedure. He writes that his wife Eve decided it was time to apply science to the nursery, in the interest of saving labor—presumably her own. The first consideration, quite properly, was the physical and psychological well-being of the child. Deborah's living quarters were spacious, providing ample room for the child and her toys. The open area in front was normally covered by a removable pane of safety glass. The floor of the compartment was covered with a sheet that could be replaced instantly by means of a roller device. Also, the child wore only a diaper, but was kept quite comfortable with no clothes, as her "home" featured temperature and humidity control.

Unconfined by clothes, Deborah was free to move her limbs in any way she wished. Compared with some babies who are restrained by clothes, she joyously exercised with all her might. The result was the development of strong back, leg, and abdominal muscles. By-products of the exercise were unusual agility of the feet and excellent hand/foot coordination. Deborah often played for hours with toys suspended from the ceiling of the box. Manipulating a music maker with her feet, the baby was able to compose her own tunes, much to the amusement of the family.

Feeding and changing the child took only about one-and-a-half hours a day, but this was only a small portion of the time devoted to her. If she wanted to play, she was entertained in her habitat or removed for interaction with the family. Far from being neglected, Deborah was the center of attention. Neighborhood children were continually parading past the box for a chance to see and play with the "baby in the box." Instead of receiving less affection than children housed in the usual way, Deborah may have received more affection of higher quality. Freed from much of the drudgery associated with caretaking, her parents had more time for affection and a stronger inclination to display it.

Some of Skinner's techniques and "suggestions for a better society" were viewed by critics as mechanical and even tyrannical (Haney, 1990). Skinner himself was seen by some as a cold, unfeeling scientist. Putting his baby in apparent isolation only confirmed these perceptions of the famous behaviorist. In fact, Skinner was a warm and responsive father to Deborah and to his other daughter Julie. They often exchanged poems and touching notes. There are many examples of tenderness and concern for his daughters in the last volume of his autobiography (Skinner, 1983b). For example, when Debs, as he called Deborah, broke a leg on a ski trip to the Deux Alps, Skinner flew to Geneva and then drove to Grenoble under dangerous winter conditions so he could care for her. When she arrived home, being confined to crutches, she was understandably cranky. A day after being somewhat unpleasant, Deborah wrote her father the following note: "Dear Pop, How are things? This is just a note to tell you I love you. Love, Debs. P.S. & that I apologize for my poor behavior of yesterday . . ." (Skinner, 1983b, p. 234). A later note to Debs contains an astounding passage for a radical behaviorist to write: "I'm not embarrassed by any supposed shortcomings of yours or afraid you will prove to the world that I am a bad psychologist. Live your own life, not mine. Be yourself. I like your Self" (p. 235). Self psychologists of the Rogers mold may take note.

And how did Debs turn out? She became an accomplished and successful artist. Julie is a professor married to a professor.

Building a Personality

Skinner wastes no opportunity to dismiss personality from the realm of science. In Chapter 1 of *Beyond Freedom and Dignity* (1971), he mocks the notion of "disturbed personality" (pp. 8 and 16) and flatly states, "We do not need to try to discover what personalities, states of mind, feelings, traits of character . . . or the other perquisites of autonomous man really are in order to get on with scientific analysis of behavior" (p. 15). Yet in that book, and in *Walden Two* (1948), he subtly, and perhaps unwittingly, indicates that people do have personalities, at least in the sense of showing individual differences in behaviors that are relatively constant across time and situations.

In *Walden Two*, the person one might think would be given even less personality than Prof. Burris is "blessed" with a rich and full repertoire of behaviors that distinguish him from others. Frazier, the founder and leader of Walden Two, is an impulsive individual whose temper flares on many occasions. He shows a great deal of self-confidence, but seems rather vulnerable underneath all the bravado. At one point, Frazier bursts forth:

> *You think I'm conceited, aggressive, tactless, selfish. You're convinced that I'm completely insensitive to my effect upon others . . . You can't see in me any of the personal warmth or the straightforward natural strength which are responsible for the success of Walden Two. My motives are ulterior and devious, my emotions warped (pp. 236–237).*

It seems that the author who condemns personality provides excellent examples of "lots of" (Frazier) and "little" personality (Burris) in his only novel. In *Beyond Freedom and Dignity* (1971), not only is it implied that people have personality, but Skinner alludes to the possibility of developing and changing personality by design.

In commemoration of the year 1984 Skinner wrote a new episode in which a resurrected George Orwell (who wrote the futuristic book *1984*) seeks admittance to Walden Two (Skinner, 1987a). Burris and Frazier appear to be their same old selves, despite the elapse of considerable time. Thus, Skinner provides testimony to the stability of personality.

Whether or not one finds Skinner's attempt to dismiss internal entities (traits) convincing, it still must be granted that his notions implicitly include individual differences in behaviors that are constant across time and situations, the popular assumption underlying personality. If the relatively constant behaviors that signify personality can be changed through environmental intervention, it should also be possible to develop a personality by design.

In fact, Skinner wrote of "Creating the Creative Artist" (1972c). In that essay he implies that the predisposition for creating art may be inborn, but will not be manifested without the development of contingencies between artistic endeavor and reinforcement.

But what exactly is reinforcing in a work of art, such as a painting? It has been argued that the content of a painting is somehow rewarding in and of itself, "intrinsically rewarding." However, if one examines popular subjects for paintings, Skinner asserts, those objects with survival value predominate (Skinner, 1983a)—"extrinsically rewarding" objects). For example, the human hand, a form of great strength and capability, is a frequent subject. Pictures of food are also common in paintings. More abstract are portraits depicting family and loved ones, themes that have been associated with survival throughout the evolutionary history of humans. Paintings are reinforcing because of their content, but it is not some intrinsic value of a picture as such. Rather, the content, food and the human form, has value because of the evolutionary history of human beings and factors from the history of the particular artist. You may find these ideas reminiscent of Jung's beliefs.

During the lifetime of each artist, there are themes embedded in his or her works that especially appeal to people in the artist's community. When depicted on canvas, these themes result in a form of reinforcement that is familiar to us all, praise. Needless to say, the artist in question will represent in her or his works those themes that are repeatedly followed by reinforcement. Thus, the artist's own history of reinforcement, as well as the history of human beings, shapes her or his behavior when confronting the canvas.

However, creativity, in the sense of an idea that no one has ever had before, is an illusion (Skinner, 1972c). True, a successful artist does not merely copy the works of other artists, but does "copy" from her or his own experience. The resultant work of art may be unique in that no one has ever expressed the experience exactly as has our hypothetical artist. However, the work is not wholly original in that it represents an experience common to many people. Further, once an artist has arrived at a form of expression that is at least an unusual rendition of some experience, and therefore is reinforced, he or she is likely to repeat that expression throughout his or her career. To support this contention, Skinner points to Picasso. Supposedly, only the first of Picasso's paintings was not derivative. All the works that followed stemmed from the first effort.

How might a community encourage the pursuit of art in general, rather than just promoting a single artist? Skinner would supply a simple answer: mass exposure to art. Widespread display of art would help to develop artists in two ways. First, there would be an increase in the number of people who would appreciate art, and thus be able to reinforce artists with praise and attention to their works. Second, large-scale exposure to art would uncover most of those people who are genetically disposed to create works of art. You cannot produce great athletes in a society where sports are not played. If the opportunity to reinforce athletic prowess is not available, athletes will not develop, even though the genetic potential is present in members of the society. Proportional to population, the former East Germany won far more Olympic medals than any other country (in absolute numbers they were often second only to the former USSR). Skinner would explain this phenomenal success by reference to the interplay of genetics and reinforcement. Rather than simply working with the same material that other countries possess and doing a better job of developing it, East Germany thoroughly exploited excellent material by making athletic opportunities readily available and by constructing contingencies between athletic performance and reinforcement.

Remaining to be specified is the kind of society that would promote such development by design. On the surface, it might seem to be a society in which "talent scouts" go on frequent quests for those characteristics that are needed by the society. To the contrary, in *Walden Two* the greatest number and variety of pursuits and accompanying reinforcements imaginable are made available to all members of the community. People receive credits for the jobs they perform daily, and, with some flexibility, they have to earn a certain number of credits per week in order to continue in the community. In contrast to real societies, Walden Two offers the most credits for tasks that are tiresome, difficult, and uninteresting (for example, collecting garbage) and the fewest credits for tasks that are enjoyable and interesting (for example, giving a lecture on a favorite topic). Under this system, medical doctors of Walden Two might receive fewer credits per unit time than laborers. Therefore, doctors would have to work longer hours than laborers to earn the same number of credits.

BOX 14.3 Skinner on Diversity and Equality of Opportunity

Skinner showed concern for culture and cultural change (Pennypacker, 1992). Not surprisingly, he thought cultures develop according to operant principles. People find themselves in a physical environment that selects certain behaviors rather than others. For example, the behaviors—planting, cultivating, and harvesting papaya—may be selected in the case of certain people living in a particular environment where papaya grow. Out of these behaviors come others: by-products of papaya are used for decoration and rituals develop relating to farming papaya.

Cultural change can also be accounted for by behaviorism. Africans brought to the United States as slaves carried rich cultural traditions with them. These included food preferences and all that goes with them as well as methods of communication. Obviously some of these behaviors relating to food no longer were reinforced: The foods were not present in the United States. Rituals regarding these foods disappeared. Other cultural traditions, however, were associated with behaviors that were selected by the new U.S. environment which provided reinforcement for them. Some Africans while still in Africa communicated with drums, using a sort of Morse code (long before Morse made his code). This communication method proved highly useful to Africans isolated on different plantations. Use of the drum code was reinforced by news of relatives and friends. Thus, change and maintenance of culture can be explained by operant principles.

Skinner has been accused of promoting totalitarian principles of control over human behavior

(Todd & Morris, 1992). If there is substance to these charges, one would expect that equal opportunity for a variety of people would not exist in a Skinnerian world: Certain people would rule (e.g., males) and certain groups of people (e.g., women and poor, uneducated people) would be excluded from power. According to Dinsmoor (1992) nothing could be further from the truth about life in a community run on Skinnerian principles. In *Walden Two* half of the Board of Governors were women. No groups were ever consigned solely to menial tasks. True, people migrated to the jobs that fit their skills and reinforcement histories best, but everybody continued to do everything: Leaders, professors, and physicians performed manual labor at least occasionally. Finally, would George Orwell, who loathed his literary creation "Big Brother," come to *Walden Two* and be welcomed if Skinnerianism did not reject totalitarian control? The answer is as obvious as Skinner's disgust with malevolent control of behavior.

Equality of intellectual potential is also Skinnerian. Lying behind programs to raise the intellectual performance of disadvantaged children is the assumption that poor performance can be improved, because it is due to impoverished environments, not innate intellectual deficiencies (Greenwood et al., 1992; Johnson & Layng, 1992). Thus, children who might otherwise be written off can experience an academic boost through manipulations of environmental contingencies.

The net result of the *Walden Two* credit system is that most people try a wide variety of pursuits, but eventually migrate to those that they are genetically disposed to perform well. "Planners," such as Frazier, presumably because of their inherited disposition to "leadership," spend much of their time planning life in the imaginary society, but sometimes they tend the garden or chop wood. Other members of the community may work at mending fences, repairing the barns, and feeding the animals on many more occasions than they are employed at teaching or serving on committees. Walden Two is an efficient society because experiences rich in number and variety are arranged, creating an environment that selects behaviors the performers are best equipped to enact. It is not necessary to search for talent.

Because the society offers the opportunity for performance and reinforcement of almost any conceivable behavior, talent simply emerges.

By the way, Walden Two is not entirely hypothetical. Some young people built a replica of Skinner's utopia near Richmond, Virginia (Kinkade, 1973). It has been successful, but might benefit from changes that Skinner would make in Walden Two, if he could do it over (see Skinner, 1983a).

Evaluation

Contributions

The number of studies that stem directly or indirectly from Skinner's research and ideas is impossible to estimate. There must be thousands. The *Journal of the Experimental Analysis of Behavior* has been, since its founding in 1958, devoted entirely to research in the Skinnerian tradition. For this reason and because you have already had a glimpse of Skinnerian research methods in the section on operant learning, this section is issue oriented: Supporting evidence for Skinner's view of the relationship between experiences of reinforcement and genetic disposition is considered and Skinner's pioneering work on behavior therapy is covered.

The Interrelationship of Genetic Disposition and Reinforcement

Gromly (1982) reports an attempt to investigate the interrelationship between the genetic disposition of individuals and the history of reinforcement during their lives. He states:

> *Although learning theory and biological viewpoints are sometimes presented as competing explanations for behavior, they are more likely complementary. This appears to be so in the development of personality traits. One direction this complementary process might take is that, within the limits of their particular environment, people tend to select experiences that suit their biological dispositions. In this way, the selection of preferred experiences by individuals acts as an amplifier of differences that already exist (p. 255).*

Skinner would likely agree with Gromly's statement, with one exception: People do not select experiences from their environment, the environment selects individuals' behavior and thus it selects the experiences that accompany the behavior. People who are genetically disposed to be articulate may end up on the debating team where their ability to articulate will be amplified, provided only that a team is available to them.

To illustrate the possible link between genetic disposition and experiences, Gromly had university fraternity men keep a log of their experiences. Essentially, "logging experiences" amounted to recording the situations encountered and the corresponding behaviors performed. A sample log entry would be "played basketball today." They also rated themselves on scales designed to assess the possibly inherited dispositions "energetic-physically active" and "sociable-extraverted, socially outgoing." Results showed a close relationship between what the men reported doing and scores on "energetic" and "sociable." Thus, measures of genetic disposition, "energetic" and "sociable," were closely related to behaviors and accompanying experiences consistent with those dispositions. In Skinner's terms, the *environment selected* energetic behaviors for those people who were genetically inclined to be energetic. It is important to note that the behaviors of "energetic" people in one environment are not likely to be the same as those of energetic people in another environment. A given environment does not simply extend and refine genetic disposition. It leads to specific and concrete behaviors that go far beyond the global and abstract genetic disposition (Skinner, 1972e).

Behavior Therapy

The phrase **behavior therapy**, psychological therapy employing behavioral techniques, first appeared in print in an article by Skinner and a colleague that described their use of the then new methods (Skinner, 1983b). Almost all of the vast number of techniques that fall under "behavior therapy" were directly suggested by behavioristic research or have been validated by that research (Skinner, 1972j). These methods include positive reinforcement, negative reinforcement, and punishment. Behavior therapy has been successfully used for everything from treatment of obesity, heavy smoking, and alcoholism to treatment of children who do not talk or relate to adults (autistic children) and treatment of psychotic adults (people who have withdrawn from reality; see Ullmann & Krasner, 1965).

It is beyond the scope of this book to consider even a small sample from the massive psychotherapeutic tool chest of behavior therapy. However, to get a flavor of behavior therapy and to see how it relates to Skinner's ideas, consider a hypothetical example suggested by Skinner (1972l). Imagine a child of five who is not psychotic or autistic, but who is so shy and withdrawn that he almost never talks or relates in any way to adult strangers. Such a child would have difficulty attending school and relating to teachers.

Behavior therapy can be beneficial. The child is placed in a room on one of two chairs positioned side by side in front of a vending machine. It has been established that candy is a good reinforcer for the child, and the machine is capable of vending the child's favorite confection. The machine is operated by an observer who is hidden behind a one-way mirror (the observer can see the child, but the child sees only his reflection). After a few minutes, an adult stranger enters the room and takes a seat next to the child. Nothing happens for a long while, and the adult leaves, returning shortly. Each entry is a trial. Several trials occur before the child finally utters a word to the stranger. Immediately, the vending machine operator presses a button, and out of the machine comes the child's favorite treat. Several more trials may occur before the child speaks again, but each episode of speech is reinforced by candy. Soon the child is talking regularly to the stranger, and the schedule is then changed to a VR(5). Later, the schedule is changed to deliver even fewer reinforcements per speech episode, and other strangers take the place of the original adult in order to spread the response to adults in general.

Whenever the child speaks to the stranger, the stranger replies. The replies occur at the same time as the candy reinforcement is being delivered. Thus, the stranger's replies become **secondary reinforcers**, stimuli that come to have all the properties of primary reinforcers (such as candy) through association with primary reinforcers (Kimble, 1961). Thereafter, replies can reinforce the child's utterances. Now the child can go out into the real world and talk to people, with each string of utterances being reinforced by people's replies: People respond to others' remarks. This feature makes it likely that the conquest of the child's shyness will generalize beyond the laboratory. If "shyness" is a trait, then the child will have undergone a "personality change."

Limitations

Perhaps Skinner has been most severely criticized for discounting thought, feeling, and other phenomena that exist "in the head" and thus cannot be directly observed (Skinner, 1971). He admitted that individuals, including himself, do have thoughts and feelings, but he argued that there is no need to consider these internal entities in order to understand people (Skinner, 1983a). He believed that feelings or emotions are by-products of behavior, not its determinants or predecessors (Skinner, 1971). According to this point of view, one flees (behavior), then is afraid (emotion). Assuming this sequence of events, emotions cannot be determinants of behavior. His easy adoption of the behavior–emotion sequence and rejection of its opposite (people are afraid and then flee) seems unwarranted. According to J. Jung (1978), the position that Skinner endorses is not amenable to testing by experimental procedures and has been subjected to severe criticism.

Emotions can be important even when divorced from behavior. A few years before his recent death, famed British actor Sir Laurence Olivier, was interviewed on TV (60 *Minutes*, January 2, 1983). He recounted that, at one point in his career, he had developed severe stage fright. While portraying Shakespeare's Othello, Olivier was so overcome with fear and thoughts of inadequacy that he had difficulty catching his breath and wondered if he could continue. Yet somehow he finished. His portrayal of the troubled Moor was shown on 60 *Minutes*. Nothing in his performance revealed even a trace of his internal agony. The critics had also noticed nothing unusual; as always, they had praised Olivier's performance. There were no external consequences to his stage fright. However, the solely internal terror suffered by the actor was recalled as one of the most notable experiences of his life. Emotions can be extremely important in the lives of people, even when unaccompanied by any external manifestations, behavioral or otherwise.

Most of us have solved a never-before-encountered mathematical problem in private. By a reasoning process, we have come up with an answer that had never occurred to us before, and thus could not have been the object of reinforcement in the past. Neither is it currently subject to reinforcement by the verbal community. This common experience, and others like it, constitute evidence that thoughts unrelated to behavior are important to everyday functioning (J. Hayes, 1978).

By his own admission, Skinner's (1989) behaviorism cannot account for the process by which we take in information through our senses and give meaning to it. Skinner and his works are virtually absent from the pages of books on sensation and perception (see comments by Matlin & Foley, 1992). But this observation highlights an important point regarding post-Skinner Skinnerianism: Radical behaviorism must change if it is to survive. Examples of this needed change abound. Just a little leaning in the mentalistic direction, such as you saw in the case of language acquisition, can allow behaviorism to reasonably account for phenomena that have been beyond its reach. This same flexibility can even extend behaviorism to the realm of perception (Schlinger, 1992). Behaviorists also must reconsider differences among species. Although Skinner did recognize differences, he did not go far enough. Rats, pigeons, and people are not equipped the same with regard to behavior potentials (Garcia, 1993; Bailey & Bailey, 1993). Finally, as you may be convinced after reading the Mischel/Rotter and Bandura chapters, humans are forward-looking, making the notion of "expectations" a needed addition to any account of human behavior (Fagen, 1993).

Conclusions

Skinner's ideas have certainly inspired numerous researchers and theorists to discover many new ways to predict and control behavior. His concepts have directed attention to specific aspects of human behavior and have stimulated a formidable amount of research, commentary, and criticism. When he died, newspapers and popular magazines were filled with acknowledgments of his contributions. Psychologist Eric Ward, who worked with Skinner, characterized Skinner's impact as so great that it has profoundly affected school teachers and parents, not just other psychologists (Hopkins, 1990). As an example, he mentioned "time out," a method now known to most teachers and parents. Originally, "time out" meant an interruption in the schedule of reinforcements while a pigeon pecked a panel other than the one connected to the food cup (that is, pecks went unreinforced). "Time out" when applied to children "involves briefly interrupting the rewards inadvertently stemming from bad behavior" (p. A9) by ignoring misbehaving children or placing them where their "bad behavior" cannot be reinforced.

As proof Skinner has continued to have great impact right up to the present time, just months before his death, articles written in praise of his position appeared in several publications, even in some that are apparently alien to behaviorism. For example, a month before his death, an article extolling his position was published in the *Humanist* (Bennett, 1990). Soon after his death, he was said to have had much in common with existentialists (Fallon, 1992).

Even if the criticisms noted above are valid in some degree, it is still probably true that Skinner's point of view is one of the most general in all of psychology. It is difficult to find an introductory psychology book that does not consider Skinner in several different chapters. Likewise, social psychology, developmental psychology, personality, and psychotherapy texts typically devote considerable space to Skinnerianism. More importantly, through his contributions to child-rearing and behavior therapy, he has had an important and positive influence on literally thousands and thousands of lives. There are those who would argue that Skinner's contributions have had more positive impact on more people than those of any other psychologist.

But has he surpassed Freud? Although Skinner at times bragged that he had passed Freud in psychological literature citations (Lattal, 1992), if he was correct at those times, his claim is no longer supported. As you may recall from the Freud chapter, no one is currently even close to Freud in number of times mentioned in the contemporary literature. However, there are other indexes of importance. When historians of psychology and chairpersons of psychology departments were asked who are the most important contributors among contemporary psychologists, Skinner topped both lists (Korn, Davis, & Davis, 1991). Chairpersons also put Skinner atop the all-time list, with Freud at the number two spot. Thus, when experts are consulted, Skinner beats Freud and everyone else.

Summary Points

1. Skinner (1904–1990) was born in Susquehanna, PA. His Ph.D. was from Harvard where he spent most of his career. As a youngster Skinner dabbled in psychology, even flirting with mentalism. However, after college, a failed attempt to be a writer, and a sojourn in Greenwich Village, he was converted to radical behaviorism. As a young man Skinner was naively overenthusiastic about his scientific contributions; as an older person he was iconoclastic. Skinner, like "Professor Burris," his alter-ego in *Walden Two*, was a straightforward academic in many respects. However, he showed a variety of behaviors and was hard to pin down in terms of personality.

2. Rather than being an S-R psychologist, Skinner emphasized that environmental consequences of responses and the process of environmental selection of behavior are parallel to "natural selection." In his book *Beyond Freedom and Dignity* he asserted that freedom is possible in a limited sense (avoid aversive control; arrange positive consequences), but dignity is an illusion. He also indicated that we can arrange our environments so that desirable consequences to our behaviors will occur. We regularly acknowledge environmental control when we attribute the cause of our own behavior to our environments. Skinner acknowledges that currently our language is replete with words that refer to internal states and cognitions, but has shown that many of these words originally referred to behavior.

3. In operant conditioning the organism operates on its environment with consequences that increase the likelihood of the operation. In positive reinforcement, a stimulus increases the likelihood of a response on which its presentation is contingent. Indexes of conditioning and the termination of it are "rate of responding" and "extinction," respectively. Shaping is done by successive approximation. In negative reinforcement the likelihood of a response increases when it is followed by the absence of an aversive stimulus. By contrast, in punishment, responses that are followed by the presentation of aversive stimuli decrease in likelihood.

4. In intermittent reinforcement, responses are reinforced (1) every so often, or (2) after some number of responses has occurred. A temporal schedule of reinforcement is based on

the amount of time between reinforced responses. Ratio schedules are based on number of responses between reinforced responses. In fixed schedules, the amount of time or number of responses is constant. Variable schedules can be temporal or ratio, but the amount of time or number of responses varies around some average, rather than being constant.

5. Skinner believed that language develops via a process through which crude utterances are reinforced by the verbal community. Chomsky offered an innate "language faculty" as a substitute for the behavioristic account. This position has at least as many flaws as the behavioristic view: It is like a little person in the head, the faculty only appreciates what is already arranged, and questions about its genetic underpinnings have been raised. Quasi-cognitive additions to behaviorism may save its account of language acquisition.

6. Skinner reared his daughter Deborah in a "box" with the following advantages: freedom from child care drudgery, more time for affection, and more opportunities for creative child play. Despite all the controversy, Deborah, and her sister Julie, turned out well and have had a warm and close relationship with their father. Skinner explicitly rejects the notion "personality," but he often supported ideas that are consistent with popular conceptions of personality. For example, some of Skinner's characters in *Walden Two* wear their personalities on their sleeves. Frazier is an illustration. Skinner has striven to show how society can promote the development of traits such as "creativity" and "leadership" by providing opportunities for reinforcement of "creative" and "leader" behaviors.

7. A culture develops through the environment's selection of the behaviors of the people inhabiting it. Culture changes with shifts in environments (e.g., certain foods no longer available). Maintenance is seen when new environments also select certain cultural behaviors (e.g., drum communication). As *Walden Two* shows, Skinner supported gender equality and he relegated no group to menial tasks. Skinnerian methods to boost academic performance assume the intellectual equality of all children.

8. Gromly's work with fraternity men who kept logs that recorded "energetic-physically active" and "sociable-extraverted, socially outgoing" behaviors supports Skinner's ideas regarding the interplay of genetic disposition and reinforcement. Men presumedly disposed to these traits, as indicated by their scores on some scales, tended to show behaviors and accompanying experiences corresponding to the traits. Skinner was a pioneer in the area of behavior therapy. Methods consistent with his work are illustrated by the case of the shy child who learns to speak with adults and who receives secondary reinforcement in the form of their replies.

9. Skinner's belief that emotions accompany or follow behavior has been criticized as scientifically untestable. His ideas have been rejected by some critics because reinforcement cannot account for solutions to problems that have never before been used by the problem solver, and emotions that remain entirely internal, but still have a profound impact on our lives. Skinner's behaviorism will survive only if it becomes flexible by adding a cognitive flavor to its account of language acquisition and if it becomes more future-oriented and acknowledges differences in species.

10. Despite the criticisms of his point of view, Skinner has inspired many fruitful theoretical and practical approaches to understanding and controlling behavior. His recent death was followed with an outpouring of testimonials to his many contributions, some from un-

expected sources. Skinner's work has influenced virtually every branch of psychology and has even touched rank and file citizens through such notions as "time out." But is Skinner # 1? Not in literature citations, but he is ahead of Freud and all others in terms of experts' endorsements.

Running Comparison

Theorist	Skinner in Comparison
Freud	Unlike Freud, he believed in external causation and condemned "mentalism."
Rogers	In private he acknowledged a self not unlike Rogers would. Also, like Rogers, he was concerned with creativity.
Jung	Like Jung, he alluded to symbols in art that reflect humans' evolutionary past.

Essay/Critical Thinking Questions

1. What was it about Skinner's early life and "character" that made a behaviorist of him?

2. Build an argument that suggests that dignity, as we commonly define it, is consistent with behaviorism after all, despite Skinner's belief to the contrary.

3. Write a list of common terms that refer to mental events—a different one than found in the book—and translate them into behavioristic terms.

4. Describe an operant conditioning experiment in which positive reinforcement is used to condition an animal to eventually press a bar on a VI(10 sec.) schedule.

5. Could punishment be used to eliminate the self-mutilative behavior of an autistic child? Would such use be ethical? How would you go about it?

6. Imagine a *Walden III*. In it create a personality that is characterized by leadership capability. How would you find people who might turn out to be fine leaders and how would you arrange the selection of their leadership behaviors?

7. How would you extinguish the gambling behavior of a compulsive gambler? Describe the schedule of reinforcement such a person would be on and then indicate an ideal way to extinguish the troublesome behavior.

8. Briefly describe a culture and tell how some significant aspect of it would change after some environmental change.

9. Describe how you might improve Skinner's "baby box." How would you make it more attractive to the public so that it might be used by them?

10. Illustrate how a disruptive child's aggressive behavior might be extinguished, and cooperative behavior shaped. Use time out.

E-mail Interaction

(Contact the author at mfbpa@wiu.edu)
Forward one of the following or phrase your own.

1. Who is really #1, Freud or Skinner?
2. How could I teach my dog to walk on its hind legs?
3. Tell me how one can justify shocking someone to help her or him change an undesirable behavior.
4. What is the single most important Skinnerian concept?
5. What do schedules of reinforcement have to do with personality?

15

HUMAN NEEDS AND ENVIRONMENTAL PRESS: HENRY A. MURRAY

- Can forbidden love become a centerpiece in a life, even eclipsing the professional goals of an ambitious man?
- Can psychological theories have more impact on the personal than the professional lives of psychologists?
- Which is more important, a person's needs, her or his environment, or some combination of the two factors?
- What happens when more than one need arises at the same time?
- Can dreams predict real life outcomes?

Henry A. Murray

You have now come round the full circle—well almost. Unconscious processes, emphasized by Freud, have been considered, as well as reactions to Freudian thought. The interpersonal approach of Sullivan and the sociopsychological orientation of Fromm have been covered. Rogers and Maslow have proposed their humanistic concepts of empathy and self-actualization. You have contemplated the cognitive constructs of Kelly and the interplay of the social environment with cognitive processes offered by Rotter, Mischel, and Bandura. Finally, the radical behaviorism of Skinner provided you with a stark contrast to the others. Next the thinking of Henry A. Murray establishes the cables and pillars for the required bridge from these several basic points of view to the orientation that has dominated modern personality research, personality traits.

In one way or another, Murray's thinking resembles that of most theorists covered so far, but, at the same time, it remains unique. Jung stimulated Murray's interest in psychology. Murray acknowledged a debt to Freud, but, like Horney, used Freudian thought as a point of departure from which he launched his own theory. Murray, like Sullivan, clearly was interpersonally oriented: Relations among people are critical in his theory. In some little-known research, Murray devoted considerable time to the dyad: relations within a group of two (Robinson, 1992). He was also sociopsychological: Though he neglected Fromm, he borrowed heavily from social psychologist Kurt Lewin. Murray was definitely also cognitive and the interplay between internal needs and the external environment were prominent in his thinking. Despite his disdain for experimental psychology, he even showed some affinity for the ideas of his contemporary B. F. Skinner. Murray states, "We may see . . . that certain effects are more fundamental to life and occur more regularly than any observed action patterns. This agrees with Skinner's conclusions" (Murray, 1981a, p. 140). Like Skinner, Murray believed it is the end effect of an action that is unique and relatively important. The action itself could be any number of behaviors. Also similar to Skinner, but unlike the social learning theorists, Murray believed that behavior is more "pushed from the rear" than "pulled from the future" (Murray, 1981a).

Murray had an intellect for all seasons. The trek across his broad mind is a journey from the first part of this book to the last.

Murray, The Person

Henry A. Murray was born in 1893 to well-to-do parents who occupied a brownstone house on the present site of Rockefeller Center, New York City (Anderson, 1988). Unlike most other theorists, he never developed a meaningful relationship with his mother. He once dreamed that she was a helpless invalid held like an infant in his arms. It was as if he longed to offer her the nurturance she denied him (Robinson, 1992). Although he did not reject his mother as did Maslow, like Maslow he felt his mother favored his older and his younger siblings. She was an emotionally bland, prim and proper socialite who rarely showed affection or concern for her middle child. Once he said to her "You make my feelings hurt me" (Anderson, 1988, p. 141). On and off throughout his life, Murray attempted, sometimes lamely, to establish a relationship with her. He once even tried to administer his Thematic Apperception Test to her. Finally he gave up and declared them "dead to each other" (p. 141). Although his overt reactions to maternal rejection were mild, as a child, and later as an adult, he must have been seething inside. Even in his late sixties, Murray still spoke of the "marrow of misery and melancholy" that plagued him through the years (p. 141). In addition he stuttered much of his life, an affliction that was more "psychological" than physiological: It diminished to a mild stammer by the 1930s and largely disappeared later in life when time lessened the hurt. By the post-World War II period, when Murray was called as an expert witness in the trial of accused traitor Alger Hiss, he faced cross-examination by the F. Lee Bailey of his day without stammering once (Robinson, 1992).

Murray described his father as "a nice guy" (Anderson, 1988, p. 142), a code for amiable dolt. Anyone he found mediocre was described similarly. The elder Murray was a disappointment for a number of reasons: He was not bright (he could not follow conversations between his physician sons); he was not self-sufficient (he married the boss's daughter); he lacked ambition; he was predictable (a conservative banker by profession); his values and way of life were commonplace and unimaginative. In fact, Murray came to see himself as the opposite of his father. Nevertheless, as he matured, the scintilla of respect Murray had granted his father increased somewhat (Robinson, 1992).

One might wonder what sort of father would have gained Murray's respect and affection. Murray had trouble sustaining admiration for anyone. He wrote James Anderson (1988) during 1981, "I'd admire someone for a while, and then it would fade, and it would be someone else. These were all tentative things" (p. 143). According to Anderson, Murray was imbued with a certain "specialness." Perhaps it was a fault, but it may have also been a virtue. Believing that his ideas had truth value and that he was the natural leader of any group to which he belonged drove Murray to conceive of original ideas and to inspire creative thinking in others (Robinson, 1992). He was narcissistic by his own declaration, and sometimes joked about it. Erik Erikson, Murray's former research associate, "imagined what Murray's fantasy would be: to put a statue of himself in place of Napoleon's on the column in the Place Vendome in Paris" (p. 169). The leader of the team that produced the timeless research reported in Murray's *Explorations in Personality* (1938) might be cast as the benevolent dictator.

While this sense of specialness may not be equivalent to arrogance, it did give him a feeling of privilege. Like many "great people," one intimate, romantic relationship was not enough. His wife, the former Josephine L. Rantoul, whom he married in 1916, was a traditional woman—a "good wife and mother"—but was insufficiently intellectual to fully satisfy Murray. Perhaps to fill the void, he became involved with Christiana Morgan, a research collaborator, confidant, friend, and lover. But in his day and time, maintaining two romantic relationships was very difficult, yet he could not give up either woman. When he became enthralled with Jungian thought, partly because of Morgan's enthusiasm for the Swiss psychiatrist, he acceded to her insistence that he visit Zurich to speak with the architect of the collective unconscious. There he found a solution to his dilemma. Jung, it turned out, had a similar problem . . . and adopted the usual solution: He arranged for his lover, Toni Wolff, to occupy a house near his own. Despite Jung's attempts to discourage him—it was very touchy business—Murray emulated his new-found Swiss colleague. Though not provided a near-by house, Morgan was usually not far away.

Christiana was much more than a mere paramour; she was the center of Murray's universe throughout most of his adult life. So intense was their passion they built a tower as a monument to their love (skeptics please see the picture in Robinson, 1992, facing p. 178). In full view of his wife Jo and her husband Will, Christiana and he carried on a stormy romance beginning soon after they met until the day she died. Because of Christiana's influence, Murray, despite protests to the contrary, never escaped the grip of Jungian thought. He and Christiana became characters out of Jungian mythology. As living reflections of anima and animus, they exchanged gender identities on occasion, but more often reveled in his "masculine" dominance and her "feminine" submission.

But Robinson (1992) contends that their attraction was more intellectual than sexual. She was the light in the background, illuminating many of Murray's most important works. She was also a source of his torment. Deep and troubled, her brooding poetry seemed to characterize the gloomy side of their romance. As they jointly tried to moderate the misery of Jo and Will—Murray was fond of Will and grieved at his death—Christiana knew she would never fully possess Murray. Her hunger for him was so great that she starved emotionally for lack of him and wasted away from drink and despair. Shortly after calling her "disgusting," he found her lifeless body face down in the surf off a Caribbean island where they were vacationing (Robinson, 1992, p. 357). It had only been a few years since Jo had succumbed to a heart attack. Murray later announced that he and Christiana were to be married only weeks hence. He had lost a part of his soul and he knew it.

Anderson (1988), through numerous communications over several years, made an in-depth analysis of Murray's personality. Besides the sense of specialness, and the narcissism that went with it, Murray had a clear recognition of his intellectual gifts. He also had a powerful need for achievement and a sense of independence that was forced on him by the lack of parental connections. While his desire for intimacy was strong, he was wary of close-ness. Nevertheless, he achieved intimacy, especially with women. With men his orientation was different. Murray searched for weaknesses in his male associates and used his findings to assert his superiority. At the same time, he had a need for heroes, but quickly found all candidates for that role to have clay feet.

Despite his sometimes bubbly enthusiasm, he had an inner core of melancholy. De-pression enveloped him at several points in his life. His gloominess even affected his lit-erary preferences: Murray's interest in the doleful classic *Moby Dick* was so intense that he became a leading authority on it. Herman Melville, its despondent and perplexing author, became Murray's alter ego (Robinson, 1992). Yet his belief in himself was undy-ing and his intellect was towering. Henry A. Murray was destined to make major con-tributions.

Murray's academic credentials were as illustrious as they were unusual. After grad-uating from one of the most exclusive Eastern boy's schools, Groton, he enrolled at Har-vard during 1911. There he did all the "right things": Murray was captain of the crew team (rowing)—equivalent in stature to football captain—and a social butterfly who was into drinking and carousing. Attaining something close to a gentleman's "C" average, he was granted an undergraduate degree in 1915 (Robinson, 1992). Following medical training at Columbia University, leading to the M.D. degree, Murray completed a twenty-month internship in surgery (Smith & Anderson, 1989). During this period he helped care for future president Franklin D. Roosevelt, who was beginning his struggle against polio, and he launched a successful career as a medical researcher (Smith & An-derson, 1989). It was in this time frame that he also experienced his first meaningful re-lationship with a woman, a frail prostitute dying of syphilis over whom he hovered with genuine compassion (Robinson, 1992). For four years Murray studied the development of the chicken embryo at the Rockefeller Institute. Twenty-one articles reporting his re-search appeared in the leading medical and biochemical journals (Anderson, 1988). His interest in biochemistry was so strong that Murray went to study at Cambridge Univer-sity in England where he received a Ph.D. in the field during 1927. By this date, he had become a respected pioneer in the fledgling field of biochemistry, but he was not satis-fied with himself.

Murray was an enigma, a tantalizing mystery. As you will see, he fell for people with a schoolboy crush, only to seemingly reject them a short time thereafter. Still, his loyalty to people who supported him was undying. He was unconsolable when Jo died. His brother's death during World War I was never fully accepted. Even his affection for Christiana's hus-band, Will, never ceased. Likewise, the deaths of close colleagues were devastating. He was insensitive and arrogant, yet soft and vulnerable; he was a confidant to Presidents, though he was a hated rival to major academic figures; he experienced limitless joy and bottomless despair. Hollywood take note: Henry A. "Harry" Murray was a remarkable person who led an extraordinary life, bordering on the incredible.

Murray's View of the Person

Early Exposure to Psychology

While an undergraduate, Murray, like Kelly and Maslow, found his first encounter with psychology anything but inspiring. Murray said of his German-trained professor of experimental psychology, "A bud of interest in psychology . . . was nipped by the chill of Professor Munsterberg's approach" (quoted in Anderson, 1988, p. 146). Later he wrote to Anderson of his dismay with Munsterberg's denial that "psychology had anything to do with people" (p. 146). Thus began a lifelong quarrel with experimental psychologists.

Even during his training as a medical researcher and biochemist, Murray was undergoing a "profound affectional upheaval" (Anderson, 1988, p. 146). "He suddenly and unexpectedly found himself 'in a blaze, a blaze which would go on for three years and eventually pressure him to embrace psychiatry and psychology'" (pp. 146–147). But just as his exposure to experimental psychology brought him no comfort, neither did his first inquiries into Freudian thought. Having overheard some students talking about Freud, Murray consulted W. Courtney, a neurologist on the faculty of the medical school and the revered father of a classmate. This academic compared Freud's ideas to vomit. In an attempt at Freudian humor, Courtney punned, "I regard [Freud's ideas] . . . as the greatest phallusy of the age" (quoted in Anderson, 1988, p. 146). Despite this rude introduction, Murray eventually gained some respect for Freud and his notions. However, Courtney's response was of little help at a time when Murray needed to embrace some psychological point of view.

It was in 1923 that Murray stumbled onto Jung's just translated *Psychological Types* (reprinted in 1961). The experience was a revelation to him and may have been a case of predestination, because he met the Jung enthusiast Morgan about the same time. It was in 1925 that Murray succumbed to Christiana's persistent urging and traveled to Zurich for three intense weeks with Jung (Smith & Anderson, 1989). Murray wrote of the experience:

> *Dr. Jung was the first full-blooded, all-encompassing, spherical human being I had ever met . . . I had only the touchstone of my own peculiar tribulation to apply to his intelligence with the importunate demand that he interpret what I presumably knew best— myself. He proved more than equal to this exacting test and within an hour my life was permanently set on a new course. In the next few days 'the great flood-gates of the wonder-world swung open' and I experienced the unconscious in that immediate and moving way that cannot be drawn out of books. . . . All this and more I owe to Dr. Jung (Murray, 1981b, pp. 80–81).*

Consistent with his personality, Murray's admiration for Jung faded—"he wasn't good with his concepts . . . he'd believed anything I told him that was along the lines that he liked . . . but he would overlook what did not fit his theories" (Anderson, 1988, p. 155). Nevertheless, his relationship with Christiana ensured that he would never abandon Jung. He continued to cite Jung and his theory reflected Jung's propensity for polarities.

In 1927 Morton Prince, recently commissioned to establish the Psychology Clinic at Harvard, wanted to hire an assistant. It was to be a psychology faculty appointment that included lecturing and duties in the clinic. Because he was absent from the United States, a friend and professor of physiology interceded on Murray's behalf, declaring to Prince, "Here's this brilliant chemist in England. You want a scientist, don't you?" (p. 149). Despite "being entirely inadequate," Murray was offered the job and accepted. Within two years Prince was dead and Murray was director of the clinic. Needless to say, his education in psychology was even more abbreviated than that of Kelly, his companion in skepticism about experimental psychology. Murray was the featured lecturer in the first psychology courses he regularly attended.

Why Did Murray Become a Psychologist?

Jung was part of the answer. Murray's disaffection with his medical and biochemical work, which he found to be rote and lifeless, was another (Anderson, 1988). His work with medical patients did give him some intimate contact with other human beings, but he described it as "necessarily brief and superficial" (p. 149). More importantly, work in medical science allowed Murray no contact "with the deeper wellsprings of his personality . . . with his own inner life" (p. 149). In the end it was the "marrow of misery and melancholy" that became the strongest magnet drawing him to psychology. Murray fit the stereotype of the maladjusted individual who becomes a psychologist to solve personal problems. But it worked. Despite not being profoundly influenced by others' theories, as Murray developed his own point of view, he grew stronger and stronger until he could be accurately described as a well-adjusted person.

Developing a Unique Approach to Understanding People

Murray at first flirted with orthodox psychoanalysis. As a leader of the Boston Psychoanalytic Society he was instrumental in recruiting Franz Alexander, a favorite of Freud's among graduates of the Berlin Psychoanalytic Institute. At the beginning of the 1930s, Alexander arrived in Boston as resident psychoanalyst and engaged Murray in training analysis. Analysis lasted nine months, six in Boston and three after Alexander moved to Chicago.

It is safe to say that Murray was not terribly impressed with psychoanalysis, at least not favorably (Anderson, 1988). He, in effect, laughed his way through analysis, never being serious about it—"I was too busy, otherwise-attached" (p. 158). Though he liked Alexander, they were never really in sync with one another. Among the few comments Murray made to Anderson about the experience was in regard to Alexander's wife: she was a blond, flamboyant, race car driver who seemed incompatible with the stout, unemotional, former student of Freud. Murray imagined that she was attracted to him.

During psychoanalysis, he did not speak of Alexander's wife, nor did he speak to the psychiatrist about matters of substance, including his own love life. Later, he was to regard the analysis experience as time not especially well spent. Learning about the contents of his unconscious did not cure his stuttering, nor did Freudianism help him understand his relationship with his parents. Because he thought of his father as a "nice guy," he was certain that the Oedipal situation did not apply to him. In the end, he dismissed Alexander as another "nice guy" and declared himself disillusioned with psychoanalysis. Again, this initial reaction did not fit his later favorable statements about psychoanalysis (Robinson, 1992).

Despite his overt reaction to psychoanalysis, there were some subtle signs that Murray was affected by the nine months with Alexander. First, there were covert signs that an underlying current of hostility flowing deep within Murray was whipped into waves. Not only was Alexander described as fat and bland, his office was said to be "very depressing, the color of feces" (Anderson, 1988, p. 159). Second, Murray must have been influenced, because thereafter he felt obligated to address Freud's notions in his own writings, though it was sometimes done in a sort of offhand manner (Murray, 1981a). He also practiced psychoanalysis, though sparingly (Anderson, 1988).

Freud's influence on Murray was evident in other ways. Murray believed in unconscious processes and often mentioned sexuality. More importantly, he liked the global, philosophical orientation of Freud, especially certain basic psychoanalytic assumptions. Prominent among these was the belief that there are complex internal processes going on that cannot be illuminated by scientific experiments. Experiments treat people like machines, cut from the same mold, with components that can be considered apart from the whole. Murray, like Maslow, came to believe that humans are dynamic wholes, not meaningfully divisible into parts and pieces. In fact, Murray believed that his most important contribution was an insistence that the whole person always be considered.

Needless to say, Murray's Harvard colleagues did not care for his complaint that subdividing psychology into the disciplines of the neuropsychology, perception, learning, and so forth, fragmented the person and thus was a serious error. He fought with them "like dragonflies" (Anderson, 1988, p. 157). When he arrived at Harvard in 1935, famed neuropsychologist Karl Lashley tried to oust Murray. Department chair E. G. Boring, warned Murray that he would be ostracized from the American Psychological Association for life if he published a paper containing comments such as "[John] Watson's proposal [is] naive, juvenile perversity" and "A budding psychologist . . . could scarcely have been disposed to adopt with zest the dogmas of those whose avowed conscious purpose was to convince us that consciousness and purpose were nonexistent . . ." (quoted in Anderson, 1988). Robinson (1992) claims that Boring literally quaked with the fear that Murray was about to puncture psychology's soft underbelly, precipitating its demise. Further, Murray persisted in opposing what he called the "scientism" of academic psychology. To him psychologists were playing at real science—of which biochemistry was an example—for the purpose of basking in the reflected glory of physical scientists. In so doing, they were failing to understand that psychology not only could not but *should not* be like the other sciences. It should be designed to study whole people and whole people cannot be fitted into test tubes or under microscopes.

Only Gordon Allport was clearly sympathetic to Murray. Allport was a social psychologist and personality theorist who spoke of studying "the individual" and of "personality traits." In preference to his colleagues' concern with "sensory elements" and "conditioned responses," Allport's ideas should have appealed to Murray. Allport did make friendly overtures to Murray, even acting with gentlemanly restraint when the two faced off in a student-arranged debate. But Allport, like most other male associates of Murray, was initially dismissed with "He thought of consciousness as large . . . and the unconscious as a little bit of a thing down there" (Anderson, 1988, p. 154). Murray emerged from his years at

Harvard with the perception of himself as a lone hero, fighting for the truth. With the dry wit that characterized him, he commented, "at departmental meetings there were five votes in favor of psychophysics and one vote in favor of " psychoanalytic theory (p. 153). Through all of this, however, Murray showed his tendency to rebound from rejection to ambivalence and even beyond. He dedicated a book to Allport and others, team-taught classes with him, and sometimes referred to Allport as a friend (Robinson, 1992).

Basic Concepts: Murray

Postulates

As his ideas about personality developed, Murray offered several basic "propositions" on which personality is founded (Murray, 1981a). Among the most crucial was the assumption that the object of study should be individual organisms, not aggregations of organisms. This premise is consistent with an even more fundamental principle: holism, studying the whole organism, not pieces of it. Another proposition was that rhythms of activity and rest are inherent in the organism and stem from internal factors. This assumption stresses that people are not just inert bodies passively responding to external stimulation. He also believed that one cannot get to know a human being by studying even a rather extended episode in her or his existence. One must study the **long unit** of the organism, its life cycle. "The history of the organism is the organism" (p. 127).

While the person is not just a tool of the environment, Murray contended that "an organism is within an environment which largely determines its behavior" (p. 127). In fact, much of what is now inside the organism was once outside—a present need for security may have originated in past threats arising in the environment. Because the internal and the external are so intimately connected, it is necessary to view the organism as a product of "creature–environment" interactions. These interactions may be considered the "short unit" of psychological inquiry. Thus, the long unit, an individual life, may be thought of as a succession of related short units or episodes.

The organism usually responds to patterns of meaningful wholes, not discrete "sense impressions." "In turn the reactions of the organism to its environment usually exhibit a **unitary trend**," activity that is organized and directional in nature, not willy nilly, trial and error (p. 128). An activity itself can be cast as an **actone**, a pattern of bodily movements in and of itself, divorced from its effect. Therefore, a certain condition of the organism, hunger, can be followed by several different actones, picking fruit, buying a meal, begging for food, each of which yields the same end effect, food in the stomach. The connection among the sub-effects associated with simple actones constitutes a trend toward some overall effect.

"Though the psychologist is unable to find identities among the episodes of an organism's life, he can perceive uniformities. For an individual displays a tendency to react in a similar way to similar situations . . . Thus there is sameness (consistency) as well as change (variability) . . ." (p. 130). In these comments, Murray recognizes that *temporal consistencies* exist—people may react similarly to similar situations encountered across time. Such consistencies are one argument for the existence of traits. Nevertheless, Murray also acknowledges that behavioral variability is a fact of the organism's life.

Neurologically based internal representations occurring early in the chain of events end in an effect. "Since, by definition, it [internal representation] is a process which follows a stimulus and precedes an actonal response, it must be located in the brain" (p. 131). **Regnant** is the name given to "dominant configurations in the brain" that correspond to internal representations. An image of a food object is the regnant response to the hunger need aroused by smells from the environment. **Regnancy** is the label for the "totality of such [brain] processes occurring during a single moment (a unitary temporal segment of brain processes)" (p. 131). These concepts were proposed by Murray to recognize the fact that everything we call "psychological" ultimately arises out of brain action. However, Murray made it clear that while "activities of nerve cells and muscle cells are necessary conditions of the whole action . . . they are not in any full sense its cause" (p. 131). Brain action enables the chain of events leading to some effect; it is not the final cause of that sequence. "Cause" lies in a complex of interrelated external and internal events that is too intricate and vast to be encompassed by a simple statement.

". . . the constituents of regnancies in man are capable of achieving consciousness (self-consciousness) . . ." (p. 132). There are brain processes that correspond to what we call consciousness; humans are able to reflect on themselves as a result of these regnancies. The conscious images we experience arise from regnant or neurological processes. On the other hand, there are unconscious regnant processes. "An unconscious process is something that must be conceptualized as regnant even though the [person] is unable to report its occurrence" (p. 132). This declaration is Murray's way of legitimizing unconsciousness by linking it to brain processes.

To further show that "nerve cells" do not cause effects at the end of the environmental event>internal processes>actone chain, Murray boldly suggested that the personality can affect the brain. Personality processes may even alter the autonomic nervous system, as in cases of neuroses that affect such vital functions as heart rate and blood pressure. Personality is not the slave of neurology; it is somewhat the other way round.

Definition of Needs

Like Maslow, Murray's most central concept is **need**, "a [physiochemical] force . . . in the brain . . . , [that] organizes perception, . . . intellection, . . . and action in such a way as to transform . . . an . . . unsatisfying situation [into a more satisfying one]" (Murray, 1981a, p. 189). Beyond this formal definition, Murray characterized a need as equivalent to a drive (he often used them interchangeably, as in the section title of his [1981a] article "The Concept of Need or Drive"). This equivalence moves the concept in a biological direction. Here Murray and Maslow differed greatly. The proposer of the "hierarchy of needs" took great pains to distinguish between "drives," which he thought to be of secondary importance, and "needs," which he emphasized.

Murray also alluded to another equation relevant to the organization of this text. His ideas provide a bridge to the later discussion of "traits," because a need can sometimes be thought of as "a more or less consistent trait of personality" (p. 142). He hastened to add that it can at times be considered a "temporary happening" (a state). Other evidence that Murray's needs are trait-like is seen in the fact that they have been transformed into one of the most frequently used personality-trait measures currently available (Paunonen, Jackson, & Keinonen, 1990).

At different points, Murray wrote of "need" in different, though not necessarily contradictory, terms (Murray, 1981a). At one point he conceived of a given need as aiming the organism toward a unique effect, different from the direction assumed by it when it is being influenced by other needs. At another point, in tune with Skinner, he indicated that "a need is a . . . 'push from the rear' rather than a 'pull from the future'" (p. 148). In still another context he "loosely" referred to "need" as "an organic . . . readiness to respond in a certain way under given conditions" (p. 142). One may conclude that a need is a (1) drive-like, and (2) sometimes trait-like, entity that is (3) associated with brain functioning, and (4) arises to transform an unsatisfactory situation through (5) readying the organism's mental and behavioral faculties to respond to "a push from the rear."

Varieties of Needs

Murray (1981a) divides needs into basic categories. The **viscerogenic needs** involve basic physiological drives, and, as such, are relatively straightforward and self-explanatory. *Positive* viscerogenic needs—characterized by an approach orientation to objects—include n Inspiration (need for oxygen), n Water, n Food, n Sentience (need to experience sensory gratification, for example, sucking and bodily contact with another person), n Sex, and n Lactation. *Negative* viscerogenic needs, characterized by an avoidant (or expellant) orientation to objects, are n Expiration (need to exhale carbon dioxide), n Urination, n Defecation, n Noxavoidance (need to get rid of noxious stimulation), n Heatavoidance, n Coldavoidance, and n Harmavoidance.

Psychogenic needs are secondary to viscerogenic needs and may be derived from them, but, being one step away from the biological side of the organism, are psychological in nature. Like the viscerogenic needs, psychogenic needs can be typed as positive or negative. Each type is associated with a **vector** which is a force with directional properties. **Adience** refers to the positive-need-promoting vectors that describe movement toward objects and people. The positive viscerogenic and psychogenic needs fit here. There are several psychogenic examples, many of them well-known to professionals, and some even known to the public. **n Achievement** indicates the drive to "overcome obstacles, to exercise power, to strive to do something difficult as well as [and as] quickly as possible" (Murray, 1981a, p. 157). **n Affiliation** refers to the desire for friendships and associations: "To greet, join, and live with others. To co-operate and converse sociably with others. To love. To join groups" (p. 159). **n Succorance** is the dependent attitude of seeking aid, protection, and sympathy by crying for mercy and help from affectionate, nurturant caretakers. This need has the flavor of unresolved Basic Anxiety, Horney's central notion. **n Order** involves arranging, organizing, and putting away objects: to be tidy, clean, and scrupulously precise. **n Dominance** is the drive to influence, control, persuade, prohibit, dictate, lead, direct, restrain others and to organize the behavior of a group. **n Exhibition** is desiring to attract attention to one's person by exciting, amusing, stirring, shocking, or thrilling others. **n Aggression** refers to an assaultive or injurious orientation to others, including to belittle, harm, blame, accuse, ridicule, punish severely, react sadistically toward, or even murder. **n Abasement** involves surrendering, complying, accepting punishment, apologizing, confessing, atoning, and generally being masochistic. This need brings to mind Horney's portrayal of people with the masochistic need for submission to a lover (Clare).

Abience is the name given to the negative-need-promoting vectors that describe movements away from objects and people. The negative viscerogenic needs fit here. There are fewer clear psychogenic examples in this category, but some of them will be familiar. **n Autonomy** is the drive to resist influence or coercion, to defy authority, seek freedom, and strive for independence. **n Inviolacy** is an attitude of attempting to prevent depreciation of self-respect, to preserve one's good name, to avoid criticism, and to maintain psychological distance. In the common parlance, it is trying not to be dissed. **n Blamavoidance** refers to avoiding blame, punishment, and ostracism by inhibiting asocial or even unconventional impulses: being a well-behaved, law-abiding citizen. Satisfying this need amounts to conforming in order to avoid alienation from others. **n Infavoidance** is an orientation to avoiding failure, shame, humiliation, or ridicule by concealing disfigurement and refraining from attempts at anything seen as beyond one's powers. Avoiding challenging circumstances fits here. **n Contrarience** is the drive to act differently from others, to be unique, to take the opposite side, and to hold unconventional views. Table 15.1 summarizes several of Murray's most central needs.

TABLE 15.1

Summary of Murray's Needs

Adience Vectors (positive needs)	Abience Vectors (negative needs)
VISCEROGENIC	
n Inspiration	n Expiration
n Water	n Urination
n Food	n Defecation
n Sentience	n Noxavoidance
n Sex	n Heatavoidance
n Lactation	n Coldavoidance
	n Harmavoidance
PSYCHOGENIC	
n Achievement	n Autonomy
n Affiliation	n Inviolacy
n Succorance	n Blamavoidance
n Order	n Infavoidance
n Dominance	n Contrarience
n Exhibition	
n Aggression	
n Abasement	

BOX 15.1   Are You Avoidant/Withdrawn or Approaching/Attached?

Murray's needs may be cast into two broad categories: *avoidant/withdrawn* (*abience*), avoiding objects and people or withdrawing from them, and *approaching/attached* (*adience*), approaching objects and people or submissively/controllingly attaching oneself to them. Examine all of the psychogenic needs and the underlined viscerogenic needs in Table 15.1: 9 Adience and 7 Abience. Honestly decide which are prominent among the needs that typically drive you. Check off all of the ones you choose. Where does the balance lie? If 66 percent or more of your choices fit in the Adience category you may score yourself as approaching/attaching. For example, if you checked 10 needs, and 7 of them (6.6 rounded up) were in the Adience category, you may be regarded as "approaching/attached." On the other hand, if 55 percent or more of your choices fall in the Abience category, you are better characterized as avoidant/withdrawn (for example, if you made 11 choices and 6 were in the Abience category). If you fail to meet either percentage criterion, you fit in neither the approaching/attached or the avoidant/withdrawing categories. Of course, this is an exercise. Attach no special meaning to being in either category; neither is necessarily good or bad. However, if you are at one extreme or the other, you may examine your behavior in the future and decide that a better balance would be better for you.

Strength of Needs, and Interactions among Them

Strength

The **strength** of a need is measured in terms of its frequency, intensity, and duration (Murray, 1981a). A need may be considered strong because it occurs under given conditions with great regularity: high frequency. It may also be considered strong if it occurs occasionally with great intensity. Of course, a need is strong if it is persistent—when it is aroused, it continues to endure for a long time in the absence of satisfaction.

Interrelation of Needs

During everyday life, an individual may experience the arousal of several needs, either all at once or in succession. Consequently, it is common to observe a person take a particular course of action that is designed to satisfy several needs. Like Maslow, Murray believed that people are complicated; they rarely do anything for just one reason.

Fusion of needs is Murray's name for a single "action pattern that satisfies two or more needs at the same time" (p. 161). An example would be an individual who gets paid to sing a solo in public (F n AcqExh; F = fusion). The person is satisfying n Acquisition—making money—while also taking care of n Exhibition—getting attention from others.

Subsidiation of needs occurs "When one or more needs are activated in the service of [one or more other needs]" (p. 161). In the following sequence, each need is subsidiary to the succeeding need, with the last mentioned need (n Achievement) being the most prominent: the one served by all the rest.

> *A politician removes a spot from his suit (n Noxavoidance) because he does not wish to make a bad impression (n Infavoidance), and thus diminish his chances of winning the approval and friendship of Mr. X (n Affiliation), from whom he hopes to obtain some*

slanderous facts (n Cognizance) relating to the private life of his political rival, Mr. Y, information which he plans to publish (n Exposition) in order to damage the reputation of Mr. Y (n Aggression) and thus assure his own election to office (n Achievement): (n Nox S n Inf S n Aff S n Cog S n Exp S n Agg S n Ach) (the need preceding the "S" is subsidiary to the one following the "S," p. 162).

Contrafactions

Contrafactions of needs are cases where needs are related to their opposites in alternating phases. For example, "A phase of Dominance is succeeded by a phase of Deference. A wave of Aggression is followed by a wave of Nurturance . . . Abstinence follows indulgence . . . etc." (p. 163). A person who is a Napoleon at work is a grovelling serf at home. These ideas are reminiscent of Jung's "equivalence" and his conception of dream content as contradicting waking orientations.

Conflict

Conflicts of needs occur when needs oppose each other "within the personality, giving rise when prolonged to harassing spiritual dilemmas" (p. 163). "A woman hesitates to satisfy her passion because of the disapproval of her family (n Sex-C-n Blamavoidance) . . . A man hesitates to satisfy his desire to fly an airplane because of fear (n Achievement-C-n Harmavoidance)" (p. 163; "C" = "conflict"). These oppositions balance needs so that one or the other does not get out of hand.

Need Integrates (Complexes)

Needs may form the core of structures that, in turn, are central components of the personality. A critical predecessor to the formation of these core structures is **cathexis**, a process by which an object evokes a need. The object may be "cathected" by the need or the person with the need. This Freudian term originally meant the investment of psychic energy in some object, as an infant may cathect its mother. If the object is present, the need is likely to be aroused. "Objects" can be either inanimate entities or people. Common cathexes, with objects listed first and the cathected (c) needs second, are: garbage (c Noxavoidance); lightning (c Harmavoidance); doctor (c Succorance); sobbing child (c Nurturance); hero (c Deference); autocrat (c Autonomy).

A **need integrate or complex** is formed when "traces (images) of cathected objects in familiar settings become integrated in the mind with the needs and emotions which they customarily excite, as well as with the images of preferred modes" (actones or other means of creating satisfaction; p. 179). Integrates are much more abstract than needs, and thus harder to put into words. They are recurrent phenomena that fill our dreams, hallucinations, illusions, and delusions. A complex may come to consciousness (or unconsciousness) because of an encounter with a real world object that resembles the image that excites the need integrated with it. For example, a bird floating effortlessly in the air may be cathected by the need to be free (n Autonomy). If so, the person with the complex would be expected to dream of birds flying and to see them as illusions when they are not actually present (in wallpaper; in the tree leaves; in sidewalk cracks). Complexes make us do something, like pursue independence from others.

BOX 15.2   Are Dreams Clairvoyant?

If complexes are at all like archetypes, they may relate to themes repeated over and over in human history. This repetition suggests that "history repeats itself." Should such be the case, manifestations of complexes, as may occur in dreams, might predict future events. Thus, past events of a certain nature that are reflected in complexes and manifested in dreams may foretell future events of the same nature. Conceivably, a case in point may be instances of kidnapping/murders. Because kidnapping/murders have occurred many times in human history, they are a part of human lore. Therefore, they may become the basis for complexes shared by people. Given this line of reasoning, people's dreams may predict the details of an actual kidnapping/murder.

Murray (1981c) capitalized on a much publicized event in order to ascertain whether dreams are clairvoyant, that is, able to predict future events. A few days after the baby of famous aviator Charles Lindbergh was kidnapped, but before any details of the crime were known to the public, Murray placed an ad in a newspaper to solicit descriptions of dreams relating to the crime. Some 1300 people responded.

The facts of the case were that the baby had *died* instantly after suffering blows to the head resulting in *three fractures of the skull*. Its *naked body* was found in a *shallow grave* in some *woods* near a *road* several miles from the Lindbergh home. An ex-convict of German extraction was later convicted of the crime (his relatives are still denying his guilt).

Of the 1300 dreams many did contain references to "foreigners" or "foreign accents." This outcome was probably due to suspicion of "aliens" that was rampant in the United States then (1932) and now. However, in only about 5 percent of the dreams did the baby appear dead. Further, only 10 dreams were at all accurate in predicting the details of the crime when those became known. Seven dreams referred to the baby as deceased, and two others implied as much. Five of the ten dreams made definite references to the wooded locale where the body was found. Five referred to a grave, two of them indicating that it was shallow. Three dreams referred to a road near where the baby was found, and another implied that a road was nearby. One dream indicated explicitly that the baby was naked, another implied nakedness, and in a third, that the baby was clothed only in a diaper. Of the 10 dreamers, 3 claimed they had their dreams before the kidnaping had even occurred. Two of the three included mention of the Lindberghs, one also referred to "woods," and the one without mention of the Lindberghs did refer to a "roadside" and "diaper only." Only 3 of the 10 dreams included death, a grave, and a wooded locale.

The very fact that the dreams were collected argues that Murray endorsed the *possibility* that dreams are clairvoyant. Therefore, it is a tribute to his objectivity that he drew negative conclusions regarding the ability of dreams to predict the future. He correctly interpreted results as due to happenstance: By chance one would expect 10 (or more) of 1300 dreams to contain some accurate information relating to the facts of the crime as revealed later.

Need integrates or complexes manifest themselves in various forms, not just in dreams. For example, complexes show up in artistic expression and creation, drama, ritual, religion, fantasies, desires and temptations, fiction, fairy tales, plays and movies, art objects, and even child (or adult) play. At a more global rather than individual level, cultures can be sources of complexes. One may see complexes manifested in the art objects, stories, and religious practices that are part and parcel of a culture. The "cross" in Christian cultures would be an example. Notice that need integrates appear to be more like the archetypes of Jung than Freud's "complexes."

TABLE 15.2 Press

p Affiliation	object is a friendly, sociable companion
p Nurturance	object is a protective, sympathetic ally
p Aggression	object is a combative person, one who censures, or one who belittles
p Rival (recognition of)	object is a competitor
p Lack (economic)	object is the condition of poverty
p Dominance	object is a restraining, prohibiting, or imprisoning person

Environmental Press

Unlike some theorists, Murray neglects nothing inside or outside the person. Thus, he devotes considerable space to the environment in which the person is embedded, although more is reserved for needs and other internal entities.

The environmental factors that influence the person are called **press**, which designates a directional tendency in the object or situation (*press* is also plural). Unlike the cathexis of an object involved with complexes, *which makes the individual do something or other*, ". . . press of an object is what it can *do to the subject* [person] or *for the subject*—the power that it has to affect the well-being of the subject in one way or another" (Murray, 1981a, p. 187). "Everything that can supposedly harm or benefit the well-being of an organism may be considered *pressive*, everything else is inert" (p. 185). A dominant person in an individual's life is a press that restricts and restrains the individual.

A press may be a sign of things to come. Individuals often actually perceive the pressive object, but they infrequently think of the object in the present tense: The object is now "doing this or that to me." Rather, the individual anticipates: "The object may do this or that to me (if I remain passive) or I may use the object in this or that way (if I become active)" (p. 185). However, Murray is quick to point out that press are not entirely anticipatory. Very often aspects of the present situation excite images of past pressive situations. These images allow the individual to operate smoothly and effectively relative to present press, because the person has past experience to act as a guide. Table 15.2 contains examples of press.

Thema

Needs and press are internal and external entities, respectively. In view of Murray's holistic position and his inclination to see all factors relating to the individual as integrated, one would expect that he would see a way to merge needs and press. Indeed he did. A **thema** is a combination of a particular need and a particular press or pressive object. In the case of thema, some object is present that holds promise to do something to the person or for the person thereby generating a need consistent with it. Examples include: a friendly sociable companion is present, resulting in the activation of n Affiliation (p Affiliation > n Affiliation); a combative, belittling person is present evoking n Aggression (p Aggression > n Aggression); a restraining, prohibiting person is present giving rise to n Dominance (p Dominance > n Dominance). Often a press leads to the activation of a need that reciprocates it, opposes it, or compensates for it: A rejecting person may inspire the rise of n Rejection resulting in reciprocity of rejection; a dominating person initiates n Autonomy; an belittling person initiates n Achievement.

Evaluation

Contributions

Needs

One of Murray's two lasting contributions to the field of personality is definitely his conception of needs. A description of the uses to which Murray's needs have been put by numerous researchers and theorists would fill an entire, separate book. Here there is space to mention only personality tests based on Murray's needs.

Douglas N. Jackson's Personality Research Form (PRF) is a personality-trait measure based on Murray's needs (Jackson, 1984). Twenty of those needs are translated rather directly into 20 trait scales. After three revisions of the PRF manual, Jackson's measure ranks "as the fourth most frequently cited personality test in the psychological research literature" (Paunonen, Jackson, & Keinonen, 1990).

Sampo Paunonen, Jackson, and Mirja Keinonen (1990) have translated the 20 trait scales into a nonverbal form consisting of stick figures depicting some trait and accompanied by the instruction "estimate the likelihood that [you] would engage in the type of behavior shown" (p. 486). To illustrate, a frowning tennis player breaking a tennis racket after having missed a return is among the figures. It is intended to measure the trait "aggression" (based on n Aggression). Subjects look at the figure and mark a scale point that represents the likelihood they would perform the behavior depicted, breaking the racket.

Paunonen and colleagues (1990) showed that the nonverbal version had respectable validity: It correlated acceptably with the verbal form of the PRF in both Canadian and Finnish subjects. Other evidence indicates that it is also reliable. The nonverbal PRF should be invaluable in the study of personality functioning in a variety of cultures, because it can be administered in the same form to people of each culture without loss and distortion due to translation into various languages. It will also be useful with children who are too young to respond to the verbal form and people who cannot read.

Work by Jefferson Singer (1990) reconceived 16 of Murray's needs as "life goals." For example, one goal statement was "I would like to be a leader and sway others to my opinion" (based on n Dominance; p. 541). Another was "I would like to have as sensual and erotic a life as possible" (based on n Sentience and n Sex combined; p. 541).

The Thematic Apperception Test (TAT)

Murray's second timeless contribution was development of a much-used projective test, the Thematic Apperception Test (TAT), an instrument for assessing a person's self-reflective perceptions (apperceptions) revealing thema that are evoked by some ambiguous pictures (Murray, 1981d). With use of the TAT, research subjects or clinical clients are told that they are participating in a "test of creative imagination" (p. 391). Then, one at a time, they are shown each of 20 (or more) pictures mounted on cards, such as a boy with a violin, a woman holding a man, and a girl with a doll. Subjects or clients are asked to "make up a plot or story" about each picture (p. 391). To assist them, they are asked some questions: "What is the relation of the individuals in the picture? What has happened to them? What are their present thoughts and feelings? What will be the outcome?" (p. 391). The TAT was and is still used to reveal Murray's needs and for other purposes (e.g., to reveal personality orientations and traits that go well beyond Murray's needs).

The advantages of the TAT revolve around the claim that the subject/client can interpret the pictures in innumerable ways, because they are inherently ambiguous. Thus, whatever the subject/client says about the pictures comes from his or her own unique mind (usually assumed to be the unconscious mind, past experiences, and needs). These advantages include extraction of responses from subjects/clients that are spontaneous and relatively uncontaminated by any cues provided by researcher or clinician. Such responses are rich with information, can be mined to great depths and may provide a glimpse of the unconscious that cannot be achieved otherwise.

The narratives provided by subjects/clients have been scored in various ways. In early uses, these stories were analyzed informally and subjectively by the test administrator (Murray, 1981d). Analysis of a card usually involved the card as a whole, rather than each individual human figure on the card. Beginning around 1949, researchers obtained data that allowed more concrete, less subjective means of analyzing narratives inspired by pictures. The most frequent responses were catalogued so that future users of the TAT could check to determine whether a client or subject was providing a typical or atypical response to a given card. Cards were rated using various scaling techniques to determine the degree to which they suggested achievement, aggression, sex, or other needs.

While these efforts helped to objectify TAT analysis, scoring was still somewhat haphazard and unsystematic. To begin improvement, Charles R. Potkay listed major problems: (1) total cards are typically considered despite the fact that a given card may contain two figures that contribute to stories in different, even opposite, ways; (2) when objective methods are used to aid analysis, scales are employed that may limit subjects' or clients' responses or suggest to them how they should respond; and (3) when more objective methods are used, they usually involve only a few concepts (for example, achievement and aggression) rather than the many concepts subjects/clients may have had in mind while making responses (Allen & Potkay, 1983a).

To remedy these deficiencies, Potkay and his colleagues had subjects generate any words that came to their minds when they looked at single figures on each card, rather than the whole card (see Potkay, Merrens, & Allen, 1979, in Allen & Potkay, 1983a). This method is called the Adjective Generation Technique (AGT). The instruction is simply "write down [some number of] adjectives" (Allen & Potkay, 1983a; Potkay & Allen, 1988). With use of the AGT, (1) single figures are considered, (2) problems with scaling techniques are avoided, and (3) subjects can use any concepts contained in their entire repertoires of words.

Sixty male and sixty female subjects viewed seventeen male and seventeen female figures featured on twenty-two cards and then described each with three adjectives. Table 15.3 contains a sampling of the figures investigated, and, for each, the three words used most frequently.

TABLE 15.3   Descriptions of Figures and Words Most Frequently Used in Description of Them (% of Subjects Using Word in Brackets)

TAT Figure	Three Most Used Adjectives
Boy with violin	bored [42], tired [32], sleepy [25]
Woman with books	pretty [18], young [18], intelligent [11]
Man working in fields	strong [43], hardworking [30], muscular [28]
Woman downcast	sad [25], upset [17], depressed [14]
Man holding woman	angry [34], mad [12], determined [10]
Woman holding man	loving [26], pleading [14], concerned [8]
Woman with back turned	old [31], sad [16], hurt [11]
Man looking down	worried [20], young [16], sad [11]
Man with pipe	angry [12], mean [8], domineering [8]
Man with gray hair	old [38], wise [22], understanding [13]
Girl with doll	young [28], bored [25], uninterested [9]
Woman daydreaming	thoughtful [19], thinking [10], wondering [10]
Woman on beach	scared [18], hurried [17], frightened [12]
Man embracing woman	loving [45], happy [14], old [10]
Boy sitting	lonely [45], young [21], poor [18]
Woman nude	dead [37], tired [13], exhausted [12]
Man silhouetted	lonely [15], searching [14], alone [13]
Man at lamp post	lonely [25], alone [18], old [10]

The entries in Table 15.3 will give you a good idea of the kinds of pictures contained in the TAT and their nature as defined by the most frequently used descriptive words. Because gender made no difference, percentages are for all 120 subjects.

Considering that subjects could choose any words from the many hundreds available to each of them, agreement among them on descriptions is remarkable. Averaged across figures, the percent of subjects who agreed on most frequently used words was twenty-eight. For second most used words it was sixteen and for words used third most it was twelve. For eight of the 34 figures agreement for most frequent words was greater than forty percent to just less than fifty percent (in one case it was fifty-two percent). Obviously subjects were seeing much the same thing in these figures, indicating that they have definite meaning to people.

There were certain themes running through responses to the figures. They tended to be old, and sad, but if they were male, they were angry and lonely, and if females, loving and nurturing (for example, motherly and concerned; remember not all the figures are included in Table 15.3). The adjectives that subjects generated were also scored on FAVorability, ANXiety, and FEMininity. "Man embracing woman" came out on top in terms of FAV. The figure reflecting the highest ANX was "woman on beach." "Woman holding man" was most FEM. Another analysis indicated that FAV and ANX were moderately, inversely related.

BOX 15.3   Clinical Analysis Using the TAT

Murray (1981d) and Christiana Morgan wrote an article illustrating the use of the TAT via reference to narratives produced by a Harvard undergraduate in response to cards. The student, called "B," was a music major who tended to be deferential and submissive to those he respected. B constantly squinted his eyes, as if in response to a photographer's flashbulb, giving him the appearance of puzzled anxiety. His overall demeanor was that of an "unobtrusive, banal" individual (p. 402). B came to the clinic because unsettling images were intruding on his reading, preventing him from retaining the meaning of the words he was reading, but not the impressions of the printed page. Thus, he lost the sense of what he was reading, but his unfailing recollection of the printed pages allowed him to get high marks on exams.

These images seemed at first glance to be as bland as the individual they tormented. He saw scenes from his distant past, such as pastures and brooks, buildings, and woods, and some from his recent past, including Harvard Square and the Boston State House. Nothing from B's autobiography, or the information he provided during the intake interview, suggested an explanation of his symptoms. He had been brought up in a proper, Southern, Methodist family by parents he regarded with equal favor. However, he tended to be more like his morally "right" father in general disposition if not in emotional intensity: The father had an explosive temper. His mother apparently nagged him often, but also showed him lavish affection. There was a younger sibling, a sister with whom he frequently quarreled. As a child he was quite timid and prone to numerous fears. B shied away from water and animals. He was fearful of automobile accidents, and periodically dreamed of being chased by a bull.

B's self-description confirmed his timidity and included sensitivity, reticence, avoidance of athletics, and feelings of inferiority. The disclosure of frequent doll-play sessions with his sister until age nine, unusual neatness, and extreme sensitivity to smells seemed an unconscious effort to portray an effeminate nature.

Thoughts of death often plagued him, particularly after seeing a man killed in a fall from a hayrack. These fears were reinforced when he was comforted at his grandmother's funeral on breaking into tears. Sex was alien to him: He did not masturbate until age eighteen, had still not experienced intercourse, and was appalled on contemplating that his parents had done what farm animals do to produce offspring. According to Murray, "He held a theory of anal intercourse. He told of several experiences of fellatio occurring at about the age of ten, but said that there had been none since" (p. 403). As a child he slept with his father while his mother slept with his sister, all on the same porch.

In response to the card "The nude figure of a man clinging to a pole," B called the figure a "sailor" who scaled his ship's mast in an escape attempt made after having been chased from his cabin because of "some morbid . . . homosexual crime" (p. 403). He is shot down by a fellow sailor. Four months later, after psychoanalysis, he altered the story by indicating that the sailor climbed the mast in an insane effort to escape the horror of his unsuccessful attempt at homosexual relations. His face "distorted and carnal," he hurled himself into the sea (p. 403). The card "man clinging to a rope" inspired similar fears of being trapped on a precariously high perch, but no allusions to homosexuality. Murray noted the "obvious" homosexual themes of the first two stories, and manifestations of B's admitted fear of heights in all three.

To the "boy with violin," B responded with a tale of musical triumph at a recital, but spoiled the achievement by declaring that the boy subsequently lost "hands or fingers" and had to abandon music. Murray depicted this latter tragedy in his thema notation: p injury > n achievement [failure] theme. After psychoanalysis, B gave a more neutral description of the boy with the violin.

When confronted with "boy huddled against a couch," B said the youngster had flown into a rage and shot a horse or dog, thus his current state of remorse. He related that, as a child, he had directly participated in brutality to animals (beatings) as well as vicariously participated (decapitation). After psychoanalysis, the emphasis in his story was less on brutality and more on the figure being remorseful and having learned a les-

Continued

BOX 15.3   Continued

son. Murray saw themes of self-punishment, castration anxiety, sadism, and bestiality in B's narrative.

To the card "girl standing alone," B responded "Girl [is] about to be attacked by a demented person. She has gone on a picnic with him. A coming storm increases the carnal instincts of the boy. He attacks the girl" (p. 404). To the card "malicious-looking man grasping the arm of a young girl [who recoils in terror]," B offered "When the time comes he takes her to attack her . . ." (p. 404). Based on this story, as well as a remembered movie in which a scientist fills a woman's veins with ossifying material, and a recollection of a movie hero's wife dying in childbirth, Murray suggested that B was prone to fantasies of women being killed during intercourse or childbirth. These stories of girls being attacked hinted at a sadistic heterosexual orientation.

B was also given some of the Rorschach Inkblots. In one he saw a man looking at a medical book in which there is an illustration of a dissected male or female. In another, a man is seen engaging in a sexual act in which the object addressed sexually is an embryo or a part of a miscarriage. Murray indicated that necrophilia is implied. B also was asked to write a story and responded with a tale of a minister who returns home to find his brother in "compromising circumstances" with a woman (p. 405).

Murray's overall conclusion regarding B was that the young man felt guilt over, and fear of, homosexuality. He also showed evidence of anal sadism, masochism, and a castration complex. His castration anxiety may have stemmed from having had his first nocturnal emission while sleeping in contact with his enormous, temperamental father, possibly the bull of his dreams. He also showed womb fantasies, sadistic trends, and necrophilia. B fantasied about pregnancy and tried to picture himself in his mother's womb. Once he dreamed of opening a woman up and filling her womb with straw. Another time he fantasied that he was pregnant. To build in masochism, just after the pregnancy fantasy, he became constipated and lay doubled up on the floor groaning with abdominal pain. The necrophilic and anal themes were manifested in his "most exciting fantasy" during which he opened one grave after another performing anal intercourse with each corpse in turn (p. 407). It seemed to Murray that birth, death, and sexual intercourse were closely linked in B's mind.

Because the TAT was developed during a time characterized by more open sexism than exists today, male and female figures were compared statistically on FAV. Contrary to expectations based on sexism, results showed that females were more favorably described.

It is interesting to note the emotional tone that emerges from the figures included on the TAT cards: They are melancholy, sad and depressed, reflective, and lonely as a whole, just as their chief selector, Murray, was afflicted by a "marrow of misery and melancholy." Once again it is clear that the TAT cards are not entirely neutral with regard to the kinds of emotions and themes that they suggest.

Box 15.3 describes an actual, clinical use of the TAT cards. It will provide you with further insight into the nature of the TAT, as well as some examples of cards, figures, and responses to them, along with Murray's analysis. You may also find the individual who is analyzed to be quite interesting.

The TAT Today
The TAT continues to be one of the most used of projective tests. The breadth of its uses attests to its flexibility and its wide applicability. A representative sample of its varied utility follows.

BOX 15.4   Diversity: Murray and the Social Class Wars

Social class is a neglected source of diversity and classism is an often ignored variety of oppression. Despite all his virtues, Murray had several deficiencies, some of which related to his affluent, upper-class status. Murray's authoritarianism may have, in part, come from assuming the upper-class license to lead, an elitist norm of his era (Robinson, 1992). Many of the young, middle-class Ph.D.'s who worked with him on the project leading to *Explorations in Personality* (1938), and the TAT, complained about his arrogance and aloofness. Some felt almost like sharecroppers on his plantation. During the 1960s, Murray took a dim view of the war in Vietnam, but he rejected hippie/protesters' defiance of authority (Robinson, 1992). While he shared their reverence for sexual freedom, especially for women, he was unsympathetic regarding their other unconventional behaviors. His social class gave him a "sense of propriety" and an understanding that elicit sex as well as illegal substance use was a private matter, not for public display.

While Murray's sense of privilege was overt, most of us are so subtle about our class assumptions that we are not conscious of them. Many of us lack the sense of concern for working men and women that characterized our parents and grandparents during the post-depression period. As a result, poor, working-class Americans suffer in silence. Even their identity is obscure. While people of color are disproportionately represented among the U.S. poor, many people do not realize that the majority of the poor are of European descent (white; Blauner, 1992). Among them is a group who can call no government program their own: young, white males who are poor. If their numbers begin to swell and their discontent expands proportionately, we will all pay for their dismal condition. Currently they are a major target of Klan, Neo-Nazi and militia recruitment campaigns. Late-middle-aged European American men who make top salaries are also being subjected to harsh treatment. Some of them are being fired a few months or years from scheduled retirement and the opportunity to collect lucrative benefits. Their dismissal is apparently related to companies' needs for convenient ways to cut costs. It is quite reasonable to argue that some of these men may have had an unfair advantage in initially getting their good jobs, but no one deserves to be cruelly dumped after years of service to their companies. These examples remind us of two diversity "principles": 1) diversity includes everyone; and 2) no group has exclusive claim to being oppressed.

In comparison to the TAT responses of non-demented psychiatric patients, Alzheimer's patients used fewer words in descriptions of pictures, tended to drift away from adherence to instructions, and gave descriptions that differed from those of other patients (Johnson, 1994). Compared to a nonsexually abused group, sexually abused child and adolescent females showed more primitive and simple characterizations of people, inability to invest in people except for need-gratification, and a tendency toward extreme and immature functioning (Ornduff et al., 1994). In another sexual abuse study, compared to a group with no abuse history, abused girls showed sexual preoccupation and, secondarily, guilt (Pistole & Ornduff, 1994).

George and Waehler (1994) used the "man clinging to rope" card to examine perceptions of climbing up versus down as indications of optimism and self-efficacy. Goal specification and goal attainment themes in descriptions related to optimism and self-efficacy, but not direction of climbing.

Other findings include the identification in TAT picture descriptions of causal explanations for "bad events" (Peterson & Ulrey, 1994), evidence for the validity of the TAT

A photo of a TAT being administered.

(Rosenberg et al., 1994; Alvardo, 1994), and a demonstration of the TAT Problem Solving Assessment Protocol's sensitivity to training in problem-solving (Ronan et al., 1995). Additionally, a recent article traced the history of each TAT picture's development (Morgan, 1995). Among several interesting disclosures were indications that Christiana Morgan was a major figure in early TAT research and the senior author of early TAT articles, but was absent from later publications. Speculative explanations ranged from "male chauvinism" to her declining health (p. 239). The TAT pictures were taken from original paintings done especially for the TAT, paintings by contemporary artists, magazine art, and drawings by Christiana.

Limitations

Shortcomings of Murray's point of view and methods fall into four categories: (1) he pulled many of his critical concepts off the top of his head without input from previous research or theory; (2) he failed to differentiate his concepts from other similar notions; (3) he attempted to explain everything; and (4) his methodologies, most especially those associated with the TAT, were loose, informal, and intuitive, rather than scientific.

Murray's narcissism apparently affected his thinking. He imbued his ideas with an aura of self-evident truth as soon as he conceived of them, even though they often seemed not to have been inspired by scientific theory or data that preexisted them. As soon as ideas occurred to him, he wrote of them as fact, without citing other sources in support, except as after-the-fact citations to confirm what he already believed (Murray, 1981a). The lone, possible exception was the case of Freud. Although often cited after-the-fact, Freud is mentioned frequently enough in regard to Murray's ideas that have a clear psychoanalytic flavor that one can readily believe Freud was at least partially the source of those notions. Excluding Freud's influence, one is left with the impression that some of Murray's important concepts came from "out of the blue," or his self-proclaimed intuitive genius, not scientific data or theory. Ideas treated as if they stem from scientific thought, but, in fact do not, may be more appropriately placed in the realm of philosophy.

At some points in his writings, Murray seems almost confused about the nature of his ideas. Are needs actually drives? Are they really traits of personality? If Murray could not decide, he was not alone. Indecision may have also characterized his followers who used his needs. As indicated earlier, Jackson (1984) thinks of needs as "traits" and Singer (1990) conceives of them as "goals." Concepts are scientifically useful only insofar as they are clearly distinct from other concepts (Allen & Potkay, 1981; 1983b). Consistent with this lack of clear differentiation among concepts, some of his ideas do not fit well into appropriate categories. For example, n Play, to relax, amuse oneself, and seek diversion and entertainment, was not included in Table 15.1, because it does not clearly fit under Adience or Abience vectors. What exactly Murray was talking about remains unclear.

Murray felt obligated to explain everything and reconcile his point of view with everyone else's position (1981a). He mentioned many of the popular concepts of his day, either rejecting them and asserting that his ideas were better or squaring them with his own. Thus, he attempted to reconcile some of his ideas with those of Skinner, but he rejected Watson's position out of hand. No theory can handle everything. Those that try almost always explain nothing very precisely.

Murray made so much of his disdain for scientism in psychology that he alienated his colleagues in experimental psychology. So thorough was his rejection of them and their methods that one wonders whether the former biochemist abandoned science altogether. The TAT is a good case in point. Murray guided his colleagues in more or less arbitrarily selecting TAT pictures. What he finally decided on were hardly the ambiguous figures appropriate to a projective test. Potkay and colleagues have shown them to be gender-biased, females favored over males, and invested with definite meaning that is shared by subjects (See Allen & Potkay, 1983a; Potkay & Allen, 1988). Further, for many years, scoring of the TAT was unsystematic to the point that the quantitative methods so dear to science could not be used. Murray himself (1981d) tended to ramble in analyzing TAT narratives, revealing no particular system and often drawing unclear conclusions. Later more systematic methods were developed, but, as Potkay indicates, these fall short of providing for fully valid and reliable interpretations.

There is irony in Murray's rejection of "scientism." Some of his own concepts have the flavor of superficial science. "Regnancy" and "strength of needs" are examples. But it seems not so ironic that the name "Henry A. Murray" is disappearing from the pages of psychology's scientific journals. A recent, informal computer search turned up no references to his name.

Conclusions

Despite his much celebrated narcissism—and it probably was real—Murray was a warm and kind person who inspired the love and admiration of countless psychologists. As a measure of his impact, tributes to him began *before* he died. It is obvious from reading them that he touched the professional and personal lives of many colleagues. True, many of his ideas may have been off the top of the head, and his needs may not have been well differentiated from other concepts. However, the measure of a theorist's contribution is often more in how much he or she inspires others to new professional heights than whether the theorist's ideas as originally proposed were without flaws. While Murray's name is not often mentioned, his needs and the TAT recently received hundreds of mentions. Perhaps Murray's name is scarce in the literature because some of the many researchers who use his ideas wish to lay claim to them: A concept may seem to originate with those who cite it, if they fail to mention the real source of it. As for the TAT, no one can deny its historical significance: it is one of the most cited and used tests ever. Rather than a fault, some would consider it a virtue that TAT output might be understood mainly by intuition. Clinical intuition may be a better tool for helping real people than all the products of scientific methodology in the world.

Summary Points

1. Henry A. Murray was the child of wealthy parents who sent him to the best preparatory school and to Harvard. Throughout most of his life he fought stammering and a "marrow of misery and melancholy." His private life and, to a degree, his professional life were heavily influenced by his mistress Christiana Morgan. Examination of their relationship reveals his great complexity. As an adult he developed a sense of "specialness" and a distinct narcissistic orientation. These inclinations led him to distrust male colleagues and dismiss others' points of view.

2. After graduating with an M.D. and a Ph.D. in biochemistry, and spending several weeks with Jung in the interim, he assisted the head of the Harvard Psychological Clinic and immediately ran afoul of his "scientistic" colleagues. Drawn to psychology because of his personal problems, he pursued his own brand of "psychoanalysis." He became a primary mover in the Boston Psychoanalytic Society and underwent psychotherapy, but got little from it except reinforcement for his belief in the unconscious.

3. Murray believed that internal representations are regnant, related to "dominant configurations in the brain." To him, a need is a force in the brain that transforms an unsatisfying situation into a more satisfying one. He considered need to be nearly synonymous with drive and also overlapping with trait. One need category is called viscerogenic, and is further segmented into positive (the adience vector)—for example, n Water, n Sentience—and negative (the abience vector)—for example, n Expiration, n Noxavoidance. The other need category is psychogenic, which is segmented into positive—for example, n Achievement and n Affiliation—and negative—for example, n Autonomy, and n Contrarience.

4. Needs can be specified in terms of strength. In fusion of needs there is an "action pattern that satisfies two or more needs at the same time." Subsidiation of needs occurs "When one or more needs are activated in the service of another need" and contrafactions of needs are cases where needs alternate with their opposites. Conflicts of needs are cases where needs oppose each other.

5. A need integrate or complex is formed when images of cathected objects become mentally integrated with the needs, emotions, and modes (actones) that they typically excite. Complexes are recurrent phenomena that fill our dreams, hallucinations, illusions, and delusions. They may also be manifested in artistic expression, drama, religion, fantasies, plays, and movies. While they may seem to allow clairvoyance through dreams, Murray found no evidence to support that connection.

6. Press "do to the subject" or "for the subject" and often are referred to in the future tense: "It may do this or that to me." A thema is a combination of a particular need and a particular press or pressive object. Jackson's much used Personality Research Form (PRF) is a trait measure based on Murray's needs. Recently it has been translated into a nonverbal form that will be useful for cross-cultural research. Murray's needs have also been profitably translated into "life goals."

7. The Thematic Apperception Test (TAT) consists of one or more human figures mounted on cards. Research subjects/clients are asked to look at each card and then tell a

story about it. Potkay and colleagues advanced previous attempts to discover information that would aid analysis of responses to the TAT cards. They used the AGT and showed that figures had definite, shared meaning for subjects: Females were more favorably depicted, and the tone of the figures was melancholy. Recent TAT research supports its validity and its applicability to diverse clinical and research problems. A history of its cards reveals the role Christiana Morgan played in card development and the origin of card-pictures.

8. Using the TAT, Murray analyzed B, a student, who came from an upright, Southern, Methodist family ruled by his large, temperamental father with whom he slept as a boy. As a child B was plagued by thoughts of death, portrayed himself as effeminate and fearful, and reported what were regarded as homosexual experiences. Themes in B's narratives evoked by TAT cards included homosexuality, anality, heterosexual sadism, masochism, and necrophilia. Murray concluded that birth, death, and sexual intercourse were closely linked in B's mind. Murray's evident classism was a source of pain for his colleagues and an explanation of his disdain for the hippie rebellion. His attitude now exists subtly in many of us.

9. Limitations of Murray's point of view include: (1) his tendency to pull concepts off the top of his head; (2) his failure to differentiate his concepts from similar notions; (3) his attempts to explain everything; and his (4) intuitive methodologies, especially regarding the TAT. Ironically he resorted to scientism himself, but it is no irony that his name is scarce in the psychological science literature.

10. Despite these shortcomings, Murray, the subject of several tributes even before his death, inspired many psychologists to develop his concepts in meaningful ways. His needs and the TAT continue to be heavily cited, even if he is rarely given credit. They stand as monuments to his intuitive genius.

Running Comparison

Theorist	*Murray in Comparison*
Freud	He used Freudian language and was a defender of psychoanalysis. He believed in the unconscious and the importance of sexuality.
Skinner	Like Skinner he emphasized the "push from the rear" and the importance of the effect of an action, not its particular form.
Horney	n Succorance is like her unresolved basic anxiety and n Abasement is like her masochistic submission.
Sullivan	Like Sullivan, he was interpersonally oriented.
Maslow	Like Maslow, he believed humans to be dynamic wholes who rarely respond to one need at a time. Need was also central to Maslow, but only Murray said need is equivalent to drive.
Jung	Need integrates were like Jung's Archetypes. He also embraced Jung's polarities and "contrafactions of needs" was like Jung's "equivalence." The contrast of waking and dream orientations was also Jungian. Generally he borrowed a great deal from Jung.

Gordon Allport   Like Allport, Murray also studied individuals rather than groups and ignored sensory elements and conditioned responses in favor of personality characteristics.

Essay/Critical Thinking Questions

1. What would Murray have been like had Christiana Morgan never entered his life?

2. Can you argue that one can solve her or his own problems by becoming a psychologist? What is the counterargument?

3. Could you argue that studying the "long unit," the entire life history of the "organism," is the best way to understand people in general? Why is it better than "taking snapshots"—working piecemeal?

4. Did Maslow borrow from Murray? His major works did follow Murray's. What is it about the viscerogenic and psychogenic needs that might have given Maslow his idea about the "hierarchy of needs"?

5. Can you choose a couple of Murray's needs and join them by fusion (fusion of needs)? In so doing, use real life examples.

6. Can you identify a need integrate or complex that is shared by so many people in our society that it shows up in books and movies? Give some examples of its manifestations in the entertainment media.

7. Can you list some press that affect us regularly? Try to list some in addition to those in Table 15.2.

8. Can you give some examples of thema that regularly are seen in your interactions with other people? Use Murray's notation.

9. What else is wrong with the TAT in addition to those problems uncovered by Potkay and his colleagues? Look at Table 15.3 to see what you can discover.

10. How might Murray have been a different person had he been middle class or working class? Would it have affected his theoretical ideas?

E-mail Interaction

(Contact the author at mfbpa@wiu.edu)
Forward one of the following or phrase your own.

1. What's the difference between Murray, who had a "girlfriend" on the side but got by with it, and behaviorist John B. Watson, whose affair cost him his academic job?

2. Murray seems to occupy the extremes of many dimensions. Tell me what he was really like.

3. What was the most important need in Murray's long list?

4. Was that Harvard student "B" really unusually weird, or would the TAT uncover strange things about most of us?

5. Which TAT cards do you find to be the most interesting?

16

THE FACTOR ANALYTIC APPROACH TO PERSONALITY TRAITS: RAYMOND CATTELL AND HANS EYSENCK

- Can people with "hard science" training do better psychological research than those whose backgrounds are entirely in psychology?
- How many kinds of intelligence are there? Is intelligence the same the world over?
- Do your genes determine your personality and your intelligence?
- Can how strongly you salivate to lemon juice say anything about your personality?
- Can personality be reduced to just three dimensions?

Raymond B. Cattell

As you have seen, Murray's needs were used as if they were traits. In fact, Murray was regarded as a trait theorist by many colleagues in personality psychology. He was, however, not nearly as dedicated a trait theorist as the two covered in this chapter. Raymond Cattell and Hans Eysenck conceive of personality rather exclusively in terms of traits or traitlike entities.

Cattell believes in isolating and reducing the raw material of personality to a manageable data pool, collecting massive amounts of data from the pool, and using intricate statistical methods to tease facts about personality from the data. Thus, he proceeds in a manner opposite to that of all the theorists considered so far, except for Skinner.

Eysenck shares many interests with Cattell. They both use the statistical technique "factor analysis" to discover a few central traits. Nevertheless, he differs from Cattell in embracing experimental psychology. Eysenck believes that researchers should take the principles developed in the psychology laboratory and relate them to personality by use of experimental procedures. Because of their differences, it is not surprising that the two personality psychologists arrive at different sets of traits to characterize personality.

Cattell, The Person

Raymond B. Cattell was born (1905) in Staffordshire, England, the son of middle-class parents (a cut above the American middle class). He labelled his father's career "design engineer," apparently in reference to the elder Cattell's role in Grandfather Field's manufacturing business (Cattell, 1974a). Raymond's father was congenial and inclined to deliver dinnertime lectures on history and current topics. The son has little more to say about the father, except to show veiled disappointment at the discovery, following the administration of IQ tests, that the "design engineer" was the intellectual inferior of his mother. She also is only briefly mentioned, but he implies a warm relationship with her and hints that the high intelligence he attributes to himself came mostly from her family. This judgment, made soon after he became a psychologist, is interesting because it shows an early orientation to conceiving of intelligence as mostly inherited.

Cattell describes his childhood as basically happy, but he is quick to add that it was "not easy" (Cattell, 1974b, p. 88). He described his parents and teachers as "exacting." One gets the feeling that the symptoms of stress Cattell showed later in his life were born of the strong drive to achieve instilled in him by the circumstances of his family's middle-class standing and the pressure exerted on him by his parents (Cattell, 1974a). Still, the claim to happiness appears to be genuine.

Three years before World War I started, he moved from England's midlands to the magnificent coast of Devonshire. There he and his brothers and friends "sailed, swam, fought group battles, explored caves, landed on rocky islands . . ." and generally enjoyed an idyllic childhood (p. 62). Even the War, when it arrived, became something of a plaything. Cattell was appointed a "sea scout" and charged with watching the coast for enemy ships. Like Fromm, Adler, and Jung, he was impressed with the destructiveness of modern warfare. "I enjoyed [the scouting] though awestricken to see the holes as big as a house that torpedo and mines could blow in steel plates. And then came the long trainloads of wounded from the Flanders . . . still in their bloodstained bandages" (p. 63). Young Cattell helped care for these stricken soldiers.

Schooling at the "selective secondary school" where Cattell was on scholarship continued despite the sacrifice of the best teachers to the war effort (p. 63). However, the headmaster at the school kept his position throughout the war. This "very intelligent and hard-driving man, a cousin of [Rudyard] Kipling [author of the *Jungle Book*] whom he closely resembled" provided Cattell with a first scholastic role-model (p. 63). The intellect and motivation of the man was not all that impressed Cattell: "He divided his time between giving me personal sessions in science and mathematics, and thrashing me for various original deviations from school regulations" (p. 63).

Cattell's connection to Freud—reflected in some of the traits he later identified—is mentioned in relation to his older brother and father. "A fine Freudian Oedipus situation [developed] between my older brother, the first born, and Father." The brother, one of two, is remembered fondly by Cattell. He recalls tagging along behind the older sibling during their daily treks to school. They were in the same grade, owing to Cattell's advanced status, and the brother's modest intellectual skills. Yet the specter of sibling rivalry was also present. He wrote, "If I admit to scars of distrustful independence . . . they . . . come from the severe stresses of maintaining my freedom of development under a powerful brother three years older, who could be outwitted, but not overcome" (p. 63).

"At fifteen, I passed the Cambridge University entrance examination (. . . in which I was granted first-class honors), but since my scientific interest indicated London University, and my parents were loath to leave me on my own in London at that age, I did not go until sixteen" (p. 64). This proclamation is interesting in that Cambridge, not London University, is world famous and especially known for its excellence in science. It seems that every institute with which Cattell was associated was a haven for intellectual giants. It may have been a way for him to say that he was himself quite brilliant. In his writings he sometimes draws analogies between his own work and that of famous scientists.

While he may be a bit of a braggart with regard to his intellectual powers, his beliefs about himself are hardly delusions. After distinguishing himself in secondary school, Cattell graduated *Magna cum Laude* in chemistry at the ripe old age of nineteen. But almost immediately he decided to apply his intellectual acumen to the pursuit of psychology. Just before he received his degree, he was enchanted by a speech concerning the work of Sir Francis Galton, a pioneer in mental testing. The speaker, Sir Cyril Burt, was soon to be one of his mentors and later to be involved in a scandal over IQ data. Immediately he was fascinated with psychological assessment. Despite protests from friends that he would go unemployed—there were only a handful of psychology chairs in all of England—he, like Murray, deserted his test tubes in favor of working with some of the most notable figures in the world of psychological measurement. In 1929 he received his Ph.D. in psychology and entered the field.

After a series of " 'fringe jobs' in psychology" (e.g., psychologist in the schools), during which there was time for research planning, but little research, Cattell spent five years gaining clinical experience (1974b, p. 90; Cattell, 1974a). Then he was elevated to director of a school psychological service in Leicester, Devonshire, England, his home territory. During this time he became convinced that intelligence is mostly inherited. In 1936 he wrote an article for the *Eugenics Review* in which he answered "yes" to the question "Is national intelligence declining?" (Loehlin, 1984). The argument began with the assumption that the higher the social class the higher the intelligence. It proceeded with the observation that lower social classes were having more children. The conclusion was that more children among the less intelligent lower classes were driving the average national intelligence down. Out of these efforts and Cattell's book, *The Fight for Our National Intelligence* (1937), came the bold prediction that England's intelligence was in for a fall.

But, alas, it did not happen. Fifteen years later, there was actually a slight increase in national intelligence (Loehlin, 1984; IQ continues to rise in England and elsewhere in the world). This disappointment did not deter Cattell from continuing his membership in the controversial Eugenics Society (Cattell, 1974a). **Eugenics** is the application of genetics to the improvement of human biological and psychological characteristics. It, of course, has animal applications. In its most benevolent form, it was dedicated to exhorting people to carefully choose spouses and monitor the number of children they produce with an eye to promoting positive traits and discouraging negative traits. In its more malevolent form, it advocates "species improvement by controlled breeding" (McGuire & Hirsch, 1977, p. 61), even to the point of calling for government programs to control human breeding.

There is evidence that Cattell has not changed his mind on eugenics and, if anything, has increased his influence regarding it. Citing lines from Cattell's 1987 book, *Beyondism: Religion from Science*, Rep. Cardiss Collins (D-ILL) charged that the NCAA (National Collegiate Athletic Association) was being influenced by a panel of psychologists that included three Beyondism Foundation Members (Associated Press, 1993). Because Beyondism, both the book and the Foundation, supports eugenics, Congresswoman Collins implies that the NCAA is listening to advocates of a eugenics support system: One plank in Beyondism's eugenic platform is academic encouragement of only the "intellectually gifted." Apparently they would reserve college scholarships for people who score high on college entrance exams and other IQ-related tests. They would deny scholarships to most others. As the NCAA is embroiled in a controversy over whether disadvantaged minorities of low academic standing ought to be allowed athletic scholarships, Collins objected to the influence of Beyondism advocates. It appears she suspected that athletic scholarships, presently dominated by students of color, will be transferred to the "academically capable," which would exclude minority students, if Beyondism advocates have their way.

This period between graduation with the Ph.D. and his first secure job in a real academic setting was a time of frustration and stress. Probably owing to long hours and laborious administrative duties, Cattell developed a "functional stomach disorder" from which "I have ever since suffered" (Cattell, 1974a, p. 68). The hard work, the stress, the stomach problem, and the low pay also took a toll on his marriage. Finally, his wife, who was accustomed to better, could stand the annual salary of $1200 and the "dark damp basement flat" no more (p. 68). She left and he yearned for a fresh start. Being frustrated with his job, and having severed his closest ties, he considered life in the United States.

Fortunately, at about this time, Edward L. Thorndike, who was the salvation of Maslow, came to Cattell's rescue (Cattell, 1974a). The author of the "law of effect" had read *The Fight for our National Intelligence* (1937) and was so impressed that he offered Cattell a position at Columbia University Teachers College in New York City. From there he moved to the G. Stanley Hall Professorship at Clark University and then to a lectureship at Harvard. After a time at Duke University, he accepted a Research Professorship at the University of Illinois where he prospered from 1945 until his retirement in 1973. He is now settled on Oahu where he is associated with the University of Hawaii at Manoa. Retirement to some is a perpetual vacation, but, like Fromm, Cattell saw it as an opportunity to produce a torrent of papers and books, guaranteeing a place for himself in the history of personality psychology.

Cattell's View of the Person

Cattell's Approach to Understanding the Person

One of the great virtues of Cattell's position is that he makes a refreshingly different basic, philosophical assumption. Unlike some other theorists, Cattell did not begin with "ideas off the top of the head," based on nothing more than simple intuition or subjective clinical observation. As an empiricist he believes that one collects data first then filters and sifts it through various statistical techniques until the facts emerge. These facts then generate hypotheses that can be tested. Thus, the proper mode of reasoning is first *inductive*, reasoning from particular observations to a more general statement of position. Then it becomes *deductive*, reasoning from a general statement to expected observations and so on. He operates along the **inductive-hypothetico-deductive spiral**, "the detecting of regularities in observational data leads to a hypothesis from which experimental consequences are deduced, [leading] to further data from which new regularities are induced, and so on in an ever-expanding spiral" (Wiggins, 1984, p. 189). This approach is the method of astronomy, and often physics and chemistry, but rarely psychology, especially personality psychology. Personologists should note Cattell's strategy: eschew "off the top of the head" theorizing in favor of careful data collection from which meaningful hypotheses will arise.

Personality Defined

Through judicious use of the inductive-hypothetico-deductive spiral, eventually a complete picture of the human personality can be painted. In straightforward fashion Cattell defines **personality** "as that which tells what a [person] will do when placed in a particular situation" (Cattell, 1966, p. 25). It is expressed in a simple formula: $R = f(S.P)$ where R stands for the "nature and magnitude of a person's behavioural response, . . . what he [or she] says, thinks, or does," which is some function (f) of S the "stimulus situation in which [the person] is placed," and P the nature of her or his personality (p. 25). While these conceptions seem delightfully simple, in fact, getting from P to R is a complicated matter.

Nature and Nurture

Cattell is noted for coming down on the nature side of the nature/nurture debate (Hirsch, 1975). Based on his own and others' research, he has argued that a number of human characteristics, most especially intelligence, are controlled to a great extent by the genes (Loehlin, 1984). Therefore, Cattell believes that the person is in large part shaped by genetic influences.

The Econetic Model

The relative emphasis on genetic influences should not be taken to mean that Cattell totally neglects the environment (Cattell, 1979, v. 1). $R = f(S.P)$ is consistent with attention to the environment(s). To express these sentiments more emphatically, Cattell has proposed the **econetic model**, a framework that integrates environmental situations with characteristics of the person, including personality components, in attempts to understand the person. When he discusses the various personality traits he has uncovered through research, he very often indicates the approximate degree to which each is controlled by the genes and how much each is controlled by the environment. For example, *self-sentiment*, a self-concept maintenance structure, is believed to be genetically determined, while *super-ego-strength* is believed to be environmentally determined, based on research findings (Cattell, Rao, & Schuerger, 1985).

Factor Analysis

One of the ways one can isolate and verify traits is by seeking quantitative support for them in patterns of statistical correlations. To uncover these patterns, Cattell uses **factor analysis**, a statistical procedure for determining the number and nature of factors underlying larger numbers of measures (Kerlinger, 1973). The basic assumption is that certain simple responses correlate, or vary together, and thus may be grouped together to define a separate psychological dimension or factor. By determining "what goes with what," factor analysis is able to reduce large amounts of data from a complex to a simpler form (Spearman, 1927).

To help gain a concrete conception of factor analysis, imagine that a psychological test made up of many questions is administered to a group of one hundred people. If one of the test items is answered in a certain way by forty people, it is possible that these same forty people will answer other items in systematically related ways. Suppose that they answer "yes" to test item #1. They might also answer "yes" to other items, let's say #26, #45, and #37, and "no" to others, say #17 and #82. At the same time, another subgroup of forty people may answer the same items in the opposite way from the first group. And, the remaining twenty people may show no definite pattern. Obviously certain items are related to certain other items, otherwise subgroups of the entire sample would not be answering them in the same way. Factor analysis identifies such sets of items and determines that the items of each set share some common denominator. The **factor** in factor analysis refers to a hypothetical construct that is applied to a data cluster (set of items) and suggests what it is measuring.

The *analysis* in factor analysis refers to the procedures used to identify factors. These methods involve computations of many intercorrelations: Each item is correlated with each other item and each with the item clusters that are identified. Once a factor has been identified, it is assigned a label, based on the researcher's best judgment about the psychological dimension the cluster of items seems to measure. Judgments are guided by the content of items making the greatest contribution to a cluster identified as a factor. In turn, contributions of items to a factor are determined by statistical **loadings**, correlations of particular items with a given factor.

Factors resulting from factor analysis are not all of the same order of comprehensiveness or generality. Some are **primary factors** which are relatively pure and narrow in scope. It can be arranged statistically that primary factors are independent (Cattell, 1966; Eysenck, 1984). Other are **secondary factors** which encompass several primary factors and are called "superfactors" or "second-order factors" (Cattell, 1966; Eysenck, 1984). Cattell (1966) and others believe that extraversion–introversion is a secondary factor that subsumes certain primary factors.

In sum, Cattell approaches understanding the person by first observing simple responses, often reactions to questionnaire items. Through the use of factor analysis, certain clusters of these items are isolated as factors. These factors may allow the development of certain theoretical statements, which, in turn, may suggest further research to refine the previously discovered factors and associated statements. Eventually, after many repetitions of this inductive-deductive cycle, a picture of human personality may emerge.

Basic Concepts: Cattell

"There are no constructs in Cattell's theory that are not related to quantitative measuring procedures" (Wiggins, 1984, p. 177). Cattell does not have "concepts" in the usual sense: theoretical statements that are somewhat removed from the research procedures used to derive or confirm them. Many of the notions covered in the preceding section were shared with other researchers, and, in all cases, were related to research procedures. However, the two ideas that are covered next are unique to Cattell. They also refer to research procedures.

Data Types

In **Q-data**, where Q stands for *questionnaire*, people are their own observers, describing their behavior and feelings through paper-and-pencil inventories, self-reports, or interviews. Endorsing, "I am sensitive" is a sample response. In **L-data** or *life-records*, ratings are "made by observers on the frequency and intensity with which specific kinds of behavior occur in the people they observe" (p. 61). An example observation would be "Maria is studious." **T-data** involves an observer's recordings of a person's behavior in some standard, contrived, laboratory-test situation. "Hakeem reacts to a light by pressing a button in .34 seconds" would be an example. Factor analysis may involve any of the three data types.

Data Collection Techniques

Only three data collection techniques are covered here because the others "appear rarely if at all in Cattell's empirical work" (Cronbach, 1984, p. 229). Cattell's most used method is called the **R-technique**, a "process of correlating behaviour measures across some hundreds of people [*tested on a single occasion*] and factoring them" (Cattell, 1966, p. 153). Thus, hundreds respond to all of many measures to see which measures cluster together. Often involving Q-data, the R-technique is more straightforwardly factor analyzed than other methods.

   The differential R or **dR-technique** is the same as the R method, except that each of the hundreds of people responding to the several measures does so two times, usually after only a short delay, and each person's score on each measure is the second response minus the first. It is useful in looking at change effects. Suppose a psychologist is interested in the effect of a tranquillizer drug on people under stress. She assesses two hundred people on forty measures relating to various aspects of anxiety and stress, some psychological and some physiological. After they have responded to the measures the first time, half of them are given the drug, and the other half get no drug, then they all respond to the same measures again. Second minus first scores are computed next. The forty change scores for each subject are factored to see which factors best account for the change. To determine the effects of the drug, the change scores of the "drug" subjects can be factored separately from those of the "no drug" subjects. Then a comparison of the two factor structures might illuminate the role of the drug in generating changes over the two measurement occasions.

   P-technique is "A factor analytic design which measures a single person on the same set of variables repeatedly over a number of different occasions" (Cattell, 1966, p. 372). The "P" is for "person" and the focus is on change over many units of time (e.g., many days). The data matrix for eight measures and twenty days is filled by having one subject respond to all eight measures on each of the twenty days. The matrix could be factor analyzed to extract factors in the category **state** or mood, a psychological entity that fluctuates or varies over time and thus is "transitory," as distinguished from traits which are "permanent" (Cattell, 1977, p. 220). Cattell has done a considerable amount of work with states, often involving his *Eight State Questionnaire*. However, most of it has employed the two-response dR technique, rather than the more appropriate multiple response P technique.

Traits

Trait Subsidiation

A **trait** is a permanent entity that does not fade in and out like a state; it is inborn or develops during the life course and regularly directs behavior. Cattell has developed quite an elaborate method for classifying traits. It springs from **subsidiation**, the idea, borrowed from Murray, that some psychological entities are subsumed under others. Thus, traits are arranged in a hierarchy, from the most general and fewest in number to the most specific and greatest in number. The **common trait** is "A trait which can be measured for all people by the same battery [of tests] and on which [the people] differ in degree rather than in form" (Cattell, 1966, p. 368). Thus, almost everyone can be given a position on a common trait dimension, varying, for example, from "extraverted" to "introverted." By contrast the **unique trait** is "so specific to an individual that no one else could be scored on [its dimension]" (p. 28). An example would be the tendency to wink on completing the expression of a question. Cattell paid very little attention to unique traits.

Second-Order Traits

At the top of the hierarchy are the most all-embracing or **second-order traits**, "superfactors" that subsume the other traits ("secondary factors" define second-order traits). That is, other traits fall under secondary traits: each secondary trait may be thought of as composed of lower order traits that all relate to the secondary trait's label. Cattell has dealt extensively with two of these higher order factors. One is **exvia-invia**, "A factorially established broad dimension within the area of behaviour popularly referred to as extraversion-introversion" (p. 369). The other second-order trait is equally familiar: **anxiety**, the feelings of tension and upset, the source of which may be difficult to identify. In addition to exvia-invia and anxiety, two of the six others he has considered appear consistently in factor analytic studies: a measure of intelligence and an index of "good upbringing" (includes having "good manners"; H. Cattell, 1994). Still Cattell continues to argue that his 16 primary factors have more predictive power than the second-order factors.

Source Traits

The **source trait** is "A [primary] factor-dimension, stressing the proposition that variations in value along it are determined by a single unitary influence or source" (Cattell, 1966, p. 374). As the definition indicates, source traits are homogeneous: each relates to a set of behaviors that resemble each other. For example, *emotionality* is a trait that refers to behaviors such as calmness, jitteriness, "cool-headedness," and "excitability."

Source traits are further broken down into three categories. An **ability trait** is reflected in "the manner of response to the complexity of a situation, [selected after] the individual is clear on what goals he wants to achieve in that situation" (p. 28). Most of Cattell's efforts in the "ability" category have been concentrated on "intelligence," a concept I will return to later. The second category is the **temperament trait**, "a general personality trait [that] is usually stylistic, in the sense that it deals with tempo, persistence, [and so forth] covering a large variety of specific responses" (p. 28). A good example of a temperament dimension is "emotional vs. stable" (same as emotionality; Wiggins, 1984).

Compared to the other two categories of source traits, Cattell devotes relatively more attention to the **dynamic trait**, which refers to motivations and interests (Cattell, 1966). This subcategory may receive more attention because it is complex, composed of three interrelated subordinate categories. Like Maslow's needs, dynamic traits are goal-directed. The most basic is the **erg**, "An innate source of reactivity, such as is often described as a drive [or instinct], directed to a certain goal and accompanied by a certain quality . . ." (p. 369). The term comes from the Greek *ergon* for work or energy. Although there are many examples of ergs, a couple of representative cases will suffice to illustrate the concept. The operation of the *sex erg* is signified by expression of such attitudes as "I want to satisfy my sexual need" (p. 190). An illustration of the *fear erg* is seen in "I want us to attack and destroy any formidable military power that actively threatens us" (p. 189).

The second dynamic trait relates to the first. An erg is manifested in an **attitude**, an expression of an ergic goal that is generally subsidiated to an erg(s). The third dynamic trait category is **sentiment**, "A *set* of attitudes the strength of which has become correlated through their being all learnt by contact with a particular social institution [such as] sentiment to school, to home, to country" (emphasis added; p. 374). Thus, sentiments organize and coordinate attitudes in the service of ergs. Illustrative sentiments are (1) *sentiment to religion*: "I want to see the standards of organized religion maintained or increased throughout our lives"; (2) *sentiment to career*: "I want to make my career in the Air Force" (pp. 191–192). Note the reference to society's institutions in both expressions.

The relationship among attitudes, sentiments, and ergs is reflected in the **dynamic lattice**, "The tracing of the subsidiation of attitudes . . . ending in the satisfaction of a number of primary ergic goals" (p. 369). A partial illustration of the dynamic lattice shows the nature of the relationship among attitudes, sentiments, and ergs (Figure 16.1). Note that, for the protection erg, the sentiment is "country" and the related attitude set includes "Armed Forces" and "President of U.S."

Surface Traits

Surface traits are "A set of personality characteristics which are correlated but do not form a factor, hence are believed to be determined by more than one influence or source" (p. 375). They are the most subordinate traits, responses to the individual test items or the specific behaviors with which the researcher begins factor analysis. Surface traits are gut-level feelings, thoughts, and actions, the atoms of the personality molecule (the quarks may be neurological events, as Murray believed). Examples are "I enjoy scuba diving" and "I practice yoga." These surface traits would fall under the source trait conservative-experiencing (to the experiencing end of the continuum). It will be helpful to look at Cattell's entire schema for classifying traits. See Figure 16.2 for trait type, factor analytic level (parenthetical statement), and examples.

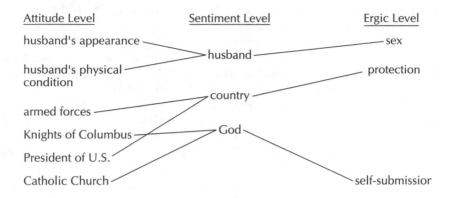

FIGURE 16.1   The Dynamic Lattice

Intelligence

Cattell endorsed the conception of intelligence fostered by Charles Spearman, an early mental tester. Spearman promoted "g," which supposedly subsumes the so-called primary mental abilities and forms a common core of general intelligence (McGuire & Hirsch, 1977). Cattell assumes that this general factor of intelligence is largely due to the genes (Cattell, 1966). In a paper read at the American Psychological Association convention, 1940, he argued that "g" fell into two categories (Cattell, 1984b). **Fluid general ability** (g_f); is "That form of general intelligence which is largely innate and which adapts itself to all kinds of material, regardless of previous experience with it" (Cattell, 1966, p. 369). Whereas he reports that early evidence indicated "g" was 80 percent inherited, he claims that g_f is nearly 100 percent inherited. Only pre-birth accidents and post-birth trauma, such as head injury, prevent g_f from being fully inherited. By contrast, **crystallized general ability** (g_c) is "A general factor, largely . . . abilities learned at school, representing . . . applications of [g_f], and amount and intensity of schooling; it appears in vocabulary and numerical ability [tests]" (p. 369). g_c is acquired intelligence that is little affected by the genes. The quality of schooling largely determines the magnitude of this ability.

The Personality of Nations

Syntality is national personality "equivalent to personality in an individual and capable of (a) predicting many behaviors and (b) by profile similarity measures permitting nations to be classified in a dozen types" (1984, p. 99). In one study, 18 families of nations were isolated from a pool of 100 nations (Cattell & Brennan, 1984). One family was composed of Canada and Australia and another of Britain, Sweden, and Switzerland. Thus, some nations form a family because their personalities are similar and different from those of other families. The notion of national personalities is similar to Fromm's "social character."

```
                          TRAITS
                          Common
    _____
                       Second Order
                        Exvia-Invia
                      (Secondary Factor)
    _____
                          Source
                      (Primary Factor)
    _____
    ability              dynamic              temperamen
    _____  _____  _____
    "I.Q." |  attitude  | sentiment | erg | emotional/stab
           | "I love sex"|  spouse  | sex |
    _____
                          Surface
               " I laugh at other people's jokes"
```

FIGURE 16.2   Cattell's Trait Classification Schema

Evaluation

Contributions

For decades, Cattell has been among the most prolific of test developers, devoted to the process of constructing, refining, and extending his measurement techniques. His work has been programmatic, undertaken systematically rather than piecemeal.

His firm belief is that individuals differ in relative locations on "permanent" trait dimensions as well as on "transitory" state dimensions and that these dimensions are assessable by means of personality questionnaires.

Assessing Personality with the 16 PF

True to his empiricist nature and his inductive-hypothetico-deductive orientation, Cattell began with the most basic, elemental reflections of personality, trait descriptive words of the English language (Wiggins, 1984). He reduced 4500 trait words from the comprehensive list produced by Gordon Allport and his colleague Odbert (1936) to 160 synonym groups. These groups were regarded as "surface clusters" and were eventually reduced to 171 terms by eliminating synonyms. The 171 *trait elements* were intercorrelated and 36 clusters of correlations were isolated. These clusters were called *surface traits*. Ten more were later added to make a total of 46 surface traits. This set was the grist for Cattell's factor analytic mill. Eventually, much refinement yielded the *16 primary factors* of the now famous 16 Personality Factors test or *16 PF*, a 16-scale test of adult personality measured in terms of 16 source traits (Cattell, Eber, & Tatsuoka, 1970). The final 16 PF was based on responses of 10,000 people. Later versions were developed for use at elementary, junior, and early high school levels.

In business and industry, the **16 PF** has served as an aid to decision-making about employee selection, efficiency, turnover, and promotion. In education, it has aided the

Label	Low Score Description		High Score Description
A	Reserved (Sizothymia)		Outgoing (Affectothymia)
B	Less Intelligent (Low "g")		More Intelligent (High "g")
C	Emotional (Low ego strength)		Stable (High ego strength)
E	Humble (Submissiveness)		Assertive (Dominance)
F	Sober (Desurgency)		Happy-go-lucky (Surgency)
G	Expedient (Low super-ego)		Conscientious (High super-ego)
H	Shy (Threctia)		Venturesome (Parmia)
I	Tough-minded (Harria)		Tender-minded (Premesia)
L	Trusting (Alaxia)		Suspicious (Protension)
M	Practical (Praxernia)		Imaginative (Autia)
N	Forthright (Artlessness)		Shrewd (Shrewdness)
O	Placid (Assurance)		Apprehensive (Guilt-proneness)
Q_1	Conservative (Conservatism)		Experiencing (Radicalism)
Q_2	Group-tied (Group adherence)		Self-sufficient (Self-sufficiency)
Q_3	Casual (Low integration)		Controlled (High Self-concept)
Q_4	Relaxed (Low Ergic tension)		Tense (Ergic tension)

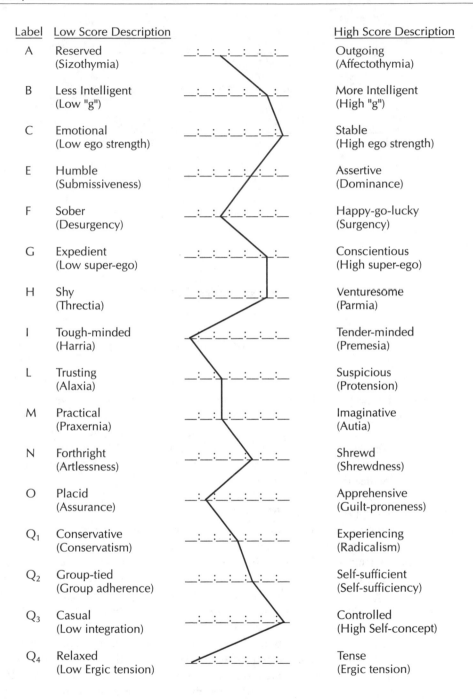

Figure 16.3   Technical (in parentheses) and Popular Labels for the 16 PF Factors A to Q4

BOX 16.1   Your Own 16 PF Profile

Your can create your own 16 PF profile by simply placing an "X" in the scale interval that you think represents your level on each factor and then drawing a line through the "Xs." Be honest with yourself; ignore the line for "John Skyman" while you are creating your own profile. After you have completed your profile, then you can compare yourself to "Skyman."

Of course, you should recognize that your perceptions of your positions on the scales would not necessarily coincide with your actual positions if you took the 16 PF. In the actual test, for each factor there are several items over which a score is computed to represent the final factor score. You would not know your positions on the factors with confidence until you responded to all of the items.

---

planning of individualized programs for students and the prediction of school achievement. Cattell's, Eber's, and Tatsuoka's (1970) handbook for the 16 PF contains 125 profiles depicting ideal trait levels for various jobs, including sales personnel, airline pilots, mechanics, teachers, school counselors, nurses, and electricians. In clinical settings, the 16 PF has aided the diagnosis of people with behavior problems, anxiety, neurosis, alcoholism, drug addiction, and delinquency. It also has been used to understand similarities and differences in personalities of married couples seeking counseling. Figure 16.3 contains the popular and technical names for the scales of the 16 PF. Study them to get a feel for the different scales.

Notice the zigzag line through the middle of the scales. It represents the personality profile of a hypothetical pilot, "John Skyman." By following the line you can see how "John" scored on each scale. "John's" profile conforms well with data derived from 360 real airline pilots. The pattern reflected in the profile is "an excellent combination for high reality contact and emotional stability under stress" (Cattell, Eber, & Tatsuoka 1970).

Identifying Developmental Trends

Another of Cattell's contributions involves the identification of trends in personality development, from childhood through adulthood. Knowledge of age trends permits the plotting of standardized growth curves. Comparisons can then be made between individuals within a given age group, and between groups of persons of different ages and gender. Results are analogous to guidelines represented by the height and weight charts used by pediatricians in assessing patterns of children's physical growth. An example personality trend reflected in 16 PF measures is superego-strength's moderate but decelerating increase with age.

Limitations

Because he depended on it so heavily, much of Cattell's theoretical structural and research interpretations rests on the validity and meaningfulness of factor analysis. Unfortunately, it is commonly said of factor analysis that researchers never get anything out of it they did not put there in the first place. This is because the results of factor analysis are extremely dependent on several biasing influences.

No Single Factor Analytic Method

Controversy continues over which specific method of factor analysis should be used (Eysenck, 1984). Eysenck points out that one of the methods used in conjunction with factor analysis can force factors to be independent of one another. Another method can force factors to agree with theory. Cattell's 16 PF work involved a third method that allows factors to be dependent or correlated with one another. This procedure makes the factors "impure," according to Eysenck. In view of this impurity, he queried, "Why not use the second order factors as they are fewer in number and more inclusive?" Regarding who is correct, Cronbach (1970) wrote, "There is no one 'right' way to do a factor analysis any more than there is a 'right' way to photograph Waikiki Beach" (p. 315).

Subjective Judgments Remain

Factor analysis only partially reduces the amount of subjective judgment involved in answering questions about "what" and "how many" dimensions are present in personality. Arbitrariness on the part of researchers enters into the picture at three points. First, researchers promote certain factor-analytic solutions rather than others partly by estimating how many factors are likely to be present in the data. Cattell (1973) and the Eysencks (Eysenck & Eysenck 1969) refer to this as "the number of factors problem." Different decisions by each theorist regarding the number of constructs underlying personality partly explains why different numbers of traits have been proposed to account for personality. Goldberg (1981) observes:

> The number of primary personality factors in Cattell's system is in the 20-to-30 range, . . . the 16 most famous [constituting the] 16 PF. When his data were made available to others, however, virtually everyone who factored those data found only 5 (pp. 156–159).

Second, sometimes the items entered into factor analysis are arbitrarily and subjectively chosen. Item selection should be based on previous research. Instead items may be chosen solely on the basis of the factor analyst's biases.

Third, once factors have been identified, cutoff values are required to establish whether an item makes a meaningful contribution to a factor. Statistical loadings of .60 to .40 on a factor are likely to be judged quite acceptable by most factor analysts. But what about .30 to .10? There is another criterion available to help decision-making, but it is also a number for which some arbitrary cutoff point must be established.

The fourth source of subjectivity is perhaps the most serious. Although statistical programs can identify various factors present in a set of data, it is the factor analyst who interprets and labels all factors. By looking at the items contained in a factor, the analyst must subjectively decide what to call them. She or he assigns labels that are consistent with his or her own theory. Other analysts might label the factors differently, according to their own theoretical biases. This helps explain why one researcher's "neuroticism" and "extraversion" (Eysenck) are another's "anxiety" and "exvia" (Cattell).

Nature–Nurture: Heritability

Cattell casts almost everything he studies according to how much of its variability is determined by the genes and how much by the environment. For example, as you recall, nearly

100 percent of the variation (individual differences) in fluid intelligence is supposedly accounted for by the genes, but the figure is much smaller for crystallized intelligence (Cattell, 1966). Among 16 PF factors some are thought to be controlled more by the genes than by the environment and some are more environmentally controlled (Cattell, Schuerger, & Klein, 1982).

Heritability popularly refers to the proportion of the variability in a trait that is accounted for by the genes. (See McGuire and Hirsch, 1977, for a discussion of the different indexes of heritability.) Heritability has been estimated in various ways, sometimes rather directly by use of correlations between the IQs of identical twins reared apart (they are rightly assumed to be genetically identical, and perhaps wrongly assumed to be reared in entirely different environments). Cattell has adopted a seemingly more complex method for estimating heritability, one that he regards as among his major achievements. It is **Multiple Abstract Variance Analysis (MAVA)**, "A research design for discovering relative proportions of environmental vs. hereditary determination for personality traits (nature-nurture ratio)" (Cattell, 1966, p. 372). For those of you who enjoy mathematics, it involves writing a series of equations, each with one unknown, either relating to heredity or environment, and solving the *set of equations simultaneously* for the unknowns (Loehlin, 1984). For those less enamored with math, MAVA is simply another way to produce heritability estimates. To his credit, Cattell has used MAVA to go beyond the limited twins method. MAVA considers not only identical or fraternal twins but also brothers and sisters and unrelated people. Although the method may seem complex, actually Cattell has kept it relatively simple by ignoring certain important considerations (Loehlin, 1984).

In an example study, heritability was estimated using MAVA for the 16 PF factors ego-strength, super-ego strength, and self-sentiment (efforts to maintain one's self-concept) (Cattell, Rao, & Schuerger, 1985). Results indicated that self-sentiment is more genetically determined and super-ego strength more environmentally determined, with ego-strength falling between the two. However, heritability estimates varied markedly depending on the method of estimation used. Also, results were not entirely in line with those of a highly similar study reported by Cattell, Schuerger, and Klein (1982). Further, Cattell's attempts at heritability estimation have come under fire for technical shortcomings. Esteemed statistician H. W. Norton wrote about one such attempt: "In conclusion, the statistical analyses reported by Cattell et al. are incorrect, and the 'results' they report should be ignored" (Norton, 1972, p. 225).

Again, to his credit, Cattell acknowledges the variations in estimations with variation in technique, but he attempts to strongly interpret results anyway. This doublethink about heritability results highlights a fact that is often ignored by Cattell and others: Heritability estimates are good only for the population used, at the time it is used (McGuire & Hirsch, 1977; Hirsch, 1975; Weizmann, Wiener, Wiesenthal, & Ziegler, 1990). They do not generalize to other populations or to another sample taken from the same population at another time. Further they are population measures; they do not apply to individuals from the populations: it is "an average statistic and *population* measure, [and] provides no information about how a given *individual* might have developed under . . . [different] conditions . . ." (Hirsch, 1975). Just as a specimen of a tree species develops differently on the top of a mountain than down in a valley, a given individual might turn out differently if reared under different conditions than those that actually existed for her or him. It is important to

---

**BOX 16.2   Intellectual Diversity: Variety and
                Relativity**

That intelligence is one thing, "g", probably constitutes a consensus among psychologists interested in mental ability. Cattell has broken it down further, but he seems only to be saying that the one thing, "g", can be conceived of as one part inherited and another part not inherited. While most psychologists may support "g," there is also a growing minority of rebels who believe that intelligence is extremely complex, not just one thing but many things.

Prominent among them is Robert Sternberg (1988) who believes that there are three broad intelligence categories, not just one called "g". One kind is like "g": It is the ability to collect information and analyze it. A second kind is sort of like creativity: It is putting pieces of information together into something entirely new. The third kind may be thought of as "street smarts": It is adapting to one's environment so as to maximize one's outcomes. The last two are not really measured on IQ tests, but do contribute to people's survival and prosperity (in terms of this broad definition, any psychological factor that makes such a contribution is a kind of intelligence).

Another rebel is Howard Gardner (1983) who believes there are seven kinds of intelligence rather than just "g". Among his intelligences are some that amount to "g", but also there is musical ability and kinesthetic ability, the latter being, roughly speaking, the "right stuff" for athletics. There are two others that may be interpreted as the ability to know oneself and the ability to know others. Most of Gardner's intelligences are not measured on intelligence tests that are designed to assess only "g". Obviously if IQ tests did include Sternberg's and Gardner's intelligences, some people's scores would go up (those

individuals with the additional intelligences) and some people's scores would go down (those without the additional intelligences).

Most psychologists who are interested in intelligence apparently think that it is absolute: the same thing the world over. It is assumed that to test the intelligence of the Australian Aborigines (native Australians) or the people of Tibet the most one needs is someone to translate the U.S. IQ test into another language. But suppose intelligence is relative: it is related to the specific socio-physical environment of a people. In one environment abilities A, B, C . . . are critically important to survival and prosperity. In that environment, people who have A, B, C . . . are intelligent and those who do not are not intelligent. But in another environment, abilities X, Y, Z . . . are critically important, because, compared to the first environment, different skills are needed for survival and prosperity. Actually, because of the barren, hilly, amorphous environment their ancestors had to master, Australian Aborigines children have stronger spatio-visual ability than Australian children of European descent (Carnes, 1994). The original Australians throughout most of their history needed this kind of intelligence to find their way in their amorphous surround. They had to be able to look at this misshapen hill or that undulating terrain and remember it or they would get lost and possibly die. Aborigines children can remember the position of each of several rocks placed in a box better than the European Australian children. If the spatio-visual ability measured on the rocks test were more heavily weighted on the IQ test, the Aborigines children's scores would go up and those of the European children would go down.

---

note that, because heritability is a population statistic, it is interpretable for the single population contributing the data from which it is estimated. For example, heritability estimates made using "whites" are meaningless when applied to "blacks."

The notion of heritability itself is suspect when used as Cattell and others have employed it. It was originally developed to estimate how successful animal breeders would be in their efforts to breed for certain desirable traits (McGuire & Hirsch, 1977; Weizmann, Wiener, Wiesenthal, & Ziegler, 1990). It was never intended to be used as a means to partition the variance in a trait into that accounted for by the genes and that accounted for by the environment. In fact, the very act of dividing up variation in a trait, whether intelligence or personality is considered, is suspect from a genetic point of view. Consider an analogy. The question "In computing the area of a rectangle, which is more important, its length or its height?" makes no sense. Likewise, asking "Which is more important, heredity or environment?" may be meaningless (Hirsch, 1975). Every genetic disposition unfolds in an environment. Likewise, one could argue that no environmental influence exerts itself apart from potential genetic input. Separating the genetic contribution to a trait from that of the environment in which it is expressed may be seen as artificial.

It seems clear that Cattell's work with heritability is at best controversial. While this possibility does not distract from his other contributions, it does suggest that his research and theory regarding heritability be viewed with considerable caution.

State-Trait

Cattell, like others, declares that state and trait are distinct (Allen & Potkay, 1981, 1983b). The index of his 1966 book refers to the distinction between state and trait. However, on turning to the indicated page, all that one finds is a declaration that they are distinct. To his credit, in a later publication (1977) he, unlike others, acknowledges the lack of a clear distinction by referring to "The fact of there being no absolute distinction between traits and states" (p. 220). Yet, like others, he has always and continues to refer to traits as "stable" and states as "transitory" without saying how "stable" a personality entity must be before it is considered a "trait" rather than a "state."

Conclusions

Even if one ignores his heritability work and the fact that his research techniques have been criticized, there is much to be admired among Cattell's many contributions. His empiricist stance is in stark contrast to the "off the top of the head" theorizing of many theorists covered in this book. Perhaps personality psychologists should be more like astronomers than chemists. Because what psychologists study is complex and difficult to "get the hands on," or even "the eyeballs," they should be cautious in forming hypotheses until after many observations are made. If psychologists consider this advice, they are following Cattell's capable lead.

As mentioned several times before, the worth of a scientific contributor is often determined as much by whether he or she inspires others to think new and useful thoughts as by his or her own ideas. Cattell has literally trained dozens of personality psychologists. Some of them, such as Jerry Wiggins and John Nessleroade, have gone on to prominence.

If one had to point to a personality measure that taps personality more completely and meaningfully than all the others, one could well vote for the 16 PF. It is perhaps the most carefully developed by use of the most sophisticated methods. It also was not "done in a day" as are some measures. It evolved over many years of careful research.

Finally, the model of scientific contribution is not to "make your mark" with a few publications based on a few studies, each done in a short time, early in a career. Cattell is still producing research. He is a contributor for life.

EYSENCK: 16=3—

CONCEIVING OF PERSONALITY

IN THREE DIMENSIONS

Eysenck and Cattell are often linked, perhaps because they both are pioneer factor analysts and both were trained in Britain. Both are associated with heavy use of complicated statistical methods. Both believe that personality and intelligence are strongly determined by the genes. Both have spent a professional lifetime trying to reduce personality to only a few dimensions. They even had the same mentor, Sir Cyril Burt. However, there are differences. In fact, in recent years they have been carrying on quite a debate. The issue? How many dimensions must one consider in order to account for personality, 16 or 3? Eysenck's argument for just "3" occupies most of the remaining pages of this chapter.

Eysenck, The Person

Hans Jurgen Eysenck

Hans Jurgen Eysenck was born in Germany on March 4, 1916 to a moderately known actor, Eduard Eysenck, and an aspiring actress, Ruth Werner (Gibson, 1981). He came of age during the deprivations of the period following World War I. After his parents' marriage was dissolved, Eysenck lived with his maternal grandmother, who raised him in a permissive atmosphere. Consequently, he was a self-willed boy, accustomed to having his own way. For example, at age eight, he bit the finger of a teacher who was trying to punish him for his adamant refusal to sing. Later, in high school, he proved a teacher wrong in his claim that Jews were lacking in military valor. Interestingly he did it with statistics: Jewish soldiers received a disproportionate number of German medals for valor during the war. In another incident, he refused to attend the lectures of a teacher who had given him less than the highest grade on an essay. This kind of behavior inspired Gibson (1981) to indicate "Eysenck appears to have . . . a very good opinion of his own abilities" and ". . . of himself . . ." (p. 18).

In fact Eysenck's hard head and tough mind have raised the ire of many people during his life. By the time he was a teenager, the Nazis were in the process of taking over Germany. It was inevitable that Eysenck would continue his education elsewhere, because, to him, Nazism was absurd. He would have had to leave in any case, because his stepfather, Max Glass, was a Jewish movie producer-director who was no longer welcome in Germany. Thus, in the summer of 1934, Hans, Max, and Ruth departed for France where Max successfully resumed his career. There Eysenck briefly pursued an advanced education, until a visit to Exeter, England in 1933 led to a love affair with Britain. At age eighteen, in the autumn of 1934, the affinity for England was still so strong that it lured him to London. There he entered University College with the intention of pursuing a "hard" science curriculum. Unfortunately, he had a deficiency in science that would have required time and money to correct. Accordingly, he enrolled in psychology, which was just beginning to be recognized as a "science."

As fate would have it, Eysenck entered what then was the most scientific psychology department in England. It was the site of intense activity in psychometrics, the measurement movement in psychology. Even as an undergraduate, he did research with Sir Cyril Burt, and Burt helped him collect the data that went into his first publication. Sir Cyril also edited the article, and, without Eysenck's permission, altered it to fit his own theories. Undismayed, Eysenck took only three years to finish his psychology doctorate with honors. The topic was experimental aesthetics.

In the same year, 1940, Britain declared war on Germany and Eysenck was labeled an enemy alien. Barred from the armed forces, he did research at the Mill Emergency Hospital, which was associated with the Maudsley Hospital, later his lifelong research center. During this period and later Eysenck was accused of being a "fascist," probably because he was a German who seemed to espouse "heredity is everything"—and thus, it seemed to follow that personality traits and intelligence cannot be changed. This position was in defiance of social programs that assumed "environment is everything"—traits and intelligence can be changed. Despite these handicaps, Eysenck moved up the academic ladder. In 1950 he was granted the position of reader at the University of London. In 1955 he became a professor, despite the opposition of Cyril Burt, who had turned against him. At the same time he was becoming a dominant figure at Maudsley. From these positions of power he defied the psychological establishment and began the long campaign for acceptance of his "Big 3" factors.

Eysenck's View of the Person

Eysenck is apparently not the warm and accepting person that Carl Rogers was (Gibson, 1981). While he is a supportive friend and colleague, his condemnation of psychotherapy, for which he narrowly escaped physical assault, may have emerged from his inability to be a therapist sympathizing with neurotic clients.

Like Cattell, he believes a continuous program of research conducted over many years is the proper approach to understanding the person, but he advocates a different research program.

> *Thus, Cattell starts from the generation of hypotheses about the major factors involved, stays [with] factor analysis . . . and assigns . . . low importance to the fact that his primary factors are intercorrelated, and give rise to superfactors . . . At each stage I follow exactly the opposite line. Starting out with a theoretical model . . . I use factor analysis to test theories rather than to originate them.* I tried to use [theory] from . . . psychology and physiology to link the factors . . . with causal hypotheses which led outside factor analysis altogether" (Eysenck, 1984, p. 335; emphasis added).

Eysenck added, "Cattell has been opposed to the current theories emerging from experimental laboratories, and has openly criticized 'brass-instruments' psychology. As a consequence his own work has little relation to the concepts which concern the classical experimentalists, or the psychophysiologists" (p. 329). By contrast, Eysenck does real experiments and relies on evidence and hypotheses from experimental psychology. Also he alternates between experimental procedures and factor analysis until he feels that he has honed and refined the concept he is working with.

Central to the difference between Eysenck and Cattell, and critical to Eysenck's uniqueness relative to other personality theorists, is the question "at what level does one find the traits that are necessary and sufficient in number and nature to account for personality?" Contrary to Cattell and his 16 factors, Eysenck believes personality can be parsimoniously understood, with no loss of thoroughness or depth, by reference to only 3 second-order factors. But neither has given an inch, as is evident in Cattell's (1986) response to Eysenck.

Basic Concepts and Contributions: Eysenck

Traits And Types in Eysenck's Theory

As with Cattell, the essence of Eysenck's theory is that personality can be described in terms of **traits** represented as statistical primary factors and defined as "theoretical constructs based on observed intercorrelations between a number of different habitual responses" (Eysenck & Eysenck, 1969, p. 41). Examples of traits relevant to Eysenck's theory include physical activity, impulsiveness, risk-taking, responsibility, worrisomeness, carefreeness, and sociability, all dating to the ancient Greeks.

Traits, in turn, are often grouped in categories called **types**, second-order dimensions made up of statistically intercorrelated primary traits. They can be thought of as superfactors, but Eysenck prefers "second-order" (1984). He has identified three such factors, reporting that they "or others remarkably similar to them" have been found repeatedly in different studies (1981, p. 6). Eysenck's three second-order factors or types are: E, Extraversion-introversion; N, Neuroticism-stability; P, Psychoticism-superego functioning. These types essentially are the same as Cattell's second-order factors exvia-invia and anxiety and his primary factor "super-ego strength" respectively (Eysenck, 1984).

Eysenck does not believe each person is either E or not-E, 100 percent N or not at all, totally P or totally not P. This means that all people show some degree of all three types. One person may show much extraversion, some neuroticism, and a little psychoticism. A second person may show very little extraversion (much introversion), some neuroticism, and some psychoticism. For most people, values fall within the average range. Since very few people fall at such extreme degrees as 0 percent or 100 percent, pure "types" are hard to find. When it comes to extraversion-introversion, most of us are **ambiverts**, people who show medium degrees of this trait, with behaviors characteristic of both aspects. Nevertheless we tend to *perceive* people as falling at the extremes. If a person is induced to be introverted, he or she will see a partner as extraverted (Alicke & Klotz, 1993).

Biological Determinism

Among psychologists, it would be difficult to find a more radical advocate of biological and genetic determinism. Eysenck has always maintained that there is a "substantial" hereditary basis to personality (Eysenck, 1990). Over the years he has also contended that intelligence is genetically determined (Eysenck, 1971, 1974). Eysenck complains that psychologists, especially those in the United States, whom he views as overemphasizing environment and learning, pay too little attention to hereditary influences on behavior. Psychology's purpose is to study the behavior of organisms, but psychologists have failed to appreciate the degree to which organisms respond differently to the same environmental stimuli, independent of learning.

> *Personality is determined to a large extent by a person's genes; . . . while environment can do something to redress the balance, its influence is severely limited. [For] Personality [and] intelligence . . . genetic influence is overwhelmingly strong, and the role of environment . . . is reduced to effecting slight changes . . . (Eysenck, 1976, p. 20).*

E, N, and P have "a strong genetic basis" (1981, p. 6). He estimates that, across all trait dimensions, including E, N, and P, about 60 percent of individual differences in personality is determined by the genes (Eysenck, 1990).

Eysenck also indicates that E, N, and P are closely tied to physiology (Eysenck, 1967; Eysenck & Eysenck, 1969, 1976). To illustrate, extraversion (E) has been linked to the brain's **ascending reticular activating system (ARAS)**, which acts as an arousal mechanism. The core of the system is the reticular formation of the brain stem. When stimulated by sensory input, it sends messages through ascending nerve fibers to arouse the cerebral cortex, the brain's upper crust that coordinates lower brain areas. In turn, the entire organism is activated. If the sensory input originates in environmental events having survival value, the cortex sends messages back down to the reticular telling it to continue promoting arousal. This feedback loop determines whether we continue to *attend to* given environmental events or not.

Eysenck links Neuroticism (N) to the limbic system, the brain's emotional center that regulates such functions as sex, fear, and aggression. Psychoticism (P) has been linked with the endocrine glands, specifically the ones that secrete sex hormones. One source of support for Eysenck's (1990) genetic position is research involving genetically identical twins and fraternal twins, who bear no more genetic similarity to one another than any two siblings. Because they are genetically identical any differences between identical twins must be due to the environment. By contrast differences between fraternal twins may be due to either the genes or to the environment (Eysenck, 1967).

Eysenck (1967, 1990) points to empirical findings that show identical twins to be much more alike in personality than fraternal twins, even when identical twins have been separated early in childhood and raised by different parents, in separate environments. Also, he contends that identical twins are more alike in criminal and neurotic behavior than fraternal twins. Further, adopted children are more similar to their biological parents than to their adoptive parents on a number of trait dimensions. Loehlin, Horn, and Willerman (1990) report partial support for Eysenck's position.

Toward a Scientific Model of Personality

Eysenck's (1981) **scientific model for studying personality** involves two interlocking components: (1) *description*, which seeks to answer questions about "what" personality is—for example, "what are the identifiable individual differences in traits and types?" and (2) *explanation*, which seeks to answer questions about "why" personality is the way it is—"What are the causes of those individual differences?" In Eysenck's model, concepts are sought that will help reduce human behavior to a small number of variables that are tied together by rules or laws. Ideally, laws should enable psychologists to explain past events and to predict future events.

Researching Traits and Types

Eysenck's model of personality is closely linked to **psychometrics**, a quantitative approach to psychological measurement. Box 16.3 will introduce you to psychometrics.

Measuring and Describing E, N, and P

Reducing Observable Events to a Few Variables

Like Cattell, Eysenck adheres to *subsidiation*, the Murray concept. Imagine a pyramid that has four levels representing the personality traits and responses falling under "extraversion." At the base of the pyramid are **specific responses (SR)**, everyday behaviors or experiences that may or may not be characteristic of an individual, such as saying "Hi" to a neighbor. At the next level up are **habitual responses (HR)**, specific responses (Cattell's surface traits) that recur under similar circumstances, such as *regularly* saying "Hi" to a neighbor. At the third level, habitual responses are organized into *primary factors*, or traits. For our extraversion example, these are sociability, impulsiveness, activity, liveliness, and excitability. Extraversion is at the top of the pyramid, the level of *secondary factors* or types. Thus, "[the four primary traits] would form a constellation of traits intercorrelating amongst themselves and giving rise to a higher order construct, the type" (H. Eysenck & S. Eysenck, 1969, p. 41). Obviously Cattell and Eysenck are very close on what is subsidiated to what, but Cattell emphasizes primary factors and Eysenck second-order factors.

The MMQ, MPI, and EPQ

The Maudsley Medical Questionnaire (MMQ) introduced the concept of neuroticism (N), the Maudsley Personality Inventory (MPI) added extraversion-introversion (E), and the Eysenck Personality Questionnaire (EPQ) added psychoticism (P) (Eysenck, 1952; Eysenck, 1959; S. Eysenck & H. Eysenck, 1968, 1976). Using the MMQ to investigate N, Eysenck found that 1000 neurotic soldiers scored twice as high on N as 1000 normal soldiers. N scores tend to decrease with age, to be higher for women than for men, and for persons in lower socioeconomic classes. High Ns are emotionally overresponsive and unstable, anxious, worrisome, moody, restless, touchy, often complain of bodily symptoms, and are prone to breakdown under stress. Persons with low N are emotionally stable, calm, carefree, even-tempered, and reliable.

The MPI, a revision of the MMQ, included E as well as N items. In general, E scores tend to be higher for men than for women, to decrease with age, and to be unrelated to socioeconomic class. Persons with high E scores tend to be sociable, popular, talkative, crav-

BOX 16.3 The Maudsley Personality Inventory (MPI), Short Form

Instructions: The following questions pertain to the way people behave, feel, and act. Decide whether the items represent your *usual* way of acting or feeling, and circle either a "Yes" or "No" answer for each. If you find it absolutely impossible to decide, circle the "?," but use this answer sparingly.

1. Do you prefer action to planning for action? YES ? NO
2. Do you sometimes feel happy, sometimes depressed, without any apparent reason? YES ? NO
3. Are you happiest when you get involved in some project that calls for rapid action? YES ? NO
4. Do you usually take the initiative in making new friends? YES ? NO
5. Are you inclined to be moody? YES ? NO
6. Would you rate yourself as a lively individual? YES ? NO
7. Are you frequently "lost in thought" even when supposed to be taking part in a conversation? YES ? NO
8. Do you have frequent ups and downs in mood, either with or without apparent cause? YES ? NO
9. Are you sometimes bubbling over with energy and sometimes very sluggish? YES ? NO
10. Are you inclined to be quick and sure in your actions? YES ? NO
11. Does your mind often wander while you are trying to concentrate? YES ? NO
12. Would you be very unhappy if you were prevented from making numerous social contacts? YES ? NO

(Adapted From Eysenck & S. Eysenck, 1969; used with permission of Hans Eysenck.)

Now try to group the items into two categories: put together the six items that seem to go together, then look at the other six items to see if they go together. If not, then categorize again until you come up with two sets of six items that seem to measure two different types. When you finish, you have performed a crude factor analysis. Categorize now before going on.

If you grouped items 2, 5, 7, 8, 9, and 11 together and labeled them as N and items 1, 3, 4, 6, 10, and 12 as E, you have done well. Obviously, if you said yes to most N items, especially numbers 2 and 8, which are loaded .75 and .74 on neuroticism, you are "high on neuroticism" (but do not take it too seriously; a six-item test result is not to be trusted without further evidence). Just as obviously, if you indicated "yes" to E items, especially numbers 6 and 12, which are loaded .68 and .64 on extraversion, you are extraverted.

ing excitement, taking chances, impulsive, practical jokers, easygoing, optimistic, on the move, short-tempered, lacking control of feelings, and unreliable. Persons with low E scores tend to be retiring, fond of books, distant except to close friends, introspective, quiet, cautious, unimpulsive, serious, organized, reserved, pessimistic, ethical, imperturbable, controlling of feelings, and reliable.

In developing the EPQ, which added P items to those assessing N and E, Eysenck (1952) wondered whether there was a clear-cut separation between "psychotic" and "normal." Contrary to psychiatric classification systems, he answered "no": Most people have at least a little "psychotic" tendency as part of their genetic makeup. Further, P is independent of N and E (S. Eysenck & H. Eysenck, 1976, pp. 17–18). Clinically "psychotic" people, especially schizophrenics, showed the highest P scores. Also high were criminals and others showing antisocial behavior. P scores tend to be higher for men, to be lower for persons in the middle socioeconomic class, and to decrease with age. Persons with high P scores are solitary, troublesome, uncooperative, hostile, cruel, unempathetic, sensation-seekers, like odd things, like films of war and horror, undervalue people, are socially withdrawn, sexually impersonal, deficient in thought and memory, distractible, devalue education, are suspicious, have mood disturbances, show motor disturbances, are suicidal, have psychotic relatives, are delusional, hallucinatory, and creative. The flavor of P is seen in Eysenck's (1970) description of a high P man, aged 21. When asked to explain his endorsement of the EPQ "liking parties" item, he answered, "Well, at parties you get free grub, free likker and a chance to screw some bird, don't you?" Then, with an angelic smile, he added, "And sometimes you can break up the place, too" (p. 427).

Supporting Evidence

The Lemon Juice Test for Arousal Shown by Extraverts (Es) and Introverts (Is)

Eysenck contends that Is have a higher level of cortical arousal through the ARAS than extraverts (Es hereafter; Corcoran, 1964; S. Eysenck & H. Eysenck, 1967). It follows that "under conditions of equal stimulation, [the reaction of nerves in the muscles and glands] would be greater for introverts" (p. 1047). Thus, the more people's scores show them to be introverts (Is hereafter), the more strongly they should salivate to lemon juice. In fact, Is do salivate more than Es when pure lemon juice is placed on their tongues.

Loud Commercials Are More Appealing to Es

As everybody knows, commercials on TV and radio are played at a louder volume than the programs surrounding them. This strategy is assumed to overwhelm resistance to persuasion, thereby increasing the likelihood that listeners will purchase the advertised products. Cetola and Prinkey (1986) found that high volume works, but only Es favored commercials played at a louder volume than the preceding program; louder volume did not matter for Is.

Bad Exam News Is Worse for Is

Based on completion of the MPI by 200 college students, Fremont, Means, and Means (1970) isolated the 30 highest scoring (Es) and the 30 lowest scoring students (Is). Each student was then given a brief written task requiring the learning of a digit-symbol code. Some Es and some Is were told they scored "higher than average," or told they scored "lower than average," or were given no information about their performance. An anxiety test was administered to all students immediately following the feedback session. When feedback was negative, Is clearly showed greater anxiety than Es. Is and Es differed under no other condition.

Drugs, Liquor, Coffee, and Tobacco

Eysenck believes that depressant drugs, such as alcohol, will have a more detrimental effect on Es, because their ARASs already put a lid on their arousal (1962). On the other hand, stimulants, such as coffee and cigarettes, will be more detrimental to Is, because their ARASs already allow them too much arousal. In partial support of the hypothesis, Jones (1974) reported that although the detrimental effect of alcohol applied to Is and Es alike, it was significantly worse for Es. Gupta and Kaur (1978) showed that a stimulant, dextroamphetamine, improved the efficiency of Es but interfered with Is's performance on a perceptual judgment task. The hypothesis also helps to resolve a dilemma: Hyperactive children are given the stimulant Ritalin. If they are "cortically underaroused" like Es, which causes them to seek stimulation, the paradox is resolved (Powell, 1981). Stimulants function to make them more physiologically like Is, allowing them to slow the desperate search for stimulation that is part and parcel of hyperactivity.

Explaining Real-Life Behavior: Mass Hysteria

In 1965 a polio epidemic dominated press coverage of a town where a British secondary school was located, causing outsiders to avoid the "polio town." Later that year, an outbreak of physical symptoms occurred among girls attending the school (Moss & McEvedy, 1966). On day 1, students attended a lengthy church ceremony, during which 20 girls fainted. The next day, new fainting began to occur during school assemblies. Fainters rested on the floor, where the sight of them generated excitement and fear, resulting in overbreathing, dizziness, headache, feeling cold or hot, shivering, nausea, and faintness. Soon the behavior resumed spontaneously at school assemblies. Medical lab findings were negative. All 25 girls who fainted on day 1 and went to school on day 2 were affected, while none of the girls absent on day 1 were affected on day 2. Also, those still suffering on later days had been among those affected on early days. Consistent with the "mass hysteria" label, the number of new occurrences was higher during school assemblies than classroom sessions. The EPQ was given to 535 of the students and results showed that affected students displayed a combination of high E and high N scores.

Extraversion: King of the Personality Concepts

Extraversion (versus introversion) may well be the most investigated and substantiated personality concept ever and Hans Eysenck is in large part responsible for its popularity and success. A few recent study outcomes illustrate the breadth and importance of Eysenck's central concept. Viken's and colleagues's (1994) study is a recent example of a long line of research that confirms the genetic underpinnings of extraversion. They found that extraversion was substantially inherited and tended to be stably so across gender and time.

As is indicated later in this chapter, there is an ongoing debate concerning which personality factors are necessary and sufficient to account for personality. However, work by Zuckerman and his colleagues (1993) supports a consensus: Extraversion will be prominent on any list of most important personality constructs. They found that extraversion was consistently represented in all three models of personality they investigated.

Extraversion's link to other important psychological variables is illustrated by McFatter (1994). He found that extraversion was related to both positive and negative affect (mood) among neurotic subjects. The research literature also links extraversion to psychological factors that have implications for people's well-being. Amirkhan and colleagues (1995) found extraversion to be positively related to "seeking social support" and optimism, two concepts known to be important in coping with stress. Magnus and colleagues (1993) found that extraversion predisposed research participants to experience positive life events.

Obviously extraversion is a core personality variable that links to many critically important psychological concepts.

Limitations

Arousal and E-I

Probably Eysenck's best known experimental contributions are wrapped up in the link between E-I and the ARAS. While there seems to be general agreement that Is are, on average, more sensitive to stimulation and react more negatively to it, this difference is being laid at the door of newly specified brain mechanisms, not ARAS (Stelmack, 1990). Despite this development, some researchers continue to support Eysenck's ARAS theory (Bullock & Gilliland, 1993).

Further, work by Gerald Matthews and his colleagues shows that the effect of extraversion on task performance is a complex function of the type of task, and surprisingly, the time of day at which the task is completed (Matthews, Davies, & Lees, 1990; Matthews, Jones, & Chamberlain, 1989). Level of arousal (high or low) affects both Es and Is in the AM, but in the PM only Is are affected by arousal level. Further, Es may have more resources available to them for use on certain kinds of tasks and "These resources are more reliably increased in subjects . . ." exposed to high arousal (Mathews, Davies, & Lees, 1990, p. 167). Thus, arousal may only facilitate what Es already have, rather than change the character of their reactions to tasks.

Genes and Controversy

Eysenck's work in behavior genetics is as suspect as Cattell's. Like Cattell, he has been scalded by some critics for applying heritability to differences between groups, such as "blacks" and "whites" (Hirsch, 1975). Furthermore, Eysenck's suggestion that personality factors are largely genetically determined is sometimes given no support or only qualified support by other researchers. For example, Loehlin, Horn, and Willerman (1990) found that the primary source of change in some personality factors, including extraversion, was *individual experience*, not the genes. However, they did report some support for the genetic hypothesis: in the case of adopted and natural children, with increased age the children were tending to change in the direction of their real parents' personalities.

It should be noted that Eysenck and Cattell are not being criticized for studying the genetics of behavior, personality, and intelligence. It would be absurd to suggest that the genes have nothing to do with these psychological entities (Hirsch, 1981). The problem is with the heritability method favored by psychologists that artificially partitions the variation in psychological traits into the portion accounted for by heredity and the portion accounted for by environment. Psychologists need to become real geneticists trained in biological laboratories so they can do genetics as it traditionally has been done, with populations, not behaviors or cognitions (Hirsch, 1964). Properly trained psychologists could directly assess the genetic underpinnings of psychological traits rather than relying solely on statistical approximations. In fact, such work is currently being done (VandeWoude et al., 1990; Brunner et al., 1993).

The Bell Curve: Race and Environment

Richard Herrnstein's and Charles Murray's *The Bell Curve* continues to cause waves on the academic pond. Critics from a variety of disciplines condemn its claim that intelligence is mostly due to the genes. Given the claim is correct, Herrnstein and Murray assert that the intellectual elite will literally inherit the technological society of tomorrow. Herrnstein and Murray also point to an IQ gap favoring European Americans over African Americans and imply that it might be "inherited." As a prologue to their race/IQ discussion, they pledged to eschew use of the word *race*, because the term has uncertain status at best, but they continued to use *race* throughout their discussion anyway. Thus, they opened themselves up to some serious problems.

Problems with comparing "whites" and "blacks" on IQ begin with those racial designations (Allen & Adams, 1992; Katz, 1995; Yee et al., 1993). One can hardly meaningfully compare two groups on anything if experts cannot agree on the criteria for separating people into the two groups. Even if there were a consensus on criteria for dividing people into racial groups, how would one show that a racial gap on IQ was "inherited"? The heritability index could not be used, because it is applicable to a single population, not comparisons of two populations. In short, "Is a 'black'-'white' IQ gap inherited?" is a bogus question.

There is a way to finesse the debate on whether intelligence—which is probably more than IQ—is "genetically determined." That environmental interventions can change the expression of genetically "determined" traits is as certain as the observation that medical science can prevent the occurrence of genetically "determined" diseases, genetically "determined" deformities can be reversed with plastic surgery, and genetically scrawny people can become strong via weightlifting.

Even if intelligence were totally "genetic," genetic input may be eclipsed by early exposure to enriched environments. It has long been known that animals bred to be "bright" and other animals bred to be "dull" turn out equally highly intelligent when reared from soon after birth in an enriched environment (e.g., a sort of animal Disney World: a very complex environment; see, for example, Cooper & Zubek, 1958). In recent years, William T. Greenough and his colleagues have shown that enrichment actually increases the complexity of nerve cells' branches, thus providing an explanation of the enrichment effect on animal intelligence (e.g., Greenough et al., 1987). What about humans? Also, in recent years, Craig T. Ramey and his colleagues exposed children, for whom the genetic prediction would be low intelligence, to environmental enrichment *beginning in infancy*. In one study, exposed children showed dramatically higher intelligence test scores relative to comparable children provided no early enrichment (Campbell & Ramey, 1994). What is more, they maintained their advantage to age 12 where the research ended. Genetic "anatomy" is not necessarily intellectual destiny. To his credit, Eysenck is now recognizing the validity of this observation (*Monitor*, 1993).

Big 5 or Big 3?

Finally, Eysenck, in effect, has shrunk personality to just three dimensions. While many trait theorists have reduced personality to just five dimensions, virtually no one agrees with Eysenck's smaller number (see the *American Psychologist*, Comments, December 1993). But is 5 enough or is 16 really required? The five are Extraversion, Emotional Stability (Neuroticism), Conscientiousness, Agreeableness, and Openness to Experience (Guastello, 1993; Kroger & Wood, 1993). Eysenck (1993) sees conscientiousness and agreeableness as collapsible into Psychoticism. Thus, it is three after all. But Big 5 advocates (e.g., Goldberg, 1993) could just as easily argue that Psychoticism is merely a confounding of conscientiousness and agreeableness. So we are back to five. On the other hand, Cattell has matched the Big Five to five of his 8 second-order factors (Guastello, 1993; H. E. P. Cattell, 1993). However, we have already seen that Cattell (1994) believes his 16 primaries have more predictive power. So where does that leave us? Perhaps we should entertain the possibility that personality is much too complex to be characterized by 3, 5, or even 16 factors (Shadel & Cervone, 1993).

Conclusions

Hans Eysenck should be a model for other trait psychologists in that he is one of the few who uses the experimental method consistently, and the only major theorist to do so. It is almost as if others are afraid to use experimentation lest they find that their "stable" traits do not remain stable when subjected to experimental manipulations. While Eysenck's work with extraversion has been qualified, it has made the concept one of the most important in the personality field. Jung conceived of extraversion, but it was Eysenck who showed that it intrudes on many aspects of human functioning.

Summary Points

1. Cattell was English-born, the son of middle-class parents. Always sold on himself, he won scholarships and honors and turned down a chance at Cambridge University. After graduating with honors from London University, he chose psychology over chemistry. Following some "fringe jobs" and stressful administrative duties, he finally ended up with E. L. Thorndike in the United States. From there he went to several prestigious professorships. Along the way, his involvement with Eugenics and Beyondism has stirred controversy.

2. Cattell follows the inductive-hypothetico-deductive spiral. Consistent with the econetic model, $R = f(S.P)$ expresses his belief that both personality and environment contribute to responses. He gives nature more weight than nurture. Factor analysis, his technique of choice, extracts primary and secondary factors and specifies loadings of items on these factors.

3. Cattell deals with three kinds of data: Q-data (questionnaire), L-data (ratings), and T-data (objective measures in lab situations). His data collection techniques are R-technique (correlating measures taken once from hundreds of people and then factored), dR-tech-

nique (same as R but with two responses), and P-technique (single person responds to same measures repeatedly). He emphasizes common traits and also studies transitory states.

4. Traits are subsidiated under one another as follows: Second-order traits; source or primary traits (ability, temperament, dynamic: attitudes, sentiments, ergs); and surface traits. He has named 8 second-order traits, but believes that his 16 primaries are better predictors. Intelligence is believed to be largely inherited and is subdivided into fluid and crystallized. Nations have personalities too: syntality.

5. Cattell's lifelong project, the 16 PF, includes emotional - stable, expedient - conscientious, trusting - suspicious, conservative - experiencing, casual - controlled. Its uses range from personnel selection, through academic achievement to clinical diagnosis. Cattell has classified tests so that their usefulness has increased. Factor analysis involves often arbitrary choices between several different procedures. Data sources are subjectively selected and so are criteria for deciding magnitude of loadings and factor labeling.

6. Cattell assesses "heritability" by several methods, each potentially yielding different values. Heritability is applicable to a single population, not to other populations, or the same one at a different time, or to group differences. Heritability inappropriately separates genetic and environmental input. Intelligence may be more than "g" (Sternberg and Gardner list 3 and 7 intelligences, respectively). Contrary to Cattell, intelligence may be regarded as relative to sociophysical environment. Also, Cattell, like others, makes no clear distinction between state and trait.

7. Eysenck was born in Germany to an actor and an aspiring actress. Reared by his grandmother, he was strong-willed. After fleeing the Nazis, Eysenck earned a Ph.D. and did research at Maudsley Hospital and as a Professor at the University of London. He believes that personality is more than adequately encapsulated by three second-order factors and that factor analysis should be used to confirm theory, not generate it. He does real experiments and uses concepts from experimental psychology and physiology. His "big 3" are extraversion - introversion (E), neuroticism–stability (N), and psychoticism - superego functioning (P). Extraversion is linked to the ARAS.

8. His scientific model for studying personality has two components: description and explanation. So does his psychometrics: sophisticated statistical techniques and objective questionnaires. Eysenck's hierarchy of traits produced through subsidiation is much like Cattell's except that specific responses are added at the bottom and surface traits are called habitual responses. People who score high on E are impulsive, optimistic, sociable and rather unreliable. High Is are the opposite. High Ns are unstable, anxious, worrisome, and moody. High Ps are solitary, troublesome, hostile, cruel, liking of oddities, sexually impersonal, and distractible. Es have underactive ARAS, but Is' are overactive.

9. Is react to stimulation more readily than Es. Is salivate more to lemon juice, react with more anxiety to bad news about test results, are deterred by stimulants, and react less strongly to alcohol. Hyperactive children may be changed in the I direction by ritalin. Mass hysteria may be explained by high E and N scores. Modern work with extraversion indicates that it is partly inherited, definitely central, and related to well-being.

10. Eysenck's postulations about heredity have been, at best, partially supported, and his assumptions about the ARAS have not been fully supported: The relation of E-I and arousal is complicated and indirect. *The Bell Curve* agrees with Eysenck: IQ is mostly inherited. But it errs in phrasing the question "Is a 'black'-'white' IQ gap inherited?" In addi-

tion, it ignores strong evidence that early enrichment may overwhelm genetic input. The argument over 3 or 5 personality dimensions may miss the point: Even 16 does not do justice to the complexity of personality. Eysenck's extraversion work is a major contribution.

Running Comparison

Theorist	Cattell in Comparison
Freud	He used many Freudian concepts.
Skinner	Like Skinner he begins with raw observations, the empirical approach.
Fromm	Fromm's social character and Cattell's syntality are similar.
Murray	He borrows Murray's subsidiation.
Maslow	Dynamic traits are like Maslow's goal direction.

Theorist	Eysenck in Comparison
Cattell	Both are concerned about the number of traits accounting for personality, but Eysenck used experimentation. Both subsidiated traits.
Skinner	Both did lab research.
Jung	He revised Jung's extraversion.
Murray	He borrows Murray's subsidiation.

Essay/Critical Thinking Questions

1. Is there something about Cattell's background that influenced his belief that traits and intelligence are primarily inherited?

2. Can you come up with another way to collect data in addition to the three defined in the text?

3. How would you draw the line between common and unique traits? That is, how unusual must a person's unique trait be before one can say that no one else can be placed on the trait's dimension? (Hint: think of the problem of differentiating trait and state or mood.)

4. How many intelligences are there? Can you name some not mentioned in the text?

5. Take another look at the 16 PF. Can you categorize the factors into temperament, ability, and dynamic trait categories? Better still, further break down the dynamic category into ergs and sentiments. Note: there appears to be no "right or wrong" answer to this question.

6. Are there sub-populations within given countries for whom intelligences other than "g" are crucial to survival and prosperity?

7. What was it about Eysenck's personality, revealed in his youth, that may account for his tendency to defy the establishment and postulate unpopular points of view?

8. Could you design a simple experiment to look at the relationship between introversion-extraversion, some other variable, and tolerance for pain (dependent variable)?

9. Look at the list of traits attributed to high E, N, and P individuals. Can you see any overlap? Specify what you see.

10. If an early enriched environment is so powerful, why are we not immersing poor, disadvantaged children in it by age one?

E-mail Interaction

(Contact the author at mfbpa@wiu.edu)
Forward one of the following or phrase your own.

1. Is Cattell a member of the radical right?
2. Give me a shortcut to understanding Cattell's theory.
3. Is intelligence inherited or not?
4. How many trait dimensions are there, 3, 5, or 16?
5. Tell me what brain functioning has to do with personality?

17

PERSONALITY DEVELOPMENT AND PREJUDICE: GORDON ALLPORT

- What would you expect from a prominent personality theorist, unbounded confidence bordering on arrogance or a sense of true humility?
- Which should be emphasized, the unique trait dimensions that each person has and does not share with others or the universal dimensions that we all share?
- Should psychologists base theories on people as a whole (on average) or each individual separately?
- Which is the clearer sign of a mature personality, a place in life and a major role to play, or insight into oneself and a genuine sense of humor?
- Are being "prejudiced," being a "racist," and harboring "racism" the same?

Gordon W. Allport

Gordon Allport is at least the equal of trait theorists Murray, Cattell, and Eysenck, but he is a different person with a different style. Murray was a self-proclaimed narcissist. Cattell and Eysenck are known for their hubris. By contrast, Allport preached and practiced humility (Allport, 1967). His point of view was broad and open, encompassing the ideas of other theorists and including room for change. Further, Allport, like Kelly, took the hard road to understanding personality. Rather than assume that all persons can be fitted to a small number of trait dimensions, he believed that each person is unique, distinguished from others by her or his own peculiar traits.

The breadth of Allport's theoretical interests exceeds that of most personality theorists. His concern for social problems led him to study diverse topics ranging from people's senses of humor to prejudice. By careful consideration of his groundbreaking work, you will be able to gain significant insight into personality development, maturity, and prejudiced thinking.

Allport, The Person

Gordon Willard Allport was born November 11, 1897 in Montezuma, Indiana, the last of three sons (Allport, 1967). While Allport's father, a physician, was "pure English," his mother, a school teacher, was a mixture of German and Scottish (p. 4). Allport's versatile father was in business before becoming a doctor and eventually combined medicine with business.

Like the atmosphere in which Rogers was reared, Allport's home life was characterized by warmth as well as "Protestant piety and hard work" (p. 4). His father's motto was, "If every person worked very hard and took only the minimum financial return required by family needs, there would be just enough wealth to go around." This "broad humanitarian outlook" dictated a philanthropic orientation that was adopted by the entire family. Because his father lacked adequate hospital facilities, the Allport house became a hospital and family members its staff. Gordon recalled tending to office work, washing bottles, and interacting with patients. Just as his family's interactions were virtually free of strife, Allport's relations with others were unburdened by conflict. He was able to work successfully with a wide variety of people, including students who relished the friendly exchange of ideas that occurred in his graduate seminars. Just as he refused to engage in verbal combat with Murray—choosing instead to emphasize their similarities—he sought common ground when interacting with others.

As a young adult Allport tried to replace his more fundamental religious beliefs with a broader humanitarian religion. In the midst of trying on one religious garb or another, and failing to find a good fit, he remarked on the essentials of any global view that he might adopt: "Humility . . . [was] indispensable for me" (p. 7). Being the baby of the family also contributed to his sense of humility. His older brothers were largely successful, especially Floyd, a Harvard-educated experimental psychologist in whose footsteps Gordon was destined to tread. Throughout his life, humility was manifested in frequent self-effacing remarks. In reference to his standing as second in his high school class of 100, he commented, "Apparently I was a good routine student, but definitely uninspired . . ." (p. 5). When he first had the opportunity to perform volunteer social service, he found it "deeply satisfying, partly because it gave me a feeling of competence (to offset a generalized inferiority feeling)" (pp. 6–7). Just before his death in 1967, as he was ruminating about his possible contributions, he expressed surprise at the numerous honors he received. Only one, his favorite, was deemed worthy of mention: His former students presented him with two volumes of their own writings inscribed "From his students—in appreciation of his respect for their individuality" (p. 24).

After Gordon graduated from high school in 1915, Harvard grad Floyd suggested his own school. With characteristic modesty, Gordon remembered "squeezing through the entrance tests" (p. 5). Despite initial experiences that were no better than Murray's, Kelly's, and Maslow's, he was attracted to psychology. Like Murray, his first psychology teacher was Munsterberg, whose appearance reminded Allport of Wotan, the god of war to whom Jung had alluded. He got no more out of the beginning class than the other three, but he was not discouraged. Neither did he falter when hostilely confronted by the professor who nearly turned Maslow away from psychology, E. B. Titchener. This relic from psychology's early years glared at Allport as he briefly described his dissertation project. Later Titchener groused to one of Allport's advisors, "Why did you let him work on [a personality] problem?" (p. 9).

During his undergraduate years, Allport took courses from many of the famous psychologists of the day. But sociology and social ethics also fascinated him. After a brief hitch in the Students' Army Training Corps during World War I, he returned to his classes full-time and began to pursue social ethics by volunteering to work in various social service capacities, such as for the Humane Society.

Allport's humanitarian orientation showed up early. In 1917, Allport's junior year, he wrote a magazine piece on the legend of former Harvard student John B. G. Rinehart (Winter, 1996). True to character, Allport reinterpreted the admittedly ambiguous facts about the Rinehart case, projecting his own benevolence onto Rinehart and other students' reactions to the legendary figure.

After finishing his undergraduate studies in 1919, Allport took a one-year job teaching English and sociology at Robert College in ancient Constantinople, Turkey. Near the end of his stay he received notice of acceptance into Harvard's psychology graduate program. Perhaps to celebrate his new status, on the way home he stopped off in Vienna to visit with Freud. With youthful audacity that later would embarrass him, Allport announced "that I was in Vienna and implied that no doubt he [Freud] would be glad to make my acquaintance" (p. 7).

Freud sent a reply "in his own handwriting inviting me to come to his office at a certain time" (p. 7). Entering Freud's office, Allport looked in wonder at the "famous red burlap room with pictures of dreams on the wall" (pp. 7–8). On being ushered into Freud's inner sanctum, the "master" remained mute, waiting for young Allport to state his business. Finding the silence awkward, Allport began to comment on the apparent dirt phobia of a

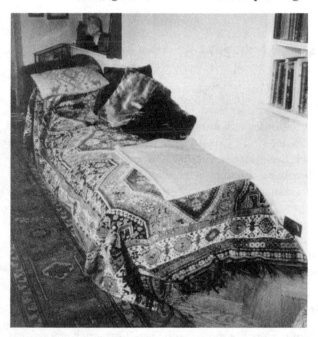

boy he encountered on the tram he rode to Freud's address. The child repeatedly complained to his mother about the "dirty man" beside whom he was forced to sit. The stern and dominant demeanor of the mother provided Allport with a ready explanation of the boy's problem. True to form, "Freud fixed his kindly therapeutic eyes" on young Allport and queried, "And was that little boy you?" (p. 8). Allport was "flabbergasted" but at the same time was "guilty" and "amused" that Freud had "misunderstood" his reasons for telling the story. He believed the therapist in Freud was probing for defenses to overcome and completely missed the "rude curiosity and youthful ambition" that was the actual motivation behind the dirt phobia story (p. 8).

Allport apparently did very well in Harvard's psychology graduate program, but as usual he managed to find some chinks in his academic armor. Though he lamented his imagined academic shortcom-

The actual couch used by Freud in the psychoanalysis of many notables.

ings, he found graduate school rather easy. After only two years of course work he received his doctorate in 1922 at the age of twenty-four. His dissertation, *An Experimental Study of the Traits of Personality: With Special Reference to the Problem of Social Diagnosis* almost certainly was one of the first major projects on personality done in the United States. Later he was to teach one of the first courses on personality.

After a fellowship in Europe, including exposure to the Gestalt view, and a lectureship in social ethics at Harvard (1924), he took a short-lived position at Dartmouth. When there was an opening in social psychology at his Alma Mater, he was offered the job and accepted without hesitation. By the end of the 1930s, Allport had become a permanent member of the staff, wrote his first book on personality (1937), and was elected President of the American Psychological Association (1939). World War II provided the opportunity to advise the government on the issue of morale and on the problem of rumors. He also became involved in attempts to understand the causes of war and methods for maintaining a lasting peace. In 1946 he participated in successful efforts to establish a multidisciplinary department, combining sociology, social psychology, clinical psychology, and social anthropology. He published his famous book on prejudice in 1954. A year and a half before his death, Allport was awarded an endowed chair in social ethics.

With typical modesty, Allport devoted considerable space to detailing his many efforts in the interest of charities and social welfare. A self-proclaimed "social reformer," he never missed an opportunity to condemn oppression and to praise social consciousness. In addition he was the epitome of the Renaissance man. No other theorist covered in this book was on the cutting edge of so many new movements or involved in such a diversity of academic pursuits.

Allport's View of the Person

Humanism?

Allport's personal warmth and social consciousness suggest a humanistic orientation. Indeed, he even occasionally referred to himself as a humanist and he authored a 1955 book partially entitled *Becoming* (DeCarvalho, 1991). Consequently it is clear that he was a humanist at least at the personal level. Less clear is whether he was a humanistic theorist, though he has been credited with coining the phrase "humanistic psychology" (DeCarvalho, 1991). On the other side, humanism is not even entered in the *Becoming*'s index, much less made the focus of a chapter. He was concerned about the self, but "self-actualization," "peak experiences," and "empathy" were not terms he often used. Further, the sociologist in him fostered an interest in groups per se, not a matter of great concern among typical humanists. Thus, it can be said that his point of view had the flavor of humanism, but was not mainstream humanism.

Emphasis on Unique Traits and Behavioral Variability

Allport was a pioneer in the study of personality traits, but he was a maverick among trait theorists (Allport, 1966; Zuroff, 1986). Whereas Cattell and Eysenck emphasized common traits at the expense of unique traits, Allport was the other way round (Allport, 1966, 1967). Like Kelly, as a personologist he preferred to look at people one at a time and found that a given person's traits were generally not applicable to other people. This orientation was in sharp contrast to that of typical trait theorists. Cattell and Eysenck are **nomothetic theorists,** inclined to derive general laws concerning how a few traits apply to all people. By contrast, Allport was more an **idiographic theorist,** inclined to study each individual's unique traits without attempting to find a place for each along a small number of trait dimensions.

The idiographic approach, although still a minority orientation, is gaining advocates. Pelham (1993) supported Allport's contention that the idiographic strategy actually provides greater predictive power. Ironically it also allows for insights into universal patterns of human behavior (an example is "all humans have anxiety that each expresses uniquely"). Schmitz and Skinner (1993) also extol the virtues of considering one person at a time.

Cross-situational behavioral consistency, so dear to the hearts of typical trait theorists, was a matter of less concern to Allport (Allport, 1966; Zuroff, 1986). He would have agreed with Huxley that "The only completely consistent people are dead" and with Ralph Waldo Emerson who proclaimed ". . . consistency is the hobgoblin of little minds." He believed that "behavior in different situations was often inconsistent, even contradictory, because different traits are aroused to different degrees in different situations" (Zuroff, 1986, p. 993). Zuroff asserted that Allport was ahead of his time in being an interactionist. By the 1960s, Allport was writing about variability of behavior from situation to situation and the possibility that a given trait is activated only in a certain situation or class of situations (Zuroff, 1986). He may well have influenced Mischel.

De-emphasizing the Freudian Unconscious

The conversation with Freud helped to convince Allport that "depth psychology . . . may plunge too deep" (Allport, 1967. p. 8). He felt then and continued to believe that psychologists would do well to look for and recognize open and obvious motivations, rather than immediately probe the dark depths of the unconscious. It was this "underemphasis" on the unconscious that irritated Murray. More generally, Allport was often critical of psychoanalysis, even parting company with his own brother when one of Floyd's books was deemed "too psychoanalytic for my taste" (p. 8).

Basic Concepts: Allport

Personality Defined

According to Allport, **personality** "is the *dynamic organization* within the individual of those *psychophysical* systems that *determine* his *characteristic behavior and thought*" (1961, p. 29; emphasis added). For Allport short definitions could not capture the complexity of personality; elaboration was needed. A system is a "complex of elements" that have the potential for activities that bond people (p. 28). *Dynamic organization* referred to the interplay of forces within an integrated system with tightly connected components. Activation of one component of the system activates others in an orderly fashion. A personality springs into integrated activity much like an orchestra: The conductor waves his baton signalling the violinists to play; when they sound a certain note, the drums begin to roll and so forth until all the components of the orchestra are active. *Psychophysical* simply "re-

BOX 17.1   The Adjective Generation Technique: A Method Inspired by Allport

Several exercises in this book involve asking you to produce adjectives, or other words, to describe someone, usually yourself. This method, formally known as the Adjective Generation Technique (AGT), was first used by the author in 1969 and was developed by Charles Potkay and me from that year to the present (Allen & Potkay, 1983a; Potkay & Allen, 1988). The original idea for the AGT came from a demonstration performed by Allport and reported in his 1961 book. A stranger simply walked into a college classroom, gave a short ambiguous speech and left. The professor then asked students to describe the stranger. "Allport's approach was to just look at the words to get a general qualitative idea of the kind of impression the visitor had made on class members" (Allen & Potkay, 1983a, p. 3). He apparently made no attempt to attach numbers to words relating to some psychological dimensions. True to Allport's open and eclectic approach, students produced the words, rather than checking words on a list or points on a dimension, either of which would be more a reflection of the assessor's orientation than the students'. They could use any descriptive words in their vocabularies. Further, they were unlikely to paint an ingratiating picture of themselves, because they performed anonymously and had no idea whether their words would be scored in any way.

Unlike Allport, Potkay and I have often scored the words in some way. Words could simply be counted to see how many are produced when people generate as many as they desire. This method tells assessors how prominent the target of descriptions was in the minds of describers: the more words, the more prominent. Words also might be categorized and their frequency in each category compiled. In one study, words most used to describe "good teachers" versus "poor teachers" were compared: Good teachers were "intelligent," "clear," and "humorous," while poor teachers were "boring," "dull," but "knowledgeable" (see M. Ward in Allen & Potkay, 1983a). In addition, each of nearly 2200 words has been assigned a value indicating degree of FAVora-bility (the desirability of a word attributed to someone), ANXiety (the amount of anxiety connoted by a word attributed to someone), and FEMininity (the femininity versus masculinity of a word attributed to someone). When people describe themselves, one can assess how FAVorable their descriptions are, how much ANXiety descriptions reflect, and how FEMinine are the describers.

Daily Log Sheet

Date:_____

Write down five (5) words to describe yourself. Use only single words that can be found in the dictionary, no sentences or phrases.

    _____

    _____

    _____

    _____

    _____

Briefly write down what happened to you that you regard as significant.

    _____

The AGT can be used to increase self-understanding. Get to know yourself a little better: make about 30 copies of the "Daily Log Sheet" and describe yourself for thirty days. It should be done at the end of the day and will take only about 5 minutes. For each day, just record self-descriptive words and briefly indicate what happened to you on that day. Just looking at the words will show you how you are evolving over days and how "what happens to you" affects your view of yourself. If you want, you can get a copy of Allen and Potkay (1983a) from your library and look up FAV, ANX, and FEM values. Notice that on a single day you will frequently use both desirable words, reflecting high FAV, low ANX, and FEM appropriate to your gender, and undesirable words. Further, you will find that the words you use differ day to day. This is quite normal and consistent with Allport's belief that different "traits"—your words may be considered trait labels—are aroused in the different situations you encounter on different days.

minds us that personality is neither exclusively mental nor . . . neural (physical)." Its organization entails "the functioning of both 'mind' and 'body' in some inextricable unity" (p. 28). *Determine* refers to the fact that the "Personality is something that does something" (p. 29). In his *characteristic behavior and thought*, use of the singular pronoun and the word *characteristic* in reference to *behavior and thought* reminds us that action and cognition are unique to a particular person.

Traits

Definition of Traits

In Allport's view, **trait** "is a neuropsychic structure having the capacity to render many stimuli functionally equivalent, and to initiate and guide equivalent . . . forms of adaptive and expressive behavior" (p. 347). In more straightforward terms, a trait "guides" a person to respond to similar but not identical elements of the environment (stimuli) in much the same way. "Hostile person" is a stimulus belonging to a category of stimuli that has members who may take on different forms—different people are hostile in different ways. But whatever the forms, similar responses are called for within a given environmental context, if the context is a formal party and the hostile person is a guest, the appropriate response would be to calm the person. On the other hand, Allport was quick to assert that a different environment would call forth a different response to functionally equivalent stimuli: In a nursery school context, regardless of which child is hostile to other children, physical restraint may be called for.

Allport proposed the following criteria for traits:

1. Has more than nominal existence
2. Is more generalized than a habit
3. Is dynamic, or at least determinative, in behavior
4. May be established empirically
5. Is only relatively independent of other traits
6. Is not synonymous with moral or social judgment
7. May be viewed either in the light of the personality which contains it, or in the light of its distribution in the population at large
8. Acts, and even habits, that are inconsistent with a trait are not proof of the nonexistence of the trait (p. 1).

There are several implications of these criteria. First, it is obvious that Allport believes that people do have traits. Second, traits of personality are not matters of moral functioning. Third, traits may determine behavior. Fourth, inconsistencies are real, but do not mean traits are nonexistent. Behavior related to "kindness" may be inconsistent across situations because only some situations call forth "kindness." Inconsistency may also be apparent because different behaviors may manifest "kindness" under different circumstances even within the same environmental context (sometimes you have to be cruel to be kind). Fifth, traits are more generalized than habits. A habit is quite specific, like the habit of not talking while one is eating (talking "with a mouth full"). A trait, by contrast is more broad, general, and variable. "Politeness" is a trait which would subsume "not talking while one is eating." Because it is subordinate, "not talking while one is eating" may be suspended in the greater interest of "politeness": If guests talk while eating, one would suspend one's intolerance for "talking with the mouth full" in the interest of being polite to the guests.

Sixth, and critical to Allport's theory, "trait" may refer to different but similar phenomena. **Common traits** "are . . . those aspects of personality in respect to which most people within a given culture can be profitably compared" (Allport, 1961, p. 340). Obviously, Cattell and Allport agree on what a "common trait" is. But Allport's de-emphasis of common traits is apparent in the reference he made to them while derogating "dimensionalism": He condemned distributing everyone along each of a few common trait dimensions.

To Allport, a **personal disposition (p.d.)** is a trait that is unique to a particular individual. P.d. means approximately the same thing as Cattell's "unique trait." In his 1961 book, Allport is careful to use "common traits" in reference to traits that all people have, but possess in varying degrees, and p.d. when referring to traits that are unique to particular persons. *Conscientiousness* has universal meaning when used in reference to a trait possessed by many, but has specific meaning when used in reference to a trait possessed by a particular person (John's conscientiousness applies to his job as a mail carrier and to his role as father of seven children). Oddly, by the time he wrote his seminal 1966 paper, Allport had lapsed into using "trait" to refer to both. Perhaps by the latter date, he assumed that readers were familiar with his theory and knew that he most often meant p.d. when he used "trait." Still, even in 1966 he periodically reminded readers about the distinction.

These reminders notwithstanding, using "trait" in reference to both "common traits" and "p.d." raises a perplexing question: How can "trait" be two things at once? The puzzle becomes more of an enigma when Allport acknowledges that the same labels may be used for both common traits and p.d.s. A person can somehow be uniquely "conscientious," yet all people can be placed on the "conscientiousness" dimension. Allport attempted to clear up this paradox by indicating that a trait label has a different *flavor* when referring to a particular person than when the reference is to people generally. For example, while most people can be cast as reflecting some degree of *anxiousness*, "Little Susan has a peculiar anxious helplessness all her own" (Allport, 1961, p. 359). Notice that more words are needed to describe "Susan's" trait than the single word *anxious*, which suffices to describe what most people show a degree of. "Anxiousness" must be qualified when applied to a particular person. Not surprisingly, Allport believed that trait labels fit common traits more readily than p.d.s.

Cardinal, Central, and Secondary P.D.s

P.d.s can vary in terms of how close they are to the core of an individual's personality. A **cardinal p.d.** is pervasive and outstanding in the life of a person. A word referring to a cardinal p.d. that a person possesses is often our choice as the sole description of him or her. Names of historical or fictional characters are often used in reference to cardinal traits: quixotic, narcissistic, sadistic, Emersonian, Falstaffian, Faustian, Christlike, or Don Juan. More common terms may also refer to cardinal p.d.s: flaky, sober, realistic, immoral, superficial, and obnoxious.

A **central p.d.** is one of the entries on the relatively large list of traits we use to summarize an individual's personality. We list central p.d.s when we write a person a letter of

---

BOX 17.2   Are Traits Specific to Situations?

Norman Endler and his colleagues hold a position that is very close to Allport's in an important way (Endler, 1983; Endler, Parker, Bagby, & Cox 1991). Consistent with Allport's view, Endler's group has scientifically demonstrated that a given trait may be activated only in certain situations (the rule seems to apply to either common traits or p.d.s). With anxiety as the sample trait, the Endler group isolated four different classes of situations that evoke anxiety. In each class, a variation of anxiety is activated that is in tune with the nature of the class of situations and different from the form of anxiety elicited by situations in the other three classes. In *social evaluation* situations, something a person does may be evaluated by other people. "Making a speech" is a good example, because it arouses social evaluation anxiety. *Physical danger* situations involve a potential for physical injury, but it is blown out of proportion. Driving on a narrow mountain road would evoke physical danger anxiety. In *ambiguous* situations, it is unclear how one should behave. Trying a new sport is an example, because anxiety due to ambiguity is likely to be aroused. The fourth kind of situation is dubbed *daily routine*, anxiety exhibited in mundane, everyday situations such as working or attending class. This last category was added as a a baseline against which anxiety in the others could be compared.

Rather than a person being generally anxious, she or he would have, say, very high social evaluation anxiety, high physical danger anxiety, and low anxiety in the other two categories. This person would be anxious in all the situations in the social evaluation category, somewhat anxious in those situations in the physical danger category, and not anxious in the situations of the other two classes. There would be "behavioral consistency" in that the individual would be anxious in all the members of the social evaluation class of situations: for example, going to a costume ball and singing in front of a group. However, there would be little consistency across classes of situations: Anxiety would peak then drop dramatically with movement from social evaluation to ambiguity situations.

You could learn more about yourself, and confirm Allport/Endler in your own mind, if you kept track of the kinds of situations in which you are anxious. The index of anxiety might be heart rate. Place the index and middle finger of the left hand just under the right jaw, in the hollow next to the Adam's Apple. Count how many pulses occur in ten seconds and multiply by six (6). The result will be number of beats per minute.

Carry a log with a listing of the four classes of situations. When you are in a certain situation, classify it into one of the four categories and take your pulse. For most people who have been sitting somewhere for 10 minutes, a heart rate of 120 would be quite high and indicative of anxiety. (You will have to become familiar with your normal heart rate, to decide what is "high" and what is "low" for you.) Taking a sample of five situations in each of the four classes should be sufficient. Average the heart rate numbers within each class for an idea of what makes you anxious and what does not.

---

recommendation. So-and-so is meticulous, thoughtful, even-tempered, and generous but shy and moody.

Even further removed from the core of personality are **secondary p.d.s**—dispositions that are "less conspicuous, less generalized, less consistent, . . . less often called into play . . . [and] more peripheral" (Allport, 1961, p. 365). Therefore, a person may be sporadically helpful, intermittently humorous, and occasionally melodramatic, thereby displaying secondary p.d.s. Unfortunately, any term might be used in reference to any of the three types of p.d.s. Allport was quick to point out that there is no distinct dividing line between one kind of p.d. and the next.

Personality Development

Allport devoted a greater proportion of his writings to personality development than most theorists. In particular, he valued the notion of "self" and wished to show how it evolves during development. Like many theorists of personality development—e.g., Freud and Sullivan—Allport is a stage theorist.

The Proprium and the Seven Stages of the Developing Self

In one of his most important written works, Allport (1961) devotes a chapter to what he calls "sense of self," formally labelled the **proprium,** "me as felt and known . . . the self as 'object' of knowledge and feeling" (p. 127). But "Why not simply [use] the term self . . ." and define it in the conventional way? (p. 127). He answered, "This chapter [in the 1961 book] has been devoted to the sense of selfhood, not the nature of selfhood. Our discussion . . . is primarily psychological, not philosophical . . . it is much easier to feel the self than to define [it]. Final definitions we leave to philosophy" (p. 137).

Early Infancy
Early infancy, the first stage, involves no sense of self. Infants initially are unable to separate themselves from their environment. They are conscious, but not self-conscious. If an infant picks up an object, the fingers and the object are one and the same. If she hurts her own foot she has no idea that it is *she* who inflicted the pain. She melts into Mother and they become fused. Later, as motor skills help the infant work out of this early phase, she crawls about and bumps into objects. In this way, she learns there are "things" that are apart from her body; she becomes aware of objects "out there" in another world. However, she does not yet know she is apart and distinct from that other world.

Bodily Self
The most primitive predecessor of selfhood emerges during the second part of the first year. Infants display signs of **bodily self,** sensations that emanate from the muscles, joints, tendons, eyes, ears, and so on. Children experience frustrations relating to the body, such as a stubbed toe or an unsatisfied hunger. These also contribute to appreciation of the bodily self which becomes the foundation of selfhood and remains with us forever. However, it is noticed only under unusual conditions. Allport (1961) suggests a way of appreciating how all your bodily parts and elements are "you": contrast swallowing your own saliva with spitting it into a cup and drinking it. Your saliva is a part of you that you take for granted, until it becomes physically separated from your body, then it is alien.

Self-Identity
The bodily self is only the first chapter in the story of the self. Emerging during the second year of life, Allport's third stage, is **self-identity,** the continuity of self over past, present, and future that results from the operation of memory. "Today I remember some of my thoughts of yesterday, and tomorrow I shall remember some of my thoughts of both yesterday and today; and I am certain that they are the thoughts of the same person—of myself" (p. 114).

Because we all are changing over time, even as adults, this feeling of continuity is essential to a sense of self. The learning of language underlies the ability to appreciate continuity. Words are what one remembers that assure him he is the same person today as yesterday. The most important of these is the child's name, a word that serves as an anchor to which the ship of self-identity is tied. Each time "Johnny" hears his name—as in "Good Johnny!" "Johnny! Do that on the toilet!"—his feeling of self-identity is strengthened.

Self-Esteem

If bodily self is the cornerstone of selfhood, and self-identity its framework, some walls and a roof must yet go up. Self-esteem has been translated literally as "the esteem in which one holds oneself." Allport is more specific: **Self-esteem** is pride in one's pursuits and accomplishments. During the third year, Allport's fourth stage, one of the child's favorite exclamations is "Let me!" "Me" has evolved beyond just a body and a sense of continuity to a feeling of instrumentality—the ability to successfully manipulate the environment. "I can do it" implies "I am what I am able to do; don't diminish me by doing for me." This prideful insistence on doing for oneself is matched by shame at having others do for one. Born with self-esteem is its fraternal twin, negativism. Allport writes of a child whose first words on arriving at his grandmother's were "Grandmother, I won't." "Reverse psychology" may well have been inspired originally by this negativism. For example, some mother may have exclaimed, "I don't want you to eat your broccoli, it's bad for you" in the hope of getting her child to eat the "gross green stuff."

Extension of Self

A sense of body, of continuity, and of pride are a great part of our self structure, but do not include the most important element of the environment, other people. During Allport's fifth stage, bounded by the years 4 to 6, the child develops a fourth aspect of selfhood, an egocentric component. Children think that Santa Claus and even God are there to serve them. However, this self-focus contains an advancement. "He" becomes not merely himself, but is extended to include all that he "possesses." It is "his dog, his house, his sister." This **extension of self** is expanding oneself to include all those significant aspects of one's environment, including people. Now, the family and the self are one. They are like an external conscience that may turn on the child should he fail.

Self-Image

Related to this fledgling relationship to others is a fugitive fifth aspect of self that also emerges during the fifth stage. The **self-image** is composed of the hopes and aspirations that develop from the perceptions and expectations that others have of oneself. Parents say the child is "good" or "naughty." Peers say that she is "smart" or "fat." She must do this, do that, be this, be that—whatever others expect. To discover whether she is living up to her developing self-image, she will compare others' expectations of how she should behave with her actual behavior.

Rational Coper

During the sixth stage (6 to 12) the self-image continues to develop, and a new aspect emerges: **rational coper**, the sense of selfhood that is not merely able to solve problems, but also can reason them through "in the head" and come up with logical solutions. The rational coper is much like Freud's "ego." It tries to efficiently satisfy the demands of the body (id), the external environment, and society (superego). As the rational coper develops, children become able to think about thinking.

Propriate Striving

During the seventh stage, adolescence, the individual continues to develop the self-image and experiences a renewed search for self-identity. Now self-identity focuses on tying together the teenager and the would-be adult. A teen may ask, "How can I be an adult and still be me?" Continuity must be maintained in the face of a major transition from one phase of life to the next. Society does little to solve teenagers' dilemma. They can join the army, but cannot legally drink. They can vote, but hold office almost nowhere. So teens experiment by rebelling. They stay out late, drink, and are sexually active—all the while hoping that their parents' restrictions on these activities will help define them. They want to become adults, but simultaneously be faithful to themselves as they were.

When thoughts turn to adult pursuits another component of selfhood comes into play: **Propriate striving** is planning for the future by setting long-range goals. During adolescence, people come to realize that success in life will depend on planning ahead. To involve effective propriate striving, goals must be reasonably, narrowly focused and in tune with people's abilities. Earlier, there may have been thoughts of being a movie star or a famous athlete. Now, to be mature, goals must be realistic and married to a step-by-step plan for attainment.

By adolescence, individuals are in an "identity crisis," a phrase borrowed from Erikson. They are trying to find their own identities apart from their parents. Adolescents try to cast off the conscience that parents, peers, and society have forced on them and build their own. At this point, conscience shifts from outside the self to within. Now, self-esteem is bolstered by doing what is "right." The self-image includes aspiring to do what ought to be done, and propriate striving encompasses plans to be a fair, kind, and otherwise a worthwhile person. As adolescence passes into adulthood, people no longer perform good deeds to avoid a vengeful conscience, but to strive actively for worthy goals that will support a mature self-image. Table 17.1 summarizes Allport's theory of personality development.

The Mature Personality

Individuals continue to evolve. Progress toward a *mature personality* is measured in terms of how well adults meet six criteria.

Extension of the Sense of Self

Extension of self is not fully formed even after the first ten years of life. At adolescence, it reaches out like the tentacles of a confused octopus. It does not know what experiences and roles to grasp for the self, and which to cast aside. With the advent of "puppy love," however, "The boundaries of self are rapidly extended" (1961, p. 283). The welfare of someone else becomes important to one's own, in fact, identical to one's own. As maturity advances, "loneliness" is reflected in "new ambitions, new memberships, new ideas, new friends, . . . new hobbies, and above all one's vocation" (p. 283). All of these new pursuits become incorporated into the self.

Not only does the self take on the new, but it transforms the old. One may continue to do what one did, but the original reasons for doing those things fade. Old pursuits may be-

TABLE 17.1   Allport's Evolving Sense of Self Proprium (the self as felt and known)

Stage	Aspect of selfhood	Definition
1	Early infancy	No sense of self
2	Bodily self	Awareness of bodily sensations
3	Self-Identity	Continuity of self
4	Self-Esteem	Pride in one's pursuits
5	Extension of self	Self includes significant aspects of environment
	Self-Image	Hopes and aspirations based on others' expectations
6	Rational coper	Reasoning and solving problems "in the head"
7	Propriate striving	Planning for the future

come detached from original motivations. Allport's name for this transformation is **functional autonomy**, a process by which a new system of motivation evolves from an older one, but stems from tensions different from those of the original.

This transformation is illustrated by reference to Kahlil, the son of a politician who initially goes into politics so that he may "follow in his father's footsteps." Later he becomes fascinated by and enmeshed in the political process; being "his father's son" no longer matters. He pursues politics for love of the process and for the power and glory of it. Allport argues that much of what we do that is important to the self has become functionally autonomous from the original motivations. The new motivations are more abstract than the old. They include "aesthetics," "intrinsic interest," and "human well-being."

One problem of maturity is to extend oneself into the spheres of one's life. Allport provides an example. Yin works in a factory, knows many people, pays union dues, drinks at the local tavern, and finds movies to be significant diversions. However, he is constantly *task-involved* and rarely *ego-involved*. "He has not extended his sense of self into any of the significant areas of his life . . . the economic, educational, recreational, political, domestic and religious. [He] passes them all by, incorporating none into his self" (p. 284). To be mature one must detach oneself from the "clamorous immediacy of the body" and find self-related reasons for doing whatever one has been doing (p. 285). Yin could become involved in his union for reasons of "fair and equitable treatment of workers," or local politics in the interest of "cleaning up the neighborhood."

Warm Relating of Self to Others

By extending the self, a person of warmth is capable of great *intimacy*. Warm relationships reflect a genuine capacity for love involving family, friends, and lovers. But mature warmth also entails *compassion*, a form of detachment. Gossip and possessiveness are avoided. Others are allowed to lead their own lives free of intrusions. "Both intimacy and compassion require that one not be a burden or nuisance to others, nor impede their freedom in finding their own identity" (p. 285).

Emotional Security (Self-Acceptance)

To Allport "self-acceptance" includes avoidance of overreaction to "drives" or gut tissue needs. Mature people are neither constantly seeking sexual gratification nor prudish and repressed about sex. They accept sexual urges as a part of themselves. Mature people do have fears and well they should: There are real dangers "out there." However, they do not recoil in terror at the thought of roaming a large city or at the prospect of confronting hostile protesters. Self-acceptance assures mature people that the exercise of reasonable prudence will allow them to successfully cope with dangers.

Self-accepting persons have high **frustration tolerance**; when things go wrong, they do not pitch a tantrum, blame others, or wallow in self-pity. Instead they accept some of the blame and find a way around the obstacle, or, failing that, resign themselves to some unpleasantness and bide their time until things get better. Part of self-acceptance is to know one is fallible, but to believe one is capable of compensating for faults.

Realistic Perceptions and Skills

"Maturity does not bend reality to fit one's needs and fantasies" (p. 289). The mature person seems to "see things" more clearly than others and, thus, has more wisdom than others. But does this mean one has to have high intelligence to be mature? Allport answers that intelligence helps in the achievement of maturity, but does not guarantee it.

Mature people are problem-solvers. "Although we often find skillful people who are immature, we never find mature people without problem-pointed skills" (pp. 289–290). Not only are mature people capable of solving task-related problems, they are capable of losing themselves in the task. They are problem-centered. "In short a mature person will be in close touch with what we call 'the real world.' He will see objects, people, and situations for what they are. And he will have important work to do" (p. 290).

Self-Objectification: Insight and Humor

Imagine someone who announces, "I'm a master of the English language and a person who knows himself well." Immediately the person apologetically adds, "I don't mean to infer that I'm more smarter than others." Allport believed that most of us are like this individual in that we believe we have insight into ourselves, but we really do not. Can we obtain what we falsely claim to possess? We can, of course, never know the "true person." Even if we assume there is a single, stable "true person"—thereby ignoring the possibility that a person is always in a state of flux—we could never know that "true person." No one is privy to all the complexities and subtleties that constitute a person, not even the person. Thus, the best we can do is to look at the discrepancy between what a person believes about her or himself and what other people believe about him or her. The less the discrepancy, the greater the insight.

In a study where subjects rated each other, the correlation between ratings of insight and sense of humor was .88. What makes a sense of humor such a close associate of insight? A **genuine sense of humor**, as opposed to an appreciation of sexual and aggressive jokes, is being able "to laugh at the things one loves (including, of course, oneself and all that pertains to oneself), and still to love them" (p. 292). Insightful people communicate that they know and accept their own limitations and deficiencies by laughing at their shortcomings. Such people are good judges of others and are accepted by them.

Perhaps the key to the close correlation between insight and humor is that a person with a good "sense of humor" communicates a match between perceptions of self by self and by others. Friends know a person's faults and find evidence for insight in the match between their knowledge of the person's deficiencies and the person's acknowledgment of those shortcomings.

The Unifying Philosophy of Life

One primary element in a unifying philosophy of life is **directedness**, having a goal or goals in life toward which one strives. The goals may change as one's life circumstances change, but they must be in place if one is to claim a mature personality. For example, goals may change after a series of "bad luck" incidents. Goals also evolve with maturity and become more realistic. For example, as a post-adolescent may have to admit, some earlier goals, becoming a corporate executive, are unlikely to be obtained. Allport points especially to the late twenties as a time of goal-shattering disillusionment accompanying the early phases of marriage and career.

Some coherent value orientation is also necessary for a unifying philosophy to take shape. Allport believed that six ideal types express value options best. These are pure values that may be adopted by people, rather than being actual people.

1. The *theoretical*. Here the dominant interest is discovery of the "truth." The inclination is toward the cognitive. People adopting this orientation are empirical, critical, and rational.

2. The *economic*. The dominant orientation is toward what is useful and what is practical. Individuals who embrace this orientation are like the "marketing type" that Fromm popularized. Their view may clash with other sets of values. The economic individual will denude the forest and pollute the rivers for present economic gain.

3. The *esthetic*. The esthetic orientation focuses on form and harmony. These values are diametrically opposed to theoretical values. Events in life are enjoyed for their own sake; truth is beauty. The interest is in people rather than the welfare of people; the trend is toward individualism and self-sufficiency.

4. The *social*. In the social orientation, the emphasis is on love of people. Being friendly, philanthropic, kind, and unselfish is valued. Power is repudiated in favor of love and selflessness.

5. The *political*. The political orientation is to seek power. The desire is for personal power, influence, and renown. The interest is narrow, confined to politics, because power is concentrated there.

6. The *religious orientation*. Unity is the magnet of the religious orientation. The quest is to become one with the cosmos, to relate to an all-embracing totality. People of this inclination "find their religious experience in the affirmation of life and in active participation therein" (Allport, 1961, p. 299).

Allport believed that a coherent *religious sentiment* is central to maturity of personality. He was not heavily invested in organized religion, but he seemed fascinated with the possibility of a higher power that is the center of human experience. He saw religious orientation as the most comprehensive and integrative of the six value orientations and believed some form of religious sentiment to be essential to the mature personality.

Religious sentiment can be immature: a deity is adopted who favors the person's immediate interests much as did Santa Claus during childhood. Another form of immature sentiment is the tribal type: "God favors my people to your people" (p. 300). In both cases the motivation is **extrinsic**—utilitarian and in the service of self-esteem maintenance. Extrinsic people (*Es*) *use* their religion (Allport & Ross, 1967).

By contrast the motivation behind a mature religious sentiment is **intrinsic**—religion is an end-in-itself, something that one surrenders to, not something to use. Intrinsics (*Is*) *live* their religion (Allport & Ross, 1967). Religious sentiment, like humor, transports life's troubles from the routine context to a perspective that is more universal and generally meaningful. Like humor, religious sentiment allows one to avoid taking things too seriously: Whatever is currently happening in life is trivial relative to the universal scheme of things.

Although rational thought is not excluded from religious sentiment, faith is the basic cognitive mode. Religious faith is unique and more comprehensive than other forms of faith. It represents a theory of life rather than being a collection of beliefs in specifics, such as that one will succeed in business. Religious faith is all-engrossing and all-encompassing.

Generic conscience is central to the development of personality and is a unifying force in personality: It lays down comprehensive guidelines for nearly all of a person's conduct. Ultimately it is the source of accepting responsibility for oneself and the wellspring of one's responsibilities to others.

Allport distinguishes the generic conscience of maturity from the "must sayer" of childhood. The child feels guilty for failure to live up to any of the immature conscience's commandments. The mature, generic conscience is not troubled by a knee-jerk need to avoid any transgression. Minor slips and sins are not the mature person's concern. Only adherence to personally selected moral standards is relevant to the self of the mature person. These standards will include some of the moral strictures of the mature person's society, but are not limited to them.

The extrinsically religious have a "spotty and inconsistent conscience readily soothed by self-justification" (p. 304). By contrast, conscience in the intrinsically religious person is a fully developed guide to behavior. Religious sentiment, therefore, is often closely tied to the generic conscience. Box 17.3 contains more about Is and Es.

Personality and Prejudice

Personality development can take unexpected turns. Witness the relationship between religion and prejudice. But just what facets of personality development—childhood (and adulthood) experiences—shape prejudice? Before seeking an answer, it is necessary to consider "prejudice" and related concepts from Allport's view and that of others he has influenced.

There are three reasons why Allport's book *The Nature of Prejudice* (1954) is perhaps the single most important work ever done on the subject of prejudice. First, it was the earliest comprehensive discussion of prejudice that was based on a significant body of scientific research. Second, it was extremely influential in shaping social scientists' thinking concerning prejudice. Third, because Allport has had so much influence on prejudice research done since 1954, it is relatively easy to fit some of today's findings regarding prejudice into his theoretical framework.

BOX 17.3   Type of Religiousness: Prejudice, Self-
            Deception, Psychological Adjustment,
            and Optimism

Allport and Ross (1967) showed that extrinsic and intrinsic orientations have implications well beyond religion per se. They found that extrinsic orientation was moderately related to prejudice toward various groups (r = [approximately] .30). Across various religious groups, *Is* were less prejudiced than *Es* who, in turn, were less prejudiced than indiscriminately pro-religious people.

Donohue (1985) did an extensive review of the literature on extrinsic/intrinsic religiousness. Allport originally thought that *E* and *I* orientations were at opposite ends of the same continuum (*E/I* is bipolar). Donohue's view of the evidence called this assumption into question. Consistent with the bipolar assumption, many studies found *E* and *I* to be mildly negatively correlated (r = [approximately] −.20). However, relations of *E* and *I* measures to other psychological measures implied the two orientations were better viewed as independent. For example, *I* tended to be unrelated to prejudice, but *E* was clearly related to prejudice (r = [approximately] .30), as Allport and Ross had found. Also, *I* tended to be unrelated to fear of death, but *E* was positively related to that fear.

Burris (1994) further pursued the relationship between *E* and *I*. He found that for people scoring above the *I* mean (average *I* score), the *E/I* relationship was indeed negative, but it was not for those scoring below the *I* mean. Thus, high *I* orientation is the opposite of *E*. Deeply and genuinely religious people are very different from those who pursue religion for external, utilitarian, self-interested reasons. But all is not well with *Is*. They show evidence of self-deception and a tendency to manipulate the impressions they make on others. *Es* have deficiencies too. High *Es* showed more depression than low *Es* and *E* orientation was associated with maladjustment.

Burris found, in effect, two types of *Is*. However, only one *I* type, those scoring above the *I* mean, truly embraced religion for its own sake. Genia (1993) isolated two types of *Es*—those who get personal benefits out of religion and those who pursue religion for social rewards. Further, measures of the two types are differently related to *I* measures. Obviously *I/E* is much more complicated than Allport originally thought.

Insofar as *Is*, at least high *Is*, are "fundamentalists," they are more optimistic than less devout religious people (Sethi & Seligman, 1993). Further, they get their optimism from the religious materials they read. Thus, deeply religious people are healthfully optimistic, compared to maladjusted, depressed high *Es*. But they are also self-deceptive impression managers. Perhaps, as implied by Bandura (1994b), painting a more highly positive picture of oneself than is warranted may be good strategy. It is what high *Is* do and it is associated with optimism—a positive correlate of physical health and a negative correlate of depression.

Prejudice Defined

According to Allport (1954), **prejudice** is felt or expressed antipathy based on a faulty and inflexible generalization and may be directed toward a group as a whole, or toward an individual because he is a member of the group. Thus, prejudice is negative feelings regarding members of some group that are sometimes just felt internally and sometimes expressed openly. It is based on the faulty generalization that most, or all, members of some group, such as Native Americans, possess certain negative traits, such as drunkenness. Such a generalization is always erroneous in the sense that no trait will apply to most, much less all, members of a large group (even skin color varies greatly among people who are called "black").

Discrimination usually has meant directing more negative behaviors toward a particular group, compared to others, but may include having more negative thoughts and feelings about some group relative to others. People can be discriminatory in regard to their feelings and thinking, just as they are in terms of their behavior ("I *hate* them [feelings] because they are *trash* [thinking]"). Many measures of prejudice amount to asking people—usually via questionnaire—how much they discriminate so their level of prejudice can be inferred. For this reason, it is possible to offer a more empirical definition of prejudice that is consistent with Allport's theoretical definition. Prejudice measures typically ask about *self-perceptions* of discrimination. Therefore, *prejudice* may be seen as the degree to which people believe that they discriminate against members of some group in terms of directing relatively more negative behaviors, as well as thoughts and feelings, toward group members. As prejudice is most often assessed with the use of questionnaires completed anonymously, people's pronouncements about their level of prejudice probably represent what they really believe.

Social Distance

Given this empirical definition, it is immediately obvious that what people believe about their level of discrimination may not be accurate. Because nobody has total insight, some people who honestly claim not to discriminate against others may do so anyway. To explore this logical conclusion, it is necessary to consider **Social Distance (SD)**, a measure of discrimination that requires individuals to indicate how close to themselves they would allow members of some group to come. Allport (1954, p. 39) listed the items of the SD scale as follows:

I would admit (members of some group)

1. To close kin by marriage
2. To my club as personal chums
3. To my street as neighbors
4. To employment in my occupation
5. To citizenship in my country
6. As visitors only to my country
7. Would exclude from my country

Notice that the social relations to which the members of some group can be admitted vary from those involving a great deal of *intimacy* with group members, *commitment* to them, and *permanency* of relationships involving them (top of list) to those involving no intimacy, commitment and permanency (bottom of list).

Not only do people who strongly claim not to discriminate against some often-disparaged group really believe themselves, these self-proclaimed "unprejudiced" people probably do not discriminate under most circumstances. Nevertheless, would they discriminate when asked to accept the same group for social relations that entail high intimacy, commitment, and the permanency? An answer to the question may tell us whether what people believe about their level of discrimination is accurate.

A number of years ago, I gave some European American college students a test to determine the degree to which they were prejudiced against African Americans (Allen, 1975).

Based on their scores, some students were classified as "unprejudiced," some as "prejudiced," and some as "ambivalent" (gave mixed signals about their level of discrimination). All of these subjects were then asked to indicate the degree of closeness they would allow African Americans by use of an SD scale composed of items 1 and 3 (Triandis, Loh, & Levine, 1966). Results showed that all categories of these white subjects, even those who claimed they did not discriminate according to race, in fact did so. When it comes to relations involving intimacy, commitment, and permanency, even "unprejudiced" subjects show racial discrimination.

Although unprejudiced European American subjects did discriminate on the SD scale, when it came to indicating who they admire, another part of my same study showed that they did not discriminate by race. In fact, they actually expressed more admiration for African Americans than for European Americans. (This so-called "reverse discrimination" effect reverted to no discrimination when subjects thought they were hooked up to a lie detector machine.)

But why do all categories of European Americans, even self-proclaimed nondiscriminators, in fact discriminate when it comes to choices for intimate, committed, permanent social relations? European Americans show great individual differences in prejudice, but they do not display great individual differences in discrimination for intimate, committed, permanent relations. Perhaps there is some underlying dimension for which individual differences are not great that explains why most such people sometimes discriminate by race.

In the case of discrimination against African Americans, such a dimension appears to exist. *Racism* is widespread negative sentiment directed toward African Americans and other people of color (Allen, 1975, 1990). It has been argued that racism is a part of the mainstream culture in this country (Gaines & Reed, 1995). When people incorporate their culture, largely through the process of identification, they swallow it whole. They ingest not only the good aspects of their culture, of which there are many, they also consume the bad . . . racism. Because most people adopt their culture, most European Americans would incorporate racism within themselves. This may be the reason that even unprejudiced European Americans show discrimination in some areas: racism rears its ugly head when it comes to choices of others for intimate, committed, permanent relations, although it fails to show up in other realms (deciding who to admire). It should be added that racism also may show up in subtle ways. By contrast, racism is reflected often in a wide spectrum of prejudiced people's expressions and behaviors. Figure 17.1 shows the degree to which racism is *incorporated* by European Americans who range across the prejudice spectrum (top) and the degree to which racism shows up in the *social choices and reactions* of European Americans who range across the prejudice spectrum (bottom). Notice that racism is incorporated by almost all European Americans, regardless of prejudice level (top). However, racism clearly and regularly shows up only in the social choices and reactions of highly prejudiced people (bottom). It shows up in the choices/reactions of low prejudiced and especially "unprejudiced" people only in terms of permanent, intimate, and committed choices and in subtle ways. Also, note that, with this schema, only high prejudiced people are considered "racist."

Consistent with this consideration of racism, Allport found that racial animosity is very widespread. After examining the polls assessing antagonism toward various groups—most frequently African Americans—Allport concluded, "These . . . studies tempt us to estimate that four-fifths of the American population harbors enough antag-

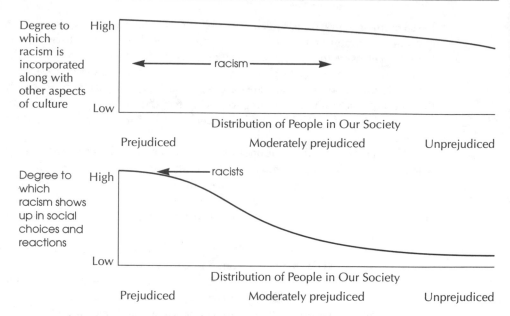

FIGURE 17.1   The relationship between racism and prejudice

onism toward minority groups to influence their daily conduct" (p. 78). Although his statement was based on polls taken many years ago, there is reason to believe that it is still accurate today. While animosity was very open in the early fifties, today, for most European Americans, it has become limited to a few social relations and it has evolved to be more underground and subtle. The reluctance of European Americans to engage in intimate, committed, permanent relations with African Americans is reflected in the still exceedingly low interracial marital rate (Allen, 1990). Also, many studies over the years have shown that careful investigation of subtle behaviors reveals definite traces of racial animosity (Allen, 1978, 1990).

"Race" Differences

Allport (1954) traces continued interest in alleged racial differences to arguments that subcategories of humans exist and can be arranged in a hierarchy from best to worst. It made thinking and life itself simpler to believe that there are big differences between one race and the next, and few differences among people of a given racial designation. It was also gratifying: One could declare one's own race "best" and view the members of other races as uniformly inferior.

Allport asserted that gender mirrors how we react to the races. "Only a small part of our human nature is differentiated by sex. . . . the vast proportion of human physical, physiological, psychological traits are not sex linked" (p. 109). Yet, despite the evidence of no difference on critical traits such as IQ, "women are regarded as inferior, kept in the home . . . [and] denied many of the rights and privileges of men. The special roles assigned to them are far in excess of what sexual genetic difference would justify. So it is with race" (p. 109). That we habitually exaggerate gender differences is the focus of much current research (Allen, 1995).

Allport, a pioneer in questioning "race," makes two important points about the concept. First, most of the world's people are of "mixed stock"; thus most do not fit any racial category. Second, "Most human characteristics ascribed to race are . . . [actually] ethnic, not racial" (p. 113). Today, the validity of "race" is again being challenged (Katz, 1995; Weizmann, Wiener, Wiesenthal, & Ziegler, 1990; Yee et al., 1993; Zuckerman, 1990). It now appears that three criteria must be met before "race" is applicable to humans: (1) consensually accepted criteria for differentiation among races must be developed and shown to actually erect clear boundaries between one "race" and the next; (2) variability within "races" must be adequately reconciled with assumptions of intraracial uniformity; (3) overlap among races must be reconciled with the assumption that "races" are meaningfully distinct (Allen & Adams, 1992).

Stereotypes

According to Allport, prejudice affects our thinking as well as our feelings. It is associated with the development of beliefs concerning the traits supposedly possessed by all or most members of a group. A belief of this sort is called a **stereotype**, an exaggerated belief that members of a group possess a certain trait: "Its function is to justify (rationalize) our conduct in relation to that [group]" (p. 191). Such beliefs may have a "grain of truth" to them. In centuries past, Jews were "money handlers" in Europe, simply because they were allowed few alternatives for making a living. The problem is that this veridical observation evolved to become "most [or all] Jews are obsessed with making money." Though there may be a "grain of truth" to a stereotype, it is almost always false to assume that most members of any large group possess any trait one can conjure up (excepting those characteristics that define the group; e.g., all Catholics are Catholic).

Stereotypes do tend to change somewhat in content over time, and the overall valence of their emotional tone may show some change in response to major events over time. Before World War II, the tone of our stereotypes of the Japanese was negative, but not strongly so. As soon as Pearl Harbor was bombed, stereotypes of the Japanese became viciously negative. As the Japanese wrought their economic miracle following the war, stereotypes became more positive. Currently, because they are viewed as beating us economically and "buying up America," stereotypes of the Japanese have become more negative.

What of the tone and content of stereotypes about African Americans? Allport lists the following stereotypes of African Americans that were held by European Americans at the time he was writing his 1954 book: unintelligent, morally primitive, emotionally unstable, overassertive, lazy, boisterous, fanatically religious, gamblers, flashy dressers, criminal, violent, reproductively prolific, occupationally unstable, superstitious, happy-go-lucky, ignorant, musical. To find out how these stereotypes might have changed, 81 European American undergraduate students were asked to each write down five words to describe African Americans (Allen, 1996). Sixty-three African American students were given the same instruction. Next the words most frequently used to describe African Americans were tallied. The results are presented in Table 17.2.

TABLE 17.2   African Americans Described by Themselves and by European Americans (% of each sample using each word)

By Themselves	By European Americans
6 misunderstood	6 boastful
6 emotional	6 fast
6 poor	6 moody
6 funny	6 poor
6 humorous	6 strong
6 inventive	7 musical
6 powerful	7 obnoxious
8 corrupt	7 prejudiced
8 determined	9 black
8 educated	9 mean
10 independent	9 smart
10 friendly	10 arrogant
11 athletic	10 funny
13 intelligent	10 independent
14 beautiful	11 corrupt
14 oppressed	11 friendly
27 strong	21 humorous
27 smart	25 loud
	40 athletic

You can see that European Americans' stereotypes of African Americans are still negative, though some content remains the same—"musical" and "loud" (boisterous)—but there have been some changes. African Americans are now seen as "humorous" and "athletic." Notice also that African Americans agree with European Americans on "independent," but mention "athletic" much less often and include "intelligent," omitted by European Americans.

Unlike the vast majority of other stereotype surveys, this one involved asking African Americans to indicate stereotypes of European Americans. (Usually African Americans are not asked, or stereotypes of various "white" ethnic groups are assessed, not "whites" in general.) Table 17.3 displays the stereotypes of European Americans.

Again, African Americans and European Americans show limited agreement. African Americans are more negative about European Americans than European Americans are about themselves. Though both agree that European Americans are "greedy" and "smart," European Americans see themselves as "lazy" and "intelligent," but African Americans do not. European Americans now ascribe "lazy" to themselves, not African Americans.

Neither these results nor those reported by Allport were produced by large, representative samples of U.S. citizens. These results, however, were produced by procedures with

TABLE 17.3 **European Americans Described by Themselves and by African American (% of each sample using each word)**

By Themselves	By African Americans
6 corrupt	6 inventive
6 free	6 competitive
6 happy	6 powerful
6 kind	6 wealthy
7 conceited	6 educated
7 educated	10 racist
7 egotistical	11 selfish
10 intelligent	11 greedy
10 prejudiced	13 rich
10 rich	16 mean
12 humorous	19 smart
12 independent	24 prejudiced
12 inventive	41 corrupt
12 lazy	
15 arrogant	
15 friendly	
19 competitive	
19 greedy	
32 smart	

certain advantages. One plus is that subjects produced the words from their own vocabularies, rather than being forced to choose from some limited, possibly biased list. This fact probably accounts for results not predicted on the basis of previous research, like European Americans being seen as "corrupt" "prejudiced," and "greedy" and African Americans as "friendly," "funny," and "humorous."

Painting the Picture of the Prejudiced Personality

The traits that highly prejudiced people share can be summarized in the phrase "threat oriented." The reference is partly to viewing the world as a threatening place. However, some of the threat comes from within. The prejudiced person "seems fearful of himself, of his own instincts, of his own consciousness, of change, and of his social environment" (p. 396). To put it another way, very prejudiced people suffer from "crippled egos." By promoting oppression of other groups, they can ensure that their own status in society is not threatened.

Covered next are some specific traits that Allport believed prejudiced people tend to have in common. This consideration is relevant to the question, "If most European Americans incorporate racism when they swallow their culture whole, why do only a relative few turn out to be racists?" (highly prejudiced). The answer may partially lie in the practices used to rear them and in their childhood experiences. These practices and experiences may act on racism, dragging it from the fringe to the core of some people's personalities, thereby pushing them into the "racist" category.

Ambivalence about Parents

As one kind of "ism" tends to resemble other kinds, Allport often used anti-Semitism as a model for the "isms." In a study of anti-Semitic women college students, ambivalence toward their parents is clearly evident. While they openly praised their parents, on projective tests these women showed hostility toward parents. Tolerant subjects were the opposite: Though they loved their parents, they were openly critical of them, but the projective tests revealed no underlying hostility toward parents. Prejudiced students' hostility toward their parents may stem from child-rearing themes of obedience, punishment, and actual or threatened rejection.

Moralism

Allport reports that very prejudiced people tend to be highly moralistic as reflected in high attention to cleanliness and good manners. When the anti-Semitic students were asked what would embarrass them the most, they "responded in terms of violations of mores and conventions in public. Whereas [the] non-prejudiced spoke more often of inadequacy in personal relations" (p. 398). Again, child-rearing practices are implicated. The prejudiced had parents who punished them severely for any show of interest in their genitals and for aggression against the parents. The result is children who are guilt-ridden and full of self-hatred due to repeatedly being reminded of their wickedness. As adults their repressed hostility explodes onto members of other groups and their rigid morality is the source of a rationale for rejecting those individuals.

Dichotomization

Highly prejudiced people literally see in black and white. There is good and there is bad; there is right and there is wrong. This orientation was forced on them by parents who dished out approval and disapproval categorically: Everything the child did was either right or it was wrong, there was no middle ground. Little wonder that as adults they see only two classes of people: Those who are acceptable and those who are not.

Need for Definiteness

Allport believed that very prejudiced people are distinguished by their unique cognitive processes. Consistent with their tendency to classify everything into two categories, they show another critical characteristic. They have little **tolerance for ambiguity**; their cognitive orientation requires that everything be clearly distinguished from everything else: Questions have definite answers, and problems have simple solutions. In short, prejudiced people want everything to be clear-cut, no gray areas. Shown an illusion involving a stationary point of light presented in darkness that appears to move, prejudiced people "reported the light as moving in a constant direction from trial to trial and to [move] a constant number of inches" (p. 401). In contrast unprejudiced people saw movement in all directions and to a variable extent. Very prejudiced people imposed clarity and order on an inherently ambiguous situation, while unprejudiced people tolerated the ambiguity.

Externalization

Allport saw very prejudiced people as lacking in self-insight. They do not see their own faults; they project them onto other people. Further, "things seem to happen 'out there' " (p. 404). In Horney's terms, they externalize. Rather than believing that they control what happens to them by use of their own resources, they believe that fate controls them. Rotter would class these people as externals. Allport explained, "It is better and safer for a person in inner conflict to avoid self-reference. It is better to think of things happening to him rather than as caused by him" (p. 404). Also, prejudiced people externalize punishment: "it is not *I* who hates and injures others; it is *they* who hate and injure me" (p. 404).

Institutionalization

Allport believed the highly prejudiced person prefers order, especially social order. He finds safety and definiteness in his institutional memberships. "Lodges, schools, churches, the nation, may serve as a defense against disquiet in his personal life. To lean on them saves him from leaning on himself" (p. 404). Also, the prejudiced are more devoted to institutions than the unprejudiced. The anti-Semitic college women were more wrapped up in their sororities and more patriotic. While patriotic people are not necessarily prejudiced, Allport referred to evidence that very prejudiced people are almost always super-patriots. He would have been unsurprised by the behavior of today's militia group members, such as the Freemen. He cites an investigation in which club members completed a lengthy belief questionnaire in return for a monetary contribution to their clubs. The large number of variables examined were reduced to only one trait held in common: *nationalism*. Allport is quick to point out that "the nation" to these people is not what it is to most people. When most people think of "the nation," it is the people, the principles of the constitution, and the lands that come to mind. Instead, prejudiced people view "the nation" as something that will protect them from people seen as unlike themselves and preserve the *status quo*.

Authoritarianism

Allport believed that very prejudiced people are uncomfortable with democracy. "The consequences of personal freedom they find unpredictable" (p. 406). It is easier to live in a power hierarchy where everyone has a place and the top spot is occupied by an all-powerful person. In a word, prejudiced people are **authoritarian**—they show high deference for authority figures, submission to the power of authority, and a need to command those seen as lower in power than themselves. Allport cites a study in which prejudiced people listed dictators like Napoleon when asked who they admired most, while low prejudiced people listed figures such as Lincoln. Authoritarianism is seen in prejudiced people's mistrust of others. Authority embedded in a strong nation can save oneself from suspected others. "To the prejudiced person the best way to control these suspicions is have an orderly, authoritative, powerful society. Strong nationalism is a good thing. Hitler [wasn't] so wrong. . . . America needs . . . a strong leader" (p. 407). This crucial concept is still receiving attention from researchers (Peterson, Doty, & Winter, 1993).

Evaluation

Contributions

Allport's more general ideas seem to have had more impact than his specific concepts or his theory as a whole. His idiographic approach is periodically mentioned to remind us that seeking general principles applicable to all people may not be the best way to understand humans (Pelham, 1993).

Personality writers have considered Allport to be the voice of moderation with regard to the matter of behavioral consistency (for example, Zuroff, 1986). While Allport did not see evidence for a high level of cross-situational behavioral consistency, he was quick to argue that there is sufficient repetition of behavior to support the existence of p.d.s. The idea of p.d.s itself is important, because it suggests that each person is even more unique than is generally recognized. Unlike many other theorists, Allport appreciated that understanding humans is very difficult, because each is so different from the others and each is extremely complex. Reading Allport reminds us that there are no easy solutions to the human puzzle. Further, Allport's notions about personality development have been highly influential. His chronicle of how the self (proprium) unfolds has provided many insights into how people come to be who they are.

The timely publication of *Nature of Prejudice* in 1954, the year of the Supreme Court's school desegregation ruling, was the most important event in the history of studying prejudice up to that time and for years after. Despite its age, the book continues to be cited and to inspire research. Allport's belief that prejudice can be reduced by positive, equal status, interracial contact supported by organizational officials and occurring in an atmosphere of cooperation is still accepted today.

While not many of Allport's specific terms are often on the lips of typical personologists, there are exceptions. "Cardinal, central, and secondary dispositions" have been given more than lip service because they point to a crucial consideration: the centrality of dispositions (traits) to the life of the individual. "Functional autonomy" represents an insight on Allport's part. It suggests how certain relatively temporary behaviors that may be of no special importance to a person can evolve into long-standing behaviors that come to characterize the individual.

Limitations

Allport's "theory" may be regarded as several mini-theories that are, at best, loosely tied together. In a sense, he seems to have jumped on his horse and ridden off in all directions at once. He does have a theory of traits and a personality development theory, but the connection between the two was not made explicit. Because he was both a personologist and a social psychologist, he wrote on diverse topics such as the proprium and prejudice. Little wonder that he was not able to tie things together very well.

Allport's emphasis on unique rather than common traits has put him out of the mainstream. The primary thrust of personality theory has been to state general principles that apply to all people and to specify traits that most people possess to some degree (the Big Five). Allport's insistence on the extreme uniqueness of each person makes the task of understanding humans look very daunting.

The boundaries between some of Allport's concepts are so indistinct as to be exceedingly hazy. The outstanding example is "cardinal, central, and secondary" p.d.s. Within a single person, there seems to be no concrete basis for deciding why one p.d. is "cardinal," another "central," and still another "secondary." Also troublesome is that a given trait can be both a common trait and a p.d. It does not help much to indicate that a trait such as "kind"

BOX 17.3   Allport and DuBois on the African American Experience and the Nature of Prejudice and Stereotyping

African American social psychologists Stanley Gaines and Edward Reed are among Allport's many admirers (Gaines & Reed, 1994, 1995). Nevertheless they feel that Allport's writings contain two serious shortcomings. He, like most European Americans, viewed the basic experiences of African Americans and European Americans as very similar. Allport also is seen by Gaines and Reed as starting the trend in social psychology of regarding prejudice and stereotyping as processes that rather naturally emerge from normal human thought patterns.

Gaines and Reed (1995) contrast Allport's view, that "black" experience is simply a variant of "white" experience, with the position of W. E. B. DuBois, a famous African American historian and student of American psychology's founder, William James. DuBois believed that a certain duality, resulting from their unique experience, characterized the self-conceptions of African Americans. African Americans see themselves as American and not American, as citizens and not citizens, and as participants in the American dream but excluded from that dream. African Americans are caused to think of themselves as "white" as well as "black": They are often enticed to "be white" by the media and by European American acquaintances, but are constantly reminded that they are "black" and, thus, not accepted in the "white" world. The conflicting poles of this duality are seen in the condemnation by African Americans of African Americans who "act white." An African American is supposed to "act black." To put this predicament into perspective, consider the question, "Wouldn't it be odd if 'whites' were supposed to 'act white'?" Speaking of oddities, weird is the way

wannabes are regarded: "white" people who "act black."

Another DuBoisian duality is collectivism, which is natural to people of African descent, and individualism, which (mostly male) European Americans hold up to African Americans as the means to "making it" in America. African Americans must figure out how to fit both of these extremes. Gaines and Reed (1995) also point out that Allport had his own duality: extropunitive—blaming others—and intropunitive—blaming oneself. Allport saw some African Americans as extropunitive and some as intropunitive. Gaines and Reed viewed Booker T. Washington, known for his attempts to appease "whites," as tending to be intropunitive and DuBois, founder of the National Association for the Advancement of Colored People (NAACP), as tending to be extropunitive. But they also felt that the dichotomy was false. Because of the oppressive circumstances of African Americans, each would reflect some mixture of extropunitive and intropunitive orientation.

As for the second shortcoming, Gaines and Reed rejected the notion attributed to Allport that prejudice and stereotyping naturally flow from normal cognitive processes. To the contrary, prejudice/stereotyping stem from slavery and its legacy of oppression, as well as attempts to justify both that cruel institution and its horrific aftermath. Racism came to America with the ingenious but imperfect culture that European Americans brought from Europe. Slavery and oppression flowed directly from the arrival of that culture (see Allen, 1978 for a historical perspective consistent with this view).

---

has a different "flavor" when found in one person as opposed to another. How is it that the same trait is different when possessed by different people? In a sense Allport argues for a lack of continuity between people. Each person is an island unto herself or himself and must be understood using principles unique to him or her. Such conceptions make the study of people very costly.

Conclusions

Some people find fault with Allport's idiographic approach. Others, including myself, believe that he has correctly understood the complexity of people and the extraordinary uniqueness of each person. These insights make it appropriate to regard any statements of general principles applicable to all humans as exceedingly difficult to support. Many personologists have acted as if understanding people is easier than understanding chemistry or physics. In fact, people are the most complicated entities on this earth. Facing up to the difficulty of explaining them is the first step in the grueling task of sorting out all that complexity.

While Allport may be criticized for creating a series of mini-theories rather than one coherent theory, does writing a grand, all-encompassing theory make sense? After all, even Einstein failed when he tried to compose a theory unifying the major physical forces. In view of human complexity, it may be naive to attempt a theory, such as Freud's, that explains most things psychological. Even theories restricted to explaining everything about personality may be too ambitious. Given the present "state of the art" methods we have in personality, mini-theories may be the best we can do.

A few of the theorists covered in this book are notable not just for their theories, but also for the persons they were. Like Kelly, Allport received a warm, genuine tribute from his students. Like Rogers, he seemed undistracted by the pursuit of fame and fortune; his concern was for the well-being of people. Allport's life is a reminder that truly meaningful psychological theorizing provides many benefits for human beings.

Summary Points

1. Allport was born into a warm and philanthropic home headed by a school teacher and a physician. Always humble, he dismissed his academic feats in high school and later. The baby of the family, he followed older brother Floyd to Harvard. There, like others, his first experience with psychology was less than positive. Still he adopted the discipline and received a doctorate from Harvard.

2. While Allport was a personal humanist, his theory was not orthodox humanistic. Unlike others, he was idiographic, inclined to study each person's unique traits. The idiographic view is currently gaining strength. He was also a forerunner of the interactionists. The Freudian unconscious was, to Allport, just as overemphasized as behavioral consistency.

3. The Adjective Generation Technique came from his tendency to abandon typical methods in favor of what works to understand people. Personality is the dynamic organization of psychophysical systems that determine characteristic behavior and thought. A trait has the capacity to render many stimuli equivalent and to guide adaptive behavior. Traits are not habits or character, but can be common or p.d.s. Traits have a different flavor when attributed to a particular person rather than to people in general.

4. Cardinal, central, and secondary p.d.s. refer to centrality of traits within the personality. Allport's stage theory of personality development is founded on the proprium, "me as felt and known, the self as 'object' of knowledge and feeling." The "bodily self" refers to sensations of the body. Self-identity is continuity of the self over time. Self-esteem is pride in one's pursuits and accomplishments.

5. In extension of self, the self expands to include important elements of the environment. Self-image is composed of hopes developing from others' expectations. The rational coper can solve problems in the head. Propriate striving involves laying plans for the future. Extension of the self in the mature personality is based on functional autonomy. Warm relating to others in maturity is founded on intimacy and compassion. Self-acceptance entails reasonable handling of urges and high frustration tolerance.

6. Realistic perceptions of useful skills, insight, and humor are essential for maturity. Laughing at ourselves tells others that we have insight. A unifying philosophy of life involves directedness. Value orientations take six different forms. Mature, intrinsically motivated, religious sentiment is also essential to maturity. Extrinsics tend to be prejudiced, but high intrinsics have traits related to good psychological and physical health, though they are self-deceptive and impression managers.

7. Generic conscience is concerned with self-selected principles, not with "sins." Prejudice is felt antipathy based on faulty generalizations directed to most members of a group. More empirically, it is what people say and write about their discrimination. Even "whites" who claim not to discriminate by race do so when making choices that entail high intimacy, commitment, and permanency. Underlying racism may be the reason why almost all majority people discriminate in some ways.

8. Race differences may be reduced to ethnic differences since "race" is a questionable concept. A stereotype, a belief that most members of a group possess a certain trait, may contain a grain of truth, but is false when applied to almost all of a large group. Stereotypes of African Americans are still negative, but have changed in content. A study of African Americans' attributions to European Americans reveals several negative stereotypes. The prejudiced personality is "threat-oriented." Prejudiced people have underlying feelings of hostility toward their parents and are highly moralistic.

9. Prejudiced people dichotomize everything, show a high need for definiteness, tend to externalize their own hostility, and are devoted to their institutions, most especially "the nation." They also show high deference for and willingness to submit to authority. Dubois casts the uniqueness of African Americans' experience in terms of dualities: being a part of America and being excluded; collectivism and individuality. He also contended that prejudice/stereotyping results from slavery and its legacy of oppression, not normal cognitive processes.

10. Allport has been the voice of moderation on "behavioral consistency" and his "personality development" has been influential. *The Nature of Prejudice* was a landmark contribution to understanding prejudice. Certain of his specific concepts have been useful, but his theory is really several mini-theories. His emphasis on p.d.s puts him out of the mainstream and the borders between the three kinds of p.d.s are murky. Also, the distinction between p.d.s and common traits is not clear. Still, his emphasis on the uniqueness and complexity of people may be realistic. His warmth and concern set him apart.

Running Comparison

Theorist	*Allport in Comparison*
Freud	He thought that Freud dug too deep too often, but saw these co-incidences: id (body), ego (environment), superego (society).
Fromm	His economic orientation and the marketing type of Fromm are similar.
Murray	He disagrees with Murray on importance of the unconscious.
Maslow	They both alluded to multiple motivations.
Kelly	Like Kelly, he adopted the "one person at a time" approach.
Cattell & Eysenck	He disagreed with them on emphasizing common traits.
Erikson	He found Erikson's "identity crisis" useful.
Rotter	His prejudiced people were like Rotter's externals.
Sullivan	Both were stage theorists.
Horney	Prejudiced people show her "externalizing."

Essay/Critical Thinking Questions

1. Sometimes children turn out just like their parents. How was Allport like his parents?

2. Can you trace Allport's greater interest in p.d.s than common traits to a deeper philosophical orientation?

3. How can highly intrinsically religious people be both self-deceptive impression managers and genuinely optimistic true-believers?

4. Could laughing at oneself be carried too far? Indicate a couple of reasons why making fun of oneself might sometimes be a mistake.

5. Besides the social relations specified on the Social Distance Scale, what other intimate, committed, permanent relations can you name?

6. Might the "change" in stereotypes of African Americans shown with recent use of the Adjective Generation Technique have something to do with the method used?

7. Can you make explicit the connection between how prejudiced people are reared and their attitudes toward their parents?

8. How does the need for "definiteness" in prejudiced people link to their prejudice?

9. Besides DuBois' dualities, what are some other ways that the daily experiences of African Americans and European Americans differ?

10. Why are mini-theories better than an all-encompassing theory?

E-mail Interaction

(Contact the author at mfbpa@wiu.edu)
Forward one of the following or phrase your own.

1. In view of his background, was Allport an elitist?
2. Tell me how unique I am. Is there anyone out there quite like me?
3. It seems that Allport was trying to promote religion. Tell me whether he was.
4. Is there a conflict between Allport's view that prejudice stems from child-rearing practices and Dubois' belief that it has its roots deep in mainstream culture?
5. If racism is a thing that is wrong with European American culture, what is right about it?

GLOSSARY

Abience is the name given to the negative-need-promoting vectors that describe movements away from objects and people.

Ability trait is reflected in "the manner of response to the complexity of a situation, [selected after] the individual is clear on what goals he wants to achieve in that situation."

Abstracting across the cleavage line occurs when whole constructs fall under superordinate emergent and under superordinate implicit poles.

Accurate empathy is Rogers's term for the ability to accurately perceive the client's internal world in a nonevaluative way.

Active imagination is a method through which patients are encouraged to simulate dream experiences by actively engaging in imagination while fully awake.

Actone is a pattern of bodily movements in and of itself, divorced from its effect.

Actual self (Horney) is who one currently is.

Adience refers to the positive-need-promoting vectors that describe movement toward objects and people.

Advantageous comparison is a cognitive mechanism by which ". . . deplored acts can be made to appear righteous by contrasting them with flagrant inhumanities."

Aesthetic needs are related to beauty, structure, and symmetry.

Alpha is press that actually exist, that is, are objectively verifiable.

Ambiverts show medium degrees of exvia-invia, with behaviors characteristic of both aspects.

Amphigenital refers to the case where one or both members of a pair, who both may be homosexual or heterosexual, take on a role that is different from their usual role.

Amplification is broadening and enriching dream or other image content through a process of directed association.

Anal-expulsive is an adult type involving an inclination to disregard widely accepted rules of cleanliness, orderliness, and "appropriate behavior, a "diarrhetic" orientation.

Anal-retentive is an adult type that is characterized by delay of final satisfactions to the last possible moment; these people save and retain, a constipated orientation.

Anal stage is a period in which sexual gratification occurs when defecation relieves the tension of a full bowel and simultaneously stimulates the anus.

Anima   is the representation of woman in man.

Animus   is man in woman.

Anxiety   (Cattell) is the feelings of tension and upset, the source of which may be difficult to identify.

Anxiety   (Freud) is a state of extremely unpleasant emotional discomfort.

Anxiety   (Kelly) is what a person experiences when his or her construction system does not apply to critical events.

Anxiety gradient   refers to "learning to discriminate increasing from diminishing anxiety and to alter activity in the direction of the latter."

Arbitrary rightness   is the strategy of people who see life as a merciless battle and, therefore, feel they must be definite and "right" about everything lest "foreign influence" control them.

Archetypes   or ancient types are preexistent forms that are innate and represent psychic predispositions that lead people to apprehend, experience, and respond to the world in certain ways.

Ascending reticular activating system   (ARAS) acts as an arousal mechanism. The core of the system is the reticular formation of the brain stem.

Assimilation   is how people acquire things.

Attitude   (Cattell) is an expression of an ergic goal that is generally subsidiated to an erg(s).

Attitude   (Jung) is a readiness of the psyche to act or react in a certain way to experience.

Authoritarians   show high deference for authority figures, submission to the power of authority, and a need to command those seen as lower in power than themselves.

Automaton conformity   is the condition that occurs when the person, out of fear of aloneness, gives up freedom for union with society, and she or he bends over backwards to maintain the union by strict adherence to social norms and conventions.

Autonomy   is independence stemming from the reasonable self-control that allows children to hold rather than restrain, to let be rather than lose.

Autophilic person   is one who manifests no preadolescent development, because it has not occurred or was attempted without success, causing the continuation self-directed love.

Awareness   is the conscious apprehension of experience.

Basic anxiety   is "an insidiously increasing, all-pervading feeling of being lonely and helpless in a hostile world."

Basic conflict   involves contradictory orientations to move toward, away from, and against others, all existing within a neurotic.

Basic mistrust   is the feeling of abandonment and helpless rage that accompanies uncertainty of satisfaction.

Basic trust   results from the infant's sense that it can count on satisfaction of its needs; the world takes on the aura of a "trustworthy realm."

Behavioral dimension   is a continuum of behavior analogous to a yardstick.

Behaviorism   is a school of psychology for which the basic subject matter is "outside"; it is overt (observable) behavior.

Behavior therapy   is psychological therapy employing behavioral techniques.

Belongingness and love needs   orient the person toward affectionate relations with people, and a sense of place in family and groups.

Beta   is press that are determined by the person's own interpretation, that is, subjectively determined.

Biophilia   is love of life.

Birth order   is the child's position relative to other siblings.

Blaming victims   for their own fate is a self-exonerative process for escaping self-blame.

Blind spot   is an area of contradiction about which the individual manages to remain unaware.

Bodily self   is sensations that emanate from the muscles, joints, tendons, eyes, ears, and so on.

Brief therapy approach   involves techniques that address and solve clients' problems in a specifiable and relatively small number of sessions.

B-Values   are ultimate or end-goals of meta-need fulfillment.

Cardinal p.d.s   are pervasive and outstanding in the life of a person.

Care   is the strength of maturity, is "the broadening concern for what has been generated by love, necessity, or accident—a concern which must consistently overcome the ambivalence adhering to irreversible obligation and the narrowness of self-concern."

Case history method   involves collecting background data about and making intensive observations on a single individual in order to discover how to treat that person or to obtain information that may apply to other people.

Castration anxiety   is a generalized fear on the part of boys that they might lose their penises, the highly prized organs of pleasure (father may cut it off).

Catharsis   is a process by which inner feelings are openly expressed in words or behaviors.

Cathexes   (Freud) are attachments of libidinous energy either to real external world objects or to fantasized inner world images.

Cathexis   (Murray) is a process by which an object evokes a need.

Central p.d.   is one of the entries on the relatively large list of traits we use to summarize an individual's personality.

Characterizing events   associated with a situation is placing them into meaningful categories.

Childhood   (birth to adolescence) is a relatively problem-free period dominated by instincts, dependency, and a psychological atmosphere provided by parents.

Childhood stage   emerges with articulate speech and ends with the appearance of the need for peers (pre-school years).

Choice   is a decision between the alternatives provided by the construct that has preempted the situation.

Circumspection phase   refers to a period of "trying on for size" the various constructs available in our personal repertory.

Cognitive needs   are motivations to know, to understand, to explain, and to satisfy curiosity.

Cognitive social learning theory   proposes that important factors are cognitive facilities rather than traits.

Cognitively complex   persons have construction systems containing constructs that are clearly differentiated, that is, distinguished one from the other.

Cognitively simple   people have construction systems for which distinctions among constructs are blurred—a poorly differentiated system.

Collective unconscious   is a storehouse of ancestral experiences dating to the dawn of humankind and common to all humans.

Commonality   is a reference to the sharing of constructs by two or more people whose experiences are similar.

Common trait   (Cattell) is "A trait which can be measured for all people by the same battery [of tests] and on which [the people] differ in degree rather than in form."

Common traits   (Allport) "are . . . those aspects of personality in respect to which most people within a given culture can be profitably compared."

Compartmentalization   is a mechanism by which individuals separate key aspects of themselves and their life situations into "logic-tight" compartments.

Compensate   is to overcome weaknesses by striving to become superior in some way.

Compensation   is the balancing of a conscious experience with an opposing unconscious representation as in observations that a dream's meaning is often just the opposite of the person's conscious experience.

Competence   is "the free exercise (unimpaired by an infantile sense of inferiority) of dexterity and intelligence in the completion of serious tasks."

Competency   embraces both the cognitive ability to size up a situation so that one understands how to operate effectively in it and the ability to perform behaviors that will lead to success in the situation.

Complexes   are mental contents in the psyche that agglutinate or stick together like the clumping of red blood cells and eventually take up residence in the personal unconscious.

Component of a situation   is some part of the total situation, such as physical characteristics, or, more importantly, factors associated with people who are present when the situation is unfolding.

Conflicts of needs   occur when needs oppose each other "within the personality, giving rise when prolonged to harassing spiritual dilemmas."

Congruence   is a state in which a person's self-concept and actual experiences relating to self are consistent.

Conscience   is the internal agent that punishes us when we do wrong.

Consequence   is an event that occurs after a response has been performed and changes the probability that the response will occur again.

Construction system   is an organization of many constructs with the more important, and often more abstract, at the top and the less important constructs at the bottom.

Constructive alternativism   is the assumption that a person's present interpretations of her or his life situation are subject to revision and replacement.

Constructs   are ways of construing events or "seeing the world" so that the future is anticipated.

Context   of a construct is composed of all those elements to which the construct applies.

Contingent   refers to a relationship in which the occurrence of event B depends on the prior occurrence of event A.

Continuous reinforcement   involves reinforcement following every response.

Contrafactions of needs   are cases in which needs are related to their opposites in alternating phases.

Correlated   refers to a condition that exists if variations in one variable correspond closely with variations in another.

Correlation coefficient is an index, designated by the letter "r," of the degree to which a relationship is linear.

Creative power of the individual is the process by which we each make original conceptions of ourselves and our world as we develop a style of life for solving the three great problems of life.

Crystallized general ability (g_c) is "A general factor, largely . . . abilities learned at school, representing . . . applications of [g_f], and amount and intensity of schooling; it appears in vocabulary and numerical ability [tests]."

Cumulative records are graphs for which responses are accumulated and plotted against time.

Cynicism is "the denying or deriding of moral values" because of a deep-seated uncertainty with regard to morality.

Defense mechanisms are internal, unconscious, and automatic psychological strategies for coping with or regaining control over threatening id instincts.

Defensive behaviors are adopted in order to cope with unpleasant events that are anticipated on future occasions.

Defensive externals are people who are highly competitive and do well on tests, but endorse external items for the apparent purpose of blaming others for their failures.

Deficiency needs or D-needs involve satisfactions that allow the person to avoid physical sickness and psychological maladjustment.

Dehumanization is a cognitive process that involves lowering the status of certain people from "human being" to "lesser being."

Delaying gratification is postponing some pleasure so that it can be enjoyed to the maximum degree or in its most optimal form.

Denial (Freud) is the process by which we refuse to think about or address whatever is too hard to bear.

Denial (Rogers) involves the inability to recognize or accept the existence of an experience that has occurred.

Dependency constructs are special constructs that revolve around the child's survival needs. A "mother" construct would be an example.

Dependent variables have values that are free to vary so that they are open to influence by the independent variables.

Despair is a feeling that time is too short for the achievement of integrity and the accompanying contribution to the connection between generations.

Diffusion of innovation occurs when models try something new and thereby display its benefits and advantages to others.

Dignity or worth is what we refer to when we give people credit for what they have done.

Directedness is having a goal or goals in life toward which one strives.

Displacement is finding a new target for some feelings, one that is less threatening than the original.

Displacement and diffusion of responsibility involves placing the blame for one's deplorable acts onto others, and spreading the responsibility for reprehensible behavior to others who are present, respectively.

Distortion involves a reinterpretation of an experience so as to make it consistent with how one wants things to be.

Diversity   refers to the numerous cultures, along with gender and sexual orientations, that characterize the population in the United States and other countries.

dR-technique   is the same as the R method, except that each of the hundreds of people responding to the several measures does so two times, usually after only a short delay, and each person's score on each measure is the second response minus the first.

Dream series   analysis involves large numbers of dreams in succession, because Jung believed that one or a few dreams did not tell the whole story.

Dream symbol   is dream content that represents some person, thing, or activity involved in unconscious processes.

Dynamic lattice   is "The tracing of the subsidiation of attitudes . . . ending in the satisfaction of a number of primary ergic goals."

Dynamic trait   refers to motivations and interests.

Dynamisms   refer to "the relatively enduring energy [units] which [periodically] characterize the organism in its duration as a living organism."

Early adolescence   erupts at puberty when the need for intimacy evolves toward lustful feelings of closeness and tenderness with a sexual partner.

Early infancy   is the first stage and involves no sense of self.

Early recollections (ERs)   indicate how a person views her or himself and other people and reveal what the person strives for in life, what he or she anticipates, and, more generally, his or her conception of life itself.

Econetic model   is a framework that integrates environmental situations with characteristics of the person—including personality components—in attempts to understand the person.

Eductive   refers to learning relationships by "pulling them out" of the entities that contain them.

Effectiveness   is the need to compensate for "being in a strange and overpowering world" by developing a sense of being able to do something that will "make a dent" in life.

Ego   (Freud) is a coherent organization of mental processes that develops out of id energy, has access to consciousness, and is devoted to contacting reality for the purpose of satisfying id needs.

Ego   (Jung) is what one thinks of oneself, the genuine me, and is the "centre of the total field of consciousness."

Ego ideal   is positive standards in the form of internal representations of idealized parental figures that can result in feelings of pride and self-respect.

Ego-strength   refers to the ability of the ego to successfully interact with reality on behalf of the id and inhibit id impulses until "safe" satisfactions are found.

Elaborative choice   is a selection of an alternative, aligned to a single construct dimension, that appears to provide the greatest opportunity for the further elaboration of a system.

Electra complex   is the dynamic corresponding to the Oedipal complex involving girls' love of father and hatred of mother.

Elements   are objects, beings, or events.

Emergent pole   is the primary and principle end of a construct, like "good" in good-bad and "intelligent" in intelligent-stupid.

Empathy   (Rogers) is sensing and participating in the emotions of others.

Empathy   (Sullivan) is "the term that we use to refer to the peculiar emotional linkage [that exists between the] infant [and] other significant people . . ."

Entropy   is the equalization of differences in order to bring about a balance or equilibrium.

Epigenesis—*epi* means "upon" and genesis means "emergence":   the stages literally emerge "one on top of another in space and time."

Equivalence   is the circumstance in which energy consumed to accommodate one intention—"say something nice"—is balanced by energy fueling an opposite intention—"say something nasty."

Erg   is "An innate source of reactivity, such as is often described as a drive [or instinct], directed to a certain goal and accompanied by a certain quality . . ."

Erogenous zones   are sensitive areas of the body from which instinctual satisfactions can be obtained.

Eros   represents energy for preserving oneself (love of self) and one's species (love of others).

Escape   simply involves jumping to the side of the shuttle box without shock.

Esteem needs   are of two kinds: 1) there are personal desires for adequacy, mastery, competence, achievement, confidence, independence, and freedom, and 2) there are desires for respect from other people, including attention, recognition, appreciation, status, prestige, fame, dominance, importance, and dignity.

Eugenics   is the application of genetics to the improvement of human biological and psychological characteristics.

Euphemistic labeling   is the cognitive process of assigning a name to deplorable behavior that makes it seem innocuous or even laudable.

Eupsychia   (Yew-sigh-key-ah) is a utopian society characterized by psychological health among all its members.

Events   are simply occurrences that are produced by components of a situation.

Excessive self-control   arises in reaction to a flood of contradictory emotions and involves holding feelings and behavior in a vice-grip.

Excitation and stimulation   is the need for the nervous system to be "exercised," that is, to experience a certain amount of excitation.

Existential needs   are needs that must be met if one's existence is to be meaningful, one's inner being is to be developed, one's talents are to be fully exploited, and abnormality is to be avoided.

Existentialism   is a philosophically based approach to understanding each person's most immediate experience and the conditions of his or her existence.

Expansive   is to be "in control," to not admit that one is incorrect (or another person is correct), and to never give an inch in a conflict.

Expectancy   (Mischel) is a belief based on past experience that provides a prediction of future outcomes.

Expectancy   (Rotter) is "the probability held by the individual that a particular reinforcement will occur as a function of a specific behavior on his part in a specific situation or situations."

Experience   (Kelly) is what one learns from the events of the past.

Experience   (Rogers) is all that is going on within the organism at any given moment that is potentially available to awareness.

Experiment   is a procedure whereby an experimenter first sets the variation in some independent variable(s) and then ascertains whether variation in some dependent variable(s) is influenced.

Exploitative   orientation involves experiencing the source of all good as outside of oneself, and taking things through force or cunning, rather than expecting to receive from others.

Extension of self   is expanding oneself to include all those significant aspects of one's environment, including people.

Extension of the cleavage line   is a reference to the observation that the poles of a person's subordinate constructs fall directly under the corresponding emergent and implicit poles of his or her superordinate constructs.

External locus of control   refers to people's belief that reinforcement of their behaviors is due more to luck, chance, fate, powerful others, or complex and unpredictable environmental forces, rather than determined by their own behaviors or characteristics.

Externalization   is the tendency to experience internal processes as if they occurred outside oneself and to hold these "exterior" factors responsible for one's difficulties.

Extinction   occurs when a previously reinforced response is no longer followed by the same reinforcement and the response eventually decreases in frequency.

Extraversion   is an "outward-turning" of libido that involves a positive movement of interest away from one's inner experience toward outer experience.

Extrinsic   (Allport) refers to an orientation to religion that is utilitarian and in the service of self-esteem maintenance.

Extrinsic rewards   are rewards originating outside the individual (money).

Exvia-invia   is "A factorially established broad dimension within the area of behaviour popularly referred to as extraversion–introversion."

Factor   in factor analysis refers to a hypothetical construct that is applied to a data cluster (set of items) and suggests what it is measuring.

Factor analysis   is a statistical procedure for determining the number and nature of factors underlying larger numbers of measures.

Favorable ratio   is the greater the magnitude of the pull to the positive pole relative to the pull of the negative pole the better.

Fear   is the experience one has when a new construct appears to be entering the system, and may become dominant.

Feeling   evaluates how experiences strike us, whether they are suitable to us or not; it is a kind of judgment that is an entirely subjective process.

Fictional finalism   is a fictional goal toward which all psychological currents flow, thereby unifying the personality.

Fidelity   is "the opportunity to fulfill personal potentialities . . . in a context which permits the young person to be true to himself and true to significant others . . . [and to] sustain loyalties . . . in spite of inevitable contradictions of value systems."

Fixation   is the impairment of development at a particular stage because satisfactions appropriate for the stage are frustrated, resulting in permanent investment of libidinal energy in the stage.

Fixed-interval (FI) schedules   are schedules for which the amount of time between one reinforced response and the next is constant.

Fixed-ratio (FR) schedules   are procedures for which the number of responses occurring between one reinforced response and the next is constant.

Fixed-role therapy   involves a client playing the role of an imaginary character who possesses constructs that are in contrast to his or her actual constructs.

Fixed schedules   are procedures for which a response is reinforced after a constant amount of time has elapsed or after a constant number of responses have been performed.

Fluid general ability   (^g_f) is "That form of general intelligence which is largely innate and which adapts itself to all kinds of material, regardless of previous experience with it."

Forbidding gestures   are negative, covert cues such as a wrinkled brow, a cold tone of voice, a too tight grasp, a hesitancy, reluctance, or even revulsion at having to interact with the infant.

Foresight   is the capacity to look ahead in search of good experiences and in the interest of avoiding bad ones.

Forethought   is anticipation of "likely consequences of . . . [future] actions."

Frame of orientation   is a cognitive "map" of people's natural and social worlds that enables them to organize and make sense of puzzling matters and allows them to operate in the arena of rational understanding.

Free association   is a process in which the person adopts a mental orientation that allows ideas, images, memories, and feelings to be expressed spontaneously.

Freedom   refers to our belief that we can choose from various behaviors, rather than having our actions controlled by an external force, the environment.

Frustration tolerance   is exhibited when things go wrong; people who have it do not pitch a tantrum, blame others, or wallow in self-pity.

Functional autonomy   is a process by which a new system of motivation evolves from an older one, but stems from tensions different from those of the original.

Fundamental postulate   is the assumption that a person's psychological processes are routed through various channels or pathways by the ways in which she or he anticipates events.

Fusion of needs   is the name Murray gave to a single "action pattern that satisfies two or more needs at the same time."

"g"   supposedly subsumes the so-called primary mental abilities and forms a common core of general intelligence.

Gambler's Fallacy   is the expectation that a failure on one attempt means that success on a subsequent attempt becomes more likely, whereas success means greater likelihood of failure in the future.

General actualizing tendency   is an inherent tendency of the organism to develop all its capacities in ways that serve to maintain or enhance the organism.

Generalized expectancy   is an expectancy that holds for a number of situations that are similar to one another.

Generativity   is "the concern with establishing and guiding the next generation."

Generic conscience   is central to the development of personality and is a unifying force in personality: it lays down comprehensive guidelines for nearly all of a person's conduct.

Genital stage   is the stage of mature sexual love, beginning at puberty, that includes directing both feelings of lust and of affection toward another person.

Genuine sense of humor—as opposed to an appreciation of sexual and aggressive jokes— is being able "to laugh at the things one loves (including, of course, oneself and all that pertains to oneself), and still to love them."

Goals   are anticipated achievements that are in line with current personal standards.

Gradualistic moral disengagement   is a process during which people slowly slip unawares into what was normally unacceptable behavior.

Growth model   emphasizes helping people to "remove whatever blocks to growth exist" so they can move beyond being normal or average.

Guilt   (Erikson) is the harness that restrains pursuit of desires, urges, and potentials; the exercise of an overzealous conscience.

Guilt   (Freud) is an intense feeling of regret over having done something wrong or evaluations of oneself as an undeserving, inadequate person.

Guilt   (Kelly) is the result of the person's perception that he or she is being dislodged from some critical role.

Habitual responses (HR)   are specific responses (Cattell's surface traits) that recur under similar circumstances, such as regularly saying "Hi" to a neighbor.

Heritability   popularly refers to the proportion of the variability in a trait that is accounted for by the genes.

Heterophilic person   "has gone through the preadolescent period and made the early adolescent change in which he has become intensely interested in achieving intimacy with members of . . . the other sex."

Hoarding   orientation is embraced by people who believe the "goods" come from the inside not the outside, themselves not others, so security is based on an attitude of saving, of letting out as little as possible.

Hope   is the enduring belief in the attainability of basic satisfactions.

Humanistic communitarian socialism   is a political system embracing economic, social, and moral functions wherein ordinary citizens interact cooperatively and are actively involved in the various functions.

Humanistic psychoanalyst—one who believes in the essential worth and dignity of each person, and in the importance of helping each person to do the most with what she or he has.

Humanistic psychology   is the school of psychology that emphasizes the present experience of the whole person, assumes the essential worth of the person, and fosters the belief that the person can solve his or her own psychological problems.

Hypercompetitiveness   is the indiscriminate need by individuals to compete and win (and to avoid losing) at any cost as a means of maintaining or enhancing feelings of self-worth.

Hysterical neurosis   is a condition in which a person who displays no medical signs of a physical disorder develops symptoms of the disorder to avoid experiences too painful or threatening for conscious consideration.

Id   is beyond conscious awareness and comprises whatever is present at birth, including everything that relates to the satisfaction of physical drives, such as sex and hunger, or primitive psychological needs, such as for comfort and for protection from danger.

Ideal self   is the self a person most values and desires to be.

Identity   (Erikson) is the accumulated confidence that the sameness and continuity one has previously cultivated are now appreciated by others, allowing, in turn, the promise of careers and lifestyles to come.

Identity   (Fromm) is the need to be aware of oneself as a separate entity, and to sense oneself as the subject of one's own actions.

Identity confusion   is the failure of previous identity developments to coalesce in such a way that it is clear what roles one is expected to play in the future.

Idiographic theorists   are inclined to study each individual's unique traits without attempting to find a place for each along relatively few trait dimensions.

Impermeable   is a reference to certain constructs that tend not to change in terms of range of convenience or place in the construction system.

Implicit pole   is the contrasting end of a construct, like *uneducated* in educated–uneducated and *not admired* in admired–not admired.

Incentive   is any circumstance, concrete or abstract, that creates an anticipation of positive outcome following the performance of a behavior.

Incongruence   reflects an inconsistency between self-concept and experiences relating to self.

Independent variables   have variation that is arranged by the person who uses the experimental method, called the experimenter.

Individual character   is the pattern of behavior characteristic of a given person—"the relatively permanent system of all noninstinctual strivings through which man relates himself to the human and natural world."

Individual differences   is a key psychological phrase generally referring to the observation that people differ in a variety of ways.

Individuality   refers to differences among construction systems both in terms of the constructs comprising the systems and in terms of how the constructs are organized.

Individual psychology   is an attempt to conceive of a unique human being as an interconnected whole, biologically, philosophically, and psychologically.

Individuation   is the process by which a person becomes a psychological "in-dividual," that is, a separate, indivisible unity or "whole."

Inductive-hypothetico-deductive spiral   is "the detecting of regularities in observational data leads to a hypothesis from which experimental consequences are deduced, [leading] to further data from which new regularities are induced, and so on in an ever-expanding spiral."

Industry   is children's absorption in the "tool world" of their culture—the workaday world—thereby preparing them "for a hierarchy of learning experiences which [they] will undergo with the help of cooperative peers and instructive adults."

Infancy stage   starts at birth and continues until the appearance of speech.

Inferiority   (Adler) is the persistent feeling that one does not measure up to society's ideals or to one's own fictional standards.

Inferiority (Erikson) occurs if children perceive their skills or status among peers to be inadequate.

Inferiority complex   is Adler's term for the consequences of an exaggerated, persistent form of inadequacy that is partly explained by a deficiency in social interest.

Initiative   is acting on one's desires, urges, and potentials.

Insight   is a method through which personally unacceptable and socially "taboo" experiences buried in the person's unconscious can be made conscious.

Instinctoid   is a reference to the instinct-like nature of needs, because of their biological, genetic, and universal characteristics.

Instincts   are inborn forces whose characteristics are both physical (bodily needs) and psychological (wishes).

Institutional safeguard   is a cultural unit that protects and promotes products of crisis resolution.

Integrity   is "an emotional integration faithful to the image bearers of the past and ready to take (and eventually renounce) leadership in the present."

Intellectualization   involves talking and thinking at an intellectual rather than an emotional level about what we do or contemplate that is threatening to us (smoker says, "the link between cancer and smoking is unproven; I've seen the studies").

Interaction point of view   is a position that emphasizes the interplay between internal entities or person factors and social situations, rather than either in isolation from the other.

Intermittent reinforcement   is a process in which responses are reinforced every so often, or after some number of responses has occurred.

Internal locus of control   is the belief that reinforcement is dependent on one's own behavior or characteristics—not fate, luck, or chance.

Interpersonal anxiety   is a tension that is alleviated in relationships with significant others or in feelings of well-being.

Interpersonal relations   are the relationships between a person and each other important person in his or her life.

Interpersonal security   is "relaxation of the tension of anxiety" that is experienced as a return to a tranquil, untroubled state.

Interpersonal trust   is a generalized expectancy that people's verbal promises are reliable.

Intimacy   "is really the ability to fuse your identity with somebody else's without fear that you're going to lose something yourself."

Intolerance for ambiguity   is the cognitive orientation requiring that everything be clearly distinguished from everything else: questions have definite answers and problems have simple solutions.

Intrinsic   (Allport) refers to religion being an end-in-itself, something that one surrenders to, not something to use.

Intrinsic motivation   refers to the desire for intrinsic rewards, leading to the pursuit of the same.

Intrinsic rewards   are rewards from within the individual (self-praise).

Introjection   is a process by which personality incorporates the norms and standards of its culture through identification with parents or other admired persons in society, such as clergy and teachers.

Introversion   is an "inward-turning" of psychic energy and involves a negative movement or withdrawal of subjective interest away from outer objects and toward one's inner experience.

Intuition   suggests where something seems to have come from and where it may be going; it is a kind of "instinctive apprehension," of unconscious origin, with no tangible basis.

Isolation   is the failure to secure close and cooperative relationships with the same and, especially, the opposite gender such that partners' identities are important to, but distinct from, one's own.

Isophilic person   is someone who "has been unable to progress past preadolescence, and continues to regard as suitable for intimacy only people who are as like himself as possible . . . that is, members of his own sex."

Jealousy   is the fear of losing a relationship that is seen as the best available means of satisfying an insatiable concern for affection and incessant demands for unconditional love.

Juvenile era   is the period ushered in with the child's need for peer companions, or "playmates rather like oneself."

L-data or *life-records*   are "made by observers on the frequency and intensity with which specific kinds of behavior occur in the people they observe."

Late adolescence   begins with the acknowledgment of an orientation regarding genital behavior and how to fit that revelation into the rest of life, then ends with "the establishment of a fully human or mature repertory of interpersonal relations."

Latency   is a quiet period between ages 6 and 12 during which children repress their attraction to parents and become sexually disinterested.

Latent content   is the underlying meaning of each dream.

Law of movement   is the direction taken by the person that originates in his or her ability to exercise free choice in fully exploiting personal capabilities and resources.

Learn by anxiety   is a process that occurs when anxiety is not severe; individuals may become acquainted with the situations in which it is present so that those circumstances may be avoided.

Libido   (Freud) is an energy variously described as "psychical desire," "erotic tendencies," "sexual desire in the broadest sense," and the "motive forces of sexual life."

Libido   (Jung) is psychic energy.

Loadings   are correlations of particular items with a given factor.

Locus of control   refers to "the degree to which persons expect that . . . reinforcement [and other outcomes] of their behavior is [dependent on their] behavior or personal characteristics versus the degree to which [they expect it is due to] chance, luck, or fate, . . . powerful others, or is simply unpredictable."

Locus of evaluation   refers to the source of evidence about values, whether it is inside oneself or outside, in others.

Loose constructs   yield varying predictability.

Long unit   is the life cycle of the individual.

Love   "is the guardian of that elusive and yet all-pervasive power of cultural and personal style which binds . . . the affiliations of competition and cooperation, procreation and production" into a "way of life."

Lust   is Sullivan's term for "certain tensions of or pertaining to the genitals," culminating in orgasm.

Make prompt statements of all that comes to mind   is a task of the patient during the interview that is enabled by trusting the "situation to the extent of expressing the thoughts that it provokes."

Mandala   or magic circle is a round object, often including an inner spiral that draws the eyes to the center of its surface.

Manifest content   is what the dreamer remembers about the dream when awakened.

Marketing   orientation is unique to the modern historical era in which exchanging goods for money, other goods, or services became the backbone of a "supply and demand" economy.

Mature love   "is union under the condition of preserving one's integrity, one's individuality . . . [it] is an active power of man."

Medical model   refers to the idea that people with psychological problems are sick and need some sort of treatment, at least analogous to medication, that will make them normal again.

Mentalism   is the belief that thoughts and feelings determine behavior, not external consequences.

Metagenital   use does not involve one's own genitals, but another person's genitals are involved.

Meta-needs or growth needs (G-needs)   are terms used "to describe the motivations of self-actualizing people."

Middle age   (age 40 to old age) brings with it the task of building a whole personality.

Model   refers to a person who performs some behavior for an audience, showing how it is done and what benefits accrue from it.

Modeling   refers to the act of performing a behavior before one or more observers.

Morality principle   is the code that concerns society's values regarding right and wrong.

Moral justification   occurs when individuals invoke religious or other moral bases to support their inhuman behavior.

Moving against people   reflects compulsive cravings for power and prestige, as well as personal ambition.

Moving away from people   reflects a person's concern with self, as seen in needs for admiration and perfectionism.

Moving toward people   reflects neurotic needs for a partner and for affection; it also involves compulsive, exaggerated modesty.

Multiple Abstract Variance Analysis (MAVA)   is "a research design for discovering relative proportions of environmental versus hereditary determination for personality traits (nature–nurture ratio)."

n Abasement   involves surrendering, complying, accepting punishment, apologizing, confessing, atoning, and generally being masochistic.

n Achievement   indicates the drive to "overcome obstacles, to exercise power, to strive to do something difficult as well [and] as quickly as possible."

n Affiliation   refers to the desire for friendships and associations; "to greet, join, and live with others."

n Aggression   refers to an assaultive or injurious orientation to others, including to belittle, harm, blame, accuse, ridicule, punish severely, react sadistically toward, or even murder.

n Autonomy   is the drive to resist influence or coercion, to defy authority, seek freedom, and strive for independence.

n Blamavoidance   refers to avoiding blame, punishment, and ostracism by inhibiting asocial or even unconventional impulses; being a well-behaved, law-abiding citizen.

n Contrarience   is the drive to act differently from others, to be unique, to take the opposite side, and to hold unconventional views.

n Dominance is the drive to influence, control, persuade, prohibit, dictate, lead, direct, restrain others and to organize the behavior of a group.

n Exhibition is desiring to attract attention to one's person by exciting, amusing, stirring, shocking, or thrilling others.

n Harmavoidance is avoidance of physical harm to one's self.

n Infavoidance is an orientation to avoiding failure, shame, humiliation, or ridicule by concealing disfigurement and refraining from attempts at anything seen as beyond one's powers.

n Inviolacy is an attitude of attempting to prevent depreciation of self-respect, to preserve one's good name, to avoid criticism, and to maintain psychological distance.

n Noxavoidance is avoidance of noxious substances.

n Order involves arranging, organizing, and putting away objects; to be tidy, clean and scrupulously precise.

n Succorance is the dependent attitude of seeking aid, protection, and sympathy by crying for mercy and help from affectionate, nurturant parents.

Necrophilous character is engrossed by death, dwells on it, and glories in it.

Need (Murray) refers to "a . . . [physiochemical] force . . . in the brain . . . , [that] organizes perception, . . . intellection, . . . and action in such a way as to transform . . . an . . . unsatisfying situation [into a more satisfying one]."

Need for self-actualization is "the desire for self-fulfillment . . . the tendency for [one] to become actualized in what [one] is potentially."

Need for tenderness differs from "love," in that it refers to relief from various tensions.

Need integrate or complex is formed when "traces (images) of cathected objects in familiar settings become integrated in the mind with the needs and emotions which they customarily excite, as well as with the images of preferred modes" (actones or other means of creating satisfaction).

Needs (Maslow) are desires for certain satisfactions that are sought by all humans, regardless of their culture, environment, or generation.

Negative correlation refers to high values on one variable corresponding to low values on the other variable.

Negative mood regulation (NMR) is a belief that one can muster the cognitive and behavioral means to alleviate a negative-affective state or bring it under control.

Negative reinforcement is a process whereby the likelihood of a response increases when it is followed by the termination, reduction, or absence of a stimulus.

Neuroses (Freud) are patterns of abnormal behavior related to an over-control of instincts.

Neuroses (Horney) are "psychic disturbance[s] brought about by fears and defenses against these fears, and by attempts to find compromise solutions for conflicting tendencies."

Neurosis (Adler) is an extreme form of reaction to shock, "a person's automatic, unknowing exploitation of the symptoms resulting from the effects of a shock."

Neurotic needs (Horney) are the coping techniques that are initiated in childhood—excessive, insatiable, and unrealistic demands developed in response to the basic anxiety that dominates the person.

Nomothetic theorists are inclined to derive general laws concerning how a small number of traits apply to all people.

Nonproductive types   are those who have at best pseudo-connection to others and at worse destructive relations with others.

Notice marginal thoughts   is paying attention to thoughts that monitor, critique, and alter speech in terms of formation and grammar, and in terms of errors that may cause incomplete or misunderstood communications to others (patient task during interview).

Noticing changes in the body   that signal decreases or increases in the tension signifying anxiety is one of the interview tasks of the patient.

Objective tests   are highly structured paper-and-pencil questionnaires such as true/false or multiple-choice, each of which can be scored with a key so that scorers all agree on the scores.

Object of devotion   is a goal that gives meaning to people's existence and position in the world.

Observational learning   is learning by observing models as they perform useful behavior.

Oedipus complex   is the constellation of feelings, desires, and strivings revolving around the boy's desire for his mother and his fearful/hateful orientation to his father.

Old age   parallels childhood because of a return to submersion in the unconscious.

Operant conditioning   is a process by which an organism operates on its environment with consequences that influence the likelihood that the operation, or behavior, will be repeated.

Operationalized   refers to translation of concepts into a form that can be quantified or expressed in numbers.

Oral or Narcissistic (self-centered) stage   is a phase that begins at birth and in which the organism's psychic activity focuses on satisfying the needs of the mouth and digestive tract, including the tongue and lips.

Oral-aggressive   is an adult type that is derived from childhood pleasures associated with the mouth, food, and eating, but with greater chewing, biting, and use of teeth.

Oral-receptive   is a personality type that is derived from childhood pleasures of receiving food in the mouth and ingesting it; it is associated with adult dependency and suggestibility.

Organismic   refers to a natural, biological, inborn predisposition reflected in the total functioning of every living being.

Origins   are the locus of their own intentions and behaviors.

Orthogenital   involves the integration of one's own genitals with the "natural receptor genitals" of the opposite sex, that is, heterosexual use of the genitals.

Overcompensate   is to bend over backwards to do or become whatever people's weaknesses have denied them.

P-technique   is "A factor analytic design which measures a single person on the same set of variables repeatedly over a number of different occasions."

Paragenital   involves use of the sex organs such that one acts to seek contact with genitals opposite one's own, but in such a way that impregnation will not occur.

Parataxic   mode is experienced as the infant becomes a child who begins to use speech, but still makes few logical connections within the sequence of its experiences (approximately the pre-school years).

Participant modeling   occurs when a person with low self-efficacy imitates a model's efficacious behavior.

Passive externals (also called "congruent") believe they are controlled by fate or chance.

Pawns are instruments of outside forces that control them.

Peak experiences are intense, mystical experiences associated with simultaneous feelings of limitless horizons, powerfulness and helplessness, a lost sense of time and place, and great ecstasy, wonder, and awe.

Penis envy refers to girls' feelings of inferiority over not having the male organ and compensatory wishes to someday obtain one of their own.

Periodicity refers to rhythms of activity and rest.

Persona or mask is the identities we assume because of the socially prescribed roles we play.

Personal agency is a condition in which people come to believe that they can make things happen that will be of benefit to themselves and to others.

Personal cognitive factors are memories of previous experiences, from the past history of an individual, that determine strategies and skills the person employs for producing behavior at the present time.

Personal disposition (p.d.) is a trait that is unique to a particular individual.

Personal unconscious "is made up essentially of contents [that] have at one time been conscious but which have disappeared from consciousness through having been forgotten or repressed . . ."

Personality (Allport) "is the dynamic organization within the individual of those psychophysical systems that determine his characteristic behavior and thought."

Personality (Cattell) "[is] that which tells what a [person] will do when placed in a particular situation."

Personality (Fromm) is "the totality of inherited and acquired psychic qualities which are characteristic of one individual and which make the individual unique."

Personality (Introduction) is a set of degrees falling along many behavioral dimensions, each degree corresponding to a trait.

Personality (Kelly) consists of an organized system of constructs that may be ranked as to importance.

Personality (Sullivan) is "the relatively enduring pattern of recurrent interpersonal situations which characterize a human life."

Personality system (Mischel) "is characterized by . . . available cognitive and affective [or feeling] units" such that "When certain configurations of situation features are experienced by the individual a . . . subset of cognitions and affects become activated."

Personality traits are internally based psychological characteristics that often correspond to adjectival labels such as "shy," "kind," "mean," "outgoing," "dominant," and so forth.

Personifications are investments of human attributes in persons or objects that do not actually possess the assigned traits, at least not in the degree to which they are applied.

Personologists are psychologists who study personality.

Phallic stage is a phase in which satisfaction is gained primarily by stimulation of the penis or clitoris, through masturbation.

Phenomenology is concerned with grasping reality as individuals perceive it, in a "fresh" manner that is free of preconceptions.

Physiological needs encompass specific biological requirements for water, oxygen, proteins, vitamins, proper body temperature, sleep, sex, exercise, and so on.

Pleasure principle   refers to the achievement of pleasurable feelings as quickly and immediately as possible through the reduction of discomfort, pain, or tension.

Positive regard   is experiencing oneself as making a positive difference in the life of another person and as receiving warmth, liking, respect, sympathy, acceptance, caring, and trust from others.

Positive reinforcement   is a process whereby some event, usually a stimulus, increases the likelihood of a response on which its presentation is contingent.

Positive self-regard   is a favorable attitude toward oneself.

Positively correlated   refers to a condition in which high values on one variable correspond to high values on the other, and low values correspond with low values.

Preadolescence   is brief, beginning with the need for interpersonal intimacy in the form of a close relationship with another person "of comparable status."

Predictability   refers to the ability to predict the future.

Preemption phase   is a period during which one construct is allowed to preempt the situation and define the pair of alternatives between which the person must make his or her choice.

Prejudice   is felt or expressed antipathy based on a faulty and inflexible generalization and may be directed toward a group as a whole, or toward an individual because he is a member of the group.

Press   designates a directional tendency in the object or situation ("press" is also plural).

Primary factors   are relatively pure and narrow in scope and it can be arranged statistically that they are independent.

Primary process   is a continual flow of events involving infantile images and wishes that demand immediate and direct satisfaction.

Productive orientation   is an attitude of relatedness to the world and oneself that encompasses all realms of human experience: reasoning, loving, and working.

Projection   protects people from threat by allowing them to literally project their own unacceptable traits onto other people.

Projective tests   present people with test items that are unstructured, ambiguous, or open-ended, thus allowing them a wide range of freedom in making responses.

Propriate striving   is planning for the future by setting long-range goals.

Proprium   is "me as felt and known . . . the self as 'object' of knowledge and feeling."

Prospective   or "anticipatory" refers to a process through which dreams may "foretell" future events and outcomes.

Prototaxic   mode is the earliest (infancy), most primitive type of experience, a state of generalized sensation or feeling, in the absence of thought.

Prototype   is the "complete goal" of the style of life that is a fiction conceived as a means of adapting to life and includes a strategy for its achievement.

Psyche   is total mentality, all of consciousness and unconsciousness.

Psychoanalysis   refers to Freud's systematic procedures for providing a patient with the insight necessary to rid the personality of its neurotic conflicts.

Psychogenic   needs are secondary to viscerogenic needs and may be derived from them, but, being one step away from the biological side of the organism, are psychological in nature.

Psychological determinism   is a belief that nothing about human behavior occurs by accident or chance; everything about personality "is determined" or has a psychological cause.

Psychological situation   is characterized in a way peculiar to a person, allowing the person to categorize it with certain other situations, as well as differentiate it from still others.

Psychometrics   a quantitative approach to psychological measurement.

Psychosexual   refers to stages conceived of as *sexual* only in the broadest sense of the word, because some stages involve organs ordinarily seen as "sexual" and other organs not popularly regarded as "sexual."

Psychosocial development   refers to a union of physical yearnings and the cultural forces that act on the individual.

Punishment   is a process in which responses that are followed by the presentation of aversive stimuli decrease in likelihood of being performed in the future.

Purpose   is "the courage to envisage and pursue valued and tangible goals guided by conscience but not paralyzed by guilt and by fear of punishment."

Q-data,   where Q stands for *questionnaire*; are a kind of data for which people are their own observers, describing their behavior and feelings through paper-and-pencil inventories, self-reports, or interviews.

R = f(S.P) where R stands for the "nature and magnitude of a person's behavioural response, . . . what he [or she] says, thinks, or does," which is some function (*f*) of S, the "stimulus situation in which [the person] is placed," and P, the nature of her or his personality.

R-technique   is a "process of correlating behaviour measures across some hundreds of people [tested on a single occasion] and factoring them."

Radical behaviorism   considers currently observable events and also potential, future events that can be observed and measured.

Range of convenience   refers to the extent and breadth of the event-category to which a construct applies.

Range of focus   refers to the events to which a construct is most readily applied.

Rate of responding,   when it becomes stable, indicates that conditioning is completed and a new response acquired.

Ratio schedules   are procedures for which some number of responses must be performed between one reinforced response and the next. *Temporal schedules* are procedures for which there must be an elapse of some amount of time between one reinforced response and the next.

Rational coper   is the sense of selfhood that is not merely able to solve problems, but can also reason them through "in the head" and come up with logical solutions.

Rationalization   allows us to excuse our threatening and unacceptable behavior and thoughts (So I lost the money. Money is not what's important in life).

Rationalization   "may be defined as self-deception by reasoning."

Real self   is the potential for growth beyond the artificial idealized image of self.

Reality principle   refers to ego's capacity to delay satisfaction of id's demands until an appropriate object is found that will allow gratification without harmful side effects.

Receptive   refers to an orientation of people who experience the source of all good as being outside themselves.

Recognition   of unconscious contents leads to synthesizing archetypes to consciousness, a process of blending conscious and unconscious into a whole, resulting in self-knowledge.

Regnancy   is the label for the "totality of such [brain] processes occurring during a single moment (a unitary temporal segment of brain processes)."

Regnant   was the name given to "dominant configurations in the brain" that correspond to internal representations.

Reinforcement   (Skinner) occurs when some event is contingent on the prior performance of some response, and the response changes in likelihood of occurrence on future occasions.

Reinforcement   (Rotter) refers to anything that has an influence on the occurrence, direction, or kind of behavior.

Reinforcement value   is the degree of preference for any reinforcement to occur if the possibilities of many different reinforcements are all equal.

Relatedness   is "the necessity to unite with other living beings . . . [that constitutes] an imperative need on the fulfillment of which man's sanity depends."

Reliability   is the degree to which test results are repeatable.

Replicate   refers to repeating a test in the hope that the results will be the same as before.

Repression   refers to a selective type of memory mode in which threatening material is unavailable for recall, because it has been pressed down into the unconscious.

Resignation   is to free oneself from the risks involved in approaching or attacking others by being an onlooker, a noncompetitor, an avoider, and a reactive person who is hypersensitive to influence attempts.

Resilience   is the ability to absorb the slings and arrows of outrageous fortune and still believe that one can accomplish what one desires to do.

Response facilitation   is a process in which nothing new is learned, but some old responses may be disinhibited as a result of watching a model's performance.

Role Construct Repertory (REP) Test   is an assessment device designed to reveal an individual's construct system.

Roles   involve behaving in ways that meet the expectations of important other people in one's life.

Rootedness   is a deep craving to maintain one's natural ties and not be "separated."

Safety needs   include security, protection, stability, structure, law and order, and freedom from fear and chaos.

Schedules of reinforcement   determine whether reinforcement is to be delivered either every so often or after some number of responses has occurred.

Scientific   refers to unbiased observations that are quantified so that systematic analyses can be performed.

Scientific model for studying personality   involves two interlocking components: 1) description, which seeks to answer questions about "what" personality is—for example, "What are the identifiable individual differences in traits and types?" and 2) explanation, which seeks to answer questions about "why" personality is the way it is—"What are the causes of those individual differences?"

Secondary factors   encompass several primary factors and are called "superfactors" or "second-order" factors.

Secondary p.d.s are dispositions that are "less conspicuous, less generalized, less consistent, . . . less often called into play . . . [and] more peripheral."

Secondary process refers to the intellectual operations such as thinking, evaluating, planning, and decision-making that test reality to determine whether certain behaviors would be beneficial.

Secondary reinforcers are stimuli that come to have all the properties of primary reinforcers (such as food) through association with primary reinforcers.

Second-order traits are the "superfactors" that subsume the other traits ("secondary factors" define secondary traits).

Security operations involve skills that allow avoidance of forbidding gestures.

Seduction thesis refers to Freud's belief that his early female patients actually had been sexually molested by their fathers, as they allegedly claimed, and that these traumas were the source of their adult hysterical neuroses.

Self (Jung) is the "total personality," the unifying core of the psyche that ensures a balance of conscious and unconscious forces.

Self (Rogers) is the organized, consistent, conceptual whole composed of perceptions of the characteristics of the 'I' or 'me,' the values attached to these perceptions, and the relationships of the 'I' or 'me' to various aspects of life.

Self-actualization (Rogers) is a person's lifelong process of realizing his or her potentialities to become a fully functioning person.

Self-actualizers (Maslow) are people who fulfill themselves by making complete use of their potentialities, capacities, and talents, who do the best they are capable of doing, and who develop themselves to the most complete stature possible for them.

Self-analysis is a process whereby people come to understand themselves better through their own efforts, often outside the context of psychotherapy.

Self-effacing is a mode of responding to others in which the person will seek accommodation at any price including backing down whenever there is an interpersonal conflict in order to avoid loss of friendship, support, or love of others.

Self-efficacy is a belief concerning one's ability to perform behaviors yielding an expected outcome that is desirable.

Self-esteem is pride in one's pursuits and accomplishments.

Self-evaluation is a process that involves assessing one's performance at various points along the way to task completion and issuing a vocal or "under the breath" judgment of its value.

Self-exonerative processes is the general name given to cognitive activities that allow people to dissociate themselves from the consequences of their actions.

Self-identity is the continuity of self over past, present, and future that results from the operation of memory.

Self-image is composed of the hopes and aspirations that develop from the perceptions and expectations that others have of oneself.

Self-recognition is coming to know one's neuroses, idealized self-image, and real self, including positive and negative attributes.

Self-regulatory plans are rules, established in advance of opportunity for behavioral performance, that act as guides for determining what behavior would be appropriate under particular conditions.

Self-regulatory processes   are internal, cognitive/affective functions that guide and govern efforts toward goal attainment.

Self-system   is "that part of personality which is born entirely out of the influences of significant others upon one's feeling of well-being."

Sensation   determines that something is present; it is the same as the sensory perceptions of sight, sound, smell, taste, and touch.

Sentiment   is "A set of attitudes the strength of which has become correlated through their being all learnt by contact with a particular social institution [such as] sentiment to school, to home, to country."

Shadow   is the underside of the personality, the inferiorities of the person that are emotional in nature and too unpleasant to willingly reveal.

Shame and doubt   is the estrangement that results from the feeling of being controlled and of losing self-control.

Shaping   is a process by which natural variability in behavior is exploited so that a new behavior is acquired by reinforcing successive approximations to it.

Shock   may be experienced when a person's fiction runs head-on into reality.

Significant others   are those people who are most meaningful to us in our lives.

Simple stimuli   generate reflexes that call for reactions more than actions, particularly surface reactions that are immediate and passive in nature.

Sixteen or 16 PF   is a 16-scale test of adult personality in terms of 16 source traits.

Slips of the tongue   are verbal errors that seem to replace neutral words with ones that supposedly emanate from the unconscious.

Social character   represents "the core of a character structure common to most people of a given culture . . . [and] shows the degree to which character is formed by social and cultural patterns."

Social comparison   is determining how well one is doing in life by comparing oneself to those who share one's life situation.

Social desirability   refers to the need to please others by displaying the characteristics that are valued in our society (for example, goodness, honesty, sincerity, and so forth).

Social Distance (SD)   is a measure of discrimination that requires individuals to indicate how close to themselves they would allow members of some group to come.

Social feeling   is a concern for the community of other human beings and a need to associate and cooperate with them.

Social interest   is individuals' efforts to develop social feeling.

Socialization   is how people relate to others.

Social learning   entails acquiring useful information through interactions with people and other elements of the environment.

Sociopsychological orientation   is the sociological study of people that sheds light on their psychological nature.

Source trait   is "A [primary] factor-dimension, stressing the proposition that variations in value along it are determined by a single unitary influence or source."

Specific responses (SR)   are everyday behaviors or experiences that may or may not be characteristic of an individual, such as saying "Hi" to a neighbor.

Stagnation   is the arrest of the ripening process that comes with inability to funnel previous development into the formation of the next generation.

State   or mood is a psychological entity that fluctuates or varies over time and thus is "transitory," as distinguished from traits which are "permanent."

Statistically significant   is a condition that is reflected in a difference between conditions so large that it is very unlikely to occur solely by chance.

Stereotype   is an exaggerated belief that members of a group possess a certain trait; "Its function is to justify (rationalize) our conduct in relation to that [group]."

Stimulus   is a very definite, well-defined component or event associated with a situation and can be either physical or behavioral.

Strength   (Erikson) is a virtue arising from dominant movement toward the positive pole.

Strength   (Murray) of a need is measured in terms of its frequency, intensity, and duration.

Striving for superiority   is a universal psychological phenomenon that parallels physical growth and involves the goal of bringing about perfection, security, and strength.

Style of life   is the individual's unique but consistent movement toward self-created goals and ideals developed beginning in childhood.

Sublimation   is a process that reorients instinctual aims in new directions that are more personally and culturally acceptable.

Submerged pole   is an implicit pole that has either never been put into word form, perhaps because the construct is new, or is being suppressed.

Subordinate   refers to constructs that are at the bottom of the construction system.

Subsidiation of needs   occurs "When one or more needs are activated in the service of [one or more other needs]."

Success   may be defined as effectively performing the behaviors that yield the outcomes that are valued by the performer.

Superego   is the representation of society in personality that incorporates the norms and standards of the surrounding culture.

Superiority complex   is Adler's term for an exaggerated, abnormal form of striving for superiority that involves "overcompensation" for personal weakness.

Superordinate   refers to constructs that are at the top of the construction system.

Superstitious behavior   is a response that is accidentally reinforced, as there is no prearranged contingency between the response and reinforcement.

Surface traits   are "A set of personality characteristics which are correlated but do not form a factor, hence are believed to be determined by more than one influence or source."

Symbiotic union   is a coupling of beings in which each meets the needs of the other while they "live 'together'" as "two, and yet one."

Symbol   is one of the emergent elements to which a construct applies that is used as the name of the construct.

Symbolic modeling   involves verbal and pictorial means used to convey information necessary for adoption of behaviors associated with rewards.

Synchronicity   is the simultaneous occurrence of two happenings that are correlated but have no direct cause-and-effect connection.

Syntality   is national personality "equivalent to personality in an individual and capable of (a) predicting many behaviors and (b) by profile similarity measures permitting nations to be classified in a dozen types."

Syntaxic   mode becomes important when the meaning of words becomes shared with most other people so that experience, judgments, and observations can be shared (approximately the early elementary school years).

Systematic eclecticism   takes the best and most effective methods and orientations from each school of thought and binds them into a comprehensive approach to understanding the person.

T-data   involves an observer's recordings of a person's behavior in some standard, contrived, laboratory test situation.

Teaching machines   are devices that run a program that teaches a topic through a step by step process involving positive reinforcement.

Teleological   means to perform with a purpose.

Temperament trait   is "a general personality trait [that] is usually stylistic, in the sense that it deals with tempo, persistence, [and so forth] covering a large variety of specific responses."

Thanatos   is the class of instincts that is aimed at returning living things to their original, nonliving state.

Thema   is a combination of a particular need and a particular press or pressive object.

Thematic Apperception Test (TAT)   is an instrument for assessing a person's self-reflective perceptions (apperceptions) revealing thema that are evoked by some ambiguous pictures.

Thinking   determines what is present and interprets its meaning; it brings ideas into connection with one another to form concepts or reach solutions.

Threat   is realization of the possibility that a person's entire construction system will be overhauled.

Tight constructs   yield unvarying predictability.

Trait   (Cattell) is a permanent entity that does not fade in and out like a state; it is inborn or develops during the life course and regularly directs behavior.

Trait   (Allport) "is a neuropsychic structure having the capacity to render many stimuli functionally equivalent, and to initiate and guide equivalent . . . forms of adaptive and expressive behavior."

Traits   (Eysenck) are represented as statistical primary factors and defined as "theoretical constructs based on observed intercorrelations between a number of different habitual responses."

Transcendence   is the act of transforming one's accidental and passive role of "creature" into that of an active and purposeful "creator."

Transference   occurs when patients relate to the psychoanalyst as if he or she were some other person from their past with whom they were continuing to experience psychological conflict.

Type   (Jung) is a habitual attitude, or a person's characteristic way.

Types   (Eysenck) are second-order dimensions made up of statistically intercorrelated primary traits. They can be thought of as superfactors, but Eysenck prefers "second-order."

Tyranny of the shoulds   is the belief that one should do this and that, whatever a good person should do, whatever is expected by others, rather than whatever one feels it is his or her nature to do.

Unconditional positive regard   is provided when other people communicate, with no strings attached, that one is accepted, valued, worthwhile, and trusted, simply for being who one is.

Undoing   involves erasing "bad" behavior by displaying behavior designed to reverse the effects of the undesirable behavior ("Forgive me for hitting you! Let me grovel at your feet, and proclaim my undying love for you, and buy you flowers").

Unique trait   is "so specific to an individual that no one else could be scored on [its dimension]."

Unitary trend   is activity that is organized and directional in nature, not willy-nilly, trial and error.

Unity   is a sense of oneness within one's self and with the "natural and human world outside."

Validity   is the degree to which a test measures what it was designed to measure.

Values of outcomes   refers to how much one prizes results of behavioral or stimulus occurrences in the ongoing situation.

Variable   refers to variation in quantity specified by numbers.

Variable-interval (VI) schedule   requires that a given amount of time elapse between one reinforced response and the next, on the average.

Variable-ratio (VR) schedules   require that, on the average, a given number of responses be performed before a response is reinforced.

Variable schedules   are procedures for which reinforcement is delivered after some X amount of time has elapsed, on the average, or after some Y number of responses have been performed, on the average.

Vector   is a force with directional properties.

Vicarious expectancy learning   involves people adopting other people's expectancies concerning future events, especially expectancies of those with whom they share relevant experiences.

Vicarious reinforcement   occurs when one observes another person being rewarded for performing a behavior.

Viscerogenic needs   involve basic physiological drives, and, as such, are relatively straightforward and self-explanatory.

Will power   is "the unbroken determination to exercise free choice as well as self-restraint in spite of the unavoidable experience of shame, doubt, and a certain rage over being controlled by others."

Wisdom   is a "detached and yet active concern with life in the face of death," not magical access to "higher knowledge."

Word Association Test   (WAT) is a Jungian method in which people are instructed to say the first word that cames to mind after hearing each of 100 words from a standardized list.

Youth   (adolescence through young adulthood) begins at puberty, at which time physiological changes are accompanied by "psychic revolution."

REFERENCES

Abramson, L., Seligman, M., & Teasdale, J. Learned helplessness in humans: Critique and reformulation. JOURNAL OF ABNORMAL PSYCHOLOGY, 1978, 87, 49–74.

Abt, L. E., & Bellak, L. (Eds.) PROJECTIVE PSYCHOLOGY, CLINICAL APPROACHES TO THE TOTAL PERSONALITY. New York: Grove Press, 1950.

Achterberg, J., and Lawlis, G. F. IMAGERY OF CANCER. Champaign, IL: Institute for Personality and Ability Testing, 1978.

Adams, P. Changing their minds. PEORIA JOURNAL STAR, 1994 (Sept. 29), p. A5.

Adler, A. STUDY OF ORGAN INFERIORITY AND ITS PSYCHICAL COMPENSATION: A CONTRIBUTION TO CLINICAL MEDICINE. New York: Nervous and Mental Diseases Publishing Company, 1907/1917.

Adler, A. Individual psychology. In C. Murchison (Ed.). PSYCHOLOGIES OF 1930. Worcester, MA: Clark University Press, 1930.

Adler, A. The structure of neurosis. In Ansbacher, H. L. and Ansbacher, R. R. (Eds.), ALFRED ADLER: SUPERIORITY AND SOCIAL INTEREST. Evanston, IL: Northwestern University Press (1964), 1932.

Adler, A. Advantages and disadvantages of the inferiority feeling. In Ansbacher, H. L. and Ansbacher, R. R. (Eds.), ALFRED ADLER: SUPERIORITY AND SOCIAL INTEREST. Evanston, IL: Northwestern University Press (1964), 1933a.

Adler, A. Religion and individual psychology. In Ansbacher, H. L. and Ansbacher, R. R. (Eds.), ALFRED ADLER: SUPERIORITY AND SOCIAL INTEREST. Evanston, IL: Northwestern University Press (1964), 1933b.

Adler, A. In H. L. Ansbacher & R. R. Ansbacher (Eds.), THE INDIVIDUAL PSYCHOLOGY OF ALFRED ADLER. New York: Basic Books, 1956.

Adler, A. SOCIAL INTEREST: A CHALLENGE TO MANKIND. New York: Capricorn Books, 1964.

Adler, A. THE PRACTICE AND THEORY OF INDIVIDUAL PSYCHOLOGY (Trans. by P. Radin). London: Routledcge & Kagan Paul, 1971/1929.

Adler, A. In H. L. Ansbacher & R. R. Ansbacher (Eds.), CO-OPERATION BETWEEN THE SEXES. New York: Norton, 1982.

Adler, K. Socialist influences on Adlerian psychology. INDIVIDUAL PSYCHOLOGY JOURNAL OF ADLERIAN THEORY, RESEARCH AND PRACTICE, 1994, 50, 131–141.

Ainsworth, M. D. S. Infant-mother attachment. AMERICAN PSYCHOLOGIST, 1979, 34, 932–937.

Alderfer, C. P. Theories reflecting my personal experience and life development. THE JOURNAL OF APPLIED BEHAVIORAL SCIENCE, 1989, 25, 351–365.

Alexander, F. G. PSYCHOSOMATIC MEDICINE,

ITS PRINCIPLES AND APPLICATIONS. New York: Norton, 1950.

Alexander, F. G., and Selesnick, S. T. THE HISTORY OF PSYCHIATRY. New York: Harper & Row, 1966.

Alicke, M. D. & Klotz, M. L. Social roles and social judgment: How an impression conveyed influences an impression formed. PERSONALITY AND SOCIAL PSYCHOLOGY BULLETIN, 1993, 19, 185–194.

Allen, B. P. Perceived trustworthiness of attitudinal and behavioral expressions. JOURNAL OF SOCIAL PSYCHOLOGY, 1973, 89, 211–218.

Allen, B. P. Social distance and admiration reactions of "unprejudiced" whites. JOURNAL OF PERSONALITY, 1975, 43, 709–726.

Allen, B. P. Race and physical attractiveness as criteria for white subjects' dating choices. SOCIAL BEHAVIOR AND PERSONALITY, 1976, 4, 289–296.

Allen, B. P. SOCIAL BEHAVIOR: FACT AND FALSEHOOD. Chicago: Nelson-Hall, 1978.

Allen, B. P. Harrower's and Miale-Selzer's use of Hjalmar Schacht in their characterizations of the Nazi leaders. JOURNAL OF PERSONALITY ASSESSMENT, 1984, 48, 257–258.

Allen, B. P. After the missiles: Sociopsychological effects of nuclear war. AMERICAN PSYCHOLOGIST, 1985, 40, 927–937.

Allen, B. P. Dramaturgical quality. JOURNAL OF SOCIAL PSYCHOLOGY, 1988a, 128, 181–190.

Allen, B. P. Beyond consistency in the definition of personality: Dramaturgical quality and value. IMAGINATION, COGNITION AND PERSONALITY, 1988b, 7, 201–213.

Allen, B. P. PERSONAL ADJUSTMENT. Pacific Grove, CA: Brooks/Cole, 1990.

Allen, B. P. Gender stereotypes are not accurate: A replication of Martin (1987) using diagnostic, self-report, and behavioral criteria. SEX ROLES, 1995, 32, 583–600.

Allen, B. P. African-Americans' and European-Americans' mutual attributions: Adjective Generation Technique (AGT) Stereotyping. JOURNAL OF APPLIED SOCIAL PSYCHOLOGY, 1996, 26, 884–912.

Allen, B. P. & Adams, J. Q. The concept "race": Let's go back to the beginning. JOURNAL OF SOCIAL BEHAVIOR AND PERSONALITY, 1992, 7, 163–168.

Allen, B. P. & Potkay, C. R. Variability of self-description on a day-to-day basis: Longitudinal use of the adjective generation technique. JOURNAL OF PERSONALITY, 1973, 41, 638–652.

Allen, B. P. & Potkay, C. R. The relationship between AGT self-description and significant life events: A longitudinal study. JOURNAL OF PERSONALITY, 1977a, 45, 207–219.

Allen, B. P. & Potkay, C. R. Misunderstanding the Adjective Generation Technique (AGT): Comments on Bem's rejoinder. JOURNAL OF PERSONALITY, 1977b, 45, 207–219.

Allen, B. P. & Potkay, C. R. On the arbitrary distinction between states and traits. JOURNAL OF PERSONALITY AND SOCIAL PSYCHOLOGY, 1981, 41, 916–928.

Allen, B. P. & Potkay, C. R. ADJECTIVE GENERATION TECHNIQUE (AGT). New York: Irvington, 1983a.

Allen, B. P. & Potkay, C. R. Just as arbitrary as ever: Comments on Zuckerman's rejoinder. JOURNAL OF PERSONALITY AND SOCIAL PSYCHOLOGY, 1983b, 44, 1046–1087.

Allen, B. P. & Smith, G. Traits, situations and their interaction as alternative "causes" of behavior. JOURNAL OF SOCIAL PSYCHOLOGY, 1980, 111, 99–104.

Allport, G. W. THE USE OF PERSONAL DOCUMENTS IN PSYCHOLOGICAL SCIENCE. New York: Social Science Research Council, 1942.

Allport, G. W. THE NATURE OF PREJUDICE. Reading, MA.: Addison-Wesley, 1954.

Allport, G. W. PERSONALITY, A PSYCHOLOGICAL INTERPRETATION. New York: Henry Holt, 1937.

Allport, G. W. BECOMING, BASIC CONSIDERATIONS FOR A PSYCHOLOGY OF PERSONALITY. New Haven: Yale University Press, 1955.

Allport, G. W. PATTERN AND GROWTH IN PERSONALITY. New York: Holt, Rinehart and Winston, 1961.

Allport, G. W. Traits revisited. AMERICAN PSYCHOLOGIST, 1966, 21, 1–10.

Allport, G. W. In E. G. Boring & G. Lindzey (Eds.). A HISTORY OF PSYCHOLOGY IN AUTO-

BIOGRAPHY (Vol. 5). New York: Appleton-Century Crofts, 1967.

Allport, G. W. THE PERSON IN PSYCHOLOGY, SELECTED ESSAYS. Boston: Beacon Press, 1968.

Allport, G. W. & Odbert, H. Trait-names: A psycholexical study. PSYCHOLOGICAL MONOGRAPHS, 1936, 47, Whole No. 211, 1–171.

Allport, G. W. & Ross, J. M. Personal religious orientation and prejudice. JOURNAL OF PERSONALITY AND SOCIAL PSYCHOLOGY, 1967, 5, 432–443.

Alpher, V. S. Comment on Skinner. AMERICAN PSYCHOLOGIST, 1988, 43, 824–825.

Alvardo, N. Empirical validity of the Thematic Apperception Test. JOURNAL OF PERSONALITY ASSESSMENT, 1994, 63, 59–79.

AMERICAN PSYCHOLOGIST. 1958 award for distinguished scientific contributions to B. F. Skinner, 1958, 13, 735–738.

AMERICAN PSYCHOLOGIST. 1980 award for distinguished scientific contributions to Albert Bandura, 1981, 36, 27–42.

AMERICAN PSYCHOLOGIST. 1982 award for distinguished scientific contributions to Walter Mischel, 1983, 38, 9–14.

American Psychological Association. A CAREER IN PSYCHOLOGY. Washington, DC: American Psychological Association, 1980.

American Psychological Association. STANDARDS FOR EDUCATIONAL AND PSYCHOLOGICAL TESTS. Washington, DC: American Psychological Association, 1974.

American Psychiatric Association. DIAGNOSTIC AND STATISTICAL MANUAL OF MENTAL DISORDERS, 3rd ed. Washington, DC: 1980.

Ames, L. B., Learned, J., Metraux, R. W., & Walker, R. N. CHILD RORSCHACH RESPONSES, DEVELOPMENTAL TRENDS FROM TWO TO TEN YEARS. New York: Harper & Row, 1952.

Amirkhan, J. H., Risinger, R. T., & Swickert, R. J. Extraversion: A "hidden" personality factor in coping? JOURNAL OF PERSONALITY, 1995, 63, 189–212.

Anastasi, A. PSYCHOLOGICAL TESTING, 5th ed. New York: Macmillan, 1982.

Anch, A. M., Browman, Carl P., Mitler, M. M., &

Walsh, J. K. SLEEP: A SCIENTIFIC PERSPECTIVE. Englewood Cliffs, NJ: Prentice-Hall, 1988.

Anderson, J. W. Henry A. Murray's early career: A psychobiographical exploration. JOURNAL OF PERSONALITY, 1988, 56, 137–171.

Angyal, A. FOUNDATIONS FOR A SCIENCE OF PERSONALITY. Cambridge: Harvard University Press, 1941.

Angyal, A. NEUROSIS AND TREATMENT, A HOLISTIC THEORY. New York: Wiley, 1965.

Ansbacher, H. L. In A. Adler, PROBLEMS OF NEUROSIS, A BOOK OF CASE HISTORIES. P. Mairet (Ed.) New York: Harper & Row Torchbooks, 1964.

Ansbacher, H. L. & Ansbacher, R. R. THE INDIVIDUAL PSYCHOLOGY OF ALFRED ADLER. New York: Basic Books, 1956.

Ansbacher, H. L. & Ansbacher, R. R. (Eds.) ALFRED ADLER: SUPERIORITY AND SOCIAL INTEREST. Evanston, IL: Northwestern University Press, 1964.

Ansbacher, H. L. Alfred Adler's influence on the three leading cofounders of humanistic psychology. JOURNAL OF HUMANISTIC PSYCHOLOGY, 1990, 30, 45–53.

APA MONITOR, Bandura's childhood shaped life interests, 1992, Aug., p. 13.

Asch, S. E. SOCIAL PSYCHOLOGY. New York: Prentice-Hall, 1952.

Associated Press. NCAA committee accused of racism. PEORIA JOURNAL STAR, 1993 (Dec., 15), p. D5.

Astin, A. W. Productivity of undergraduate institutions. SCIENCE, 1962, 136, 129–135.

Astrachan, B. M. The "Seasons of a Man's Life" by Daniel J. Levinson (1920–1994), APS OBSERVER (American Psychological Society), 1994 (July/August), p. 36.

Backteman, G., & Magnusson, D. Longitudinal stability of personality characteristics. JOURNAL OF PERSONALITY, 1981, 49, 148–160.

Bacciagaluppi, M. Eric Fromm's views on psychoanalytic "technique." CONTEMPORARY PSYCHOANALYSIS, 1989, 25, 226–243.

Bailey, M. B. & Bailey, R. E. "Misbehavior": A case history. AMERICAN PSYCHOLOGIST, 1993, 48, 1157–1158.

Bailey, M. J., Gaulin, S., Agyei, Y., & Gladue, B. A. Effects of gender and sexual orientation on evolutionarily relevant aspects of human mating psychology, JOURNAL OF PERSONALITY AND SOCIAL PSYCHOLOGY, 1994, 66, 1081–1093.

Baillargeon, J. & Danis, C. Barnum meets the computer: A critical test. JOURNAL OF PERSONALITY ASSESSMENT, 1984, 48, 415–419.

Bales, J. Skinner gets award, ovations at APA talk. MONITOR OF THE AMERICAN PSYCHOLOGICAL ASSOCIATION, 1990, 21(10), 1 & 6.

Bandura, A. AGGRESSION: A SOCIAL LEARNING ANALYSIS. Englewood Cliffs, NJ: Prentice-Hall, 1973.

Bandura, A. SOCIAL LEARNING THEORY. Englewood Cliffs, NJ: Prentice-Hall, 1977.

Bandura, A. The psychology of chance encounters and life paths. AMERICAN PSYCHOLOGIST, 1982, 37, 747–755.

Bandura, A. Social cognitive theory. ANNALS OF CHILD DEVELOPMENT, New York: Jai Press, Inc., 1989a, Vol. 6, 1–60.

Bandura, A. Human agency in social cognitive theory. AMERICAN PSYCHOLOGIST, 1989b, 44, 1175–1184.

Bandura, A. Effect of perceived controllability and performance standards of self-regulation of complex decision making. JOURNAL OF PERSONALITY AND SOCIAL PSYCHOLOGY, 1989c, 56, 805–814.

Bandura, A. Perceived self-efficacy in the exercise of personal agency. APPLIED SPORT PSYCHOLOGY, 1990a, 2, 128–163.

Bandura, A. Mechanisms of moral disengagement. In W. Reich (Ed.), ORIGINS OF TERRORISM: PSYCHOLOGIES, IDEOLOGIES, STATES OF MIND (pp. 161–191). Cambridge, England: Cambridge University Press, 1990b.

Bandura, A. Social cognitive theory of self-regulation. ORGANIZATIONAL BEHAVIOR AND HUMAN DECISION MAKING PROCESSES, 1991a, 50, 248–287.

Bandura, A. Social cognitive theory of moral thought and action. In W. M. Kurtines and Jacob L. Gerwirtz (Eds.), HANDBOOK OF MORAL BEHAVIOR AND DEVELOPMENT, vol. 1: THEORY. Hillsdale, NJ: Lawrence Erlbaum Assoc., 1991b.

Bandura, A. Perceived self-efficacy in cognitive development and functioning. EDUCATIONAL PSYCHOLOGIST, 1993, 28, 117–148.

Bandura, A. Reflections on human agency. Keynote address presented at the IV European Congress of Psychology, 1995, July 2–7, Athens, Greece.

Bandura, A. Social cognitive theory of mass communication. In J. Bryant and Dolf Zillmann (Eds.), MEDIA EFFECTS: ADVANCES IN THEORY AND RESEARCH, pp. 61–90. Hillsdale, NJ: Lawrence Erlbaum Assoc. 1994a.

Bandura, A. Self-efficacy. In V. S. Ramachaudran (Ed.), ENCYCLOPEDIA OF HUMAN BEHAVIOR, vol. 4, pp. 71–81. New York: Academic Press, 1994b.

Bandura, A. & McDonald, F. The influence of social reinforcement and the behavior of models in shaping children's moral judgments. JOURNAL OF ABNORMAL AND SOCIAL PSYCHOLOGY, 1963, 67, 274–281.

Bandura, A., Reese, L., & Adams, N. Microanalysis of action and fear arousal as a function of differential levels of perceived self-efficacy. JOURNAL OF PERSONALITY AND SOCIAL PSYCHOLOGY, 1982, 43, 5–21.

Bandura, A., Ross, D., & Ross, S. Imitation of film-mediated aggressive models. JOURNAL OF ABNORMAL AND SOCIAL PSYCHOLOGY, 1963, 66, 3–11.

Bandura, A. & Wood, R. Effect of perceived controllability and performance standards on self-regulation of complex decision making. JOURNAL OF PERSONALITY AND SOCIAL PSYCHOLOGY, 1989, 56, 805–814.

Barber, T. X. "Hypnosis," suggestions, and psychosomatic phenomena: New look from the standpoint of recent experimental studies. In J. Fosshage and P. Olsen (Eds.), HEALING: IMPLICATIONS FOR PSYCHOTHERAPY (pp. 269–297). New York: Human Sciences Press, 1978.

Barnes, H. E. Translator's introduction. In J-P. Sartre, BEING AND NOTHINGNESS. New York: Philosophical Library, 1953, viii–xliii.

Barnet, H. S. Divorce stress and adjustment model: Locus of control and demographic predictors. JOURNAL OF DIVORCE, 1990, 13, 93–109.

Barry, H., Child, I., & Bacon, M. Relation of child rearing to subsistence economy. AMERICAN ANTHROPOLOGIST, 1959, 61, 51–64.

Baum, W. M. & Heath, J. L. Behavioral explanations and intentional explanations in psychology. AMERICAN PSYCHOLOGIST, 1992, 47, 1312–1317.

Beck, J. E. Testing a personal construct theory model of the experiential learning process—A. The impact of invalidation on the construing processes of participants in sensitivity training groups. SMALL GROUP BEHAVIOR, 1988, 19, 79–102.

Bell, P. A., and Byrne, D. Repression-Sensitization. In H. London and J.E. Exner, Jr. (Eds.), DIMENSIONS OF PERSONALITY. New York: Wiley, 1978, 449–485.

Bem, D. J. Predicting more of the people more of the time: Some thoughts on the Allen-Potkay studies of intraindividual variability. JOURNAL OF PERSONALITY, 1977, 45, 327–332.

Bem D. J. & Allen, A. On predicting some of the people some of the time: The search for cross-situational consistencies in behavior, PSYCHOLOGICAL REVIEW, 1974, 81, 506–520.

Bem, D. J. & Funder, D. C. Predicting more of the people more of the time: Assessing the personality of situations. PSYCHOLOGICAL REVIEW, 1978, 85, 485–501.

Bem, S. L. The measurment of psychological androgeny. JOURNAL OF CONSULTING AND CLINICAL PSYCHOLOGY, 1974, 42, 155–162.

Bender, L. A VISUAL MOTOR GESTALT TEST AND ITS CLINICAL USE. New York: American Orthopsychiatric Association, 1938.

Benesch, K. F. & Page, M. M. Self-construct systems and interpersonal congruence. JOURNAL OF PERSONALITY, 1989, 57, 137–173.

Benjamin, L. T. A history of teaching machines. AMERICAN PSYCHOLOGIST, 1988, 43, 703–712.

Bennett, C. M. A Skinnerian view of human freedom. THE HUMANIST, 1990 (July/August), 18–20, 30.

Bentler, P. M., Jackson, D. N., and Messick, S. Identification of content and style: A two-dimensional interpretation of acquiescence. PSYCHOLOGICAL BULLETIN, 1971, 76, 186–204.

Bexton, W., Heron, W., & Scott, T. The effects of decreased variation in the sensory environment. CANADIAN JOURNAL OF PSYCHOLOGY, 1954, 8, 70–76.

Biancoli, R. Radical humanism in psychoanalysis or psychoanalysis as art, COMTEMPORARY PSYCHOANALYSIS, 1992, 28, 695–731.

Bieri, J. Cognitive complexity—simplicity and predictive behavior. JOURNAL OF ABNORMAL AND SOCIAL PSYCHOLOGY, 1955, 51, 61–66.

Binswanger, L. BEING-IN-THE-WORLD, SELECTED PAPERS OF LUDWIG BINSWANGER (J. Needleman, Trans.). New York: Harper and Row, 1963.

Binswanger, L. The case of Ellen West: An anthropological-clinical study. In R. May, E. Angel, and H. F. Ellenberger (Eds.). EXISTENCE, A NEW DIMENSION IN PSYCHIATRY AND PSYCHOLOGY. New York: Basic Books, 1958, 237–364.

Bixler, R. H. Carl Rogers, "counseling," and the Minnesota point of view. AMERICAN PSYCHOLOGIST, 1990, 45, 675.

Blake, M. J. F. Relationship between circadian rhythm of body temperature and introversion-extraversion. NATURE, 1967, 215, 896–897.

Blake, M. J. F. Temperament and time of day. In W. P. Colquhoun (Ed.), BIOLOGICAL RHYTHMS AND HUMAN PERFORMANCE. New York: Academic Press, 1971.

Blau, G. Testing the relationship of locus of control to different performance dimensions. JOURNAL OF OCCUPATIONAL AND ORGANIZATIONAL PSYCHOLOGY, 1993, 66, 125–138.

Blauner, R. The ambiguities of racial change. In M. L. Andersen and P.H. Collins (Eds.), RACE, CLASS, AND GENDER. Belmont, CA: Wadsworth Publishing Company, 1992.

Blechner, M. J. Projective indentification, countertransference, and the "maybe-me." CONTEMPORARY PSYCHOANALYSIS, 1994, 30, 619–631.

Block, J. THE Q-SORT METHOD IN PERSONALITY ASSESSMENT AND PSYCHIATRIC RESEARCH. Springfield, IL: Charles C. Thomas, 1961.

Block, J. & Ozer, D. Two types of psychologists: Remarks on the Mendelshon, Weiss, and Feimer Contribution. JOURNAL OF PERSONALITY AND SOCIAL PSYCHOLOGY, 1982, 42, 1171–1181.

Blum, G. The Blacky Test. GENETIC PSYCHOLOGY MONOGRAPHS, 1949, 39, 13–22.

Blum, G. THE BLACKY PICTURES: A TECH-NIQUE FOR THE EXPLORATION OF PER-SONALITY DYNAMICS. New York: Psychological Corporation, 1950.

Blum, G. The Blacky Test-Sections II, IV, and VII. In R. Birney & R. Teevan (Eds.), MEASURING HUMAN MOTIVATON. New York: Van Nostrand, 1962, 119–144.

Blum, G. PSYCHOANALYTIC THEORIES OF PERSONALITY. New York: McGraw-Hill, 1964.

Boring, E. A HISTORY OF EXPERIMENTAL PSYCHOLOGY, 2nd ed. New York: Appleton-Century-Crofts, 1957.

Bornstein, R. F. Radical behaviorism, internal states, and the science of psychology: A reply to Skinner. AMERICAN PSYCHOLOGIST, 1988, 43, 819–821.

Boss, M. PSYCHOANALYSIS AND DASEINS-ANALYSIS, L. B. LeFebre, Trans. New York: Basic Books, 1963.

Bosselman, B. C. SELF-DESTRUCTION: A STUDY OF THE SUICIDAL IMPULSE. Springfield, IL: Charles C. Thomas 1958.

Bottome, P. ALFRED ADLER: APOSTLE OF FREEDOM. London: Faber & Faber, 1939.

Bowers, K. Situationism in psychology: An analysis and a critique, PSYCHOLOGICAL REVIEW, 1973, 80, 307–336.

Bowlby, J. MATERNAL CARE AND MENTAL HEALTH. New York: Schocken Books, 1969.

Bozarth, J. D. The evolution of Carl Rogers as a therapist. Special issue: Fiftieth anniversary of the person-centered approach. PERSON CENTERED REVIEW, 1990, 387–393.

Bozarth, J. D. & Brodley, B. T. Actualization: A functional concept in client-centered therapy. Special issue: Handbook of self-actualization. JOURNAL OF SOCIAL BEHAVIOR AND PERSONALITY, 1991, 6, 45–59.

Breuer, J. & Freud, S. STUDIES IN HYSTERIA. Boston: Beacon Press, 1985/1950.

Brigham, J. SOCIAL PSYCHOLOGY. Boston: Little, Brown, 1986.

Brody, B. Freud's case-load. PSYCHOTHERAPY: THEORY, RESEARCH AND PRACTICE, 1970, 7, 8–12.

Bromberg, P. M. "Obsessions and/or obsessionality: Perspectives on a psychoanalytic treatment": Comment and Erratum. CONTEMPORARY PSYCHOANALYSIS, 1993, 29, 372.

Bronfen, E. The lady vanishes: Sophie Freud and beyond the Pleasure Principle. THE SOUTH ATLANTIC QUARTERLY, 1989, 88 (Fall), 961–991.

Brunner, H. G., Nelen, M., Breakefield, X. O., Ropers, B. A., & van Oost, B. A. Abnormal behavior associated with a point mutation in the structural gene for monoamine oxidase A. SCIENCE, 1993 (Oct., 22), 262, 570–578.

Brunswick, E. Representative design and probabilistic theory in a functional psychology. PSYCHOLOGICAL REVIEW, 1955, 62, 193–217.

Buber, M. I AND THOU, 2nd ed. New York: Scribner's, 1958.

Bugental, J. F. T. The third force in psychology. JOURNAL OF HUMANISTIC PSYCHOLOGY, 1964, 4, 19–25.

Buhler, C. VALUES IN PSYCHOTHERAPY. New York: Free Press of Glencoe, 1962.

Buhler, C. Some observations on the psychology of the third force, JOURNAL OF HUMANISTIC PSYCHOLOGY, 1965, 5, 54–55.

Bullock, W. A. & Gilliland, K. Eysenck's arousal theory of introversion–extraversion: A converging measures investigation, JOURNAL OF PERSONALITY AND SOCIAL PSYCHOLOGY, 1993, 64, 113–123.

Burks, H. F. MANUAL FOR BURKS' BEHAVIOR RATING SCALES. Huntington Beach, CA: Arden Press, 1971.

Burnell, G. M., & Solomon, G. F. Early memories and ego function. ARCHIVES OF GENERAL PSYCHIATRY, 1964, 11, 556–567.

Burris, C. T. Curvilinearity and religious types: A second look at intrinsic, extrinsic, and quest relations. THE INTERNATIONAL JOURNAL FOR THE PSYCHOLOGY OF RELIGION, 1994, 4, 245–260.

Bussey, K. & Bandura, A. Self-regulatory mechanisms governing gender development. CHILD DEVELOPMENT, 1992, 63, 1236–1250.

Butcher, J. N. (Ed.) OBJECTIVE PERSONALITY ASSESSMENT. New York: Academic Press, 1972.

Butler, J. M., and Haigh, G. V. Changes in the relation between self-concepts and ideal concepts consequent upon client-centered counseling. In C. R.

Rogers and R. F. Dymond (Eds.). PSY-CHOTHERAPY AND PERSONALITY CHANGE. Chicago: University of Chicago Press, 1954, 55–75.

Buttle, F. The social construction of needs, PSYCHOLOGY AND MARKETING, 1989, 6, 199–207.

Byrne, D. The Repression-Sensitization Scale: Rationale, reliability, and validity. JOURNAL OF PERSONALITY, 1961, 29, 334–349.

Cameron, N. THE PSYCHOLOGY OF THE BEHAVIOR DISORDERS. Boston: Houghton Mifflin, 1947.

Campbell, D. P. MANUAL FOR THE STRONG-CAMPBELL INTEREST INVENTORY, revised ed. Stanford, CA: Stanford University Press, 1977.

Campbell, D. T. On the conflicts between biological and social evolution and between psychology and moral tradition. AMERICAN PSYCHOLOGIST, 1975, 30, 1103–1126.

Campbell, D. T., & Fiske, D. W. Convergent and discriminant validation by the multitrait-multimethod matrix. PSYCHOLOGICAL BULLETIN, 1959, 56, 81–105.

Campbell, F. A. & Ramey, C. T. Effects of early intervention on intellectual and academic achievement: A follow-up study of children from low-income families. CHILD DEVELOPMENT, 1994, 65, 684–698.

Cannon, W. G. WISDOM OF THE BODY. New York: Norton, 1932.

Cantor, N. & Mischel, W. Traits as prototypes: Effects on recognition memory. JOURNAL OF PERSONALITY AND SOCIAL PSYCHOLOGY, 1977, 35, 38–48.

Cantor, N., Mischel, W., & Schwartz, J. C. A prototype analysis of psychological situations. COGNITIVE PSYCHOLOGY, 1982, 14, 45–77.

Carkhuff, R. R. HELPING AND HUMAN RELATIONS: A PRIMER FOR LAY AND PROFESSIONAL HELPERS, vols. I and II. New York: Holt, Rinehart and Winston, 1969.

Carlson, R. Personality. In M. R. Rosensweig and L. W. Porter (Eds.). ANNUAL REVIEW OF PSYCHOLOGY. Palo Alto, CA: Annual Reviews, 1975, 26, 393–414.

Carlson, J. Brief therapy for health promotion. INDIVIDUAL PSYCHOLOGY, 1989, 45, 220–229.

Carlyn, M. An assessment of the Myers-Briggs Type Indicator. JOURNAL OF PERSONALITY ASSESSMENT, 1977, 41, 461–473.

Carnes, J. Judy Carnes on "Culture and intelligence." A segment of THE BRAIN: THE UNIVERSE WITHIN. Discovery Communications, Discovery Enterprises Group, Bethesda, Maryland 20814, 1994.

Carskadon, T. G. Use of the Myers-Briggs Type Indicator in psychology courses and discussion groups. TEACHING OF PSYCHOLOGY, 1978, 5, 140–142.

Carson, R. C. INTERACTION CONCEPTS OF PERSONALITY. Chicago: Aldine, 1969.

Carson, R. C. & Butcher, J. N. ABNORMAL PSYCHOLOGY AND MODERN LIFE. New York: Harper Collins, 1992.

Catina, A. & Tschuschke, V. A summary of empirical data from the investigation of two psychoanalytic groups by means of repertory grid technique. GROUP ANALYSIS, 1993, 26, 443–447.

Cartwright, D., DeBruin, J., & Berg, S. Some scales for assessing personality based on Carl Rogers' theory: Further evidence of validity. PERSONALITY AND INDIVIDUAL DIFFERENCES, 1991, 12, 151–156.

Catanzaro, S. J. & Mearns, J. Measuring generalized expectancies for negative mood regulation: Initial scale development and implications, JOURNAL OF PERSONALITY ASSESSMENT, 1990, 54, 546–563.

Cattell, H. E. P. Comment on Goldberg. AMERICAN PSYCHOLOGIST, 1993, 48, 1302–1303.

Cattell, R. B. "Is national intelligence declining?" EUGENICS REVIEW. 1936–1937, 28, 181–203.

Cattell, R. B. THE DESCRIPTION AND MEASUREMENT OF PERSONALITY. New York: World Book, 1946.

Cattell, R. B. THE SIXTEEN PERSONALITY FACTOR QUESTIONNAIRE 1st ed. Champaign, IL: Institute for Personality and Ability Testing, 1949.

Cattell, R. B. The nature and measurement of anxiety. SCIENTIFIC AMERICAN, 1963, 208, 96–104.

Cattell, R. B. PERSONALITY: A SYSTEMATIC, THEORETICAL AND FACTUAL STUDY. New York: McGraw-Hill, 1950.

Cattell, R. B. THE SCIENTIFIC ANALYSIS OF

PERSONALITY. Baltimore, MD: Penguin Books, 1966 (1965).

Cattell, R. B. PERSONALITY AND MOOD BY QUESTIONNAIRE. San Francisco: Jossey-Bass, 1973.

Cattell, R. B. Raymond B. Cattell. In G. Lindzey (Ed.), A HISTORY OF PSYCHOLOGY IN AUTOBIOGRAPHY. Engelwood Cliffs, NJ: Prentice-Hall, 1974a.

Cattell, R. B. Travels in psychological hyperspace. In T. S. Krawiec (Ed.), vol. 2, THE PSYCHOLO-GISTS. New York: Oxford University Press, 1974b.

Cattell, R. B. STRUCTURED PERSONALITY-LEARNING THEORY: A HOLISTIC MUL-TIVARIATE RESEARCH APPROACH. New York: Praeger, 1983.

Cattell, R. B. HUMAN MOTIVATION AND THE DYNAMIC CALCULUS. New York: Praeger, 1984a (1985).

Cattell, R. B. PERSONALITY AND LEARNING THEORY, vols. 1 & 2. New York: Springer Publishing, 1979.

Cattell, R. B. The voyage of a laboratory, 1928–1984. MULTIVARIATE BEHAVIORAL RE-SEARCH, 1984b, 19, 121–174.

Cattell, R. B. & Brennan, J. The cultural types of modern nations, by two quantitative classification methods. SOCIOLOGY AND SOCIAL RE-SEARCH, 1984, 68, 208–235.

Cattell, R. B. The 16 PF personality structure and Dr. Eysenck. JOURNAL OF SOCIAL BEHAVIOR AND PERSONALITY, 1986, 1, 153–160.

Cattell, R. B. Constancy of global, second-order personality factors over a twenty-year-plus period. PSYCHOLOGICAL REPORTS, 1994, 75, 3–9.

Cattell, R. B., Eber, H. W., & Tatsuoka, M. M. HANDBOOK FOR THE SIXTEEN PER-SONALITY FACTOR QUESTIONNAIRE. Champaign, IL: Institute for Personality and Ability Testing, 1970.

Cattell, R. B. & Kline, P. THE SCIENTIFIC ANALYSIS OF PERSONALITY AND MO-TIVATION. New York: Academic Press, 1977.

Cattell, R. B., Rao, D. C., Schuerger, J. M. Heritability in the personality control system: Ego strength (C), super ego strength (G) and the self-sentiment (Q3); by the MAVA mode, Q-data, and Maximun likelihood analyses. SOCIAL BEHAVIOR AND PERSONALITY, 1985, 13, 33–41.

Cattell, R. B. & Scheier, I. H. THE MEANING AND MEASUREMENT OF NEUROTICISM AND ANXIETY. New York: Ronald Press, 1961.

Cattell, R. B., Schuerger, J. M., & Klein, T. W. Heritabilities of ego strength (factor C), super ego strength (factor G), and self-sentiment (factor Q3) by multiple abstract variance analysis. JOURNAL OF CLINICAL PSYCHOLOGY, 1982, 38, 769–779.

Cattell, R. B. & Warburton, F. W. OBJECTIVE PERSONALITY & MOTIVATION TESTS, A THEORETICAL INTRODUCTION AND PRACTICAL COMPENDIUM. Urbana: University of Illinois Press, 1967.

Cautela, J. R., & Upper, D. THE BEHAVIORAL IN-VENTORY BATTERY: THE USE OF SELF-REPORT MEASURES IN BEHAVIORAL ANALYSIS AND THERAPY. In M. Hersen & A. S. Bellack (Eds.), BEHAVIORAL ASSESS-MENT: A PRACTICAL HANDBOOK. New York: Pergamon Press, 1976.

Cetola, H. & Prinkey, K. Introversion-extraversion and loud commercials. PSYCHOLOGY AND MARKETING, 1986, 3, 123–132.

Chapman, A. H. HARRY STACK SULLIVAN: HIS LIFE AND HIS WORK. New York: Putnam, 1976.

Cherian, V. I. Birth order and academic achievement of children in Transkei. PSYCHOLOGICAL RE-PORTS, 1990, 66, 19–24.

Chiesa, M. Radical behaviorism and scientific frameworks: From mechanistic to relational accounts. AMERICAN PSYCHOLOGIST, 1992, 47, 1287–1299.

Chomsky, N. A review of VERBAL BEHAVIOR by B. F. Skinner, LANGUAGE, 1959, 35, 26–58.

CHRISTIAN SCIENCE MONITOR. Editorial. December 4, 1978, p. 32.

Churchill, J. C., Broida, J. P., & Nicholson, N. L. Locus of control and self-esteem of adult children of alcoholics, JOURNAL OF STUDIES ON AL-COHOL, 1990, 51, 373–376.

Cialdini, R. B. INFLUENCE: SCIENCE AND PRACTICE. Glenview, IL: Scott, Foresman.

Ciminero, A. R., Calhoun, K. S., & Adams, H. E. (Eds.) HANDBOOK OF BEHAVIORAL AS-SESSMENT. New York: Wiley, 1977.

Cioffi, F. Was Freud a liar? THE LISTENER, 1974, 91, 172–174.

Clark, K. B. The psychology of the ghetto. In DARK GHETTO. New York: Harper & Row, 1965, 63–80.

Cohen, D. PSYCHOLOGISTS ON PSYCHOLOGY. New York: Taplinger Publishing, 1977.

Collins, B. & Hoyt, M. Personal responsibility for consequences: An integration and extension of the "forced" compliance literature, JOURNAL OF EXPERIMENTAL SOCIAL PSYCHOLOGY, 1972, 8, 558–593.

Colm, H. N. The affirmation of distance and closeness in psychotherapy. REVIEW OF EXISTENTIAL PSYCHOLOGY AND PSYCHIATRY, 1961, 1, 33–43.

Combs, A. W. Some observations on self-concept research and theory. In M. D. Lynch, A. A. Norem-Hebeisen, & K. J. Gergen. (Eds.) SELF-CONCEPT, ADVANCES IN THEORY AND RESEARCH. Cambridge, MA: Ballinger, 1981, 5–16.

Conci, M. Harry Stack Sullivan and the training of the psychiatrist. CONTEMPORARY PSYCHIATRY, 1993, 29, 530–540.

Conn, J. H. & Kanner, L. Children's awareness of sex differences. JOURNAL OF CHILD PSYCHIATRY, 1947, 1, 3–57.

Cooper, R. & Zubek, J. Effects of enriched and restricted environments on the learning ability of bright and dull rats. CANADIAN JOURNAL OF PSYCHOLOGY, 1958, 12, 159–164.

Conway, F. & Siegelman, J. SNAPPING, AMERICA'S EPIDEMIC OF SUDDEN PERSONALITY CHANGE. New York: Lippincott, 1978.

Corcoran, D. W. J. The relation between introversion and salivation. AMERICAN JOURNAL OF PSYCHOLOGY, 1964, 77, 298–300.

Corsini, R. J. CURRENT PSYCHOTHERAPIES, 3rd Ed. Itasca, IL: F. E. Peacock, 1984.

Cousins, N. ANATOMY OF AN ILLNESS AS PERCEIVED BY THE PATIENT. New York: Norton, 1979.

Cramer, P. WORD ASSOCIATION. New York: Academic Press, 1968.

Crandall, J. E. Adler's concept of social interest: Theory, measurement, and implications for adjustment. JOURNAL OF PERSONALITY AND SOCIAL PSYCHOLOGY, 1980, 39, 481–495.

Cronbach, L. J. The two disciplines of scientific psychology. AMERICAN PSYCHOLOGIST, 1957, 12, 671–684.

Cronbach, L. J. ESSENTIALS OF PSYCHOLOGICAL TESTING, 3rd Ed. New York: Harper & Row, 1970.

Cronbach, L. J. A research worker's treasure chest, MULTIVARIATE BEHAVIORAL RESEARCH, 1984, 19, 223–240.

Crow, L., and Crow, A. (Eds.) READINGS IN GENERAL PSYCHOLOGY. New York: Barnes & Noble, 1954.

Crumbaugh, J. & Maholick, L. MANUAL OF INSTRUCTIONS FOR THE PURPOSE IN LIFE TEST. Munster, IN: Psychometric Affiliates, 1969.

Curran, C. A. PERSONALITY FACTORS IN COUNSELING. New York: Grune & Stratton, 1945.

Dalton, P. & Dunnett, G. A PSYCHOLOGY FOR LIVING: PERSONAL CONSTRUCT THEORY FOR PROFESSIONALS AND CLIENTS. New York: John Wiley and Sons, 1992

Daly, M. & Wilson M. Is parent-offspring conflict sex-linked? Freudian and Darwinian models. JOURNAL OF PERSONALITY, 1990, 58, 163–190.

Damico, S. B. & Scott, E. S. Role of extracurricular activities in the promotion of cross-race contact by white students from high school to college. URBAN REVIEW, 1984, 16, 165–176.

Danto, A., & Morgenbesser, S. PHILOSOPHY OF SCIENCE. Cleveland: Meridan, 1960.

Darley, J. & Zanna, M. Making moral judgments. AMERICAN SCIENTIST, 1982, 70, 515–521.

Das, A. K. Beyond self-actualization. INTERNATIONAL JOURNAL FOR THE ADVANCEMENT OF COUNSELING, 1989, 12, 13–17.

Davidson, P. O., & Costello, C. G. (Eds.) N = 1: Experimental studies of single cases. New York: Van Nostrand Reinhold, 1969.

Davis, C. & Cowles, M. Automated psychological testing: Method of administration, need for approval, and measures of anxiety. EDUCATIONAL AND PSYCHOLOGICAL MEASUREMENT, 1989, 49, 311–320.

Davis, W. & Phares, E. Parental antecedents of internal-external control of reinforcement. PSYCHOLOGICAL REPORTS, 1969, 24, 427–436.

Davison, G. C., & Neale, J. M. ABNORMAL PSYCHOLOGY, AN EXPERIMENTAL CLINI-

CAL APPROACH 3rd ed. New York: Wiley, 1982.

Dawidowicz, L. S. THE WAR AGAINST THE JEWS. New York: Bantam, 1975.

DeAngelis, T. Not just a good theory: Transference is proven. MONITOR OF THE AMERICAN PSYCHOLOGICAL ASSOCIATION, 1994 (October), 56.

DeAngelis, T. Loving styles may be determined in infancy. MONITOR OF THE AMERICAN PSYCHOLOGICAL ASSOCIATION, 1994 (October), 21.

DeAngelis, T. Jung's theories keep pace and remain popular. MONITOR OF THE AMERICAN PSYCHOLOGICAL ASSOCIATION, 1994 (July), 41.

de Bonis, M., and Delgrange, C. A psycholinguistic approach to the measurement of anxiety. In C. D. Spielberger and I. G. Sarason, (Eds.), STRESS AND ANXIETY (vol. 4). New York: Wiley, 1977, 67–76.

DeCarvalho, R. J. Contributions to the history of psychology: LXIX. Gordon Allport on the problem of method in psychology. PSYCHOLOGICAL REPORTS, 1990, 67, 267–275.

DeCarvalho, R. J. Gordon Allport and humanistic psychology. JOURNAL OF HUMANISTIC PSYCHOLOGY, 1991, 31, 8–13.

DeCarvalho, R. J. The humanistic paradigm in education. THE HUMANISTIC PSYCHOLOGIST, 1991, 19, 88–104.

deCharms, R., & Moeller, G. H. Values expressed in American children's readers: 1800–1950. JOURNAL OF ABNORMAL PSYCHOLOGY, 1962, 64, 136–142.

deCharms, R. Personal causation training in the schools. JOURNAL OF APPLIED SOCIAL PSYCHOLOGY, 1972, 2, 95–113.

deCharms, R., & Muir, M. S. Motivation: Social approaches. In M. R. Rosenzweig and L. W. Porter, (Eds.), ANNUAL REVIEW OF PSYCHOLOGY (vol. 29). Palo Alto, CA: Annual Reviews, 1978, 91–113.

Deci, E. & Ryan, R. M. INTRINSIC MOTIVATION AND SELF-DETERMINATION IN HUMAN BEHAVIOR. New York: Plenum, 1975.

Dement, W. C. SOME MUST WATCH WHILE SOME MUST SLEEP. New York: Norton, 1976.

Demorest, A. P. & Siegel, P. F. Personal influences on professional work: An empirical case study of B. F. Skinner. JOURNAL OF PERSONALITY, 64, 1996, 241–261.

DePaulo, B. & Rosenthal, R. Telling lies. JOURNAL OF PERSONALITY AND SOCIAL PSYCHOLOGY, 1979, 37, 1713–1722.

Deutsch, H. THE PSYCHOLOGY OF WOMEN. vol. II. New York: Grune & Stratton, 1945.

Diener, E. & Wallbom, M. Effects of self-awareness on antinormative behavior. JOURNAL OF RESEARCH IN PERSONALITY, 1976, 10, 107–111.

Dinkmeyer, D. & Sherman, R. Brief Adlerian family therapy. INDIVIDUAL PSYCHOLOGY, 1989, 45, 148–158.

Dinsmoor, J. A. Setting the record straight: The social views of B. F. Skinner. AMERICAN PSYCHOLOGIST, 1992, 47, 1454–1463.

Dixon, N. SUBLIMINAL PERCEPTION: THE NATURE OF A CONTROVERSY. London: McGraw-Hill, 1971.

Doherty, W. Impact of divorce on locus of control orientation in adult women: A longitudinal study. JOURNAL OF PERSONALITY AND SOCIAL PSYCHOLOGY, 1983, 44, 834–840.

Dollard, J., Doob, L., Miller, N., Mowrer, O., & Sears, R. FRUSTRATION AND AGGRESSION. New Haven: Yale University Press, 1939.

Dollard, J. & Miller, N. PERSONALITY AND PSYCHOTHERAPY. New York: McGraw-Hill, 1950.

Dolliver, R. H. Classifying the personality theories and personalities of Adler, Freud, and Jung with introversion/extroversion. INDIVIDUAL PSYCHOLOGY JOURNAL OF ADLERIAN THEORY, RESEARCH, AND PRACTICE, 1994, 50, 192–202.

Donohue, M. J. Intrinsic and extrinsic religiousness: Review and meta-analysis. JOURNAL OF PERSONALITY AND SOCIAL PSYCHOLOGY, 1985, 48, 400–419.

Dreikurs, R. Family counseling: a demonstration. JOURNAL OF INDIVIDUAL PSYCHOLOGY, 1972a, 28, 207–222.

Dreikurs, R. Technology of conflict resolution. JOURNAL OF INDIVIDUAL PSYCHOLOGY, 1972b, 28, 203–206.

Dry, A. THE PSYCHOLOGY OF JUNG: A CRIT-

ICAL INTERPRETATION. New York: Wiley, 1961.

Duval, S., & Wicklund, R. A. A THEORY OF OBJECTIVE SELF AWARENESS. New York: Academic Press, 1972.

Duval, S., & Wicklund, R. A. Effects of objective self awareness on attribution of causality. JOURNAL OF EXPERIMENTAL SOCIAL PSYCHOLOGY, 1973, 9, 17–31.

Eaves, L. J. & Eysenck, H. J. The nature of extraversion: A genetical analysis. JOURNAL OF PERSONALITY AND SOCIAL PSYCHOLOGY, 1975, 32, 102–112.

Eckardt, M. H. In K. Horney, THE ADOLESCENT DIARIES OF KAREN HORNEY. New York: Basic Books, 1980.

Eckardt, M. H. Feminine psychology revisited: A historical perspective. Special issue: (Karen Horney). AMERICAN JOURNAL OF PSYCHOANALYSIS, 1991, 51, 235–243.

Eckardt, M. H. Fromm's concept of biophilia. JOURNAL OF THE AMERICAN ACADEMY OF PSYCHOANALYSIS, 1992, 20, 233–240.

Ekman, P. & Friesen, W. Detecting deception from the body and face, JOURNAL OF PERSONALITY AND SOCIAL PSYCHOLOGY, 1974, 29, 288–298.

Eldredge, P. R. A granddaughter of violence: Doris Lessing's good girls as terrorists, Special Issue: Interdisciplinary applications of Horney, AMERICAN JOURNAL OF PSYCHOANALYSIS, 1989, 49, 225–238.

Ellenberger, H. THE DISCOVERY OF THE UNCONSCIOUS: THE HISTORY AND EVOLUTION OF DYNAMIC PSYCHIATRY. New York: Basic Books, 1970.

Ellis, A. Rational-Emotive Theory. In A. Burton (Ed.), OPERATIONAL THEORIES OF PERSONALITY. New York: Brunner/Mazel, 1974a, 308–344.

Ellis, A. Experience and rationality: The making of a Rational-Emotive therapist. PSYCHOTHERAPY: THEORY, RESEARCH AND PRACTICE, 1974b, 11, 194–198.

Endler, N. S. The person versus the situation—A pseudo issue? A response to Alker. JOURNAL OF PERSONALITY, 1973, 41, 287–303.

Endler, N.S. Persons, situations, and their interactions. In A. I. Rabin, J. Aronoff, A. M. Barclay & R. A.

Zucker (Eds.), FURTHER EXPLORATIONS IN PERSONALITY. New York: Wiley-Interscience, 1981, 114–151.

Endler, N. S. Interactionism: A personality model, but not yet a theory. In M. Page & R. Dienstbier. NEBRASKA SYMPOSIUM ON MOTIVATION, 1982: PERSONALITY—CURRENT THEORY AND RESEARCH. Lincoln: University of Nebraska Press, 1983.

Endler, N. S. & Hunt, J. McV. S-R inventories of hostility and comparisons of the proportions of variance from persons, responses, and situations for hostility and anxiousness. JOURNAL OF PERSONALITY AND SOCIAL PSYCHOLOGY, 1968, 9, 309–315.

Endler, N. S., & Hunt, J. McV. Generalizability of contributions from sources of variance in the S-R Inventory of Anxiousness. JOURNAL OF PERSONALITY, 1969, 37, 1–24.

Endler, N. S., & Okada, M. A multidimensional measure of trait anxiety: The S-R Inventory of General Trait Anxiousness. JOURNAL OF CONSULTING AND CLINICAL PSYCHOLOGY, 1975, 43, 319–329.

Endler, N. S., Parker, J. D. A., Bagby, R. M., & Cox, B. J. Multidimensionality of state and trait anxiety: Factor structure on the Endler Multidimensional Anxiety Scales. JOURNAL OF PERSONALITY AND SOCIAL PSYCHOLOGY, 1991, 60, 919–926.

Engleman, E. BERGGASSE 19: SIGMUND FREUD'S HOME AND OFFICES, VIENNA 1938. New York: Basic Books, 1976.

Engelhard, G. Gender differences in performance on mathematics items: Evidence from the United States and Thailand. CONTEMPORARY EDUCATIONAL PSYCHOLOGY, 1990, 15, 13–26.

English, H. B., & English, A. C. A COMPREHENSIVE DICTIONARY OF PSYCHOLOGICAL AND PSYCHOANALYTICAL TERMS. New York: Longmans, Green, 1958.

Epstein, L. H. Psychophysiological measurement in assessment. In M. Hersen & A. S. Bellack (Eds.), BEHAVIORAL ASSESSMENT, A PRACTICAL HANDBOOK. New York: Pergamon, 1976, 207–232.

Epstein, R. Skinner, creativity, and the problems of spontaneous behavior. PSYCHOLOGICAL SCIENCE, 1991, 2, 362–370.

Epstein, S. The nature of anxiety with emphasis upon its relationship to expectancy. In C. D. Spielberger, (Ed.), ANXIETY, CURRENT TRENDS IN THEORY AND RESEARCH (vol. 2). New York: Academic Press, 1972, 291–337.

Epstein, S. Traits are alive and well. In D. Magnusson & N. Endler (Eds.), PERSONALITY AT THE CROSSROADS: CURRENT ISSUES IN INTERACTIONAL PSYCHOLOGY. Hillsdale, NJ: Erlbaum, 1977.

Eric Erikson: The quest for identity. NEWSWEEK, 1970 (December 21), 84–89.

Erikson, E. CHILDHOOD AND SOCIETY. New York: Norton, 1950.

Erikson, E. Womanhood and the inner space. In E. H. Erikson. IDENTITY, YOUTH AND CRISIS. New York: Norton, 1968a, 261–294.

Erikson, E. Life cycle. In D. Sills (Ed.), INTERNATIONAL ENCYCLOPEDIA OF THE SOCIAL SCIENCES. New York: Macmillan & Free Press, 1968b, vol. 9, 286–292.

Erikson, E. LIFE HISTORY AND THE HISTORICAL MOMENT, DIVERSE PRESENTATIONS. New York: Norton, 1975.

Esterson, A. SEDUCTIVE MIRAGE: AN EXPLORATION OF THE WORK OF SIGMUND FREUD. New York: Open Court, 1993.

Estes, K. An experimental study of punishment. PSYCHOLOGICAL MONOGRAPHS, 1944, 47, No. 263, 40.

Evans, R. I. CONVERSATIONS WITH CARL JUNG, AND REACTIONS FROM ERNEST JONES. Princeton, NJ: van Nostrand, 1964.

Evans, R. I. DIALOGUE WITH ERIK ERIKSON. New York: Harper & Row, 1967.

Evans. R. I. CARL ROGERS, THE MAN AND HIS IDEAS. New York: E. P. Dutton, 1975.

Evans, R. I. THE MAKING OF PSYCHOLOGY. New York: A.A. Knopf, 1976.

Eysenck, H. J. THE SCIENTIFIC STUDY OF PERSONALITY. New York: Macmillan, 1952.

Eysenck, H. J. SENSE AND NONSENSE IN PSYCHOLOGY. Baltimore, MD: Penguin Books, 1957.

Eysenck, H. J. MANUAL OF THE MAUDSLEY PERSONALITY INVENTORY. London: University of London Press, 1959.

Eysenck, H. J. THE MAUDSLEY PERSONALITY INVENTORY MANUAL. San Diego: Educational and Industrial Testing Service, 1962.

Eysenck, H. J. THE BIOLOGICAL BASIS OF PERSONALITY. Springfield, IL: Charles C. Thomas, 1967.

Eysenck, H. J. A dimensional system of psychodiagnosis. In A. R. Mahrer (Ed.), NEW APPROACHES TO PERSONALITY CLASSIFICATION. New York: Columbia University Press, 1970.

Eysenck, H. J. THE I.Q. ARGUMENT: RACE, INTELLIGENCE AND EDUCATION. New York: The Library Press, 1971.

Eysenck, H. J. THE INEQUALITY OF MAN. London: Temple Smith, 1974.

Eysenck, H. J. (Ed.). THE MEASUREMENT OF PERSONALITY. Baltimore, MD: University Park Press, 1976.

Eysenck, H. J. Hans Jurgen Eysenck. In G. Lindzey, A HISTORY OF PSYCHOLOGY IN AUTOBIOGRAPHY (vol. VII). San Francisco: W. H. Freeman, 1980, 153–187.

Eysenck, H. J. (Ed.). A MODEL FOR PERSONALITY. New York: Springer-Verlag, 1981.

Eysenck, H. J. Cattell and the theory of personality. MULTIVARIATE BEHAVIORAL RESEARCH, 1984, 19, 323–336.

Eysenck, H. J. Genetic and environmental contributions to individual differences: The three major dimensions of personality. JOURNAL OF PERSONALITY, 1990, 58, 245–261.

Eysenck, H. J. Comment on Goldberg. AMERICAN PSYCHOLOGIST, 1993, 48, 1299–1300.

Eysenck, H. J. & Eysenck, S. B. G. PERSONALITY STRUCTURE AND MEASUREMENT. San Diego, CA: Robert R. Knapp, 1969.

Eysenck, H. J. & Eysenck, S. B. G. PSYCHOTICISM AS A DIMENSION OF PERSONALITY. New York: Crane, Russak & Company, 1976.

Eysenck, H. J. & Levey, A. Conditioning, introversion-extraversion and the strength of the nervous system. In V. D. Nebylitsyn & J. A. Gray (Eds.), BIOLOGICAL BASES OF INDIVIDUAL BEHAVIOR. New York: Academic Press, 1972, 206–220.

Eysenck, S. B. G. & Eysenck, H. J. Salivary response to lemon juice as a measure of introversion. PERCEPTUAL AND MOTOR SKILLS, 1967, 24, 1047–1053.

Eysenck, S. B. G. & Eysenck, H. J. The measurement of psychoticism: A study of factor analytic stability and reliability. BRITISH JOURNAL OF SOCIAL AND CLINICAL PSYCHOLOGY, 1968, 7, 286–294.

Eysenck, S. B. G. & Eysenck, H. J. PERSONALITY STRUCTURE AND MEASUREMENT. New York: Crane, 1976.

Fagen, J. W. Reinforcement is not enough: Learned expectancies and infant behavior. AMERICAN PSYCHOLOGIST, 1993, 48, 1153–1155.

Falbo, T. Relationships between birth category, achievement and interpersonal orientation, JOURNAL OF PERSONALITY AND SOCIAL PSYCHOLOGY, 1981, 41, 121–131.

Falbo, T. & Polit, D. Quantitative review of the only child literature: Research evidence and theory development. PSYCHOLOGICAL BULLETIN, 1986, 100, 176–189.

Fallon, D. An existential look at B. F. Skinner. AMERICAN PSYCHOLOGIST, 1992, 47, 1433–1440.

Fairbairn, W. R. D. AN OBJECT-RELATIONS THEORY OF PERSONALITY. New York: Basic Books, 1954.

Farber, A. Freud's love letters: Intimations of psychoanalytic theory. THE PSYCHOANALYTIC REVIEW, 1978, 65, 167–189.

Farberow, N. L. A society by any other name. JOURNAL OF PROJECTIVE TECHNIQUES AND PERSONALITY ASSESSMENT, 1970, 34, 3–5.

Feldman, B. Jung's infancy and childhood and its influence upon the development of analytical psychology. JOURNAL OF ANALYTICAL PSYCHOLOGY, 1992, 37, 255–274.

Fenichel, O. THE PSYCHOANALYTIC THEORY OF NEUROSIS. New York: Norton, 1945.

Ferenczi, S. CONTRIBUTIONS TO PSYCHOANALYSIS. Boston: Badger, 1916.

Ferguson, E. Rotter's locus of control scale: A ten-item two-factor model, PSYCHOLOGICAL REPORTS, 1993, 73, 1267–1278.

Ferguson, E. D. Adler's motivational theory: An historical perspective on belonging and the fundamental human striving. INDIVIDUAL PSYCHOLOGY, 1989, 45, 354–362.

Festinger, L. A theory of social comparison processes. HUMAN RELATIONS, 1954, 2, 117–114.

Festinger, L. & Carlsmith, J. M. Cognitive consequences of forced compliance. JOURNAL OF ABNORMAL AND SOCIAL PSYCHOLOGY, 1959, 58, 203–210.

Finchilescu, G. Interracial contact in South Aftica within the nursing context. JOURNAL OF APPLIED SOCIAL PSYCHOLOGY, 1988, 18, 1207–1221.

Findley, M. & Cooper, H. Locus of control and academic achievement: A literature review. JOURNAL OF PERSONALITY AND SOCIAL PSYCHOLOGY, 1983, 44, 419–427.

Fischer, W. F. THEORIES OF ANXIETY. New York: Harper & Row, 1970.

Fischl, D. & Hoz, R. Stability and change of conceptions about teacher education held by teacher educators. Special issue: International conference on teacher thinking: II. JOURNAL OF STRUCTURAL LEARNING, 1993, 12, 53–69.

Fiske, D. W. MEASURING THE CONCEPTS OF PERSONALITY. Chicago: Aldine, 1971.

Fletcher, J. SITUATION ETHICS, THE NEW MORALITY. Philadelphia: Westminster Press, 1966.

Fliegel, Z. Half a century later: Current status of Freud's controversial view on women. THE PSYCHOANALYTIC REVIEW, 1982, 69, 7–28.

Frank, L. K. Projective methods for the study of personality. JOURNAL OF PSYCHOLOGY, 1939, 8, 389–413.

Frank, J. D. PERSUASION AND HEALING, A COMPARATIVE STUDY OF PSYCHOTHERAPY. New York: Schocken Books, 1961.

Frank, J. D. Therapeutic factors in psychotherapy. AMERICAN JOURNAL OF PSYCHOTHERAPY, 1971, 25, 350–361.

Frankl, V. E. Dynamics, existence and values. JOURNAL OF EXISTENTIAL PSYCHIATRY, 1961, 2, 5–16.

Frankl, V. E. THE DOCTOR AND THE SOUL, AN INTRODUCTION TO LOGOTHERAPY. New York: Knopf, 1960.

Frankl, V. E. PSYCHOTHERAPY AND EXISTENTIALISM, SELECTED PAPERS ON LOGOTHERAPY. New York: Simon and Schuster, 1968.

Frankl, V. E. MAN'S SEARCH FOR MEANING, AN INTRODUCTION TO LOGOTHERAPY. New York: Washington Square Press, 1963.

Franz, C. E., McClelland, D. C., & Weinberger, J.

Childhood antecedents of conventional social accomplishment in midlife adults: A 36–year prospective study. JOURNAL OF PERSONALITY AND SOCIAL PSYCHOLOGY, 1991, 60, 586–595.

Fredericksen, N. Toward a taxonomy of situations. AMERICAN PSYCHOLOGIST, 1972, 27, 114–123.

Fremont, T., Means, G. H. & Means, R. S. Anxiety as a function of task performance feedback and extraversion-introversion. PSYCHOLOGICAL REPORTS, 1970, 27, 455–458.

Freud, A. Changes in psychoanalytic practice and experience. INTERNATIONAL JOURNAL OF PSYCHO-ANALYSIS, 1976, 57, 257–260.

Freud, A. THE EGO AND THE MECHANISMS OF DEFENSE, Rev. Ed. New York: International Universities Press, 1936/1967.

Freud, E. (Ed.). LETTERS OF SIGMUND FREUD. New York: Basic Books, 1961.

Freud, S. THE EGO AND THE ID. London: Hogarth, 1923.

Freud, S. THE PROBLEM OF ANXIETY. New York: Norton, 1923/1936.

Freud, S. MOSES AND MONOTHEISM, K. Jones, Trans. New York: Knopf, 1939a.

Freud, S. CIVILIZATION AND ITS DISCONTENTS. London: Hogarth, 1939b.

Freud S. AN OUTLINE OF PSYCHOANALYSIS. New York: Norton, 1940/1949.

Freud, S. CIVILIZATION AND ITS DISCONTENTS, J. Riviere, Trans. London: Hogarth, 1953.

Freud, S. Leonardo da Vinci and a memory of his childhood. In J. Strachey (Ed.), THE STANDARD EDITION OF THE COMPLETE PSYCHOLOGICAL WORKS OF SIGMUND FREUD, VOL. 11. London: Hogarth Press, 1910/1957.

Freud, S. THE INTERPRETATION OF DREAMS. New York: Basic Books, 1900/1958.

Freud, S. Some psychological consequences of the anatomical distinction between the sexes. In J. Strachey (Ed.), THE COLLECTED PAPERS OF SIGMUND FREUD, vol. 5. New York: Basic Books, 1925/1959, 186–197.

Freud, S. CIVILIZATION AND ITS DISCONTENTS. In Standard edition, vol. XXI. London: Hogarth Press, 1930/1961.

Freud, S. Analysis of a phobia in a five-year-old boy. In

S. Freud, THE SEXUAL ENLIGHTENMENT OF CHILDREN. New York: Collier, 1909/1963, 47–138.

Freud, S. THREE CASE HISTORIES. New York: Collier, 1963.

Freud, S. PSYCHOPATHOLOGY OF EVERYDAY LIFE. New York: Mentor (New American Library), 1901/1965.

Freud, S. NEW INTRODUCTORY LECTURES ON PSYCHOANALYSIS. New York: Norton, 1933/1965.

Freud, S. Why war? In E. I. Megargee and J. E. Hokanson (Eds.). THE DYNAMICS OF AGGRESSION. New York: Harper & Row, (1932)1970, 10–21.

Freud, S. INTRODUCTORY LECTURES ON PSYCHOANALYSIS. New York: Norton, 1920/1977.

Freud, S. INHIBITION, SYMPTOMS AND ANXIETY, Alix Strachey, Trans., James Strachey, Ed. New York: Norton, 1977.

Freud, S., & Bullit, W. C. THOMAS WOODROW WILSON, A PSYCHOLOGICAL STUDY. New York: Avon, 1966.

Friedman, R. C. & Downey, J.I. Homosexuality. NEW ENGLAND JOURNAL OF MEDICINE, 1994 (Oct. 6), 331, 923–930.

Fromm, E. ESCAPE FROM FREEDOM. New York: Holt, Rinehart and Winston, 1941.

Fromm, E. MAN FOR HIMSELF, AN INQUIRY INTO THE PSYCHOLOGY OF ETHICS. New York: Holt, Rinehart and Winston, 1947.

Fromm, E. THE SANE SOCIETY. New York: Rinehart, 1955.

Fromm, E. THE ART OF LOVING. New York: Harper & Brothers, 1956.

Fromm, E. Values, psychology and human existence. In A. H. Maslow (Ed.), NEW KNOWLEDGE IN HUMAN VALUES. Harper & Brothers, 1959, 151–164.

Fromm, E. MAY MAN PREVAIL? Garden City, New York: Doubleday, Anchor Books, 1961.

Fromm, E. BEYOND THE CHAINS OF ILLUSION, MY ENCOUNTER WITH MARX AND FREUD. New York: Pocketbooks, 1962.

Fromm, E. THE HEART OF MAN, ITS GENIUS FOR GOOD AND EVIL. New York: Harper & Row, 1964.

Fromm, E. On the sources of human destructiveness. In

L. Ng. (Ed.), ALTERNATIVES TO VIO-LENCE. New York: Time-Life Books, 1968, 11–17.

Fromm, E. THE ANATOMY OF HUMAN DE-STRUCTIVENESS. New York: Holt, Rinehart and Winston, 1973.

Fromm, E. TO HAVE OR TO BE? New York: Harper & Row, 1976.

Fromm, E. THE GREATNESS AND LIMITA-TIONS OF FREUD'S THOUGHT. New York: Harper & Row, 1980.

Fromm, E., and Maccoby, M. SOCIAL CHARAC-TER IN A MEXICAN VILLAGE, A SOCIOPSYCHOANALYTIC STUDY. Engle-wood Cliffs, NJ: Prentice-Hall, 1970.

Frosch, J. The New York psychoanalytic civil war. JOURNAL OF THE AMERICAN PSYCHO-ANALYTIC ASSOCIATION, 1991, 39, 1037–1064.

Funder, D. C., & Ozer, D. Behavior as a function of the situation. JOURNAL OF PERSONALITY AND SOCIAL PSYCHOLOGY, 1983, 44, 107–112.

Funk, R. ERICH FROMM: THE COURAGE TO BE HUMAN. New York: Continuum, 1982.

Gabriel, M. T., Critelli, J. W., & Ee, J. S. Narcissistic illusions in self-evaluations of intelligence and at-tractiveness. JOURNAL OF PERSONALITY, 1994, 62, 143–155.

Gaines, S. O. & Reed, E. S. Prejudice: From Allport to DuBois. AMERICAN PSYCHOLOGIST, 1995, 50, 96–103.

Gaines, S. O. & Reed, E. S. Two social psychologies of prejudice: Gordon W. Allport, W.E.B. Du Bois and the legacy of Booker T. Washington. JOUR-NAL OF BLACK PSYCHOLOGY, 1994, 20, 8–29.

Garcia, J. Misrepresentations of my criticisms of Skin-ner. AMERICAN PSYCHOLOGIST, 1993, 48, 1158.

Gardner, H. FRAMES OF MIND: THE THEORY OF MULTIPLE INTELLIGENCES. New York: Basic Books, 1988.

Garfield, E. The hundred most cited authors. CUR-RENT CONTENTS, 1978, 45, 5–15.

Garrison, M. A new look at Little Hans. THE PSY-CHOANALYTIC REVIEW, 1978, 65, 523–532.

Gelman, D. & Hager, M. Finding the hidden Freud. NEWSWEEK, November, 30, 1981, 64–70.

Gendlin, E. T. EXPERIENCING AND THE CRE-ATION OF MEANING. New York: Free Press, 1962.

Gendlin, E. T. Experiencing: A variable in the process of therapeutic change. AMERICAN JOURNAL OF PSYCHOTHERAPY, 1961, 15, 2.

Gendlin, E. T., and Rychlak, J. F. Psychotherapeutic processes. In P. H. Mussen and M. R. Rosenzweig (Eds.), ANNUAL REVIEW OF PSYCHOL-OGY, 1970, 21, 155–190.

Gendlin, E. T. Carl Rogers (1902–1987). AMERI-CAN PSYCHOLOGIST, 1988, 43, 127–128.

Gendlin, E. T. & Tomlinson, T. M. The process of con-ception and its measurement. In C. R. Rogers (Ed.), THE THERAPEUTIC RELATIONSHIP AND ITS IMPACT: A STUDY OF PSY-CHOTHERAPY WITH SCHIZOPHRENICS. Madison, WI: University of Wisconsin Press, 1967.

Genia, V. A psychometric evaluation of the Allport-Ross I/E scales in a religiously heterogeneous sam-ple. JOURNAL FOR THE SCIENTIFIC STUDY OF RELIGION, 1993, 32, 284–290.

George, B. L. & Waehler, C. A. The ups and downs of TAT card 17BM. JOURNAL OF PERSONAL-ITY ASSESSMENT, 1994, 63, 167–172.

Gerard, L. SIGMUND FREUD: THE MAN AND HIS THEORIES. New York: Fawcett, 1962.

Gibson, H. B. HANS EYSENCK, THE MAN AND HIS WORK. London: Peter Owen, 1981.

Gilberstadt, H. & Duker, J. A HANDBOOK FOR CLINICAL AND ACTUARIAL MMPI IN-TERPRETATION. Philadelphia: W.B. Saunders, 1965.

Gill, M. Special book review: A new perspective on Freud and psychoanalysis. THE PSYCHOANA-LYTIC REVIEW, 1981, 68, 343–347.

Gilligan, C. IN A DIFFERENT VOICE. Cambridge, MA: Harvard University Press, 198.

Goble, F. G. THE THIRD FORCE: THE PSY-CHOLOGY OF ABRAHAM MASLOW. New York: Brossman Publishers, 1970.

Goldberg, L. R. Language and individual differences: The search for universals in personality lexicons. In L. Wheeler (Ed.), REVIEW OF PERSONAL-ITY AND SOCIAL PSYCHOLOGY, 1981, Beverly Hills, CA: Sage, 141–165.

Goldberg, L. R. Author's reactions to the six com-ments. AMERICAN PSYCHOLOGIST, 1993, 48, 1303–1304.

Goldstein, K. THE ORGANISM. New York: American Book Company, 1939.

Golub, S. Coping with cancer: Freud's experiences. THE PSYCHOANALYTIC REVIEW, 1981, 68, 191–200.

Gordon, J. E. Interpersonal prediction of repressors and sensitizers. JOURNAL OF PERSONALITY, 1957, 25, 686–698.

Gorlow, L., Simonson, N. R., & Krauss, H. An empirical investigation of the Jungian typology. BRITISH JOURNAL OF SOCIAL AND CLINICAL PSYCHOLOGY, 1966, 5, 108–117.

Gorman, C. Are gay men born that way? TIME, 9/9/1991, 60–61.

Gough, H. G., & Heilbrun, A. B., Jr. THE ADJECTIVE CHECK LIST MANUAL, Rev. Ed. Palo Alto, CA: Consulting Psychologists Press, 1980.

Gould, P. & White, R. MENTAL MAPS. Baltimore, Maryland: Penguin Books, 1974.

Graf, C. On genuineness and the person-centered approach: A Reply to Quinn. JOURNAL OF HUMANISTIC PSYCHOLOGY, 1994, 34, 90–96.

Graham, W. K., and Balloun, J. An empirical test of Maslow's need hierarchy theory. JOURNAL OF HUMANISTIC PSYCHOLOGY, 1973, 13, 97–108.

Gray, J. A. A critique of Eysenck's theory of personality. In H.J. Eysenck (Ed.), A MODEL FOR PERSONALITY. New York: Springer-Verlag, 1981, 246–276.

Gray, J. A. The psychophysiological basis of introversion-extraversion: A modification of Eysenck's theory. In V.D. Nebylitsyn & J.A. Gray (Eds.), THE BIOLOGICAL BASES OF INDIVIDUAL BEHAVIOR. New York: Academic Press, 1972, 182–205.

Green, C. W. Operationalizing contact theory: Measuring student attributes toward desegregation. Paper presented at the Annual Convention of the American Psychological Association, Los Angeles, August, 1981.

Greene, J. N., Plank, R. E., & Fowler, D. G. Compugrid: A program for computing, sorting, categorizing, and graphing multiple Bieri grid measurements of cognitive complexity. EDUCATIONAL AND PSYCHOLOGICAL MEASUREMENT, 1989, 49, 623–626.

Greenough, W. T., Black, J. E., & Wallace, C. S. Experience and brain development. CHILD DEVELOPMENT, 1987, 58, 539–559.

Greenwald, A. G. New look 3: Unconscious cognition reclaimed. AMERICAN PSYCH0LOGIST, 1992, 47, 766–779.

Greenwood, C. R., Carta, J. J., Hart, B., Kamps, D., Terry, B., Arreaga-Mayer, C., Atwater, J. Walker, D., Risley, T., & Delquadri, J. C. Out of the laboratory and into the community: 26 years of applied behavior analysis at the Juniper Gardens Children's Project. AMERICAN PSYCHOLOGIST, 1992, 47, 1464–1474.

Greever, K. B., Tseng, M. S., & Friedland, B. U. Development of the Social Interest Index. JOURNAL OF CONSULTING AND CLINICAL PSYCHOLOGY, 1973, 41, 454–458.

Grey, A. L. The dialectics of psychoanalysis: A new synthesis of Fromm's theory and practice. CONTEMPORARY PSYCHOANALYSIS, 1993, 29, 645–672.

Griffin, D. & Bartholomew, K. Models of self and other: Fundamental dimensions underlying measures of adult attachment. JOURNAL OF PERSONALITY AND SOCIAL PSYCHOLOGY, 1994, 67, 430–445.

Gromly, J. Behaviorism and the biological viewpoint of personality. BULLETIN OF THE PSYCHONOMIC SOCIETY, 1982, 20, 255–256.

Gross, O. DIE ZEREBRALE SEKUNDARFUNKTION. Leipzig, Germany: 1902. Referenced in H. J. Eysenck (Ed.), A MODEL FOR PERSONALITY. New York: Springer-Verlag, 1981.

Guastello, S. J. A two-(and-a-half)-tiered trait taxonomy. AMERICAN PSYCHOLOGIST, 1993, 48, 1298–1299.

Guilford, J. P. & Zimmerman, W. S. Fourteen dimensions of temperament, PSYCHOLOGICAL MONOGRAPHS, 1956, 70, Whole No. 417.

Guilford, J. P. PERSONALITY. New York: McGraw-Hill, 1959.

Guilford, J. P. THE NATURE OF HUMAN INTELLIGENCE. New York: McGraw-Hill, 1967.

Gupta, B. S. & Kaur, S. The effects of dextroamphetamine on kinesthetic figural after effects. PSYCHOPHARMACOLOGY, 1978, 56, 199–204.

Gurman, A. S., and Razin, A. M. (Eds.) EFFECTIVE PSYCHOTHERAPY, A HANDBOOK OF RESEARCH. New York: Pergamon Press, 1977.

Haan, N. Two moralities in action contexts. JOURNAL OF PERSONALITY AND SOCIAL PSYCHOLOGY, 1978, 36, 286–305.

Hafner, J. L., Fakouri, M. E., & Labrentz, H. L. First memories of "normal" and alcoholic individuals. INDIVIDUAL PSYCHOLOGY, 1982, 38, 238–244.

Hakmiller, K. L. Threat as a determinant of downward comparison. JOURNAL OF EXPERIMENTAL SOCIAL PSYCHOLOGY, 1966, Supplement No. 1, 32–39.

Hall, C. & Nordby, V. J. A PRIMER OF JUNGIAN PSYCHOLOGY. New York: Mentor Books, 1973.

Hall, C. & Van de Castle, R. An empirical investigation of the castration complex in dreams. JOURNAL OF PERSONALITY, 1965, 33, 20–29.

Hall, C. S., & Lindzey, G. THEORIES OF PERSONALITY, 3rd Ed. New York: Wiley, 1978.

Hall, E. A. conversation with Erik Erikson. PSYCHOLOGY TODAY, June, 1983, 35–42.

Hall, M. H. The psychology of universality. PSYCHOLOGY TODAY, 1968, 2, 34–37; 54–57.

Haney, D. O. Psychologist B. F. Skinner dies at 86. PEORIA JOURNAL STAR (ASSOCIATED PRESS), 1990 (AUGUST 20), p. B1.

Hanly, C. Review of The assault on truth: Freuds's suppression of the seduction theory by J. Masson. INTERNATIONAL JOURNAL OF PSYCHOANALYSIS, 1987, 67, 517–519.

Harlow, H. F. Love in monkeys. SCIENTIFIC AMERICAN, 1959, 200, 68–74.

Harlow, H.F. The nature of love. AMERICAN PSYCHOLOGIST, 1958, 13, 673–685.

Harlow, H. F., & Harlow, M. K. The young monkeys. In J. B. Maas, (Ed.), READINGS IN PSYCHOLOGY TODAY, 3rd Ed. Del Mar, CA: CRM Books, 1974, 198–203.

Harper, H., Oei, T. P. S., Mendalgio, S., & Evans, L. Dimensionality, validity, and utility of the I-E scale with anxiety disorders. JOURNAL OF ANXIETY DISORDERS, 4, 1990, 89–98.

Harrington, D. M., Block, J. H., & Block, J. Testing aspects of Carl Rogers' theory of creative environments: Child-rearing antecedents of creative potential young adolescents. JOURNAL OF PERSONALITY AND SOCIAL PSYCHOLOGY, 1987, 52, 851–856.

Harris, M. E., & Greene, R. L. Students' perception of actual, trivial, and inaccurate personality feedback. JOURNAL OF PERSONALITY ASSESSMENT, 1984, 48, 179–184.

Hart, J. T., and Tomlinson, T. M. NEW DIRECTIONS IN CLIENT-CENTERED THERAPY. Boston: Houghton Mifflin, 1970.

Hartl, E., Monnelly, E., & Elderkin, R. PHYSIQUE AND DELINQUENT BEHAVIOR. New York: Academic Press, 1982.

Hartmann, H. EGO PSYCHOLOGY AND THE PROBLEM OF ADAPTATION. New York: International Universities Press, 1958.

Harvey, R. J. & Murry, W. D. Scoring the Myers-Briggs Type Indicator: Empirical comparison of preference score versus latent-trait methods. JOURNAL OF PERSONALITY ASSESSMENT, 1994, 62, 116–129.

Haslam, D. R. & Thomas, E. A. C. An optimum interval in the assessment of pain threshold. QUARTERLY JOURNAL OF EXPERIMENTAL PSYCHOLOGY, 1967, 19, 54–58.

Haslam, D. R. Individual differences in pain threshold and level of arousal. BRITISH JOURNAL OF PSYCHOLOGY, 1967, 58, 139–142.

Hastorf, A. H., Schneider, D. J., & Polefka, J. PERSON PERCEPTION. Menlo Park, CA: Addison-Wesley, 1970.

Hathaway, S. R., & McKinley, J. C. MANUAL FOR THE MINNESOTA MULTIPHASIC PERSONALITY INVENTORY. New York: Psychological Corporation, 1943.

Hathaway, S. R., & McKinley, J. C. THE MINNESOTA MULTIPHASIC PERSONALITY INVENTORY MANUAL, Rev. Ed. New York: Psychological Corporation, 1967.

Hausdorff, D. ERIC FROMM. New York: Twayne Publishers, 1972.

Havassy-De Avila, B. A critical review of the approach to birth order research. THE CANADIAN PSYCHOLOGIST, 1971, 12, 282–305.

Hayes, C. Changes in MAACL Anxiety scale scores during 11 class meetings. Cited in M. Zuckerman and B. Lubin, MANUAL FOR THE MULTIPLE AFFECT ADJECTIVE CHECK LIST. San Diego, CA: Educational and Industrial Testing Service, 1965, 7–9.

Hayes, G. E. Empathy: A conceptual and clinical deconstruction. PSYCHOANALYTIC-DIALOGUES, 1994, 4, 409–424.

Hayes, J. COGNITIVE PSYCHOLOGY, THINKING AND CREATING. Homewood, IL: Dorsey Press, 1978.

Hayes, S. C. & Hayes, L. J. Verbal relations and the evolution of behavior analysis. AMERICAN PSYCHOLOGIST, 1992, 47, 1383–1395.

Hebb, D. O. THE ORGANIZATION OF BEHAVIOR. New York: John Wiley, 1949.

Heckhausen, H. & Krug, S. Motive modification. In A. J. Stewart, (Ed.), MOTIVATION AND SOCIETY. San Francisco: Jossey-Bass, 1982, 274–318.

Heidegger, M. AN INTRODUCTION TO METAPHYSICS, R. Manheim, Trans. New Haven: Yale University Press, 1959.

Heidegger, M. EXISTENCE AND BEING. Chicago: Henry Regnery, 1949.

Heider, F. THE PSYCHOLOGY OF INTERPERSONAL RELATIONS. New York: Wiley, 1958.

Hempel, C. & Oppenheim, P. Problems of the concept of general law. In A. Danto & S. Morgenbesser (Eds.), PHILOSOPHY OF SCIENCE. New York: World Publishing, 1960.

Henry, W. E. THE ANALYSIS OF FANTASY. New York: Wiley, 1974.

Hermann, B. P., Whitman, S. W., Wyler, A. R., Anton, M. T., & Vanderzwagg, R. Psychosocial predictors of psychopathology in epilepsy, BRITISH JOURNAL OF PSYCHIATRY, 1990, 156, 98–105.

Hermans, H. J. M., Kempen, H. J. G., & van Loon, R. J. P. The dialogical self: Beyond individualism and rationalism. AMERICAN PSYCHOLOGIST, 1992, 47, 23–33.

Heron, W. The pathology of boredom. In S. Coopersmith (Ed.), FRONTIERS OF PSYCHOLOGICAL RESEARCH. San Francisco: W. H. Freeman and Company, 1966 (originally appeared in SCIENTIFIC AMERICAN, January 1957, 82–86).

Herrnstein, R. J. & Murray, C. THE BELL CURVE: INTELLIGENCE AND CLASS STRUCTURE IN AMERICAN LIFE. New York: Free Press, 1994.

Hersen, M., & Bellack, A. S. BEHAVIORAL ASSESSMENT: A PRACTICAL HANDBOOK. New York: Pergamon Press, 1976.

Heylighen, F. A cognitive-systemic reconstruction of Maslow's theory of self-actualization. BEHAVIORAL SCIENCE, 1992, 37, 39–58.

Heymans, G. Uber einige psychische Korrelationen. Z ANGEW PSYCHOLOGIE, 1908, 1, 313–381. Referenced in H.J. Eysenck (Ed.), A MODEL

FOR PERSONALITY. New York: Springer-Verlag, 1981.

Hill-Hain, A. & Rogers, C. R. A dialogue with Carl Rogers: Cross-cultural challenges of facilitating person-centered groups in South Africa, JOURNAL OF SPECIALISTS IN GROUP WORK, 1988. 13, 62–69.

Hineline, P. N. A self-interpretive behavior analysis. AMERICAN PSYCHOLOGIST, 1992, 47, 1274–1286.

Hirsch, J. Genes and behavior: A reply. SCIENCE, 1964, 144, 891.

Hirsch, J. Jensenism: The bankruptcy of "science" without scholarship. EDUCATIONAL THEORY, 1975, 25, 1–27.

Hirsch, J. To "unfrock the charlatans." SAGE RACE RELATIONS ABSTRACTS, 1981, 6 (May), 1–67.

Hoban, P. Psychodrama: The chilling story of how the Sullivanian cult turned a utopian dream into a nightmare. NEW YORK (June, 19, 1989), 41–55.

Hoffman, E. THE RIGHT TO BE HUMAN. Los Angeles: Jeremy P. Tarcher, 1988.

Hoffman, L. E. Erikson on Hitler: The origins of "Hitler's imagery and German youth." PSYCHOHISTORY REVIEW, 1993, 22, 69–86.

Hogan, R. A socioanalytic theory of personality. In M. Page & R. Dienstbier, NEBRASKA SYMPOSIUM ON MOTIVATION, 1982: PERSONALITY—CURRENT THEORY AND RESEARCH. Lincoln: University of Nebraska Press, 1983.

Hogan, R. Moral conduct and moral character. PSYCHOLOGICAL BULLETIN, 1973, 79, 217–232.

Hogan, R. PERSONALITY THEORY, THE PERSONOLOGICAL TRADITION. Englewood Cliffs, NJ: Prentice-Hall, 1976.

Holland, J. & Skinner, B. THE ANALYSIS OF BEHAVIOR. New York: McGraw-Hill, 1961.

Hollander, J. & Yeostros, S. The effect of simultaneous variations of humidity and barometric pressure on arthritis. BULLETIN OF THE AMERICAN METEOROLOGICAL SOCIETY, 1963, 44, 489–494.

Holmes, T. H. & Masuda, M. Life change and illness susceptibility, SEPARATION AND DEPRESSION, 1973, American Association for the Advancement of Science, Publication No. 94, 161–186.

Holmes, T. H., & Rahe, R. H. The Social Readjustment Rating Scale. JOURNAL OF PSYCHOSOMATIC RESEARCH, 1967, 11, 213–218.

Holmstrom, R. W., Karp, S. A., & Silber, D. E. The apperceptive personality test and locus of control. PSYCHOLOGICAL REPORTS, 1991, 68, 1071–1074.

Holtzman, W. Thorpe, J., Swartz, J., & Herron, E. INKBLOT PERCEPTION AND PERSONALITY: HOLTZMAN INKBLOT TECHNIQUE. Austin: The University of Texas Press, 1961.

Hopkins, E. The impact of B. F. Skinner. PEORIA JOURNAL STAR, September 11, 1990, p. A9.

Horney, K. The flight from womanhood: The masculinity complex in women as viewed by men and by women. INTERNATIONAL JOURNAL OF PSYCHO-ANALYSIS, 1926, 7, 324–329.

Horney, K. NEW WAYS IN PSYCHOANALYSIS. New York: Norton, 1939.

Horney, K. THE NEUROTIC PERSONALITY OF OUR TIME. New York: Norton, 1937.

Horney, K. SELF ANALYSIS. New York: Norton, 1942.

Horney, K. OUR INNER CONFLICTS, A CONSTRUCTIVE THEORY OF NEUROSIS. New York: Norton, 1945.

Horney, K. ARE YOU CONSIDERING PSYCHOANALYSIS? New York: Norton, 1946.

Horney, K. NEUROSIS AND HUMAN GROWTH, THE STRUGGLE TOWARD SELF-REALIZATION. New York: Norton, 1950.

Horney, K. FEMININE PSYCHOLOGY. New York: Norton, 1967.

Horney, K. THE ADOLESCENT DIARIES OF KAREN HORNEY. New York: Basic Books, 1980.

Houle, G. R. The diagnostic conference planning questionnaire for speech–language pathology. LANGUAGE, SPEECH, AND HEARING SERVICES IN SCHOOLS, 1990, 21, 118–119.

Huber, R. J., Widdifield, J. K., & Johnson, C. L. Frankenstein: An Adlerian Odyssey. INDIVIDUAL PSYCHOLOGY, 1989, 45, 267–278.

Hull, C. L. A BEHAVIOR SYSTEM. New Haven: Yale University Press, 1952.

Hull, C. L. Principles of Behavior. New York: Appleton-Century-Crofts, 1943.

Hunt, J. Mc V. Psychological development: Early experience. In Rosenzweig, M., & Porter, L., ANNUAL REVIEW, vol. 30, 1979, 103–144.

Husserl. E. IDEAS, W. R. Boyce Gibson, Trans. New York: Collier Books, 1961.

Hyer, L., Woods, M. G., & Boudewyns, P. A. Early recollections of Vietnam veterans with PTSD. INDIVIDUAL PSYCHOLOGY, 1989, 45, 300–312.

Iaccino, J. F. PSYCHOLOGICAL REFLECTIONS ON CINEMATIC TERROR: JUNGIAN ARCHETYPES IN HORROR FILMS. London: Praeger, 1994.

Inkeles, A., & Levinson, D. National character: The study of modal personality and sociocultural systems. In G. Lindzey & E. Aronson (Eds.), THE HANDBOOK OF SOCIAL PSYCHOLOGY, 2nd Ed. London: Addison-Wesley 1969, 418–506.

Ionedes, N. S. Social interest psychiatry. INDIVIDUAL PSYCHOLOGY, 1989, 45, 416–422.

Ishiyama, F. I., Munson, P. A., & Chabassol, D. J. Birth order and fear of success among midadolescents. PSYCHOLOGICAL REPORTS, 1990, 66, 17–18.

Ittelson, W. & Kilpatrick, F. Experiments in perception. SCIENTIFIC AMERICAN, 1951, 185, 50–55.

Iversen, I. H. Skinner's early research: From reflexology to operant conditioning. AMERICAN PSYCHOLOGIST, 1992, 47, 1318–1328.

Jackson, D. B., & Paunonen, S. V. Personality structure and assessment. In M.R. Rosenzweig and L.W. Porter (Eds.). ANNUAL REVIEW OF PSYCHOLOGY, 1980, 31, 503–551.

Jackson, D. N. PERSONALITY RESEARCH FORM MANUAL, 3rd Ed. Port Huron, MI: Sigma Assessment Systems, 1984.

Jackson, D. N. PERSONALITY RESEARCH FORM MANUAL. Goshen, NY: Research Psychologists Press, 1967.

Jackson, M. & Sechrest, L. Early recollections in four neurotic diagnostic categories. JOURNAL OF INDIVIDUAL PSYCHOLOGY, 1962, 18, 52–56.

Jacobi, J. THE PSYCHOLOGY OF C. G. JUNG, Rev. Ed. New Haven: Yale University Press, 1962.

James, W. THE PRINCIPLES OF PSYCHOLOGY, vol. I & II. New York: Dover Publications, 1890/1950.

James, W. THE VARIETIES OF RELIGIOUS EXPERIENCE. New York: Mentor Books, 1958.

Jankowicz, A. D. Whatever became of George Kelly? Applications and implications. AMERICAN PSYCHOLOGIST, 1987, 42, 481–487.

Jarman, T. L. THE RISE AND FALL OF NAZI GERMANY. New York: Signet, 1961.

Jensen, A. R. How much can we boost IQ and scholastic achievement? HARVARD EDUCATIONAL REVIEW, 1969, 39, 1–123.

Jensen, A. R. Sir Cyril Burt in perspective. AMERICAN PSYCHOLOGIST, 1978, 33, 499–503.

Johnson, E. E., Nora, R. M., & Bustros, N. The Rotter I-E scale as a predictor of relapse in a population of compulsive gamblers. PSYCHOLOGICAL REPORTS, 1992, 70, 691–696.

Johnson, J. L. The Thematic Apperception Test and Alzheimer's Disease. JOURNAL OF PERSONALITY ASSESSMENT, 1994, 62, 314–319.

Johnson, K. R. & Layng, T. V. J. Breaking the structuralist barrier: Literacy and numeracy with fluency. AMERICAN PSYCHOLOGIST, 1992, 47, 1475–1490.

Jones, E. THE LIFE AND WORK OF SIGMUND FREUD. Garden City, NY: Anchor Books, 1953/1963.

Jones E. THE LIFE AND WORK OF SIGMUND FREUD, vol. II. New York: Basic Books, 1955.

Jones, B. M. Cognition performance of introverts and extraverts following acute alcohol ingestion. BRITISH JOURNAL OF PSYCHOLOGY, 1974, 65, 35–42.

Jones, B. M., Hatcher, E., Jones, M. K., & Farris, J. J. The relationship of extraversion and neuroticism to the effects of alcohol on cognitive performance in male and female social drinkers. In F.A. Seixas (Ed.), CURRENTS IN ALCOHOLISM. New York: Grune & Stratton, 1978.

Jordan, E. W., Whiteside, M. M., and Manaster, G.J. A practical and effective research measure of birth order, INDIVIDUAL PSYCHOLOGY, 1982, 38, 253–260.

Joseph, E. Presidential address: Clinical issues in psychoanalysis. INTERNATIONAL JOURNAL OF PSYCHO-ANALYSIS, 1980, 61, 1–9.

Jourden, F. J., Bandura, A., & Banfield, J. T. The impact of conceptions of ability on self-regulatory factors and motor skill acquisition. JOURNAL OF SPORT & EXERCISE PSYCHOLOGY, 1991, 8, 213–226.

Joy, S. & Wise, P. Maternal employment, anxiety, and sex differences in college students' self-descriptions. SEX ROLES, 1983, 9, 519–525.

Jung, C. G. The association method. AMERICAN JOURNAL OF PSYCHOLOGY, 1910, 21, 219–269.

Jung, C. G. THE DEVELOPMENT OF PERSONALITY, R. F. C. Hull, Trans. New York: Pantheon Books, 1954.

Jung, C. G. THE ARCHETYPES AND THE COLLECTIVE UNCONSCIOUS, R. F. C. Hull, Trans., Collected Works (Vol. IX, Part I). Princeton, NJ: Princeton University Press, 1959a.

Jung, C. G. THE ARCHETYPES AND THE COLLECTIVE UNCONSCIOUS, R. F. C. Hull, Trans., Collected Works (Vol. IX, Part 2). Princeton, NJ: Princeton University Press, 1959b.

Jung, C. G. MEMORIES, DREAMS, REFLECTIONS, A. Jaffe, Ed. New York: Pantheon Books, 1963.

Jung, C. G. MAN AND HIS SYMBOLS. New York: Dell, 1964.

Jung, C. G. PSYCHOLOGICAL TYPES, R. F. C. Hull, Trans., Collected Works (Vol. VI). Princeton, NJ: Princeton University Press, 1921/1971.

Jung, C. G. FLYING SAUCERS, A MODERN MYTH OF THINGS SEEN IN THE SKIES, R. F. C. Hull, Trans. Princeton, NJ: Princeton University Press, 1978.

Jung, J. UNDERSTANDING HUMAN MOTIVATION. New York: MacMillan, 1978.

Kaiser, W. Adler and C. G. Jung: The history of their meetings. ZEITSCHRIFT FÜR INDIVIDUAL PSYCHOLOGIE, 1994, 19, 3–19.

Kal, E. F. Survey of contemporary Adlerian clinical practice. INDIVIDUAL PSYCHOLOGY, 1972, 28, 261–266.

Kanfer, F. H., & Goldstein, A. P. (Eds.). HELPING PEOPLE CHANGE, A TEXTBOOK OF METHODS, 2nd Ed. New York: Pergamon Press, 1980.

Katz, S. H. Is race a legitimate concept for science? UNESCO RACE STATEMENT. Available from S. H. Katz, Anthropology, University of Pennsylvania, 1995.

Kelley, H. H. Attribution theory in social psychology. In D. Levine (Ed.), NEBRASKA SYMPOSIUM ON MOTIVATION, Vol. 15. Lincoln: University of Nebraska Press, 1967, 52–81.

Kelley, H. H. The process of causal attribution.

AMERICAN PSYCHOLOGIST, 1973, 28, 107–128.

Kelly, G. A psychology of the optimal man. In A. W. Landfield and L. M. Leitner (Eds.), PERSONAL CONSTRUCT PSYCHOLOGY: PSYCHOTHERAPY AND PERSONALITY. New York: Wiley, 1980.

Kelly, G. A THEORY OF PERSONALITY: THE PSYCHOLOGY OF PERSONAL CONSTRUCTS. New York: Norton, 1963.

Kelly, G. THE PSYCHOLOGY OF PERSONAL CONSTRUCTS, (two vols.). New York: Norton, 1955.

Kelly, G. The autobiography of a theory. In B. Maher (Ed.), CLINICAL PSYCHOLOGY AND PERSONALITY: THE SELECTED PAPERS OF GEORGE KELLY. New York, 1969, 40–65.

Kelman, H. Introduction. In K. Horney, FEMININE PSYCHOLOGY. New York: Norton, 1967.

Kendall, P. Anxiety: States, traits—situations? JOURNAL OF CONSULTING AND CLINICAL PSYCHOLOGY, 1978, 46, 280–287.

Kendall, P. C., Finch, A., Auerbach, S., Hooke, J., & Mikulka, P. The state–trait anxiety inventory: A systematic evaluation. JOURNAL OF CONSULTING AND CLINICAL PSYCHOLOGY, 1976, 44, 406–412.

Kendler, H. H. Behavioral determinism: A strategic assumption? AMERICAN PSYCHOLOGIST, 1988, 43, 822–823.

Keniston, K. Remembering Erikson at Harvard. PSYCHOLOGY TODAY, June, 1983, 29.

Kerlinger, F. N. FOUNDATIONS OF BEHAVIORAL RESEARCH, 2nd Ed. New York: Holt, Rinehart and Winston, 1973.

Kelleher, K. The afternoon of life: Jung's view of the tasks of the second half of life. PERSPECTIVES IN PSYCHIATRIC CARE, 1992, 28, 25–28.

Kern, C. W. & Watts, R. E. Adlerian counseling. Special Issue: Counselor educators' theories of counseling. TCA JOURNAL, 1993, 21, 85–95.

Kern, R. M. LIFE-STYLE SCALE. Coral Springs, FL: Communication and Motivation Training Institute, 1986.

Kierkegaard, S. FEAR AND TREMBLING, AND SICKNESS UNTO DEATH, W. Lowrie, Trans. Garden City, NY: Doubleday Anchor Books, 1954.

Kimble, G. HILGARD AND MARGUIS' CONDI-

TIONING AND LEARNING. New York: Appleton-Century-Crofts, 1961.

Kinkade, K. Commune: A Walden-Two experiment. PSYCHOLOGY TODAY, 1973, 6, 35.

Kirschenbaum, H. ON BECOMING CARL ROGERS. New York: Delacorte Press, 1979.

Kirschenbaum, H. Denigrating Carl Rogers: William Coulson's last crusade. JOURNAL OF COUNSELING & DEVELOPMENT, 1991, 69, 411–413.

Kirschenbaum, H., & Henderson, V.L. (Eds.). The Carl Rogers Readers. Boston: Houghton Mifflin, 1989.

Kishton, J. M. Contemporary Eriksonian theory: A psychobiographical illustration. GERONTOLOGY AND GERIATRICS EDUCATION, 1994, 14, 81–91.

Klein, G. PERCEPTIONS, MOTIVES AND PERSONALITY. New York: Knopf, 1970.

Klein, M. NARRATIVE OF A CHILD ANALYSIS. New York: Delta, 1961.

Klein, M. THE PSYCHOANALYSIS OF CHILDREN. London: Hogarth, 1932.

Kleinmuntz, B. PERSONALITY AND PSYCHOLOGICAL ASSESSMENT. New York: St. Martin's Press, 1982.

Kline, P. FACT AND FANTASY IN FREUDIAN THEORY. London: Methuen, 1972.

Klopfer, B., Meyer, M. M., & Brawer, F. B. (Eds.). DEVELOPMENTS IN THE RORSCHACH TECHNIQUE, vol. III. New York: Harcourt Brace Jovanovich, 1970.

Knapp, R. R. HANDBOOK FOR THE PERSONAL ORIENTATION INVENTORY. San Diego: EdITS Publishers, 1976.

Koestler, A. THE ROOTS OF COINCIDENCE. New York: Vintage, 1972.

Koffka, K. PRINCIPLES OF GESTALT PSYCHOLOGY. New York: Harcourt, 1935.

Kohlberg, L. A cognitive-developmental analysis of children's sex-role concepts and attitudes. In E.E. Maccoby (Ed.), THE DEVELOPMENT OF SEX DIFFERENCES. Stanford, CA: Stanford University Press, 1966, 82–173.

Kohlberg, L. Moral stages and moralization. In T. Lickona (Ed.), MORAL DEVELOPMENT AND BEHAVIOR-THEORY RESEARCH, AND SOCIAL ISSUES. New York: Holt, 1976, 31–53.

Kohlberg, L. THE MEANING AND MEASURE-

MENT OF MORAL DEVELOPMENT. Worchester, MA: Clark University Press, 1981.

Kohlberg. L. Stage and sequence: The cognitive-developmental approach to socialization. In D. Boslin (Ed.), HANDBOOK OF SOCIALIZATION THEORY AND RESEARCH. Chicago: Rand McNally, 1969.

Kohler, W. GESTALT PSYCHOLOGY: AN INTRODUCTION TO NEW CONCEPTS IN PSYCHOLOGY. New York: Liveright, 1947.

Kohn, A. The birth-order myth. HEALTH, (January, 1990), 34–35.

Kohut, H. THE ANALYSIS OF THE SELF. New York: International Universities Press, 1971.

Koppitz, E. M. THE BENDER GESTALT TEST FOR YOUNG CHILDREN, VOLUME II, RESEARCH AND APPLICATION, 1963–1973. New York: Grune & Stratton, 1975.

Korn, J. H., Davis, R., & Davis, S. F. Historians' and chairpersons' judgments of eminence among psychologists. AMERICAN PSYCHOLOGIST, 1991, 46, 789–792.

Kowaz, A. M. & Marcia, J. E. Development of and validation of a measure of Eriksonian industry. JOURNAL OF PERSONALITY AND SOCIAL PSYCHOLOGY, 1991, 60, 390–397.

Krane, R. & Wagner, A. Taste aversion learning with a a delayed shock US: Implications for the "generality of the laws of learning." JOURNAL OF COMPARATIVE AND PHYSIOLOGICAL PSYCHOLOGY, 1975, 88, 882–889.

Kratochwill, T. R. (Ed.). SINGLE SUBJECT RESEARCH, STRATEGIES FOR EVALUATING CHANGE. New York: Academic Press, 1978.

Kretschmer, E. PHYSIQUE AND CHARACTER, W. J. H. Spratt Trans. New York: Harcourt, 1921/1925.

Krippner, S., Achterberg, J., Bugental, J. F. T., Banathy, B., Collen, A., Jaffe, D. T., Hales, S., Kremer, J., Stigliano, A., Giorgi, A., May, R., Michael, D. N., Salner, M. Whatever happened to Scholarly discourse? A reply to B. F. Skinner. AMERICAN PSYCHOLOGIST, 1988, 43, 819.

Kroger, R. O. & Wood, L. A. Reification, "Faking," and the Big Five, AMERICAN PSYCHOLOGIST, 1993, 48, 1297–1298.

Krueger, R. F., Caspi, A., Moffitt, T. E., White, J., & Stouthamer-Loeber, M. Delay of gratification, psychopathology, and personality: Is low self-con-

trol specific to externalizing problems? JOURNAL OF PERSONALITY, 64, 1996, 107–129.

Kuhn, T. S. THE STRUCTURE OF SCIENTIFIC REVOLUTIONS. Chicago: University of Chicago Press, 1962.

Lamb, D. H. Anxiety. In H. London & J. E. Exner, Jr. (Eds.), DIMENSIONS OF PERSONALITY. New York: Wiley, 1978, 37–83.

Lamiell, J. Toward an idiothetic psychology of personality. AMERICAN PSYCHOLOGIST, 1981, 36, 276–289.

Langer, W. C. THE MIND OF ADOLPH HITLER, THE SECRET WARTIME REPORT. New York: Signet, 1972.

Las Heres, A. Psychosociology of Jung's parapsychological ability, JOURNAL OF THE SOCIETY FOR PSYCHICAL RESEARCH, 1992, 58, 189–193.

Latané, B., & Darley, J. THE UNRESPONSIVE BYSTANDER: WHY DOESN'T HE HELP? New York: Appleton-Century-Crofts. 1970.

Lattal, K. A. B. F. Skinner and Psychology: Introduction to the special issue. AMERICAN PSYCHOLOGIST, 1992, 47, 1269–1272.

Lawrence, A. The voice of Sigmund Freud, an audio tape. PSYCHOANALYTIC REVIEW, 1938.

Leak, G. K. & Gardner, L. E. Sexual attitudes, love attitudes, and social interest. INDIVIDUAL PSYCHOLOGY JOURNAL OF ADLERIAN THEORY, RESEARCH AND PRACTICE, 1990, 46, 55–60.

Leak, G. K., & Williams, D. E. Relationship between Social Interest and perceived family environment. INDIVIDUAL PSYCHOLOGY, 1989a, 45, 362–368.

Leak, G. K. & Williams, D. E. Relationship between Social Interest alienation, and psychological hardiness. INDIVIDUAL PSYCHOLOGY, 1989b, 45, 369–375.

Lebowitz, M. Religious immoralism. KENYON REVIEW, 1990 (Spring), 154–156.

Lee, D. E., & Ehrlich, H. J. Sensory alienation and interpersonal constraints as correlates of cognitive structure, PSYCHOLOGICAL REPORTS, 1977, 40, 840–842.

Lee, V. Transdermal interpretation of the subject matter of behavior analysis. AMERICAN PSYCHOLOGIST, 1992, 47, 1337–1343.

Lesser, R. M. Frommian therapeutic practice: "A few

rich hours." CONTEMPORARY PSYCHO-ANALYSIS, 1992, 28, 483–494.

Leupold–Lowenthal, H. The emigration of Freud's family. PARTISAN REVIEW, 1989, 56 (Winter), 57–64.

Leventhal, H. Findings and theory in the study of fear communications. In L. Berkowitz (Ed.), ADVANCES IN EXPERIMENTAL SOCIAL PSYCHOLOGY, Vol. 5. New York: Academic Press, 119–186.

Levine, D. Why and when to test: The social context of psychological testing. In A.I. Rabin (Ed.), ASSESSMENT WITH PROJECTIVE TECHNIQUES. New York: Springer, 1981, 265–295.

Levinson, D. THE SEASONS OF A MAN'S LIFE. New York: Knopf, 1978.

Levinson, D. THE SEASONS OF A WOMAN'S LIFE. New York: Knopf, 1996.

Levy, M. R., & Fox, H. M. Psychological testing is alive and well. PROFESSIONAL PSYCHOLOGY, 1975, 6, 420–424.

Lewin, K. PRINCIPLES OF TOPOLOGICAL PSYCHOLOGY. New York: McGraw-Hill, 1936.

Lewis, A. Problems presented by the ambiguous word 'anxiety' as used in psychopathology. In G. D. Burrows and B. Davies, (Eds.) *Handbook of Studies on Anxiety*. New York: Elsevier/North-Holland Biomedical Press, 1980, 1–15.

Liddell, H. S. The role of vigilance in the development of animal neurosis. In P. H. Hoch & J. Zubin (Eds.), ANXIETY. New York: Hafner, 1964, 183–196.

Lifton, R. J. (Ed.). EXPLORATIONS IN PSYCHOHISTORY, THE WELLFLEET PAPERS. New York: Simon & Schuster, 1974.

Lilly, J. C. THE CENTER OF THE CYCLONE. New York: Bantam, 1973.

Lilly, J. C. THE DEEP SELF. New York: Warner Books, 1977.

Linder, D., Cooper, J., & Jones, E. E. Decision freedom as a determinant of the role of incentive magnitude in attitude change. JOURNAL OF PERSONALITY AND SOCIAL PSYCHOLOGY, 1967, 6, 245–254.

Lindzey, G. L. & Aronson, E. THE HANDBOOK OF SOCIAL PSYCHOLOGY, 2nd Ed. London: Addison-Wesley Publishing, 1969.

Lindzey, G. L., & Aronson, E. THE HANDBOOK OF SOCIAL PSYCHOLOGY, 3rd Ed. New York: Random House, 1985.

Lindzey, G. L. (Ed.). THE HANDBOOK OF SOCIAL PSYCHOLOGY. London: Addison-Wesley, 1954.

Linville, P. The complexity-extremity effect and age-based stereotyping, JOURNAL OF PERSONALITY AND SOCIAL PSYCHOLOGY, 1982, 42, 293–211.

Liptzin, B. B.F. Skinner: An example of adaptive aging. JOURNAL OF GERIATRIC PSYCHIATRY, 1994, 27, 35–40.

Loehlin, J. C. R. B. Cattell and behavior genetics. MULTIVARIATE BEHAVIORAL RESEARCH, 1984, 19, 337–343.

Loehlin, J. C., Horn, J. M., & Willerman, L. Heredity, environment, and personality change: Evidence from the Texas adoption project, JOURNAL OF PERSONALITY, 1990, 58, 221–244.

Loehlin, J. C. COMPUTER MODELS OF PERSONALITY. New York: Random House, 1968.

Loftus, E. F. EYEWITNESS TESTIMONY. Cambridge, MA: Harvard University Press, 1979.

Loftus, E. F. The reality of repressed memories. AMERICAN PSYCHOLOGIST, 1993, 48, 518–537.

Lopez Ibor, J. J. Basic anxiety as the core of neuroses. In G. D. Burrows & B. Davies, (Eds.), HANDBOOK OF STUDIES ON ANXIETY. New York: Elsevier/North-Holland Biomedical Press, 1980, 17–20.

Lorenz, K. ON AGGRESSION. New York: Harcourt, Brace & World, 1966.

Lothane, Z. Special book review: A new perspective on Freud and Psychoanalysis. THE PSYCHOANALYTIC REVIEW, 1981, 68, 348–361.

Loutitt, C. M., & Browne, C. G. Psychometric instruments in psychological clinics. JOURNAL OF CONSULTING PSYCHOLOGY, 1947, 11, 49–54.

Lubin, B., Wallis, R. R., & Paine, C. Patterns of psychological test usage in the United States: 1935–1969. PROFESSIONAL PSYCHOLOGY, 1971, 2, 70–74.

Lynch, M. D., Norem-Hebeisen, A. A., & Gergen, K. J. SELF-CONCEPT, ADVANCES IN THEORY AND RESEARCH. Cambridge, MA: Ballinger, 1981.

Lynn, R. & Eysenck, H. J. Tolerance for pain, extraversion and neuroticism. PERCEPTUAL AND MOTOR SKILLS, 1961, 12, 161–162.

MacDonald, A. P., Jr. Birth order and personality. JOURNAL OF CONSULTING AND CLINICAL PSYCHOLOGY, 1971, 36, 171–176.

Maddi, S. PERSONALITY THEORIES: A COMPARATIVE ANALYSIS. Homewood, IL: Dorsey Press, 1968.

Magnus, K., Diener, E., Fujita, F., & Pavot, W. Extraversion and neuroticism as predictors of objective life events: A longitudinal analysis. JOURNAL OF PERSONALITY AND SOCIAL PSYCHOLOGY, 1993, 65, 1046–1053.

Maier, N. R. F. FRUSTRATION: THE STUDY OF BEHAVIOR WITHOUT A GOAL. New York: McGraw-Hill, 1949.

Manaster, G. J. & Perryman, T. B. MANASTER-PERRYMAN MANIFEST CONTENT EARLY RECOLLECTION SCORING MANUAL. In H. A. Olson, 1979, 347–353.

Mandler, G. & Sarason, S. B. A study of anxiety and learning, JOURNAL OF ABNORMAL AND SOCIAL PSYCHOLOGY, 1952, 47, 166–173.

Mann, L. The baiting crowd in episodes of threatened suicide. JOURNAL OF PERSONALITY AND SOCIAL PSYCHOLOGY, 1981, 41, 703–709.

Mansfield, E. D., & McAdams, D. P. Generativity and themes of agency and communion in adult autobiography. PERSONALITY AND SOCIAL PSYCHOLOGY BULLETIN, 1996, 22, 721–731.

Mariotto, M. J., & Paul, G. L. A multimethod validation of the Inpatient Multidimensional Psychiatric Scale with chronically institutionalized patients. JOURNAL OF CONSULTING AND CLINICAL PSYCHOLOGY, 1974, 42, 497–509.

Martens, R. & Landers, D. M. Motor performance under stress: A test of the inverted-U hypothesis, JOURNAL OF PERSONALITY AND SOCIAL PSYCHOLOGY, 1970, 16, 29–37.

Martin, A. R. Karen Horney's theory in today's world. AMERICAN JOURNAL OF PSYCHOLOANALYSIS, 1975, 35, 297–302.

Maslow, A. H. Resistance to acculturation. JOURNAL OF SOCIAL ISSUES, 1951, 7, 26–29.

Maslow, A. H. MOTIVATION AND PERSONALITY. New York: Harper & Row, 1954.

Maslow, A. H. Psychological data and value theory. In A. H. Maslow (Ed.), NEW KNOWLEDGE IN HUMAN VALUES. New York: Harper & Row, 1959, 119–136.

Maslow, A. H. Lessons from the peak-experiences. JOURNAL OF HUMANISTIC PSYCHOLOGY, 1962, 2, 9–18.

Maslow, A. H. EUPSYCHIAN MANAGEMENT. Homewood, IL: Dorsey Press, 1965.

Maslow, A. H. THE PSYCHOLOGY OF SCIENCE, A RECONNAISSANCE. New York: Harper & Row, 1966.

Maslow, A. H. A theory of metamotivation: The biological rooting of the value-life. JOURNAL OF HUMANISTIC PSYCHOLOGY, 1967, 7, 93–127.

Maslow, A. H. TOWARD A PSYCHOLOGY OF BEING. Princeton, NJ: D. Van Nostrand, 1968.

Maslow, A. H. Toward the study of violence. In L. Ng (Ed.), ALTERNATIVES TO VIOLENCE. New York: Time-Life Books, 1968, 34–37.

Maslow, A. H. Toward a humanistic biology. AMERICAN PSYCHOLOGIST, 1969, 24, 724–735.

Maslow, A. H. MOTIVATION AND PERSONALITY, 2nd Ed. New York: Harper & Row, 1970.

Maslow, A. H. THE FARTHER REACHES OF HUMAN NATURE. New York: Viking Press, 1971.

Maslow, B. G. (Ed.). ABRAHAM H. MASLOW: A MEMORIAL VOLUME. Monterey, CA: Brooks/Cole, 1972.

Masserman, J. H. BEHAVIOR AND NEUROSIS. Chicago: University of Chicago Press, 1943.

Massey, R. F. The philosophical compatability of Adler and Berne. INDIVIDUAL PSYCHOLOGY, 1989, 45, 323–334.

Masson, J. M. THE ASSAULT ON TRUTH. Toronto: Colins Publishers, 1984.

Mathes, E. W. FROM SURVIVAL TO THE UNIVERSE, VALUES AND PSYCHOLOGICAL WELL-BEING. Chicago: Nelson-Hall, 1981.

Mathes, E. W., Adams, H., & Daves, R. Jealousy: Loss of relationship rewards, loss of self-esteem, depression, anxiety and anger. JOURNAL OF PERSONALITY AND SOCIAL PSYCHOLOGY, 1985, 48, 1552–1556.

Mathes, E. W., Zevon, M. A., Roter, P. M., & Joerger, S. M. Peak experience tendencies: Scale development and theory testing. JOURNAL OF HUMANISTIC PSYCHOLOGY, 1982, 22, 92–108.

Matlin, M. W. & Foley, H. J. SENSATION AND PERCEPTION. Boston: Allyn & Bacon, 1992.

Matthews, G., Davies, D. R., & Lees, J. L. Arousal, extraversion, and individual differences in resource availability. JOURNAL OF PERSONALITY AND SOCIAL PSYCHOLOGY, 1990, 59, 150–168.

Matthews, G., Jones, D. M., & Chamberlin, A. G. Interactive effects of extraversion and arousal on attentional task performance: Multiple resources or encoding processes? JOURNAL OF PERSONALITY AND SOCIAL PSYCHOLOGY, 1989, 56, 629–639.

Maurer, A. Did Little Hans really want to marry his mother? JOURNAL OF HEALTH PROFESSIONS, 1964, 4, 139–148.

May, R. Contributions of existential psychotherapy. In R. May, E. Angel, & H. F. Ellenberger (Eds.), EXISTENCE, A NEW DIMENSION IN PSYCHIATRY AND PSYCHOLOGY. New York: Basic Books, 1958, 37–91.

May, R. THE MEANING OF ANXIETY. New York: Ronald Press, 1950.

May, R., Angel, E., & Ellenberger, H. F. (Eds.). EXISTENCE, A NEW DIMENSION IN PSYCHIATRY AND PSYCHOLOGY. New York: Basic Books, 1958.

McAdams, D. P., Ruetzel, K., & Foley, J. M. Complexity and generativity at mid-life: Relations among social motives, ego development, and adults' plans for the future. JOURNAL OF PERSONALITY AND SOCIAL PSYCHOLOGY, 1986, 50, 800–807.

McCelland, D. C. THE ACHIEVING SOCIETY. New York: Free Press, 1961.

McEwan, K. L. & Devins, G. M. Is increased arousal in social anxiety noticed by others? JOURNAL OF ABNORMAL PSYCHOLOGY, 1983, 92, 417–421.

McFatter, R. M. Interactions in predicting mood from extraversion and neuroticism. JOURNAL OF PERSONALITY AND SOCIAL PSYCHOLOGY, 1994, 66, 570–578.

McClatchey, L. An investigation into the uniqueness of educational psychologist competences. EDUCATIONAL AND CHILD PSYCHOLOGY, 1994, 11, 63–74.

McGrath, J. E. SOCIAL AND PSYCHOLOGICAL FACTORS IN STRESS. New York: Holt, Rinehart and Winston, 1970.

McGraw-Hill Films. PERSONALITY. New York: CRM Educational Films Collection, 1971.

McGuire, T. R. & Hirsch, J. General intelligence (g) and heritability (H^2, h^2). In I. C. Uzgiris and F. Weizmann (Eds.), THE STRUCTURING OF EXPERIENCE. New York: Plenum, 1977, 25–72.

McGuire, W. (Ed.). THE FREUD/JUNG LETTERS, R. Manheim & R. F. C. Hull, Trans. Princeton, NJ: Princeton University Press, 1974.

McGuire, W., & Hull, R. F. C. (Eds.). C. G. JUNG SPEAKING, INTERVIEWS AND ENCOUNTERS. Princeton, NJ:Princeton University Press, 1977.

McIntosh, D. The empirical bearing of psychoanalytic theory. INTERNATIONAL JOURNAL OF PSYCHO-ANALYSIS, 1979, 60, 405–431.

Mead, M. BLACKBERRY WINTER, MY EARLIER YEARS. New York: PocketBooks, 1975.

Mead, M. On Freud's view of female psychology. In J. Strouse, (Ed.), WOMEN AND ANALYSIS: DIALOGUES ON PSYCHOANALYTIC VIEWS OF FEMININITY. New York: Grossman, 1974, 95–106.

Mearns, J. Coping with a breakup: Negative mood regulation expectancies and depression following the end of a romantic relationship. JOURNAL OF PERSONALITY AND SOCIAL PSYCHOLOGY, 1991, 60, 327–334.

Meehl, P. F. Wanted—A good cookbook. AMERICAN PSYCHOLOGIST, 1956, 11, 263–272.

Meltzoff, J. & Kornreich, M. RESEARCH IN PSYCHOTHERAPY. New York: Atherton Press, 1970.

Mendelsohn, G., Weiss, D., & Feimer, N. Conceptual and empirical analysis of the typological implications of patterns of socialization and femininity. JOURNAL OF PERSONALITY AND SOCIAL PSYCHOLOGY, 1982, 42, 1157–1170.

Menninger, K. THE VITAL BALANCE, THE LIFE PROCESS IN MENTAL HEALTH AND ILLNESS. New York: Viking, 1963.

Menninger, W. C. PSYCHIATRY IN A TROUBLED WORLD. New York: Macmillan, 1948.

Merleau-Ponty, M. THE STRUCTURE OF BEHAVIOR, A. L. Fisher, Trans. Boston: Beacon Press, 1963.

Merrens, M. R., & Richards, W. S. Acceptance of generalized versus "bona fide" personality interpretation. PSYCHOLOGICAL REPORTS, 1970, 27, 691–694.

Miley, C. H. Birth order research 1963–1967: Bibliography and index. JOURNAL OF INDIVIDUAL PSYCHOLOGY, 1969, 25, 64–70.

Milgram, S. OBEDIENCE TO AUTHORITY. New York: Harper & Row, 1974.

Miller, N. The frustration-aggression hypothesis. PSYCHOLOGICAL REVIEW, 1941, 48, 337–342.

Miller, P. C., Lefcourt, H. M., Holmes, J. G., Ware, E. E., & Saleh, W. E. Marital locus of control and marital problem solving. JOURNAL OF PERSONALITY AND SOCIAL PSYCHOLOGY, 1986, 51, 161–169.

Millon, T. On the Renaissance of personality assessment and personality theory. JOURNAL OF PERSONALITY ASSESSMENT, 1984, 48, 450–466.

Mirels, H. L. & Garrett, J. B. The Protestant Ethic as a personality variable. JOURNAL OF CONSULTING AND CLINICAL PSYCHOLOGY, 1971, 36, 40–44.

Mischel, W. PERSONALITY AND ASSESSMENT. New York: Wiley, 1968.

Mischel, W. Toward a cognitive social learning reconceptualization of personality. PSYCHOLOGICAL REVIEW, 1973, 80, 252–283.

Mischel, W. On the future of personality measurement. AMERICAN PSYCHOLOGIST, 1977, 32, 246–254.

Mischel, W. Convergences and challenges in the search for consistency. AMERICAN PSYCHOLOGIST, 1984, 39, 351–364.

Mischel, W. & Ebbesen, E. Selective attention to the self: Situational and dispositional determinants. JOURNAL OF PERSONALITY AND SOCIAL PSYCHOLOGY, 1973, 27, 129–142.

Mischel, W., Ebbesen, E., & Zeiss, A. Cognitive and attentional mechanisms in delay of gratification. JOURNAL OF PERSONALITY AND SOCIAL PSYCHOLOGY, 1972, 21, 204–218.

Mischel, W. & Peake, P. Analysing the construction of consistency in personality. In M. Page & R. Dienstbier (Eds.), NEBRASKA SYMPOSIUM ON MOTIVATION, 1982: PERSONALITY—CURRENT THEORY AND RESEARCH. Lincoln: University of Nebraska Press, 1982a.

Mischel, W., & Peake, P. Beyond déjà vu in the search for cross-situatonal consistency. PSYCHOLOGICAL REVIEW, 1982b, 89, 730–733.

Mischel, W. & Shoda, Y. Personality psychology has two goals: Must it be two fields? PSYCHOLOGICAL INQUIRY, 1994, 5, 156–158.

Mischel, W. & Shoda, Y. A cognitive-affective system theory of personality: Reconceptualizing situations, dispositions, dynamics, and invariance in personality structure. PSYCHOLOGICAL REVIEW, 1995, 102, 246–268.

Mischel, W., Shoda, Y., & Rodriguez, M. L. Delay of gratification in children. SCIENCE, 1989, 933–938.

Mischel, W., Shoda, Y., & Wright, J. C. Intraindividual stability in the organization and patterning of behavior: Incorporating psychological situations into the ideographic analysis of personality. JOURNAL OF PERSONALITY AND SOCIAL PSYCHOLOGY, 1994, 67, 674–687.

Mitchell, K.M., Bozarth, J. D., & Krauft, C. C. A reappraisal of the therapeutic effectiveness of accurate empathy, nonpossessive warmth and genuineness. In A. S. Gurman and A. M. Razin (Eds.), EFFECTIVE PSYCHOTHERAPY, A HANDBOOK OF RESEARCH. New York: Pergamon, 1977, 482–499.

Mittelman, W. Maslow's study of self-actualization: A reinterpretation. JOURNAL OF HUMANISTIC PSYCHOLOGY, 1991, 31, 114–135.

Molière, J. LE BOURGEOIS GENTILHOMME. (1670) In I.A. Gregory (Ed.), THREE LAST PLAYS. New York: G.P. Putnam, 1928.

MONITOR OF THE AMERICAN PSYCHOLOGICAL ASSOCIATION, Opening addresses. 1993 (Nov.), pages 1 & 12.

Morgan, W. G. Origin and history of the Thematic Apperception Test images. JOURNAL OF PERSONALITY ASSESSMENT, 1995, 65, 237–254.

Morris, M. & Peng, K. Culture and cause: American and Chinese attributions for social and physical events. JOURNAL OF PERSONALITY AND SOCIAL PSYCHOLOGY, 1994, 67, 949–971.

Morrow, L. "I spoke . . . as a brother." TIME, 1984, 123 (2), 26–33.

Mosak, H. H. Early recollections: Evaluation of some recent research. JOURNAL OF INDIVIDUAL PSYCHOLOGY, 1969, 25, 56–63.

Mosak, H. H. & Kopp, R. R. The early recollections of Adler, Freud, and Jung. JOURNAL OF INDIVIDUAL PSYCHOLOGY, 1973, 24, 157–166.

Moss, P. D. & McEvedy, C. P. An epidemic of over-breathing among schoolgirls. BRITISH MEDICAL JOURNAL, 1966, 2, 1295–1300.

Motley, M. T. Slips of the tongue. SCIENTIFIC AMERICAN, 1985 (March) 253, 116–127.

Motley, M. T. What I mean to say. PSYCHOLOGY TODAY, (February, 1987), 24–28.

Mowrer, O. H. On the dual nature of learning—a reinterpretation of "conditioning" and "problem solving." HARVARD EDUCATIONAL REVIEW, 1947, 17,102–148.

Moxley, R. A. From mechanistic to functional behaviorism. AMERICAN PSYCHOLOGIST, 1992, 47, 1300–1311.

Mullahy, P. (Ed.). THE CONTRIBUTIONS OF HARRY STACK SULLIVAN. New York: Science House, 1952.

Mullahy, P. OEDIPUS, MYTH AND COMPLEX. New York: Grove Press, 1948.

Mullahy, P. THE BEGINNINGS OF MODERN AMERICAN PSYCHIATRY, THE IDEAS OF HARRY STACK SULLIVAN. Boston: Houghton Mifflin, 1970.

Muller, R. Karen Horney's "resigned person" heralds DSM-III-R's borderline personality disorder. COMPREHENSIVE PSYCHIATRY, 1993, 34, 264–272.

Mummendey, H., Wilk, W., & Sturm, G. Die erfassung retrospektiver selbstbildanderungen erwachsener mit der Adjektiv-beschreibungs-technik (AGT). BIELEFELDER ARBEITEN ZUR SOZIALPSYCHOLOGIE, April, 1979, 1–16.

Murray, H. A. THEMATIC APPERCEPTION TEST MANUAL. Cambridge: Harvard University Press, 1943.

Murray, H. A. EXPLORATIONS IN PERSONALITY. New York: Science Editions, 1938/1962.

Murray, H. A. Proposals for a theory of personality. In E.S. Shneidman (Ed.), ENDEAVORS IN PSYCHOLOGY: SELECTIONS FROM THE PERSONOLOGY OF HENRY A. MURRAY. New York: Harper & Row, 1981a, 125–203.

Murray, H. A. Jung: Beyond the Hour's most exacting expectation. In E. S. Shneidman (Ed.), ENDEAVORS IN PSYCHOLOGY: SELECTIONS FROM THE PERSONOLOGY OF HENRY A. MURRAY. New York: Harper & Row, 1981b, 79–81.

Murray, H. A. A note on the possible clairvoyance of dreams. In E. S. Shneidman (Ed.), ENDEAVORS IN PSYCHOLOGY: SELECTIONS FROM THE PERSONOLOGY OF HENRY A. MURRAY. New York: Harper & Row, 1981c, 563–566.

Murray, H. A. A method for investigating fantasies: The Thematic Apperception Test (with Christiana D. Morgan). In E. S. Shneidman (Ed.), ENDEAVORS IN PSYCHOLOGY: SELECTIONS FROM THE PERSONOLOGY OF HENRY A. MURRAY. New York: Harper & Row, 1981d, 390–408.

Murstein, B. I. (Ed.). HANDBOOK OF PROJECTIVE TECHNIQUES. New York: Basic Books, 1965.

Murstein, B. I. Normative written TAT responses for a college sample, JOURNAL OF PERSONALITY ASSESSMENT, 1972, 36, 109–147.

Murstein, B. I. THEORY AND RESEARCH IN PROJECTIVE TECHNIQUES: EMPHASIZING THE TAT. New York: Wiley, 1963.

Mussen, P., Conger, J., & Kagan J. CHILD DEVELOPMENT AND PERSONALITY. New York: Harper & Row, 1979.

Myers, I. B. MYERS-BRIGGS TYPE INDICATOR MANUAL. Palo Alto, CA: Consulting Psychologists Press, 1962.

Naisbett, J. MEGATRENDS. New York: Warner Books, 1984.

Nash, H. Thinking about thinking about the unthinkable, BULLETIN OF THE ATOMIC SCIENTISTS, 39 (October 1983), 39–42.

Nathan, P. E., & Harris, S. L. PSYCHOPATHOLOGY AND SOCIETY. New York: McGraw-Hill, 1975.

Nay, W. R. MULTIMETHOD CLINICAL ASSESSMENT. New York: Gardner Press, 1979.

Needleman, H. L., Leviton, A., & Bellinger, D. Lead-associated intellectual deficit. NEW ENGLAND JOURNAL OF MEDICINE, 1982, 360–367.

Neher, A. Maslow's theory of motivation: A critique. JOURNAL OF HUMANISTIC PSYCHOLOGY, 1991, 31, 89–112.

Nesselroade, J. R. Concepts of intraindividual variability and change: Impressions of Cattell's influence on lifespan developmental psychology. MULTIVARIATE BEHAVIORAL RESEARCH, 1984, 19, 269–286.

Neuman, M. Was Jung anti-Semite? SIHOTDIA-

LOGUE ISRAEL JOURNAL OF PSY-CHOTHERAPY, 1991, 5, 201–208.

Newman, L. S., Higgins, E. T., & Vookles, J. Self-guide strength and emotional vulnerability: Birth order as a moderator of self affect relations. PERSONALITY AND SOCIAL PSYCHOLOGY BULLETIN, 1992, 18, 402–411.

NEWSWEEK. Erik Erikson: The quest for identity, December 21, 1970, 84–89.

New York Times Service. Scholar denied access to Jung papers. CHICAGO TRIBUNE, 1995 (June 4)., Sec. 1, p. 6.

Nisbett, R. N. The trait construct in lay and professional psychology. In L. Festinger (Ed.), RETROSPECTIONS ON SOCIAL PSYCHOLOGY. New York: Oxford University Press, 1980.

Noll, R. THE JUNG CULT: ORIGINS OF A CHARISMATIC MOVEMENT. Princeton, NJ: Princeton University Press, 1994.

Norman, W. T. Toward an adequate taxonomy of personality attributes: Replicated factor structure in peer nomination personality ratings. JOURNAL OF ABNORMAL AND SOCIAL PSYCHOLOGY, 1963, 66, 574–583.

Norton, H. W. Blood groups and personality traits. AMERICAN JOURNAL OF HUMAN GENETICS, 1972, 23, 225–226.

Nunnally, J. C. An investigation of some propositions of self-conception: The case of Miss Sun. JOURNAL OF ABNORMAL AND SOCIAL PSYCHOLOGY, 1955, 50, 87–92.

Ochse, R. & Plug C. Cross-Cultural investigation of the validity of Erikson's theory of personality development. JOURNAL OF PERSONALITY AND SOCIAL PSYCHOLOGY, 1986, 50, 1240–1252.

O'Connor, K. P., Gareua, D., & Blowers, G. H. Changes in construals of tic-producing situations following cognitive and behavioral therapy. PERCEPTUAL AND MOTOR SKILLS, 1993, 77, 776–778.

Oliviero, P. Social communication of biological materials: Blood, semen, organs, and cadaver. CAHIERS INTERNATIONAUX de PSYCHOLOGIE SOCIALE, 1993, June (# 18), 21–51.

Olson, H. A. (Ed.). EARLY RECOLLECTIONS, THEIR USE IN DIAGNOSIS AND PSYCHOTHERAPY. Springfield, IL: Charles C. Thomas, 1979.

Orlov, A. B. Carl Rogers and contemporary humanism, JOURNAL OF RUSSIAN AND EAST EUROPEAN PSYCHOLOGY, 1992, 30, 36–41.

Ormel, J. & Schaufeli, W. B. Stability and change in psychological distress and their relationship with self-esteem and locus of control: A dynamic equilibrium model. JOURNAL OF PERSONALITY AND SOCIAL PSYCHOLOGY, 1991, 60, 288–299.

Ornduff, S. R., Freedenfeld, R. N., Kelsey, R. M., & Critelli, J. W. Object relations of sexually abused female subjects: A TAT analysis. JOURNAL OF PERSONALITY ASSESSMENT, 1994, 63, 223–238.

Osgood, C. E., Suci, G. J., and Tannenbaum, P. THE MEASUREMENT OF MEANING. Urbana, IL: University of Illinois Press, 1957.

Ozer, E. M. & Bandura, A. Mechanisms governing empowerment effects: A self-efficacy analysis. PERSONALITY AND SOCIAL PSYCHOLOGY, 1990, 472–486.

Paige, K. E. Women learn to sing the menstrual blues. PSYCHOLOGY TODAY, 1973 (Sept.), 32–37.

Palmer, D. C. & Donahoe, J. W. Essentialism and selectionism in cognitive science and behavior analysis. AMERICAN PSYCHOLOGIST, 1992, 47, 1344–1358.

Parisi, T. Why Freud failed: Some implications for neurophysiology and sociobiology. AMERICAN PSYCHOLOGIST, 1987, 42, 235–245.

Park, B., Ryan, C. S., & Judd, C. Role of meaningful subgroups in explaining differences in perceived variability for in-groups and out-groups. JOURNAL OF PERSONALITY AND SOCIAL PSYCHOLOGY, 1992, 63, 553–567.

Parrish, T. S. Examining teachers' perceptions of children's support systems. JOURNAL OF PSYCHOLOGY, 1990, 124, 113–118.

Pasley, S. The Social Readjustment Rating Scale: A study of the significance of life events in age groups ranging from college freshmen to seventh grade. Unpublished paper, Chatham College, Pittsburgh, Pennsylvania, 1969.

Patterson, C. H. The self in recent Rogerian theory. JOURNAL OF INDIVIDUAL PSYCHOLOGY, 1961, 17, 5–11.

Paunonen, S. V., Jackson, D. N., & Keinonen, M. The structured nonverbal assessment of personality. JOURNAL OF PERSONALITY, 1990, 58, 481–502.

Pavlov, I. P. CONDITIONED REFLEXES. London: Oxford, 1927.

Pavlov, I. P. EXPERIMENTAL PSYCHOLOGY. New York: Philosophical Library, 1957.

Pearl, R. A. Some dangers of using personality questionnaires to study personality. PSYCHOLOGICAL BULLETIN, 1982, 92, 572–580.

Pelham, B. W. The idiographic nature of human personality: Examples of the idiographic self-concept. JOURNAL OF PERSONALITY AND SOCIAL PSYCHOLOGY, 1993, 64, 665–677.

Pennypacker, H. S. Is behavior analysis undergoing selection by consequences? AMERICAN PSYCHOLOGIST, 1992, 47, 1491–1498.

Perls, F. S. GESTALT THERAPY VERBATIM. Lafayette, CA: Real People Press, 1969.

PEORIA JOURNAL STAR. Psychoanalyst Erik Erikson dead at 91, 1994 (May 13), C8.

Perry, H. S. PSYCHIATRIST OF AMERICA, THE LIFE OF HARRY STACK SULLIVAN. Cambridge: Harvard University Press, 1982.

Perry, W., Sprock, J., Schaible, D., McDougall, A., Minassian, A., Jenkins, M., & Braff, D. Amphetamine on Rorschach measures in normal subjects. JOURNAL OF PERSONALITY ASSESSMENT, 1995, 64, 456–465.

Pervin, L. A. Personality: Current controversies, issues, and directions. In M. R. Rosenzweig and L. W. Porter, (Eds.), ANNUAL REVIEW OF PSYCHOLOGY, 1985, 36, 83–114.

Peterson, B. E., Doty, R. M., & Winter, D. G. Authoritarianism and attitudes toward contemporary social issues. PERSONALITY AND SOCIAL PSYCHOLOGY BULLETIN, 1993, 19, 174–184.

Peterson, B. E. & Stewart, A. J. Generativity and social motives in young adults. JOURNAL OF PERSONALITY AND SOCIAL PSYCHOLOGY, 1993, 65, 186–198.

Peterson, C. & Ulrey, L. M. Can explanatory style be scored from TAT protocols? PERSONALITY AND SOCIAL PSYCHOLOGY BULLETIN, 1994, 20, 102–106.

Phares, E. Perceptual threshold decrements as a function of skill and chance expectancies. JOURNAL OF PSYCHOLOGY, 1962, 53, 399–407.

Phares, E. LOCUS OF CONTROL IN PERSONALITY. Morristown, NJ: General Learning Press, 1976.

Phares, E. J. & Lamiell, J. T. Personality. In M. R. Rosenzweig and L. W. Porter, (Eds.), ANNUAL REVIEW OF PSYCHOLOGY, 1977, 28, 113–140.

Phillips, W. M., Watkins, J. T., & Noll, G. Self-actualization, self-transcendence, and personal philosophy. JOURNAL OF HUMANISTIC PSYCHOLOGY, 1974, 14, 53–73.

Piaget, J. THE MORAL JUDGMENT OF THE CHILD. Glencoe, IL: Free Press, 1948.

Pierce, D. L., Sewell, K. W., & Cromwell, R. L. Schizophrenia and depression: Construing and constructing empirical research. In R. A. Niemeyer and G. J. Neimeyer (Eds.), ADVANCES IN PERSONAL CONSTRUCT PSYCHOLOGY vol. 2. Greenwich, CT: JAI Press, 1992.

Pistole, D. R., & Ornduff, S. R. TAT assessment of sexually abused girls: An analysis of manifest content. JOURNAL OF PERSONALITY ASSESSMENT, 1994, 63, 211–222.

Pogrebin, L. GROWING UP FREE. New York: Bantam, 1980.

Potkay, C. R. THE RORSCHACH CLINICIAN, A NEW RESEARCH APPROACH AND ITS APPLICATION. New York: Grune & Stratton, 1971.

Potkay, C. R. The role of personal history data in clinical judgment: A selective focus. JOURNAL OF PERSONALITY ASSESSMENT, 1973, 37, 203–212.

Potkay, C. R. Using the word association test "to catch a thief," PROFESSIONAL PSYCHOLOGY, 1974, 5, 446–447.

Potkay, C. R. Current issues in projective and personality assessment, in the schools. SCHOOL PSYCHOLOGY IN ILLINOIS, NEWSLETTER OF THE ILLINOIS SCHOOL PSYCHOLOGISTS ASSOCIATION, 1982, 3, 9–11.

Potkay, C. R., & Allen, B. P. The Adjective Generation Technique (AGT): Assessment via Word Descriptions of Self and Others. In C. D. Spielberger and J. N. Butcher (Eds.), ADVANCES IN PERSONALITY ASSESSMENT. Hillsdale, NJ: Lawrence Erlbaum Association, 1988.

Potkay, C. R., Allen, B. P., & Merrens, M. R. Adjective Generation Technique descriptions of Kohoutek: A comet that fizzled. Paper presented at the annual convention of the American Psychological Association, Chicago, Illinois, September, 1975.

Potkay, C. R. & Merrens, M. R. Sources of male chauvinism in the TAT. JOURNAL OF PERSONALITY ASSESSMENT, 1975, 39, 471–479.

Potkay, C. R., Merrens, M. R., & Allen B. P. AGT descriptions of TAT figures: "Loving" females more favorable than "lonely" males. Paper presented at the Annual Meeting of the Midwestern Psychological Association, Chicago, 1979.

Potkay, C. E., Potkay, C. R., Boynton, G., & Klingbeil, J. Perceptions of male and female comic strip characters using the Adjective Generation Technique (AGT). SEX ROLES, 1982, 8, 185–200.

Powell, G. E. A survey of the effects of brain lesions upon personality. In H.J. Eysenck (Ed.), A MODEL FOR PERSONALITY. New York: Springer-Verlag, 1981, 65–87.

Powell, R. A. & Boer, D. P. Did Freud mislead patients to confabulate memories of abuse? PSYCHOLOGICAL REPORTS, 1994, 74, 1283–1298.

Powell, R. A. & Boer, D. P. Did Freud misinterpret reported memories of sexual abuse as fantasies? PSYCHOLOGICAL REPORTS, 1995.

Purton, C. The person-centered Jungian. PERSON-CENTERED REVIEW, 1989, 4, 403–419.

Quinn, R. H. Confronting Carl Rogers: A developmental-interactional approach to person-centered therapy. JOURNAL OF HUMANISTIC PSYCHOLOGY, 1993, 33, 7–23.

Quinn, S. A MIND OF HER OWN: THE LIFE OF KAREN HORNEY. New York: Addison-Wesley, 1988.

Rabin, A. I. (Ed.). ASSESSMENT WITH PROJECTIVE TECHNIQUES. New York: Springer, 1981.

Rahe, R. H. Life changes and near-future illness reports. In L. Levi (Ed.), EMOTIONS—THEIR PARAMETERS AND MEASUREMENT. New York: Raven Press, 1975, 511–529.

Rank, O. WILL THERAPY AND TRUTH AND REALITY. New York: Knopf, 1945.

Raskin, R. & Shaw, R. Narcissism and the use of personal pronouns. JOURNAL OF PERSONALITY, 1988, 56, 393–404.

Ravizza, K. Peak experiences in sport. JOURNAL OF HUMANISTIC PSYCHOLOGY, 1977, 17, 35–40.

Revusky, S. & Garcia, J. Learned associations over long delays. In G. Bower (Ed.), THE PSYCHOLOGY OF LEARNING AND MOTIVATION, Vol. 4. New York: Academic Press, 1970.

Roazen, P. FREUD AND HIS FOLLOWERS. New York: Knopf, 1974.

Roazen, P. ERIK H. ERIKSON: THE POWER AND LIMITS OF A VISION. New York: Free Press, 1976.

Roback, A. A. A HISTORY OF AMERICAN PSYCHOLOGY, Rev. Ed. New York: Collier Books, 1964.

Robbins, A. D. Harry Stack Sullivan: Neo-Freudian or not? CONTEMPORARY PSYCHOANALYSIS, 1989, 25, 624–640.

Robinson, F. G. Love's story told: A life of Henry A. Murray. Cambridge, MA: Harvard University Press, 1992.

Rockwell, W. T. Beyond determinism and indignity: A reinterpretation of operant conditioning. BEHAVIOR AND PHILOSOPHY, 1994, 22, 53–66.

Rodriquez, M. L., Mischel, W., & Shoda, Y. Cognitive variables in the delay of gratification of older children at risk. JOURNAL OF PERSONALITY AND SOCIAL PSYCHOLOGY, 1989, 57, 358–367.

Rogers, C. R. COUNSELING AND PSYCHOTHERAPY, NEWER CONCEPTS IN PRACTICE. Boston: Houghton Mifflin, 1942.

Rogers, C. R. Some observations on the organization of personality. AMERICAN PSYCHOLOGIST, 1947, 2, 358–368.

Rogers, C. R. The case of Mrs. Oak: A research analysis. In C. R. Rogers and R. F. Dymond (Eds.), PSYCHOTHERAPY AND PERSONALITY CHANGE. Chicago: University of Chicago Press, 1954, 259–348.

Rogers, C. R. The necessary and sufficient conditions of therapeutic personality change. JOURNAL OF CONSULTING PSYCHOLOGY, 1957, 21, 95–103.

Rogers, C. R. A theory of therapy, personality, and interpersonal relationships, as developed in the client-centered framework. In S. Koch (Ed.), PSYCHOLOGY: A STUDY OF A SCIENCE. New York: McGraw-Hill, 1959, 184–256.

Rogers, C. R. ON BECOMING A PERSON, A THERAPIST'S VIEW OF PSYCHOTHERAPY. Boston: Houghton Mifflin, 1961.

Rogers, C. R. FREEDOM TO LEARN: A VIEW OF WHAT EDUCATION MIGHT BECOME. Columbus, OH: Charles Merrill, 1969.

Rogers, C. R. CARL ROGERS ON ENCOUNTER GROUPS. New York: Harper & Row, 1970.

Rogers, C. R. BECOMING PARTNERS: MARRIAGE AND ITS ALTERNATIVES. New York: Delacorte Press, 1972.

Rogers, C. R. My philosophy of interpersonal relationships and how it grew. JOURNAL OF HUMANISTIC PSYCHOLOGY, 1973, 13, 3–15.

Rogers, C. R. In retrospect: Forty-six years. AMERICAN PSYCHOLOGIST, 1974, 29, 115–123.

Rogers, C. R. In R. I. Evans., CARL ROGERS, THE MAN AND HIS IDEAS. New York: E. P. Dutton, 1975.

Rogers, C. R. CARL ROGERS ON PERSONAL POWER. New York: Delacorte Press, 1977.

Rogers, C. R. A WAY OF BEING. Boston: Houghton Mifflin, 1980.

Rogers, C. R. Personal communication, January 4, 1983.

Rogers, C. R. The foundations of the Person-Centered approach. EDUCATION, 1979, 100, 98–107. Reprinted in T. H. Carr and H. E. Fitzgerald (Eds.), PSYCHOLOGY 83/84. Guilford, CT: Dushkin, 1983, 227–233.

Rogers, C. R. The underlying theory: Drawn from experience with individuals and groups. COUNSELING AND VALUES, 1987a, 32, 38–46.

Rogers, C. R. Inside the world of the Soviet professional. COUNSELING AND VALUES, 1987b, 32, 66.

Rogers, C. R. Comments on the issue of equality in psychotherapy. JOURNAL OF HUMANISTIC PSYCHOLOGY, 1987C, 27, 38–39.

Rogers, C. R. Steps Toward Peace, 1948–1986: Tension reduction in theory and practice. COUNSELING AND VALUES, 1987d, 32, 12–15.

Rogers, C. R. What I learned from two research studies. In H. Krischenbaum and V. L. Henderson (Eds.), THE CARL ROGERS READER. Boston: Houghton Mifflin, 1989a.

Rogers, C. R. A psychologist looks at nuclear war. In H. Krischenbaum & V. L. Henderson (Eds.), THE CARL ROGERS READER. Boston: Houghton Mifflin, 1989b.

Rogers, C. R. & Dymond, R. F. (Eds.) PSYCHOTHERAPY AND PERSONALITY CHANGE. Chicago: University of Chicago Press, 1954.

Rogers, C. R. & Malcolm, D. The potential contribution of the behavioral scientist to world peace. COUNSELING AND VALUES, 1987, 32, 10–11.

Rogers, C. R. & Ryback, D. One alternative to nuclear planetary suicide. COUNSELING PSYCHOLOGIST, 1984, 12, 3–11.

Rogers, C. R. & Sanford, R. Reflections on our South African experience (January-February 1986). COUNSELING AND VALUES, 1987, 32, 17–20.

Rogers, R., Flores, J., Ustad, K., & Sewell, K. W. Initial validation of the Personality Assessment Inventory-Spanish Version with clients from Mexican American communities. JOURNAL OF PERSONALITY ASSESSMENT, 1995, 64, 340–348.

Rohrbaugh, J. WOMEN: PSYCHOLOGY'S PUZZLE. New York: Basic Books, 1979.

Ronan, G. F., Date, A. L., & Weisbrod, M. Personal problem-solving scoring of the TAT: Sensitivity to training. JOURNAL OF PERSONALITY ASSESSMENT, 1995, 64, 119–131.

Roodin, P. & Hoyer, W. A framework for studying moral issues in later adulthood. Paper read at the American Psychological Association Convention, Washington, D.C., 1982.

Rorer, L. G. & Widiger, T. A. Personality structure and assessment. In M. R. Rosenzweig and L. W. Porter (Eds.), ANNUAL REVIEW OF PSYCHOLOGY, 1983, 34, 431–463.

Rorschach, H. PSYCHODIAGNOSTICS, A DIAGNOSTIC TEST BASED ON PERCEPTION. New York: Grune & Stratton, 1942/1951.

Rosch, E. Principles of categorization. In E. Rosch & B. B. Lloyd (Eds.), COGNITION AND CATEGORIZATION. Hillsdale, NJ: Erlbaum, 1978.

Rosenberg, S. D., Blatt, S. J., Oxman, T. E., McHugo, G. J., & Ford, R. Q. Assessment of object relatedness through a lexical content analysis of the TAT. JOURNAL OF PERSONALITY ASSESSMENT, 1994, 63, 345–362.

Rosenhan, D. L. On being sane in insane places. SCIENCE, 1973, 179, 365–369.

Rosenhan, D. L. & Seligman, M. E. P. ABNORMAL PSYCHOLOGY. New York: Norton, 1995.

Rosenthal, R. The "file drawer problem" and tolerance for null results. PSYCHOLOGICAL BULLETIN, 1979, 86, 638–641.

Ross, L. The intuitive psychologist and his shortcomings: Distortion in the attribution process. In L. Berkowitz (Ed.), ADVANCES IN EXPERIMENTAL SOCIAL PSYCHOLOGY, Vol. 10. New York: Academic Press, 1977.

Rotter, J. SOCIAL LEARNING AND CLINICAL PSYCHOLOGY. New York: Prentice-Hall, 1954.

Rotter, J. Generalized expectancies for internal versus external control of reinforcement. PSYCHOLOGICAL MONOGRAPHS: GENERAL AND APPLIED 1966, Vol. 80, No. 1, Whole No. 609, 1–28.

Rotter, J. A new scale for the measurement of interpersonal trust. JOURNAL OF PERSONALITY, 1967, 35, 651–665.

Rotter, J. Some problems and misconceptions related to the construct of internal versus external control of reinforcement. JOURNAL OF CONSULTING AND CLINICAL PSYCHOLOGY, 1975, 43, 56–67.

Rotter, J. THE DEVELOPMENT AND APPLICATION OF SOCIAL LEARNING THEORY. New York: Praeger, 1982.

Rotter, J. Internal versus external control of reinforcement. AMERICAN PSYCHOLOGIST, 1990, 45, 489–493.

Rotter, J. Cognates of personal control: Locus of control, self-efficacy, and explanatory style. APPLIED AND PREVENTIVE PSYCHOLOGY, 1992, 1, 127–129.

Royce, J. R. & Mos, L. P. HUMANISTIC PSYCHOLOGY, CONCEPTS AND CRITICISMS. New York: Plenum, 1981.

Rubin, T. I. Horney, here and now: 1991, Special Issue: (Karen Horney). AMERICAN JOURNAL OF PSYCHOANALYSIS, 1991, 51, 313–318.

Ruble, D. N. Premenstrual symptoms: A reinterpretation. SCIENCE, 1977, 197, 291–292.

Rudman, F. W. & Ansbacher, H. L. Anti-war psychologists: Alfred Adler. PSYCHOLOGISTS FOR SOCIAL RESPONSIBILITY NEWSLETTER, 1989, 8(#4), 8.

Ryan, R. M. & Grolnick, W. S. Origins and pawns in the classroom: Self-report and projective assessments of individual differences in children's perceptions. JOURNAL OF PERSONALITY AND SOCIAL PSYCHOLOGY, 1986, 50, 550–558.

Rychlak, J. F. A PHILOSOPHY OF SCIENCE FOR PERSONALITY THEORY. Boston: Houghton Mifflin, 1968.

Rychlak, J. F. Is a concept of "self" necessary in psychological theory? In A. Wandersman, P. Poppen, and D. Ricks (Eds.), HUMANISM AND BEHAVIORISM: DIALOGUE AND GROWTH. New York: Pergamon, 1976, 121–143.

Rychlak, J. F. INTRODUCTION TO PERSONALITY AND PSYCHOTHERAPY. Boston: Houghton Mifflin, 1981.

Ryckman, R. M., Thornton, B., & Butler, J. C. Personality correlates of the Hypercompetitive Attitude Scale: Validity tests of Horney's theory of neurosis. JOURNAL OF PERSONALITY ASSESSMENT, 1994, 62, 84–94.

Sabatelli, R., Buck, R., & Dreyer, A. Locus of control, interpersonal trust, and nonverbal communication accuracy. JOURNAL OF PERSONALITY AND SOCIAL PSYCHOLOGY, 1983, 44, 399–409.

Sagan, C. Where did TV come from? PARADE MAGAZINE, 1995 (Sept. 17), 10 & 12.

Salzinger, K. B. F. Skinner (1904–1990), OBSERVER (of the American Psychological Society) (September 3, 1990), 1, 3, & 4.

Samuels, A. New material concerning Jung, anti-Semitism, and the Nazis. JOURNAL OF ANALYTICAL PSYCHOLOGY, 1993, 38, 463–470.

Sanitioso, R., Kunda, Z., & Fong, G. T. Motivated recruitment of biographical memories. JOURNAL OF PERSONALITY AND SOCIAL PSYCHOLOGY, 1990, 59, 229–241.

Sanna L. J. & Pusecker, P. A. Self-efficacy, valence of self-evaluation, and performance. PERSONALITY AND SOCIAL PSYCHOLOGY BULLETIN, 1994, 20, 82–92.

Sapir, E. LANGUAGE, AN INTRODUCTION TO THE STUDY OF SPEECH. New York: Harcourt, Brace and Company, 1921.

Sarason, I. G. Anxiety and self-preoccupation. In C. D. Speilberger and I. G. Sarason (Eds.), STRESS AND ANXIETY, Vol. 2. New York: Wiley, 1975, 27–44.

Sarason, I. G., Smith, R. E., & Diener, E. Personality research: Components of variance attributed to the person and the situation. JOURNAL OF PERSONALITY AND SOCIAL PSYCHOLOGY, 1975, 32, 199–204.

Sarbin, T. Metaphorical encounters of the fourth kind.

Paper presented at the American Psychological Association Convention, Washington, D.C., 1982.

Sartre, J-P. BEING AND NOTHINGNESS, AN ESSAY ON PHENOMENOLOGICAL ONTOLOGY, H. Barnes, Trans. New York: Philosophical Library, 1956.

Sartre, J-P. EXISTENTIALISM AND HUMAN EMOTIONS. New York: Philosophical Library, 1957.

Scarr, S., Webber, P., Weinberg, R., & Wittig, M. Personality resemblance among adolescents and their parents in biologically related and adoptive families. JOURNAL OF PERSONALITY AND SOCIAL PSYCHOLOGY, 1981, 40, 885–898.

Schafer, R. A NEW LANGUAGE FOR PSYCHOANALYSIS. New Haven: Yale University Press, 1976.

Schlinger, H. D. Theory in behavior analysis: An application to child development. AMERICAN PSYCHOLOGIST, 1992, 47, 1396–1410.

Schmitz, B. & Skinner, E. Perceived control, effort, and academic performance: Interindividual, intraindividual, and multivariate time-series analyses. JOURNAL OF PERSONALITY AND SOCIAL PSYCHOLOGY, 1993, 64, 1010–1028.

Schooler, C. Birth order effects: Not here, not now! PSYCHOLOGICAL BULLETIN, 1972, 78, 161–175.

Schroeder, D. J. & Pendleton, M. G. The adjective generation technique: Consistency of self-description in psychiatric patients. JOURNAL OF PERSONALITY, 1983, 51, 631–639.

Schwartz, B. PSYCHOLOGY OF LEARNING AND BEHAVIOR. New York: Norton, 1978.

Sears, R. R. STUDIES IN PERSONALITY. New York: McGraw-Hill, 1942.

Sears, R. R. SURVEY OF OBJECTIVE STUDIES OF PSYCHOANALYTIC CONCEPTS. Bulletin 51. New York: Social Science Research Council, 1943.

Sechrest, L. & Jackson, D. N. Social intelligence and accuracy of interpersonal predictions. JOURNAL OF PERSONALITY, 1961, 29, 167–182.

Seligman, M. E. P. HELPLESSNESS: ON DEPRESSION, DEVELOPMENT, AND DEATH. San Francisco: Freeman, 1975.

Seligman, M. E. P. On the generality of the laws of learning. PSYCHOLOGICAL REVIEW, 1970, 77, 406–418.

Selye, H. THE STRESS OF LIFE, Rev. Ed. New York: McGraw-Hill, 1978.

Sethi, S. & Seligman, M. E. P. Optimism and fundamentalism. PSYCHOLOGICAL SCIENCE, 1993, 4, 256–260.

Shadle, W. G. & Cervone, D. The Big Five versus nobody? AMERICAN PSYCHOLOGIST, 1993, 48, 1300–1302.

Shafter, R. Women and masochism: An introduction to trends in psychoanalytic thinking. ISSUES IN EGO PSYCHOLOGY, 1992, 15, 56–62.

Shaver, P. & Hazan, C. Being lonely and falling in love: Perspectives from attachment theory. In M. Hojat & R. Crandall (Eds.), Loneliness: theory, research and applications, a special issue of JOURNAL OF SOCIAL BEHAVIOR AND PERSONALITY, 1987, 2(2, Pt. 2), 105.

Shaver, P. Being lonely, falling in love: Perspectives from attachment theory, 1986 (August). Paper presented at the American Psychological Association Convention, Washington, D.C.

Sheehy, G. PASSAGES. New York: Bantam, 1977.

Sheldon, W. H. THE VARIETIES OF HUMAN PHYSIQUE: AN INTRODUCTION TO CONSTITUTIONAL PSYCHOLOGY. New York: Harper, 1940.

Shelley, M. W. FRANKENSTEIN: A MODERN PROMETHEUS. New York: Dell, 1965.

Sherrill, C., Gench, B., Hinson, M., Gilstrap, T., Richir, K., & Mastro, J. Self-actualization of elite blind athletes: An exploratory study. JOURNAL OF VISUAL IMPAIRMENT & BLINDNESS, 1990, 84, 55–60.

Shirer, W. L. THE RISE AND FALL OF THE THIRD REICH. Greenwich, CT: Fawcett Crest, 1960.

Shlien, J. M. Phenomenology and personality. In J. T. Hart and T. M. Tomlinson (Eds.), NEW DIRECTIONS IN CLIENT-CENTERED THERAPY. Boston: Houghton Mifflin, 1970, 95–128.

Shlien, J. M. & Zimring, F. M. Research directives and methods in client-centered therapy. In J. T. Hart and T. M. Tomlinson (Eds.), NEW DIRECTIONS IN CLIENT-CENTERED THERAPY. Boston: Houghton Mifflin, 1970, 33–57.

Shneidman, E. S., Farberow, N. L., & Litman, R. E. THE PSYCHOLOGY OF SUICIDE. New York: Science House, 1970.

Shoda, Y. & Mischel, W. Cognitive social approach to dispositional inferences: What if the perceiver is a cognitive social theorist? PERSONALITY AND SOCIAL PSYCHOLOGY BULLETIN, 1993, 19, 574–585.

Shoda, Y., Mischel, W., & Peake, P. K. Predicting adolescent cognitive and self-regulatory competencies from preschool delay of gratification: Identifying diagnostic conditions. DEVELOPMENTAL PSYCHOLOGY, 1990, 26, 978–986.

Shoda, Y., Mischel, W., & Wright, J. C. Intuitive interactionism in person perception: Effects of situation-behavior relations on dispositional judgments. JOURNAL OF PERSONALITY AND SOCIAL PSYCHOLOGY, 1989, 56, 41–53.

Shoda, Y., Mischel, W., & Wright, J. S. The role of situational demands and cognitive competencies in behavior organization and personality coherence. JOURNAL OF PERSONALITY AND SOCIAL PSYCHOLOGY, 1993, 65, 1023–1035.

Shostrom, E. FREEDOM TO BE, EXPERIENCING AND EXPRESSING YOUR TOTAL BEING. New York: Bantam, 1972.

Shostrom, E. L. (Ed.). THREE APPROACHES TO PSYCHOTHERAPY: ROGERS, PERLS AND ELLIS. Orange, CA: Psychological Films, 1965.

Shostrom, E. L. EITS MANUAL FOR THE PERSONAL ORIENTATION INVENTORY. San Diego: Educational and Industrial Testing Service, 1966.

Signell, K. Cognitive complexity in person perception and nation perception: A developmental approach. JOURNAL OF PERSONALITY, 1966, 34, 517–537.

Silva-Garcia, J. Fromm in Mexico: 1950–1973. CONTEMPORARY PSYCHOANALYSIS, 1989, 25, 244–257.

Silverman, L. An experimental technique for the study of unconscious conflict. BRITISH JOURNAL OF MEDICAL PSYCHOLOGY, 1971, 44, 17–25.

Silverman, L. Psychoanalytic theory: "The reports of my death are greatly exaggerated." AMERICAN PSYCHOLOGIST, 1976, 31, 621–637.

Simonton, O. C. & Simonton, S. Belief systems and management of the emotional aspects of malignancy. JOURNAL OF TRANSPERSONAL PSYCHOLOGY, 1975, 7, 29–48.

Simpson, P. W., Bloom, J. W., Newlon, B. J., & Arminio, L. Birth order proportions of the general population in the United States. INDIVIDUAL PSYCHOLOGY JOURNAL OF ADLERIAN THEORY, RESEARCH AND PRACTICE, 1994, 50, 173–182.

Singer, J. A. Affective responses to aubiographical memories and their relationship to long-term goals. JOURNAL OF PERSONALITY, 1990, 58, 535–563.

Singer, J. ANDROGENY, TOWARD A NEW THEORY OF SEXUALITY. Garden City, NY: Anchor Books, 1977.

Singer, J. L. & Singer, D. G. Personality. In P. H. Mussen & M. R. Rosenzweig (Eds.), ANNUAL REVIEW OF PSYCHOLOGY, 1972, 23, 375–412.

Skinner, B. F. WALDEN TWO. New York: McMillan, 1948.

Skinner, B. F. VERBAL BEHAVIOR. New York: Appleton-Century-Crofts, 1957.

Skinner, B. F. BEYOND FREEDOM AND DIGNITY. New York: Knopf, 1971.

Skinner, B. F. (Ed.). CUMULATIVE RECORD: A SELECTION OF PAPERS, THIRD EDITION. New York: Appleton-Century-Crofts, 1972.

Skinner, B. F. A lecture on "having" a poem. In B. Skinner (Ed.), CUMULATIVE RECORD : A SELECTION OF PAPERS, THIRD EDITION. New York: Appleton-Century-Crofts, 1972a, 345–358.

Skinner, B. F. The design of cultures. In B. Skinner (Ed.), CUMULATIVE RECORD: A SELECTION OF PAPERS, THIRD EDITION. New York: Appleton-Century-crofts, 1972b, 39–50.

Skinner, B. F. Creating the creative artist. In B. Skinner (Ed.), CUMULATIVE RECORD: A SELECTION OF PAPERS, THIRD EDITION. New York: Appleton-Century-Crofts, 1972c, 333–344.

Skinner, B. F. Freedom and the control of men. In B. Skinner (Ed.), CUMULATIVE RECORD: A SELECTION OF PAPERS, THIRD EDITION. New York: Appleton-Century-Crofts, 1972d, 3–24.

Skinner, B. F. The operational analysis of psychological terms. In B. Skinner (Ed.), CUMULATIVE RECORD: A SELECTION OF PAPERS, THIRD EDITION. New York: Appleton-Century-Crofts, 1972e, 370–384.

Skinner, B. F. Baby in a box. In B. Skinner (Ed.), CUMULATIVE RECORD: A SELECTION OF PAPERS, THIRD EDITION. New York: Appleton-Century-Crofts, 1972f, 567–573.

Skinner, B. F. "Superstition" in the pigeon. In B. Skinner (Ed.), CUMULATIVE RECORD: A SELECTION OF PAPERS, THIRD EDITION. New York: Appleton-Century-Crofts, 1972g, 236–256.

Skinner, B. F. Some relations between behavior modification and basic research. In B. Skinner (Ed.), CUMULATIVE RECORD: A SELECTION OF PAPERS, THIRD EDITION. New York: Appleton-Century-Crofts, 1972h, 276–282.

Skinner, B. F. What is psychotic behavior? In B. Skinner (Ed.), CUMULATIVE RECORD: A SELECTION OF PAPERS, THIRD EDITION. New York: Appleton-Century-Crofts, 1972i, 257–275.

Skinner, B. F. Reflection on a decade of teaching machines. In B. Skinner (Ed.), CUMULATIVE RECORD: A SELECTION OF PAPERS, THIRD EDITION. New York: Appleton-Century-Crofts, 1972j, 194–207.

Skinner, B. F. Contingency management in the classroom. In B. Skinner (Ed.), CUMULATIVE RECORD: A SELECTION OF PAPERS, THIRD EDITION. New York: Appleton-Century-Crofts, 1972k, 225–235.

Skinner, B. F. Why we need teaching machines. In B. Skinner (Ed.), CUMULATIVE RECORD: A SELECTION OF PAPERS, THIRD EDITION. New York: Appleton-Century-Crofts, 1972l, 171–193.

Skinner, B. F. PARTICULARS OF MY LIFE. New York: Knopf, 1976a.

Skinner, B. F. ABOUT BEHAVIORISM. New York: Vintage Books, 1976b.

Skinner, B. F. THE SHAPING OF A BEHAVIORIST. New York: Knopf, 1979.

Skinner, B. F. Orgins of a behaviorist. PSYCHOLOGY TODAY, September, 1983a.

Skinner, B. F. A MATTER OF CONSEQUENCES. New York: Knopf, 1983b.

Skinner, B. F. UPON FURTHER REFLECTION. Englewood Cliffs,NJ: Prentice-Hall, 1987a.

Skinner, B. F. Whatever happened to psychology as the science of behavior? AMERICAN PSYCHOLOGIST, 1987b, 42, 780–786.

Skinner, B. F. The origins of cognitive thought. AMERICAN PSYCHOLOGIST., 1989, 44, 13–18.

Skinner, B. F. & Vaughan, M. E. ENJOY OLD AGE. New York: Norton, 1983.

Smith, B. On self-actualization: A transambivalent examination of a focal theme in Maslow's psychology. JOURNAL OF HUMANISTIC PSYCHOLOGY, 1973, 13, 17–33.

Smith, M. B. & Anderson, J. W. Henry A. Murray (1893–1988). AMERICAN PSYCHOLOGIST, 1989, 44, 153–154.

Smith, M. L. & Glass, G. V. Meta-analysis of psychotherapy outcome studies. AMERICAN PSYCHOLOGIST, 1977, 32, 752–760.

Smith, S. L. Extraversion and sensory threshold. PSYCHOPHYSIOLOGY, 1968, 5, 293–299.

Snyder, M. & Monson, T. Persons, situations, and the control of social behavior. JOURNAL OF PERSONALITY AND SOCIAL PSYCHOLOGY, 1975, 32, 637–644.

Snyder, M. The self-monitoring of expressive behavior. JOURNAL OF PERSONALITY AND SOCIAL PSYCHOLOGY, 1974, 30, 526–537.

Solomon, R. & Wynne, L. Traumatic avoidance learning: Acquisition in normal dogs. PSYCHOLOGICAL MONOGRAPHS, 1953, 67, No. 354, 19.

Spearman, C. ABILITIES OF MAN. New York: Macmillan, 1927.

Spearman, C. "General intelligence" objectively determined and measured. AMERICAN JOURNAL OF PSYCHOLOGY, 1904, 15, 201–293.

Speer, A. INSIDE THE THIRD REICH. New York: Avon, 1970.

Spence, J. T. (Ed.). ACHIEVEMENT AND ACHIEVEMENT MOTIVES, PSYCHOLOGICAL AND SOCIOLOGICAL APPROACHES. San Francisco: W.H. Freeman, 1983.

Spence, K. W. A theory of emotionally based drive (D) and its relation to performance in simple learning situations. AMERICAN PSYCHOLOGIST, 1958, 13, 131–141.

Spence, K. W. Anxiety (drive) level and performance in eyelid conditioning. PSYCHOLOGICAL BULLETIN, 1964, 61, 129–139.

Spence, K. W. BEHAVIOR THEORY AND CONDITIONING. New Haven: Yale University Press, 1956.

Spielberger, C. D. (Ed.). ANXIETY, CURRENT TRENDS IN THEORY AND RESEARCH, Vol. 1. New York: Academic Press, 1972.

Spielberger, C. D. Anxiety: State-trait-process. In C. D. Speilberger & I. G. Sarason (Eds.), STRESS AND ANXIETY, Vol. 1. New York: Wiley, 1975, 115–143.

Spielberger, C. D., Gorsuch, R. L., & Lushene, R.E. MANUAL FOR THE STATE-TRAIT ANXIETY INVENTORY. Palo Alto, CA: Consulting Psychologists Press, 1970.

Spitz, R. A. Hospitalism: An inquiry into the genesis of psychotic conditions in early chldhood. In PSYCHOANALYTIC STUDY OF THE CHILD, Vol. II. New York: International Universities Press, 1946.

Spivack, G., & Levine, M. The Devereux Child Behavior Rating Scales: A study of symptom behaviors in latency age atypical children, AMERICAN JOURNAL OF MENTAL DEFICIENCY, 1964, 68, 700–717.

Standal, S. The need for positive regard: A contribution to client-centered theory. Unpublished doctoral dissertation, University of Chicago, 1954.

Stanovich, K. E. HOW TO THINK STRAIGHT ABOUT PSYCHOLOGY, 2nd ed. Glenview, IL: Scott, Foresman, 1989.

Station WQED, Pittsburgh. BECAUSE THAT'S MY WAY. (film) Lincoln: GPI Television Library, University of Nebraska, 1971.

Steinem, G. Womb envy, testyria, and breast castration anxiety. MS., 1994 (March/April), 49–56.

Stelmack, R. M. Biological bases of extraversion: Psychophysiological evidence. JOURNAL OF PERSONALITY, 1990, 58, 291–311.

Stepansky, P. E. IN FREUD'S SHADOW, ADLER IN CONTEXT. Hillsdale, NJ: Erlbaum, 1983.

Stephenson, W. THE STUDY OF BEHAVIOR. Chicago: University of Chicago Press, 1953.

Steele, R. S. Freud and Jung: Conflicts of Interpretation. London: Routledge, 1982.

Stern, P. J. C. G. JUNG, THE HAUNTED PROPHET. New York: Delta, 1976.

Sternberg, R. J. THE TRIARCHIC MIND: A NEW THEORY OF HUMAN INTELLIGENCE. New York: Viking, 1988.

Stevens, R. ERIK ERIKSON: AN INTRODUCTION. New York: St. Martin's Press, 1983.

Stokes, D. Chance can play key role in life, psychologist says. CAMPUS (Stanford University), 1986a (June 4), (Profile).

Stokes, D. It's no time to shun psychologists, Bandura says. CAMPUS (Stanford University), 1986b (June 11), (Profile).

Stolorow, R. D. & Atwood, G. E. FACES IN A CLOUD, SUBJECTIVITY IN PERSONALITY THEORY. New York: Jason Aronson, 1979.

Stuttaford, G. Review of "Freud on women: A reader" by Elisabeth Young–Bruehl. PUBLISHER'S WEEKLY, 237 (June), 1990, 54.

Sullivan, H. S. CONCEPTIONS OF MODERN PSYCHIATRY. New York: Norton, 1947.

Sullivan, H. S. PERSONAL PSYCHOPATHOLOGY. New York: Norton, 1972.

Sullivan, H. S. SCHIZOPHRENIA AS A HUMAN PROCESS. New York: Norton, 1962.

Sullivan, H. S. THE INTERPERSONAL THEORY OF PSYCHIATRY. (H.S. Perry & M.L. Gawel, Eds.) New York: Norton, 1953.

Sullivan, H. S. THE PSYCHIATRIC INTERVIEW. (H. S. Perry & M. L. Gawel, Eds.) New York: Norton, 1954.

Sullivan, H. S. The onset of schizophrenia. AMERICAN JOURNAL OF PSYCHIATRY, 1994 (1927), 151, (6, supplement), 135–139.

Sundberg, N. D. ASSESSMENT OF PERSONS. Englewood Cliffs, NJ: Prentice-Hall, 1977.

Sundberg, N. D. The practice of psychological testing in clinical services in the United States. AMERICAN PSYCHOLOGIST, 1961, 16, 79–83.

Sundberg, N. D., & Tyler, L. E. CLINICAL PSYCHOLOGY: AN INTRODUCTION TO RESEARCH AND PRACTICE. New York: Appleton-Century-Crofts, 1962.

Suomi, S. J. & Harlow, H. F. Social rehabilitation of isolate-reared monkeys, DEVELOPMENTAL PSYCHOLOGY, 1972, 6, 487–496.

Suomi, S. J., Collins, M. L., Harlow, H. F., & Ruppenthal, G. C. Effects of maternal and peer separations on young monkeys. JOURNAL OF CHILD PSYCHOLOGY AND PSYCHIATRY, 1976, 17, 101–112.

Super, D. E. Comment on Carl Rogers' Obituary. AMERICAN PSYCHOLOGIST, 1989, 44, 1162–1163.

Sutich, A. J. Transpersonal psychology: An emerging force. JOURNAL OF HUMANISTIC PSYCHOLOGY, 1968, 7, 77–78.

Suzuki, D. T. AN INTRODUCTION TO ZEN BUDDHISM. New York: Causeway, 1974.

Symonds, A. Gender issues and Horney's theory. Special Issue: (Karen Horney). AMERICAN JOURNAL OF PSYCHOANALYSIS, 1991, 51, 301–312.

Szasz, T. S. LAW, LIBERTY AND PSYCHIATRY. New York: Macmillan, 1963.

Szasz, T. S. The myth of mental illness. AMERICAN PSYCHOLOGIST, 1960, 15, 113–118.

Szent-Gyoergyi, A. Drive in living matter to perfect itself. SYNTHESIS, 1974, 12–24.

Tanner, O. STRESS. New York: Time-Life Books, 1976.

Taylor, J. A. The relationship of anxiety to the conditioned eyelid response. JOURNAL OF EXPERIMENTAL PSYCHOLOGY, 1951, 41, 81–92.

Taylor, J. A. A personality scale of manifest anxiety. JOURNAL OF ABNORMAL AND SOCIAL PSYCHOLOGY, 1953, 48, 285–290.

Taylor, J. A. Drive theory and manifest anxiety. PSYCHOLOGICAL BULLETIN, 1956, 53, 303–320.

Taylor, M. & Hall, J. Psychological androgyny: Theories, methods, and conclusions. PSYCHOLOGICAL BULLETIN, 1982, 92, 347–366.

Taylor, S. E. Adjustment to threatening events: A theory of cognitive adaptation. AMERICAN PSYCHOLOGIST, 1983, 38, 1161–1173.

Tetlock, P. E., Armor, D., & Peterson, R. S. The slavery debate in antebellum America: Cognitive style, value conflict, and the limits of compromise. JOURNAL OF PERSONALITY AND SOCIAL PSYCHOLOGY, 1994, 66, 115–126.

Tetlock, P. E., Peterson, R. S., & Berry, J. M. Flattering and unflattering personality portraits of integratively simple and complex managers. JOURNAL OF PERSONALITY AND SOCIAL PSYCHOLOGY, 1993, 64, 500–511.

Teplov, B. M. Problems in the study of general types of higher nervous activity in man and animals. In J. A. Gray (Ed.), PAVLOV'S TYPOLOGY. New York: Pergamon Press, 1964, 3–153.

Thompson, G. George Alexander Kelly (1905–1967). JOURNAL OF GENERAL PSYCHOLOGY, 1968, 79, 19–24.

Thorne, B. Carl Rogers and the doctrine of original sin. Special Issue: Fiftieth anniversary of the person-centered approach. PERSON CENTERED REVIEW, 1990, 5, 394–405.

Thorne, F. C. CLINICAL JUDGMENT, A STUDY OF CLINICAL ERRORS. Brandon, VT: Journal of Clinical Psychology, 1961.

Thunedborg, K., Allerup, P., Bech, P., & Joyce, C. R. Development of the Repertory Grid for measurement of individual quality of life in clinical trials. INTERNATIONAL JOURNAL OF METHODS IN PSYCHIATRIC RESEARCH, 1993, 3, 45–56.

Thurstone, L. L. Primary mental abilities. PSYCHOMETRIC MONOGRAPHS, 1938, No. 1.

Tillich, P. THE COURAGE TO BE. New Haven: Yale University Press, 1952.

TIME. In the dock, The Popieluszko trial begins. January 7, 1985, 72.

Timnick, L. Chowchilla's kidnapped kids—Five years later. In Chicago SUNDAY SUN-TIMES, January 25, 1981, p. 52.

Todd, J. T. & Morris, E. K. Case histories in the great power of steady misrepresentation. AMERICAN PSYCHOLOGIST, 1992, 47, 1441–1453.

Toffler, A. FUTURE SHOCK. New York: Random House, 1970.

Toland, J. ADOLF HITLER. New York: Ballantine Books, 1976.

Tomkins, S. S., and Izard, C. E. AFFECT, COGNITION AND PERSONALITY. New York: Springer, 1965.

Tosi, D. J. & Hoffman, S. A factor analysis of the Personal Orientation Inventory. JOURNAL OF HUMANISTIC PSYCHOLOGY, 1972, 12, 86–93.

Triandis, H., Loh, W., & Levine, L. Race, status, quality of spoken English, and opinion about civil rights as determinants of interpersonal attitudes. JOURNAL OF PERSONALITY AND SOCIAL PSYCHOLOGY, 1966, 3, 468–472.

Truax, C. B., & Carkhuff, R. R. TOWARD EFFECTIVE COUNSELING AND PSYCHOTHERAPY: TRAINING AND PRACTICE. Chicago: Aldine, 1967.

Truax, C. B., & Mitchell, K. M. Research on certain therapist interpersonal skills in relation to process and outcome. In A. E. Bergin and S. L. Garfield. (Eds.) HANDBOOK OF PSYCHOTHERAPY AND BEHAVIOR CHANGE: AN EMPIRICAL ANALYSIS. New York: Wiley, 1971, 299–344.

Tucibat, J. The effect of similarity of a braggart on self-esteem. Unpublished Masters Thesis, Department of Psychology, Western Illinois University, 1986.

Tudge, J. R. H. & Winterhoff, P. A. Vygotsky, Piaget, and Bandura: Perspectives on the relations between the social world and cognitive development. HUMAN DEVELOPMENT, 1993, 36, 61–81.

Turco, R., Toon, T., Ackerman, T., Pollack, J., & Sagan, C. Nuclear winter: Global consequences of multiple nuclear explosions. SCIENCE, 1983, 222, 1283–1292.

Tyler, K. The ecosystemic approach to personality. EDUCATIONAL PSYCHOLOGY, 1994, 14, 45–58.

Uhlemann, M. R., Lee, D. Y., & Hasse, R. F. The effects of cognitive complexity and arousal on client perception of counselor nonverbal behavior. JOURNAL OF CLINICAL PSYCHOLOGY, 1989, 45, 661–664.

Ullmann, L. & Krasner, L. (Eds.). CASE STUDIES IN BEHAVIOR MODIFICATION. New York: Holt, Rinehart and Winston, 1965.

Ulrich, R. E., Stachnik, T. J., & Stainton, N. R. Student acceptance of generalized personality interpretations. PSYCHOLOGICAL REPORTS, 1963, 20, 831–834.

Vaihinger, H. THE PHILOSOPHY OF 'AS IF': A SYSTEM OF THE THEORETICAL, PRACTICAL AND RELIGIOUS FICTIONS OF MANKIND. New York: Harcourt, Brace, 1925.

Valins, S. & Nisbett, R. ATTRIBUTION PROCESSES IN THE DEVELOPMENT AND TREATMENT OF EMOTIONAL DISORDERS. Morristown, NJ: General Learning Press, 1971.

VandeWoude, S., Richt, J. A., Zink, M. C., Rott, R., Narayan, O., & Clements J. E. A borna virus cDNA encoding a protein recognized by antibodies in humans with behavioral diseases. SCIENCE, 1990, 250, 1278–1281.

Van Kaam, A. Existential psychology as a comprehensive theory of personality, REVIEW OF EXISTENTIAL PSYCHOLOGY AND PSYCHIATRY, 1963, 3, 11–26.

Van Kaam, A. Existential and humanistic psychology. REVIEW OF EXISTENTIAL PSYCHOLOGY AND PSYCHIATRY, 1965, 5, 291–296.

Van Kaam, A. EXISTENTIAL FOUNDATIONS OF PSYCHOLOGY. New York: Image Books, 1969.

Viken, R. J., Rose, R. J., Kaprio, J., & Koskenvuo, M. A developmental genetic analysis of adult personality: Extraversion and neuroticism from 18 to 59 years of age. JOURNAL OF PERSONALITY AND SOCIAL PSYCHOLOGY, 1994, 66, 722–730.

Viney, L. L., Benjamin, Y. N., & Preston, C. Mourning and reminiscence: Parallel psychotherapeutic processes for elderly people. INTERNATIONAL JOURNAL OF AGING AND HUMAN DEVELOPMENT, 1989, 28, 239–249.

Vinokur, A. & Selzer, M. L. Desirable versus undesirable life events: Their relationship to stress and mental distress. JOURNAL OF PERSONALITY AND SOCIAL PSYCHOLOGY, 1975, 32, 329–337.

Vockell, E. L., Felker, D. W., & Miley, C. H. Birth order literature 1967–1971: Bibliography and index. JOURNAL OF INDIVIDUAL PSYCHOLOGY, 1973, 29, 39–53.

Wade, T. C., & Baker, T. B. Opinions and use of psychological tests: A survey of clinical psychologists. AMERICAN PSYCHOLOGIST, 1977, 32, 874–882.

Wallace, J. An abilities conception of personality: Some implications for personality measurement. AMERICAN PSYCHOLOGIST, 1966, 21, 132–138.

Watkins, C. E. Adlerian-oriented early memory research: What does it tell us? JOURNAL OF PERSONALITY ASSESSMENT, 1992, 59, 248–263.

Watkins, M. M. WAKING DREAMS. New York: Harper Colophon Books, 1976.

Watson, D. L., & Tharp, R. G. SELF-DIRECTED BEHAVIOR, SELF-MODIFICATION FOR PERSONAL ADJUSTMENT, 2nd ed. Monterey, CA: Brooks/Cole, 1977.

Watson, J. BEHAVIORISM. Chicago: University of Chicago Press, 1930.

Watson, J. & Rayner, R. Conditioned emotional reactions. JOURNAL OF EXPERIMENTAL PSYCHOLOGY, 1920, 3, 1–14.

Watts, A. PSYCHOTHERAPY EAST AND WEST. New York: Pantheon, 1961.

Watts, R. E. & Holden, J. M. Why continue to use "fictional finalism"? INDIVIDUAL PSYCHOLOGY, 1994, 50, 161–163.

Weber, M. THE PROTESTANT ETHIC AND THE SPIRIT OF CAPITALISM, T. Parsons, Trans. New York: Scribner's, 1904/1930.

Wehr, G. AN ILLUSTRATED BIOGRAPHY OF C. G. JUNG. Boston: Shambhala, 1989.

Weinberger, D. A., Schwartz, G. E. & Davidson, R. J. Low-anxious, high-anxious and repressive coping styles: Psychometric patterns and behavioral and physiological responses to stress. JOURNAL OF ABNORMAL PSYCHOLOGY, 1979, 88, 369–380.

Weiss, D., Mendelsohn, G., & Feimer, N. Reply to the comments of Block and Ozer. JOURNAL OF PERSONALITY AND SOCIAL PSYCHOLOGY, 1982, 42, 1182–1184.

Weizmann, F., Wiener, N. I., Wiesenthal, D. L., & Ziegler, M. Differential K theory and racial hierarchies. CANADIAN PSYCHOLOGY, 1990, 31, 1–13.

Wessman, A. E. & Ricks, D. F. MOOD AND PERSONALITY. New York: Holt, Rinehart and Winston, 1966.

Wexler, D. A., & Rice, L. N. INNOVATIONS IN CLIENT-CENTERED THERAPY. New York: Wiley, 1974.

Wheeler, L. Motivation as a determinant of upward comparison. JOURNAL OF EXPERIMENTAL SOCIAL PSYCHOLOGY, 1966, Supplement No. 1, 27–31.

Wheeler, L., Deci, E., Reis, H., & Zuckerman, Miron. INTERPERSONAL INFLUENCE. Boston: Allyn & Bacon, 1978.

White, C., Flatley, D., & Janson, P. Moral reasoning in adulthood: Increasing consistency or contextual relativism? Paper presented at the American Psychological Association Convention, Washington, D. C., 1982.

White, D. E. Studies on Hysteria: Case histories and the case against history. MODERN LANGUAGE NOTES, 1989, 104, 1034–1048.

Whitworth, R. H. & McBlaine, D. D. Comparison of the MMPI and MMPI-2 administered to Anglo- and Hispanic-American University Students. JOURNAL OF PERSONALITY ASSESSMENT, 1993, 61, 19–27.

Wicker, F. W., Brown, G., Wiehe, J. A., Hagan, A. S., & Reed, J. L. On reconsidering Maslow: An examination of the deprivation/domination proposition. JOURNAL OF RESEARCH IN PERSONALITY, 1993, 27, 118–133.

Wicker, F. W., Wiehe, J. A., Hagen, A. S., & Brown, G. From wishing to intending: Differences in salience of positive versus negative consequences. JOURNAL OF PERSONALITY, 1994, 62, 347–368.

Wiedenfeld, S. A., O'Leary, A., Bandura, A., Brown, S., Levine, S., & Raska, K. Impact of perceived self-efficacy in coping with stressors on components of the immune system. JOURNAL OF PERSONALITY AND SOCIAL PSYCHOLOGY, 1990, 39, 1082–1094.

Wiesel, E. NIGHT. New York: Pyramid Books, 1961.

Wiggins, J. S. Cattell's system from the perspective of mainstream personality theory. MULTIVARIATE BEHAVIORAL RESEARCH, 1984, 19, 176–190.

Will, O. A. Introduction. In H.S. Sullivan, 1954, ix–xxiii.

Williams, D. E. & Page, Monte, M. M. A Multi-dimensional measure of Maslow's hierarchy of needs. JOURNAL OF RESEARCH IN PERSONALITY, 1989, 23, 192–213.

Williams, J. & Morland, J. Comment on Bank's "White preference in blacks: A paradigm in search of a phenomenon." PSYCHOLOGICAL BULLETIN, 1979, 86, 28–32.

Williams, J. H. PSYCHOLOGY OF WOMEN, BEHAVIOR IN A BIOSOCIAL CONTEXT, 2nd ed. New York: Norton, 1983.

Wilson, G. D. Personality and social behavior. In H. J. Eysenck (Ed.), A MODEL FOR PERSONALITY. New York: Springer-Verlag, 1981, 210–245.

Wilson, S., & Barber, T. The fantasy prone personality: Implications for understanding imagery, hypnosis, and parapsychological phenomena. In A. Sheikh (Ed.), IMAGERY: CURRENT THEORY, RESEARCH AND APPLICATION. New York: Wiley, 1982.

Winter, D. A. Repertory grid technique as a group psychotherapy research instrument. GROUP ANALYSIS, 1992, 25, 449–462.

Winter, D. G. Gordon Allport and the legend of "Rinehart." JOURNAL OF PERSONALITY, 1996, 64, 263–273.

Wolff, P. THE DEVELOPMENTAL PSYCHOLOGIES OF JEAN PIAGET AND PSYCHOANALYSIS (Psychological Issues Monograph 5). New York: International Universities Press, 1960.

Wolman, B. B. CONTEMPORARY THEORIES AND SYSTEMS IN PSYCHOLOGY, 2nd ed. New York: Plenum, 1981.

Wolpe, J. THE PRACTICE OF BEHAVIOR THERAPY, 3rd ed. New York: Pergamon, 1982.

Wolpe, J., & Rachman, S. Psychoanalytic evidence: A critique based on Freud's case of Little Hans. JOURNAL OF NERVOUS AND MENTAL DISEASES, 1960, 131, 135–145.

Wong, P. T. P. & Weiner, B. When people ask "why" questions, and the heuristics of attributional search. JOURNAL OF PERSONALITY AND SOCIAL PSYCHOLOGY, 1981, 40, 650–663.

Wood, R. & Bandura, A. Impact of conceptions of ability on self-regulatory mechanisms and complex decision making. JOURNAL OF PERSONALITY AND SOCIAL PSYCHOLOGY, 1989, 56, 407–415.

Woodward, K. L. An identity of wisdom. NEWSWEEK, 1994 (May 23), 56.

Woodward, K. L. How they bend minds. NEWSWEEK, December 4, 1978, 92 (#23), 72 77.

Woody, R. H. ENCYCLOPEDIA OF CLINICAL ASSESSMENT, VOLUMES I AND II. San Francisco: Jossey-Bass, 1980.

Wortis, J. FRAGMENTS OF AN ANALYSIS WITH FREUD. New York: Charter, 1954.

Wright, J. C. & Mischel, W. Conditional hedges and the intuitive psychology of traits. JOURNAL OF PERSONALITY AND SOCIAL PSYCHOLOGY, 1988, 55, 454–469.

Wylie, R. THE SELF-CONCEPT, A REVIEW OF METHODOLOGICAL CONSIDERATIONS AND MEASURING INSTRUMENTS, Vol. I, Rev. Ed. Lincoln: University of Nebraska Press, 1974.

Wylie, R. THE SELF-CONCEPT: THEORY AND RESEARCH ON SELECTED TOPICS, Vol. 2, Rev. ed. Lincoln: University of Nebraska Press, 1979.

Yee, A. H., Fairchild, H. H., Weizmann, F., & Wyatt, G. E. Addressing psychology's problems with race. AMERICAN PSYCHOLOGIST, 1993, 48, 1132–1140.

Young, P. T. The experimental analysis of appetite. PSYCHOLOGICAL BULLETIN, 1941, 38, 129–164.

Young, P. T. Appetite, palatability and feeding habit: A critical review. PSYCHOLOGICAL BULLETIN, 1948, 45, 289–320.

Young-Bruehl, E. FREUD ON WOMEN: A READER. New York: Norton, 1990.

Zajonc, R. B. The decline and rise of the Scholastic Aptitude Scores: A prediction derived from the confluence model. AMERICAN PSYCHOLOGIST, 1986, 41, 862–867.

Zajonc, R. B. & Markus, G. B. Birth Order and intellectual development. PSYCHOLOGICAL REVIEW, 82, 1975, 74–88.

Zhurbin, V. I. The notion of psychological defense in the conceptions of Sigmund Freud and Carl Rogers. SOVIET PSYCHOLOGY, 1991, 29 (#4, July-Aug.), 58–72.

Zimbardo, P. The human choice: Individuation, reason, and order versus deindividuation, impulse, and chaos. In W. Arnold & D. Levine (Eds.), NEBRASKA SYMPOSIUM ON MOTIVATION. Lincoln: University of Nebraska Press, 1970.

Zimmerman, B. J., Bandura, A., & Martinez-Pons, M. Self-motivation for academic attainment: The role of self-efficacy beliefs and personal goal setting. AMERICAN EDUCATIONAL RESEARCH JOURNAL, 1992, 29, 663–676.

Zuckerman, M. Some dubious premises in research and theory on racial differences: Scientific, social, and ethical issues. AMERICAN PSYCHOLOGIST, 1990, 12, 1297–1303.

Zuckerman, M. The distinction between trait and state scales is NOT arbitrary: Comments on Allen and Potkay's "On the Arbitrary distinction between traits and states." JOURNAL OF PERSONALITY AND SOCIAL PSYCHOLOGY, 1983, 44, 1083–1086.

Zuckerman, M. & Lubin, B. MANUAL FOR THE MULTIPLE AFFECT ADJECTIVE CHECK LIST. San Diego, CA: Educational and Industrial Testing Service, 1965.

Zuckerman, M., Kuhlman, D. M., Joireman, J., Teta, P., & Kraft, M. A comparison of three structural models for personality: The Big Three, the Big Five, and the Alternative Five. JOURNAL OF PERSONALITY AND SOCIAL PSYCHOLOGY, 1993, 65, 757–768.

Zuckerman, Miron, & Wheeler, L. To dispel fantasies about the fantasy-based measure of fear of success, PSYCHOLOGICAL BULLETIN, 1975, 82, 932–946.

Zuroff, D. Person, situation, and person-by-situation interaction components in person perception. JOURNAL OF PERSONALITY, 1982, 50, 1–14.

Zuroff, D. S. Was Gordon Allport a trait theorist? JOURNAL OF PERSONALITY AND SOCIAL PSYCHOLOGY, 1986, 51, 993–1000.

Zweig, S. Wider horizons on Freud. In Gerard, L. (Ed.), SIGMUND FREUD: THE MAN AND HIS THEORIES. New York: Fawcett, 1962.

NAME INDEX

Abraham, K. 100
Achterberg, J. 65
Adams, N. 322, 324–325
Adams, H. 114
Adams, J.Q. 289, 419, 445
Adams, P. 331
Addams, Jane 237
Adler, A. 4, 73–97, 99, 101, 109, 111,
    115, 123, 126, 142, 209, 225, 229,
    230, 254, 282, 394
Adler K. 75, 77
Adler, R. 74
Agyei, Y. 103
Ainsworth, M.D.S. 138
Alderfer, C.P. 228, 240, 245
Alexander, F. G. 75, 372
Ali, M. 330
Alicke, M. 412
Allen, A. 305
Allen, B. P. 36, 42, 103, 109, 159, 208,
    217, 254, 289, 383, 419, 442 443
Allen, Woody 143
Allerup, P. 270
Allport G. 2, 147, 152, 154, 156, 181,
    199, 205, 218, 296, 373, 403,
    425–455
Alvardo, N. 387
American Psychologist 41, 46
Amirkhan, J.H. 417
Anch, A.M. 182
Anderson, J.W. 368–373
Anderson, S. 40
Angel, E. 203
Angyal, A. 203
Ansbacher, H. L. 75, 76, 77, 89
Ansbacher, R. R. 76, 89
Anthony, S.B. 237, 330
Anthony, Susan B. 458

Anton, M.T. 288
APA Monitor 596
Arminio, L. 83, 93
Armor, D. 267
Aronson, E. 193, 194
Asch, S. 542
Astrachan, B.M. 163
Bacciagaluppi, M. 191
Bagby, R.M. 433
Bailey, F. Lee. 368
Bailey, M.B. 361
Bailey, M.J. 103
Bailey, R.B. 361
Balloun, J. 241
Bandura, A. 10, 91, 168, 261, 309–335,
    441
Banfield, J.T. 327
Barnet, H.S. 289
Bartholomew, K. 115
Bates, Norman 56
Baum, W.M. 327, 338, 342
Bech, P. 270
Beethoven, L. 318
Bem, D.J. 305
Benesch, K.F. 261, 265
Benjamin, Y. N. 265
Bennett, C. M. 361
Berg, S. 218
Berry, J.M. 267
Biancoli, R. 190, 194, 195
Bieri, J. 265–266
Binswanger, L. 203
Bixler, R. 203
Blau, G. 288
Blauner, R. 387
Blechner, M.J. 130
Block, J. 216, 218
Block, J. H. 216, 218

Bloom, J.W. 83, 93
Blum, G. 39
Boer, D. 44, 45
Boring, E.G. 373
Boss, M. 203
Bosselman, B.C. 138
Boudewyns, P. A. 84, 88
Bowers, G.H. 270
Bowlby, J. 138, 142
Bozarth, J.D. 213, 218, 220
Braff, D. 9
Braun, E. 23
Brennan, J. 402
Breuer, J. 38
Brodley, B.T. 213
Brody, B. 43
Broida, J.P. 289
Bromberg, P.M. 134
Bronfen, E. 24
Browman, C.P. 182
Brown, S. 324
Brown, G. 242
Bruce, Lenny 143
Brucke, E. 22
Brunner, H.G. 419
Buck, R. 292
Buddha 244–245
Bugental, J. F. T. 203, 204
Buhler, C. 203
Bullock, W. A. 418
Burnell, G. M. 88
Burris, C.T. 441
Burt, Cyril 395, 411
Bussey, K. 327
Bustos, N. 289
Butcher, J.N. 143
Butler, J.C. 118
Buttle, F. 245

Bryan, Herbert (Rogers recorded client) 216
Campbell, Ben Lighthorse 317
Campbell, D. T. 63
Campbell, F.A. 419
Cannon, W. 234
Carkhuff, R. R. 218
Carlson, J. 91–92, 93
Carlyn, M. 64
Carnes, J. 408
Carskadon, T. G. 64
Carson, R.C. 143
Cartwright, D. 218
Cartwright, R. 201
Caspi, A. 301
Catanzaro, S.J. 292
Catina, A. 270
Cattell, R. B. 2, 4, 9, 10, 199, 393–409, 411, 412, 414, 425, 428, 432
Cattell, H.E.P. 420
Cervone, D. 420
Cetola, H. 416
Chabassol, D. J. 84
Chamberlain, A.G. 418
Chapman, A. H. 125, 142
Chavez, Cesar 237
Cherian, V.I. 84
Chiesa, M. 343
Chomsky, N. 353
Churchill, J.C. 289
Cialdini, R.B. 297
Cioffi, F. 45
Clare, case of 4, 116–118, 377
Clinton, Bill 317
Collins, B. 331
Collins, Cardiss, U.S. Rep. (D-IL) 396
Collins, M.L. 138
Conci, M. 125
Conger, J. 46
Conn, J. H. 43
Cooper, J. 331
Cooper, H. 289
Cooper, R. 419
Corcoran, D. W.J. 416
Cornell University 125
Costello, C. G. 3
Coulson, W. 220
Cowles, M. 293
Cox, B.J. 433
Crandall, J.E. 89
Cramer, P. 69
Critelli, J.W. 40
Cromwell, R.L. 271
Cronbach, L.J. 399
Crumbaugh, J. 243
cummings, e.e. 317
Curie, Pierre 339
Curie, Marie 339
Czar 175
Dalton, P. 262, 270

Daly, M. 40, 42, 43
Danielsen, Berndt Henrik 99
Darley, J. 329
Darwin, C. 46, 67, 340
Das, A.K. 244–245
Davidson, P.O. 3
Davies, D. R. 418
Davies, R. 114
Davis, W. 290
Davis, C. 293
Davis, R. 362
Davis, S.F. 362
de Unamuno, Miguel 188
Dean, James 124
DeAngelis, T. 40, 69, 112
DeBruin, J. 218
DeCarvalho, R.J. 205, 1991
DeCharms, R. 290
Deci, E.L. 331
Dement, W. 23, 32, 37
Demorest, A.P. 339
Demosthenes 81
DePaulo, B. 292
Deutsch, H. 73
Didrikson, Mildred "Babe" 237
Dinkmeyer, D. 76, 92
Dinsmoor, J. A. 339, 341, 357
Dixon, N. 39
Doherty, H. 289
Dollard, J. 41
Dolliver, R.H. 60, 75
Donahoe, J.W. 353
Donohue, M.J. 441
Doty, R.M. 449
Douglass, Frederick 237
Downey, J.I. 103
Dr. Jekyll 56, 105
Dreyer, A. 292
DuBois, W.E.B. 451
Dunnett, G. 262, 270
Eber, H. W. 403, 404
Eck, D. 150
Eckardt, M.H. 177, 190, 194
Ee, J.S. 40
Einstein, Albert 43, 143, 237
Ekman, P. 291
Eldredge, P.R. 110, 111
Elijah 51
Ellenberger, H. F. 203
Ellis, A. 115
Emerson, Ralph Waldo 342, 429
Endler, N.S. 433
Epstein, R. 345
Epstein, S. 305
Erikson, E. 73, 124, 147–170, 173, 369, 435
Erkardt, M.H. 102
Esterson, E. 44, 45
Estes, C.P. 69
Evans, L. 294

Evans, R. I. 56, 60, 150, 151. 152, 154, 155, 157, 159, 207
Eysenck, H. 2, 4, 9, 10, 199, 393, 398, 406, 410–423, 425, 428
Eysenck, S. 406, 412, 414, 415,416
Fagen, J.W. 688
Fairchild, H.H. 289
Fakouri, M. E. 88
Falbo, T. 82, 83, 93
Fallon, D. 361
Feldman, B. 50
Felker, D.W. 83
Fenichel, O. 56, 73
Ferdinand, Waldo Demara 310
Ferguson, E.D. 76
Ferguson, E. 293
Festinger, L. 320
Findley, M. 289
Fischl, D. 271
Fliess, W. 24, 43, 44, 45, 150
Flores, J. 13
Foley, J.M. 163
Foley, M. 230, 312, 361
Fong, G. T. 87
Foster, Jodie 127
Frank, L.K. 11
Frankenstein, V. 4, 57, 85, 181
Frankl, V. E. 203, 243
Franz, C.E. 166
Fremont, T. 416
Freud, Anna 23, 27, 43, 44, 148, 151
Freud, Amalie 21
Freud, J. 21, 24
Freud Museum 22, 38
Freud, Phyllis 35
Freud, S. 4, 21–48, 49, 51, 68, 73, 74, 90, 99, 101, 102, 108, 110, 111, 115, 123, 126–127, 142, 143, 147, 148, 151, 173, 174, 176, 199, 209, 215, 225, 229, 251, 252, 295, 362, 367, 371, 388, 427, 429
Friedland, B. U. 89
Friedman, R.C. 103
Friesen, W. 291
Fromm, E. 4, 73, 100, 101, 111, 147, 154, 173–198, 227, 230, 254, 394, 402
Frosch, J. 101
Frost, R. 338
Funk, R. 173, 174
Gabriel, M.T. 40
Gaines, S.O. 443, 451
Galton, F. 395
Gandhi, M. 77, 150, 235
Garcia, J. 361
Gardner, H. 408
Gardner, L.E. 90
Gareau, D. 270
Garrison, M. 32
Gaulin, S. 103

Gendlin, E. T. 201, 203, 215, 218
Genia, V. 441
George, B.L. 387
Gibran, Kahlil 237
Gibson, H. B. 410–411
Gilligan, C. 36
Gilliland, K. A. 418
Gladue, B.A. 103
Gloria (Rogers client) 215, 219
Goble, F. 234
Goddard, Robert 317
Goethe 50
Goldberg, L. 406
Goldstein, K. 203, 241, 295
Golub, S. 23
Gorlow, L. 64
Graf, C. 220
Graf, Steffi 258, 261
Graham, W.K. 241
Greenough, W.T. 419
Greenwald, A. 41
Greenwood, C.R. 357
Greever, K. B. 89
Grey, A.L. 178
Griffin, D. 115
Grolnick, W.S. 291
Gromly, J. 358–359
Guastello, S.J. 420
Gupta, B.S. 416
Hafner, J. L. 88
Hagan, A.S. 242
Hall, C.S. 40, 56, 62
Hall, E. 148, 154, 157, 159
Hall, M. 246
Haney, D. O. 354
Hanly, C. 44
Hans Vaihinger's H. 79
Harlow, H.F. 138, 139, 142, 228, 229
Harlow, M.K. 139
Harper, H. 294
Harrington, D. M. 216, 218
Harris, S.L. 38
Harvey, R.J. 64
Hasse, R. F. 267
Hausdorff, D. 174, 175, 176, 179
Havassy-De Avila, B. 93
Haydn 318
Hayes, G.E. 128
Hayes, J. 360
Hayes, L.J. 348, 348
Hayes, S.C. 348, 353
Hazan, C. 112
Heath, J.L. 327, 338, 342
Hebb, D.O.182
Hegel, Georg 152
Heidegger, M. 203, 204
Hempel, C. 253
Henderson, V.L. 219
Hermann, B.P. 288
Hermaphrodite 61

Herrnstein, R. 419–420
Heron, W. 182
Heylighen, F.A. 244
Higgins, E.T. 93
Hill-Hain, A. 202, 204, 217
Himmler, H. 192
Hinckley, John 127
Hineline, P.N. 343
Hirsch, J. 289, 395, 397, 402, 407, 408–408, 418
Hitler, A. 4, 23, 149, 150, 167, 179, 189, 192, 230, 329, 449
Hoban, P. 125
Hoffman, S. 244
Hoffman, E. 226, 229
Hoffman, L.E. 158
Hogan, R. 62
Holden, J.M. 79
Holland, J. 344, 346, 348
Holmes, J.G. 290
Holmstrom, R.W. 293
Homburger 148
Hopkins, E. 361
Horn, J.M. 413, 418
Horney, K. 4, 69, 73, 99–122, 123, 127, 142, 143, 174, 177, 185–186, 227, 230, 254, 376
Horney, Oscar 100, 104
Houle, G. R. 240
Hoyt, M. 331
Hoz, R. 271
Huber, R. J. 85
Hugo, V. 109
Hull, C. 228
Hunt, J. McV 39
Hussein, Saddam 190
Husserl, E. 204
Huxley, A. 429
Hyer, L. 84, 88, 93
Iaccino, J. 56
Ionedes, N. S. 75
Ishiyama, F.I. 84
Iversen, I.H. 339, 340, 345
Jackson, D. N. 375, 382, 388
Jackson, M. 88, 266
Jackson, Michael 57
Jacobi, J. 59, 66
James, William 238, 451
Jankowicz, A. D. 261, 270
Jefferson, Thomas 237
Jenkins, M. 9
Jim and Joan (Kelly) 256–258
Joerger, S.M. 243, 245
Johnny Cochran 299
Johnson, C.L. 85
Johnson, E.E. 289, 290, 294
Johnson, J.L. 387
Johnson, K.R. 357
Jones, B.M. 416
Jones, D.M. 418

Jones, E. 22, 24
Jones, E.E. 331
Jordan, Barbara 153
Jordan, E.W, 93
Joseph, E. 42
Jourden, F.J. 327
Joyce, C.R. 270
Joyce, James 317
Judd, C. 267
Juan, Don 33, 42, 432
Jung, C. 4, 21, 46, 49–71, 73, 99, 115, 123, 142, 151, 177, 180, 209, 355, 369, 371–272, 394, 420, 426
Jung, J. 360
Kagan, J. 46
Kaiser, W 74
Kal, E. F. 90
Kanner, L. 43
Karp, S.A. 293
Katcher, A. 43
Katz, S.H. 419, 445
Kaur, S. 416
Keinonen, M. 375, 382
Kelleher, K. 62, 63
Kelly, G. A., 4, 10, 228, 251–279, 282, 295, 313, 371, 425, 426, 428
Kendler, H. 343
Keniston, K. 148
Kennedy family 126
Kerlinger, F.N. 398
Kern, C.W. 76, 90, 91
Kierkegaard, S. 203
Kimble, G. 343, 360
King, Martin Luther 237, 330
King, Steven 56
Kinkade, K. 358
Kipling, Rudyard 394
Kirschenbaum, H. 199, 201, 205, 219, 220
Kishton, J.M. 167
Klein, G. 41
Klein, T.W. 407
Klotz, M. L. 412
Kobler, F. 77
Koffka, K. 228, 230
Kohlberg, L. 36, 43
Kohler, W. 203
Kohn, A. 93
Korn, J.H. 362
Kowaz, A.M. 164
Krasner, L. 359
Krauft, C. C. 218
Krauss, H. 64
Kroger, R.O. 420
Krueger, R.F. 301
Kunda, Z. 87
Labrentz, H. L. 88
Lamarck, C. 67
Lamiell, J. 2
Lance Ito 299

Landers, Ann 115
Las Heras, A 57
Lashley, K. 373
Latane, B. 329
Lattal, K.A. 362
Lawlis, G. F. 65
Layng, T.V.J. 357
Leak, G.K. 89, 90
Lebowitz, M. 50, 60
Lee, D. Y. 267
Lee, V. 344
Lees, J. 418
Lefcourt, H.M. 290
Lesser, R.M. 178
Leupold-Loewenthal, H. 23
Leventhal, H. 321
Levine, L. 443
Levine, S. 324
Levinson, D. 162–163
Lewin, K. 282, 367
Lincoln, A. 237
Lincoln, Abraham 158
Lindbergh, C. 4, 380
Linder, D. 331
Lindzey, G. 193, 194
Linville, P. 266
Liptzin, B. 338
Little Anna, 4, 58
Little Hans, 4, 32
Loehlin, J.C. 395, 397, 407, 413, 418
Loftus, E. 44
Loh, W. 443
Luther, Martin 150
Lyle, W. H. 264, 273
Maccoby, M. 192
MacDonald, A. P. 93
Machiavelli, N. 231
Maddi, S. 39
Magnus, K. 417
Maholick, L. 243
Malcolm X 161, 237
Malcolm, D. 201, 217
Mann, L. 330
Mansfield, E.D. 165
Manaster, G. J. 87, 93
Marcia Clark 299
Marcia, J.E. 164
Markus, G. B. 83, 93
Marshall, Thurgood, 14
Martin, A.R. 115
Martinez-Pons, M. 315
Marx, K. 173, 174, 176
Maslow, A. 62, 69, 94, 181, 183, 199, 203, 220, 225–249, 254, 282, 368, 371, 373, 375, 396, 401, 426
Maslow, Rose 226
Masson, J. 43, 44
Mathes, E.W. 113, 114, 243, 245
Matlin, M. 230, 312, 361
Matthews, G. 418

Maxwell, James Clerk 317
May, R. 203
McAdams, D.P. 165, 166
McBlaine, D. D. 13
McCarthy, Eugene 176
McCarthy, Senator Joe 283
McClatchey, L. 271
McClelland, D.C. 166
McDougall, A. 9
McEvedy, C.P. 417
McFatter, R.M. 417
McGuire, T.R. 395, 402, 407, 408
Mead, M. 101
Means, R.S. 416
Means, G.H. 416
Mearns, J. 292
Melville, H. 370
Mendalgio, S. 294
Menninger, K. 205
Merleau-Ponty, M. 203
Merrens, M. 383
Miley, C.H. 83
Milgram, S. 330
Millan Astray, Spanish Civil War General 188
Miller, N. 41, 310
Miller, P.C. 290
Minassian, A. 9
Mischel, W. 2, 193, 281, 294–307, 309, 361, 367, 429
Mitchell, K. M. 215, 218
Mitler, M.M. 182
Mittelman, W. 244
Moffitt, J.E. 301
Monroe, Estella 4 and in the Instructor's Manual
Morgan, C. 369–371, 388
Morgan, W.G. 388
Morris, M.W. 304
Morris, E.K. 344, 357
Mosak, H. H. 88
Moss, P.D. 417
Motley, M. 41
Moxley, R.A. 340
Mozart, W. 318
Mr. Hyde 56, 105
Mullahy, P. 128–129
Muller, R. 107
Munson, P.A. 84
Munsterberg, H. 371, 426
Murray, H.A. 2, 4, 10, 11, 94, 148, 165, 183, 231, 232, 296, 367–392, 393, 414, 425, 426, 429
Murray, C. 419
Murry, W. D. 64
Mussen, P. 46
Mussolini, B. 189
Myers, I. B. 64
Napoleon 369
Nathan, P.E. 38

Neher, A. 246
Nessleroade, J.R. 409
Neulon, B.J. 83, 93
Neuman, M. 68
Newman, L. S. 93
Nicholson, N.L. 289
Noll, G. 243
Noll, R. 68
Nora, R.M. 289
Nordby, V. J. 56, 62
Norton, H.W. 407
O'Connor, K.P. 270
O'Leary, A. 324
Ochse, R. 160, 164, 167
Odbert, H. 2, 403
Oei, T.P.S. 294
Olivier, Sir Laurence 360
Oliviero, P. 271
Olson, H.A. 88
Oppenheim, P. 143, 253
Oppenheimer, Robert 280
Orlov, A.B. 211
Ormel, J. 288
Ornduff, S.R. 387
Orwell, George 175, 355, 357
Page, M.M. 241–242, 246, 261, 265
Paige, K.E. 213
Palmer, D.C. 353
Parisi, T. 22, 24
Park, B. 267
Parker, J.D.A 433
Parrish, T. S. 84
Paunonen, S.V. 375, 382
Pavlov, I.P. 252, 338
Peake, P. 301
Pelham, B.W. 429, 450
Peng, K. 304
Pennypacker, H.S. 357
Perls, F. 69, 203
Perry, W. 9
Perry, H. S. 123–126
Perryman, T. B. 87
Peterson, B.E. 165
Peterson, R.S. 267
Peterson, C. 387
Pharaoh, 37
Phares, E.J. 281, 283, 288, 290, 291
Phillips, W.M. 243, 244
Picasso 356
Pierce, D.L. 271
Pistole, D.R. 387
Plug, C. 160, 164, 167
Pol Pot 189
Polit, D. 82
Potkay, C. R. 3, 11, 193, 201, 208, 276, 296, 297, 339, 383, 389, 430
Powell, R. 44, 45
Powell, Colin 317
Powell, G.E. 417
Preston, C. 265

Prince, M. 371–372
Prinkey, K. 416
Pryor, Richard 143
Purton, C. 209
Pusecker, P.A. 325
Quinn, Anthony 317
Quinn, S. 99–100, 104, 105, 119
Quinn, R.H. 219, 220
Rachman, S. 32
Ramey, C.T. 419
Rantoul, J.L. [Mrs. H.A. Murray] 369
Rao, D.C. 397, 407
Raska, K. 324
Raskin, R. 40
Ravizza, K. 243, 245
Reagan, Ronald 127
Reed, E.S. 443, 451
Reed, J.L. 242
Reese, L. 322, 324–325
Reik, T. 174
Rice, L. N. 216
Rinehart, John B. G. 427
Roazen, P. 65, 148, 149, 150, 151
Robbins, A.H. 143
Robeson, Paul 237
Robinson, F.G. 367–370, 373–374, 387
Rockwell, W.T. 342, 343
Rodin, Auguste 317
Rodriguez, M.L. 301, 304
Rogers, C. 4, 62, 65, 69, 94, 181,
    199–224, 225, 229, 239, 246, 254,
    261, 354, 411, 425
Rogers, R. 13
Rohrbaugh, J. 43, 111
Romeo and Juliet 235
Ronan, G.F. 388
Roosevelt, Eleanor 237
Roosevelt, Franklin 370
Rorschach, H. 9, 11
Rosenberg, S.D. 387
Rosenhan, D.L. 3
Rosenthal, R. 292
Ross, J.M. 440–441
Roter, P.M 243, 245
Rotter, J. 2, 89, 227, 281–294, 309, 361,
    367
Rubin, T.I. 119
Ruble, D.N. 312
Rudmin, F.W. 77
Ruetzel, K. 165
Ruppenthal, G.C. 138
Russell, B. 338
Ryan, C.S. 267
Ryan, R.M. 291, 331
Ryback, D. 201, 217
Rychlak, J. 25, 51, 53, 58, 61, 65, 66, 67,
    75, 78, 79, 215
Ryckman, R.M. 118
Sabatelli, R. 292
Sach, H. 174

Sagan, C. 317
Saleh, W.E. 290
Salmon, D. 271
Salome 51
Salzinger, K. 337, 339, 340, 341
Samuels, A. 68
Sanford, R. 201
Sanitioso, R. 87
Sanna, L.J. 325
Saroyan, W. 317
Sartre, J-P. 204
Schaible, D. 9
Schaufeli, W.B. 288
Schlinger, H.D. 343, 361
Schmitz, B. 429
Schooler, C. 93
Schuerger, J.M. 397, 407
Schumann, K. 81
Schweitzer, Albert 237
Sears R. 311
Sechrest, L. 88, 266
Selesnick, S. T. 75
Seligman, M. E. P 3, 441
Sethi, S. 441
Sewell, K. W. 13, 271
Shadel, W.G. 420
Shafter, R. 103
Shakespeare, W. 360
Shapiro, D.H. 292, 294
Shaver, P. 112–115, 119, 138
Shaw, H. 40
Shaw, George Bernard 338
Sheehy, G. 162,163–164
Shelley, M. 4, 85, 181
Sherman, R. 76, 92
Sherrill, C. 240, 245
Shirer, W. L. 23
Shlien, J. M. 207
Shoda, Y. 294, 295, 297, 298, 299,
    300–301, 302, 304, 305
Shostrom, E.L. 215, 240, 241, 243
Siegel, P.F. 339
Signell, K. 266
Silber, D.E. 293
Silva-Garcia, J. 195
Silverman, L. 39
Simmel, G. 110
Simonson, N. R. 64
Simonton, O.C. 65
Simonton, S. 65
Simpson, P.W. 83, 93
Singer, J. 382, 388
Sitting Bull 237
Skinner, B.F. 4, 181, 199, 215, 239, 261,
    295, 312, 337–365, 368, 376, 389,
    393, 429
Skutnik, L. 330
Smith, M.B. 243, 370, 371
Smith, G.F. 254, 301
Solomon, G. F. 88

Spearman, C. 398, 402
Speer, A. 189, 329
Spence, K. 310
Spielberger, Steven 339
Spitz, R. A. 138
Sprock, J. 9
Stack, Ella 124, 126
Stalin, J. 77, 186, 189
Standal, S. 408
Stanovich, K. E. 42
Steele, R. 45
Stein, Gertrude 317
Steimen, G. 35
Stepansky, P. E. 74
Sternberg, R. 408
Stevens, R. 148, 149
Stevenson, Adlai 237
Steward, A.J. 165
Stelmack, R.M. 418
Stokes, D. 310
Stouthamer-Loeber, M. 301
Stuttaford, G. 36
Sullivan, H.S. 73, 101, 123–146, 226,
    227, 228, 239, 254, 367
Suomi, S.J. 138, 139
Sun Phallus Man 68
Super, D. E. 203, 205
Symonds, A. 110
Tatsuoka, M.M. 403, 404
Teresa, Mother 237, 330
Tetlock, P.E. 267
Tiffany family 148
Thompson, C. 124
Thompson, G. 252, 253
Thorndike, E.L. 143, 229, 396
Thorne, B. 200
Thornton, B. 118
Thunedborg, K. 270
Titchener, E.B. 228, 426
Todd, J.T. 344, 357
Toland, J 23
Tomlinson, T. M. 218
Tosi, D.J. 244
Travis, L. 282
Triandis, H. 443
Truax, C. B. 215, 218
Truth, Sojourner 237
Tschuschke, V. 270
Tseng, M. S. 89
Tubman, Harriet 237
Tucibat, J. 82
Tudge, J.R.H. 332
Tyler, K. 261, 265
Tyson, Mike 82
Uhlemann, M. R. 267
Ullmann, L. 359
Ulrey, L. M. 387
Ustad, K. 13
Van de Castle, R. L. 40
Van Gogh 143, 317

Vanderzwagg, R. 288
VandeWoude, S. 419
Van Kaam, A. 203
Van Ronzelen, Clothilde (Sonni) 99, 124
Van Ronzelen, Wilhelmine (Minna) 100
Viken, R.J. 417
Viney, L. L. 265
Vockell, E.L. 83
Vookles, J. 93
Waehler, C.A. 387
Walsh, J.K. 182
Walters, R. 311
Ward, E. 361
Ward, M. 430
Ware, E.E. 290
Washington, Booker T. 451
Watkins, C.E. 66, 88, 93, 94
Watkins, E. 172
Watkins, J.T. 243
Watkins, M.M. 131
Watson, J.B. 204, 228, 338, 373, 389
Watts, R.E. 76, 79, 90
Wehr, G. 49, 50, 51
Weinberger, J. 166
Weizmann, F. 289, 407, 407, 408–409, 445

Wells, H.G. 338
Wertheimer, M. 445
Wexler, D. A. 216
Wheeler, L. 331
White, D.E. 27
White, J. 301
Whiteside, M.M. 93
Whitman, S.W. 288
Whitworth, R. H. 13
Wicker, F.W. 242, 246
Widdifiel, J. 85
Wiedenfeld, S.A. 324–325
Wiehe, J.A. 242
Wiener, N. 407, 409, 445
Wiener, N.I. 838
Wiesenthal, D.L. 407, 409, 445
Wiggins, J. 397, 398, 401, 403, 409
Willerman, L. 413, 418
Williams, D. E. 89, 241–242, 246
Williams, J. H. 111
Wilson, M. 40, 42, 43
Winter, D.A. 270
Winter, D.G. 427, 449
Winterhoff, P.A. 332
Wolf Man 31
Wolff, P. 41
Wolff, T. 369
Wolpe, J. 32

Wood, R. 326
Wood, L.A. 420
Woods, M. G. 84, 88
Woodward, K.L. 147, 148, 150, 152
Wortis, J. 42
Wright, Frank Lloyd 317
Wright, J.C. 298, 301
Wu, Harry 237
Wundt, W. 228
Wyatt, G.E. 289
Wyler, A.R. 288
Yee, A. 289, 419, 445
York, Sergeant 329
Young, P.T. 234, 236, 239
Young-Bruehl, E. 36, 46
Zajonc, R. 83, 93
Zevon, M.A. 243, 245
Zhurbin, V.I. 209
Ziegler, M. 407, 408, 445
Zimmerman, B.J. 315
Zubek, J. 419
Zuckerman, M. 417, 445
Zuroff, D.C. 428, 429, 450
Zweig, S. 22

SUBJECT INDEX

abience 377, 389
ability trait 400
abstracting across the cleavage line 260
accurate empathy 212
acquirable skill 326, 327
activating stimuli 182
active imagination 66
actones, 374
actual self 109, 208
adience 376, 389
Adjective Generation Technique
  (AGT) 302, 383, 430
Adler, A. 73–97
  birth order, 82, 83, 84, 93
  brief therapy approach, 91–92
  compensate, 81
  creative power of the individual, 79
  Early recollections (ERs) 84, 86, 87,
    88, 93
  fictional finalism 79
  individual psychology, 78
  Inferiority complex 75, 76, 80
  inferiority, 80
  law of movement 79
  love, 78
  neurosis 80
  overcompensate, 81
  prototype, 79
  shock 80
  social feeling, 78, 85
  social interest 75, 78, 85, 89, 90, 127
  society 78
  striving for superiority, 76, 81, 86, 87
  style of life 78, 79, 86
  Superiority complex 75, 76, 81
  teleological 79
  work 78
Adlerian therapy 90

adolescence 156
adulthood stage 159
advantageous comparison 329, 331
aesthetic needs 238, 437
Africa 158, 357
African Americans 54, 153, 202, 289,
  290, 304, 317, 419, 442–447, 451
aggression 309, 311, 382
alcohol effects 416
alcoholics 192, 289, 310
Alcoholics Anonymous 65
alcoholism 65, 192, 289, 310, 359
alienation 293
Allport 425–455
  authoritarian 449
  bodily self, 343
  cardinal p.d. 432, 450
  central p.d. 432, 450
  common traits 432
  directedness 439
  early infancy, 434
  extension of self 435, 436
  extrinsic religious orientation
    440–441
  frustration tolerance, 438
  functional autonomy, 437, 450
  Generic conscience 440
  genuine sense of humor, 438
  idiographic theorist, 429, 449–450
  intrinsic motivation 437
  nomothetic theorists, 429
  personal disposition (p.d.) 432
  personality 429
  prejudice 425, 441
  prejudiced personality 447–449
  propriate striving 436
  proprium, 17, 434
  rational coper, 435

  secondary p.ds. 433, 450
  self-esteem 435
  self-identity, 434
  self-image 435
  Social Distance (SD) 442
  stereotype, 445–447
  tolerance for ambiguity, 448
  trait 431
  unified philosophy of life 439
ambiverts 412
amphigenital 136
amplification 66
anal stage 30, 155
anal-expulsive 31
anal-retentive 30
anima 55, 63, 67
animus 55
anti-Semitism 22–23, 68, 174, 194,
  226–227, 448–449
anxiety 26, 128, 140, 400, 433
anxiety (Cattell) 400
anxiety (Freud) 26
anxiety (Kelly) 259
anxiety gradient 133
approaching/attached 378
arbitrary rightness 109
archetypes 54, 55, 56, 61, 62, 67
ascending reticular activating system
  (ARAS) 413, 416, 418
Asians 158, 182, 291, 304
assimilation 185
athletic performance and self-efficacy
  327
athletics, genes, and the environment
  356, 396
attachment 113–114, 138
attachment Styles 113–114, 138
attitude 401

attitude (Jung) 60
attractiveness 319
Australian Aborigines 54, 408
authoritarianism 191, 449
autistic children 359
automaton conformity 178
autonomy 154, 167
autophilic person 136
autosexual 136
avoidance conditioning 346
avoidant/withdrawn 378
awareness 207

Baby in a Box 354
bad news 416
Bandura 309–335
    advantageous comparison 329, 331
    blaming victims 329
    Defensive behaviors 321
    Dehumanization 328, 331
    Diffusion of innovation 318–319
    Displacement and diffusion of re-
        sponsibility 329
    euphemistic labeling 329, 331
    extrinsic rewards, 319
    forethought 313
    goals 316, 320–321
    gradualistic moral disengagement,
        330
    incentive, 315
    intrinsic motivation 319, 331
    model 314, 315
    modeling 314
    moral justification 329
    observational learning, 311
    participant modeling 318
    personal agency, 313
    resilience 317
    response facilitation 318
    self-efficacy, 316–317, 319, 321–326
    self-evaluation 320, 325, 330
    self-exonerative processes 328
    self-regulatory processes 316, 317,
        326, 327
    social cognitive theory 311, 331
    social comparison, 320
    symbolic modeling 314
    vicarious expectancy learning 318
    vicarious reinforcement 320
basic anxiety 104, 376
basic conflict 107
basic mistrust 153
basic trust 153
basketball shooting 350
being 203
behavior therapy 359
behavioral alternatives 328
behavioral avoidance test 322, 324
behavioral consistency 294, 296–297,
    302–303, 429, 431, 433, 450

behavioral dimension 1
behaviorism 337
Bell Curve 419–420
belongingness and love needs 233
Beyondism 396
Big Five 420
biophilia 190
birth order 82, 83, 93
bisexual 201, 245
blaming victims 631
blind spot 109
bodily self 434
Bolsheviks, 77
borderline personality 107
braggart 81, 82
brain and environmental enrichment 419
brainwashing 354
brief therapy approach 91
business and industry 326–327
B-Values 238

caffeine 179
cardinal p.d. 432, 450
Care 160
case history method 2
case of Jim 91
castration anxiety 32, 39, 40, 386
castrative tendencies 198
catalytic exteriorization phenomenon
    49
catharsis 37
cathexes 34
cathexis (Murray) 379
Cattell 393–409
    "g" 763
    16 PF, 403–405, 409
    ability trait 400
    anxiety, 400
    attitude, 401
    common trait 400
    crystallized general ability (^g_c) 402
    dR-technique 399
    dynamic lattice, 401
    dynamic trait 401
    econetic model, 397
    erg, 401
    Eugenics 395–396
    exvia-invia, 400
    factor 398
    factor analysis 393, 397–398, 406
    Fluid general ability (^g_f) 402
    heritability 406–409
    inductive-hypothetico-deductive spi-
        ral, 397
    L-data 399
    loadings, 398
    Multiple Abstract Variance Analysis
        (MAVA), 407
    P-technique 399
    personality 397

primary factors 398
Q-data 399
R = f(S.P) 397
R-technique, 399
second-order traits, 400
secondary factors 398
sentiment, 401
source trait 400
state 399
subsidiation (of traits) 400
surface traits 401
Syntality 402
T-data 399
temperament trait 401
trait 400
unique trait 400
central p.d. 432, 450
cerebral cortex 781
chance 283, 310
characterizing events 298
childhood 216
childhood (Jung) 62
childhood stage (Sullivan) 132
children 216, , 290315
child rearing practices 216, 290,
    352–354, 419
choice (kelly) 264
chum 134
circumspection phase 264
clairvoyance 380
Clare, case of 116–118
class (social) 327–328, 387
client centered 201, 205
client centered therapy 213
cognitive dissonance theory 331
cognitive factors 311–313, 314
cognitive needs 238
cognitive social learning theory (Mis-
    chel) 295
cognitively complex 265–267
cognitively simple 265–267
collective unconscious 52, 67, 99
collectivistic culture 194
commitment 442
common traits 400, 432
common traits (Allport) 432
commonality 259, 265
communism 74, 77, 138, 150, 176
compartmentalization 109
compeers 134
compensate 81
compensation 56, 59, 81
competence 156, 167
competency 16, 298
complex 65, 76
complexes (Jung) 65
component of a situation 298
conflict 105, 379
conflict of needs 379
conflict resolution 202

conflicts of needs 718
conformity 178, 288
congruence 209, 212
conscience 28
consciousness 27, 51, 53
consensual validation 129
consequences 340, 343
consistency in child rearing 134
consistency of behavior 294, 296–
    297, 302–303, 429, 431, 433,
    450
consistent pattern of behavior 303
construction system 258
constructive alternativism 260
constructs 255, 265
context 260
contingent 344
continuous reinforcement 347
contrafaction of needs 379
control 292
controlling person 107
correlated 4, 9
correlation coefficient 6,
Costa Rican hummingbirds 340
counseling 203
countertransference 39, 215
C-P-C Cycle 263
craft-idiocy 156
creativity 143, 181, 216, 318, 355–356
creativity fostering environment (CFE)
    216
creative power of the individual 79
crime 327–328, 415
crystallized general ability ($^{g}_{c}$) 402
cult 126
cumulative records 348
cynicism 109

defense mechanisms 26, 27, 108
defensive behaviors 327
defensive externals 293
deficiency needs 234
dehumanization 328, 331
delay of gratification 300–301
de-illusionment 162
denial (Freud) 26
denial (Rogers) 210
dependency constructs 262
dependent variables 9
Despair 160, 161
detachment 138
dextro-amphetamine 16
diffusion of innovation 318–319
dignity 342–343
dimensionalism 814
directedness (Allport) 439
discrimination 442
displacement 32
displacement and diffusion of responsi-
    bility 329

distortion (Rogers) 210
Diversity 13, 54, 77, 110, 125, 158, 192,
    202, 227, 244–245, 271, 304, 327–
    328, 357, 387, 408, 419, 451
affirmative action 150
Africa 84, 158, 357
African Americans 54, 153, 202, 289,
    290, 304, 317, 419, 442–447, 451
African culture 158, 164, 357, 451
African heritage 54, 357, 451
African societies 84, 158, 357
African-American therapy clients 202
Africans 54, 357
Ali, Muhammad 330
Anthony, Susan B 237
anti-Semitism 22–23, 68, 227, 448–449
Asian 158, 180, 182
Asian Culture 158, 194
Asian societies 158
Asians 158, 291, 304
Australian Aborigines 54, 408
bisexuals 103, 125
black and white South Africans 164,
    167, 201, 202, 217
Blacky Test 39
Budda 244
Catholic 65, 126, 189, 217, 445
children of the world 150
Chinese 54, 304
classism 328, 387
collectivistic culture 194, 291
cultural identity 349
culture 106, 194, 271, 471
culture-bound 296, 271
diversity principles 387
DuBois, W.E.B. 451
Eastern religions 52, 63, 243–244
Egyptian culture 54
ethnicity 306
Europeans 340
European Jews 226, 226, 329, 410
European Americans 54, 102, 110,
    304, 387, 408, 419, 442–447
extrinsic and intrinsic religious orien-
    tations 440–441
feminists 67
gangs 227
gay people 46, 124–126
gay/lesbian 46, 103, 113
gender bias 327, 331, 386, 389, 444
gender differences 324, 327, 386
fascism 177
Holocaust 329
homeless people 451, 456
homosexuality 46, 103, 124–126,
    136, 385
Indian Hindus 304
intelligence and heredity 395–396,
    402, 406–407, 408–408, 412–413,
    418

intelligences 408
interracial relations 202
individualistic culture 194, 291
Irish 126, 217, 329
Irish Republican Army (IRA) 329
Japanese 304, 445
Jehovaha's Witnesses 23
Jewish people 43, 74, 126, 174,
    226–227, 329, 410, 445
Jordan, Barbara 300
King, Martin Luther 237
Klansmen 328
Latina author 136
Latino 22, 180, 317
Malcolm X 161, 237
Marshall, Thurgood 13
Mexican-Americans 22
Mexicans 192, 194
Muslims 190
Native American 54, 149, 152,180,
    317,329, 441
Northern European ancestry 107
poor people 327–328, 387
prejudice 425, 441–442
prejudice and religion 440–441
prejudiced personality 841
protestant 217
race 306, 377, 419, 443–446
race and intelligence 408, 419
racism 419, 443–444, 447, 451
racist 443–444
relativity of intelligence 408
religion 200, 244–245, 380, 426
religious sentiment 401, 439
sexism 66
sexual orientation 46, 103
Sioux 149, 152
slavery 357, 451
social class 387
South Africa 84, 201, 202
South American 158
South American societies 164
Spanish Personality Assessment In-
    ventory (PAI) 13
stereotype 202, 445–447
teen gangs 227
wannabes 848
Washington, Booker, T. 451
white males 387
women 66, 77, 110, 111, 151, 163,
    330–331, 357
women's movement 111
women, battering of 331
Vikings 54
Yiddish language 226
Yurok 149, 152
divorce 163, 289
dR-technique 399
dream analysis 23, 37, 59, 66, 116, 117,
    181–182, 189, 380

dream series 66, 69
dream symbol 37, 38
drive 375
Dungeons and Dragons 189
dynamic lattice 401
dynamic trait 401
dynamisms 131
dysfunctional family 180

early infancy (Allport) 434
early memories 183
early childhood stage 154–155
early recollections (ERs) 84, 86, 87, 88, 93
Eastern religions 52, 63, 244–245
econetic model 397
economic orientation 439
eductive 133
effectiveness 181
ego 25, 26, 28, 37, 51, 53, 76, 132
ego (Jung) 53
ego ideal 28
ego-strength 33
Egypt 54
Eight State Questionnaire 400
elaborative choice 263
electra complex 31, 33
elements 260
elusiveness 109
emergent pole 259
emotionality 400
empathy (Rogers) 202, 204
empathy (Sullivan) 128
entropy 53
environmental enrichment 419
environmental determinism 311–312, 340–341–381, 419
epigenesis 152, 160, 164, 167
equivalence 53, 379
erg 401
Erikson 147–170
    adolescence stage 156
    adulthood stage 159
    autonomy 154, 167
    basic mistrust, 153
    Basic trust 153
    Care, 160
    Competence, 156, 167
    despair, 160, 161
    early childhood stage 154–155
    epigenesis 152, 160, 164, 167
    favorable ratio, 153
    fidelity, 157, 167
    generativity 159, 165–166
    guilt, 155, 167
    hope, 154
    identity confusion, 157
    identity, 153, 157
    industry, 156, 164–165
    infancy stage 153–154

inferiority, 156
inherited ideas 67
initiative, 155
institutional safeguard, 154
Integrity 160
Intimacy 159, 164
isolation, 159
love 159
old age stage 160
play stage 155
psychosocial development 152
purpose, 155
school age stage 156
Shame and doubt 154, 167
stagnation 159
strength, 152
will power, 155, 167
wisdom, 161, 167
young adulthood stage 158–159, 167
erogenous zones 28
eros 25, 29, 34, 55
esteem needs 233
esthetic orientation 439
Eugenics 395–396
euphemistic labeling 329, 331
Eupsychia 239–240
European American 54, 102, 110, 304, 387, 408, 419, 442–447
events (Mischel) 298
excessive self-control 109
excitation and stimulation 181
existential needs 177
existentialism 203–204
existential psychology (Rogers) 203
expansive 107
expectancies 281, 299, 318
expectancy (Mischel) 299
expectancy (Rotter) 281, 285
experience 205, 207, 259
experience (Kelly) 259
experiment 9
experimental method 9
experimenter 9
exploitative orientation (Fromm) 186, 192
extension of self 435, 436
extension of the cleavage line 260
external locus of control 89, 286–291
externalization (Horney) 108, 118
externalization (Allport) 448
extinction 339, 345
extrasensory perception (ESP) 57
extraversion 60, 63, 87, 412, 417
extraversion (Jung) 60, 63, 87
extraversion-introversion (Eysenck) 412–417, 420
extrinsic religious motivation 440–441
extrinsic rewards 319
extrinsically rewarding 319
extropunitive-intropunitive 451

exvia-invia 400
Eysenck 410–423
    ambiverts, 412
    ascending reticular activating system 413, 416, 418
    extraversion-introversion 412–417, 420
    habitual responses (HR), 414
    neuroticism 412–416, 420
    psychometrics, 414
    psychoticism 412–416, 420
    scientific model for studying personality 413
    specific responses (SR) 414
    traits 412
    types, 412

facade 209
factor 398
factor analysis 393, 397–397, 406
false memory syndrome 44
family 191
fantasy abuse 43
fate 283, 310
favorable ratio 153
fear 210, 259
fear (Kelly) 259
feeling 61, 64, 273
fictional finalism 79
fidelity 157, 167
figure-ground 230
fixation 30
fixed interval schedule 348
fixed ratio (FR) schedule 348–349
fixed role therapy 271
fixed schedule 348
fluid general ability (g_f) 402
forbidding gestures 131
foresight 141
forethought 313
frame of orientation 177
free association 37, 38, 66, 191
free will, 313
freedom 204, 341
Freud 21–48
    anal stage 30
    anal-expulsive 31
    anal-retentive 30
    anxiety, 26
    castration anxiety 32, 39, 40
    catharsis, 37
    cathexes, 34
    conscience, 28
    countertransference 39
    defense mechanisms 26, 27
    deny 26
    displacement, 32
    dream analysis 23, 37
    dream symbol 37, 38
    ego 25, 26, 27, 28, 29

ego ideal, 28
ego-strength, 33
Electra complex 31, 33
erogenous zones, 28
eros 25, 29, 34
fixation, 30
free association 37, 38, 66
genital stage 34
guilt, 28
hysterical neurosis, 27
id 25, 26, 28, 29, 33
insight, 38, 65
instincts, 25
intellectualize 27
introjection 33
latency 33
latent content 37, 58
libido, 25, 28
manifest content 37, 58
morality principle, 28
narcissistic 29, 40
neuroses 27
Oedipus complex 31, 32, 33, 45
oral or narcissistic (self-centered)
    stage 29, 40
oral-aggressive 30
oral-receptive 30
penis envy, 32, 39, 40, 110
phallic stage 31, 33
pleasure principle, 25
primary process, 25
Projection 26
Psychoanalysis 38, 43
Psychoanalytic Theory 39, 41, 42
psychological determinism, 23
psychosexual 29, 34
rationalization 26
reality principle 50
regression, 30
repression, 26
secondary process, 26
seduction thesis, 83
slips of the tongue, 78
sublimation 33
superego, 27, 28, 29, 33
Thanatos 25
transference 38, 40
undoing 27
Freud couch 427
frigidity 103, 104
Fromm 173–198
    activating stimuli 182
    assimilation, 185
    automaton conformity, 178
    biophilia 190
    effectiveness, 181
    excitation and stimulation 181
    existential needs, 177
    exploitative 186
    frame of orientation, 177

hoarding 187, 192
humanism 199
humanistic communitarian socialism,
    176
humanistic psychoanalyst, 177
identity 180, 181
individual character 184
marketing 187, 193
mature love 179
necrophilous character 188
object of devotion, 178
personality 184
productive orientation 185–190
receptive 185, 192, 193
relatedness, 178
rootedness, 179
simple stimuli 182
social character 184, 193
socialization, 185
sociopsychological orientation, 173
symbiotic union, 178, 185
transcendence 181
unity 180
frustration tolerance 438
functional autonomy 437, 450
fundamentalists (religion) 441
fundamental postulate 255
fusion of needs 378

gambler's fallacy 283
gambling addiction 351
Gemeinschaftsgefuhl 75, 237
gender bias 327, 331, 386, 389, 444
gender roles 327, 386
general actualizing tendency 206
generalized expectancies 549
generalized expectancy 285–286
generalized expectancy for negative
    mood regulation NMR 292
generativity 159, 162, 165–166
generic conscience 440
genes and personality 358
genetics 340, 358, 395, 406–409,
    412–413, 418–419
genital stage 34
genuine sense of humor 438
Gestalt 203, 228, 230, 241, 282, 295,
    427
Gestapo 22
goal-directed 76
goals 178, 231, 316, 321, 325, 387, 389,
    436, 439
goal setting 321, 325, 326, 436
gradualistic moral disengagement
    330
Great Depression 229, 252, 282
growth model 201
guilt 28, 155, 167, 263
guilt (Freud) 28
guilt (Kelly) 263

habitual responses 414
here and now 209
heritability 407–409
Hermaphrodite 61
heterophilic person 266
hierarchy of needs 233–235, 238,
    241–241, 245, 375
hoarding orientation 187, 192
holism 69, 203, 230
homeostasis 234
homosexuality 46, 103, 124–126, 385
hope 154
Horney 99–122
    actual self 109
    Arbitrary rightness 109
    basic anxiety 104
    Basic conflict 107
    blind spot 109
    compartmentalization, 109
    conflict 105
    Cynicism 109
    Elusiveness, 109
    Excessive self-control 109
    expansive 107
    externalization, 108, 118
    hyper-competitiveness 107, 118
    idealized image of self, 108, 109, 115,
        116
    jealousy 112–115, 118
    Moving against people 107
    Moving away from people 107
    Moving toward people 106
    neurotic needs, 105, 106
    rationalization 109
    real self 108, 109, 116, 118
    resignation 107
    self-analysis 115–118
    self-effacing 106, 107
    self-recognition, 116, 118
    tyranny of the shoulds, 115
horror movies (jung) 55–56
humanistic communitarian socialism
    176
humanistic education 205, 220
humanistic psychoanalyst 177
humanistic psychology (Rogers) 199,
    203
humanists 204, 225, 426, 428
hyperactive children 417
hypercompetitiveness 107, 118
hypnosis 178, 338
hysterical neuroses 27

I_1 141
I_2 141
iceberg (Freud) 26
id 25, 26, 28, 29, 33, 37, 51, 76, 102
ideal self (Rogers) 208, 213
idealized image of self 108, 109, 115,
    116

identity 153, 157, 181, 436
identity (Fromm) 180
identity crisis 147, 148, 152, 153, 160, 164, 436
identity confusion 157
idiographic theorist 205, 429, 449–450
I-E Scale 286–288
immunological status and self-efficacy 324–325
impermeable 259
implicit pole 259, 272
impression managers 441
incentive 315
incongruence 212
independent variables 9
individual character (Fromm) 184
individual differences 1, 78
individual psychology 78
individualistic 194
individuality 259
individuation 61, 67, 162
inductive-hypothetico-deductive spiral 397
industry 156, 164
infancy 130, 153
infancy stage 153–154
inferiority 76, 80, 156, 426
inferiority (Erikson) 156
inferiority complex 76, 80, 426
initiative 155
insight (Freud) 38, 51, 65, 115, 191
instinct 25, 236
instinctoid 236
institutional safeguard 154
integrity160
intellectualization 27
intelligence 83, 394–395, 401, 402, 406–407, 408
interaction point of view 295, 301, 304, 433
interactionism 304, 433
intermittent reinforcement 348
internal locus of control 286–291
internal representation 315
interpersonal anxiety 127
Interpersonal Jealousy Scale 113–114
interpersonal relations 123
interpersonal security 128
interpersonal trust 291
intimacy 159, 164, 437, 442
intimacy needs 136
intimate, committed, permanent relations 442
instincts 25
intrinsic motivation 319, 331
intrinsic religious motivation 440–441
intrinsically religious person 440–441
intrinsic rewards 319
introduction
  behavioral dimension 1

case history method 3
correlated 4
correlation coefficient 10
dependent variables 9
experiment, 15
human diversity 21
independent variables 9
individual differences 1
negative correlation 6
nil correlation 8
objective tests 12
personality 2
personality traits 1
personologists 1
positively correlated 6
projective test 11
reliability, 10
Rorschach inkblots 9, 10, 11, 12
scientific 3
statistically significant 10
variable 4
introjection 33
introversion 60, 64, 87, 90
introversion/extraversion 60, 63, 64, 90
intuition 61, 64
I.Q. 83, 84, 394, 395–396, 408, 419–420, 444
isolation 159
isophilic 136

jealousy 112–115, 118
Jehovaha's Witnesses 23
Jim and Joan (Kelly) 256–258
Jim, case of 91
Jung, C. 49–71
  active imagination 66
  amplification, 66
  anima 55, 63, 67
  animus 55
  archetypes 54, 55, 56, 61, 62, 67
  attitude 60
  Childhood 62
  collective unconscious, 52, 67
  compensation 56, 59
  complexes, 129
  dream analysis 59, 66
  dream series 66, 69
  ego 53
  Entropy 53
  equivalence 53
  extraversion 60
  feeling 61, 64
  individuation, 61, 67
  introversion 60, 63, 64
  intuition 61, 64
  libido 53
  mandala 56
  Middle age 62
  old age 63

persona, 53, 62, 209
personal unconscious 52
prospective 59
psyche 53
recognition 62
self, 52, 53
sensation 61
shadow 54, 55, 62, 67
synchronicity, 57
Thinking 61, 64
transcendental function, 61
type 60
Word Association Test 65, 69
Youth 62
juvenile era 134

katasexual 136
Kelly 251–279
  abstracting across the cleavage line, 260
  anxiety, 259
  choice, 264
  Circumspection phase 264
  cognitively complex 265–267
  cognitively simple 265–267
  commonality, 259, 265
  construction system 258
  constructive alternativism, 260
  constructs, 255, 265
  context 260
  C-P-C Cycle 263–264
  dependency constructs, 262
  elaborative choice, 263
  elements 260
  emergent pole 259, 272
  experience 259
  extension of the cleavage line, 260
  fear, 259
  fixed role therapy 271
  fundamental postulate 255
  guilt, 263
  impermeable, 259
  implicit pole 259, 272
  individuality 259
  Jim and Joan 256-258
  loose constructs 262
  Personal Construct Theory (PCT) 255, 264, 274
  personality 255
  Predictability 262
  preemption phase, 264
  range of convenience, 259
  range of focus 259
  replicate, 260
  role 263
  Role Construct Repertory (REP) Test, 267–270, 273–276
  submerged pole 272
  subordinate 258
  superordinate 258

symbol 260
threat, 259
tight construct 262
Ku Klux Klan 328, 387

L-data 399
late adolescence 137
latency stage 33, 156
latent content 37, 58
Latino 22, 180, 317
law and order 155
law of movement 79
learn by anxiety 133, 135
legacy 163
lemon juice 416
Les Miserables 211
libido 25, 28, 53
limbic system 781
loadings 398
locus of control 286
locus of evaluation 212
logos 55
long unit 374
loose constructs 262
loud commercials 416
love 78, 159, 181, 231, 235
lust 265

Machiavellians 118
maladjustment 288
mandala 56
manifest content 37, 58
marasmus 138
marketing of products 270
marketing orientation 187,193
marital conflict 290
Marshal, Thurgood 24
Maslow 225–249
   aesthetic needs 238
   B-Values 238
   belongingness and love needs 233
   cognitive needs, 238
   deficiency needs or D-needs 234
   esteem needs 233
   Eupsychia 239–240
   hierarchy of needs 233–235, 238,
      241–242, 245
   instinctoid, 236
   meta-needs or growth needs (G-
      needs), 234, 238
   need for self-actualization, 225, 233,
      236, 240–240, 243–244
   needs 231
   peak experiences, 238, 243, 245
   Physiological needs 233
   safety needs 233
   self-actualizers, 237, 240–241
masochistic 179, 386
mass hysteria 417
mature love 179

mature personality 147, 190, 436–440
Maudsley Personality Inventory (MPI)
   414–415
maybe me 130–131
medical model 201
menstural cycle 312
mentalism 338, 342
metagenital 136
meta-needs or growth needs (G-Needs)
   234, 238
methodological behaviorism 204, 337
Mexicans 192
middle age (Jung) 62
midlife crisis 162–164
midlife transition 162
militia 328, 387, 449
Minnesota Multiphasic Personality Inventory (MMPI) 13, 241
Mischel 294–307
   Characterizing events 298
   cognitive social learning theory 295
   competency 298
   component of a situation 298
   delay of gratification 300
   events 298
   expectancy 299
   interaction point of view, 295, 301,
      304
   personal cognitive factors 295
   self-regulatory plans, 300
   stimulus 299
   success 300
   values of outcomes 300
MMPI 22
model 314, 315
modeling 314
Montessori 148–149
moralism 448
moral justification 329
morality principle 28
mother, bad 130
mother, good 130
mothering one 126–128, 133
motivation 231
moving against people 107
moving away from people 107, 185
moving toward people 106, 185
Multiple Abstract Variance Analysis
   (MAVA) 407
Murray 367–392
   abience 377, 389
   actone, 374
   adience 376, 389
   cathexis 379
   conflicts of needs 379
   contrafactions of needs 379
   fusion of needs 378
   long unit 374
   n Abasement 376
   n Achievement 376

n Affiliation 376
n Aggression 376
n Autonomy 377
n Blamavoidance 377
n Contrarience 377
n Dominance 376
n Exhibition 376
n Infavoidance 377
n Inviolacy 377
n Order 376
n Succorance 376
need integrate or complex 379
need, 375
press 381
psychogenic needs 376
regnancy 375
regnant 375
strength 378
subsidation of needs 378
thema 381
Thematic Apperception Test (TAT),
   11, 12, 165, 368, 382, 387–388,
   389
unitary trend, 374
vector 376
viscerogenic needs 376
Myers Briggs Type Indicator (MBTI)
   64

n Abasement 376
n Achievement 376
n Affiliation 376
n Aggression 376
n Autonomy 377
n Blamavoidance 377
n Dominance 376
n Exhibition 376
n Harmavoidance 377
n Inviolacy 377
n Noxavoidance 377
n Order 376
n Succorance 376
narcissistic 29, 40, 118, 136, 432
nationalism 158, 449
Native Americans 54, 149, 152, 180,
   317, 329, 441
nature-nurture 397, 406–407
Nazis 23, 68, 75, 77, 158, 177, 235, 329,
   410
necrophilia 386
necrophilous character 188
need 183, 193, 231, 375
need (Maslow) 231
need (Murray) 375
need for self-actualization (Maslow)
   225, 233, 236, 240–241
need for tenderness 127
need integrate or complex 379
negative correlation 6
negative reinforcement 346

neglected child 81
Neo-Freudian 73
Neo-Nazi 387
neurobiology 311–312, 375
neurosis (Adler) 80
neuroses (Freud) 27
neurotic needs 105, 106
neuroticism 412–416, 420
nil correlation 8,
nomothetic theorists 429
non-directive approach 219
nonproductive 184
Northern European heritage 107
notice changes in the body 141
notice marginal thoughts 141

object of devotion 178
objective personality test 21
objective tests 12
observational learning 311
Oedipus complex 31, 32, 33, 45, 74, 81, 101, 112, 174, 191, 372
old age (Jung) 63
old age stage 160, 167
old testament 174
operant conditioning 343–353
optimism 387, 441
oral fixation (Adler) 177
oral or Narcissistic (self-centered) stage 29, 40, 118, 191
oral dynamism 132
oral-aggressive 30
oral-receptive 30
organ inferiority 80
organismic approach 203, 205, 207, 239
origins 290
orthogenital 136
overcompensate 81

P-technique 399
paragenital 136
parapsychology 113
parataxic 129, 132
participant modeling 318
passive externals 293
pawns 290
peak experiences 238, 243, 245
penis envy 32, 39, 40, 51, 102, 110
performance accomplish 318
permanency 442
persona 53, 62, 209
personal agency 313
personal cognitive factors 295
Personal Construct Theory (PCT) 255, 264, 274
personal disposition (p.d.) 432
personal unconscious 52
personality (Allport) 429
personality (Cattell) 397
personality (Fromm) 184

personality (Intro) 2
personality (Kelly) 255
personality (Sullivan) 249
personality and heredity 406–407, 412–413, 416–418
Personality Assessment Inventory (PAI) 22
personality development 818
Personality Orientation Inventory or (POI) 240–241, 243, 244
Personality Research Form (PRF) 382
personality traits 1, 281, 373, 375, 428
person centered 202, 205
person centered therapy 213–214, 215
person factors 295, 311
personification 130, 132
personologist 2
PH balance 92
phallic stage 31, 33
phenomenologists 204
phenomenology 204
phobia 32, 322, 427
physiological needs (Maslow) 233
play stage 155
pleasure principle 25
POI 240–241, 243, 244
political orientation 439
positive regard 211
positive reinforcement 344–345
positive self-regard 16, 212, 213
positively correlated 6
Posttraumatic Stress Disorder (PTSD) 88
preadolescence 134
preconscious 27
predictability 262
preemption phase 264
prejudice 441–442
prejudiced personality 447–449
press 381
primary factors (Cattell) 398
primary process 25
productive orientation 185, 190
productive love 190
productive reasoning 190
productive work 190
projection 26, 108
projection (Jung) 108
projective tests, 11, 65
propriate striving, 436
proprium 17, 434
prospective 59, 86
prototaxic 128, 130
prototype 79
psyche (Jung) 53
psychiatric interview (Sullivan) 139–142
psychoanalysis 38, 43, 201
Psychoanalytic Theory (PT) 39, 41, 42, 199, 429
psychogenic needs 376

psychological adjustment 441
psychological determinism 45
psychological situation 285
psychometrics 414
psychopath 415–416
psychosexual 29, 34, 102, 191
psychosocial development 152
psychotherapy 37, 38, 65, 90, 213, 217, 254–255
psychoticism 412–416, 420
punishment 346–347
Puritan ethic 187
Puppet Masters 189
purpose 155
Pyramids 107

Q-data 399

R = f(S.P) 397
R-technique 399
race 443–446
race and intelligence 408, 419
racism 443–444, 447
racist 443–444
radical behaviorism 337, 341
range of convenience 259
range of focus 259
rapid eye movements 353
rate of responding 345
ratio schedule 348
rational coper 435
rationalization 26, 109
real abuse 43
real self 108, 109, 116, 118, 208
reality principle 50
receptive 185, 192, 193
reciprocal casusation 311
recognition 62
regnancy 375
regnant 375
regression 30, 179
reinforcement 285, 315, 344
reinforcement (Rotter) 285
reinforcement (Skinner) 344
reinforcement value (Rotter) 285
reinforcer 344
relatedness 178
relativity of intelligence 408
reliability 10
religion 200, 244–245, 380, 426
religious orientation 180, 244–245
religious sentiment 439
REM 182
replicate 260
resilience 317
resignation 107
respondent conditioning 338
response facilitation 318
reverse discrimination 443

Rogers 199–224
  accurate empathy 212
  awareness 207
  client centered 201, 202, 205
  client centered therapy 213, 217
  congruence 209, 212
  denial 210
  distortion 210
  empathy 202, 204
  existentialism 203–204
  experience, 205, 207
  general actualizing tendency, 206
  growth model 201
  Humanistic psychology 199, 203
  ideal self 208, 213
  incongruence 212
  locus of evaluation, 212
  medical model, 201
  organismic approach, 203, 205
  person centered 201, 202, 205
  person centered therapy 213–214,
    215
  phenomenology 204, 215
  positive regard 211
  positive self-regard 16, 212, 213
  self, 207
  self-actualization 211
  unconditional positive regard 211
role (Kelly) 263
Role Construct Repertory (REP) Test,
    267–270, 273–274, 274–276
Remote Association Test (RAT)
    325–326
rootedness 179
Rorschach inkblot 11, 12, 386
Rotter 281–294
  Defensive externals 293
  expectancy 281, 285
  external locus of control 286–291
  Gambler's Fallacy, 283
  generalized expectancy 285–286
  I-E Scale 286–288
  internal locus of control 286–291
  interpersonal trust, 291
  locus of control 286
  negative mood regulation 292
  origins 290
  passive externals 293
  pawns 290
  psychological situation 285
  reinforcement 285
  reinforcement value 285
  social desirability, 293
  social learning 281

sadist 179, 386
SANE 176
sanity in child rearing 134
safety needs 233
schedule of reinforcement 348

schizophrenia 125, 126, 142, 415
school age stage 156
science 23, 254–255
scientific 3, 6, 254–255
scientific model for studying personal-
    ity 413
scientism 10, 373
second-order traits 400
secondary factor (Cattell) 398
secondary p.ds. 433, 450
secondary process 26
secondary reinforcers 360
security operations 141
seduction thesis 83
selective inattention 132
self 53, 207, 434, 436
self (Jung) 53
self (Rogers) 207
self-actualization (Rogers) 81, 207, 211
self-actualization (Maslow) 81, 225,
    236, 240–241, 243–244
self-actualizers, 237, 240–241, 243–244
self-analysis 23, 51, 65, 115–118
self-concept 210, 219, 242
self-deceptive 441
self-directing 238–239
self-effacing 106, 107
self-esteem 154, 231, 232, 435
self-esteem (Allport) 435
self-evaluation 320, 325, 330
self-exonerative processes 328
self-fulfilling prophecy 111
self-identity 434
self-image 435
self-influence 325
self-realization 69, 204, 244–245
self-deception 831
self-efficacy 91, 316–317, 318,
    321–326, 387
self-recognition 116, 118
self-regulatory plans 300
self-regulatory mechanisms 317, 326
self-regulatory processes 316, 317, 326,
    327
self-sentiment 397, 407
self-system 127, 132, 141
self-actualizers 237, 240, 243–244
self (Rogers) 401
sensation 61
Sensation Seeking 230
sensitivity training groups 202, 217
sentiment 401
sexual expression 103–104, 231–232
sexual orientation 46, 103
sexually abused females 732
shadow 54, 55, 62, 67
shame and doubt 154, 167
shaping 345
shock 80
short-term psychotherapy 65, 91

significant others 126–127
simple stimuli 182
Sixteen 16 PF 403–405, 409
sizing up a situation 298–299
skill 283
skin color 441
Skinner 337–365
  behavior therapy, 359
  behaviorism 337
  consequence 340, 343
  contingent 344
  continuous reinforcement, 347
  cumulative records, 348
  dignity 342–343
  escapes 664
  extinction 339, 345
  fixed schedule, 348
  fixed-interval (FI) schedule 348
  fixed-ratio (FR) schedule 348
  freedom 341
  intermittent reinforcement, 348
  mentalism 338–342
  negative reinforcement 346
  operant conditioning 343, 344–353
  positive reinforcement 344–345
  punishment 346–347
  radical behaviorism 327, 341
  rate of responding 345
  ratio schedule 348
  reinforcement 344
  schedule of reinforcement 348
  secondary reinforcers, 360
  shaping 345
  temporal schedule 348
  variable schedule 349
  variable-interval (VI) schedule
    349–350, 359
  variable-ratio (VR) schedule 351
Skinner Box 344, 345
slips of the tongue 40, 41
smoking cessation 91–92, 359
Social character 184, 193
social choices and reactions 443–444
social cognitive theory 311, 331
social comparison 320
social desirability 293
Social Distance (SD) 442
social feeling 78, 85
social interest 75, 78, 85, 89, 90, 127
Social Interest Scale (SIS) 89
"social law of relativity" 244
social learning (Rotter) 281
social orientation 439
socialism 175–176
socialization 102, 185
social situations 281
sociopsychological orientation 173
source trait 400
Soviet Union 201
spacing of children and I.Q. 84

Spanish Personality Assessment Inventory (PAI) 13
specific responses 414
speech development 352–353
speech-language pathologist 465
spider phobics 322–323
spirit possession 295
spoiled child 81, 85, 88
stable entitiy 326
stagnation 159, 162
state 399, 409
state-trait distinction 409
statistically significant 10
stereotype 202, 445–447
stimulus (Mischel) 299
stimulus-response (S-R) 340
strength 152, 378
strength of conditioning 345
striving for superiority 81, 86, 87
Structuralism 441
student centered teaching 205, 220
style of life 78, 86
subjective experience 205
sublimation, 33, 133
submerged pole 272
subordinate 258
subsidiation of needs 378
subsidiation of traits 400, 414
superordinate 258
substance abuse 289, 416
success (Mischel) 300
successive approximation 345
Sullivan 123–146
    Amphigenital 136
    anxiety gradient, 133, 140
    autophilic person, 136
    childhood stage 132
    detailed inquiry 140
    dynamisms 131
    Early adolescence 136
    eductive 133
    empathy, 128
    forbidding gestures 131
    foresight, 141
    heterophilic person 136
    infancy 130
    Interpersonal anxiety 127
    interpersonal relations. 123
    interpersonal security 128
    interruption 140
    isophilic person 136
    juvenile era 134
    Late adolescence 137
    learn by anxiety 133, 140
    lust 136
    make prompt statements of all that comes to mind 141

Metagenital 136
need for tenderness 127
notice changes in the body 141
notice marginal thoughts, 141
Orthogenital 136
paragenital 136
parataxic 129, 132
personality 249
personifications, 130
preadolescence 134
prototaxic 128, 130
reconnaissance 140
security operations, 274
self-system 127, 132, 141
significant others 126–127
sublimation 133
syntaxic 129, 134
termination 140
the inception 140
Sun Phallus Man 68
super-patriots 449
superego 27, 28, 29, 33, 102, 132
superiority complex 76, 81
surface traits 401
symbiotic union 178, 185
symbol (Kelly) 260
symbolic modeling 314
symbolic representation 314
synchronicity 57
syntality 402
syntaxic 129, 134

Taoistic 464
TAT pictures (figures) 384, 385
T-data 399
teleological 51, 79
temperament trait 401
temporal schedule 348
temporal stability 296, 374
Thanatos 25
thema 381
Thematic Apperception Test (TAT) 11, 12, 165, 368, 382, 387–388, 389
theoretical orientation 439
thinking 61, 64
threat 210, 259
threat (Kelly) 259
tight constructs 262
time competent 207
time out 361
tolerance for ambiguity 448
trial and error 133, 135
trial and success 133, 135
trait 281, 294, 343, 373, 375, 389, 393, 412, 431
trait (Allport) 431

trait (Cattell) 400
trait (Eysenck) 412
transference 38, 40, 103, 191
transcendence 181
transcendental function 161
Type E 118
types (Eysenck) 412
type (Jung) 60
tyranny of the shoulds 115, 211

UFO 56
unconscious 27, 51, 53, 429
unconditional positive regard 211
undoing 27
unidentified flying objects 110
unified philosophy of life 439
unique trait (Cattell) 400
unique trait (Allport) 432
unitary trend 374
unity 180
"unprejudiced," 442

validity 11
variable 4
variable schedule 349
variable-interval (VI) schedule 349–350
variable-ratio (VR) schedule 351
vicarious expectancy learning 318
vicarious reinforcement 320
Viking 54
vector 376
Vietnam 176, 329
values of outcomes 300
viscerogenic needs 375

Walden Two 337, 338, 343, 355, 356–357, 358
wannabes 848
well-being 369
will power 23, 155, 167
wisdom, 161, 167
withdrawal 185
womb envy 110
women 151, 163, 330–331, 357
women's movement 111
Word Association Test 65, 69
World War I 51, 75, 175, 329, 370, 394, 410, 427
World War II 56, 175, 246, 428, 445

yin and yang 123
young adulthood stage 158–159, 167
youth (Jung) 62